The Russian Revolution and Bolshevik Victory

PROBLEMS IN EUROPEAN
CIVILIZATION SERIES

The Russian Revolution and Bolshevik Victory

Visions and Revisions

Revised and Edited by
Ronald Suny
University of Michigan

Arthur Adams
Professor Emeritus
Ohio State University

D. C. HEATH AND COMPANY
Lexington, Massachusetts   Toronto

Cover: The workers of the Petrograd arms-manufacturing plant at the demonstration of July 1917. (Novosti from Sovfoto)

Published simultaneously in Canada.

Printed in the United States of America.

International Standard Book Number: 0-669-20877-9

Library of Congress Catalog Card Number: 89-84256

10 9 8 7 6 5 4 3 2 1

Preface

The Russian Revolution continues to fascinate scholars, students, and general readers of history. This small contribution to the growing literature on 1917 brings together some of the most interesting authors (but by no means all) who have written on the overthrow of tsarism and the victory of Bolshevism. We have included a variety of views, in order to provide the reader with a range of the debates that have divided historians. We hope that this collection will stimulate further reading and research on the elusive contours of the revolutionary years.

A few technical matters should be addressed at the outset. Various authors use different spellings in transliterating from Russian; we have retained the choices of the authors rather than trying to make the spelling of Russian names consistent throughout the volume. Petrograd, of course, was the wartime name of St. Petersburg, the capital of Russia from 1703 to 1918, and after Lenin's death its name was changed again, to Leningrad, which it is still called today. Most of the authors collected here use the dating system based on the Julian calendar, which was still employed in Russia at the time of the Revolution; by the twentieth century this calendar lagged thirteen days behind the Gregorian calendar used in the West. The Chronology of Events on page xi gives both the Old Style and New Style dates.

Finally, we thank Geoff Eley, Ara Sarafian, Philip Skaggs, and our editors at D. C. Heath, James Miller and Bryan Woodhouse, for their assistance and suggestions in the preparation of this volume.

R. S.
A. A.

Contents

Chronology of Events, 1917

Julian date	Gregorian date	
February 22–March 2	March 7–15	The February/March Revolution
February 27	March 12	Formation of the Duma Committee and the Petrograd Soviet
March 2	March 15	Abdication of Nicholas II and formation of First Provisional Government
April 3	April 16	Lenin arrives in Petrograd
May 2	May 15	Milyukov's resignation as minister of foreign affairs
May 5	May 18	Organization of First Coalition Government
June 18	July 1	The Kerensky Offensive
July 3–5	July 16–18	The July Days: unsuccessful Bolshevik demonstrations
July 24	August 6	Kerensky becomes prime minister in Second Coalition Government
August 25–30	September 7–12	The Kornilov revolt
September 1	September 14	Kerensky establishes the Directorate of Five
September 23	October 6	Trotsky becomes president of Petrograd Soviet
September 25	October 8	Formation of Third Coalition Government

October 12	October 25	Military Revolutionary Committee of the Soviet placed under Trotsky's direction
October 25	*November 7*	*Seizure of power in Petrograd*
October 26	November 8	Organization of the Bolshevik Government

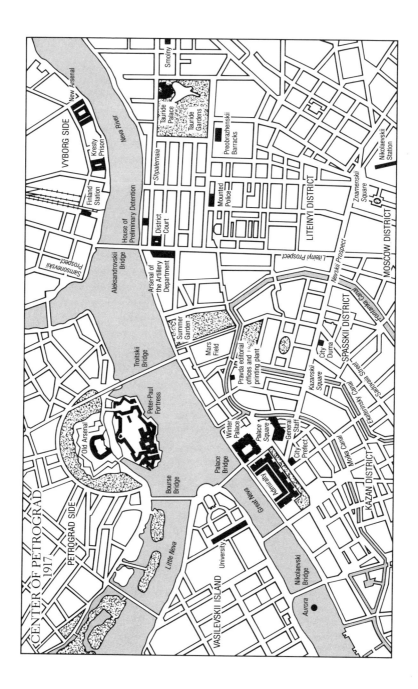

CENTER OF PETROGRAD 1917

VYBORG SIDE

New Arsenal

Kresty Prison

Finland Station

Neva River

Smolny

Tauride Palace

Tauride Gardens

Shpalernaia

Preobrazhenskii Barracks

House of Preliminary Detention

District Court

Samsonevskii Prospect

Aleksandrovskii Bridge

Arsenal of the Artillery Department

Mounted Police

LITEINYI DISTRICT

Liteinyi Prospect

Nevskii Prospect

Znamenskii Square

Nikolaevskii Station

MOSCOW DISTRICT

PETROGRAD SIDE

Old Arsenal

Troitskii Bridge

Peter-Paul Fortress

Summer Garden

Mars Field

Pravda editorial offices and printing plant

Fontanka Canal

SPASSKII DISTRICT

City Duma

Sadovaia Street

Bourse Bridge

Palace Bridge

Winter Palace

Palace Square

General Staff

City Prefect

Kazanskii Square

Ekaterinskii Canal

Moika Canal

KAZAN DISTRICT

Little Neva

Great Neva

Admiralty

VASILEVSKII ISLAND

University

Nikolaevskii Bridge

Aurora

The Russian Revolution and Bolshevik Victory

Introduction

As time and distance dim the memories and passions associated with the Russian revolutions of 1917, new sources and more specialized research have opened fresh perspectives and offered new interpretations. Each generation of historians since 1917, as well as their readers, has had access to more primary material, more complex and varied analyses with which to think through the Revolution and come up with its own understanding. Initially that history was written by the participants themselves, men like Sukhanov and Trotsky, Kerensky and Chernov, or by foreign observers sympathetic or hostile, such as John Reed, Albert Rhys-Williams, and George Buchanan.[1] Often limited by partisanship and self-justification, these original accounts became the sources and targets of successive generations of university-trained scholars, creating an intense dialogue with the ghosts of 1917 that has hardly subsided more than seventy years after the events took place.

In the Soviet Union a Bolshevik historiography in the 1920s, which argued for the necessity, even inevitability, of the October Revolution, was quickly supplanted in the following decade by a narrow reading that created a heroic, operatic fiction that condemned all opponents (and even most close associates) of Lenin in order to lay an ideological cornerstone for the dictatorial edifice of Stalinism. With the infamous *Short Course* in the history of the Communist Party (1939) the Stalinist interpretation became the required version for all historians. The slightest deviation from the official view of history could mean imprisonment or worse. Only after the death of Stalin in 1953 did Soviet historians hesitantly begin to break out of the fetters of the prescribed version. Yet attempts to return to the relative historiographic freedom of the 1920s,

---

[1] N. N. Sukhanov, *The Russian Revolution, 1917: Eyewitness Account*, 2 vols. (London: Oxford University Press, 1955); Leon Trotsky, *History of the Russian Revolution*, 3 vols. (Ann Arbor: University of Michigan Press, 1967); A. F. Kerensky, *The Prelude to Bolshevism* (New York, 1919) and *The Crucifixion of Liberty* (New York, 1934); Victor Chernov, *The Great Russian Revolution* (New Haven: Yale University Press, 1936); John Reed, *Ten Days that Shook the World* (New York: Boni & Liveright, 1919); Arthur Rhys-Williams, *Through the Russian Revolution* (London, 1923); George Buchanan, *My Mission to Russia and Other Diplomatic Reminiscences*, 2 vols. (London and Boston, 1923).

1

like that made by Eduard Burdzhalov in the late 1950s, were suppressed, and in the latter years of Khrushchev's rule (1953–1964) and the long period of conservative stabilization under Brezhnev (1964–1982), few historians were able to produce anything but politicized and hagiographic writing. Only in the mid-1980s, with the coming to power of Mikhail Gorbachev and his program of *perestroika* and *glasnost'*, did scholars begin again, at first quite tentatively, to try to re-examine the sacred truths forced on them by older "historians."

In the absence of a native historiography that commanded respect abroad, a handful of Western writers has been extraordinarily influential in shaping Western attitudes about 1917. In the atmosphere of anti-Soviet hostility that prevailed in the first decades after the revolution, Western views were determined more by lurid journalism than by the liberal and socialist emigres, like Pavel Miliukov, Leon Trotsky, and the Mensheviks around the *Sotsialisticheskii vestnik (Socialist Herald)*, who produced serious studies of their own experience.[2] But as interest in the Soviet experiment grew in the 1930s, scholars and scholar-journalists, such as Michael Florinsky, Sir Bernard Pares, Sir John Maynard, and William Henry Chamberlin, provided broader, less partisan studies that gave general readers well-told narratives based on the available printed sources.[3] Chamberlin's two-volume work, in particular, was a singular achievement, regarded by many as the most authoritative history of the revolution and civil war for nearly half a century. For all their considerable strengths, however, these histories suffered from the lack of specialized studies of the constituent social groups that made the revolution and tended to focus instead on politics and personalities such as Rasputin, Kerensky, and Lenin.

The emergence of the USSR as a Great Power in the chilling years of the Cold War changed Western attitudes toward the Soviet Union dramatically. Fear of Soviet expansionism was compounded by ignorance about the internal dynamics of the Soviet political system. To understand what could not be readily observed, analysts elaborated a

---

[2] Pavel N. Miliukov, *Istoriia vtoroi russkoi revoliutsii*, 3 parts (Sofia, 1921–1924). *Sotsialisticheskii vestnik* was issued by Menshevik emigres from 1922 to 1965, first in Berlin and later in Paris and New York.

[3] Michael T. Florinsky, *The End of the Russian Empire* (1931: New York: Collier Books, 1961); Bernard Pares, *The Fall of the Russian Monarchy: A Study of the Evidence* (New York: Knopf, 1939); John Maynard, *Russia in Flux before October* (1941: New York: Collier Books, 1962); William Henry Chamberlin, *The Russian Revolution*, 2 vols. (New York: Macmillan, 1935).

model of totalitarianism that equated the USSR with Nazi Germany and contrasted both unfavorably with pluralistic democracies. The origins of totalitarianism were sought by some writers in the ideology of Marxism-Leninism, by others in Russian backwardness and Stalin's drive to power, and by still others in the process of the revolution itself. The Cold War created a need to "know the enemy," and Soviet studies were rapidly expanded and professionalized. With the establishment of institutes of Russian studies and the sudden availability of funding for language training and research, a generation of "fathers"—Leonard Schapiro, G. T. Robinson, Michael Karpovich, and Merle Fainsod among them—laid the foundations of the postwar renaissance in Soviet studies.

Yet in those Cold War years the consensus shared by much of the academic community—that Russia could be best understood as a variant of totalitarianism—limited interest in deep research into the specifics of the Revolution. The boldest initiatives came from an odd trio of brilliant writers—E. H. Carr, Isaac Deutscher, and Bertram D. Wolfe—who either were outside academia altogether or came to university teaching late in life. In a steady progression until his death in 1982, Carr turned out volume after volume of a mammoth history of Soviet Russia from the Revolution to the Stalin years.[4] Deutscher, a veteran of both the Communist and Trotskyist movements who maintained his commitment to Marxism, won a wide public with his beautifully crafted biographies of Trotsky and Stalin.[5] Wolfe, who had left the Communist movement and become an implacable enemy of Marxism, contributed a best-selling triple biography of Lenin, Trotsky, and Stalin.[6]

In the late 1950s and through the 1960s, as Cold War orthodoxies gradually dissipated and Soviet archives and libraries opened to Western scholars, a new generation of historians took up aspects of the Revolution as topics of their dissertations. In the process they challenged established interpretations and eventually reconceptualized the nature and progress of the Revolution. Though no uniform consensus embraced the scholarly community, the major historiographic fractures that divided the older generations and the new revisionist scholarship were more clearly exposed.

[4] The first three volumes of E. H. Carr's monumental *History of Soviet Russia* were concerned with the revolutionary period: *The Bolshevik Revolution, 1917–1923* (New York: Macmillan, 1951–1953).

[5] Isaac Deutscher, *Stalin: A Political Biography* (London and New York: Oxford University Press, 1949); *Trotsky: The Prophet Armed* (New York: Oxford University Press, 1954).

[6] Bertram D. Wolfe, *Three Who Made a Revolution* (Boston: Beacon Press, 1948).

Arthur Adams' first collection of writings on 1917 (published in 1960) necessarily relied on the classic texts of Pares, Trotsky, and Chamberlin, and even his second edition (1972) only replaced Miliukov with George Kennan, Victor Chernov with Adam B. Ulam, Merle Fainsod with Robert V. Daniels. The specialized literature by Western-born scholars trained in the twilight years of the Cold War began to appear only in the fifth decade after the Revolution. Necessarily shaped by the more equivocal attitudes toward both superpowers in the age of "Peaceful Coexistence," destalinization, and the American intervention in Southeast Asia, it coexisted uneasily with work by older historians who had lived through the darkest days of Stalinism and Soviet expansion into East Central Europe. Yet the effect of the explosion of research transformed the landscape of revolutionary studies. The volumes by Oliver Radkey on the Socialist Revolutionaries, Alexander Rabinowitch on the Bolsheviks, Rex Wade on the Provisional Government, and William G. Rosenberg on the Kadets, initiated an impressive parade of monographs that shifted emphasis from outstanding personalities to larger political institutions.[7] Arthur Adams, Firuz Kazemzadeh, Alexander Park, Richard Pipes, Donald J. Raleigh, John Reshetar, Ronald Grigor Suny, and others expanded the focus from Petrograd and Moscow to the peripheries of the empire.[8] Research was redirected from the top of society toward the social matrix of the lower

[7] Oliver Radkey, *The Agrarian Foes of Bolshevism: Promise and Default of the Russian Socialist Revolutionaries, February to October 1917* (New York: Columbia University Press, 1958); Alexander Rabinowitch, *Prelude to Revolution: The Petrograd Bolsheviks and the July 1917 Uprising* (Bloomington: Indiana University Press, 1968); *The Bolsheviks Come to Power: The Revolution of 1917 in Petrograd* (New York: W. W. Norton, 1976); Rex Wade, *The Russian Search for Peace, February-October, 1917* (Stanford: Stanford University Press, 1969); William G. Rosenberg, *Liberals in the Russian Revolution: The Constitutional Democratic Party, 1917–1921* (Princeton: Princeton University Press, 1974).

[8] Arthur E. Adams, *Bolsheviks in the Ukraine: The Second Campaign, 1918–1919* (New Haven: Yale University Press, 1963); Firuz Kazemzadeh, *The Struggle for Transcaucasia, 1917–1921* (New York: Philosophical Library, 1951); Alexander G. Park, *Bolshevism in Turkestan, 1917–1927* (New York: Columbia University Press, 1957); Richard Pipes, *The Formation of the Soviet Union: Communism and Nationalism, 1917–1923* (Cambridge: Harvard University Press, 1957); Donald J. Raleigh, *Revolution on the Volga: 1917 in Saratov* (Ithaca: Cornell University Press, 1986); John S. Reshetar, *The Ukrainian Revolution, 1917–1920* (Princeton: Princeton University Press, 1952); Ronald Grigor Suny, *The Baku Commune, 1917–1918: Class and Nationality in the Russian Revolution* (Princeton: Princeton University Press, 1972).

classes. After decades of scholarship that treated the workers and soldiers of Russia as the victims of Bolshevik manipulation and deception, the work of Mark Ferro, David Mandel, Diane Koenker, S. A. Smith, Ziva Galili, William G. Rosenberg, and Allan K. Wildman[9] showed that these groups had their own aspirations and organizational capabilities.

This collection brings to undergraduates and graduate students selections from various kinds of writings on the Russian Revolution—eyewitness accounts by participants (Sukhanov, Trotsky, Tsereteli); Soviet interpretations (Lenin, Burdzhalov); histories concerned with politics and personalities (Pares, Katkov, Daniels); and examples of broader social history (Smith, Mandel, Keep, and Koenker among others).[10] No single interpretation can be insisted upon, for the scholarship on 1917 is divided along many axes (as the Variety of Opinion sections demonstrate). The excerpts selected for this book show the lines of development from political to social history: from Russocentric studies of the capitals to multiethnic studies of the peripheries, and from demonization of the revolutionaries to a more complex appreciation of the imperatives faced by all the participants.

[9]Marc Ferro, *The Russian Revolution of February 1917* (Englewood Cliffs, N. J.: Prentice-Hall, 1972); *October 1917: A Social History of the Russian Revolution* (London, Boston and Henley: Routledge & Kegan Paul, 1980); David Mandel, *The Petrograd Workers and the Fall of the Old Regime: From the February Revolution to the July Days, 1917* (New York: St. Martins Press, 1983; *The Petrograd Workers and the Soviet Seizure of Power: From the July Days, 1917 to July 1918* (New York: St. Martins Press, 1984); Diane Koenker, *Moscow Workers and the 1917 Revolution* (Princeton: Princeton University Press, 1981); S. A. Smith, *Red Petrograd: Revolution in the Factories, 1917–1918* (Cambridge: Cambridge University Press, 1983); Ziva Galili, *The Menshevik Leaders in the Petrograd Soviet: Social Realities and Political Strategies* (Princeton: Princeton University Press, 1989); William G. Rosenberg, *Liberals in the Russian Revolution: The Constitutional Democratic Party, 1917–1921* (Princeton: Princeton University Press, 1974); Allan K. Wildman, *The End of the Russian Imperial Army: The Old Army and the Soldiers' Revolt, March–April 1917)* (Princeton: Princeton University Press, 1980); *The End of the Russian Imperial Army: The Road to Soviet Power and Peace* (Princeton: Princeton University Press, 1987).

[10]Irakli Tsereteli, *Vospominaniia o fevral'skoi revoliutsii*, 2 vols. (Paris: 1963); E. N. Burdzhalov, *Vtoraia russkaia revoliutsiia: Vosstanie v Petrograde* (Moscow: Nauka, 1967); *Russia's Second Revolution: The February 1917 Uprising in Petrograd*, translation by Donald J. Raleigh (Bloomington: Indiana University Press, 1987); George Katkov, *Russia 1917: The February Revolution* (New York: Harper & Row, 1967); Robert V. Daniels, *Red October: The Bolshevik Revolution of 1917* (New York: Scribners, 1967); John L. H. Keep, *The Russian Revolution: A Study in Mass Mobilization* (New York: W. W. Norton, 1976).

Tsar Nicholas II (reigned 1894–1917) and His Wife Aleksandra Fedorovna.
(Culver Pictures)

PART

I

The February Revolution

Variety of Opinion

While the empress's letters wipe clean away all the scandalous charges made against her character . . . they also prove that she and, through her, Rasputin were the prime authors of the collapse of the empire and of Russia.

Sir Bernard Pares

By 1914 a dangerous process of polarization appeared to be taking place in Russia's major urban centers between an obshchestvo *(society) that had now reabsorbed the vast majority of the once alienated elements of its intelligentsia (and which was even beginning to draw to itself many of the workers' own intelligentsia) and a growing discontented and disaffected mass of industrial workers, now left largely exposed to the pleas of an embittered revolutionary minority.*

Leopold H. Haimson

Western accounts usually overlook that the war greatly exacerbated the traditional social cleavages, particularly as its burdens fell chiefly on the politically powerless sectors of the population, whose sense of alienation was rapidly building up to a breaking point in the months before the February Revolution. While the educated and enfranchised social layers ("census Russia") were primarily concerned about the incompe-

tence of the tsarist administration in the conduct of the war, the work-
ers, peasants, and poorer meshchantsvo [lower middle class in towns],
whether in uniform or not, were becoming profoundly impatient with
the war itself.

Allan K. Wildman

The growth of the strike movement was not entirely spontaneous . . . .
Strikes required organizers who planned strategy, agitators who ap-
pealed to the workers, orators who spoke at factory rallies, and a net-
work of communications that coordinated activities with other factories.
. . . Although no single political group could claim exclusive leadership
of the workers' movement and it is impossible to measure accurately the
influence of the underground revolutionary activists, it is certain that it
was the underground activists at the factory level who provided the
workers' movement with important leadership and continuity.

Tsuyoshi Hasegawa

The mass street movement in the February days revealed no sort of
purposefulness, nor was it possible to discern in it any kind of proper
leadership. In general, as is always the case, the organized Socialist
centres were not controlling the popular movement or leading it to any
definite political goal.

N. N. Sukhanov

The assumption that there was a particular quality of "spontaneity"
which explains the scope and strength of the February demonstrations
in Petrograd is wholly gratuitous. The theory of "spontaneity" only
serves to cover up our ignorance. . . . We know now for certain that from
the very beginning of the war the German government consistently
pursued in Russia a Revoliutionierungspolitik, *an essential element of*
which was the support of an economic strike movement capable, so it
was hoped, of gradually escalating into a political revolution.

George Katkov

To the question, Who led the February Revolution? we can . . . answer
definitely enough: Conscious and tempered workers educated for the
most part by the party of Lenin. But we must here immediately add:
This leadership proved sufficient to guarantee the victory of the insurrec-
tion, but it was not adequate to transfer immediately into the hands of
the proletarian vanguard the leadership of the revolution.

Leon Trotsky

The vanguard elements among the Petrograd proletariat, led by the
Bolsheviks, continued to battle for establishing power of the revolution-

ary people. The majority of workers and soldiers, however, having won major concessions from the bourgeoisie and broad democratic rights, accepted bourgeois power and banked on placing it under the Soviet's control. They followed their petit bourgeois leaders, who called upon them to show their faith in the new government insofar as it implemented the program it agreed to with the Soviet.

Eduard Burdzhalov

The Issues

Significantly less attention has been turned toward the outbreak of the February Revolution than to analysis of the ultimate collapse of the regime it produced. Yet if one accepts that great revolutions do not have accidental or trivial causes, then one must consider whether the fall of tsarism was the result of historical processes of long duration or the unfortunate (for the monarchy) confluence of weak personalities and a devastating war. For seventy-odd years historians have disagreed about the weight to be given structures like the autocratic state, the noble estate, and the economy, or to processes like peasant impoverishment, state-initiated modernization, and the formation of an alienated working class, or to contingencies like Bolshevik conceptions of party organization, the war, and the personality of Nicholas II. "Who will be bold enough to determine which was the factor that played the leading part in bringing about the Revolution?" asked Michael Florinsky more than fifty years ago. "Was it the folly of the Emperor and the Empress? the decay of the Government? military losses? the secular grievances of the peasants? the starving conditions of the cities? the weariness with the war?"[1] The many debates on major and minor issues can for convenience be grouped into four principal issues:

- *How important are the long-term contradictions between the nature of the imperial state and the world in which it found itself in the early twentieth century? Was there a fundamental incompatibility between autocracy and the emergence of capitalism?*
- *What was the impact of the war on the creation of the final revolutionary situation for tsarism? If imperial Russia had been able to avoid World War I, would a constitutional order have survived?*

[1] Florinsky, *The End of the Russian Empire*, p. 247.

- *What were the immediate reasons for the February revolt? Was the revolution largely spontaneously generated or was it the product of conscious organization by revolutionary political parties or (in the most extreme variant of conscious intervention by outsiders) by German agents?*
- *Why were two centers of power (dvoevlastie) — the Soviet and the Provisional Government — established in early March 1917 instead of a unitary revolutionary government? Why did workers and soldiers neither take full power into their own hands nor concede exclusive authority to the government of "privileged society"?*

In an elegant, extended essay that became a most influential book, Theodore H. Von Laue dealt with some of these questions by placing the fate of tsarist Russia in the comparative context of global modernization. He argued that Russian backwardness, combined with its precarious international position, forced a most dangerous policy on the autocracy: state-initiated industrialization that exacerbated the already-existing gulf between the government and the people. Industrialization required a common effort by those in power and their subjects. Instead, the imposition of economic modernization created "a relentless rebellion against autocracy."[2] For Von Laue, Russia's fate was unenviable, something forced upon her by her relative backwardness in a global power competition. "Russia's defeats from the Crimean War to Brest-Litovsk compelled imitation, and imitation in turn predetermined the course of Russia's development."[3] "Russia was a Great Power, set, as part of its harsh destiny, into the cross currents of European and global power politics. No Russian government, regardless of its ideology or class basis, could have abdicated from that role."[4]

Von Laue's study is in the tradition of modernization theory — the notion that the transformation of societies from primarily rural and agrarian to predominantly urban and industrial is a linear, evolutionary, and generally progressive development.[5] His highly deterministic,

[2] Theodore H. Von Laue, *Why Lenin? Why Stalin? A Reappraisal of the Russian Revolution, 1900–1930* (Philadelphia and New York: J. B. Lippincott, 1964), p. 65.
[3] Ibid., p. 223.
[4] Ibid., p. 76.
[5] See, for example: Cyril E. Black, et al., *The Modernization of Japan and Russia: A Comparative Study* (New York: The Free Press, 1975); Raymond Grew, "Modernization

even fatalistic, interpretation (peppered with words like "destiny," "fate," "inevitable," "necessities," and "no alternative but") shifted focus from emperors and revolutionaries to basic processes like industrialization and the international competition. This healthy corrective to views of older historians, like Sir Bernard Pares, however, sacrificed the human agents of resistance and change almost entirely. The dominant class of prerevolutionary Russia, the landed nobility, was treated largely as an intimate ally of tsarism. Although Lenin's manipulation of Marxism was examined, there was no sense of the Bolshevik influence in the labor movement or, indeed, the power and radicalism of that movement on the eve of the war.

Shortly after the publication of Why Lenin? Why Stalin?, *a two-part article by Leopold H. Haimson appeared in the principal American journal of Soviet studies,* Slavic Review, *and effectively changed the terms of the debate over the causes of the revolution.[6] The social cleavage that eventually would bring down the Provisional Government and propel the Bolsheviks into power, Haimson contends, predated the cataclysm of the First World War and was the product of a dual polarization that had flowed from the defeat of the revolution of 1905. At the top of society all but the closest allies of tsarism moved away from support of the autocracy, as at the same time workers, particularly those in large firms such as the metallurgical plants of St. Petersburg, pulled away from the liberal intelligentsia, the moderate socialists, and the politicians of the Duma (parliament), as well as the autocratic state. The separation of these two revolutionary processes briefly permitted the survival of the autocratic regime, even as it was undermining it fundamentally.*

In the articles, and in his subsequent work, Haimson disputed those historians, such as Alexander Gerschenkron, Arthur Mendel, and others, who believed that late imperial industrialization was creating

---

and Its Discontents," *American Behavioral Scientist,* XXI (1977), pp. 289–312; and his "More on Modernization," *Journal of Social History,* XIV (1981), pp. 179–187. For a critical view, see Dean C. Tipps, "Modernization Theory and the Comparative Study of Societies: A Critical Perspective," *Comparative Studies in Society and History,* XV, 2 (March 1973), pp. 199–266.

[6] Leopold H. Haimson, "The Problem of Social Stability in Urban Russia, 1905–1917," *Slavic Review,* XXIII, 4 (December 1964), pp. 619–642; XXIV, 1 (March 1965), pp. 1–22.

*greater social stability or that the constitutional autocracy established by
the October Manifesto of 1905 was viable until assaulted by the catastrophic defeats of World War I. The post-1905 political regime, with its
indirectly elected Duma overrepresenting propertied Russia (tsentsovoe
obshchestvo) and largely disenfranchising the majority of the people, did
grant the tsar's subjects limited civil rights, but at the same time extraordinary powers were retained by a monarch who lived uneasily with
compromises on autocracy and by a landed nobility that rejected any
further reforms. Moreover, industrialization in the last years before the
war resulted in more, not less, labor protest, and the Bolsheviks, who
historians like Leonard Schapiro had contended were an isolated sect by
1914, were in fact the principal heirs of this new labor militancy. A
liberal or moderate solution to the growing revolutionary crisis was increasingly less likely as Russia entered the war.*

*Haimson followed his initial investigations of urban instability with
a collective volume written with several of his students on rural Russia
between 1905 and 1914.[7] Again, instead of successful modernization
the evidence revealed "the growing psychological distance — indeed the
growing chasm — between the political cultures that were still prevalent
in the Russian countryside, among the many millions of the communal
peasantry but also among the* pomeshchiki *[noble landlords] who lorded
over them, and the more modern political cultures that were now so
rapidly emerging among the lower as well as the upper strata of urban,
commercial, industrial Russia."[8] Though much of Russia's history since
the eighteenth century had seen the steady encroachment of the bureaucratic state on the powers of the landholding nobility, after 1905 the
landed nobility, newly self-conscious and organized, were disproportion-
ately powerful in the new representative institutions granted by the tsar.
"Precisely as a result of Russia's post-1905 political constitution — of the
emergence of the reorganized State Council [upper house of the legisla-
ture], but also of the State Duma [lower house] . . . as well as of . . . the
Council of Local Economy of the Ministry of Internal Affairs — a
minute group of Russian society, amounting to little more than thirty
thousand nobles of the countryside, found itself in a better position to
resist the government's administrative and legislative initiatives in the*

[7] Leopold H. Haimson (ed.), *The Politics of Rural Russia, 1905–1914* (Bloomington and
London: Indiana University Press, 1979).
[8] Ibid., p. vii.

last decade of the tsarist regime than it had been since the late eighteenth century."[9]

Though few historians would question the disaster visited upon tsarist Russia by its uneven struggle with the Central Powers, the optimistic view that a constitutional monarchy might have survived had the war not intervened has been steadily assaulted by researchers since Haimson's initial presentation of the issues. In a conference organized at Harvard University to mark the fiftieth anniversary of the revolution, the eminent diplomat and historian George F. Kennan confessed his own shift to a more pessimistic reading of the prewar possibilities. "Neither the tardiness in the granting of political reform," he said, "nor the excesses of an extravagant and foolish nationalism, nor the personal limitations of the imperial couple began with the war or were primarily responses to the existence of the war."[10] The tsarist record was an ambivalent one that allowed both for hope and despair, but Kennan concluded that the "impressive program of social, economic, and cultural modernization of a great country [was] being conducted, somewhat incongruously, under the general authority of a governmental system that was itself in the advanced stages of political disintegration."[11]

The structural contradictions within tsarism have been examined more recently by two historical sociologists, who arrived at quite different conclusions. In a comparative study of social revolutions Theda Skocpol argued that the Old Regime states in Russia, China, and France were both preservers of social order and competitors with the landed nobility for a share of the agricultural output. But under foreign pressure the state was required to initiate reforms and thus found itself in conflict with the interests of the dominant classes. The question then became whether state officials would be able to overcome noble resistance to reform in order to preserve the social order. In Russia, however, the nobility was relatively weak, Skocpol claimed, and therefore her elegant theorem — foreign pressure plus dominant-class resistance to reform leads to the political crisis of the state — had to be supplemented. "In

[9] Ibid., p. 9. For fuller discussions of the nobility at the end of the empire, see Roberta Thompson Manning, *The Crisis of the Old Order in Russia: Gentry and Government* (Princeton: Princeton University Press, 1982); and Seymour Becker, *Nobility and Privilege in Late Imperial Russia* (Dekalb: Northern Illinois University Press, 1985).

[10] George F. Kennan, "The Breakdown of the Tsarist Autocracy," in Richard Pipes (ed.), *Revolutionary Russia* (Cambridge, MA: Harvard University Press, 1968), p. 15.

[11] Ibid.

Russia, a weak landed nobility could not block reforms from above. Yet the agrarian economy and class structure served as brakes upon state-guided industrialization, thus making it impossible for tsarist Russia to catch up . . . with Imperial Germany."[12] Like Von Laue, Skocpol underlines the importance of Russia's unfortunate and uneven competition with Germany and concludes that "in Russia, the revolutionary crisis of autocratic rule and dominant-class privilege was due to the over-whelming stress of World War I upon an early-industrializing economy fettered by a backward agrarian sector. . . . The Russian Revolution broke out only because — and when — the tsarist state was destroyed by the impact of prolonged involvement and repeated defeats in World War I."[13]

Skocpol's analysis, for all of its suggestiveness, left out many of the particulars of the Russian experience drawn out by social historians of Russia. She did not recognize, for example, the reemergence of noble power in the post-1905 period that Haimson and his students have claimed. Nor did she place much weight on the role of the workers. "The revolts of urban workers," she wrote, "constituted intervening moments in the processes by which the French and Russian Old Regimes were under-mined (although the fundamental causes were the international pressures and dominant class/state contradictions discussed in depth)."[14] These were not accidental omissions but flowed from her highly structuralist approach to revolution. Actors and ideologies were not given much weight, and ultimately workers and Bolsheviks were incidental to her story.

A second historical sociologist, Tim McDaniel, attempted to remedy some of the problems in Skocpol's work by centering his analysis on the working class. McDaniel began by noting the anomaly of Russia's working class in the history of European labor. Whereas elsewhere in Europe capitalist industrialization led not to revolution but to greater accommodation within capitalism, in Russia the "industrial labor movement was the pivotal revolutionary actor and . . . the process of industrialization was the wellspring of revolution."[15] McDaniel proposed that the tsarist state's goals — the promotion of economic and social modernization on the one hand and the maintenance of the stability of autocratic power on the other — ultimately contradicted one another. "Autocracy and capi-

---

[12] Theda Skocpol, *States and Social Revolutions: A Comparative Analysis of France, Russia, and China* (Cambridge: Cambridge University Press, 1979), p. 99.

[13] Ibid., p. 207.

[14] Ibid., p. 113.

[15] Tim McDaniel, *Autocracy, Capitalism, and Revolution in Russia* (Berkeley and Los Angeles: University of California Press, 1988), p. 2.

talism, in their fateful interdependence, undermined each other and thus prepared the ground for a revolution against both."[16] Capitalist industrialization weakened autocracy by subverting patriarchal norms and creating dangerous antagonists, namely the industrialists and the workers. At the same time autocracy undermined capitalism by not adequately guaranteeing property rights, by preventing a rule of law, and by undermining trust, the basis of contract. This strange hybrid, which McDaniel called "autocratic capitalism," in turn eliminated the differentiation between economic and political issues, escalating the former into the latter, and led to radicalization of the labor movement.

Whether one sees the particularities of the labor opposition or the contradictions of state policy as the primary catalyst, the focus for most historians and social scientists has moved from personalities and conspiracies toward broader considerations of political and social structures and the prewar and wartime conjunctures of state impotence and lower-class militance. By 1914 the autocratic state was unable any longer to effectively manage the consequences of the social and economic changes in Russian society that it had done so much to initiate. The war may have been the final, unsustainable burden that broke the back of tsarism, but it was neither wholly exogenous to Russia nor unexpected. Russia's ambitious engagement in Balkan and Near Eastern politics was an important ingredient in the international rivalries that led to war. Moreover, powerful groups in Russian society — at court, among the liberals in the Duma, in the circles of the Moscow industrialists, and elsewhere — were prepared to accept (some were even enthusiastic about) the coming test of arms.[17] The tsar and most of his opponents were surprised by the sudden demise of the three-hundred-year-old Romanov monarchy, but there were those who, even before the war began, understood that the antique props of the autocracy would not withstand the blows of a great war. Early in 1913 Lenin wrote to the writer Maxim Gorky, "A war between Austria and Russia would be a very useful thing for the revolution (throughout all of Eastern Europe), but it is hardly possible that Franz-Joseph and Nicky would give us this pleasure."[18]

[16] Ibid., p. 16.
[17] On the Duma, see Geoffrey Hosking, *The Russian Constitutional Experiment* (Cambridge: Cambridge University Press, 1973); on the industrialists, see Lewis H. Siegelbaum, *The Politics of Industrial Mobilization in Russia, 1914–17: A Study of the War-Industries Committees* (London and Basingstoke: Macmillan, 1983).
[18] V. I. Lenin, *Polnoe sobranie sochinenii*, 5th ed. (Moscow: Political Literature, 1970), XLVIII, p. 155.

Bernard Pares

Rasputin and the Empress Alexandra

After graduating from Cambridge University, the young Bernard Pares (1867–1949) traveled to Russia to view the site of the Battle of Borodino. A lifelong love for Russia and her people developed, and Pares became a pioneer in the study of Russia in the English-speaking world — indeed its first university professor of Russian history. His major books — *Russia Between Reform and Revolution* (1907), *The History of Russia* (1926), and *The Fall of the Russian Monarchy* (1939) — and his services as a founder of the School of Slavonic Studies at the University of London led to his being knighted. A friend of the liberal historian and politician Pavl Miliukov, Pares had hoped in vain for a constitutional monarchy in Russia. Late in life he became an advocate for rapproachement with Soviet Russia and was denounced as an apologist by some. In this selection Pares stresses personal factors in the fall of the empire. His biographical approach was an early contribution to the tradition of painting portraits of the imperial family that lead to Robert K. Massie and his *Nicholas and Alexandra* (1967).

The publication of the letters of the tsaritsa to her husband for the first time showed in black and white Rasputin's enormous political significance. But those who took the trouble to wade through that mass of loose English were probably too overcome by the sweep of the vast tragedy to realize at first the unique importance of the letters as historical material. It is to this aspect of the subject that this article is devoted.

The Rasputin tragedy passed at the time behind closed doors, except for Rasputin's own entire indifference to public scandal. By now almost every one of the persons who could give valuable firsthand evidence on the subject has said his word. M. Gilliard, tutor to the tsarevich, a man of great good sense and good feeling, has given a beautiful picture of the home life of the imperial family, the accuracy

From Sir Bernard Pares, "Rasputin and the Empress: Authors of the Russian Collapse." Reprinted by permission from *Foreign Affairs*, October 1927. Copyright by the Council on Foreign Relations, Inc., New York.

of which has been confirmed both by the Provisional and the Soviet governments. We have for what it is worth the Apologia of Madame Vyrubov, the only person who was with the family continually, and Rasputin's chosen go-between for his communications with the empress. A slighter record is given by another friend of the empress, Madame Lili Dehn. The head of the Police Department, Beletsky, has told a typical story of ministerial intrigue centered round Rasputin. The French ambassador, M. Paléologue, has issued a current record of events, evidently touched up for publication, which gives the atmosphere of grand ducal and higher society, but also connects Rasputin at point after point with political events of the most critical importance. Now we have also the important record of the president of the Third and Fourth Dumas, Mr. Michael Rodzianko, prepared in exile without many materials but preserving the details of his various conversations with the emperor, which were evidently written down with care at the time.

Rasputin, who was under fifty at the time of his death, was born in the village of Pokrovskoe on the Tura, near Tobolsk in Siberia. Like many peasants he had no surname; Rasputin, which means "dissolute," was a nickname early given him by his fellow peasants. He suddenly went off to the Verkhne-Turski Monastery near his home, where were several members of the *Khlysty,* a sect who mingled sexual orgies with religious raptures and who were emphatically condemned by the Orthodox Church. On his return he became a *strannik,* or roving man of God, not a monk, not in orders, but one with a self-given commission from heaven, such as have often appeared in Russian history, especially at critical times. Meanwhile, he lived so scandalous a life that his village priest investigated it with care. That he habitually did much the same things as the *Khlysty* is conclusively proved; but that he was actually one of the sect has not been definitely established. Certainly to the end of his life he alternated freely between sinning and repenting, and professed the view that great sins made possible great repentances. He seduced a large number of women, several of whom boasted of the fact, or repented and confessed it to others. The village priest reported him to Bishop Antony of Tobolsk, who made a more thorough inquiry and found evidence which he felt bound to hand over to the civil authorities. During the inquiry Rasputin disappeared. He went to St. Petersburg, and as a great penitent secured the confidence of Bishop Theophan, head of the Petersburg Religious Academy, and confessor to the empress, a man whose personal sanctity has been recognized by everyone. He secured also the patronage of the Grand Duchess Militsa, daughter of King Nicholas of Montenegro, a lady with a strong taste for the sensational, and also that of her future brother-in-law, the Grand Duke Nicholas. It was these who introduced him to the palace.

The Empress Alexandra, formerly Princess Alix of Hesse Darmstadt, was a daughter of the English Princess Alice and a favorite granddaughter of Queen Victoria, from whom she may be said to have taken all the ordinary part of her mental environment. The unusual feature in her character was her strong mysticism. Her family was scourged with the hemophilic ailment; all the male children of her sister Princess Irene of Prussia suffered from it. It does not appear in females, but is transmitted by them to males. Its effect is that the slightest accident may set up internal bleeding, which there is no known way of arresting. Children suffering from it may die at any moment, and on almost any occasion, though if they live to the age of thirteen they may in some measure overcome it; Rasputin prophesied such an issue for the Tsarevich Alexis. Much of the tragedy in the position of the empress lay in the fact that after she had given birth to four charming and healthy daughters, her only son, the long-desired heir to the throne, suffered from this scourge, and that she well knew that his disease came through herself.

In every other domestic respect the family was ideally happy. Husband and wife literally adored each other; the children were equally united with them and with each other. The empress was the pillar of the house, their actual nurse and attendant in time of sickness. She brought them up entirely in English ideas; they had cold baths and slept on camp beds; they talked largely in English. The family as a whole, in its clean-minded life, represented a veritable oasis in the corruption which was so prevalent in higher Russian society, and we may imagine that with that world this aspect of their isolation was one of their chief offenses. They lived almost as much apart from it as if they were settlers in Canada.

The empress's nature was singularly narrow and obstinate; Rodzianko rightly describes her as "essentially a creature of will." She had a fondness for her first "little home" at Hesse Darmstadt, but a strong antipathy for the Emperor William; indeed the Prussian monarchy found many of its bitterest critics among the smaller reigning German families. She regarded herself as essentially English, but she had frankly embraced the country of her adored husband, and more than that, she had embraced the Russian autocracy. She repeatedly speaks of herself as "anointed by God," and once as "Russia's mother." There is on record a conversation between her and Queen Victoria in which she put very strongly this difference between the English monarchy and the Russian. For her, Russia was the Russian people, above all the peasantry. Society she identified with the general corruption which she saw around her. She was always, we may be sure, entirely against the Duma and against the concession of a Russian constitution. Any such suggestion she regarded as a direct wrong to her son, and denounced [it] in the strongest language.

When she married, three of her husband's last five ancestors had perished by assassination. Her first appearance before the Russian public was in the funeral procession of her father-in-law, and the reign from start to finish was soaked in an atmosphere of fatality. She had an antipathy to all court ceremonies. The slightest accident filled her with apprehension. In the period when her most ardent desire was to give an heir to the throne, she met in France a charlatan soul doctor, Philippe, who was brought to Russia but expelled, despite her protection, for meddling in politics during the Japanese War. Philippe gave her a bell as a token that she was to scare away all other counsellors from her husband. She refers to this several times in her letters. Bishop Theophan, when he introduced Rasputin to the court, appears only to have thought that he was substituting a Russian influence for a foreign.

Rasputin at first kept quiet and studied his ground. He saw the imperial family infrequently, and his presence was sought only to comfort the nerves of the empress and her husband, and to reassure them as to the health of their son. M. Gilliard, who was nearly all day with his charge, saw him but once. The meetings ordinarily took place at the little house of Madame Vyrubov outside the palace. Soon, however, Rasputin went on openly with his earlier scandalous life. Toward the end of 1911 sensational happenings attracted public attention to him. Among his former supporters had been the robust bishop of Saratov, Hermogen, a very strong monarchist, and the Monk Heliodor, a notable and popular preacher, also very conservative. An attempt was made to push through the Synod an authorization to ordain Rasputin a priest. This was defeated in view of his well-known dissoluteness. Hermogen was one of its most vigorous opponents. Direct interference from the court obtained at least a partial reversion of the decision of the Synod.

Hermogen again was most vigorous in his protests. He and Heliodor, acting together, arranged a meeting with Rasputin which resulted in threats on both sides; Rasputin threw himself on the bishop as if to strangle him, and when pulled off departed threatening vengeance. Hermogen was then banished to his diocese by order of the emperor and, as he still refused to submit, both he and Heliodor were ultimately relegated to monasteries. The emperor had acted illegally in imposing such a sentence on a bishop without trial by a church court.

This was not the end. Shortly afterwards one Novoselov, a specialist on Russian sects who lectured at the Religious Academy near Moscow, issued a pamphlet giving full details of Rasputin's seductions, which seemed to be numberless. The book was immediately suppressed, but was widely quoted by Russian newspapers beginning with "The Voice of Moscow," the organ of Guchkov. He was leader of the Duma, and for a short time its president, and he had at first hoped to play the part of tribune of the people at the palace and to carry the emperor with him for reform. But he had been severely rebuffed, and chose this ground for attack. The papers were now forbidden to speak of Rasputin. At this time the preliminary censorship no longer existed, and such orders by the government were therefore illegal. Fines could be imposed after publication, but fines in this case the newspapers were ready to pay. Guchkov led a debate in the Duma on this infraction of the law. Rodzianko, who tried to limit and moderate the debate as much as possible, obtained an audience from the emperor, and speaking with absolute plainness laid a number of data before him. "I entreat you," he ended, "in the name of all that is holy for you, for Russia, for the happiness of your successor, drive off from you this filthy adventurer, disperse the growing apprehensions of people loyal to the throne." "He is not here now," said the emperor. Rodzianko took him up, "Let me tell everyone that he will not return." "No," said Nicholas, "I cannot promise you that, but I fully believe all you say. I feel your report was sincere, and I trust the Duma because I trust you." Next day he authorized Rodzianko to make a full investigation, and the plentiful material in the possession of the Synod was handed over to him. The empress tried to get these papers back, but Rodzianko gave a stout refusal to her messenger, saying that she was as much the subject of the emperor as himself. When he was ready with his conclusions he asked for another audience, but Nicholas put him off. He threatened to resign, and was invited to send in a report. Later he heard that it had been studied by Nicholas and the grand duke of Hesse, brother of the empress, while they were together at Livadia in Crimea. The grand duke, as is known, in no way supported the attitude of the empress.

For the time Rasputin disappeared. In the summer of 1912, while the imperial family was at a hunting box in Poland, the tsarevich fell on the gunwale of a boat; the bruise set up internal bleeding and for some weeks his life was despaired of. All the family were distracted with grief. The best doctors declared themselves impotent. The empress then ordered a telegram to be sent to Rasputin, who replied: "This illness is not dangerous; don't let the doctors worry him." From the time of the reception of the telegram the boy rapidly recovered. There is no doubt as to these facts, which were testified to unanimously by various witnesses. Nor is there evidence of any kind for the supposition that the illness was artificially created.

Stolypin before his death in 1911 had reported in the strongest language against Rasputin. The attitude of his successor, Count Kokovtsev, was practically the same. The empress when she met him turned her back on him, and he was curtly dismissed from the post of premier in January 1914. The aged Goremykin who succeeded him, and who possessed throughout the complete confidence of the empress, summed up the question to Rodzianko in the words, "C'est une question clinique."

When war broke out, Rasputin was lying dangerously ill at Tobolsk, where one of his female victims had tried to assassinate him. He sent a telegram to Madame Vyrubov, "Let papa (the emperor) not plan war. It will be the end of Russia and of all of us. We shall be destroyed to the last man." The emperor was very annoyed at this, and never was he more at one with his people than when he appeared on the balcony of the Winter Palace and the vast crowd kneeled in front of him. For the first period of the war the empress devoted herself to hospital work, and spared herself no labor or unpleasantness in the care of the sick; on matters of administration she only ventured tentative and timid opinions.

The discovery of gross munition scandals in the early summer of 1915 roused a wave of national indignation, and seemed at first to bring Russia nearer to an effective constitution than ever before. It must be understood that the constitutional question was still unsettled. The Duma had come to stay, as even the empress at this time admitted. In spite of a manipulated and limited franchise, it had more and more come to represent the nation. The limits on its competence, however, remained; it had once succeeded by moral pressure in removing a minister (Timiriazev), but the ministers were not responsible to it. As is clear from the emperor's talks with Rodzianko, he certainly did not recognize his famous edict of October 30, 1905, which gave full legislative powers to the Duma, as the grant of a constitution, and the Duma's rights had been whittled down since then both by limitations imposed at the outset in the fundamental laws of 1906, and also in practice ever since.

The emperor was in entire agreement with his people as to the needs of his army. He appealed for the utmost efforts, and at Rodzianko's request he established a War Industries Committee on which the Duma was to be represented. The Alliance itself worked in the same direction, for democratic France and England desired to see as hearty as possible a cooperation of the Russian people in the prosecution of the war. The war minister, Sukhomlinov, who had been at least criminally negligent, was dismissed; the emperor also got rid of those of his ministers who were at best half-hearted about the war, Nicholas Maklakov, Shcheglovitov and Sabler, and replaced them by men who had the confidence of the country. It looked as if the movement would go a good deal further. The bulk of the Duma, containing nearly all its best brains, had practically formed into one party under the name of the Progressive Bloc, and it asked for the definite adoption of the principle that the ministry as a whole should be such as to possess the public confidence. Those of the ministers who were of the same view, at this time a majority in the cabinet, went even further; they wrote a letter to the sovereign asking that the aged and obviously incompetent prime minister should be changed. If things had not stopped here, Russia would have done what all her Allies were doing at the same time, namely have formed a national and patriotic Coalition Ministry; but, beyond that, she would also have completed the process toward a constitution which, though often interrupted, had been going on since the emancipation of the serfs in 1861.

It was here that the empress intervened, with the assistance and advice of Rasputin. She got the emperor back to Tsarskoe Selo for several weeks and persuaded him to dismiss from the chief command the Grand Duke Nicholas, who was popular with the Duma and the country. This both she and Rasputin regarded as the most essential victory of all. She then obtained the prorogation of the Duma, and its president and the delegates of other public bodies who begged the emperor to reverse this decision were met with the most chilling refusal. She then persuaded her husband that all the ministers who had, so to speak, struck work against Premier Goremykin should be replaced as soon as possible. We thus enter the critical period which changed the war from being an instrument for producing a Russian constitution into the principal cause of the Russian Revolution. From now till the final collapse Russia was governed by the empress, with Rasputin as her real prime minister.

Two incidents in the summer and autumn sharpened the conflict between the court and the public over the influence of Rasputin. In the summer Rasputin varied his dissolute orgies with a severe course of repentance and visited the tombs of the Patriarchs in Moscow. Presumably he overdid the repentance, for he followed it up with a visit to a notorious resort, the Yar, where he got drunk and behaved in the most scandalous way. His proceedings were recorded in detail by the police, who were present, and were reported by them to one of the most loyal servants of the emperor, General Dzhunkovsky, at this time commander of the palace guard. Dzhunkovsky presented the report without comment to the emperor. Next day he was dismissed from all appointments, and the protest of another intimate friend of the Emperor, Prince Orlov, had the same result. The empress flatly refused to believe such reports and persisted in regarding them as machinations of the police.

In 1915 the emperor was starting with his son for the front when the tsarevich was taken violently ill in the train, which thereupon returned to Tsarskoe Selo. Rasputin was summoned at once and from the time of his visit the boy recovered, as in 1912. Rasputin often played on this theme. Once he fell into fervent prayer and when he had ended declared that he had saved the emperor from assassination. He made many happy guesses, some of which were almost uncanny. On the other hand, the empress herself gives several instances, some of them conspicuous, of predictions which went all wrong.

Neither the emperor nor the empress had at this time any thought whatsoever of a separate peace; the emperor, we know, never entertained such an idea even after abdication. Up till December 30, the date of the last of the empress's letters, we know that she regarded victory in the war as a foregone conclusion, that her chief anxiety was that Russian influence might be overshadowed by British when the victorious peace was made, and that her main desire was that the victory of Russia should be entirely the triumph of her husband. Nicholas at times spoke tentatively of reforms, but throughout this period insisted that they could only follow after the war.

In going to the front the emperor had *ipso facto* more or less abandoned the administration to his wife, who definitely describes herself as his "wall in the rear," speaks even of "wearing the trousers" in the struggle against internal enemies, recalls the time when Catherine the Great (who had much more drastically disposed of her husband) received the ministers, and in the end is absolutely certain that she is "saving Russia." Rasputin, who had on several occasions pushed suggestions as to the war, gradually became the ultimate factor in all decisions. Practically no minister could be appointed except on his recommendation or after accepting allegiance to him.

He initiated the period of his power by making himself absolutely supreme in all church affairs. Let me sum up his principal achievements in this domain. He dismisses an adverse minister of religion, Samarin, who had been the elected marshal of the Moscow nobility; he dismisses his successor, Volzhin, appointed at his own desire; he practically appoints a third minister, Raiev; he commands a public prayer-giving throughout the country, insisting that the order should not pass through the Synod; he appoints as metropolitan of Petrograd, Pitirim, a contemptible sycophant of his own; he negatives a project of the Synod to create seven Metropolitan Sees in Russia; through one of his subordinates and in violation of all rules he creates a new saint, St. John of Tobolsk.

But there was hardly any other department of administration with which he did not interfere. He settles at various times and in various ways the administration of the food supply; he orders an absurdly simplified way of dealing with the question of rations; he confers repeatedly with the minister of finance, whose resignation he at first demands and then defers, and he insists on the issue of an enormous loan. He secures that the whole passenger transport of the country should be suspended for six days for the passage of food — a measure which is made futile by the failure to collect the food supplies at the proper places for transport. He repeatedly interferes both in military appointments and in military operations; he secures the suspension of Sukhomlinov's trial; he secures the dismissal of his successor, Polivanov, who according to all military evidence, including that of Hindenburg, in his few months of office brought about a wonderful recovery of the efficiency of the Russian army; he orders an offensive; he countermands an offensive; he dictates the tactics to be followed in the Carpathians; he even demands to be informed in advance of all military operations, and to know the exact day on which they are to begin, in order that he may decide the issue by his prayers; he arranges the details of the future military entry into Constantinople. He removes the foreign minister, Sazonov, who in Russia was the main arch of the alliance, the trusted friend of the British and French ambassadors. He adjourns and opposes any execution of the emperor's promise to give autonomy to Poland. He dictates telegrams to the King of Serbia and to the King of Greece.

While the empress's letters wipe clean away all the scandalous charges made against her personal character, while they show that up to Rasputin's death she was a fervent Russian patriot who had no thought of a separate peace with Germany, they also prove that she and, through her, Rasputin were the prime authors of the collapse of the empire and of Russia.

The Bolshevist leaders were far away in Switzerland or Canada, and their not numerous followers were out of the picture. The leaders of the Duma, largely in answer to the pressure of Russia's Allies, were doing all that they could to postpone the explosion till after the war. Up to the intervention of the fatal pair in the late summer of 1915, it seemed that the war itself was only bringing nearer what practically all Russia desired. Apart from the terrible depression that followed on the disillusionment of 1915, Russia was then confronted with a monstrous regime which would have seemed impossible in some small duchy in the Middle Ages. In the midst of a world-wide struggle, in a time of the closest collaboration with the best brains of Western statesmanship, the Russian ministers were selected by an ignorant, blind, and hysterical woman on the test of their subservience to an ignorant, fantastic, and debauched adventurer, a test which they could only satisfy by open-eyed self-abasement or at the best by cynical passivity, and the supreme commands of the adventurer permeated every detail of government in every branch of the administration. Meanwhile, in his drunken revels he babbled publicly of his influence over the empress, held a daily *levée* attended by the worst financial swindlers, and preached views both on the war and on the government of the country, which were shared only by the avowed friends of Germany, who evidently had easier access to him than any one else.

It was under the leadership of such a government that the lives of millions of peasants were thrown into the furnace of the World War.

Leopold H. Haimson

Dual Polarization in Urban Russia, 1905–1917

Trained at Harvard University by Michael Karpovich, Leopold Haimson is recognized by many scholars as the preeminent mentor of a generation of historians of late imperial and revolutionary Russia. Early in his career he worked with the distinguished anthropologist Margaret Mead. His first major work — *The Russian Marxists and the Origins of Bolshevism* (1955) — traced the psychological and political influences on the early trajectories of the Russian Social Democrats Martov, Axelrod, Plekhanov, and Lenin. For many years he was the director of the Inter-University Project on the History of Menshevism, from which dozens of publications emerged. Turning from the study of the radical intelligentsia, Haimson began a fundamental revision of the history of the late imperial working class and the crisis of the prerevolutionary period. In the articles presented in edited form here, he demonstrates the double confrontation of society with the tsar and the working class with more moderate social elements.

When a student of the origins of 1917 looks back through the literature that appeared on the subject during the 1920's and early 1930's, he is likely to be struck by the degree of consensus in Soviet and Western treatments of the problem on two major assumptions. The first of these, then almost as widely entertained by Western as by Soviet historians,

Text by Leopold H. Haimson from *Slavic Review*, Vol. XXIII, No. 4 (Dec. 1964) and from Vol. XXIV, No. 1 (March 1965).

was that, just like other "classical" revolutions, the Revolution of 1917 had to be viewed, not as a historical accident or even as the product of immediate historical circumstances, but as the culmination of a long historical process — stretching back to the abolition of serfdom, if not to the appearance at the beginning of the nineteenth century of the Russian revolutionary intelligentsia. The second, balancing, assumption, which even Soviet historians were then still usually prepared to accept, was that, notwithstanding its deep historical roots, this revolutionary process had been substantially accelerated by the additional strains imposed on the Russian body politic by the First World War.

To be sure, even the sharing of these two assumptions allowed for a range of conflicting interpretations and evaluations of the Revolution and its background. Yet it made, however tenuously, for a common universe of discourse, transcending the insuperable values that were already supposed to separate "Marxist" and "bourgeois" historians. The years of the Stalin era and the Cold War have seen the disappearance of this common universe of discourse, and the emergence in its stead — particularly in Soviet and Western representations of the decade immediately leading up to the Revolution of 1917 — of two almost completely incongruent, and almost equally monolithic, points of view.

The first of these, which Soviet historians have advanced to demonstrate the *zakonomernost'*, the historical logic (and therefore the historical legitimacy) of October, distinguishes in the years immediately preceding the First World War the shape of a new, rapidly mounting "revolutionary upsurge." According to the periodization that has become established for this stereotype, the first modest signs that the period of "reaction" that had descended on Russian society with the Stolypin coup d'état had come to an end appeared as early as 1910–11. At first, the new revolutionary upsurge built up only very slowly, and it was only in April–May, 1912, in the wake of the Lena goldfields massacre, that it really began to gather momentum. From this moment on, however, the revolutionary wave is seen as mounting with such dramatic swiftness that by the summer of 1914 the country was ripe for the decisive revolutionary overturn for which the Bolsheviks had been preparing since the summer of 1913. In this scheme, obviously, the war is not viewed as contributing decisively to the unleashing of the revolutionary storm. On the contrary, it is held that by facilitating the suppression of Bolshevik Party organizations and arousing, however briefly, "chauvinistic" sentiments among the still unconscious elements in the laboring masses, its outbreak temporarily retarded the inevitable outcome. It was only in late 1915 that the revolutionary movement resumed the surge which two years later finally overwhelmed the old order.

Partly as a response to this Soviet stereotype and to the gross distortions of evidence that its presentation often involves, we have witnessed during the past quarter of a century the crystallization in many Western representations of the origins of 1917 of a diametrically different, and equally sweeping, point of view. It is that between the Revolution of 1905 and the outbreak of the First World War a process of political and social stabilization was under way in every major sphere of Russian life which, but for the extraneous stresses that the war imposed, would have saved the Russian body politic from revolution — or at least from the radical overturn that Russia eventually experienced with the Bolshevik conquest of power.

It is important to note that not all the data on which these conflicting Western and Soviet conceptions rest are as radically different as their composite effects suggest. Indeed, as far as the period stretching from the Stolypin coup d'état to 1909–10 is concerned ("the years of repression and reaction," as Soviet historians describe them), it is possible to find in Soviet and Western accounts a rough consensus *on what actually happened*, however different the explanations and evaluations that these accounts offer of the events may be.

For example, even Soviet historians are prepared to recognize the disintegration that the revolutionary movement underwent during these years: the success, even against the Bolshevik underground, of the government's repressive measures; the "desertion" of the revolutionary cause by so many of the hitherto radical members of the intelligentsia; the sense of apathy that temporarily engulfed the masses of the working class. Soviet historians also recognize the new rationale inherent in the Regime of the Third of June — the government's attempt to widen its basis of support by winning the loyalties of the well-to-do sector of the city bourgeoisie. And they emphasize, even more than is warranted, the willingness of these elements of the "counterrevolutionary" bourgeoisie to seek, within the framework of the new institutions, an accommodation with the old regime and its gentry supporters. To be sure, Soviet historians are less prepared than their Western confrères to concede the progress that was actually achieved during the Stolypin period in the modernization of Russian life. But the basic trends that they detect during these years — in both government policy and public opinion — are not, for all that, so drastically different.

Where the minimal consensus I have just outlined completely breaks down is in the interpretation of the period stretching from 1910–11 to the outbreak of the First World War. What is basically at stake, as we have seen, is that while Soviet historiography discerns, beginning in the waning days of the Third Duma, the onset of a new, rapidly mounting, revolutionary upsurge, most Western historians are not prepared to concede the validity of any such periodization. On the contrary, with the growing impact of the Stolypin reforms in the Russian countryside and the increasing vitality displayed by the zemstva and other institutions of local self-government, they find the processes of modernization and westernization which they see at work in the earlier period now sweeping even more decisively into the rural and provincial corners of national life. To be sure, many Western historians do recognize the alarming note introduced on the eve of the war by the growing clash between the reactionary attitudes of government circles and the liberal expectations of society (a crisis often excessively personalized in their accounts as a consequence of Stolypin's assassination). But most of them are drawn to the conclusion that in the absence of war this crisis could and would have been resolved without deep convulsions, through the more or less peaceful realization by the liberal elements of Russian society of their long-standing demand for genuine Western parliamentary institutions.

Oddly enough, the completely different representations entertained by Western and Soviet historians of the immediate prewar years rest, in part, on inferences drawn from a phenomenon on which both schools of thought concur — the fact that beginning in 1910–11, the industrial sector of the Russian economy recovered from the doldrums into which it had fallen at the turn of the century and underwent a new major upsurge. Soviet historians are less apt to emphasize the more self-sustained and balanced character that this new industrial upsurge assumes in comparison with the great spurt of the 1890's, and they are less sanguine about its long-range prospects, but they do not deny the fact of the spurt itself. On the contrary, they consider it the major "objective factor" underlying the revival of the Russian labor movement and the recovery of the Bolshevik Party that they distinguish during these years.

It is here that we come to the root of the disagreement between Western and Soviet historians on the dynamics of the prewar period

and, more broadly, on the origins of the Russian Revolution. Even as
cautious and sophisticated a historian as Alexander Gerschenkron sees
in Russia's economic development on the eve of the war, in contrast to
the admittedly socially onerous industrial growth of the 1890's, a factor
making for social and political stabilization. And what is really the crux
of the issue — if only because it involves the core of the Soviet historians' case — Gerschenkron and other Western commentators find this
stabilizing effect of Russia's economic progress on the eve of the war
reflected in a perceptible lessening of social and political tensions in
both the countryside and the working class districts of the cities. "To
be sure," he concedes, "the strike movement of the workers was again
gaining momentum" since April, 1912. But the economic position of
labor was clearly improving, and "in the resurgence of the strike movement, economic problems seemed to predominate." Gerschenkron recognizes that "in the specific conditions of the period any wage conflict
tended to assume a political character because of the ready interventions
of police and military forces on behalf of management. . . . But this did
not mean that the climate of opinion and emotion within the labor
movement was becoming more revolutionary. As shown by the history
of European countries (such as Austria and Belgium), sharp political
struggles marked the period of formation of labor movements that in
actual fact, though not always in the language used, were committed to
reformism. There is little doubt that the Russian labor movement of
those years was slowly turning toward revision and trade unionist lines."

Against this alleged background of the growing moderation of the
Russian labor movement, the picture that Western accounts usually
draw of the fortunes of the Bolshevik Party during the immediate prewar
years is a dismal one. Thus, for example, Leonard Schapiro's treatment
of this period lays primary stress on the state of political paralysis to
which Lenin and his followers appear to have driven themselves by
July, 1914: on the isolation of the Bolshevik faction within the political
spectrum of the RSDRP, as demonstrated by the line-up at the conclusion of the Brussels Conference called in July, 1914, by the International, at which the representatives of all other factions and nationality
parties in the RSDRP with the single exception of the Latvians sided
against the Bolsheviks; on the havoc wrought in Bolshevik Party cadres
by periodic police arrests, guided by Okhrana agents successively hidden at all levels of the party apparatus; on the alleged permanent loss of
popularity that the Bolsheviks suffered among the workers beginning in

the fall of 1913 as a result of their schismatic activity, particularly in the Duma; on the ultimate blow to the Bolsheviks' prestige inflicted by the exposure of their most popular spokesman in Russia, Roman Malinovsky, as just another *agent provocateur.* . . .

In substance, like many other Western historians, Schapiro considers that by July, 1914, a death sentence had been pronounced against the Bolshevik Party, which but for the outbreak of war would shortly have been carried out.

The contrast between this picture and the accounts of Soviet historians is, of course, quite startling. It is not only that their conception of the twenty-seven months leading up to the war is dominated by the image of a majestically rising strike movement which month by month, day by day, became more political in character and revolutionary in temper. It is also that they see this movement as one dominated, in the main, by a now mature, "class conscious," hereditary proletariat, hardened by the experience of the Revolution of 1905 and the years of reaction, and directed by a revived Bolshevik Party to whose flag, at the beginning of 1914, "four-fifths of all the workers of Russia" had rallied. To be sure, the party was faced in its unswerving drive toward revolution by the opposition of various factions of Russian Social Democracy. But according to the Soviet view, these factions represented by the summer of 1914 little more than empty shells resting mainly on the support of "bourgeois opportunist" *intelligenty* in Russia and the emigration. The correctness of the party's course since the Prague Conference of January, 1912, and the Krakow and Poronin Conferences of 1913 — of rejecting any compromise with these "bourgeois opportunist" elements, of combining economic and political strikes and mass demonstrations in a single-minded drive toward an "all-nation political strike leading to an armed uprising" — is considered amply confirmed by the evidence that in July, 1914, such an all-nation strike was already "under way" and an armed uprising "in the offing." Indeed, Soviet historians allege, the revolutionary upsurge had reached such a level by the beginning of 1914 that even the leading circles of the "counter-revolutionary" bourgeoisie had come to realize the irreparable "crash" of the Regime of the Third of June.

What are the realities submerged beneath these harshly conflicting representations? Any careful examination of the evidence in contemporary primary sources suggests, it seems to me, that the vision advanced by some Western historians of the growing moderation of the Russian labor movement can be even partially upheld only for the period stretching from the Stolypin coup d'état to the spring and summer of 1912. This, almost up to its conclusion, was a period of relative labor tranquillity, as in a context of economic stagnation the masses of the Russian working class relapsed into apathy, after the defeat of their great expectations of 1905.

It was in this ultimately deceptive setting of labor peace, and of the futile and increasingly degrading spectacle of the Bolsheviks' collapsing underground struggle (this was the classic period of Bolshevik "expropriations"), that the leaders of the Menshevik faction began to articulate the philosophy and programs of an open labor party and labor movement. The current task of Social Democracy, they insisted, was not to pursue in the underground, under the leadership of a handful of intelligentsia conspirators, now clearly unattainable maximalist objectives. It was to outline for the labor movement goals, tactics, and organizational forms which, even within the narrow confines of the existing political framework, would enable the masses of the working class to struggle, day by day, for tangible improvements in their lives and to become through the experience of this struggle "conscious" and responsible actors — capable of making their own independent contribution to the vision of a free and equitable society. Not only did the Menshevik "Liquidators" articulate this vision of an open labor party and labor movement during these years but they appeared to be making progress in erecting the scaffolding of the institutions through which the vision was to be realized. They were seeking to organize open trade unions, cooperatives, workers' societies of self-improvement and self-education, and workers' insurance funds: organs intended not only to help the worker but also to enable him to take his life into his own hands. Even more significantly, the Menshevik "Liquidators" appeared to be succeeding during this period in developing, really for the first time in the history of the Russian labor movement, a genuine workers' intelligentsia animated by their own democratic values, which, it seems, would have been far more capable than any self-appointed intelligentsia leadership of eventually providing an effective bridge between educated society and the masses of the workers, thus fulfilling at long last Akselrod's and Martov's dream of "breaking down the walls that separate the life of the proletariat from the rest of the life of this country."

To be sure, in 1910–11, the Mensheviks' workers' intelligentsia still appeared very thin, and the number and size of their open labor unions pitifully small in comparison with the size of the labor force, or indeed with the level that the organization of the working class had reached on the eve of the Stolypin coup d'état. And even these puny shoots were being periodically cut down by the authorities, with only the feeblest echoes of protest from the still somnolent labor masses. . . .

The news of the [Lena goldfields] massacre provoked a great outburst of public protest and, what was more important, a veritable explosion in the Russian working class. Between April 14 and 22, close to 100,000 workers struck in Petersburg alone, and the total number of strikers in the country as a whole probably reached about 250,000. This wave of protest strikes and demonstrations persisted almost without interruption through mid-May. May Day, 1912, saw nearly half a million workers out on the streets, the highest number since 1905, and this was a correct augury of the incidence and scope of political strikes and demonstrations during the balance of the year. Even the official statistics compiled by the Factory Inspectors of the Ministry of Trade and Industry, which undoubtedly were seriously underestimated, recorded that close to 550,000 workers had participated in political strikes during 1912, a level well below that of the revolutionary years 1905–6 but much higher than that of any other previous years in the history of the Russian labor movement. . . .

Indeed, it appears that from the Lena massacre to the outbreak of war, the progress of the strike movement was characterized by an almost continuous flow in which political and economic currents were inextricably mixed: quite often, even the ostensible objectives of individual strikes combined political and economic demands; and even more notably, the individual waves of "economic" strikes and "political" strikes and demonstrations proved mutually reinforcing, each seemingly giving the next additional impetus, additional momentum. By the beginning of the summer of 1914, contemporary descriptions of the labor scene forcibly suggest, the workers, especially in Petersburg, were displaying a growing spirit of *buntarstvo* — of violent if still diffuse opposition to all authority — and an instinctive sense of class solidarity, as they encountered the repressive measures of state power and what appeared to them the indifference of privileged society. . . .

If the Mensheviks were originally inclined to consider this mutual confrontation of workers and society a positive indication of the growing class maturity of both, they were soon to change their minds.

The first signs of alarm were sounded within a few months, with the returns, in the fall of 1912, of the elections to the Fourth Duma. In these elections, as Lenin and his followers untiringly emphasized thereafter, Bolshevik candidates won in six of the nine labor curiae in Russia, including all six of the labor curiae in the major industrial provinces. In their published commentaries on the election returns the Menshevik leaders pointed out (most often quite accurately) the major flaws in the Bolshevik claims to a sweeping victory, but in their private correspondence, they conceded more readily that, whatever the extenuating circumstances, the results of the elections in the labor curiae had been a definite setback. Martov observed in a letter to Potresov: "The failure of the Mensheviks in the labor curiae (partially compensated by [their] moral victory in Petersburg) shows once more that Menshevism caught on too late to the reviving danger of Leninism and overestimated the significance of its temporary wholesale disappearance."

The developments on the labor scene in 1913, and especially during the first six months of 1914, would amply confirm Martov's estimate of the significance of these election returns. Not only were these eighteen months generally characterized by a steady rise in the spirit of *buntarstvo*, of the elemental, revolutionary explosiveness of the strike movement, particularly in the capital. Not only were they marked by a growing responsiveness on the part of the amorphous and largely anonymous committees in charge of the strikes, as well as of the workers' rank and file, to the reckless tactics of the Bolsheviks and to their "unmutilated" slogans of a "democratic republic," "eight-hour day," and "confiscation of gentry lands." They also saw the Mensheviks lose control of the open labor organizations they had struggled so hard to build. From the spring and summer of 1913, when the Bolsheviks, heeding the resolutions of the Krakow and Poronin Conferences, began to concentrate their energies on the conquest of the open labor organizations, the pages of the Mensheviks' journals and their private correspondence were filled with the melancholy news of the loss of one position after another — by the very Menshevik-oriented workers' intelligentsia in which the wave of the future had once been discerned.

To note but a few of the major landmarks:

In late August, 1913, the Mensheviks were routed by their Bolshevik opponents from the governing board of the strongest union in Petersburg, the Union of Metalworkers (*Soiuz metallistov*). In January, 1914, an even more bitter pill for the Menshevik initiators of the labor insurance movement, the Bolsheviks won, by an equally decisive vote, control of the labor representation on both the All Russian Insurance Council and the Petersburg Insurance Office (*Stolichnoe strakhovoe prisutstvie*). Even more surprising, by late April, 1914, they could claim the support of half the members of the newly re-elected governing board of that traditional citadel of Menshevism in the Petersburg labor movement, the Printers' Union (*Soiuz pechatnikov*). In July, 1914, when the Bolsheviks laid their case before the Bureau of the Socialist Internationale for being the only genuine representatives of the Russian working class, they claimed control of 14½ out of 18 of the governing boards of the trade unions in St. Petersburg and to 10 out of the 13 in Moscow. . . .

To what source was the new mood of the labor movement to be traced? The Bolsheviks had a simple explanation: The workers' new mood was merely a reflection of the growth to consciousness of a now mature hereditary Russian proletariat — recovered from the defeats of 1905, hardened by the years of reaction, and rallied solidly behind the Bolshevik Party. Needless to say, Menshevik commentators found this explanation wanting. Indeed, in their writings of the period we find them groping for precisely an opposite answer: The laboring masses which had crowded into the new labor movement during the years of the new industrial upsurge — and of the new explosive strike wave — were in the main no longer the class-conscious, mature proletariat of 1905. Some of the most acute Menshevik observers (Martov, Levitsky, Gorev, Sher) pointed specifically to the social and political effects of the influx into the industrial working class of two new strata.

The first of these was the younger generation of the working class of the cities, the urban youths who had grown to working age since the Revolution of 1905 — without the chastening experience of the defeats of the Revolution, or the sobering influence of participating in the trade unions and other labor organizations during the years of reaction. It was these youths, "hot-headed and impulsive," "untempered by the lessons of the class struggle," who now constituted the intermediary link between the leading circles of the Bolshevik Party and the laboring masses. It was they who now provided, in the main, the correspondents and distributors of Bolshevik newspapers, who instigated the workers' resolutions and petitions in support of Bolshevik stands, and who dominated the amorphous, *ad hoc* strike committees which were providing whatever leadership still characterized the elemental strike wave. More recently, in the spring and summer of 1913, it had been these green youths who had begun to flow from the strike committees into the open trade unions and had seized their leadership from the older generation of Menshevik trade unionists. "Here," noted one observer, "the representatives of two different periods, [men] of different habits, different practical schools — two forces of workers, "young" and "old" — have encountered one another for the first time . . . [the takeover] which occurred extremely quickly, for many almost unexpectedly, took place in an atmosphere of patricidal conflict."

Of course, the cadres of the new generation of the hereditary working class of the cities would have remained leaders without followers had it not been for the influx into the labor force of a second, much more massive, new stratum. These were the recruits, usually completely unskilled, who, from 1910 on — the year of the "take-off" of the new industrial upsurge and of the turning point in the Stolypin agrarian reforms — had begun to pour into the labor armies of the cities from the countryside. It was these many thousands of ex-peasants, as yet completely unadapted to their new factory environment, "driven by instincts and feelings rather than consciousness and calculation," who gave the mass movement "its disorganized, primitive, elemental character," noted Martov's younger brother, Levitsky. Naturally, these "unconscious" masses proved most responsive to the extremist objectives and tactics advocated by the Bolsheviks: to their demands for "basic" as against "partial" reforms, to their readiness to support any strikes, regardless of their purpose and degree of organization. Above all, the Bolshevik "unmutilated" slogans of an eight-hour day, "complete democratization," "confiscation of gentry lands" — and the basic vision underlying these slogans of a grand union of workers and peasants arrayed against all of society, "from Purishkevich to Miliukov" — were calculated to sound a deep echo among these new elements of the working class, which combined with their current resentments about factory life the still fresh grievances and aspirations that they had brought from the countryside. . . .

We know, of course, that the increasingly explosive strike wave broadly coincided with an industrial upsurge which saw the Russian industrial labor force grow from some 1,793,000 in January, 1910, to approximately 2,400,000 in July, 1914, a rise of over 30 percent. And obviously this sharp and sudden increase in the labor force could be achieved only if to the recruitment of a new generation of urban workers was added the massive inswell into the urban labor market of landless and land-poor peasants, freed of their ties to the land by the Stolypin legislation — particularly by the arbitrary provisions of the statutes of 1910 and 1911. The literature of this period is replete with reports of the influx of these raw recruits into the industrial army. But let us refine the analysis, and focus our attention on those sectors of the Russian labor force which appear to lead the contemporary strike movement, and especially those strikes which bear a distinctly political character. One can easily distinguish two such sectors. The first of these may be defined geographically: it is the labor force of the province and particularly the city of Petersburg and suburbs, which in the first six months of 1914 contributed close to 50 per cent of the total of 1,254,000 strikers estimated for the country as a whole, and almost two-thirds of the 982,000 strikers listed as political. Secondly, when one compares strike statistics for different industries (as against different regions) it becomes apparent that by far the heaviest incidence of strikers, particularly of political strikers — in Petersburg just as in the country as a whole — is to be found among the workers in the metalworking industry.

It is notable, and undoubtedly significant, that these two sectors of the labor force — which we have singled out because of their exceptional revolutionary explosiveness — underwent during the years of the new industrial upsurge an expansion well above that of the Russian labor force as·a whole: they grew by an average of roughly 50 percent as against the national average of less than 30 percent. If we consider the necessity of allowing for replacement as well as increases in the labor force, we may assume that by 1914 well over half of the workers in Petersburg, as well as in the metalworking industry in the country as a whole, were persons who at best had undergone a very brief industrial experience. It has already been noted that while some of these recruits were urban youths who reached working age during these years, most had to be drawn from outside the cities. In this connection, one further observation appears relevant: It is that since the beginning of the century a marked shift in the pattern of labor recruitment from the countryside into the Petersburg labor force had been taking place. As the labor supply available in Petersburg province and in other provinces with relatively developed manufacturing or handicraft industries declined, a growing percentage of the recruits into the Petersburg labor force had to be drawn from the almost purely agricultural, overpopulated, central provinces of European Russia — the very provinces in which the dissolution of repartitional tenure, achieved as often as not under irresistible administrative and economic pressure, was making itself most heavily and painfully felt.

A vast mass of workers who combined with their resentments about the painful and disorienting conditions of their new industrial experience a still fresh sense of grievance about the circumstances under which they had been compelled to leave the village. A new generation of young workers of urban origin to lead them — impatient, romantic, singularly responsive to maximalist appeals. Our puzzle would appear to be resolved if it were not for a disconcerting fact. The conditions I have so far described, except perhaps for the presence of a somewhat lower percentage of young workers of urban origin, also largely obtained in other areas and sectors of the Russian labor force, which remained, however, less animated than the ones we have singled out by the spirit of *buntarstvo* of which we have been seeking the roots. These conditions probably obtained, for example, almost as much in the Donbas as in Petersburg; and for workers in chemicals as much as for those in the metalworking industry. This is why we necessarily have to add one further element which, for obvious reasons, was generally absent in most contemporary Menshevik analyses: the role exercised by Bolshevik party cadres — workers and *intelligenty* alike. If the Petersburg workers displayed greater revolutionary explosiveness, and especially greater responsiveness to Bolshevik appeals, than the workers of the Donbas, it was undoubtedly in part because of the Petersburg workers' greater exposure to Bolshevik propaganda and agitation. Similarly, if the workers in the metalworking industry were so much more agitated politically than the workers in other industries, it was partly because the labor force in the metalworking industry consisted of a peculiar combination of skilled and unskilled, experienced and inexperienced, workers — the older and more skilled workers contributing in their contacts with the young and unskilled a long-standing exposure to revolutionary, and specifically Bolshevik, indoctrination. It is not accidental that so many of the major figures in the Bolshevik Party cadres of the period — Voroshilov, Kalinin, Kiselev, Shotman, to cite but a few — had been workers with a long *stazh* in the metalworking industry. . . .

And all this anger and bitterness now struck a responsive chord in the masses of the working class. Given this correspondence of mood, given the even more precise correspondence between the image of state and society that the Bolsheviks advanced and the instinctive outlook of the laboring masses, the Bolshevik Party cadres were now able to play a significant catalytic role. They succeeded, as we have seen, in chasing the Menshevik "Liquidators" out of the existing open labor organizations. They transformed these organizations into "fronts" through which they managed to absorb, if not to control, the young workers who headed the Petersburg strike movement. Through the pages of *Pravda*, through the verbal appeals of their deputies in the Duma, by leaflet and by word of mouth, they managed to stir up and exploit the workers' embittered mood. Thus, it seems fair to say that by the outbreak of war the Bolshevik center in Petersburg, and particularly its open organizations, had developed into an organism whose arms, while still very slender and vulnerable, were beginning to extend into many corners of the life of the working class. . . .

If I might summarize my own, and to some degree, Martov's argument, it is that by 1914 a dangerous process of polarization appeared to be taking place in Russia's major urban centers between an *obshchestvo* that had now reabsorbed the vast majority of the once alienated elements of its intelligentsia (and which was even beginning to draw to itself many of the workers' own intelligentsia) and a growing discontented and disaffected mass of industrial workers, now left largely exposed to the pleas of an embittered revolutionary minority.

This is not to suggest that by the outbreak of war the Bolshevik Party had succeeded in developing a secure following among the masses of the working class. The first year of the war would show only too clearly how fragile its bonds to the supposedly conscious Russian proletariat still were. Indeed, it bears repeating that the political threat of Bolshevism in 1914 stemmed primarily not from the solidity of its organizations nor from the success of its efforts at ideological indoctrination, but from the workers' own elemental mood of revolt. . . .

Two and a half months before the outbreak of the war, Lenin already detected the chief immediate threat to his party's fortunes not to his "right" but to his "left" — in the possibility of premature, diffuse, revolutionary outbreaks by the Russian working class.

The elements of strength and weakness in the Bolshevik leadership of the labor movement on the eve of war and the relative significance of this movement as a revolutionary force are graphically illustrated by the contrast between the general strike which broke out in the working class districts of Petersburg in the early days of July, 1914, and the nature of the mutual confrontation of the workers and educated society that had characterized the high tide of the Revolution of 1905. On the earlier historical occasion — in September and October, 1905 — the workers of Petersburg and Moscow had rejoined, however briefly, the world of Russian educated and privileged society. Flocking out of their tawdry factory districts, they had descended into the hearts of the two capitals to join in society's demonstrations, to shout its slogans, to listen in the amphitheaters of universities and institutes to the impassioned speeches of youthful intelligentsia agitators. This had been the background of the awesome spectacle of the truly general strikes which paralyzed Petersburg and other cities of European Russia during the October days, driving the frightened autocracy to its knees.

In July, 1914, in protest against the brutal suppression by police detachments of a meeting of the Putilov workers called in support of the strike in the Baku oil fields, a strike as massive and explosive as any that had erupted among the workers in 1905 swept the outlying working class districts of Petersburg. (A call for such a general strike had been issued by the Bolsheviks' Petersburg Party Committee on the evening of July 3.) On July 7, three days after the opening of the strike, Poincaré arrived in Petersburg on a state visit to dramatize the solidity of the Franco-Russian alliance against the Central Powers. By this time, according to official estimates, over 110,000 workers had joined in the strikes. Almost all the factories and commercial establishments in the working class districts of the city were now closed, and many thousands of workers were clashing in pitched battles with Cossacks and police detachments. The news of the growing international crisis and the accounts of Poincaré's visit had crowded the reports of labor unrest out of the front pages. But even during the two days of Poincaré's stay, newspaper readers were told in the inside columns that workers were demonstrating in the factory districts, throwing rocks at the police and being fired upon in return, tearing down telegraph and telephone poles, attacking street cars, stoning their passengers, ripping out their controls, and in some cases dragging them off the rails to serve as street barricades.

It was also during the two days of Poincaré's visit that some workers' demonstrations, brandishing red flags and singing revolutionary songs, sought to smash their way out of the factory districts into the center of the capital. But Cossacks and mounted police blocked their access to the bridges of the Neva as well as on the Petersburg side, and the heart of the capital remained largely still. . . .

In a two-page review of the strike, published on July 12, the reporters whom *Riech'* had sent out to the factory districts described some of the scenes they had witnessed during the preceding three days. The biggest clashes, they agreed, had occurred on the night of July 9 and during the succeeding day. Many thousands of workers had then clashed with the police — at times fighting them with clubs, or hailing them with rocks from behind improvised barricades. Women and children had joined in building these barricades — out of telephone and telegraph poles, overturned wagons, boxes, and armoires. No sooner was a demonstration dispersed, or a barricade destroyed, than the workers, after evacuating their wounded, would regroup, and clashes would start all over again. Whole districts were without light, their gas and kerosene lamps having been destroyed. Most commercial establishments were closed, particularly the wine shops and taverns which the workers themselves had shut to maintain and demonstrate the discipline in their ranks. By the evening of the twelfth, the peak of the violence was over, as army and police detachments, with drawn bayonets, patrolled the now largely deserted streets. One of the *Riech'* reporters recorded these sights (the likes of which he said he hadn't seen since 1905), and noted the general background of devastation: the shattered street lights, the uptorn telegraph poles, the deserted barricades, the trolley cars abandoned or overturned, the closed factories and stores. "And on the Petersburg side, the usual traffic, the usual life, and the trolleys are moving about as usual."

It was not until July 15, four days before the outbreak of the war, that order in the factory districts of Petersburg was fully restored.

The unfolding of the Petersburg strike had given rise to sympathy strikes and demonstrations in other industrial centers: in Moscow and Warsaw, . . . , Riga, and Tallin, Kiev, Odessa, even Tiflis. But nowhere, not even in Warsaw and Moscow, had these strikes displayed a degree of massiveness and revolutionary intensity comparable to that of the Petersburg movement.

Yet another factor was even more crucial: the inability of the Petersburg workers to mobilize, in time, active support among other groups in society. To be sure, by July 12–14 shocked editorials had begun to appear, not only in liberal organs such as *Riech'* and *Russkiia viedomosti* but even in the conservative *Novoe vremia*, attacking the government for its last-minute declaration of a state of siege, condemning its labor policies as calculated only to exacerbate further the workers' already "monstrous anger and despair," arguing that only complete legalization of the open labor organizations could possibly restore domestic tranquillity. But perhaps partly because of the gathering international crisis, these appear to have been the only articulate expressions of the concern of educated society. No demonstrations, no public meetings, no collective petitions — no expressions of solidarity even barely comparable to those that Bloody Sunday had evoked were now aroused. Thus, in the last analysis, the most important source of the political impotence revealed by the Petersburg strike was precisely the one that made for its "monstrous" revolutionary explosiveness: the sense of isolation, of psychological distance, that separated the Petersburg workers from educated, privileged society.

Where does this analysis leave us with respect to the general problem of political and social stability in Russian national life on the eve of the war that we posed at the beginning of this discussion? Clearly, it seems to me, the crude representations to be found in recent Soviet writings of the "revolutionary situation" already at hand in July, 1914, can hardly be sustained. Yet when one views the political and social tensions evident in Russian society in 1914 in a wider framework and in broader perspective, any flat-footed statement of the case for stabilization appears at least equally shaky. . . .

By July, 1914, along with the polarization between workers and educated, privileged society, . . . a second process of polarization — this one between the vast bulk of privileged society and the tsarist regime — appeared almost equally advanced. Unfolding largely detached from the rising wave of the labor movement, this second process could not affect its character and temper but was calculated to add a probably decisive weight to the pressure against the dikes of existing authority. By 1914 this second polarization had progressed to the point where even the most moderate spokesmen of liberal opinion were stating publicly, in the Duma and in the press, that an impasse had been reached between the state power and public opinion, which some argued could be resolved only by a revolution of the left or of the right.

Perhaps the most dramatic symptom of this growing political crisis was the progressive disintegration of existing intra- and inter-party alignments, particularly on the political spectrum of the liberal center. This political *bouleversement*, which finally came to general public notice in late 1913 and early 1914 as "the crisis of the parties," actually appears to have been developing, largely behind the scenes, from the opening days of the Fourth Duma. . . .

In a long wail of despair, Peter Struve, the most eloquent spokesman in Russian liberalism for an "evolutionary orientation," described in [an] issue of *Russkaia mysl'* the course of collision with society which the government and its fanatic supporters appeared to be setting. Ever since the failure of the Stolypin experiment, he recalled, the state power had been engaged in an increasingly bitter struggle against the very legal order that it had sanctioned with the October Manifesto. The state power recognized the legal existence of the Duma; yet with every weapon at their command its agents sought to stifle the existence of the majority of the parties represented in it. It purportedly recognized society's right to representation; yet its bureaucracy zealously struggled to suppress society's organs of local self-government. Given these basic contradictions in the Russian body politic, there was a superficial logic to the "shameless propaganda" now circulating in higher official circles about the need for new violations of the Fundamental Laws, for a counterrevolution of the right which at a minimum should reduce the Duma to a purely consultative organ. But the pursuit of such a course, Struve desperately argued, would inevitably lead in short order to a radical revolutionary overturn. The only real salvation for the state power lay in its own restoration to health, a restoration which could be achieved only through the abandonment of its suicidal struggle against society. "Never was the country so much in need of what one calls a healthy *vlast'*, and never was the real state of affairs so distant from the realization of such a healthy, or normal, *vlast'*." . . .

Indeed, many signs of economic and social progress could be found in the Russian province of the year 1914 — the introduction of new crops, new techniques and forms of organization in agriculture, and the industrialization of the countryside; the growing literacy among the lower strata and invigorated cultural life among the upper strata of provincial society. But no more than in the major cities were these signs of progress and change in the localities to be viewed as evidence of the achievement or indeed the promise of greater political stability. Even Gessen, generally a professional optimist, felt compelled to note the all-pervasive and increasingly acute conflict in provincial life between "society," seeking to organize, to strengthen its bonds, and local bureaucratic administrative organs. Under the immediate stimulus of the Beilis affair, the fissure in provincial circles between officialdom and educated society had been revealed to be as deep and as unbridgeable as in the two capitals. An article published by S. Elpatevsky in *Russkoe bogatstvo* in January, 1914, strikingly described the two almost hermetically separated worlds that were now apparent in most provincial towns:

> *There is taking place a kind of gathering on the opposing sides of the wall which is dividing Russia. On one side have gathered the united* dvorianstvo, *the united bureaucracy, office-holders — generally the people who, in one way or another, "are feeding at the public trough." On the other side have gathered the plain citizens* [obyvateli], *the crowd of provincial society.*

. . .

One paradoxical aspect of the polarization between state and society under these gathering clouds of revolution and counterrevolution deserves to be considered further, for its examination will lead us to some of the distinctive and essential dimensions of the historical situation that has been discussed throughout this essay. It is clear that in many respects the Russian state — on the eve of the First World War just as in February, 1917 — was ripe, indeed overripe, for a takeover by a new *pays réel*: by new would-be ruling groups and institutions ready to assume formal control of national life.

The fumes of the Beilis case, the brewing scandal of the Rasputin-shchina, the striking absence in official circles of men capable of governing provided dramatic evidence of the advanced state of decomposition of the tsarist regime: of the disintegration of its intellectual and moral resources and of its loss of support among any of the viable social elements in the country at large. At the same time, it appeared that in the proliferating organs of self-expression and independent activity of educated society — in the political and journalistic circles surrounding the State Duma and the local organs of self-government, in the cooperative societies of city and country, in the various societies of public enlightenment and the now more militant associations of big business and industry — a whole organized structure of order and potential authority had now crystallized, far better prepared to take and effectively exercise power than had been the case, say, of any of their institutional counterparts on the eve of the French Revolution. . . .

The character, although not necessarily the gravity, of the political and social crisis evident in urban Russia by the eve of the war is more reminiscent of the revolutionary processes that we shall see at work during Russia's second revolution than of those that had unfolded in Russia's first. Or to put the matter in the form of a "vérité de La Palisse," that, as we knew all along, 1914 is, if only approximately, a half-way station between 1905 and 1917. What the war years would do was not to conceive, but to accelerate substantially, the two broad processes of polarization that had already been at work in Russian national life during the immediate prewar period.

On the one hand, these years would witness not only a sharpening of the dissatisfaction of educated society with the inept, helpless tsarist regime but also the further crystallization — in the State Duma, the Zemskii Soiuz, the Soiuz Gorodov, the War-Industrial Committees, and other central and local organs of public expression and activity — of a seemingly effective network of new organization, new order, new authority, fully prepared to take over and hold the reins of power as soon as the old state power fell.

But these same years witnessed as well the further progress of the other process of polarization that we have already observed in the prewar period — the division between the educated, privileged society and the urban masses — a process which would sap the new regime of much of its potential effectiveness, its authority, its legitimacy, even before it actually took over. Underlying the progress of this second polarization were not only the specific economic deprivations caused by the war but also the substantial acceleration of the changes in the character and temper of the industrial working class that we already noted in the immediate prewar years: the influx at an even more rapid tempo of new elements into the industrial army under the impact of the war boom and of the army's drafts.

Some of these new workers were women, some were adolescent or under-age boys, some (in the metalworking industry, for example) were older industrial workers shifted from nonstrategic to strategic industries, but most, we presume, continued to be drawn to the industrial army from the countryside — in the first order, from the overpopulated agricultural provinces of Central European Russia, which in 1913–14 had already provided such suitable recruits for Bolshevik agitation. The experience of 1917 would show only too clearly, if admittedly under the stresses of war, what a few more months of this agitation could do.

To be sure, the experience of the first eighteen months of the war temporarily obscured the workings of these disruptive processes. These months witnessed an indubitable crack-up of the Bolshevik Party under the combined blows of police arrests and of the draft of Bolshevik Party workers. Indeed, they saw a brief rally of public opinion under the spell of the national emergency which unquestionably affected not only educated society but also substantial elements of the "laboring masses." Even more notably, this period saw an accentuation, or at least a sharper articulation, of the desire already displayed in the pre-war period by the older, Menshevik-oriented, labor intelligentsia to rejoin the framework of national life. Left momentarily at the center of the Russian labor scene, many of the most prominent figures in this workers' intelligentsia now joined the Labor Groups of the War-Industrial Committees. Some did so with the undivided purpose of supporting the war effort; others, admittedly, with a more complex mixture of "defensist" sympathies and revolutionary hopes — both elements, however, articulating and solidifying by their participation in these organs of "society" more conciliatory attitudes toward the liberal elements represented in them.

But the political and social significance of these phenomena was proven, all too quickly, to be ephemeral. By late 1915–early 1916, some of the leaders of "advanced opinion" already resumed, this time in earnest, plots for the overthrow of the tsarist regime. By 1916, the wave of labor unrest once again began to swell. And within another year, the Menshevik workers' intelligentsia, whose stature had been so suddenly and dramatically magnified by the special conditions of war, would demonstrate an equally dramatic inability to influence, even minimally, the course of events. One of the most notable phenomena of 1917, which became evident almost from the very first days of the Revolution, was the failure of any of the leaders of the Workers' Group in the Central War-Industrial Committee to strike any responsive chord among the rank and file of their own working class, and to play a political role even comparable to that of their nonproletarian, but more radically inclined, confrères in the Menshevik Party. By this time the wall of mutual incomprehension that had come to separate this workers' intelligentsia from the rank and file of the laboring masses rose almost as high as the wall that these masses perceived between themselves and "bourgeois" society. This was to be one of the most startling features of 1917, the sorry outcome of the Mensheviks' long effort in the aftermath of 1905 to build in Russia a genuinely Europeanized labor movement.

As a historian's eyes follow the unfolding of the revolutionary processes that have been outlined in this essay, they may well search for the illumination to be derived from comparative historical perspectives — from the comparisons that we have already implicitly drawn of the revolutionary situations in Russia in 1905, 1914, and 1917; from comparisons between the character of the labor disorders in Petersburg on the eve of the First World War and that of contemporary labor unrest in other European capitals; from the even bolder and broader comparisons that might be drawn between the prehistory of the great Revolution of 1917 and that of the great Revolution of 1789. Yet, it seems to me, the differences that any of these comparisons might bring out would loom far larger than the similarities.

There is an obvious singularity about the decade leading up to 1917 in the perspective of contemporary Western experience. This singularity lies, at least in part, in the fact that these years incorporate and compress to such an extraordinary degree the two sharply distinct revolutionary processes that I have discussed — processes which in the history of other European countries are not to be found coinciding, with such intensity, in any single phase of historical development. The nearest equivalent to the political and social attitudes displayed by the Russian workers in 1914 is probably to be found on the prewar European scene among elements of the French working class, which manifested at least a comparable sense of alienation from the existing political order and the prospering world of other strata of French society. But even if this state of affairs had led by the eve of the war to a serious crisis in the system of the Third Republic, the crisis was not further complicated and aggravated by the remaining presence on the stage of substantial vestiges of an old order and an Old Regime. By the same token, if vestiges of an Old Regime may be argued to be far more visible on the German political and social scene of 1914, and to have contributed to an unresolved deadlock between the Imperial Government and the Reichstag, it surely would be difficult to claim that the social attitudes that the German working class contributed to this crisis are even barely comparable to those of the stormy Russian proletariat.

If we view the prehistory of 1917 in the perspective of the decade in Russia's development leading up to 1905, its singularity does not lie so much in the range of groups and attitudes represented among the opposition and revolutionary forces. After all, the all-nation movement which finally emerged in October, 1905 — only to disintegrate even more quickly than it had come together — was marked by an even greater heterogeneity of constituent elements: gentry, professional men, and belatedly aroused big businessmen and industrialists; workers and peasants, or, more precisely, would-be representatives of a peasant movement; Bolsheviks, Mensheviks, Socialist Revolutionaries, and that grab bag of political tendencies gathered under the umbrella of the Soiuz Osvobozhdeniia.

And all these groups and tendencies were animated by quite different underlying attitudes toward the economic and social processes that were at work in national life. Some were driven to revolutionary opposition by their impatience for a clearer and fuller articulation in Russian life of the values and institutional forms attendant on their vision of a modern world. Others were filled with resentment largely by the very forces that were at work in this modernization, or at least by the forms that this modernization had assumed during the Witte experiment: by the sufferings and deprivations that weighed on the countryside, the darkness and strangeness of life in the barracks and hovels of the industrial slums, the gross and offensive sight of the new rule of money. And even the members of the intelligentsia, who had contributed so much to patching this coalition together, had temporarily succeeded in doing so precisely because so many of them — drawn as they were from many of these sharply separated corners of Russian society — actually combined in themselves, beneath the flimsy logical constructions of ideologies, the maelstrom of chaotic and conflicting attitudes represented in national life.

While this heterogeneity of the constituent groups in the all-nation opposition to absolutism at the beginning of the century, and of the underlying attitudes of the members of the intelligentsia who led them (Liberals, Marxists, and Populists alike), ultimately accounts for the rapidity of the disintegration that this coalition underwent in the crucible of 1905, it also explains, of course, the irresistible power that it briefly manifested. If only for a flickering historical moment, the autocracy was confronted by the outline of a new and seemingly united nation. For this flickering moment, the intelligentsia, which had emerged as the prototype — the microcosm — of this united nation, managed to induce the groups under its sway to bury the long-standing differences of interests, outlook, and values that had separated them and to agree to a common set of discrete political objectives, to a common vision, however partial and abstracted, of Russia's immediate future if not of her ultimate destiny.

The potential significance of this achievement of getting different groups to agree on a limited set of political objectives — of finding a common denominator for some interests and suspending, postponing the clash of others — should not be underestimated, since it constituted the essential prerequisite for the successful launching of that great French Revolution of 1789 whose image possessed the political imagination of so much of Russia's intelligentsia in 1905: for in the prerevolutionary years 1787–88 the opposition to the *ancien régime* drew much of its strength not only from the "progressive" aspirations of the Third Estate but also from the resentments of nobles and churchmen rebelling, in the name of thinly disguised feudal liberties, against the administrative innovations of a haltingly modernizing state. To be sure, in the France of 1789, the balance between "progressive" and "reactionary" forces had been far more heavily weighted in favor of the former than turned out to be the case in the Russia of 1905. Still, if any even partially valid historical analogy is to be sought between the French and Russian prerevolutionary experiences, it should be drawn, it seems to me, between the French prerevolution and the years in Russian life leading up to 1905, not to 1917.

Indeed, it is difficult to escape the conclusion that the failure of Russia's first revolution, and the repudiation that it induced among so many in the intelligentsia of their traditional revolutionary ethos, substantially contributed to the character and pattern of the second. For if the intelligentsia's sense of messianic mission, which its *Vekhi* critics so bitterly deplored, had unquestionably contributed to the growth of revolutionary tendencies and thus to the instability of the existing political order, it had also made — particularly from the 1890's, when both Populists and Marxists had been converted to the cause of political freedom — for the translation of the new feeling of mobility in national life into a somewhat greater sense of social cohesion; for the bridging, however slow and precarious, of the psychological chasms that had hitherto divided Russia's society of estates.

By the same token, it may well be argued that the failure of the intelligentsia to secure these bridges in 1905 — even in the minimal form of a political and social framework temporarily acceptable to a broad spectrum of Russian society — and the decline in subsequent years of its sense of messianic mission substantially contributed to the character and gravity of the divisions in Russian life that we have examined in this essay. For, as it turned out, a brief historical interval, the

partially reformed political order gained a new lease on life. But this
brief measure of *political stability* was achieved in part at the price of
the promise of greater *social cohesion*, greater *social stability*, which, for
urban Russia at least, had been contained in the turbulent years leading
up to 1905. The tensions and strains which earlier had been largely
contained in the channels of common political objectives would eventually be polarized into separate revolutionary processes, each adding to
the pressures against the tsarist regime but also contributing — by their
separation — to the eventual disintegration of the whole fabric of national life.

Thus it was that 1917 would witness the collapse of an ancient old
order at the same time that it would see an industrial working class and
eventually a peasant mass, impelled by an amalgam of old and new
grievances, combine against a stillborn bourgeois society and state.
Thus it was, finally, that in the throes of these two separate revolutions,
Russia would not manage for many years to recover a new historical
equilibrium — to find its own Thermidor.

Tsuyoshi Hasegawa

The February Revolution

Equally at home in the academic worlds of Japan and the United States,
Tsyoshi Hasegawa was trained at Tokyo University and the University of
Washington. He has taught at the State University of New York at Oswego
and Hokkaido University. His monograph on the February Revolution was
the first Western study of the fall of tsarism that utilized archival materials
housed in the Soviet Union. He contended with the views of Florinsky and
Pares that looked upon the liberals as unsung heroes, rejected the conspiratorial thesis of George Katkov, and questioned the inflated role ascribed to the Bolsheviks by many Soviet historians. In the conclusion to his
book he argues that the February Revolution was a conjunction of the
revolt of the masses and the liberal opposition of the middle classes.

Text by Tsuyoshi Hasegawa from *The February Revolution: Petrograd 1917*, Chapter 29
("Conclusion"), pp. 569–586. Reprinted by permission of University of Washington
Press, 1981.

The February Revolution was the explosion of the two fundamental contradictions in Russia — the revolt of the masses against established order and the irreconcilable conflict between "society" and "state." The process of what Haimson describes as dual polarization had steadily progressed after 1905 under the impact of the successful modernization undertaken by Russia. The outbreak of the First World War at first appeared to halt this process — the liberals pledged to support the government in its effort to win the war and the "sacred union" seemed to close the gap between state and society. The workers' strike movement that had appeared to be approaching a clash with the regime was silenced at the outbreak of war. But internal peace did not last more than a year. Once a crack appeared in the monolith after the first humiliating defeat of the Russian army, the war that had initially cemented all segments of society together began to rip them apart with ferocious force.

The working class provided the most important source of social instability in Russia. Never integrated into the established order, workers lived segregated geographically as well as culturally and socially. At the outbreak of war, the modicum of independence that had existed previously had been brutally taken away. Unlike other classes in society that had formed national organizations to advance their class interests, workers were deprived of such privilege. Whatever modest legal organizations they maintained during the war were severely curtailed by the police. And yet the workers' labor lay at the foundation of the war effort. As Russian industry rapidly expanded and created a shortage of skilled workers, the workers' confidence grew in proportion. It was precisely the combination of resentment stemming from their exclusion from privileged society and their growing pride as a distinct and vital class that made the working class in Russia explosively dangerous.

The strike movement was suddenly revitalized in the summer of 1915, and from then on grew in size and militancy. It was by no means a linear development constantly moving upward toward a climax, but characterized by peaks and valleys. But as time went on peaks became constantly higher and valleys less deep. At the vanguard of the strike movement stood the metalworkers in factories that employed between 1,000 and 8,000 workers, and it was the metalworkers in the Vyborg District who provided the major impetus. Workers in the largest munition plants and in large textile factories participated in economic strikes, but they generally stayed out of political strikes until the end of

1916. As the new wave of strikes began in January 1917, even these workers merged with the militant metalworkers in Vyborg District in strikes for political reasons. Moreover, the new wave began to involve workers who had not participated in strikes since the war began. The basic trend of the wartime strike movement — to grow ever larger and wider — culminated in the February Revolution.

Wartime conditions had changed the composition of the working class in Petrograd. But in accounting for the sharp rise in the strike movement during the war, it must be stressed that changes were less drastic in Petrograd than elsewhere in Russia. The skilled metalworkers, from whom the major source of working-class radicalism in Petrograd came, were highly urban, literate, relatively highly paid, and confident and proud of their abilities. Even with the enormous influx of new labor and the rapid expansion of the number of workers, more than half of the workers in Petrograd in January 1917 had been working since the prewar period. To this core of the proletariat were added the displaced skilled workers from Poland and the Baltic provinces, the urban youths who had grown into adulthood during the war, and the women who had returned to work after the war began. Thus, Petrograd workers maintained an urban outlook despite the enormous influx into their ranks. Whether the newly recruited peasants contributed to the radicalism of the workers' movement is difficult to ascertain. Although they might have stayed out of the strike movement, it is possible to assume that the militant workers might have influenced them in a radical direction. An element of *buntarstvo* became apparent by the end of 1916 and in the beginning of 1917, not in the strike movement itself, but in the attacks on food stores. It is plausible that these attacks were made by those unorganized segments of workers and artisans who had found no way to express their pent-up anger. The organized strike movement and the *buntarstvo* were to merge into one in the February Revolution.

Just as the workers themselves were alienated from the existing order of society, the workers' movement developed independent of the conflict within established society. With the exception of a brief moment immediately after the declaration of war, the workers on the whole were relatively indifferent to its outcome. What drove them out of the factories in the first major strike during the war was not the defeat of the Russian army but the massacre of fellow workers in Ivanovo. The prorogations of the Duma and the government's other repressive measures against liberal organizations had little effect on the workers' move-ment. But the workers showed their class solidarity in the January 9 strikes and in a series of sympathy strikes in protest against the arrest of their leaders.

No doubt such wartime miseries as decline in real wages, inflation, long working hours, deterioration of working conditions, and above all food shortage contributed to the development of the strike movement. But these were only the immediate manifestations of the established order, and it was toward that established order that their deep-seated resentment was directed. There was no possibility of establishing a united front between the liberal opposition and the workers' movement during the war. All such attempts made either by the leaders of the workers' movement or by the liberals ended in failure.

The growth of the strike movement was not entirely spontaneous. In fact, it would be impossible to organize "spontaneously" such strikes as happened in August and September 1915, January, March, and October 1916, and January and February 1917. These strikes involved many factories in the entire city. Strikes required organizers who planned strategy, agitators who appealed to the workers, orators who spoke at factory rallies, and a network of communications that coor-dinated activities with other factories. Amorphous grievances of the workers had to be defined in simple slogans. Demonstrations had to be directed to a certain destination through specific routes. Although no single political group could claim exclusive leadership of the workers' movement and it is impossible to measure accurately the influence of the underground revolutionary activists, it is certain that it was the underground activists at the factory level who provided the workers' movement with important leadership and continuity. Although activ-ists who were official members of the revolutionary parties were few, they were assisted by nonparty sympathizers who came to support the hard-core activists. The government's repressive measures did not eradi-cate such activists, but created more of them.

During the war the revolutionary parties were basically split into two groups: the antiwar alliance of left-wing Socialists centered around the Bolsheviks and the moderate Socialists that gravitated toward the workers' group of the Central War Industries Committee. The differ-ences between the two groups revolved around two issues. On the issue of war the antiwar group took a militant internationalist position, while the workers' group qualified that position by allowing a possibility of national defense against aggression. A more important difference was their respective methods for achieving a revolution. While the Bolsheviks advocated a revolution carried out by the workers and the soldiers alone, the workers' group conceived revolution to be a united struggle against tsarism by all segments of society, one in which the liberal opposition was to play a leading role. The workers' movement should be subordinated to the broader struggle of the entire society. For two fundamental reasons the workers' groups' concept of revolution did not correspond to Russian reality. First, the Russian liberals, on whom the sole hope of the workers' group for revolution rested, had ceased to be revolutionary. They were frightened by the prospect of revolution from below and were more willing to accommodate themselves to the tsarist regime than to form a united front with the workers against it. Second, the workers' movement developed outside the liberal forces in society. They had no common ground on which to establish a united front.

In the latter half of 1916 the Bolsheviks and the antiwar alliance intensified their influence among the Petrograd workers at the expense of the workers' group. This is not to say that the Bolshevik programs were wholeheartedly accepted by the masses of workers. But it does indicate that the Bolsheviks' most militant antiwar stand and their equally militant rejection of the established order were beginning to strike a responsive chord among the worker-activists. As wartime reality hit the workers hard, the Bolsheviks' antiwar propaganda was not incomprehensible to the workers. The Bolsheviks' insistence on the insurrection of the masses without the help of any other class in society appealed to the workers' sense of independence and was compatible with their resentment of privileged society.

Alarmed by the loss of influence, the workers' group finally turned in a radical direction in December 1916. It began a massive campaign appealing to the workers to take action to overthrow the tsarist regime. The workers' group's new direction was taken still in the framework of the over-all struggle of the entire society against the tsarist regime. But the drastic shift from its previous policy restraining the workers' radicalism into one that encouraged the workers' action against the regime had a significant implication. On the eve of the February Revolution both groups that influenced the workers' movement advocated violent action against the regime. In this sense, the conflict between the two groups did not hinder, but rather hastened the development of the revolutionary crisis.

The workers' group also created an important buffer between the liberals and the workers — a buffer that deceptively concealed the basic antagonism between the two. The liberal movement and the workers' movement during the war and subsequent developments after the February Revolution amply demonstrated that the two were fundamentally in opposition. The liberals desperately tried to the last moment to avoid a revolution from below. The existence of the workers' group, however, contributed to the liberals' psychological acceptance of the revolution, if a revolution were inevitable. Instead of choosing a course of a civil war against the workers' movement, the liberals could count on the moderating influence of the workers' group to contain the revolution within acceptable limits. In this sense, the workers' group provided a vital link between the liberals and the revolution.

Although the workers' strike movement developed during the February Revolution into a general strike that involved virtually all the workers in Petrograd, it did not ensure the victory of the insurrection by itself. One of the crucial differences between the 1905 Revolution and the February Revolution was the soldiers' loyalty. In 1905 there were sporadic attempts by the soldiers to rise against the regime, but on the whole they remained loyal. But the impact of the world war drastically changed the morale of the officers as well as the soldiers.

The reasons for the soldiers' insurrection were not identical with those for the workers' strike movement. If the workers demanded bread, peace, and the overthrow of tsarism, the soldiers' grievances were more immediate and were directed against the officers and military discipline. The barrier between soldiers and officers — common in any military force — was even more magnified in the Russian army because of the peculiar social tensions that existed outside the military units. Barracks life reminded the soldiers — mostly "peasants in uniform" — of the servile life on the landlords' estates in pre-Emancipation days. They were at the mercy of the officers, subject to beatings, theft, and extortion by them, and detailed more often to act as servants in the officers' club or their households than to actual military training. Officers treated soldiers as landlords treated serfs. Officers had little contact with the soldiers, did not speak the same language, and did not understand them. Left alone, the soldiers managed their barracks life by forming their own self-governing communal organizations without much interference from the officers.

The morale of the reserve units was low. Unlike the front, where there was a possibility of establishing a common bond between officers and soldiers in the face of danger, boredom and regimentation in the rear made the reserve soldiers restless. The influx of older recruits and the existence of sick and wounded soldiers who had been temporarily removed from the front also contributed to declining morale. Moreover, the government's policy of drafting strike organizers into the army was like throwing matches around on a dry field. But organized revolutionary activities in the military units were negligible, although revolutionary literature was occasionally smuggled into the barracks. More significant was the influence of the general political deterioration in the rear. The trial of Miasoedov, the arrest of Sukhomlinov, rumors of the government's treason, and sensational tales of Rasputin and the empress eroded the hypnotic hold of the sacred oath of allegiance to the tsar. As Colonel Engelhardt observed, soldiers in the reserve battalions became "rather reserves of flammable material than a prop of the regime . . . capable at any moment of exercising their own will and their demands." In fact, there were some instances during the war in which the soldiers openly supported demonstrators against the police. Though sporadic, these instances foreshadowed the danger in the future.

If the oath of allegiance ceased to have magical hold over the soldiers, prestige of officers — another important factor to tie the soldiers to discipline — had declined. The most capable officers of the Russian army had either been killed in the first few months of the war or sent to the front where they were most needed. The shortage of officers contributed to the creation of a host of newly commissioned officers with dubious qualifications. It also meant the influx of a new breed of officers who brought into the military units acute political consciousness. Unlike the professional officers of the old generation, they could no longer be indifferent to political developments outside the military. Many openly sympathized with the liberal opposition, and even a few revolutionaries were in the officers' corps. The "transfer of allegiance" had taken place among the officers long before the February Revolution.

Crucial to the soldiers' loyalty to the regime at the time of crisis was the attitude of noncommissioned officers, since unlike the officers, NCOs had daily contact with the soldiers and the detachments designed to train the NCOs were supposed to be the main instrument of suppression of disturbances. It is known that the NCOs treated the soldiers most brutally, but at the same time they were much closer to the soldiers in their social and cultural background. Just as the workers who came closest to the established order of society most resented it, the NCOs were more keenly conscious of the oppressive wall that separated them from the officers. Combined with this resentment was initiative and leadership — attributes that had led them to NCO status and that made them particularly dangerous.

But the revolt of the masses was but one aspect of the February Revolution. If the basic confrontation in the February Revolution was between the masses and privileged society, why did it not immediately lead to a civil war? The answer lies in another aspect of wartime politics: the relationship between state and society. The revolution from below provided the general framework, but the specific course of the February Revolution was determined by the conflict within established society.

The internal peace that the liberal opposition had promised at the outbreak of war did not last beyond the summer of 1915. After the Russian army suffered a humiliating defeat, the liberals began criticizing the government. The voluntary organizations became increasingly involved in political questions, while in the Duma liberals formed the Progressive Bloc. After the political crisis of the summer of 1915, the liberals and the tsarist government drifted apart. But contrary to what Katkov claims, the liberals never attempted to take over the tsarist government apparatus. In fact, they never wished a far-reaching political reform in the time of war. The most the Progressive Bloc wished to accomplish was the formation of a ministry of confidence. The mainstream of liberal opposition led by Miliukov had persistently refused to take drastic action against the government, partly because they feared that such action might provoke a revolution from below, and partly because during the war, despite political animosity, the liberals and the bureaucracy had created a web of interdependent organizations in support of the war effort. The liberals and the government hated and distrusted each other, but they needed each other for survival. Faced with the growing movement from below, the government's intransigence from above, and constant danger of internal split within the fragile liberal coalescence, the liberals remained inactive and powerless. Only a minority attempted to break away from this impasse. The radical wing of the liberals had insisted upon the need of an alliance with the mass movement to keep it within reasonable bounds. At the lower level a certain cooperation was achieved between liberal activists and the moderate Socialists in the practical work of labor exchange, cooperative movements, and food supply committees. But these liberals had no tangible influence on the masses of workers. Another group of liberals became involved in a conspiracy for a palace coup to forestall the outbreak of revolution. But this course was not accepted by the majority of liberals as a viable alternative, and even those who advocated it did not seriously attempt to implement it.

From the very beginning of the war Nicholas excluded two radical actions he might have taken in dealing with the liberal opposition. On one hand, he never seriously entertained the proposal made by his reactionary advisors (including his wife and Nikolai Maklakov) that he should break completely with the liberals. On the other, he adamantly stood on his imperial prerogatives, refusing to yield to public pressure to grant a ministry of confidence willing to cooperate with the Duma. Nicholas's political actions during the war were skilled maneuvers in the narrow passage between these two extremes. When liberals raised their voices, Nicholas gave them concessions sufficient to defuse their radicalism. Dismissals of unpopular ministers, the creation of special councils, the opening of the Duma in the spring and the summer of 1915, Goremykin's dismissal and Stürmer's appointment in the aftermath of Miliukov's "stupidity or treason" speech, and even Protopopov's appointment as acting minister of internal affairs — each of these measures was taken at a time the liberals heightened the tone of criticism. And each time these measures succeeded in keeping the conservative elements of the Progressive Bloc clinging to the illusion that more concessions would follow. But Nicholas never intended to grant what the liberals wanted. As soon as he weathered a storm, he would return to reaction. Instead of forming a ministry of confidence in the summer of 1915 (which he could have done easily by replacing Goremykin with Krivoshein), he fired the "rebellious" ministers one by one. By assuming supreme commandership, he let the Aleksandra-Rasputin clique influence the appointments and dismissals of ministers. He never agreed to drop Protopopov, and never listened to the advice from various quarters to get rid of the unsavory influence of his wife and her spiritual advisor. As soon as the Duma quietly accepted the prorogation, Trepov was dismissed. Thus, in his struggle with the liberal opposition, Nicholas took the upper hand and won many tactical victories. These maneuvers themselves had a great deal to do with the liberals' powerlessness.

But these small victories ultimately led to Nicholas's downfall. The *krizis verkhov* (the crisis of power) was further deepened by them. It would be a mistake to characterize the entire tsarist cabinet as inept and corrupt — to the last moment it included capable ministers. But there was no question that following the crisis in the summer of 1915 the over-all quality of the government declined sharply. "Ministerial leap-frogging" was but one manifestation of the erosion of the government's competency. Such scandals as Khvostov's plot to assassinate Rasputin and the arrest of Manasevich-Manuilov lowered the prestige of the government. Rasputin's frolicking and the unfounded, sensational rumors about Rasputin, the empress, and the "dark forces" fed the basest popular imagination and invited the indignation of the decent public. It is true that the liberals were incapacitated by Nicholas's maneuvers. But psychologically they deserted the government. Nicholas and his government thus irretrievably alienated an ally with whom they could have combated the approaching storm from below.

The crack in the dike that let in a deluge was the supply of food. The crisis was the result of a panic rather than a real shortage of bread itself. After the news of the introduction of the ration system was announced, the number of food riots suddenly increased. At the same time the workers' strikes also sharply increased. On the eve of the February Revolution the Putilov Factory and the Izhora Factory were closed, and numerous other factories began economic strikes.

The February Revolution began with the strike in the textile mills in the Vyborg District when women workers went out into the streets with a single demand — "bread" — on February 23, to commemorate International Women's Day. The strike immediately spread to neighboring metal factories, and its leadership was quickly taken over by more experienced activists. At least 78,000 workers of fifty factories joined the strike. Although the total number of strikers was much smaller than the January 9 and February 14 strikes of this year, and the strike movement was limited in the main to the Vyborg District, its militancy far surpassed any of the previous wartime strikes. The strikers systematically employed a tactic of forcible removal, not allowing other workers to continue working. Almost all the major factories in Vyborg District employing more than 1,000 workers were shut. The strikers staged a massive demonstration in the major streets in Vyborg District, but the police succeeded in dispersing the demonstrators who attempted to cross the Neva to the center of the city.

On the second day, February 24, the strike was no longer confined to Vyborg District, but spread to all the districts in Petrograd. At least 158,000 workers participated and 131 factories were struck, more than doubling the size of the strike on the previous day. Almost all the metal and textile factories with more than 100 workers were struck, and for the first time in the war workers of other branches of industry — paper, printing, wood processing, mineral processing, leather, food process-ing, tobacco, and chemicals — joined the strike. For the first time during the war massive demonstrations were staged along Nevskii Pros-pekt. The demonstrators no longer passively waited for police assault, but instead, counterattacked. Although on this day as well, the police and the Cossacks still managed to disperse the crowds, the demon-strators became more difficult to deal with. The Cossacks were not enthusiastic in fulfilling the order to attack.

The general strike on February 25 paralyzed normal functions in the capital. The strike participants surpassed 200,000, the largest figure since the 1905 Revolution. Almost all factories were closed. Newspa-pers did not come out, trams and cabs stopped, many stores, restau-rants, and cafes were closed, banks did not open, and schools were canceled. The demonstrators became more vicious in their attacks on the police. Revolver shots were fired, bombs thrown, and police chiefs Shalfeev and Krylov were brutally murdered. Cossacks and soldiers remained halfhearted in their task of suppressing the demonstration. In some cases soldiers openly sympathized with the crowd and attacked the police. For the first time since February 23 the crowds completely controlled Nevskii Prospekt. Political rallies were held continuously on Kazan and Znamenskaia Squares, where orators spoke freely, without much harassment from the police. The demonstrators boldly hoisted red banners lettered with "Down with the War," "Down with the Gov-ernment." The workers' strike movement induced unorganized workers to come into the streets. Suddenly an element of *buntarstvo* was in-jected into the movement. Some demonstrators, mostly youths and women, rampaged in the streets, "trashing" stores along the way. Armed robberies, including one spectacular bank robbery, were com-mitted in the heart of the city.

Who led the revolution? Was it spontaneous, as often claimed by Western historians? Or was it led by the Bolshevik party as Soviet historians argue? It would be a mistake to characterize the February Revolution, as Chamberlin does, as "one of the most leaderless, spontaneous, anonymous revolutions of all time." Historians in the West have long considered the Russian mass movement as controlled by *stikhiia* — that mysterious, savage, elemental force that defies rational analysis. This belief has led them to refrain from examining the dynamics of the mass movement. But on the other hand, it is difficult to subscribe to the theory of Bolshevik leadership. The Bolshevik party as a whole failed to react to the workers' strike movement quickly and imaginatively. The Russian Bureau led by Shliapnikov was constantly behind the developing events and grossly underestimated the revolutionary potentialities of the movement. The Petersburg Committee was more actively involved in leadership of the strike and demonstration, but it, too, failed to exert strong influence among the masses, partly because its attempt to expand the movement met constant objections from the Russian Bureau, and partly because it lacked the resources and a close communication network to coordinate the activities in various districts. On the night of February 25 a majority of the Petersburg Committee was arrested and it became defunct. Thus, the 3,000 Bolsheviks scattered around Petrograd were left pretty much on their own to interpret the significance of events and exert their influence among the workers without much direction from above.

Nonetheless, in such an explosive situation as the February Revolution the existence of 3,000 committed revolutionaries cannot be easily dismissed. The most important Bolshevik organization, the one that exerted a significant influence on the workers, was the Vyborg District Committee. Headed by militant Chugurin and led by such experienced party activists as Kaiurov and Sveshnikov, the Vyborg District Committee had placed its 500 to 600 members in strategically important factories. It met frequently from the beginning of the strike movement on February 23, and from the very beginning worked to expand the movement to its maximum limit. They were the strike organizers at the factory level, stood at the head of the demonstrations, talked the Cossacks out of punitive action against the demonstrators, and led the attack on the police. Considering the important role played by the metal factories in the Vyborg District, these Vyborg Bolsheviks must have contributed to the rapid acceleration of the strike movement. In this sense, Trotskii was partially correct in stating that the February Revolution was led by the lower-rank Bolshevik activists.

However, the Bolsheviks were but one part of a much larger group of activists. There were 400 to 500 members of the initiative group, 150 Mezhraiontsy, and 500 to 600 left-wing Socialist Revolutionaries who were scattered in various factories. These activists formed a united front with the Bolsheviks and took concerted action. Not only these antiwar activists but also the moderate Socialists who supported the workers' group actively organized the strike movement. Despite ideological differences, there emerged a common goal among the activists at the factory level: the transformation of labor unrest into a revolution against the tsarist regime. Trotskii was wrong to exclude such activists from the role of leadership.

To be sure, the February Revolution was not organized in the sense that the revolution in October was. There existed no central headquarters from which all directives emanated. Nor did these activists control all aspects of the movement. But it is important to recognize the existence of these activists, who had acquired experience in strike organization under the difficult repression that existed in wartime and whose concern was no longer the solution of immediate economic problems but the ultimate overthrow of the tsarist regime itself. Moreover, these activists with affiliations with the revolutionary parties were not isolated from the masses of workers, although their number was small. Surrounding this core of activists were those nonparty activists who had not committed themselves to join the underground revolutionary parties, but who were sympathetic with the causes they espoused. Beyond these activists there were the rank-and-file workers. But many of them already had experience in strikes during the war. Taking these factors into consideration, one must reject the "spontaneity theory," according to which the masses of workers poured onto the streets spontaneously, trusting only their own destructive instincts.

It is true, however, that the February Revolution gave many workers the opportunity to join the strike movement for the first time. Certainly the sudden appearance of great numbers of workers who had been thrust into the political movement injected an element of "spontaneity" in the sense that these newcomers were more difficult for the seasoned veteran organizers to control. The uncertainty of their political allegiances contributed to the blurring of the distinct social content of the February Revolution.

By February 25 the strike movement had reached its height. But it did not lead to a revolution. It became clear that the workers' movement alone was insufficient to overthrow the regime. On February 26 security authorities in Petrograd, having adopted a stance of restraint for the three days, changed to active suppression of the unrest. Government troops systematically fired upon the demonstrators. This measure seemed successful. Demonstrators disappeared from Nevskii Prospekt. Even the veteran leaders of the strike movement pessimistically predicted that the movement was coming to an end. But the firing order inevitably pushed the soldiers to a choice between conscience and obedience. On the night of February 26, the Fourth Company of Pavlovskii Regiment revolted. This was still isolated and easily put down, but it was an ominous sign.

On February 27 the revolt of the Volynskii Regiment led by a few noncommissioned officers quickly spread to the Preobrazhenskii and Lithuanian Regiments and the Sixth Engineers Battalion. The soldiers' insurrection had begun. Insurgent soldiers crossed the Neva and were united with the workers in Vyborg District who, on their own, had attacked weapon factories and the police station. The insurgents soon occupied the entire Vyborg District. They attacked Kresty Prison, occupied Finland Station, burned the police station, and armed themselves after they occupied the weapon factories. While insurgents continued to attack the barracks of the Moscow Regiment and the Bicycle Battalion, others crossed the Neva and marched to the Tauride Palace. On their way they occupied the Arsenal, seized enormous quantities of weapons and ammunition, and burned the Circuit Court. From then on the insurrection spread to all parts of the city, and by late night almost all the reserve battalions in the city joined or were forced to join the insurrection. Lawlessness and chaos reigned in the streets. Trucks, automobiles, and armored cars full of soldiers with red armbands zoomed madly around the city, while people armed to the teeth experimented with their newly acquired toys.

The ineptitude of the security authorities contributed to the insurrection's quick spread. Khabalov lost his nerve and stood aimless and ineffectual. The punitive detachment under the command of Colonel Kutepov was isolated from the other loyal troops and disintegrated by evening. Beliaev meddled in the commanding hierarchy and heightened the confusion by issuing conflicting orders. While the insurrection spread in the city, Khabalov, Beliaev, and Zankevich moved the loyal troops that had gathered to defend the government aimlessly back and forth between the Winter Palace and the Admiralty. Disgusted by the ineptitude of the commanding hierarchy, the loyal troops disappeared; some marched to the Tauride Palace to join the insurrection. But the greatest mistake made by Khabalov and Beliaev was that they concealed the extent of the crisis in Petrograd from the Stavka until it was too late. By the time the Stavka realized the necessity of dispatching troops from the front, Petrograd was under the control of the insurgents.

The insurrection had triumphed in Petrograd. Cabinet ministers were arrested and loyal troops disintegrated. But the revolution was far from over. Nicholas II was still alive and well in Mogilev, determined to suppress the revolution by force, and the Stavka wholeheartedly endorsed his decision. In the meantime, the insurrection created anarchy in the streets, but not a revolutionary government to consolidate its gains.

One of the most curious characteristics of the February Revolution was that the insurgents who revolted against the old regime failed to create their own revolutionary government. The two organs that came into being — the Petrograd Soviet and the Duma Committee — had little to do with the insurrection itself. The masses of insurgents still continued to influence the course of events, but their influence was no longer direct. Their continued existence and radical actions provided the general framework, which the political leaders could neither ignore nor defy, but the specific course of the revolution was now determined by groups other than the insurgents themselves.

The Petrograd Soviet was created at the initiative of the Menshevik leaders, whose goal was to form a center for the movement to coordinate and organize the activities of the insurgent masses. Despite the strong left-wing preponderance in the Executive Committee, the anti-war groups were not united on the question of power. Particularly important was the confusion of the Bolshevik leadership. As a result the most important policy of the Soviet Executive Committee was formulated by Sukhanov, Steklov, and Sokolov. These Socialist intellectuals were ideologically more Left than the workers' group, but on the question of power they consistently maintained that a provisional government to be created by the revolution ought to be a bourgeois government composed of the representatives of the liberal opposition. This basically Menshevik notion that had been most persistently pursued by the workers' group during the war and that seemed to have gradually lost relevancy in the wartime political reality was ironically espoused by a majority of the Petrograd Soviet leaders and infected even the Bolshevik leaders like Shliapnikov. The new situation created by the revolution seemed to these leaders to justify the plan to transfer power to the "bourgeoisie." There was a basic confrontation between the masses and established order, and this confrontation became even clearer as the revolution became older. But the Petrograd Soviet leaders accurately judged that revolutionary power emanating solely from the insurgent masses could not possibly survive. It seemed foolhardy to rest the future of the revolution on those soldiers roaming around the street defying all order and discipline and the armed workers who did not even know how to use weapons. A civil war, if initiated by an organized military unit, would surely crush the young revolution. The leaders of the Soviet Executive Committee thus concluded that, for its survival, the revolution would have to be expanded to include the rest of society. Although its basic content was the social conflict between the masses and privileged society, the revolution would have to make itself appear *obshchestvennyi* — a political revolution involving all segments of society against the tsarist regime.

The challenge to this notion came from two different directions. First, the overwhelming support that the Petrograd Soviet received from the insurgent masses began to transform its nature into something more than the initiators had envisaged. The masses supported the Soviet, not the Duma Committee, thereby accentuating the social content of the revolution. The workers' militia in the workers' districts effectively established its police power, and the district soviets were quickly extending their self-governing authority. The soldiers formed soldiers' committees in their units, controlled weapons and the economy of their units, and began electing their officers. In other words, the insurgent masses began taking care of administrative matters on their own without reference to any outside authority. The source of "dual power" was derived, not from the conflict between the Provisional Government and the Petrograd Soviet, but from the most fundamental conflict — between the insurgents' self-assumed authority and the authority emanating from the privileged element of society. The majority of insurgents, however, had not yet begun to translate their feelings into conscious revolutionary programs. They could not offer an alternative to the Executive Committee's policy toward the problem of power, despite occasional manifestations of their latent radicalism on a number of specific issues.

The second threat to the Soviet leaders' policy toward the problem of power came from a small group of radical antiwar Socialists led by the Bolshevik Vyborg District Committee and Mezhraiontsy. From the moment the insurrection triumphed, this group called for the establishment of a provisional revolutionary government in the form of a soviet, and after the Petrograd Soviet was formed, they advocated the transformation of the Soviet into a revolutionary government. Unlike the Bolshevik leaders led by Shliapnikov, who considered the establishment of a provisional revolutionary government a task of the distant future, these activists proposed this as one of the most urgent tasks of the moment. Although the Vyborg Bolsheviks and the Mezhraiontsy were still isolated from the masses of insurgents, there were signs that their proposal might receive wide acceptance. Alarmed by this possibility, the Soviet leaders decided to hasten the formation of a bourgeois provisional government by negotiating directly with the liberal representatives before the military insurgents could push them into a position where they would have no choice but to assume power.

The liberals played a crucial role in the February Revolution. During the war, pushed by two conflicting forces — the government's intransigence and the approaching storm from below — the liberal opposition was rendered powerless. But when the revolution came, it was the liberals who tipped the balance between the two forces and who had the most telling effect on the specific course of events during the Revolution.

The liberals had attempted to avoid a revolution at any cost during the war, but when the revolution became a reality, their goal was not to crush it but to contain it. As the insurrection threw the capital into chaos, and eliminated all sources of authority, the liberals formed the Duma Committee, which was forced to assume power to restore order. From that moment, at first gingerly and later more actively, the liberals became involved in the revolutionary process. The revolutionary situation no longer allowed the liberals to stand in the neutral territory between the old regime and the revolution. But the actions of the liberals during the February Revolution represented their desperate but ultimately futile effort to create such a middle ground. The two courses of action that the liberals had rejected during the war were adopted during the revolution. First, they accepted the revolution as legitimate to prevent further intensification of the revolutionary process. Second, they reactivated the plan for a palace coup.

The most difficult question that the liberals faced during the February Revolution was the problem of legitimacy of the Provisional Government. On the one hand, they sought to make the revolution itself the source of legitimacy. In fact, they had to take some revolutionary actions despite themselves to contain the further intensification of the revolution. The Duma Committee sanctioned the arrest of the former ministers, officials, and the police, while it took over the government apparatus in the name of the revolution but actually to ensure the continuity of government functions. It created the city militia to replace the old police, which had disappeared, and took over the Military Commission created by the Petrograd Soviet to exert its influence among the insurgent soldiers. Nevertheless, because there existed an unbridgeable class barrier between the liberals and the insurgents and more importantly because their ultimate goals — the restoration of order and the prevention of further intensification of revolution — were basically contradictory to the aspirations of the insurgents, they failed to gain their acceptance. It was for this reason that they chose to negotiate with the leaders of the Petrograd Soviet for the conditions of the transfer of power in the hope that the Soviet would persuade the insurgents to support the Provisional Government.

But the Duma Committee's plan to use the Soviet leaders as agents for the Provisional Government failed. Its basic assumption that the insurgents could be swayed by the mere directives of the Soviet Executive Committee proved to be false. The insurgents were not robots moving in any direction that their leaders ordered but unmistakably imposed their will on their leaders. Despite their intention to help out the Provisional Government, the Soviet leaders could not give it their unconditional support without risking the loss of their own prestige among the masses. What the insurgents wanted was not crystallized into political programs, but on specific issues they unceremoniously overruled the Executive Committee's policy and enforced their will without much consideration of the leaders' intentions and ideological niceties. The process in which the soldiers issued Order No. 1, the insurgents' reaction to the question of weapon control, and the reaction of the workers' militia to the merger with the city militia all indicated the futility of the Provisional Government's reliance on the Soviet leaders to gain the support of the insurgents.

On the other hand, the liberals sought legitimacy for the Provisional Government in legal and institutional continuity with the old regime. A palace coup was conceived as the last defense against the intensification of the revolution and as a measure to ensure that continuity. In dealing with the tsar and military leaders the liberals always presented themselves as defenders of law and order against anarchy. They never demanded Nicholas's abdication in the name of revolution, but for the purpose of stopping the revolution. Ultimately it proved impossible to pursue two contradictory policies. The middle ground that they sought between the old regime and the revolution did not exist. The Provisional Government did not gain the full endorsement of the Petrograd Soviet. The insurgents were effectively expanding their self-governing authority in the factories and the military units, thereby undermining the authority of the Provisional Government. But the Provisional Government could not even muster the strength of privileged society, since they were forced to accept the abolition of the monarchical system. The tsarist government and the liberals had needed each other for their mutual survival. Forced to remove the monarchical system surgically, the liberals were left in a vacuum, with no solid foundation.

Another important factor that prevented a civil war in the February Revolution was the action of the military leaders. They had refused to be involved in internal politics prior to the revolution, but even among the highest leaders in the military the "transfer of allegiance" had been slowly taking place. At the beginning of the revolution the military supported Nicholas's counterrevolutionary measures, because they believed that the capital had been taken over by radical elements. But as soon as they were assured that power had been transferred to the liberal forces, they fully cooperated with the Duma Committee — some like Ruzskii and Brusilov, because they agreed with their general goals; others, like Alekseev, because they were outwitted by the Duma Committee's manipulation of information. What ultimately determined the actions of the military leaders was their concern with the continuation of war and the preservation of the fighting capacities of the armed forces. For these goals they were willing to sacrifice the monarchical system. Fearing that forceful intervention by the military to suppress the revolution might provoke the expansion of revolution in the armed forces, the military leaders were also willing to accept the revolution to contain it. What they did not foresee was that the February Revolution was in its essence directed against the integrity of the armed forces themselves. They did not receive the news of the issuance of Order No. 1 until after the February Revolution.

Nicholas had to pay the price for his intransigence. He had irretrievably alienated the forces that could have come to his rescue against the threat of revolution. When he allowed the creation of a responsible ministry under the collective pressure of the commanders and against all his moral and religious convictions, Nicholas was already a broken man. The acceptance of his abdication demanded by the liberals and supported by the military leaders was easier for Nicholas after that concession. Once Nicholas accepted his abdication, it was impossible in the revolutionary crisis for other members of the dynasty to attempt to preserve the monarchical system. It was indicative of the extent of the erosion of tsarist authority that during the entire course of the revolution only one military commander declared his willingness to sacrifice his life for the tsar. Despite its three centuries of history, tsarism had failed to create a mystical symbol of the tsar even among its most faithful subjects.

The February Revolution was complete. The old regime no longer existed, but all the important issues — now out in the open — remained unsolved. The February Revolution was thus merely the beginning of a more violent revolutionary process.

N. N. Sukhanov

Prologue

One of the most valuable sources on the February Revolution is the memoirs of Nikolai Nikolaevich Himmer, better known by his pen name Sukhanov. Originally a Socialist Revolutionary (the propeasant party), Sukhanov joined the Menshevik-Internationalists, led by Martov, in mid-1917. From the first days of the Petrograd revolt Sukhanov found himself at the center of revolutionary events. He was one of the architects of the dual power arrangement and remained a critic of the subsequent coalition government. He continued to live in Russia after the Bolshevik victory and worked for the Soviet government until his arrest and trial in 1931. Despite

From *The Russian Revolution 1917: A Personal Record* by N. N. Sukhanov, edited and translated by Joel Carmichael, 1955, pp. 3–33. Reprinted by permission of Oxford University Press.

his loyalty to the new regime, he was condemned as a Menshevik and languished for many years in prison. His ultimate fate is obscure. In this excerpt from his seven-volume *Zapiski o russkoi revoliutsii* (Notes on the Russian Revolution) (Berlin, 1922–1923), Sukhanov explains the evolution of dual power and the spontaneous nature of the February revolt.

February 21st–26th, 1917

I had been banished from St. Petersburg by May 10, 1914. At that time I was editor of the non-party but Left-wing *Sovremennik* (Contemporary), which took an internationalist line during the war, to the great dissatisfaction of its "defensist" Petersburg contributors but the equal satisfaction of its *émigré* contributors, most of whom had rallied to the banner of Zimmerwald.[1] Though under sentence of banishment, I spent most of my time, up to the revolution itself, living underground in the capital — sometimes on a false passport, sometimes sleeping in a different place every night, sometimes slipping past the night-porter in the shadows as a "frequent visitor"[2] to my own flat, where my family was living.

From November 1916 on I was on the staff of Maxim Gorky's *Letopis* (Chronicle), and practically its principal contributor, keeping the entire magazine going under the Damocles' sword of police repression. Moreover, my illegal position did not stop me from working as an economist, under my own name, in a government department, the Ministry of Agriculture, in a section that dealt with the irrigation of Turkestan.

Such were my official position, rank, and titles when the revolution of 1917 overtook me.

Tuesday, February 21st. I was sitting in my office in the Turkestan section. Behind a partition two typists were gossiping about food difficulties, rows in the shopping queues, unrest among the women, an attempt to smash into some warehouse.

---

[1] A symbol of Socialist internationalism during the war, from the programme of the Conference of International Socialists opposed to the war that was held in Zimmerwald, Switzerland, in 1915.

[2] i.e., not on the list of tenants all porters were obliged to keep for the police.

"D'you know," suddenly declared one of these young ladies, "if you ask me, it's the beginning of the revolution!"

These girls didn't understand what a revolution was. Nor did I believe them for a second. But in those days, sitting over my irrigation systems and aqueducts, over my articles and pamphlets, my *Letopis* manuscripts and proofs, I kept thinking and brooding about the inevitable revolution that was whirling down on us at full speed.

In this period of the agony of Tsarism, the attention of Russian, or at any rate of Petersburg "society," and of political circles in the capital revolved primarily around the State Duma[3] convened on February 14th. By some people — the more conservative Left (Socialist) elements — the workers' street demonstrations under the slogans of "Bread!" and "Down with the Autocracy!" were linked to this date. Elements further to the Left, including myself, spoke out at various party meetings *against* tying up the workers' movement with the Duma. For bourgeois Duma circles had given proof enough, not only of their inability to join the proletariat even against Rasputin, but also of their mortal fear even of utilizing the strength of the proletariat in the struggle for a constitutional régime or for "carrying on the war to total victory."

This fear was completely justified. It was possible, of course, to summon up a spirit, but to force it into one's own service — never. And the Progressive Bloc[4] of the Duma, which embodied the attitude of the entire propertied bourgeoisie,[5] was in favour only of sharpening its weapons for use against the proletarian movement. Miliukov,[6] its

---

[3] This was the Fourth Duma (Parliament), elected in 1912. The State Duma, created by the October Manifesto of 1905, was the lower house of the legislature and (except for the representatives of five large cities) was indirectly elected. The Ministers, who were appointed by the Tsar, were not responsible to the Duma, and its powers and influence, limited enough in theory, were in practice almost non-existent.

[4] A patriotic oppositional majority, including all the Duma fractions as well as national groups (Poles, Lithuanians, Jews, Muslims, etc.). On the Left the Social-Democrats and the Trudoviks were out, on the Right the Black Hundred.

[5] i.e., the bourgeoisie whose right to vote was based on a rather high property qualification (Russian *tsenz, tsenzovoy*).

[6] Miliukov, Pavel Nikolayevich (1859–1943): leader and one of the founders (in 1905) of the "Cadets," [usually spelled *Kadets*] a colloquial name for the Constitutional Democrats (taken from the Russian initials), later also called "Party of the People's Freedom." This was a large liberal party that favoured a constitutional monarchy, or even, eventually, a republic. It was roughly the party of progressive landowners, the middle class, and middle-class intellectuals. Miliukov was a member of the Third and Fourth Dumas.

leader, had declared not long before that he was ready to renounce even his "total victory," even the Dardanelles, even the service of the gallant Allies, if all these were attainable only at the price of a revolution. And now, in view of the rumours about the forthcoming workers' demonstration, this same Miliukov published his memorable address to the workers, in which every wartime movement of theirs against the Government was declared to have been fomented by the Secret Police and by *provocateurs*.

Finally, the burning question for the Petersburg politicians was the transfer to the Town Council of the task of provisioning the capital. For the Petersburg liberal and democratic[7] circles this was the catchword of the moment.

Not one party was preparing for the great upheaval. Everyone was dreaming, ruminating, full of foreboding, feeling his way . . .

These philistine girls whose tongues and typewriters were rattling away behind the partition didn't know what a revolution was. I believed neither them, nor the inflexible facts, nor my own judgement. Revolution — highly improbable! Revolution! — everyone knew this was only a dream — a dream of generations and of long laborious decades. Without believing the girls, I repeated after them mechanically:

"Yes, the beginning of the revolution."

On Wednesday and Thursday — February 22nd and 23rd — the movement in the streets became clearly defined, going beyond the limits of the usual factory meetings. At the same time the feebleness of the authorities was exposed. They were plainly not succeeding — with all the machinery they had been building up for decades — in suppressing the movement at its source. The city was filled with rumours and a feeling of "disorders."

As far as scale went, similar disorders had taken place scores of times in our day. And if there was anything distinctive here it was just this irresolution of the authorities, who were obviously neglecting to deal with the movement. But these were "disorders" — there was still no revolution. A favourable outcome was not only not discernible as yet, but not one of the parties was even steering towards it; they merely strove to exploit the movement for agitational purposes.

---

[7] Sukhanov uses the words "democracy," "democratic," etc., essentially in contrast to the old Tsarist régime, and not *necessarily* to the bourgeoisie, though sometimes he narrows them to refer to the peasantry and working class together.

On Friday the 24th the movement swept over Petersburg like a great flood. The Nevsky and many squares in the centre were crowded with workers. Fugitive meetings were held in the main streets and were dispersed by Cossacks and mounted police — but without any energy or zeal and after lengthy delays. The Petersburg military commander, General Khabalov, got out a proclamation, which essentially only served to reveal the impotence of the authorities, pointing out that repeated warnings had been without effect and promising to take the sternest measures — in the future. Naturally this had no result, but it was another sign of helplessness.

The movement was plainly out of hand. A new situation, distinct from the previous disorders, was apparent to every attentive observer. On Friday I began categorically maintaining that we were dealing with a revolution, as an accomplished fact. However, I was waved aside as an optimist.

It seemed to me the evidence was already sufficient, and my thoughts were already turning in another direction, towards the *political problem*.

We had to aim at a radical political overturn. That was clear. But what was to be its programme? Who was to be the successor of the Tsarist autocracy? This was the point on which my attention was focused that day.

I won't say this enormous problem presented many difficulties to me at the time. Later I pondered over it much more and felt some doubt as to whether its solution at the time had been correct. During the shilly-shallyings of the Coalition and the smothering of the revolution by the Kerensky–Tereshchenko–Tsereteli policies in August–September 1917, and also after the Bolshevik insurrection, it often seemed to me that the solution of this problem in the February days could have, and for that matter should have, been different. But at the time I decided this problem of "high policy" almost without any hesitation.

The Government that was to take the place of Tsarism must be exclusively bourgeois. Trepov[8] and Rasputin could and should be replaced only by the bosses of the Progressive Bloc. This was the solution

[8] A non-political, personal friend of the Tsar's, who had been called upon, and failed, to save the situation. He was the son of D. F. Trepov, a founder of the Black Hundred and former Governor-General of St. Petersburg.

to be aimed at. Otherwise the overturn would fail and the revolution perish.

My starting-point was the complete disintegration of democratic Russia under the autocracy. At that time the democratic movement had control of no strong organization, whether political, trade-union, or municipal. And in its state of disintegration the proletariat, isolated as it was from other classes, could create only fighting organizations which, while representing a real force in the class struggle, were not a genuine element of State power.

This disintegrated democratic movement, moreover, if it were to make an attempt to govern, would have had to accomplish the impossible: the technique of State administration in the given conditions of war and destruction was far beyond the capacity of the democratic movement in isolation. The destruction of the State and its economic organism was already immense. Industry, transport, and supply had been enfeebled by the autocracy. The capital was starving. Not only could the State machine not stand idle for a single moment, but it had to find new energy and increased resources, without loss of time, for a colossal technical task. And if the Government were one which was incapable of setting in motion all the cogs of the State mechanism, the revolution would not hold out.

The entire available state machinery, the army of bureaucrats, the *Zemstvos*[9] and municipalities, which had had the cooperation of all the forces of the democracy, could obey Miliukov, but not Chkheidze.[10] There was, however, and could be, no other machinery.

But all this was, so to speak, *technique*. The other aspect of the matter was *political*. Setting up a democratic Government and by-passing the Progressive Bloc not only meant not utilizing at the critical moment the only state apparatus available, it also meant rallying the whole of propertied Russia against the democratic movement and the revolution. The whole of the bourgeoisie as one man would have

---

[9]*Zemstvos*: established in 1864 as one of Alexander II's Great Reforms. An autonomous elected institution with a high property qualification. The *Zemstvos* were important culturally and economically; they established throughout Russia schools, hospitals, etc., and created cadres of *Zemstvo* intellectuals — statisticians, physicians, teachers — who constituted the so-called Third Estate, and played a very important role in the Russian revolutionary movement. They were dissolved after the October Revolution.

[10]Chkheidze, Nikolai Semyonovich (1864–1926): a Georgian, leader of the Menshevik fraction of the Social-Democratic Party in the Third and Fourth Dumas.

thrown all the strength it had in the scales on the side of Tsarism and formed with it a strong and united front — against the revolution. It would have roused up against the revolution the entire middle class and the press at a time when hunger and disorganization were threatening to smash the revolution at any moment and Nicholas II was still at liberty and calling himself Tsar of all the Russias. In these circumstances a Socialist seizure of power would mean the inevitable and immediate failure of the revolution. At that moment, in February, the first revolutionary Government could only be a bourgeois one.

There was also another argument, of narrower scope but to me equally convincing. During the war I was one of the two or three writers who managed to advocate the anti-defensist Zimmerwald position in the legal press. And in particular, during the first days of the war, when patriotic enthusiasm seemed universal and people with a correct estimate of the meaning of the war and Tsarist Russia's place in it were absolutely impossible to find even amongst the Socialists then in Russia (Gorky was an exception), I resolutely spurned all "Patriotic" notions. On the contrary, at that time I was guilty of something else — namely, a simplification of the proletarian class position (later taken at Zimmerwald), debasing it somewhat in the direction of that primitive "defeatism" that characterized broad strata of Russian society during the Japanese war of 1905. In any case from the beginning of the war and up to the revolution every public action of mine was as far as possible a *struggle against the war*, a struggle for its liquidation.

And now, at the first thunder-clap of the revolutionary tempest, I was pulled up short before the practical impossibility of creating a purely democratic Government, for the reason — among others — that this would have meant the *immediate liquidation of the war* by the Russian democracy. For of course I considered it impossible for a democratic Government to continue the war, since the contradiction between participation in an imperialist war and victory for the democratic revolution seemed to me fundamental. But I thought it out of the question to add an immediate radical change in foreign policy, with all its unforeseeable consequences, to all the difficulties of a revolution. Moreover, any peace policy worthy of the "dictatorship of the proletariat" must involve all the colossal tasks of demobilization and the transfer of industry to a peace-time basis, with the consequent large-scale shutting down of factories and mass unemployment at a moment when the national economy was completely disorganized.

It seemed to me absolutely indispensable to lay the problems of foreign policy temporarily on the shoulders of the bourgeoisie, in order to create the possibility of a struggle for the most rapid and painless liquidation of the war under a bourgeois Government that was carrying on the military policy of the autocracy. The *creation of the conditions* for the liquidation of the war, and not the liquidation itself — that was the fundamental problem of the overturn. And for this a bourgeois, not a democratic, Government was essential.

In general the solution of the problem of power seemed to me self-evident. And during the first revolutionary upsurge, February 24th–25th, my attention was taken up not by the programmatic aspect, so to speak, of this political problem, but by its other, *tactical* side.

Power must go to the bourgeoisie. But was there any chance that they would take it? What was the position of the propertied elements on this question? Could they and would they march in step with the popular movement? Would they, after calculating all the difficulties of their position, especially in foreign policy, accept power from the hands of the revolution? Or would they prefer to dissociate themselves from the revolution which had already begun and destroy the movement in alliance with the Tsarist faction? Or would they, finally, decide to destroy the movement by their "neutrality" — by abandoning it to its own devices and to mass impulses that would lead to anarchy?

This again was just one aspect of the matter. The other was: what was the position in this question of the Socialist parties, which ought to assume control of the movement that had now begun? Would all the Socialist groups unite in the solution of the problem of power, or might the unleashed elemental forces be exploited by a few of them for some insanely infantile attempt to establish the dictatorship of the proletariat and divide up at once the spoils that were still unwon?

And naturally, having put these questions, one must go further. If the correct solution of the problem of power could be wrecked from either side, was it not possible to take an active part now in the suitable manipulation of social forces, if only by seeking an appropriate compromise?

So on Friday the 24th, as the street movement swept in an ever-broadening flood through Petersburg, and when the revolution had become an objective fact and only its outcome was obscure, I scarcely listened to the uninterrupted accounts of street incidents. All my attention was directed at what was going on in the Socialist centres on the one hand and in the bourgeois circles, especially amongst the Duma fractions, on the other.

I knew a great many people in the most varied strata of the capital, but since there was almost no public opinion in Petersburg at that time and because of my illegal situation and my responsible literary work, I could not consider myself familiar with the moods of the various groups, who had been confronted with completely new problems during these days. I felt myself to be out of contact with the basic channel or channels where events now seemed to be forming. This sensation of isolation and helplessness, a longing to be near some sort of crucible of events, an unsatisfied desire to fling myself into the matrix of the revolution in order to do what I could, were my dominant feelings in those days.

The first thing to do was to collect information about this "high policy." It was necessary to visit those centres of both camps where one could get trustworthy intelligence. On Friday evening I 'phoned a well-known Petersburg political lawyer, traditionally considered a Bolshevik but more closely connected with the Petersburg radical groups — the ubiquitous and omniscient N. D. Sokolov, one of the principal personalities of the first period of the revolution. We arranged to convoke the representatives of different groups on the following day, Saturday, at 3 o'clock, in his apartment in the Sergiyevsky, to discuss the situation. At this conference I hoped to clear up for myself the position of the propertied as well as of the leading democratic elements. At the same time, as a representative of the Socialist Left I hoped to speak forcefully, if need arose, in support of a purely bourgeois revolutionary Government, and also to demand a compromise as indispensable in the interests of forming such a Government.

The character and limits of this compromise were clear. The mass street movement in the February days revealed no sort of purposefulness, nor was it possible to discern in it any kind of proper leadership. In general, as is always the case, the organized Socialist centres were not controlling the popular movement or leading it to any definite political goal. Of course our traditional, one might say ancient, national slogan, "Down with the Autocracy," was on the lips of all the many street orators from the Socialist parties. But this was not yet a political programme; it was a negative idea that was taken for granted. The problem of *government* had not yet been put before the masses.

And in particular the slogan of a "Constituent Assembly," not being on the order of the day, but merely part of the general programme of all the Socialist parties, was left completely in the shadow during those days.

On the other hand, the street agitators developed at great length another slogan, with extremely grave and far-reaching implications. This was "Down with the War," which dominated all the meetings of the February days.

The development of this slogan was quite inevitable. Russian Socialism, and the thinking Russian proletariat, unlike the Socialists of the Western European warring countries (with the exception of Italy), were for the most part resolutely against supporting the imperialist war. In the course of the war years our proletariat had been educated, as far as conditions allowed, in the spirit of Zimmerwald and the war against war. The defensist groups who had made themselves a niche in both capitals and here and there in the provinces had no authority whatever amongst the masses. There was nothing surprising or unexpected in the fact that a revolution against Tsarism should, at least amongst the proletariat of the capital, coincide with a movement in favour of peace. On the contrary, nothing else could have been expected of the street movement during the February days.

But at the same time it was quite clear that precisely this character of the movement must determine the attitude of the entire bourgeoisie towards it and the whole revolution. If these elements could accept the idea of liquidating Tsarism at all they could do so primarily to win the war. And this was precisely what the struggle against Tsarism of all our liberal groups had degenerated into in the course of the war. The liquidation of the Rasputin régime had come to be conceived of by the entire bourgeoisie merely as a means of strengthening our military power.

Hence it was evident that the bourgeoisie could have nothing in common with a movement that undermined the idea of "war to complete victory." It saw, or at least spoke of, any such movement as simply the result of German provocation. All propertied circles must have decisively dissociated themselves from it, and not merely left it to its own devices but felt obliged to hand it over to be destroyed by the forces of Tsarist reaction, and themselves take what share they could in that destruction.

It was clear then *a priori* that if a bourgeois Government and the adherence of the bourgeoisie to the revolution were to be counted on, it was temporarily necessary to *shelve the slogans against the war,* and furl for a time the banner of Zimmerwald, which had become the banner of the Russian, and especially of the Petersburg, proletariat. This was self-evident to me — a Zimmerwaldite.

At the same time, if the creation of a propertied Government was plainly impossible without such a compromise, it was still quite unclear whether this compromise would suffice to attain its objective. *Without it* the bourgeoisie together with Tsarism would crush the movement, but would it by itself ensure a different outcome for the revolution? Would it at least secure the formation of a bourgeois Government?

Information concerning this was indispensable. What were the plans of the Miliukov–Guchkov[11] camp? It was also necessary to know just what the opposite camp thought about all this; it was impossible to conceal from oneself that the advanced Socialists were being burdened with an extraordinary heavy task, and perhaps one beyond their capacity, which demanded not only a deep understanding of events, but also a restraint and submission to circumstances which to the outsider's eye might look like a betrayal of their basic principles and be misunderstood by the masses they were leading.

First of all a careful reconnaissance of the moods of both camps had to be made. The reports which came to me from both sides equally were extremely vague. In Duma circles, the question of a revolutionary Government had not even been raised. I could not see the slightest sign of any awareness among the parties or their leaders that the movement might end with a radical overturn. I could see only fear of the "provocative" movement and the intention of coming to the aid of Tsarism and liquidating the "disorders" with the "full authority" of the Duma. I could see also an attempt by the bourgeois groups to use the movement as a counter in coming to terms with Tsarism for a joint struggle — at the cost of any concessions in politics and the organization of the Government.

---

[11] Guchkov, Alexander Ivanovich (1862–1936): a wealthy Moscow capitalist, monarchist, and leader of the Octobrist Party, named for its support of the Imperial Manifesto of October 1905 that established the Duma. The Octobrist Party was the party of substantial commercial, industrial, and landowning interests. Though the party was monarchist, Guchkov was opposed to the dynasty during the First World War on patriotic grounds. He was an organizer of the palace revolution against the Tsar which the February Revolution prevented from maturing. He emigrated after the October Revolution.

The bourgeoisie was frightened by the movement and was not with it; therefore it was against it. But it could not afford to ignore it and make no use of it. *During these days the political slogan of the bourgeoisie, to which the entire radical intelligentsia also subscribed, was "a Ministry responsible to the Duma."*

At the same time attempts were made at a niggling solution of various urgent problems, attempts quite independent of the movement of the proletarian masses and, in the general situation, merely obscuring the issues with which our "society" was confronted. Thus on Saturday a meeting of the Town Council with various public organizations and workers' representatives proposed, in an almost revolutionary manner, to take the business of supplying Petersburg into their own hands.

In sum, looked at from the bourgeois side, hardly anything was clear on Friday the 24th, and what was clear was rather inauspicious. A session of the Duma Steering Committee, to which great significance was ascribed, was called for the next day. I counted on hearing a report of the results at Sokolov's.

In the other camp representatives of the Bolsheviks and the Socialist-Revolutionaries[12] of the Zimmerwald complexion had to be interviewed. Conversations with them gave me the same unfavourable impression. First of all the complete shapelessness of the movement and the absence of any strong, really authoritative centres were confirmed. Then I found complete indifference to the problems that were preoccupying me. Attention was wholly concentrated on immediate agitation based on general slogans and the immediate furtherance of the movement. Finally, my attempts to direct the thoughts of my interlocutors towards a concrete programme, and even more my propaganda for the creation of a revolutionary Government — even by way of a radical compromise — were received in a very sceptical and unfriendly spirit.

[12] The Socialist-Revolutionaries (SRs): a party that arose in the beginning of the 20th century as a development of earlier Populist parties; it regarded terrorism as the most effective method of struggle against the autocracy, but also engaged in propaganda amongst the workers and peasants. It boycotted the elections to the First Duma, although a number of sympathisers took part in them and in the First Duma formed the fairly substantial Trudovik group, controlled largely by Populists and SRs. They took a negative stand on the October Revolution, with the exception of the so-called Left SRs, who split from the party. The party was finally dissolved after the SR trial of 1920.

And yet, if these underground organizations could count on exercising any influence at all, it was just the Zimmerwaldite centres which could principally influence the movement. Thus the information obtainable both from this side and from the democratic camp was neither very specific nor very encouraging.

The movement of the Petersburg proletariat during those days and hours was not, however, confined to party agitation, factory meetings, and street demonstrations. There were attempts to create inter-party centres, there were joint conferences of active members of the various branches of the workers' movement — Duma deputies and representatives of the parties and of various trades and co-operatives. Meetings of this kind were held on Thursday and Friday. I was not present, but people who were told me afterwards that the discussions were chiefly devoted to the food question, or at any rate began with it. Afterwards, of course, they went on to the general situation, bringing to light only the bewilderment and confusion of the organizations. Reliable reporters said that Chkheidze, who was present, was indecision personified, and could only urge them to keep in step with the Duma. He represented the Right wing of the meetings and was disinclined to believe in the wide range of the movement. The Left, on the contrary, hailed the revolution with delight, and held that it was vital and urgently necessary to create fighting organizations of workers in the capital. F. A. Cherevanin, the old liquidator[13] and defensist, who was one of those who represented this Left view, also originated, so I was told, the idea of holding immediate elections in the Petersburg factories for a *Soviet of Workers' Deputies.*

In any case instructions for the elections were issued by this meeting. These instructions were instantly taken up by the party organizations and, as is known, successfully carried out in the factories of the capital.

---

[13] i.e., one of those who after the dissolution of the Second Duma (1907) had held that the conspiratorial and revolutionary activities of the Social-Democrats should be abandoned and the legal workers' organisations be built up until they were strong enough to defend their economic and social interests. Lenin bitterly attacked those who took this view as "Liquidators."

But I know that the *political* problem was never officially raised or resolved at these meetings. They have great historical merit for having prepared the *technique and organization* of the revolutionary forces, but no more. As for the political position of their participants, there was a preponderance of Menshevik defensists, and there could be no doubt that when they put the problem to themselves the majority of them would decide in favour of a bourgeois Government. The only trouble was that they had no serious influence on the masses.

Meanwhile the movement kept growing. The impotence of the police machinery became more evident with every hour. Meetings were already taking place almost with permission, and the military units, in the person of their commanding officers, were failing to take active steps against the growing crowds that filled the main streets. Unexpectedly the Cossack units displayed special sympathy with the revolution at various points, when in direct conversations they emphasized their neutrality and sometimes showed a clear tendency to fraternize. And on Friday evening they were saying in the city that elections were being held in the factories for the Soviet of Workers' Deputies.

On Saturday the 25th Petersburg seethed in an atmosphere of extraordinary events from the morning on. The streets, even where there was no concentration of people, were a picture of extreme excitement. I was reminded of the 1905 Moscow insurrection. The entire civil population felt itself to be in one camp united against the enemy — the police and the military. Strangers passing by conversed with each other, asking questions and talking about the news, about clashes with and the diversionary movements of the enemy.

But something else was noticeable that hadn't existed in the Moscow insurrection: the wall between the two camps — the people and the authorities — was not so impenetrable; a certain diffusion could be felt between them. This increased the excitement and filled the masses with something like enthusiasm.

Khabalov's proclamations were quite openly torn down from the walls. Policemen suddenly vanished from their posts.

Factories were at a standstill. No trams were running. I don't remember whether any newspapers appeared that day, but in any case events had far outstripped anything the half-stifled press of the day could have conveyed to the people.

That morning I proceeded as usual to my Turkestan office at the end of the Kamenno-ostrovsky Prospect, but naturally not for any reason connected with the irrigation of Turkestan. I rang up A. V. Peshekhonov,[14] inviting him to come to the Sergiyevsky, to N. D. Sokolov's, at 3 o'clock. In accordance with the conspiratorial habits well known to every Russian intellectual, he asked for no details — neither why, nor who else would be there; he promised to come himself or send one of his associates.

Before 2 o'clock, after having invited by telephone still another representative of a Left-wing organization, I went along to the Sergiyevsky, to an apartment as well known to all radical and democratic Petersburg as to the whole of the police force . . .

On the way, I dropped in at the editorial offices of the *Letopis* in the Monetny. No one, either on the editorial staff or in the office, was doing any work. They were all full of the events and the news. I was told which districts of the city were cordoned off by police and troops, and which was the best way to get through to the Tauride Gardens. But these accounts turned out to be false — for the reason that the actions of the authorities showed no trace of determination and still less of planning. Districts were cordoned off and released without any system or sense. In general the movement swept through the streets quite freely, and even the most thorough-going pessimists began to be persuaded of the impotence of the Khabalovs and Trepovs.

Near the entrance to the *Letopis* offices, at the gates of the neighbouring factory, I met a small group of civilians, workers by the look of them.

"What do they want?" said one grim-looking fellow. "They want bread, peace with the Germans, and equality for the Yids."

"Right in the bull's eye," I thought, delighted with this brilliant formulation of the programme of the great revolution.

---

[14] Peshekhonov, Alexei Vasilyevich (1867–1934): a prominent Populist journalist, later to become Supply Minister in the Provisional Government. The Populists were revolutionists with Socialist ideals who were, however, indifferent or hostile to Marxist theory. They thought the peasants rather than the working class should lead in the overthrow of Tsarism and the transformation of Russia. The word refers both to the terrorists who hoped to destroy Tsarism and rouse the peasants by the "propaganda of the deed," and to the gentlest and most idealistic Socialists who hoped to transform Russia by "going to the people."

A disappointment awaited me at N. D. Sokolov's. The meeting bore no resemblance to a representative gathering of organized groups or democratic fractions. It had a quite haphazard and at the same time uniform character. Most of those who came were representatives of the radical Populist intelligentsia. In this sort of meeting even a theoretical examination of the questions which interested me didn't have much point.

Sokolov was expecting some authorized representatives of the Bolsheviks, but not one of them turned up. In their place Kerensky[15] appeared; he had come straight from a session of the Steering Committee of the Duma, and naturally could be a unique source of information about the mood and plans of the leading political circles of the bourgeoisie.

Kerensky, as always excitable, emotional, and somewhat theatrical, spoke for the most part of the panic and confusion of the mass of the bourgeois deputies. As far as the leading circles were concerned, all their thoughts and efforts boiled down, not to shaping the revolution, or joining it and trying to make themselves the crest of the wave, but exclusively to avoiding it. Attempts were being made at deals with Tsarism; the political game was in full swing. All this was not only independent of the popular movement but as its expense and obviously aimed at its destruction.

At this moment the position of the bourgeoisie was quite clear: it was a position on the one hand of keeping their distance from the revolution and betraying it to Tsarism, and on the other of exploiting it for their own manoeuvres. But this was far from a position of *alliance* with it, even in the form of patronizing it.

Since Kerensky's account had given me no information on those aspects of the matter that specially interest me, I made a few hopeless efforts to clear up the problem for myself by direct and indirect questioning. Kerensky himself, of course, might have some relevant information, through his uninterrupted contact with various Duma circles.

---

[15] Kerensky, Alexander Fyodorovich (1881–1970): at this time leader of the Trudoviks (Labourites) in the Duma, later to become Premier. The Trudoviks were a group of Populist intellectuals who defended the peasants as against the landowners. They were not, however, much more radical than the Cadets. Kerensky escaped from Petrograd after the October Revolution and eventually settled in the United States, where he died.

But these efforts of mine elicited nothing except a bewilderment which showed that for Kerensky, as well as for some of his supporters who were present, my way of formulating the problems of the future Government seemed futile and, in any case, ill-timed and irrelevant. I came up against the same mood in these people that I had encountered the day before amongst the Left (Zimmerwald) groups and that I also encountered later on, up to the very moment of the formation of the first revolutionary Government.

Kerensky assumed the polemical tone usual in his conversations with me and soon began to lose his temper; I preferred to cut short a conversation which had not aroused enough interest in those present.

New people kept coming to Sokolov's flat bringing with them reports, all agreeing, of the unprecedented scale of the movement in the streets. The central districts looked like a continuous mass-meeting, and the populace seemed specially drawn to Znamensky Square. There, from the plinth of the statue of Alexander III, speakers of the Left parties spoke uninterruptedly and without any interference. The basic slogan was, as before, "Down with the War," which together with the autocracy was interpreted as the source of all misfortunes and especially of the breakdown in supplies.

The reports spoke also of the growing demoralization of the police and troops. Mounted and unmounted police and Cossack units in great numbers were patrolling the streets, slowly pushing their way through the crowds. But they took no action, and this immensely cheered the demonstrators. The police and troops limited themselves to removing red banners wherever this was technically convenient and could be done without a scuffle.

At this time there was the first report about a symptomatic "excess" in some Cossack unit. A police inspector, on horseback at the head of a police detachment, attacked some flag-bearer or orator with his sabre, whereupon a Cossack nearby flew at the inspector and slashed off his hand. The inspector was carried off, but the incident had no sequel in the street.

Our conference finally took on the character of a haphazard private conversation. I remember Sokolov telling me in particular something I appreciated only later on. As a defensist he indicated the danger of the anti-war slogans around which the popular movement was revolving and on which the party orators were chiefly concentrating the attention of the masses; however, he did not emphasize the aspect of the question that occupied me all this time — the inevitable refusal of the bourgeoisie to join the revolution in such circumstances — but referred to the inevitability of a split on this ground within the democratic movement itself and even within the proletariat. At that time I ascribed no importance to this point, merely because I had too strong a belief (perhaps exaggerated) in the exclusive rule over the masses of those parties and groups represented by the Socialist minority in Germany or France. Moreover the character of the approaching revolution was completely obscure; in particular no one could foresee the role in it of the army, made up as it was of officers and peasants. But a split within the most active revolutionary proletarian army cadres rapidly proved to be really a most important factor, in the light of which the entire "military" policy of the revolutionary democracy had to be guided. At that time, however, I had no interest in this aspect of the matter, devoting most of my attention to the attitude of the *haute* bourgeoisie and their relations with the revolution.

As it happened, though, in our practical conclusions Sokolov and I were in complete agreement. As a man who had come out against the war more than others and more definitely, and as a writer who had a fairly solid reputation as a defeatist, an internationalist, and a hater of patriotism, I was urged by Sokolov to speak out now as decisively as possible against the anti-war slogans and to collaborate in seeing to it that the movement did not proceed under the cry of "Down with the War." He said that the appropriate arguments, coming from me, would be devoid of any counter-revolutionary character and be more convincing to the leaders of the movement. For if it began as a movement against the war, the revolution would quickly be undone by internal dissensions.

Whatever my attitude towards this argument, I was in wholehearted sympathy with its final conclusions and promised my full cooperation with the defensists and radical groups against consistent internationalist class principles — in fact against my own principles.

However, I felt myself completely cut off from the centres of the revolution and completely powerless to do anything. I did not claim for myself the slightest influence on the controlling centres of the movement. I must recall here that from 1906 or 1907 on I had no formal connexion with any party or organization. My "wild" position naturally excluded the possibility of any direct activity in practical Socialism, to say nothing of leadership. I was primarily a writer. But nevertheless my literary work was closely tied up with the movement, and during the war, owing to accidental circumstances, my writings enjoyed wide popularity amongst active Socialists and served as material for their practical work. At the same time, without having any formal ties I was in fact, by virtue of personal acquaintance and professional connexions, linked to many, one might say all, the Socialist parties and organizations of Petersburg.

It is of no interest to describe my position among the parties and explain its causes. I shall simply say that from the time when I was editor of the *Sovremennik* — which I unquestionably succeeded in making a non-party literary centre for prominent Socialists of all shades — I had maintained rather close contacts with all the Socialist groups. Party centres knew me quite well and often made use of me. And in particular as an editor of the *Letopis* I kept up the closest relations with the literary Socialist *émigrés* of various tendencies. During the war people were always trying to attract me into various illegal literary enterprises of an internationalist complexion. Moreover, probably not one attempt of the inter-party blocs at unification or coalition during those last years was made without my participation. This was my situation during the revolution also.

At the time of the revolution this undoubtedly had some advantages from the point of view of ease of personal relationship and of mobility between those points which had the greatest importance and interest, but it deprived me of the advantages of being a party man and leader, for everybody still considered me "wild" and an outsider.

Nevertheless it is essential to emphasize at this point the great difference between the Petersburg party centres at that time and those that sprang up during the revolution. This was that *there were no authoritative leaders on the spot* in any of the parties, almost without exception. They were in exile, in prison, or abroad. In the positions of the responsible heads of the great movement, at its most important moments, there were absolutely second-rate people, who may have been clever organizers but nevertheless were routine party hacks of the days of the autocracy. It was impossible to expect of them, in the great majority of cases, a proper political perspective in the new situation or any real political guidance of events. Placed beside such leaders of the movement I felt competent and useful. But I was cut off from the work they were doing; and at the time of my conversation with Sokolov there was nothing in my mind but a consciousness of my inability to influence events in any way.

The gathering began to disperse, some going off into the streets, some into other rooms, some home. Kerensky rushed off, saying he was returning to the Duma, which was crowded with deputies from morning to night, and invited Zenzinov[16] and me to visit him in roughly an hour's time to hear the latest news. After talking about various topics for another half-hour at Sokolov's, Zenzinov and I quietly proceeded to Kerensky's. We were remembering Moscow in 1905, and going over scenes from the December uprising, in which both of us had taken part. But the district round the Sergiyevsky and the Tversky, and the Tauride Gardens, were quiet and empty. There is some interest in recording this. The people *were not gravitating toward the Duma*, had no interest in it, and did not think of making it the centre of the movement either politically or technically. Our liberal politicians later spent all their energies representing the Duma as the banner, and its fate as the cause, of the movement. But these attempts were all completely implausible.

We did not, however, find Kerensky at home. In the hall his two little boys, who knew what was going on, ran out to us and told us that "Papa had just rung up from the Duma." He had said there was shooting along the Nevsky, and a great many casualties.

At this point Kerensky's wife, Olga Lvovna, came back from her work. She was employed in some social institute or other, located around the centre of Nevsky Prospect near Kazansky Square. She had just seen from her windows a big demonstration making for Kazansky Square; it had been fired on, the shooting had gone on for a few minutes, and there had been a fight. But just which army unit had done the firing, and what the casualties were, it had been impossible either to see in the dusk or to find out.

Things were coming to a head. It was no longer thinkable for the

---

[16]Zenzinov, Vladimir Mikhailovich (1881–1953): an SR from 1903; adherent of the terrorist wing of the party. Member of the Ex. Com. in 1917 and ardent partisan of Kerensky's. He was elected to the Constituent Assembly in 1918, and after its dissolution took up arms against the Bolsheviks. An *émigré* since 1921, first in France, then in the United States. He died in New York.

authorities not to make some effort to suppress the disorders. That would mean the irrevocable laying down of their arms and being confronted by an accomplished fact — the defeat of the "existing order." The authorities, without losing a single hour, *had to* find a suitable army or police unit and push it into action. Vacillation or procrastination was obviously and literally equivalent to death. The moment was decisive for the fate of age-old Tsarism . . . Just which unit fired on the Nevsky demonstration that evening of February 25th, I don't know to this day. But one way or another the authorities had gone over to the offensive. This was the turning point of events, which had entered a new phase.

If there had been adequate forces for an offensive, if it had been possible to terrorize the unarmed and still scattered populace and drive them home, then the movement might have been liquidated (though not for long) as "disorders" had been liquidated dozens of times before. It was important to pass beyond the dead point, and with one stunning blow simultaneously destroy the morale of the masses and check any tendency to disintegration within the army. A risky, desperate, and perhaps final attempt had to be made without delay. It was made — and it proved to be the last.

When Zenzinov and I left Kerensky's it was already almost completely dark. After walking the length of the Tversky from Smolny,[17] past the dimly lit Tauride Palace and its silent square, we went along the Shpalerny. I made my way home to the Petersburg Side.

No shooting could be heard. Nearer the Liteiny, where we separated, we met a few small groups of workers who passed on rumours of the beginning of the offensive: bloody, though small, fights had begun somewhere in the working-class suburbs. A few of the biggest factories had been occupied, others were besieged by troops. Here and there the attackers had met with resistance — some pistol-shots from young workers, but mostly stones thrown by youths.

On the Vyborg Side, passers-by said, barricades were being constructed of tram-cars and telegraph poles.

---

[17]The Smolny Institute, a building designed by Quarenghi. From 1808 to the middle of 1917 an exclusive college for the education of the young daughters of the nobility. The Petersburg Soviet and the Central Executive Committee of the Soviet of Workers' and Soldiers' Deputies moved there on August 4th, 1917.

After cutting across the ice on the empty Neva, from the Liteiny to Trinity Bridge, I called on Gorky in the Kronvergsky. I found a small group there, including the other editors of the *Letopis* — Bazarov and Tikhonov, with whom, in discussing what was happening, I quickly got into a violent argument. Like the others I had spoken to, they refused to agree with me in placing the problem of the organization of the revolutionary Government in the forefront and were chiefly interested in the actual course of events, which they judged far more pessimistically than I; and they teased me for seeing mirages.

One after another people both known and unknown, to Gorky himself as well as to me, kept coming in. They came in for consultation, to share their impressions, to make inquiries, and to find out what was going on in various circles. Gorky naturally had connexions throughout Petersburg, from top to bottom. We began to talk, and we, the editors of the *Letopis*, soon set up a united front against representatives of the Left, the internationalist representatives of our own views, heedless of the charges of betrayal of our old watchwords at the decisive moment.

Meanwhile some fairly responsible Bolshevik leaders came along. And their flatfootedness or, more properly, their incapacity to think their way into the political problem and formulate it, had a depressing effect on us. But it must be said that our own arguments were not without some influence on these people, who had appeared straight from the turbulent excitement of workers' centres or party committees. In those days they were completely absorbed in a different kind of work, serving the technical needs of the movement, forcing a decisive set-to with Tsarism, and organizing propaganda and the illegal press. And our arguments compelled them to think about what was new in the vast problems which they now consciously confronted for the first time.

In these conversations Gorky took the most active part. Apart from the Bolsheviks, with whom Gorky traditionally had closer ties than with the other Socialist organizations, others came in too; a few of these in two more days were to be my colleagues on the Executive Committee. Gorky's flat had begun to be the natural centre, if not of any organization, at least of information, which attracted various elements involved in one way or another in the movement. We arranged to meet there the following day about noon.

Towards the time when house-gates in Petersburg were usually locked, I left Gorky's house to go home, to give myself as usual time to slip past the house-porter and into my apartment unnoticed, by the back way. The streets were quiet. As before consciousness of my helplessness never left me; I felt a longing for more immediate activity.

The next day, Sunday, February 26th, I went over to Gorky's again. The streets were hung with General Khabalov's new proclamations, and others, torn down and crumpled, littered the ground. Publicly admitting in them his own helplessness and implying that his previous warnings had been of no avail, he was once again threatening decisive measures and a resort to arms against disorders and mobs.

And Sunday really was given over to decisive measures and a resort to arms. The last desperate throw was being made. What was at stake was the age-old régime, embodying not merely the bric-à-brac of old privileges but also the hopes of the bourgeoisie, who scented a more dangerous enemy. The day was passed in the last grapple, amid the sound of firing and the smoke of powder. Nightfall showed that the game was lost: by evening the card had been trumped.

The siege of factories and working-class districts continued and was intensified. Great numbers of infantry units were moved out into the streets: they cordoned off bridges, isolated various districts, and set about a thorough-going clearance of the streets.

Around 1 o'clock the infantry trained rifle-fire of great intensity on the Nevsky. The Prospect, strewn with corpses of innocent passers-by, was cleared. Rumours of this flew swiftly about the city. The inhabitants were terrorized, and in the central parts of the city the movement in the streets was quelled.

Towards 5 o'clock it might well have seemed that Tsarism had again won the throw and that the movement was going to be suppressed.

However, even in these critical hours the atmosphere in the streets was completely different from what must very often have been observed during the crushing of "disorders." And in spite of the panic of the urban population and the inevitable psychological reaction of the conscious democratic groups, this atmosphere continued to give every reason for the most legitimate optimism.

The difference from the previous "disorders" consisted in the composition and the whole outward aspect of the troops, Cossacks, and even police, who were suppressing the movement. One of these units, perhaps of army cadets, was ordered to fire, and so terrorized the unarmed, scattered crowd. Others obediently formed dense cordons around a few points. Still others, also obeying orders, went around the city in groups as patrols. But all this had a rather casual, unserious, and unreal character. Both the cordons and the patrols looked as though they were hoping for organized attacks on themselves and seeking an occasion to surrender. Single policemen had long since completely vanished. The patrols, who were not marching but strolling around the city, were as a matter of fact disarmed in many places without offering serious resistance. Into every crowd and group an enormous number of soldiers' grey greatcoats had been "organically assimilated."

Around 2 or 3 o'clock a small group of us from Gorky's went out into the streets to see for ourselves.

From the Petersburg Side we tried to make our way to the Nevsky. As we went toward Trinity Bridge the crowd got denser and denser. Blocking the squares, the Kamenno-ostrovsky Prospect, and the gardens at the end of Trinity Bridge, it was breaking up into a multitude of groups, clustering round people who had returned to the Petersburg Side from the city.

Independently of sex, age, or condition, they were excitedly discussing the shooting of the casual, unorganized, and non-demonstrating crowd in the main streets of the centre. All the eye-witnesses agreed in their impression of the bewildered and terrified state of mind of the units involved who, a great distance away from the "enemy," had opened up a disorderly fire down the length of the streets. They spoke of an enormous number of casualties, although of course their figures varied from a few dozen to many thousands.

We made our way to the bridge. There was a lively bustle on the wall of the Peter-Paul Fortress and armed detachments of infantry could be seen around the guns. The crowd expected some aggressive action from there and watched with curiosity, but it did not disperse.

On the bridge, shoulder to shoulder and barring the way, stood a cordon of Grenadiers. In spite of the presence of an officer, they were standing easy and conversing animatedly with the crowd on political topics. Agitators were haranguing them in quite unambiguous terms. Some soldiers were chuckling, others were listening in attentive silence.

They refused to let anyone pass through the line on to the bridge, but a few individuals filtered through without being turned back. There was no direct insubordination, but they were obviously unsuitable material for any active operations, and there was clearly nothing for the officers to do but turn a blind eye on this scene of "corruption."

For this detachment to take aim and open fire on the people it had been conversing with was unthinkable, and no one in the crowd believed for a moment that it was possible. On the contrary, the soldiers obviously would not have objected if their front were broken through, and many of them would probably have shared their arms with the crowd. But the crowd had no such intentions.

We went back to Gorky's; he was talking on the 'phone to various representatives of the bourgeois and bureaucratic world. His basic impression was of the same perplexity and bafflement prevailing among them. Strangely enough the rifle-fire had a great effect on the entire situation; it made an extremely strong impression not only on the man in the street, but also on political circles, where voices were heard demanding "the most energetic steps." The firing had obviously produced a Leftward reaction among the whole crowd of bourgeois politicians.

I telephoned a great many Left writers and deputies at home, but for the most part without success. At Kerensky's I caught Sokolov, who was sitting with Olga Lvovna expecting some information from the Duma, but he could not tell me anything important.

In general, however, "high policy" in these hours proceeded as before — not under the banner of revolution and the overthrow of Tsarism, but on the basis of an accord with it founded on minor concessions. Some telephone reports said that various districts of the city had been isolated and that it was impossible to get to the centre; others denied this. But there was no definite goal to warrant an excursion anywhere. None of the deputies left the Duma, which was impossible to get into. People kept coming to Gorky's as before and information kept accumulating, and however little this could alleviate the strain and my longing to be in the crucible of events I had to stay there.

The time passed in interrogation, fruitless speculations, and arguments which had become tedious and nerve-wracking. There were reports that in the working-class districts street demonstrations and meetings were continuing. From Vyborg, the most militant, later a Bolshevik district, came reports of serious action by workers against police and troops. From time to time distant rifle-fire was heard.

Between 7 and 8 o'clock Gorky 'phoned Chaliapine,[18] among others, to find out what was known in his circle. Chaliapine had a strange story to tell. He had just been rung up by Leonid Andreyev,[19] whose flat was on the Champ de Mars on the same side as the Pavlovsky barracks. From the window Andreyev had personally seen an infantry unit systematically firing for a long time from the Champ de Mars at the Pavlovsky barracks. Andreyev could report nothing further, and as for the meaning of it all, Chaliapine said, they were both completely at a loss. It seemed impossible to doubt the reliability of these reports, but there really was no way of making sense of them.

I intensified my 'phoning. Luckily I quickly got in touch with Kerensky, who had come home from the Duma for a short time. Kerensky told me, in the most categorical terms, that the *Pavlovsky Regiment had mutinied*. Most of them had come out into the street and begun skirmishing with the minority who had stayed behind in the barracks. It was this skirmish that Andreyev had seen from his window.

Events had all at once taken a new turn, which presaged victory. The revolt of a regiment, in the general framework of the last few days, meant almost to a certainty that the Tsarist card was trumped. But Kerensky was exaggerating.

It became clear later that what had happened was this: A small detachment of mounted police had orders to disperse a crowd that had collected along the Catherine Canal; for safety's sake the police began to fire on it from the opposite bank, across the canal. Just then a detachment of Pavlovskys was passing along the bank that was occupied by the crowd. It was then that an historic incident took place that marked an abrupt break in the course of events and opened up new perspectives for the movement: seeing this shooting at unarmed people and the wounded falling around them, and finding themselves in the zone of fire, the Pavlovskys opened fire at the police across the canal.

This was the first instance of a massive open clash between armed

[18] Chaliapine, Fyodor Ivanovich (1873–1938): the celebrated *basso*.
[19] Andreyev, Leonid Nikolayevich (1874–1919): belletristic writer, playwright, and journalist.

detachments. It was described to us in detail by a friend who came to Gorky's later on; he had been walking along the Catherine Canal at the time and had personally seen the wounded policemen and their blood-stained horses. Then the Pavlovskys, now "mutineers" who had burnt their boats, returned to their barracks and appealed to their comrades to join them. This was when the firing took place between the loyal and the rebel parts of the regiment. How far all this was deliberate on the part of the Pavlovskys and how far it was the result of momentary instinct, nervous impulse, and simple self-defense, it is impossible to say. But the objective importance of this affair at the Catherine Canal was enormous and quite unmistakable. In any case, to the Pavlovsky Regiment belongs the honour of having performed the first revolutionary act of the military against the armed forces of Tsarism.

It was obvious that there could be no talk of a conclusive victory for the revolution without a victory over the army and the transference of the greater part of it to the side of the revolutionary populace. And the Pavlovsky Regiment had made a beginning on the evening of February 26th.

This was a terrible breach in the stronghold of Tsarism. Now, after a period of depression, we were all seized anew by a spirit of optimism, even enthusiasm, and our thoughts turned again to the political problems of the revolution. For events had again shifted our course towards revolution, making us disdain all attempts to liquidate the movement by a rotten compromise with the Rasputin régime . . .

Kerensky as before failed to sum up the political situation in any practical way. The Progressive Bloc of the Duma was growing hourly more Leftist — that was all Kerensky had to report. The people at his place were already dispersing, nor for that matter did they promise anything substantial in the way of information. There was no sense in going over there at the risk of getting held up by some police barrier.

Before 11 o'clock I rang up the Duma, intending to speak to the first Left deputy who could be found. Skobelev[20] came to the telephone and told me the Tauride Palace was already empty. Everyone had gone away confused, shaken, and worn out. A session had been called for the following day, but rumours, quasi-reliable, were going around that

[20] Skobelev, Matvei Ivanovich (1885–1930?): Menshevik member of Fourth Duma. Joined the Bolsheviks in 1922, holding many posts in planning institutions.

the next morning an ukase dissolving the Duma would be published. Skobelev had nothing more to tell.

We sat around Gorky's conversing deep into the night. Events were clearly developing favourably. There was news of the defection of other military units.

I made my way home without troubling to choose my time, boldly woke the porter by ringing the bell, and went in by the front door.

The streets were quiet.

A Word about Kerensky

By way of a footnote to the above it may be in place to say something here about Kerensky, simply as a commentary to this exposition, which in my opinion would otherwise lose a great deal of its lucidity.

I had known Kerensky for quite a long time, since my return from exile in Archangel at the very beginning of 1913. From that time on my relations with him, social, professional, and personal, constituted if not a very close sequence at least an uninterrupted one. I had seen him in every possible guise, from his advocate's frock-coat in court, his morning coat in the Duma, and his lounge suit at meetings large and small, to the dazzlingly striped Turkestani dressing-gown he had brought from his own part of the country.

I had seen him on dozens of minor and major occasions — as an orator in the Duma, as a political *rapporteur*, in conversation with friends, as one of an intimate group of not more than half a dozen people, and finally as a paterfamilias, with his wife and two boys.

During the time I was underground I had spent many, many nights at his flat, and often after he had made up a bed for me in his study the two of us would fall into a real, long-drawn-out Russian conversation lasting into the small hours. More than once he turned up at the *Sovremennik* to see me, usually bursting into the ante-chamber like a tornado, leaving his ubiquitous pair of "shadows" keeping watch at the entrance and making me redouble my precautionary measures afterwards.[21]

---

[21] Kerensky's nickname among the Secret Police was "Speedy." He did, in fact, rush headlong through the streets, and leap in and out of moving trams. The police spies couldn't keep up with him: in addition to two of them on foot, Kerensky was always followed by another in a droshky. Keeping the future Premier under observation cost the

Our conversations always started out with information or stories from Kerensky, who as a deputy had been at the very heart of things, the fountain-head of the news and the poverty-stricken public opinion of the time. But these stories always developed quickly into the most venomous disputes and desperate wrangling. Though these quarrels had no effect on our personal relations, no intimacy could for a moment blot out the awareness that we did not agree on anything, that we approached any party (or rather inter-party) or socio-political question from opposite poles, and thought about it on different planes, and that consequently we were in opposite camps politically, and temperamentally inhabited different worlds . . .

It was a heavy load that history laid upon feeble shoulders. I used to say that Kerensky had golden hands, meaning his supernatural energy, amazing capacity for work, and inexhaustible temperament. But he lacked the head for statesmanship and had no real political schooling. Without these elementary and indispensable attributes, the irreplaceable Kerensky of expiring Tsarism, the ubiquitous Kerensky of the February–March days could not but stumble headlong and flounder into his July–September situation, and then plunge into his October nothingness, taking with him, alas! an enormous part of what we had achieved in the February–March revolution.

But it was clear to me that it was precisely Kerensky with his "golden hands," with his views and inclinations, and with his situation as a deputy and his exceptional popularity who, by the will of fate, had been summoned to be the central figure of the revolution, or at least of its beginnings.

Not very long before the February days I remember visiting him on a holiday, during his illness. He was sitting alone in his study in a thick grey sweater, trying to warm himself in the cold room. He had the latest issue of *Letopis* in his hands, and lost no time in coming down on me with some polemical sarcasms. But then the conversation unexpectedly took a peaceful, speculative turn about approaching events and revolutionary perspectives. And I recall that I gently reproached him for his pernicious views, and seriously and without heat exposed what appeared

---

Government quite a lot. From the windows of the *Sovremennik*, after putting out the lights, we would watch the "shadows," having caught sight of Kerensky running out of the entrance, hurriedly climb into the droshky and start out after him . . .

to me to be his weak points. My starting-point in all this was that in the near future he would have to become the head of the State. Kerensky did not interrupt; he listened in silence. Perhaps at this time he was only *dreaming* about a Kerensky ministry; but he may also have been seriously preparing for it . . . Alas! it was indeed a heavy load that history laid upon feeble shoulders!

Now, when Kerensky is a political corpse and there is almost no hope of his resurrection (for his importance in all spheres has completely dwindled away), nothing is easier than to throw one more stone on this political tomb and soothe oneself with the consciousness of having been correct in this historical evaluation. But I am not particularly tempted by such laurels. I was a convinced political opponent of Kerensky's from the day of our first meeting and throughout the time of his greatest power, and to this day I have not changed my opinions, unlike thousands of his champions who later lost no time in selling their worthless swords.

But now that his political reputation is ruined this gives me all the greater right to emphasize his brighter side, with all the greater satisfaction and hope of being believed. This is only just.

And above all, in the face of Bolshevism now triumphant and reviling Kerensky, in the face of his incontestable alliance with the forces of bourgeois reaction against democracy, despite the Kerensky–Kornilov affair, in spite of the fact that he really did do his best to strangle the revolution and did, more than anyone else, lead it to Brest-Litovsk, I maintain that he was a sincere democrat and fighter for revolutionary victory — as he understood it. I know he was incapable of realizing his good intentions, but you cannot wring blood from a stone. That is a matter of his inadequate objective resources as a statesman, not his subjective characteristics as a man. I reaffirm: Kerensky was really persuaded that he was a Socialist and a democrat. He never suspected that by conviction, taste, and temperament he was the most consummate middle-class radical.

But he believed in his providential mission to such an extent that he could not separate his own career from the fate of the contemporary democratic movement in Russia. This was why Kerensky saw himself not only as a Socialist but also as a little bit of a Bonaparte.

His tempestuous Turkestan temperament made him grow dizzy almost immediately, simply from the grandiose events of the revolution and his own role in them. And his indubitable innate inclination to pomposity, preciosity, and theatricality completed the process before he became Premier.

'Kerensky the Little Braggart' — this epithet of Lenin's is, of course, by no means an exhaustive description of Kerensky's character, but it does hit the mark and schematize the picture by simplifying it. All this is incontestable. But none of it shakes in any way my conviction that Kerensky was a sincere democrat. For if he naïvely failed to distinguish between his personality and the revolution, he could never have *consciously* sacrificed the interests of democracy to himself and his place in history.

He sincerely believed in the correctness of his line and equally sincerely hoped that his course would bring the country to the triumph of democracy. He was cruelly mistaken. And I personally, even at the time, did all I could to expose him and his cruel errors publicly. But Kerensky, feeble politician as he was, without the schooling or wisdom of a statesman, was sincere in his delusions and plunged in all good faith into his anti-democratic policies, and so, as far as his influence was effective, interred the revolution, together with himself.

Leon Trotsky

Conscious and Tempered Workers

Born in the Ukraine in 1879, Leon Trotsky was an early convert to Marxism. Never completely comfortable with either the Menshevik or Bolshevik wings of the party, Trotsky staked out his own unique positions. In 1905–1906 he elaborated the theory of "permanent revolution" that held that even in a backward country like Russia a revolution could begin as a "bourgeois-democratic" revolution and metamorphose into a socialist one. He joined the Bolsheviks in mid-1917, and in September was elected chairman of the Petrograd Soviet. As head of the Military-Revolutionary

From Leon Trotsky, *The History of the Russian Revolution*, translated by Max Eastman, 3 vols. (New York: Simon & Schuster, 1936). Reprinted by permission of Max Schachtman.

Committee of the Soviet, he played a leading role in the Bolshevik seizure of power. Second only to Lenin in the first five years of the Soviet government, Trotsky was the first Commissar of Foreign Affairs and later Commissar of War. He is credited with organizing the Red Army that won the Civil War (1918–1921). With Lenin's illness and early death in 1924, Trotsky found himself isolated within the ruling Politburo of the Communist party. He consistently rejected the notion, later proposed by Stalin, that socialism could be completely constructed in one country. In the 1920s Trotsky was defeated by Stalin in a protracted political struggle and forced into exile. In 1940 he was murdered by a Stalinist agent in Mexico. A brilliant theorist and polemical writer, Trotsky wrote a classic three-volume treatise on the revolution that combines Marxist analysis with his own partisan judgments. In the selection offered here he attempts to refute the argument for spontaneity and proposes that Bolshevik-inspired workers played the key role in the February revolt.

Lawyers and journalists belonging to the classes damaged by the revolution wasted a good deal of ink subsequently trying to prove that what happened in February was essentially a petticoat rebellion, backed up afterwards by a soldiers' mutiny and given out for a revolution. Louis XVI in his day also tried to think that the capture of the Bastille was a rebellion, but they respectfully explained to him that it was a revolution. Those who lose by a revolution are rarely inclined to call it by its real name. For that name, in spite of the efforts of spiteful reactionaries, is surrounded in the historic memory of mankind with a halo of liberation from all shackles and all prejudices. The privileged classes of every age, as also their lackeys, have always tried to declare the revolution which overthrew them, in contrast to past revolutions, a mutiny, a riot, a revolt of the rabble. Classes which have outlived themselves are not distinguished by originality.

Soon after the 27th of February attempts were also made to liken the revolution to the military coup d'état of the Young Turks, of which, as we know, they had been dreaming not a little in the upper circles of the Russian bourgeoisie. This comparison was so hopeless, however, that it was seriously opposed even in one of the bourgeois papers. Tugan-Baranovsky, an economist who had studied Marx in his youth, a Russian variety of Sombart, wrote on March 10 in the *Birzhevye Vedomosti* [Stock Exchange News]:

The Turkish revolution consisted in a victorious uprising of the army, prepared and carried out by the leaders of the army; the soldiers were merely obedient executives of the plans of their officers. But the regiments of the Guard which on February 27 overthrew the Russian throne, came without their officers . . . Not the army but the workers began the insurrection; not the generals but the soldiers came to the State Duma. The soldiers supported the workers not because they were obediently fulfilling the commands of their officers, but because . . . they felt themselves blood brothers of the workers as a class composed of toilers like themselves. The peasants and the workers — those are the two social classes which made the Russian revolution.

These words require neither correction, nor supplement. The further development of the revolution sufficiently confirmed and reenforced their meaning. In Petrograd the last day of February was the first day after the victory: a day of raptures, embraces, joyful tears, voluble outpourings; but at the same time a day of final blows at the enemy. Shots were still crackling in the streets. It was said that Protopopov's Pharaohs, not informed of the people's victory, were still shooting from the roofs. From below they were firing into attics, false windows and belfries where the armed phantoms of tzarism might still be lurking. About four o'clock they occupied the Admiralty where the last remnants of what was formerly the state power had taken refuge. Revolutionary organizations and improvised groups were making arrests throughout the town. The Schlüsselburg hard-labor prison was taken without a shot. More and more regiments were joining the revolution, both in the capital and in the environs.

The overturn in Moscow was only an echo of the insurrection in Petrograd. The same moods among the workers and soldiers, but less clearly expressed. A slightly more leftward tendency among the bourgeoisie. A still greater weakness among the revolutionary organizations than in Petrograd. When the events began on the Neva, the Moscow radical intelligentsia called a conference on the question [of] what to do, and came to no conclusion. Only on the 27th of February strikes began in the shops and factories of Moscow, and then demonstrations. The officers told the soldiers in the barracks that a rabble was rioting in the streets and they must be put down. "But by this time," relates the soldier Shishilin, "the soldiers understood the word rabble in the opposite sense." Toward two o'clock there arrived at the building of the City Duma many soldiers of various regiments inquiring how to join the revolution. On the next day the strikes increased. Crowds flowed toward the Duma with flags. A soldier of an automobile company, Muralov, an old Bolshevik, an agriculturist, a good-natured and courageous giant, brought to the Duma the first complete and disciplined military detachment, which occupied the wireless station and other points. Eight months later Muralov will be in command of the troops of the Moscow military district.

The prisons were opened. The same Muralov was driving an automobile truck filled with freed political prisoners: a police officer with his hand at his vizor asked the revolutionist whether it was advisable to let out the Jews also. Dzerzhinsky, just liberated from a hard labor prison and without changing his prison dress, spoke in the Duma building where a soviet of deputies was already formed. The artillerist Dorofeev relates how on March 1 workers from the Siou candy factory came with banners to the barracks of an artillery brigade to fraternize with the soldiers, and how many could not contain their joy, and wept. There were cases of sniping in the town, but in general neither armed encounters nor casualties: Petrograd answered for Moscow.

In a series of provincial cities the movement began only on March 1, after the revolution was already achieved even in Moscow. In Tver the workers went from their work to the barracks in a procession and having mixed with the soldiers marched through the streets of the city. At that time they were still singing the "Marseillaise," not the "International." In Nizhni-Novgorod thousands of workers gathered round the City Duma building, which in a majority of the cities played the role of the Tauride Palace. After a speech from the mayor the workers marched off with red banners to free the politicals from the jails. By evening, eighteen out of the twenty-one military divisions of the garrison had voluntarily come over to the revolution. In Samara and Saratov meetings were held, soviets of workers' deputies organized. In Kharkov the chief of police, having gone to the railroad station and got news of the revolution, stood up in his carriage before an excited crowd and, lifting his hat, shouted at the top of his lungs: "Long live the revolution. Hurrah!" The news came to Ekaterinoslav from Kharkov. At the head of the demonstration strode the assistant chief of police carrying in his hand a long saber as in the grand parades on saints' days. When it became finally clear that the monarchy could not rise, they began cautiously to remove the tzar's portraits from the government institutions and hide them in the attics. Anecdotes about this, both authentic and imaginary, were much passed around in liberal circles, where they had not yet lost a taste for the jocular tone when speaking of the revolution. The workers, and the soldier barracks as well, took the events in a very different way. As to a series of other provincial cities (Pskov, Orel, Rybinsk, Penza, Kazan, Tzaritsyn, and others), the *Chronicle* remarks under date of March 2: "News came of the uprising and the population joined the revolution." This description, notwithstanding its summary character, tells with fundamental truth what happened.

News of the revolution trickled into the villages from the near-by cities, partly through the authorities, but chiefly through the markets, the workers, the soldiers on furlough. The villages accepted the revolution more slowly and less enthusiastically than the cities, but felt it no less deeply. For them it was bound up with the question of war and land.

It would be no exaggeration to say that Petrograd achieved the February Revolution. The rest of the country adhered to it. There was no struggle anywhere except in Petrograd. There were not to be found anywhere in the country any groups of the population, any parties, institutions, or military units which were ready to put up a fight for the old regime. This shows how ill-founded was the belated talk of the reactionaries to the effect that if there had been cavalry of the Guard in the Petersburg garrison, or if Ivanov had brought a reliable brigade from the front, the fate of the monarchy would have been different. Neither at the front nor at the rear was there a brigade or regiment to be found which was prepared to do battle for Nicholas II.

The revolution was carried out upon the initiative and by the strength of one city, constituting approximately about 1/75 of the population of the country. You may say, if you will, that this most gigantic democratic act was achieved in a most undemocratic manner. The whole country was placed before a fait accompli. The fact that a Constituent Assembly was in prospect does not alter the matter, for the dates and methods of convoking this national representation were determined by institutions which issued from the victorious insurrection of Petrograd. This casts a sharp light on the question of the function of democratic forms in general, and in a revolutionary epoch in particular. Revolutions have always struck such blows at the judicial fetishism of the popular will, and the blows have been more ruthless the deeper, bolder, and more democratic the revolutions. It is often said, especially

in regard to the great French Revolution, that the extreme centralization of a monarchy subsequently permits the revolutionary capital to
think and act for the whole country. That explanation is superficial. If
revolutions reveal a centralizing tendency, this is not in imitation of
overthrown monarchies, but in consequence of irresistible demands of
the new society, which cannot reconcile itself to particularism. If the
capital plays as dominating a role in a revolution as though it concentrated in itself the will of the nation, that is simply because the capital
expresses most clearly and thoroughly the fundamental tendencies of
the new society. The provinces accept the steps taken by the capital as
their own intentions already materialized. In the initiatory role of the
centers there is no violation of democracy, but rather its dynamic realization. However, the rhythm of this dynamic has never in great revolutions coincided with the rhythm of formal representative democracy.
The provinces adhere to the activity of the center, but belatedly. With
the swift development of events characteristic of a revolution this pro-
duces sharp crises in revolutionary parliamentarism, which cannot be
resolved by the methods of democracy. In all genuine revolutions the
national representation has invariably come into conflict with the dynamic force of the revolution, whose principal seat has been the capital.
It was so in the seventeenth century in England, in the eighteenth in
France, in the twentieth in Russia. The role of the capital is determined
not by the tradition of a bureaucratic centralism, but by the situation of
the leading revolutionary class, whose vanguard is naturally concentrated in the chief city: this is equally true for the bourgeoisie and the
proletariat.

When the February victory was fully confirmed, they began to
count up the victims. In Petrograd they counted 1443 killed and
wounded, 869 of them soldiers, and 60 of these officers. By comparison
with the victims of any battle in the Great Slaughter these figures are
suggestively tiny. The liberal press declared the February Revolution
bloodless. In the days of general salubrity and mutual amnesty of the
patriotic parties, nobody took the trouble to establish the truth. Albert
Thomas,[1] a friend of everything victorious, even a victorious insurrection, wrote at that time about the "sunniest, most holiday-like, most
bloodless Russian revolution." To be sure, he was hopeful that this
revolution would remain at the disposal of the French Bourse. But after

---

[1] Moderate French Socialist who supported participation in World War I.

all Thomas did not invent this habit. On the 27th of June 1789, Mirabeau exclaimed: "How fortunate that this great revolution will succeed without evil-doing and without tears! . . . History has too long been telling us only of the actions of beasts of prey. . . . We may well hope that we are beginning the history of human beings." When all the three estates were united in the National Assembly the ancestors of Albert Thomas wrote: "The revolution is ended. It has not cost a drop of blood." We must acknowledge, however, that at that period blood had really not yet flowed. Not so in the February days. Nevertheless the legend of a bloodless revolution stubbornly persisted, answering the need of the liberal bourgeois to make things look as though the power had come to him of its own accord.

Although the February Revolution was far from bloodless, still one cannot but be amazed at the insignificant number of victims, not only at the moment of revolution but still more in the first period after it. This revolution, we must remember, was a paying-back for oppression, persecution, taunts, vile blows, suffered by the masses of the Russian people throughout the ages! The sailors and soldiers did in some places, to be sure, take summary revenge upon the most contemptible torturers in the person of their officers, but the number of these acts of settlement was at first insignificant in comparison with the number of the old bloody insults. The masses shook off their good-naturedness only a good while later, when they were convinced that the ruling classes wanted to drag everything back and appropriate to themselves a revolution not achieved by them, just as they had always appropriated the good things of life not produced by themselves.

Tugan-Baranovsky is right when he says that the February Revolution was accomplished by workers and peasants — the latter in the person of the soldiers. But there still remains the great question: Who led the revolution? Who raised the workers to their feet? Who brought the soldiers into the streets? After the victory these questions became a subject of party conflict. They were solved most simply by the universal formula: Nobody led the revolution, it happened of itself. The theory of "spontaneousness" fell in most opportunely with the minds not only of all those gentlemen who had yesterday been peacefully governing, judging, convicting, defending, trading, or commanding, and today were hastening to make up to the revolution, but also of many professional politicians and former revolutionists, who having slept through the revolution wished to think that in this they were not different from all the rest.

In his curious *History of the Russian Disorders*, General Denikin, former commander of the White Army, says of the 27th of February: "On that decisive day there were no leaders, there were only the elements. In their threatening current there were then visible neither aims, nor plans, nor slogans." The learned historian Miliukov delves no deeper than this general with a passion for letters. Before the revolution the liberal leader had declared every thought of revolution a suggestion of the German Staff. But the situation was more complicated after a revolution which had brought the liberals to power. Miliukov's task was now not to dishonor the revolution with a Hohenzollern origin, but on the contrary to withhold the honor of its initiation from revolutionists. Liberalism therefore has wholeheartedly fathered the theory of a spontaneous and impersonal revolution. Miliukov sympathetically cites the semi-liberal, semi-socialist Stankevich, a university instructor who became political commissar at the headquarters of the Supreme Command: "The masses moved of themselves, obeying some unaccountable inner summons . . . " writes Stankevich of the February days. "With what slogans did the soldiers come out? Who led them when they conquered Petrograd, when they burned the District Court? Not a political idea, not a revolutionary slogan, not a conspiracy, and not a revolt, but a spontaneous movement suddenly consuming the entire old power to the last remnant." Spontaneousness here acquires an almost mystic character.

This same Stankevich offers a piece of testimony in the highest degree valuable: "At the end of January, I happened in a very intimate circle to meet with Kerensky. . . . To the possibility of a popular uprising they all took a definitely negative position, fearing lest a popular mass movement once aroused might get into an extreme leftward channel and this would create vast difficulties in the conduct of the war." The views of Kerensky's circle in no wise essentially differed from those of the Cadets. The initiative certainly did not come from there.

"The revolution fell like thunder out of the sky," says the president of the Social Revolutionary party, Zenzinov. "Let us be frank: it arrived joyfully unexpected for us too, revolutionists who had worked for it through long years and waited for it always."

It was not much better with the Mensheviks. One of the journalists

Leon Trotsky (1879–1940) in Moscow, 1923.

of the bourgeois emigration tells about his meeting in a tramcar on February 21 with Skobelev, a future minister of the revolutionary government: "This Social Democrat, one of the leaders of the movement, told me that the disorders had the character of plundering which it was necessary to put down. This did not prevent Skobelev from asserting a month later that he and his friends had made the revolution." The colors here are probably laid on a little thick, but fundamentally the position of the legal Social Democrats, the Mensheviks, is conveyed accurately enough.

Finally, one of the most recent leaders of the left wing of the Social Revolutionaries, Mstislavsky, who subsequently went over to the Bolsheviks, says of the February uprising: "The revolution caught us, the party people of those days, like the foolish virgins of the Bible, napping." It does not matter how much they resembled virgins, but it is true they were all fast asleep.

How was it with the Bolsheviks? This we have in part already seen. The principal leaders of the underground Bolshevik organization were at that time three men: the former workers Shliapnikov and Zalutsky, and the former student Molotov. Shliapnikov, having lived for some time abroad and in close association with Lenin, was in a political sense the most mature and active of these three who constituted the Bureau of the Central Committee. However, Shliapnikov's own memoirs best of all confirm the fact that the events were too much for the trio. Up to the very last hour these leaders thought that it was a question of a revolutionary manifestation, one among many, and not at all of an armed insurrection. Our friend Kayurov, one of the leaders of the Vyborg section, asserts categorically: "Absolutely no guiding initiative from the party centers was felt . . . the Petrograd Committee had been arrested and the representative of the Central Committee, Comrade Shliapnikov, was unable to give any directives for the coming day."

The weakness of the underground organizations was a direct result of police raids, which had given exceptional results amid the patriotic moods at the beginning of the war. Every organization, the revolutionary included, has a tendency to fall behind its social basis. The underground organization of the Bolsheviks at the beginning of 1917 had not yet recovered from its oppressed and scattered condition, whereas in the masses the patriotic hysteria had been abruptly replaced by revolutionary indignation.

In order to get a clear conception of the situation in the sphere of revolutionary leadership it is necessary to remember that the most authoritative revolutionists, the leaders of the Left parties, were abroad and, some of them, in prison and exile. The more dangerous a party was to the old regime, the more cruelly beheaded it appeared at the moment of revolution. The narodniks had a Duma faction headed by the non-party radical Kerensky.[2] The official leader of the Social-Revolutionaries, Chernov, was abroad. The Mensheviks had a party faction in the Duma headed by Chkheidze and Skobelev; Martov was abroad; Dan and Tseretelli, in exile. A considerable number of socialistic intellectuals with a revolutionary past were grouped around these Left factions — narodnik and Menshevik. This constituted a kind of political staff, but one which was capable of coming to the front only after the victory. The Bolsheviks had no Duma faction: their five worker-deputies, in whom the tzarist government had seen the organizing center of the revolution, had been arrested during the first few months of the war. Lenin was abroad, Zinoviev with him; Kamenev was in exile; in exile also, the then little known practical leaders: Sverdlov, Rykov, Stalin. The Polish social-democrat, Dzerzhinsky, who did not yet belong to the Bolsheviks, was at hard labor. The leaders accidentally present, for the very reason that they had been accustomed to act under unconditionally authoritative supervisors, did not consider themselves and were not considered by others capable of playing a guiding role in revolutionary events.

But if the Bolshevik party could not guarantee the insurrection an authoritative leadership, there is no use talking of other organizations. This fact has strengthened the current conviction as to the spontaneous character of the February Revolution. Nevertheless the conviction is deeply mistaken, or at least meaningless.

The struggle in the capital lasted not an hour, or two hours, but five days. The leaders tried to hold it back; the masses answered with increased pressure and marched forward. They had against them the old state, behind whose traditional façade a mighty power was still assumed to exist, the liberal bourgeoisie with the State Duma, the Land and City Unions, the military-industrial organizations, academies, universities, a highly developed press, and finally the two strong socialist parties who

[2] In the late nineteenth century Russian intellectuals developed an agrarian socialist philosophy which placed great weight upon the importance of the peasant and his institutions and upon the moral duty of the intellectual to help the peasants improve their lives. This *narodnik* (populist) philosophy gave rise to a series of important revolutionary movements in the nineteenth century and served as a basis for the new party of Socialist Revolutionaries in the twentieth century. Contrary to Trotsky's assertion here, Kerensky was a member of the Socialist Revolutionary party.

put up a patriotic resistance to the assault from below. In the party of the Bolsheviks the insurrection had its nearest organization, but a headless organization with a scattered staff and with weak illegal nuclei. And nevertheless the revolution, which nobody in those days was expecting, unfolded, and just when it seemed from above as though the movement was already dying down, with an abrupt revival, a mighty convulsion, it seized the victory.

Whence came this unexampled force of aggression and self-restraint? It is not enough to refer to bitter feelings. Bitterness alone is little. The Petersburg workers, no matter how diluted during the war years with human raw material, had in their past a great revolutionary experience. In their aggression and self-restraint, in the absence of leadership and in the face of opposition from above, was revealed a vitally well-founded, although not always expressed, estimate of forces and a strategic calculation of their own.

On the eve of the war the revolutionary layers of the workers had been following the Bolsheviks, and leading the masses after them. With the beginning of the war the situation had sharply changed: conservative groups lifted their heads, dragging after them a considerable part of the class. The revolutionary elements found themselves isolated, and quieted down. In the course of the war the situation began to change, at first slowly, but after the defeats faster and more radically. An active discontent seized the whole working class. To be sure, it was to an extent patriotically colored, but it had nothing in common with the calculating and cowardly patriotism of the possessing classes, who were postponing all domestic questions until after the victory. The war itself, its victims, its horror, its shame, brought not only the old, but also the new layers of workers into conflict with the tzarist regime. It did this with a new incisiveness and led them to the conclusion: we can no longer endure it. The conclusion was universal; it welded the masses together and gave them a mighty dynamic force.

The army had swollen, drawing into itself millions of workers and peasants. Every individual had his own people among the troops: a son, a husband, a brother, a relative. The army was no longer insulated, as before the war, from the people. One met with soldiers now far oftener; saw them off to the front, lived with them when they came home on leave, chatted with them on the streets and in the tramways about the front, visited them in the hospitals. The workers' districts, the barracks, the front, and to an extent the villages too, became communicating vessels. The workers would know what the soldiers were thinking and feeling. They had innumerable conversations about the war, about the people who were getting rich out of the war, about the generals, government, tzar and tzarina. The soldier would say about the war: "To hell with it!" And the worker would answer about the government: "To hell with it!" The soldier would say: "Why then do you sit still here in the center?" The worker would answer: "We can't do anything with bare hands; we stubbed our toe against the army in 1905." The soldier would reflect: "What if we should all start at once!" The worker: "That's it, all at once!" Conversations of this kind before the war were conspirative and carried on by two's; now they were going on everywhere, on every occasion, and almost openly, at least in the workers' districts.

The tzar's intelligence service every once in a while took its soundings very successfully. Two weeks before the revolution a spy, who signed himself with the name Krestianinov, reported a conversation in a tramcar traversing the workers' suburb. The soldier was telling how in his regiment eight men were under hard labor because last autumn they refused to shoot at the workers of the Nobel factory, but shot at the police instead. The conversation went on quite openly, since in the workers' districts the police and the spies preferred to remain unnoticed. " 'We'll get even with them,' the soldier concluded." The report reads further: "A skilled worker answered him: 'For that it is necessary to organize so that all will be like one.' The soldier answered: 'Don't you worry, we've been organized a long time. . . . They've drunk enough blood. Men are suffering in the trenches and here they are fattening their bellies!' . . . No special disturbance occurred. February 10, 1917. Krestianinov." Incomparable spy's epic. "No special disturbance occurred." They will occur, and that soon: this tramway conversation signalizes their inexorable approach.

The spontaneousness of the insurrection Mstislavsky illustrates with a curious example: When the "Union of Officers of February 27," formed just after the revolution, tried to determine with a questionnaire who first led out the Volynsky regiment, they received seven answers naming seven initiators of this decisive action. It is very likely, we may add, that a part of the initiative really did belong to several soldiers, nor is it impossible that the chief initiator fell in the street fighting, carrying his name with him into oblivion. But that does not diminish the historic importance of his nameless initiative. Still more important is another side of the matter which will carry us beyond the walls of the barrack room. The insurrection of the battalions of the Guard, flaring up a complete surprise to the liberal and legal socialist circles, was no surprise at all to the workers. Without the insurrection of the workers the Volynsky regiment would not have gone into the street. That street encounter of the workers with the Cossacks, which a lawyer observed from his window and which he communicated by telephone to the deputy, was to them both an episode in an impersonal process: a factory locust stumbled against a locust from the barracks. But it did not seem that way to the Cossack who had dared wink to the worker, nor to the worker who instantly decided that the Cossack had "winked in a friendly manner." The molecular interpenetration of the army with the people was going on continuously. The workers watched the temperature of the army and instantly sensed its approach to the critical mark. Exactly this was what gave such inconquerable force to the assault of the masses, confident of victory.

Here we must introduce the pointed remark of a liberal official trying to summarize his February observations:

> It is customary to say that the movement began spontaneously, the soldiers themselves went into the street. I cannot at all agree with this. After all, what does the word "spontaneously" mean? . . . Spontaneous conception is still more out of place in sociology than in natural science. Owing to the fact that none of the revolutionary leaders with a name was able to hang his label on the movement, it becomes not impersonal but merely nameless.

This formulation of the question, incomparably more serious than Miliukov's references to German agents and Russian spontaneousness, belongs to a former procuror who met the revolution in the position of a tzarist senator. It is quite possible that his experience in the courts permitted Zavadsky to realize that a revolutionary insurrection cannot arise either at the command of foreign agents, or in the manner of an impersonal process of nature.

The same author relates two incidents which permitted him to look as through a keyhole into the laboratory of the revolutionary process. On Friday, February 24, when nobody in the upper circles as yet expected a revolution in the near future, a tramcar in which the senator was riding turned off quite unexpectedly, with such a jar that the windows rattled and one was broken, from the Liteiny into a side street, and there stopped. The conductor told everybody to get off: "The car isn't going any farther." The passengers objected, scolded, but got off. "I can still see the face of that unanswering conductor: angrily resolute, a sort of wolf look." The movement of the tramways stopped everywhere as far as the eye could see. That resolute conductor, in whom the liberal official could already catch a glimpse of the "wolf look," must have been dominated by a high sense of duty in order all by himself to stop a car containing officials on the streets of imperial Petersburg in time of war. It was just such conductors who stopped the car of the monarchy and with practically the same words — this car does not go any farther! — and who ushered out the bureaucracy, making no distinction in the rush of business between a general of gendarmes and a liberal senator. The conductor on the Liteiny Boulevard was a conscious factor of history. It had been necessary to educate him in advance.

During the burning of the District Court a liberal jurist from the circle of that same senator started to express in the street his regret that a roomful of judicial decisions and notarial archives was perishing. An elderly man of somber aspect dressed as a worker angrily objected: "We will be able to divide the houses and the lands ourselves, and without your archives." Probably the episode is rounded out in a literary manner. But there were plenty of elderly workers like that in the crowd, capable of making the necessary retort. They themselves had nothing to do with burning the District Court: why burn it? But at least you could not frighten them with "excesses" of this kind. They were arming the masses with the necessary ideas not only against the tzarist police, but against liberal jurists who feared most of all lest there should burn up in the fire of the revolution the notarial deeds of property. Those nameless, austere statesmen of the factory and streets did not fall out of the sky: they had to be educated.

In registering the events of the last days of February the Secret Service also remarked that the movement was "spontaneous," that is, had no planned leadership from above; but they immediately added: "with the generally propagandized condition of the proletariat." This appraisal hits the bull's-eye: the professionals of the struggle with the revolution, before entering the cells vacated by the revolutionists, took a much closer view of what was happening than the leaders of liberalism.

The mystic doctrine of spontaneousness explains nothing. In order correctly to appraise the situation and determine the moment for a blow at the enemy, it was necessary that the masses or their guiding layers should make their examination of historical events and have their criteria for estimating them. In other words, it was necessary that there should be not masses in the abstract, but masses of Petrograd workers and Russian workers in general, who had passed through the revolution of 1905, through the Moscow insurrection of December 1905, shattered against the Semenovsky Regiment of the Guard. It was necessary that throughout this mass should be scattered workers who had thought over the experience of 1905, criticized the constitutional illusions of the liberals and Mensheviks, assimilated the perspectives of the revolution, meditated hundreds of times about the question of the army, watched attentively what was going on in its midst — workers capable of making revolutionary inferences from what they observed and communicating them to others. And finally, it was necessary that there should be in the troops of the garrison itself progressive soldiers, seized, or at least touched, in the past by revolutionary propaganda.

In every factory, in each guild, in each company, in each tavern, in the military hospital, at the transfer stations, even in the depopulated villages, the molecular work of revolutionary thought was in progress. Everywhere were to be found the interpreters of events, chiefly from among the workers, from whom one inquired, "What's the news?" and from whom one awaited the needed words. These leaders had often been left to themselves, had nourished themselves upon fragments of revolutionary generalizations arriving in their hands by various routes, had studied out by themselves between the lines of the liberal papers what they needed. Their class instinct was refined by a political criterion, and though they did not think all their ideas through to the end, nevertheless their thought ceaselessly and stubbornly worked its way in a single direction. Elements of experience, criticism, initiative, self-sacrifice, seeped down through the mass and created, invisibly to a superficial glance but no less decisively, an inner mechanics of the revolutionary movement as a conscious process. To the smug politicians of liberalism and tamed socialism everything that happens among masses is customarily represented as an instinctive process, no matter whether they are dealing with an anthill or a beehive. In reality the thought which was drilling through the thick of the working class was far bolder, more penetrating, more conscious, than those little ideas by which the educated classes live. Moreover, this thought was more scientific: not only because it was to a considerable degree fertilized with the methods of Marxism, but still more because it was ever nourishing itself on the living experience of the masses which were soon to take their place on the revolutionary arena. Thoughts are scientific if they correspond to an objective process and make it possible to influence that process and guide it. Were these qualities possessed in the slightest degree by the ideas of those government circles who were inspired by the Apocalypse and believed in the dreams of Rasputin? Or maybe the ideas of the liberals were scientifically grounded, who hoped that a backward Russia, having joined the scrimmage of the capitalist giants, might win at one and the same time victory and parliamentarism? Or maybe the intellectual life of those circles of the intelligentsia was scientific, who slavishly adapted themselves to this liberalism, senile since childhood, protecting their imaginary independence the while with long-dead metaphors? In truth here was a kingdom of spiritual inertness, specters, superstition and fictions, a kingdom, if you will, of "spontaneousness." But have we not in that case a right to turn this liberal philosophy of the February Revolution exactly upside down? Yes, we have a right to say: At the same time that the official society, all that many-storied superstructure of ruling classes, layers, groups, parties and cliques, lived from day to day by inertia and automatism, nourishing themselves with the relics of worn-out ideas, deaf to the inexorable demands of evolution, flattering themselves with phantoms and foreseeing nothing — at the same time, in the working masses there was taking place an independent and deep process of growth, not only of hatred for the rulers, but of critical understanding of their impotence, an accumulation of experience and creative consciousness which the revolutionary insurrection and its victory only completed.

To question, Who led the February Revolution? we can then answer definitely enough: Conscious and tempered workers educated for the most part by the party of Lenin. But we must here immediately add: This leadership proved sufficient to guarantee the victory of the insurrection, but it was not adequate to transfer immediately into the hands of the proletarian vanguard the leadership of the revolution.

E. N. Burdzhalov

Dual Power

The son of a middle-class Armenian family, Eduard Burdzhalov (1906–1985) became a loyal son of the Communist party through the years of the Stalinist dictatorship. By the early 1950s he had nearly reached the pinnacle of the historical profession, having been appointed assistant editor of the historical journal V*oprosy istorii* (Problems of History). In the reform years after Stalin's death Burdzhalov began to question the exaggerations and distortions in Soviet historiography, and when he published several controversial articles deflating the Bolshevik presence in February 1917 he was dismissed from his post. His career went into eclipse, but Burdzhalov continued to write. In 1967 the first volume of his history of the February Revolution appeared. In this excerpt from the translation by Donald J. Raleigh, Burdzhalov explores the complex negotiations between the Soviet, the Duma Committee, and the tsar that led to the formation of the Provisional Government.

> The highly remarkable feature of our revolution is that it has brought about a *dual power*.   V. I. *Lenin*

The Formation of the Provisional Government

The bourgeoisie had been preparing a new Russian government for a long time. It wanted the tsar to grant a "responsible ministry" or at least a "ministry of confidence." Lists of candidates for the new ministers circulated already back in 1915, and were even published. During the first days of the revolution the Duma leaders likewise insisted on a new government. The tsar procrastinated, however, when Rodzianko began negotiating with members of the Romanov dynasty, located at Tsarskoe

Text by E. N. Burdzhalov from *Russia's Second Revolution: The February Uprising in Petrograd*, trans. by Donald J. Raleigh, pp. 262–281, 295–299, 306–307, 309–311, 319–326. Reprinted by permission of Indiana University Press.

Selo and in Petrograd, to find a mutually acceptable way out of the situation.

Rodzianko had contacted the tsar's uncle, Grand Prince Pavel Aleksandrovich, commander of the guards. Rodzianko's aide, the lawyer N. I. Ivanov, relayed messages between the Tauride Palace and Pavel Aleksandrovich at Tsarskoe Selo. Since it was known that Nicholas II had left headquarters for Tsarskoe Selo, Pavel Aleksandrovich agreed to be the first to explain to him why it was necessary "to grant" a ministry responsible to the Duma and thereby lay the foundation for a constitutional system. It was proposed to shroud the tsar's concession in the form of a manifesto, which was already being drawn up. Fearing that Aleksandra Fedorovna would somehow convince her husband to act otherwise, the initiators of this venture wanted to speak with the tsar before he saw his wife.

But time lapsed and the tsar did not show up or send any orders. Nicholas II had been unable to break through to the capital where, in the meanwhile, events had become extremely threatening for the monarchy. It was decided to send under the tsarina's and grand princes' signatures a draft manifesto to the tsar at Supreme Headquarters regarding a "responsible ministry." Although Aleksandra Fedorovna rejected the scheme, the three oldest grand princes approved it.

The manifesto document said that the tsar had intended to reorganize the government on a broad popular basis as the war drew to a close, but that recent events made it necessary to introduce reforms sooner. Not supported by legislative institutions, the government had failed to foresee and prevent the unrest occurring in Petrograd. The manifesto called the growing revolution a "disturbance" and expressed the hope that it would be quelled. In the name of the tsar the manifesto proclaimed: "We grant the Russian government a constitutional system and decree the resumption of the State Council and State Duma session, which had been interrupted. We entrust the chairman of the State Duma to form a provisional cabinet at once that enjoys the country's confidence and which, in agreement with us, will convoke a legislative assembly needed to consider the government's urgent proposal for new fundamental laws for the Russian empire."

Pavel Aleksandrovich endorsed the draft manifesto of March 1. He signed it, crossed himself, and exclaimed: "What a coincidence. Today is the anniversary of my brother's death!" Such thoughts must have haunted Pavel, for on March 1, 1881, members of the People's Will[1] had killed his brother Alexander II. I wish you "Good Luck!" Pavel Nikolaevich said to Ivanov, who sped off to Mikhail Aleksandrovich and Kirill Vladimirovich in Petrograd, next in line to succeed to the throne.

"I am in complete agreement that this is absolutely necessary," Kirill said, affixing his signature. "I also believe there is no other way out and such a measure is necessary," Mikhail Aleksandrovich declared while signing. On February 28 he informed his wife, M. Brasova: "Our minds aren't given a moment's peace. It is imperative for us to make arrangements with the [provincial] authorities where we rent an estate. " The next day Mikhail wrote his wife less elusively. "Events are developing with dreadful speed. . . . I signed a manifesto that His Majesty should have signed. On it are the signatures of Pavel Aleksandrovich and Kirill and now mine, the oldest of the grand princes. This manifesto marks a new beginning for Russia."

A new beginning for Russia was indeed underway, but it had nothing to do with the manifesto. On March 1 the document was presented to the Duma, apparently for its approval and dispatch to the tsar. Unable to deliver it by car, Ivanov walked through the streets that were packed with people and realized that the manifesto would not satisfy the embittered masses. He wrote:

> I carried the manifesto to the Provisional Committee, and with each step I became more and more convinced that the Romanov cause was lost, that Rodzianko would not escape with his cabinet, and that the masses needed a bigger sacrifice. This time Rodzianko did not appear as a solemn triumvir in the revolutionary chariot, but as a helpless driver who lost the reins. He even seemed to have outwardly given up. "I think this is too late," I said about the manifesto. "I am of the same opinion," he answered. "I will give the manifesto to Miliukov and he will confirm its receipt."

. . .

---

[1]One of the more colorful and historically significant populist groups in nineteenth-century Russia. Its goals were to overthrow the autocracy and establish a democratic republic based on "the people's will." Believing a political struggle was necessary to achieve their goals, they advocated the use of individual terror.

Events pushed the Duma leaders further than they had intended to go. To save the monarchy, they had to sacrifice Nicholas himself. The State Duma Committee back on February 28 had discussed a long-existing plan for Nicholas II's abdication in favor of his son Aleksei, under Mikhail Aleksandrovich's regency. The Duma protocols read: "The rush of events, the mood of the army units, of their commanding officers and of the masses would indicate that Nicholas II's abdication is unavoidable." When the Duma Committee drafted this abdication document on February 28, the committee discussed sending Rodzianko and Shidlovskii to present it to the tsar. At first the Duma leaders decided to postpone the trip, as no one knew where the tsar was. Then the Soviet's opposition to the trip became known, and without its sanction, railwaymen would not provide trains. Thus, Rodzianko's actions were duplicitous — he negotiated with Pavel Aleksandrovich to preserve the throne for Nicholas II, yet at the same time planned to secure the tsar's abdication.

Shidlovskii's memoirs confirm the official version of the discussion of the abdication. According to him, the Provisional Duma Committee decided to demand Nicholas II's abdication and to send Shidlovskii and Rodzianko to the tsar. "Our proposed trip was poorly planned. The possibility of our arrest was not considered, nor that troops loyal to the tsar might resist. On the other hand, we discussed arresting the tsar, but not where to take him or what to do with him. In general the undertaking was amateurish. I began to await our departure. One o'clock came, two, three. We phoned the Nikolaevskii Railway Station repeatedly and asked whether a train was ready, but to no avail. For some reason none were."

The situation in Petrograd had become even more alarming and dangerous for the bourgeoisie. The Duma Committee lacked authority. The insurgent people did not trust it and were obeying the Soviet instead. In view of this, Duma leaders continued their efforts to contact the tsar but decided to organize a government before receiving his sanction. On March 1, 1917, the Provisional Duma Committee resolved: "To stave off anarchy and restore public order following the overthrow of the old regime, the Provisional Committee of the State Duma has decided to organize a new government before convocation of a constituent assembly that will determine the future form of government of the Russian state. For this purpose the Provisional Committee has set up a Provisional Council of Ministers composed of the following individuals, whose former civic and political activities ensure them the country's trust."

Membership in "the ministry of trust" was based on the list compiled before the revolution. Prince G. L'vov, named prime minister, was summoned from Moscow without delay. On March 1 he met with the Duma Committee. Miliukov subsequently wrote that this conversation disappointed him greatly. "We did not sense a leader before us. The prince, evasive and cautious, responded to events with vague formulations and generalities." "He is weak-willed and unresourceful," Miliukov said of him afterward. The character alone of the future chairman of the Provisional Government, however, cannot explain L'vov's behavior at this meeting. The bourgeoisie's precarious situation also contributed to L'vov's submissiveness and caution.

In organizing a government, the Provisional Duma Committee counted on the bourgeoisie, whose organizations expressed complete trust in the Duma Committee and approved its efforts to establish a government. In an appeal to the people of Russia, the Central War Industries Committee said that creation of a single provisional authority was now necessary, that "such an authority can emanate only from the State Duma, for it alone can muster authority in the eyes of the entire country, the entire army, and our valorous allies." The bourgeois statesmen heading the War Industries Committee enjoined the population to place power at the State Duma's disposal, and not to tolerate reprisals, disagreements, and uncoordinated actions.

The Duma Committee welcomed the support of the industrial barons united in the Congress of Representatives of Trade and Industry. On March 2 the congress declared "it is placing itself at the complete disposal of the Provisional Duma Committee. It regards the committee's orders and instructions as obligatory, until the creation of a new state administration." The congress called on "Russia's entire merchant-industrial class to forget party and social differences that can now only benefit the enemies of the people, and to unite more cohesively around the Provisional Duma Committee and place all of our resources at its disposal."

Such support did not prevent the Duma from recognizing it was treading water. It lacked real power. The armed worker and soldier masses believed in and followed only the Soviet. That is why, after deciding to form a government, the Duma Committee failed to do so without the Soviet's support. Up until this point the bourgeoisie had favored reaching an agreement with the tsar. Now, after it was no longer advantageous to do so, the bourgeoisie had to reorient itself and find other allies. Up until this point the bourgeoisie had waited for the tsar to form a ministry of trust. Now it had to form such a ministry with the autocracy's enemies.

The Provisional Duma Committee began conferring with the Soviet Executive Committee over the formation of a government. Duma leaders challenged the Soviet either to support the government that the Duma would create, or take power itself. Yet the Soviet leaders were not about to seize power. Maintaining that the revolution was bourgeois in nature, they believed that power must belong to the bourgeoisie, and they therefore looked upon creation of a government by the Duma Committee as altogether natural. SR and Menshevik leaders said that without the bourgeoisie it was impossible to defeat tsarism, govern the country, end economic ruin, etc. The Soviet's support of the Provisional Government created by the Duma Committee signified in essence a voluntary capitulation to the bourgeoisie, a transfer of power to it that had been won by the people. Sukhanov averred that in salvaging the revolution, fortifying its victory over tsarism, and establishing a democratic regime, the victorious people would have to "transfer power to their class enemies, to the privileged bourgeoisie."

The Soviet, without any reservations or strings attached, carried resolutions to do just this. The majority of Soviet leaders held, however, that in yielding power to the bourgeoisie they must demand limits upon the bourgeoisie's authority and political rights and freedoms for the population. The Soviet leaders maintained that, in transferring power to the bourgeoisie, they must neutralize bourgeois power and not give it the opportunity to be used against the people. Moreover, the Soviet leaders feared that workers' excessive demands would frighten the bourgeoisie, whose refusal to take power would be catastrophic. This is why the Soviet Executive Committee did not present socioeconomic demands to the future government, did not bring up such matters as the eight-hour workday or confiscation of landlords' estates, did not question the state's foreign policy, or raise the question of ending the war. The Soviet leaders especially tried to skirt this last concern, even removing it from the agenda, for it was most likely to provoke disagreement with Duma leaders.

The Soviet Executive Committee discussed the question of power on March 1. The protocol of this meeting has been lost and memoir accounts must be consulted to reconstruct what took place. Urgent matters interrupting discussion of the question of power kept the committee from the main business. Although the Executive Committee reached relative agreement while discussing military, technical, and organizational questions, it was rent by discord while debating the question of power. Sharp disagreements between the parties of the revolutionary proletariat and the petit bourgeois groups now surfaced. In accord with the manifesto of the Central Committee Bureau of the RSDRP, the Bolsheviks proposed that the revolutionary democracy seize the country's administration and form a provisional revolutionary government from among members of the Soviet. According to Shliapnikov, eight of the thirty members of the Executive Committee championed this view: A. Shliapnikov, P. Zalutskii, V. Molotov, K. Shutko, A. Paderin, A. Sadovskii, P. Aleksandrovich, and I. Iurenev. The Bolshevik proposal stemmed from the entire course of events; the revolution had brought the insurgent people to the point of realizing a provisional revolutionary government. The armed masses of workers and soldiers supported the Soviet, whose Executive Committee had absolute revolutionary authority at its disposal. The Soviet could have removed the bourgeoisie from power easily.

"We proposed to the Executive Committee," wrote Shliapnikov, "to form a provisional revolutionary government from those parties that had joined the Soviet. The implementation of the minimum demands of both socialist parties' [Bolshevik and Menshevik — D. J. R.] programs, as well as ending the war, must be its agenda." This was exactly what the SRs and Mensheviks who made up the majority in the Executive Committee did not want. Wishing to maintain good relations with the Duma Committee, they dissociated themselves from the Bolsheviks' antibourgeois and antiwar policies and spoke out against revolutionary power. The Soviet Executive Committee advocated a transfer of power to the bourgeoisie and formation of a bourgeois government.

But should representatives of the democracy take part in such a government? Some Mensheviks, SRs, and Bundists backed participation in the bourgeois government. They argued that the revolution otherwise would not be brought "to a favorable end," and that the old authorities would not be completely swept away. On the day the Executive Committee met, March 2, an article appeared in *Izvestiia*, "The

Democracy's Participation in the Provisional Government," which articulated this point of view. It noted that, in entering the government, representatives of the democracy would prevent the bourgeois parties and Duma Committee from compromising with the old order, and would not give the Provisional Government the opportunity to stop at half reforms, but would encourage it to call a constituent assembly and create a republican order. According to the article, a rupture between the Soviet and Provisional Government would set the bourgeoisie back, and the democracy alone could not create a state apparatus. The democracy "alone in the struggle with the coalition of all bourgeois elements was not yet strong enough to carry out state-organizational work of such colossal magnitude."

The question of the socialists' entry into the Provisional Government was a practical one. The Duma Committee offered the Ministry of Labor to Chkheidze and the Ministry of Justice to Kerensky. Chkheidze refused the office, but Kerensky wavered at first and then accepted the post. The Soviet Executive Committee did not want representatives of the democracy to join the Provisional Government, and favored preserving its strictly bourgeois character. As Sukhanov reported, this decision was carried by a vote of thirteen against seven or eight. Rafes also noted that a significant majority of the Executive Committee opposed participation in the government, but added that the committee postponed final resolution of this matter until the views of the ruling party committees were clarified. The Soviet Executive Committee decided to leave the appointment of ministers completely to the Duma Committee, merely insisting that it be notified of the candidates; where appropriate, it retained the right to reject the most unacceptable of them.

In transferring power to the bourgeois government, the Soviet Executive Committee demanded the Duma Committee and government carry out three political reforms: the declaration of political freedoms, a complete and general political amnesty, and the speedy convocation of a constituent assembly. Proposals were carried to extend all civil rights to soldiers, to abolish the police and replace it with a decentralized people's militia, and to democratize organs of local government through general elections as soon as possible. To defend the revolution, it was proposed to pressure the government not to disarm and remove from Petrograd military units that had taken part in the revolution. . . .

Although the Duma Committee for the most part found the Soviet

Executive Committee deputies' demands acceptable, many of the claims prompted the bourgeois leaders' objections. They argued it was impossible both to hold elections to the constituent assembly during the war and to undertake sweeping democratization of the army. Discussion of the form of the new state order sparked the sharpest debate. Miliukov, proposing to present the throne to Aleksei under Mikhail's regency, favored preserving the monarchy. He declared the Romanovs no longer dangerous: Nicholas was out of the picture, Aleksei was a sick child, and Mikhail was a fool. Chkheidze and Sokolov found Miliukov's plan unacceptable and utopian in view of the universal hatred toward the monarchy. They said that an attempt to save the Romanovs was "totally absurd, senseless, and in general would amount to nothing. . . . But the bourgeois leader was implacable. Seeing the futility of the argument, he addressed the remaining points."

The contracting parties left the question of the form of the state administration unresolved and instead discussed the other points in the government's declaration. The reorganization of the army ignited a major controversy. The Duma leaders rejected a radical democratization of the army and election of officers, but were forced to recognize the extension to soldiers of political rights granted to the citizens of Russia, and to agree with the Soviet's demands not to disarm and remove military units from Petrograd that had taken part in the revolution. They made this and other concessions in order to enlist the Soviet's support, without which their authority meant nothing.

The Duma leaders accepted the Soviet Executive Committee's plan and asked it to take the necessary measures to restore order in the city, to call on soldiers to obey officers, and to declare that the Soviet agrees to the Provisional Government's formation, trusts it, and supports its program. The Soviet complied. It was then decided to issue two declarations, one by the Provisional Government, the other by the Soviet, and publish them side by side so they could be read together. By morning, March 2, both sides had agreed to most points. They broke up to draw up their separate declarations and then assembled again to confirm them.

A serious hitch owing to Guchkov took place at this concluding phase of the negotiations. He had left for the military units and had not participated in talks with the Soviet's representatives, returning to the Tauride Palace after an agreement on the declaration of a government had already been reached. Guchkov objected to several points in the agreement accepted by the Duma members, in particular to extending political rights to soldiers. He did not want to break off even temporarily agitation for the continuation of the imperialist war. On March 2 a leaflet appeared under Guchkov's signature, as chairman of the Military Commission, which called for war to total victory. This appeal conflicted with the agreement that had been concluded, which had postponed resolution of the question of how to relate to the war. When the Soviet's Executive Committee banned dissemination of this leaflet, Guchkov threw a scandal. Sukhanov recalled: "Both the real strength of our forces and the government's weakness were revealed, and this clearly shook Guchkov. The incident involving this proclamation demoralized him greatly, for it was both unexpected and unbearable. He refused to take part in a government that could not express itself on the cardinal question of its future policies and could not issue a simple proclamation."

Members of the Duma Committee objected to the Soviet's draft declaration, written by Sokolov, on the formation of the Provisional Government. Although it mentioned the need to establish "contact" between soldiers and officers, the document actually called upon the rank and file not to trust the command. Duma Committee members grew alarmed when they read Sokolov's document and declared it impossible to achieve unity if the Soviet held such a position. A serious threat thus jeopardized the agreement just reached.

An outraged Kerensky protested, maintaining that the ill-considered actions of several Executive Committee members undermined the agreement with the Duma and would result in the triumph of anarchy. But Kerensky's apprehensions were exaggerated: the bourgeoisie was not about to jeopardize its relations with the Soviet. It understood that it could control the chaotic elemental revolutionary activity and come to power only with the Soviet's help. The Soviet's and Duma Committee's desire to create a bourgeois government forced them to search for a compromise that would end the negotiations satisfactorily. After rejecting Sokolov's draft, both sides in close cooperation began composing a new one. Steklov wrote the first paragraph of the Soviet's declaration, Sukhanov the second, and Miliukov the third.

At 2:00 P.M. on March 2 the Soviet of Workers' and Soldiers' Deputies discussed the question of power. The Executive Committee was to have reported to the Soviet on the outcome of the negotiations with the Duma Committee. Danger from the left and right threatened the Soviet leaders' efforts to establish bourgeois power on conditions agreed upon with the Duma leaders. The danger from the left alarmed the Executive Committee leaders the most. Sukhanov noted that the Bolsheviks' rejection of transferring power to the bourgeoisie

> could easily have been fortified by taking the struggle to the street — if Bolshevik and Left SR groups had shown sufficient resolve and energy. It would have been extremely hard if not impossible to overcome a movement of this sort by "internal" means, through influence or persuasion . . . . To defend the interests of the "privileged" before the masses, before the Soviet, which possessed real power, was uncommonly difficult. The excitement and alarm of the soldier masses magnified this difficulty tenfold. When the privileged refused to part with the monarchy and dynasty they doomed, if a street movement had started up, the entire "combination" to failure.

The Executive Committee's spokesman, Steklov, exhaustively reported to the Soviet on the negotiations with the Duma. He said the Soviet's representatives had entered into the talks, striving to avoid a conflict with the Duma members and to prevent skinning a live bear. He mentioned that the Soviet's Executive Committee had demanded a number of concessions on behalf of workers and soldiers and wanted to place the new government under popular supervision.

At first, Executive Committee representatives insisted on the immediate promulgation of a democratic republic, but then agreed to postpone doing so until the formation of a constituent assembly, whose convocation was the new government's most urgent task. The Executive Committee proposed the Soviet call upon the population to support the incipient Provisional Government "only insofar as" (postol'ku, poskol'ku) it proceeded to undertake the aforementioned tasks. Thus, for the first time, the well-known formula of support for the Provisional Government, "only insofar as," was enunciated, which was the basis of the Soviet majority's conciliatory policies.

Steklov reported that the Executive Committee debated whether the democracy should take part in the Provisional Government. The majority opposed participation, arguing they did not want to be bound by or assume direct responsibility for the future government's domestic and foreign policies. The Executive Committee saw to it that especially odious individuals, well known for their opposition to the revolutionary movement, did not enter the government, and that the most important ministries went to progressive people.

As already mentioned, Kerensky disagreed with the Executive Committee's decision on banning socialists from entering the government. He longed for power and strove at all costs to receive a ministerial portfolio. Failing to elicit a sympathetic response from the Executive Committee, Kerensky turned for support to the Soviet plenum, despite the Executive Committee's decision. Steklov had barely finished his report when Kerensky asked to be recognized. The auditorium turned to him, applause broke out, and the future minister resorted to his skilled demagogy to persuade the masses. Raising, then lowering his voice, he posed pithy questions, designed to generate applause. "Do you trust me?" Kerensky asked. "We trust you," resounded the reply. "I am speaking, comrades, from the bottom of my heart. I am ready to die if necessary," Kerensky exclaimed and then continued. "Because a new government had already been formed, I had to respond at once whether or not I would accept the offer made to me to become minister of justice, without waiting for your formal sanction. Comrades, representatives of the old authorities were in my hands, and I could not bring myself to release them. . . . I first ordered the immediate freeing of all political prisoners without exceptions, and the dignified return from Siberia of our comrade Duma deputies who had represented the democracy." Kerensky thus took credit for what the people had accomplished — the arrest of government officials and release of political prisoners.

Kerensky's account greatly impressed those present and, as the newspapers wrote, elicited "stormy applause and general enthusiasm." Inspired by success, he continued: "Insofar as I accepted the responsibilities of minister of justice before receiving formal authorization from you to do so, I hereby resign as deputy chairman of the Soviet of Workers' Deputies. I am prepared, however, to resume this office should you deem it necessary." Enthusiastic applause and cries broke out, "Yes, please." Then Kerensky tried to convince those assembled that, as a proponent of a democratic republic, he would represent the democracy within the government. Protests broke out in the auditorium that Kerensky had accepted the ministerial portfolio without the Soviet's sanction, but cries of approval drowned them out. Kerensky's performance at the Soviet ended.

Kerensky quit the Soviet meeting and almost never showed up there again afterward. Interpreting the Soviet majority's applause as a sign of approval, Kerensky settled down in the Provisional Government. The Soviet leaders could not bring themselves to speak out against Kerensky's actions, even though the overwhelming majority opposed coalition government. Yet silence is a sign of approval. In reacting to Kerensky's speech as they had, they in effect upheld his entry into the capitalist government. . . .

The Soviet also dealt with the controversial question of the monarchy's future. The report that the bourgeoisie had not rejected tsarism but wanted to continue it under Aleksei and Mikhail aroused the deputies' irate protests. The Soviet denounced the monarchy. In wishing to reach an agreement with the Duma, however, it did not demand the immediate establishment of a democratic republic in Russia and agreed that the question of Russia's political future should be left to the constituent assembly.

The Soviet deputies pointed out that the new government's program lacked such an elementary demand as the abolition of governmental restrictions on the rights of nationalities and insisted on its inclusion in the program.

The Soviet did not create a provisional revolutionary government. An overwhelming majority approved the Executive Committee's transfer of power to the government formed by the Duma Committee and also the government's program worked out during negotiations with the Duma members. The Soviet merely introduced corrections and additions in the government's program: "1) The Provisional Government agrees to carry out all of the enumerated reforms despite the war; 2) The Manifesto of the Provisional Government must be signed by both Rodzianko and the Provisional Government; 3) The Provisional Government's program will grant all nationalities the right of national and cultural self-determination; 4) The Soviet of Soldiers' and Workers' representatives will form a committee to monitor the Provisional Government."

Although the Soviet's resolution laid the basis for concluding an agreement with the Duma Committee, serious obstacles remained. While the Soviet agreed to postpone the demand for a democratic republic and leave the question of the form of the country's administration to the constituent assembly, the Duma leaders fought doggedly to preserve the formal political structure, still hoping that replacing the monarch would save the monarchy. A March 1 *Izvestiia* article called reaching an agreement with the old authorities inadmissible. "The question must be posed clearly and boldly: either a new government or a compromise with the old." Appealing for clarity and decisiveness, the newspaper purposefully expressed itself vaguely on this very issue: "We intentionally have not yet dotted all the i's. But we shall do so next time if the ambiguity continues."

It did. A compromise with the former authorities took shape in the form of Nicholas II's abdication, declaration of Aleksei as tsar, and establishment of a regency under Mikhail. *Izvestiia* insisted only a constituent assembly had the right to resolve the question of the country's state order. In an article, "The Regency and the Constituent Assembly," the newspaper wrote that "the Provisional Government does not have the right to determine any permanent form of administration. To protect the people from counterrevolutionary machinations and to help it consummate the revolution before convocation of a constituent assembly is the entire purpose of the Provisional Government." The establishment of a regency would unleash civil war, for the democracy would interpret it "as a counterrevolutionary measure, as a dangerous encroachment on the gains of the revolution."

It was Miliukov who heralded the regency. In a conversation with representatives of the Reuters News Agency and Associated Press on March 2, he stated that "the new government holds that the abdication has officially taken place and that a regency has temporarily been established under Grand Prince Mikhail Aleksandrovich. Such is our decision and we consider it impossible to change it."

In midday on March 2, Miliukov addressed a large mass of soldiers and workers in the Catherine Hall of the Tauride Palace. In this well thought-out speech the bourgeois leader announced the formation of the new government. Miliukov spared no derogatory words or bitter epithets in referring to the old authorities. "History," he said, "knows no other government that has been so stupid, so dishonest, so cowardly, and so treacherous as this one. The deposed government has disgraced itself, has deprived itself of all support and respect." What would the policies of the new authorities be? Mentioning that the Provisional Government's program was under discussion by the Soviet, Miliukov avoided sensitive questions that would alarm the masses and did not say a word about the government's attitude toward the war. He proposed to avoid temporarily all political arguments and disagreements among separate parties and groups and to establish normal relations between soldiers and officers. Miliukov spoke on behalf of unity, which was advantageous to the bourgeoisie.

The crowd asked Miliukov: "Who elected you?" And he arrogantly responded: "No one elected us, for if we had waited for popular elections we could not have seized power from the enemy. The Russian Revolution elected us." Miliukov announced that the people who had entered the government were sacrificing themselves and that as soon as they were told the nation no longer needed them, they would resign, but "we will not give up power now, when it's needed to consolidate the people's victory." Applause interrupted Miliukov's speech, but the more he spoke the louder the cries of indignation and the more biting the questions became. "Who are the new ministers?" rang out from the hall. Miliukov began naming them, giving a short description of each. "We have placed at the head of our ministry a man whose very name signifies organized Russian society," he said. Cries of "privileged society" resounded in reply. "Prince L'vov, head of the Russian Zemstvo, will be our example." "Privileged," the crowd answered once again. Miliukov cautioned those at the meeting: "Now I will mention a name I know will arouse objections." He named Guchkov. In order to sweeten the pill he added: "Right now, while I am in this hall speaking to you, Guchkov is in the streets of the capital consolidating our victory." In fact, however, Guchkov at this time was not consolidating any sort of victory, but had gone with Shul'gin to the tsar to save the monarchy.

His speech ended, Miliukov answered a question that had provoked especially vituperative discussion — the fate of the dynasty. "You ask about the royal family," Miliukov said. "I know in advance that my answer will not please everyone, but I will tell you anyway. The former despot who brought Russia to the brink of ruin will either voluntarily abdicate or will be deposed (applause). Power will be transferred to the regent, Grand Prince Mikhail Aleksandrovich (continuous, indignant cries and exclamations: 'Long live the republic!' 'Down with the dynasty!' Weak applause, drowned out by a new explosion of indignation). The heir to the throne will be Aleksei (shouts: 'that's the old dynasty')." Miliukov was forced to back off in order to calm passions. Declaring himself a supporter of a constitutional monarchy, he announced that the form of the state order was not being decided conclusively now, but would be resolved by the constituent assembly. Yet no stipulations could help anymore. Miliukov had laid all of his cards on the table.

Similar antimonarchy moods prevailed at other political rallies taking place at the time in Petrograd. Sukhanov recalled that "from the porch onto which I had barely managed to go out, I saw a crowd the likes of which I had never seen before in my life. The endless faces and heads looking at me filled the entire courtyard, square, street; the people carried banners, placards, flags. . . . I recounted how the Executive Committee had resolved the question of power, I named the main ministers who had been proposed, and I spelled out the program the Soviet dictated to the L'vov-Miliukov government." But they soon began to interrupt Sukhanov with questions about the monarchy and dynasty. "And I personally," observed Sukhanov, "had not given the matter much thought until now and for the first time saw how important it was to the masses. In reply to the clamor, I told how the disagreement between the privileged ones and the Executive Committee over the monarchy had not yet been resolved. I expressed confidence that the entire nation would favor a democratic republic. . . . An enormous, but at the same time peaceful, demonstration against the dynasty and on behalf of a republic then took place."

The account of officer Tugan-Baranovskii, a member of the Military Commission, confirmed the masses' support for a democratic republic. "On March 2," he said, "a difficult situation arose in the Duma. Placards bearing the inscription 'Down with the Romanovs' appeared. The crisis came to a head. I had to speak with the deputies and answer whether the Romanovs would continue to reign or whether we would have a republic. I had to reply in generalities because exact information was unavailable. The situation became impossible."

Miliukov's report on keeping the monarchy and establishing a regency caused a storm of indignation and protest among workers and soldiers. The insurgent people had fought to topple the tsarist regime, not for a change in tsars. They rejected an absolute, constitutional, or any other form of monarchy. Late in the evening of March 2, a group of infuriated officers announced to the Duma Committee in the Tauride Palace that officers would be unable to return to their units if Miliukov did not repudiate what he had said. Rodzianko asked Miliukov to do this, and he was compelled to declare in print that the proposal to offer the throne to Aleksei under Mikhail's regency was simply his personal opinion. "This, of course, was untrue, for in all previous discussions the question was considered to have been resolved jointly, as Miliukov had set forth. The Provisional Committee, however, frightened by the growing ferment, silently disavowed its former stance." . . .

Rodzianko's dedication to the tsar aside, neither he nor anyone else could keep Nicholas II on the throne. He had to be sacrificed. Rodzianko wrote to Mikhail Aleksandrovich: "It is too late. Only abdication on behalf of the heir under your regency can pacify the country. I beseech you to use your influence so that this will come to pass voluntarily, then things will calm down. I personally am dangling by a thread and can be arrested and hanged at any moment. . . . You cannot turn down the regency. May God help you take my advice — convince His Majesty."

That same day the Duma leaders realized it was impossible to limit itself to this concession. The insurgent people demanded a democratic republic. Supporters of the monarchy feared the Duma Committee would take this step under pressure from the people. On March 2 a group of officers addressed a memorandum to the State Duma Committee. "The Provisional Government does not have the right to follow the instructions of individual groups of people. . . . The Provisional Government must clearly and precisely express its intention to let the people themselves choose a form of government through a constituent assembly, which can be convoked only after establishing complete order in the country, so necessary for proper elections." . . .

When things were most critical, on the evening of March 2, the Provisional Government released a statement to the population, not waiting for the publication of a joint declaration. It said: "The Provisional Government formed by the State Duma Committee hereby announces that the government's program includes convocation of a constituent assembly on the basis of universal, direct, equal, and secret suffrage, which will determine the country's form of government." This appeal, signed by Prince L'vov, Miliukov, and Kerensky, was immediately given to the Soviet and the Military Commission and was widely disseminated in Petrograd.

Other points in the government's declaration did not cause controversy. The Duma members accepted the Soviet's amendment, and the text of the declaration was edited for the last time and signed by the members of the Provisional Government and Rodzianko. The Soviet's proclamation in regard to the formation and announcement of the Provisional Government was also approved.

Soviet representatives did not interfere in the appointment of ministers, which was left exclusively to the Duma Committee. The Soviet's Executive Committee did not utilize its right to remove "especially objectionable individuals." It saw none. Rafes noted that only Guchkov's candidacy met with protests, but that they were not universal and categorical. The Soviet merely asked whether Guchkov would receive any special powers in the Provisional Government. Miliukov answered in the negative, stating that the entire Provisional Government was responsible for Guchkov's actions. "The question of personality was thus eliminated."

The Provisional Duma Committee appointed the following individuals ministers to "the first public cabinet": chairman of the Council of Ministers and minister of internal affairs, Prince G. E. L'vov; minister of foreign affairs, P. N. Miliukov; minister of war and of the navy, A. I. Guchkov; minister of communications, N. V. Nekrasov; minister of trade and industry, A. I. Konovalov; minister of finance, M. I. Tereshchenko; minister of education, A. A. Manuilov; procurator of the Hold Synod, V. N. L'vov; minister of agriculture, A. I. Shingarev; minister of justice, A. F. Kerensky; state comptroller, I. V. Godnev. The new government was thus unquestioningly made up of capitalists and landowners. Four of the ministers — Miliukov, Manuilov, Nekrasov, and Shingarev — were Kadets. G. L'vov sympathized with them; Guchkov and Godnev were Octobrists; Konovalov was a Progressist; V. L'vov belonged to the center. Tereshchenko considered himself nonaligned, but he, too, was close to the Kadets. Finally, Kerensky — leader of the Trudovik faction in the Duma — declared himself an SR during the revolution.

The Provisional Government's declaration determined which considerations would guide its activities. In the course of negotiations, representatives of the Duma Committee and Soviet had agreed on eight points.

> 1) *complete and immediate amnesty for all political and religious prisoners, including those incarcerated for terrorism, mutiny, agrarian crimes, etc.; 2) freedom of speech, union, assembly, and the right to strike, with the extension of political freedoms to the armed forces prescribed by military-technical considerations; 3) the lifting of all class, religious, and national restrictions; 4) immediate preparations for the convocation of a constituent assembly on the basis of universal, equal, direct, and secret suffrage, which will determine the form of government*

and the country's constitution; 5) replacement of the police by a people's militia with elected leaders, subordinate to organs of local administration; 6) elections to organs of local administration also on the basis of four-tailed suffrage; 7) no disarmament and no withdrawal from Petrograd of army units that had taken part in the revolution; 8) the extension to soldiers of all public rights enjoyed by civilians and the preservation of strict military discipline in formation and in carrying out military service.

In accord with the Soviet's proposal, the Provisional Government concluded that "henceforth it did not intend to use the war as an excuse for postponing the aforementioned reforms and undertakings."

Rodzianko informed the high command that the Duma leaders made significant concessions to the Soviet in forming a new government. He told Ruzskii:

As a result of lengthy negotiations with deputies from the workers I was able to reach some sort of agreement only by evening today. It called for convocation of a constituent assembly so that the people could express their opinion about the form of government. It was only then that Petrograd sighed with relief and the night passed calmly.

Rodzianko reported to Lukomskii at Supreme Headquarters on March 3 in the same vein:

Yesterday we had to reach an agreement with the leftist parties, establish several basic guidelines, and secure their promise to end all disorders. Downright anarchy has set in, indiscriminate and uncontrollable, and much more intensive than in 1905. . . . To avoid bloodshed, we made up our mind to reach an agreement, the main point of which was recognition of the need to elect a constituent assembly.

Thus the bourgeoisie received state power from the Soviet in exchange for several important concessions. The Provisional Government's declaration stated that it was formed by the Provisional Duma Committee in agreement with the Soviet. . . .

The Soviet Executive Committee's statement (*Izvestiia*, March 3) said that the broad democratic circles must welcome the reforms decreed by the new government made up "of society's socially moderate strata." "To the extent that the new government moves to implement these obligations and to struggle decisively with the old authorities, the democracy must support it." In this manner the formula "only insofar as," adopted by the Soviet Executive Committee the night before, was confirmed. The announcement spoke of the inadmissibility of "disunity and anarchy" and the need to stop all excesses, robberies, property damage, arbitrary seizures of institutions, etc., at once. The Soviet Executive Committee appealed to soldiers to "work together with officers in a concerted and friendly manner, not stigmatizing the entire officer corps for the foolish behavior of a few individuals, and to show patience and ignore immaterial breaches against the democracy by those officers who have resolutely joined in the final struggle you are leading against the old regime.". . .

The second revolutionary wave ebbed with the publication of the Provisional Government's declaration and the Soviet Executive Committee's announcement calling for a constituent assembly. The vanguard elements among the Petrograd proletariat, led by the Bolsheviks, continued to battle for establishing power of the revolutionary people. The majority of workers and soldiers, however, having won major concessions from the bourgeoisie and broad democratic rights, accepted bourgeois power and banked on placing it under the Soviet's control. They followed their petit bourgeois leaders, who called upon them to show their faith in the new government insofar as it implemented the program it agreed to with the Soviet. . . .

Guchkov and Shul'gin arrived in Pskov late on the evening of March 2. Guchkov wanted to meet with Ruzskii first, but the colonel who met Guchkov and Shul'gin at the station informed them the tsar wanted the deputies to come to him at once. Shul'gin recalled that he went to the tsar with the ominous feeling that the most horrible thing conceivable was taking place and that it was impossible to avert it. "Still one more stupid thought" bothered him: "It was awkward for me to appear before the tsar unshaven, in a crumpled collar and jacket."

At 10:00 P.M. on March 2 the discussion on the imperial train began. Guchkov spoke first. Quite upset, he avoided making eye contact with the tsar and detailed unpersuasively what had occurred in Petrograd. Judging by the protocols kept by the head of the field office, K. A. Naryshkin, Guchkov said that he had arrived with Shul'gin to apprise the emperor of the real conditions in Petrograd and to seek advice on measures that could save the situation. Guchkov reported the state of affairs in Petrograd was extremely threatening, the disorders had spread to the outlying regions, there was not a single reliable unit, troops arriving from the fronts promptly sided with the insurgents, and although a Provisional Duma Committee had been formed, it lacked power. Moreover, extremist elements considered the moderate Duma members traitors and were fighting to eliminate the monarchy and establish a socialist republic. "Besides us, a committee of the workers' party is meeting and we are under its influence and censorship. . . . The leftist elements are already beginning to sweep us away. Their slogan is: proclaim a socialist republic. The movement has infected the lower classes and even the soldiers, who are promised land." Guchkov pointed out that the contagion might spread to the front, that in view of the army's present mood it was impossible to preserve the throne for Nicholas. The only way out is to transfer power to others — the abdication of Nicholas II in favor of his son under a regency of Mikhail and the formation of a new government was the only way "to save the monarchical order, to save the dynasty."

Guchkov subsequently recalled that Ruzskii supported him, confirming that "there is not a single unit reliable enough to be sent to suppress the revolution. The tsar looked completely unshaken. The only thing that could be read on his face was that this long speech was unnecessary." And, in fact, the question of abdication had been resolved before the arrival of the Duma Committee's representatives. The protocols of the abdication compiled by Naryshkin state that Nicholas, having heard Guchkov out, commented: "I thought about this during the morning and in the name of general well-being, peace, and Russia's salvation, I was ready to abdicate in favor of my son, but now, reconsidering the situation, I have come to the conclusion that because of his illness I must abdicate at the same time both for my son and for myself, since I cannot part with him."

Nicholas abdicated in favor of his brother Mikhail. The Duma representatives, arriving with a proposal to make Mikhail regent, not tsar, had not anticipated such a decision. They asked that they be given the opportunity to reflect on the "new terms" of the abdication. Then Guchkov announced they did not oppose the tsar's recommendation. Their confederates in the Duma subsequently criticized Guchkov's and Shul'gin's acceptance of Mikhail's candidacy. Attempting to justify his behavior, Shul'gin observed: "How could we have disagreed? . . . We had arrived to tell the tsar the Duma Committee's opinion . . . which coincided with the tsar's. . . . And if it hadn't, what could we have done? . . . We could have returned [to Petrograd] if they let us . . . for we, after all, had not resorted to 'clandestine violence' as was done in the eighteenth and the beginning of the nineteenth centuries. . . ." Shul'gin wrote that whether Aleksei or Mikhail would be tsar was, in the final analysis, a mere detail and that Mikhail's candidacy actually had some advantages. Mikhail could swear allegiance to a constitution to pacify the people, and if need be, he could renounce the throne like his brother, something a minor such as Aleksei could not do. The main thing was that time would be won.

Guchkov gave the tsar the draft abdication manifesto. Nicholas left, returned shortly, and handed a paper to Guchkov. It was the document previously formulated at headquarters, and not the one presented by the Duma delegates. They had wanted Nicholas's successor to grant a constitution. They had argued that the greatest danger came from the leftist elements who were striving to declare a republic, and that if the new tsar were bound by a constitution this would weaken the position of those advocating a republic. As Shul'gin said: "We are preserving the country's symbol. . . . It's hell in the Duma, a real madhouse. We'll have to get embroiled in a decisive fight with the leftist elements and some sort of basis is necessary for this. . . . Should your brother Mikhail Aleksandrovich as the legitimate monarch swear to uphold a new constitution upon his ascension to the throne, this would contribute to a general pacification." In accordance with this request, a phrase was added to the abdication manifesto that the new emperor must take an inviolable oath to govern in concert with the people's representatives.

The tsar's manifesto said that "it has pleased God to lay on Russia a new and painful trial," that the newly arisen popular domestic disturbances imperil the successful prosecution of the war, which must be carried out to a victorious end no matter what happens. The document read: "In agreement with the State Duma, we think it best to abdicate the throne of the Russian State and lay down the supreme power. Not wishing to be separated from our beloved son, we hand down our inheritance to our brother, Grand Prince Mikhail Aleksandrovich, and give him our blessing on ascending the throne of the Russian State. We enjoin our brother to govern in concert and harmony with the people's representatives in legislative institutions on such principles as they shall deem fit to establish, and to bind himself by oath in the name of our beloved country."

The Duma delegates did not wish to create the impression they had extorted the manifesto from the tsar. Although it was approaching midnight, the tsar, at the deputies' request, dated the manifesto 3:00 P.M. The document was typed in two copies, signed by Nicholas II in pencil, and countersigned by the court minister. N. Vishniakov, a bourgeois activist and Moscow City Duma deputy, gave an interesting interpretation of this curious detail. "The pitiful excuse for a tsar could not even see fit to sign his abdication in ink like a real man, but did so in pencil. It was as if he were so indifferent to it all, as others are when they scribble notes in pencil to a friend or make a list of dirty laundry. What despicable people! And it was precisely they who had controlled the fate of a great empire for centuries.". . .

Had the victorious revolution resulted in the tsar's abdication or deposition? The latter, of course. The revolution had overthrown Nicholas II, and only afterward was this presented as a voluntary resignation. Nicholas II had not stepped down in the first days of the revolution when he still intended to drown the unarmed people in blood with the help of troops from the front. The tsar abdicated when the unreliability of these units became manifest, when the revolution had spread to Moscow and other cities, when the tsar's cause had failed and all options had closed. The insurgent people had dethroned Nicholas themselves, and the "voluntary abdication" merely legalized this act by antedating it. Former subjects of the Russian tsar said he had abdicated himself long ago from the people.

Not for nothing did the bourgeoisie give the tsar's dethronement the form of a voluntary act. As Guchkov put it, "I was afraid that in the event he had refused to renounce the throne, the Soviet of Workers' and Soldiers' Deputies would depose Nicholas II."

The tsar's so-called voluntary abdication freed the army from its oath and made it easier for it to join the revolution. It paralyzed the reactionary officers corps's opposition as well as that of other supporters of the old regime. Monarchists would not be able to defend the throne if it were vacant, if no one agreed to wear the crown knocked from Nicholas II's head. They had to accept the fall of the monarchy, at least temporarily.

The form in which the autocrat's abdication was presented, however, kept the path open for the monarchy's restoration. Calling for the abolition of the monarchy and establishment of a democratic republic, *Izvestiia* rightly noted that the dethronement was shrouded in such a manner that the possibility existed it would be overruled, that the path to restoring the monarchy was not closed. Nicholas's resignation on behalf of his brother and the latter's on behalf of the Provisional Government (see below) preserved the continuity of power and created more favorable conditions for the restoration of the monarchy than the direct deposition of the tsar and proclamation of a republican order.

Supporters of the autocracy depicted the tsar's abdication as a noble gesture, as a sacrifice he made for the well-being of the fatherland. They subsequently maintained that this measure, forced upon them, was illegal, that Nicholas II was not empowered to act for his son and that therefore the Romanov dynasty had not lost its rights to the Russian throne. Aleksandra Fedorovna held that things would return to normal. Believing that all it would take was granting a responsible ministry and constitution, she wrote her husband: "If you are forced to make concessions, you are not obliged to carry them out, since they were wrung from you. . . . It's absolutely criminal that you were compelled to do this simply because you lacked an army. Such a promise will no longer be valid when power is in your hands again. . . . God will save you and restore all of your rights to you." Aleksandra Fedorovna continued to believe this even after Nicholas II had abdicated. On March 3 she wrote the former tsar: "I swear we shall see you once again on your throne which you will ascend with your people and troops for the glory of your reign.". . .

At their very first meeting on March 2, the Provisional Government's ministers already admitted that in view of present conditions the Provisional Government must take the Soviet's opinion into account, but that the Soviet's interference in the government's affairs amounted to dual power which was unacceptable. Therefore the Provisional Government "must familiarize itself with the Soviet's intentions at its private meetings before examining these questions at official meetings of the Council of Ministers." The Provisional Government could advocate familiarizing itself with the Soviet's intentions, but could not eliminate its interference in governmental affairs.

The second revolutionary wave had not achieved its main goal. The bourgeoisie remained in power, a provisional government had been formed, and the basic demands of the minimum programs of the RSDRP were yet to be realized. Nonetheless, the new revolutionary onslaught did not recede without leaving a trace. It overthrew the tsarist monarchy and strengthened the organ of genuine popular authority —

the Soviet of Workers' and Soldiers' Deputies, and this was of paramount importance for the revolution's further development. . . .

The Soviet's Activities

During its first three days of sessions, the Petrograd Soviet evolved into a powerful force. By March 3 the number of deputies had swelled to thirteen hundred. Because tiny room number 13 located in the left wing of the Tauride Palace could no longer accommodate them, the Soviet moved that day to the palace's White Hall, where the State Duma had met for eleven years. New individuals now occupied the seats so familiar to the Provisional Government's ministers. Showing up in tattered fur and cloth coats and soldiers' greatcoats, the Soviet's deputies and guests packed the auditorium. The reading of the abdication manifesto electrified the audience. A gilded frame still hung over the chairman's desk, but because the tsar's portrait had been removed from it, it gaped vacantly. . . .

The Soviet's composition and activities reflected the working people's level of consciousness and organization. The worker and soldier masses' poor understanding of their own class interests and the influence of petit bourgeois elements stirred by the revolution shaped the alignment of forces within the Soviet. The majority of its deputies were under the authority of the Mensheviks and SRs; the Bolsheviks turned out to be in the minority. Many authors maintain the Mensheviks' and SRs' strength within the Soviet was attributable to the unfair norms of representation established by the Executive Committee. Each thousand workers sent one deputy to the Soviet. Workers from enterprises with fewer than one thousand workers jointly elected deputies or participated in elections by profession, according to the same norm of one deputy per one thousand workers. In some instances, though, factories with fewer than five hundred workers independently elected deputies.

Lack of coordination naturally meant there could not be complete conformity in the elections held at large, middle-sized, and smaller enterprises. Nevertheless, it is incorrect to maintain that delegates from the largest factories floundered among those from smaller handicraft enterprises, or that "at the time of the Petrograd Soviet's formation, SRs and Mensheviks granted the large factories and plants of Petrograd, whose indigenous proletariat supported the Bolsheviks, as many places in the Soviet as the small enterprises whose workers sprang from a petit

First Session of the Petrograd Soviet, March 1917. The tsar's portrait has been removed from the frame behind the speaker. (Culver Pictures)

bourgeois milieu." In reality, the majority of workers' deputies in the Soviet represented the capital's large and middle-sized enterprises. The six largest factories in Petrograd alone sent about one hundred deputies to the Soviet. Menshevik and SR influence predominated then even at these enterprises. The majority of Soviet deputies from the Putilov, Pipe, Baltic, Metalworks, and several other of the largest factories supported the Mensheviks and SRs for deep-lying reasons, especially owing to changes in the composition of the working class during the war, when workers from the petite bourgeoisie infiltrated the largest industrial enterprises.

Soldiers made up an even broader base of support for the SRs and Mensheviks. Politically inexperienced and incited by the revolution to active struggle for the first time, they backed the SRs and Mensheviks, and believed their assertions for the need to establish national unity and continue the war to defend the revolution from German militarism. Soldiers were well represented in the Soviet and numerically dominated the workers' deputies. Soldiers elected one deputy to the Soviet from each company, the basic unit of military organization during the revolution (in reserve battalions, which composed a major part of the Petrograd garrison, companies contained one thousand to fifteen hundred soldiers). The principle of representation by company was established not only by the Provisional Executive Committee in the Soviet's address of February 27 but also by the appeal issued that day by the Vyborg Bolsheviks and published within a day as Order No. 1.

Not only companies sent one deputy each to the Soviet but also staff commands, military hospitals, storehouses, and other support groups that included an insignificant number of soldiers. As Zalezhskii noted, "among the smaller units no revolutionary work had been conducted until now and political consciousness was quite low. It therefore is natural that these units elected as deputies 'chatterboxes,' such as clerks, educated persons serving on privileged conditions, officer trainees, and others from the petit bourgeois ranks. These deputies were attracted to the SR and Menshevik parties, which were psychologically more kindred to them." Although Bolshevik influence was greater in the largest military units, petit bourgeois influence also predominated in them with rare exception.

As already noted, another circumstance told on the Soviet's membership. The Bolsheviks struggling on the streets of the capital did not participate actively enough in electing deputies, so many people were elected to the Soviet by chance. "The most progressive, active members," wrote Shliapnikov, "were involved in all sorts of revolutionary work and in the heat of passion ignored the elections." As Bolshevik Putilovite F. Lemeshev put it, "in the first days of the revolution all party members were in the streets . . . not enough attention was given to elections to the Soviet of Workers' Deputies." This explains the petit bourgeois wave that swelled in the aftermath of the workers' uprising, carrying SRs and Mensheviks at its crest, and placing them at the leadership of the Soviet. The Soviet's activities reflected SR and Menshevik influence: leaders of the Petrograd Soviet appealed to the proletariat not to drive away the bourgeoisie. Since power had been transferred to the Provisional Government, the Soviet's Executive Committee strove to avoid encroaching upon the government's territory. It advised, asked, sometimes even demanded, but tried not to resolve, order, or instruct. However, it was difficult to hold this line, for the struggle compelled the Soviet to take independent actions. In the revolutionary atmosphere of those days, in which the Soviet was under intense pressure from the masses, the Soviet and its Executive Committee discussed the most diverse problems and often acted as organs of power. They published orders for the garrison, appointed commissars to military units, commandeered printing offices, determined the makeup of the police, prohibited the shipment of Black Hundred literature, carried resolutions to arrest leaders of the old regime, to replace individuals, etc. Without the Soviet's sanction it was impossible to put out newspapers, resume work at factories, reassign military units, and implement an array of other measures. . . .

Petrograd after the Overthrow of the Monarchy

The overthrow of the monarchy gave the revolutionary forces burrowed in the underground the opportunity to carry out legal activity. On February 28, when the battle had not yet abated in the streets and shooting was still breaking out at the barracks of the bicycle battalion, members of the Vyborg Committee of the RSDRP, representatives of the Central Committee Bureau, and party workers newly released from prison gathered in Kaiurov's apartment on Bolshoi Sampsonievskii Prospekt, not far from the barracks. They decided to organize a Petersburg Bolshevik Committee at once from among former members and to let the Vyborg Committee resume its own responsibilities. One of the first steps of the Vyborg District Committee was creation of an agitational board. At the time Zhenia Egorova, Semen Roshal', and M. Latsis ("Uncle"), and others conducted especially active agitational work in the district.

The transportation breakdown during the revolutionary chaos made it difficult to restore the all-city party committee and establish ties among separate neighborhoods of the expansive city. "We were up to our necks in work," Latsis recalled.

> *Everyone was running around; we were as busy as bees. Streetcars weren't running and there were no horses or automobiles. They were available, but not to us. During the first couple of days the authorities could not figure out what was going on and sometimes let us have them. Now the authorities no longer provide the party committee with any because it has shown its true revolutionary character. . . . We're*

all dead tired and hungry. And then there's the spring slush. In crushed boots we trample from one factory to another. Automobiles rush past . . . the victors are going for a ride.

The Bolsheviks recently released from prison or those returning from the underground and drawn into the revolution were unable to link forces immediately. On March 10, N. Tolmachev wrote from Petrograd to his relatives in Rostov-on-the-Don.

Dear ones, congratulations on Russia's glorious emancipation. In these days of general amnesty, grant amnesty to me for my criminal silence. Swept up into the revolutionary movement, I thought of nothing and of no one, I forgot everyone and everything. . . . While going to work on the 27th, I became so involved in a demonstration, some 20,000-people strong, that I simply could not come to my senses until the last couple of days. I was everywhere: in the first demonstrations, at the shootings, at the soldiers' uprising, and then, together with soldiers in the Peter-Paul arsenal, I seized revolvers, rifles and drove in an automobile to arrest the police. I was at rallies, at meetings. I, myself, spoke. It was impossible to be on the sidelines. I just now came to my senses. After falling into the whirlpool of events, you become an insignificant bit of debris caught up in the whirling vortex.

V. Shmidt related:

We old PCs (members of the Petersburg Committee — E.B.) released from prison got lost in the crowd. Somehow we searched each other out; some ran off to the neighborhoods to restore old ties, others to set up legal printing presses or to find lodging. Although we agreed to meet the next day to form a Petersburg committee, we succeeded in doing so only on March 2.

The first meeting of the Petersburg Committee of the RSDRP took place on March 2 at the city Stock Exchange, a place workers knew well and which was headed by the Bolshevik L. Mikhailov (Politikus). By this time ten district party committees already existed in Petrograd as well as a students' Social Democratic organization. Not all of them were represented at this meeting. Present were delegates from the Vyborg, Narva, and Vasilevkii Island regions, the Latvian Social Democrats, the Social Democrats of Poland and Lithuania and from several workers' organizations, old party workers, in all forty people. Those present felt they did not have the right to create a permanent party committee and therefore elected a Provisional Petersburg Committee, which included authorized district representatives and also former committee members. Zalezhskii, Kalinin, Avilov, Shutko, Podvoiskii, Orlov, Antipov, and other comrades joined the Petersburg Committee. Mikhailov was elected chairman, and Shmidt, secretary. Antipov was empowered to form an agitators' board and Shutko a commission responsible for party literature. The committee proposed that Orlov, who was responsible for organizational matters, establish ties at once with the neighborhoods and invite delegates from districts still not represented to join the committee.

The Petersburg Committee of the RSDRP saw its major task in strengthening and broadening the party's ranks and establishing the widest possible contact with the worker and soldier masses. It launched a recruitment drive and resolved to agitate workers and to infiltrate the barracks in order to agitate soldiers. The Petersburg Committee instructed Bolshevik speakers to explain to the masses the need to continue the revolutionary struggle to achieve the total abolition of the monarchical order and the speedy convocation of a constituent assembly. It decided to issue party literature, leaflets, and appeals to workers and soldiers, to publish the program and statutes of the RSDRP as well as posters, and to set up a library.

Shmidt noted that work went well, that ties to the neighborhoods were quickly reestablished. Nonetheless, the first days of the revolution had been lost, and the Mensheviks had taken advantage of this. People constantly crowded into the low, stuffy rooms of the upper floor of the Stock Exchange that accommodated the Petersburg Bolshevik Committee. The Petersburg Committee and its executive commission were almost in continuous session. "Shmidt was the main organizer, carrying out the responsibilities of secretary, and Podvoiskii maintained contact with the neighborhoods and with party visitors from whom there was no respite. He issued directives to agitators and maintained ties with the editorial offices of *Pravda* (all information about us was channeled there through him); Vladimir (Zalezhskii — E.B.) enthusiastically participated in the constant discussion of tactical questions, and also fulfilled representative functions, speaking on behalf of the Petrograd Committee at large rallies and representing the party to nonparty organizations." The Petersburg Committee drew its support from local district and factory organizations. On March 5 *Pravda* observed that "the district organizations of the party are growing not by the day, but by the hour. Organized workers are not satisfied with organizations at the district level and are forming party cells at the subdistrict level and even at individual factories."

The Central Committee Bureau of the RSDRP, the temporary national party center, also carried on important party work. During the first days of the revolution it had settled down in the Tauride Palace, where its members set up a duty schedule and organized its small staff. E. D. Stasova, who had returned to Petrograd from exile shortly before the revolution, had been arrested by the tsarist authorities on the eve of February 25. Freed from police detention by the insurgent people, she now headed the secretariat of the Central Committee Bureau. Stasova wrote: "My responsibilities included receiving comrades, answering their questions on all aspects of party activities, and supplying them with literature. Second, I kept the minutes of the Orgbureau [Organizational Bureau — D.J.R.]. Third, I wrote and circulated all of the Central Committee directives. Fourth, I managed finances."

The members of the Central Committee Bureau who had emerged from the underground (Shliapnikov, Zalutskii, Molotov) could not cope with the enormous volume of work without help. Because it was impossible to wait for a party congress or conference to elect party leaders, the Central Committee Bureau began to co-opt party workers released from prison or exile. On March 7, 1917, it passed a resolution. "In view of the need to enlarge the Central Committee Bureau, as the present membership cannot handle all of the work at the moment and because the former members had just been released from prison, it has been decided to include K. Eremeev, K. Shvedchikov, M. Kalinin, K. Shutko, and M. Khakharev." Zalezhskii, G. Bokii, responsible for maintaining ties with the provinces, A. I. Elizarova, M. I. Ul'ianova, M. Ol'minskii, and others also joined the bureau. At its March 12 meeting it ratified the principle of co-opting new members. "The Central Committee Bureau recruited individuals considered useful, based on their political reliability, but it did not make membership dependent on fulfilling some specific function. The Bureau invited valuable theoreticians into its staff and only then divided up work among them."

After emerging from the underground, the Central Committee Bureau and Petersburg Committee of the RSDRP hastened to renew publication of *Pravda*. K. Eremeev, A. Gertik, N. Poletaev, K. Shvedchikov, S. Zaks-Gladnev, D. Arskii, and other old Pravdists ardently undertook this mission. With a mandate from the Soviet Executive

Committee and a small detachment of soldiers, they appeared at the printing office of the newspaper *Sel'skii vestnik* (Village Herald), which belonged to the Ministry of Internal Affairs, to utilize it for printing *Pravda*. The manager read the Executive Committee's order and announced that it said nothing about paper. "But Eremeev interrupted him. 'So you think it's possible to print a newspaper on something other than paper?' This argument had an effect on the manager, not so much because of its logic, as because of the armed patrol of Pavlovites. Cringing, the frightened manager hastened to inform us that the paper reserve totaled 16,000 poods." Shortly thereafter, Fabrikevich (Gnevich), N. Podvoiskii, V. Molotov, and others showed up and began to plan the first issue.

Zaks-Gladnev wrote that the first issue of *Pravda* was composed with difficulty.

> *We revolutionaries had forgotten how to write for a newspaper. Besides, the feverish events of the last few days had not yet taken on meaning for us, thoughts had not yet taken concrete shape, formulas had not yet crystallized. . . . Collective creativity played a tremendous role in composing the first issue. I myself wrote two articles. From the first, I remember, they kept one phrase and tacked it on to somebody else's article. My second essay — on our party's program and statutes — made it into the paper, only heavily abridged and edited. A similar fate befell other authors' work. . . . There were almost no technical workers. Many of us stayed around to work as proofreaders, distributors, etc. . . . There was no one to sell the paper in the morning, and there was no one to post the first issue to the provinces.*

Appearing on March 5, 1917, the first edition of *Pravda* was distributed free to Petrograd's factories, plants, and barracks and was sent to other cities. The lead editorial spoke the celebrated words: "The working class after years of struggle and thousands of victims, supported by the revolutionary army, has won freedom. *Pravda* was correct. Freedoms for which the workers' paper fought are being realized by the powerful force of the working class. The dawn of a new era has set in and a workers' paper is being revived. . . . Just as the workers' newspaper *Pravda* served as the organ of the revolutionary working class during the difficult days of the autocracy, the workers' newspaper *Pravda* will serve the working class in time of revolution and freedom."

Molotov, Eremeev, Kalinin, and A. I. Elizarova, in the capacity of secretary of the editorial board, joined *Pravda*'s first editorial staff. M. I. Ul'ianova also helped put out the paper. The seasoned party journalist M. Ol'minskii, summoned from Moscow to work on it, soon made his influence on the paper felt. His articles, sometimes two or three at a time, appeared in the first issues of *Pravda*. As before the revolution, workers' contributions financed the paper. The first issue of *Pravda* beseeched: "Comrade workers! Remember that now, just as in the past, the workers' press can exist only on the financial resources of the workers themselves." The newspaper proposed to launch a donation drive for a special operating fund.

The party of the revolutionary proletariat addressed the difficult question of how it should relate to the Soviet. At a March 2 meeting Petersburg Bolshevik Committee members sharply criticized the Soviet. They argued that Mensheviks, who had usurped places in it, did not represent the mood of the majority of conscious workers, that *Izvestiia* did not promote a revolutionary point of view, and that the Soviet's leaders were trailing behind the Duma Committee, which was trying to make a deal with the deposed tsar. The Bolsheviks proposed to carry out agitation more extensively in the districts, to criticize the Soviet's actions, to pressure it from below, and to advance their position more consistently at Soviet meetings.

The Bolsheviks did not criticize the Petrograd Soviet aggressively enough. Gathering after the Soviet had adopted the resolution on rendering conditional support to the Provisional Government, the Central Committee Bureau decided to continue the struggle to create a genuine revolutionary government capable of executing the people's demands. However, it did not enumerate the forms of this struggle and did not rule out the possibility that the masses might influence bourgeois power. On March 3 the bureau carried a resolution on its relationship to the Provisional Government and introduced it to the Petersburg Committee so that the latter could recommend the Petrograd Soviet adopt it. It read:

> *Insofar as the Provisional Government represents the interests of the prominent bourgeoisie and large landowners and is trying to reduce the impact of a real democratic revolution by substituting one ruling clique for another, and therefore is incapable of implementing the basic revolutionary demands of the people, the Soviet of Workers' and Soldiers' Deputies believes that: 1) the major task is to struggle for formation of a*

provisional revolutionary government which is the only one able to carry out these fundamental demands; 2) the Soviet of Workers' and Soldiers' Deputies must reserve complete freedom to determine how to carry out the basic demands of the revolutionary people and, in particular, to select ways of influencing the Provisional Government; 3) establishing control over the Provisional Government in the form of a special Soviet Control Commission is a palliative measure that does not achieve the recognized aim of controlling the implementation of the basic demands of the revolutionary democracy.

Molotov proposed this resolution at the March 3 meeting of the Petersburg Committee of the RSDRP on behalf of the Central Committee Bureau. It evoked lively debate and opinions were divided. A minority supported the Central Committee Bureau's resolution (Shutko, Kalinin, Tolmachev, and others). A majority (including Zalezhskii, Shmidt, Mikhailov, Antipov, Fedorov, and others) voted it down and decided to support a policy more in line with that of the Soviet majority. The resolution carried at this meeting read: "The Petersburg Committee of the RSDRP, taking into account the resolution on the Provisional Government passed by the Soviet, announces that it will not oppose the authority of the Provisional Government insofar as its actions further the interests of the proletariat and of the broadest democratic masses of people, but will struggle mercilessly against efforts by the Provisional Government to restore the monarchy in any form." This resolution ended talk of creating a provisional revolutionary government and gave rise to the illusion that the actions of the bourgeois authorities could "further the interests of the proletariat and of the broadest strata of people."

On March 5 the Petersburg Committee again discussed its relationship to the Provisional Government. A representative of the Vyborg Bolsheviks introduced a resolution that "our present task is to form a provisional revolutionary government, based on the union of local soviets of workers', peasants', and soldiers' deputies from all of Russia." The resolution called for the partial seizure of power in the provinces to facilitate a complete seizure of power in Petrograd. The Petrograd Committee rejected this resolution as it had the one of the Bureau of the Central Committee and confirmed its resolution on the Provisional Government, adopted on March 3. After rejecting the Vyborg Bolsheviks' resolution, the Petersburg Committee did not raise the question of eliminating bourgeois power and did not dissociate itself from the formula of conditional support for the Provisional Government, advanced by the SR-Menshevik majority in the Petrograd Soviet.

The complicated political situation after the overthrow of the monarchy prevented the leaders of the Petrograd Bolshevik Organization from adopting a correct tactical position. They failed to form, or to develop in accord with the new situation, the notion of a revolutionary-democratic dictatorship of the proletariat and peasantry and creation of a provisional revolutionary government, which the Bolshevik party had promoted since 1905. They likewise failed to devise a tactic that would guarantee the most favorable conditions for the transfer to a socialist revolution.

The Mensheviks and SRs did not promote a socialist revolution. They considered socialism a matter of the distant future and limited the struggle of the working people to the confines of the capitalist order. In *Izvestiia* on March 1 the Menshevik Organizational Committee entreated the masses to join forces for the decisive defeat of the old authorities and for formation of a provisional government that would create "conditions for the organization of a new, free Russia." Who was to compose the government and what sort of new Russia would it create? The Menshevik appeal did not answer these and many other questions. The Organizational Committee emphasized that if the proletariat would unite and organize its forces it "would be able to overthrow the old regime and also win for itself the strongest situation possible under the new order." Toward this aim the Menshevik leaders called upon workers to struggle during the revolution. They continued to do so after tsarism had been overthrown.

The central Menshevik organ *Rabochaia gazeta* (Workers' Newspaper), the first issue of which appeared on March 7, held that Russia faced a long period of capitalist development, during which state power must remain in the hands of the bourgeoisie. It explained that the Soviet could not take power because it did not enjoy the support of the bourgeoisie, which played the leading role in the country's economy. Soviet power would be "illusory power, power that would immediately lead to civil war." *Rabochaia gazeta* adjured the democracy not to remove the Provisional Government from power, but to apply to it "maximum pressure to carry out democratic demands," to help it take the bourgeois revolution to its natural conclusion. The newspaper advised the Provisional Government itself to act in the interests of the democracy. And then "it will unquestioningly enjoy the trust of the people and the struggle will be conducted on a single front against the mutual enemy — the legacy of the old order."

The SRs conducted a similar policy. There existed in Petrograd at the time a group of SR Internationalists who occupied leftist positions, which included P. Aleksandrovich, S. Maslovskii, and others. During the revolution this group, together with the Interdistrictites, urged the people not to give power to the bourgeoisie but to form a government of the revolutionary people. Kerensky, Zenzinov, and other SR leaders condemned these appeals. On March 2 a Petrograd Conference of SRs was held, which was attended by only twenty to twenty-five individuals. One SR activist, S. Postnikov, admitted that "the party in the real sense of the word did not yet exist in March 1917. During this month the process of mustering party forces, which up until now had been disorganized, took place." The conference of SRs dissociated themselves from the position of the SR Internationalists, registered its support for cooperating with the Provisional Government, and approved Kerensky's entry into it. According to the resolution that was adopted, the pressing need was to "support the Provisional Government insofar as it carries out the political program it itself declared." The conference called for a struggle "against all efforts that undermine the organizational work of the Provisional Government for the realization of political provisions put forward by it."

Close to the SRs on tactical matters, the Trudoviks occupied the far right flank of the democracy. This faction called upon the population to support the Provisional Government wholeheartedly and to obey its decrees. As a Trudovik appeal to the population of March 4 put it: "At present there is no room, nor can there be, for party quarrels or misunderstandings in the ranks of the insurgent people. Arm-in-arm, all those sympathetic to the cause of the people's emancipation must storm the last strongholds of power, selflessly obeying the Provisional Government organized by the State Duma." The March 5 edition of the daily newspaper *Den'* expressed the position of the populist parties and groups (SRs, Trudoviks, and Popular Socialists): "We will support the Provisional Government, but will not give up our right and obligation to criticize its mistakes. As the workers' and democratic organizations' unity and internal discipline grow, we will seek confirmation that the Provisional Government remains firmly committed to the country's revolutionary transformation on which it has embarked." The newspaper believed that the Provisional Government "was on top of things." It censured the Bolsheviks' *Pravda* and approved of the Petrograd Soviet "for its deep understanding of the moment, its political farsightedness and moderation in dealing with the Provisional Government." . . .

George Katkov

Was There a Revolution?

Western appreciations of Russia have consistently been influenced by the experience and analysis of émigrés from the Soviet Union. George Katkov, born in Moscow in 1903, personifies the fate of many forced by political circumstances to move westward. In 1921 his family left Russia for Czechoslovakia, where Katkov studied philosophy and graduated from the University of Prague. Forced to migrate to Britain in 1939, he developed an early interest in the history of his native country. For many years he taught at Oxford and, in the fiftieth-anniversary year of the revolution, he published a major study of the February revolt. His controversial thesis that German political intervention was a major factor in the revolution is a challenge to the more generally accepted view that the revolution was largely spontaneously generated.

1. Was There a Revolution?

With the renunciation of the throne by Grand Duke Michael and the publication of the document which formed the constitutional basis for the Provisional Government for the next eight months, what is known as the February Revolution in Russia, that is the transition from the autocracy of Nicholas II to the dictatorship of the Provisional Government, was completed. From the point of view of liberals of the type of Milyukov or Maklakov or Nolde, the revolution had taken place and was finished. For revolutionaries of the type of Kerensky, however, it had hardly begun.

The question whether there was a February Revolution in Russia in 1917 is, therefore, not entirely whimsical, except perhaps for people who might think of it as a question of the type: "Was there a blizzard in Petrograd in February 1917?" This can be answered in the indicative mood, and would express a matter of fact. A simple "yes" or "no" to the question: "Was there a revolution?" is not of the same character as a "yes" or "no" to the question: "Was there a blizzard?" It does not tell us whether certain events took place or not, but rather what the person answering felt about them, i.e., whether he believed that his political hopes and aspirations (or perhaps fears and apprehensions) had been fulfilled by what had happened, or not. It expresses a deep-seated emotional attitude towards the surrounding political and social realities of the time rather than the momentary state of jubilation which affected almost everybody at that moment. The almost universal elation which followed the announcement of the two abdications and of the formation of the Provisional Government, and which spread all over Russia (so that the Tsar's ADC Governor-General in Tashkent, Kuropatkin, could describe his feelings in almost the same terms as the SR intellectual Zenzinov in Petrograd) by no means reflected a uniform attitude to the February events. For many it was a sign of relief that the whole business had not ended in massacre; while for others it was an expression of joy at the prospect of things to come. The latter confidently expected that the masses of the people, freed from their age-old shackles, were about to play their part, not only in Russia but also in the political life of humanity at large, in particular in international affairs. It is therefore misleading to say that people accepted or welcomed the February revolution of 1917. What they accepted and welcomed they often had not had the opportunity to formulate or think about articulately. Without an analysis in depth of such emotional attitudes, we cannot understand the peculiar, dream-like terminology of revolutionary pronouncements concerning the "defence of the conquests of the revolution," the appeals for "a deepening of the revolution," etc., etc. But this was not part of our task in writing this book. This belongs to the sad and tragic history of the Provisional Government of Russia, which began on 4 March 1917 and ended on 26 October with its arrest and the seizure of power by Lenin and his henchmen.

But it must be said that the same emotionalism seriously affected the perception of events by those who were closest to them in the February days. When Prince Lvov, Rodzyanko or Milyukov claimed in the announcement which they signed jointly on 2 March that the Provisional Committee of the State Duma had won a victory over the dark forces of the old régime, with the assistance [*sic*] and the sympathy of the capital's garrison and population, they must have known very well that as a statement of fact this was simply not true. And yet the statement fairly reflects their desire to become the leading factor in the popular rising, which they had neither initiated nor directed until the crowds of workers, soldiers and intelligentsia beleaguered and invaded the Tauride Palace and demanded to be heard, harangued, organised and made use of politically. It took some years for Milyukov to moderate the effects of revolutionary phrase-mongering on his historical analysis. In his *History of the Russian Revolution*, written in the spring and summer of 1918, he still claimed that it was the Duma that had deposed the monarchy. Years later he corrected this statement, but it would obviously have taken him many more years to free his historical thinking of the influence of the political jargon which dominated his mind in February 1917. Possibly this is beyond human powers in general, although another historian of the Russian revolution, S. P. Melgunov, more conscious of the dangers facing an eye-witness who writes history, came very near to freeing himself completely from such influences and to dealing objectively with such pseudofactual statements as: "The revolution became victorious in the Petrograd streets late in the evening of 27 February." He has done splendid work in clarifying and exposing the origins of many a legend. But even he clings to one fatal misconception about the revolution which unfortunately has conquered the imagination of Western historians of the revolution as well, and which it is particularly important to clear up: this is the notion of the "spontaneity" of the Russian revolution which has been the point of departure for many histories of it.

2. Spontaneity

Paradoxically, those who regarded the February events as the fulfilment of their prophecies of revolution disclaimed both the responsibility and the honour of bringing them about. This applies in particular to the revolutionary parties, including the few Bolsheviks then active underground in Russia. It was their denials on this score which prompted the theory of the *spontaneous* nature of the February revolution. Thus in a passage introducing his account of the events of 1917, in his book *The Bolshevik Revolution 1917–1923*, E. H. Carr writes:

> *The February Revolution of 1917 which overthrew the Romanov dynasty was the spontaneous outbreak of a multitude exasperated by the privations of the war and by manifest inequality in the distribution of burdens. It was welcomed and utilized by a broad stratum of the bourgeoisie and of the official class, which had lost confidence in the autocratic system of government and especially in the persons of the Tsar and of his advisers; it was from this section of the population that the first Provisional Government was drawn. The revolutionary parties played no direct part in the making of the revolution. They did not expect it, and were at first somewhat nonplussed by it.*

We agree with Carr about the passive attitude of the revolutionary parties in February 1917. But does this justify his assumption of a spontaneous mass movement, i.e., one not instigated from outside?

The Russian word *"stikhiyny,"* of which — in this context — "spontaneous" is the translation, suggests to an even greater degree than its English counterpart that the "exasperations and privations" suffered by the masses during the war led to the degree of cohesion and purposefulness necessary for effective political action. "Spontaneous" in Carr's context indicates an inherent tendency — a predisposition — of the masses to react to such grievances as 'a manifest inequality of the distribution of burdens' by organised mass demonstrations on the scale of the Petrograd rising. Had such a disposition for concerted and deliberate action existed, it would have manifested itself in some perceptible way in other parts of Russia, where there was exactly the same inequality in the distribution of burdens. Moreover, had such inherent tendencies really existed among the Petrograd proletariat, they would surely have led to the same purposeful and coordinated action among the workers in the months subsequent to the revolution as well. In fact what we observe during the war, apart from Petrograd and perhaps one or two other industrial centres, is precisely the absence of any disposition among the working masses for sustained and purposeful political action, just as in the months following the revolution we see no sign of any such inherent tendency in the Petrograd population as a whole. The assumption that there was a particular quality of "spontaneity" which explains the scope and strength of the February demonstrations in Petrograd is wholly gratuitous. The theory of "spontaneity" only serves to cover up our ignorance.

3.   Conspiracies, Real and Imaginary

Several explanations less negative than the notion of "spontaneity" have been advanced for the success of the rising. We may instance three of these.

According to the first theory, the rising could be attributed largely to a satanic plan of the Tsarist police under Protopopov. He is supposed to have played the same trick as his predecessor Durnovo, who was alleged to have provoked the workers' rebellion of 1905 in order to suppress it by military force. This idea is linked with the legend of the Protopopov machine-guns, said to have been mounted on the roofs of Petrograd houses to mow down workers' demonstrations. We have already commented on this tenacious legend. No demonstrators were, of course, mown down by machine-gun fire from the house-tops during the February days. The number of casualties resulting from what Lenin described as "a week of bloody battles between workers and the Tsarist police" was relatively small if one considers the many hundreds of thousands of people involved, and most of these casualties can be put down to the few clashes that took place between the military and the crowd from 26 to 28 February. The Protopopov machine-guns never existed. With them vanishes the whole story of police provocation as a major causative factor in the Petrograd demonstrations.

This is not to say that the police were not equipped for provocation. The various revolutionary committees were penetrated and were kept under observation, and to some extent under control. But the plans of the Minister of the Interior for using the apparatus of police control in workers' circles were quite different from what this theory assumes. Protopopov, through his agents, did encourage among the workers of the WICs[1] extremist, indeed defeatist, ideas on the pattern of the resolutions of the Zimmerwald and Kienthal Conferences. But this he did in order to strike — when the time was ripe — at the WICs themselves. He thought that defeatist propaganda among the workers would reflect on the leadership of the WICs as a whole and discredit it in the eyes of the

---

[1] War Industry Committees, set up during the war to help the government in supplying the military.

public. There was no plan to bring the workers out on the streets and the police [were] not prepared for such an eventuality. On the contrary, the Ministry of the Interior dreaded the thought of casualties on the streets of Petrograd.

Indirectly, however, the action of the Minister of the Interior did contribute to the outbreak of these demonstrations. By arresting the leaders of the Labour Group of the WICs he removed the very people who, in February 1916, had succeeded in halting the strike movement in Petrograd. Deprived of the authority and guidance of the Mensheviks in the Labour Group and goaded to further impatience by their arrest, the working masses became even more susceptible to strike propaganda from whatever quarter it might come.

Some students of the February revolution incline to believe that it was brought about by the very circles which pressed for constitutional reform, when they despaired of achieving their aim through legal political means. This school of thought holds that the Petrograd rising was precipitated and facilitated by their wholesale denunciation of the imperial government, and in particular of the Tsar, his family, and his closest advisers. There is little evidence to support this view, although general considerations make it less fantastic than might at first appear. The rivalry between the government and the liberal circles for power had reached its climax. The liberals, whose political aspirations had once been favoured by the fortunes (or rather misfortunes) of war, were beginning to lose ground. Should victory, with Allied help, be won during 1917 all their forecasts would be disproved, and it would be easy for the government to turn the tables on them.

But here again the "conspiratorial" explanation for the Petrograd rising fails. Not only is there no evidence of any liberal group appealing directly to the workers to strike; but there is proof that they had made preparations for direct political action unconnected with the mass rising in Petrograd, and which were actually forestalled by it. Guchkov and his friends had worked out a complete plan for a palace coup, which would have put him in power in circumstances far more favourable from his point of view than those in which he became minister after the rising. The coup was planned for the middle of March, but the February events took its organisers by surprise. This project, like others of its kind, was in itself incompatible with a popular rising of the sort that actually took place. But, albeit indirectly and unintentionally, the plotting of the palace coup promoted the success of the mass movement. By stepping up their anti-government propaganda, reinforcing popular rumours of treason in high places, whipping up mass hysteria and directing it against the "German woman" and the Tsar, liberal circles both in the Duma and the Voluntary Organisations had built up among the newspaper-reading public an atmosphere of such unbearable tension that the fall of the autocratic régime was welcomed like a cleansing thunderstorm.

Guchkov must have contributed in an even more direct way to the success of the popular rising. As we have seen, a military demonstration by units of the Petrograd garrison was part of his plan. This demonstration was to support a new government of "popular confidence," and was to neutralise any resistance by the old régime, after the Tsar had been forced to sign the act of abdication, or its equivalent, at some obscure stop on the railway line between Petrograd and Mogilev. The involvement of some of the officers of the Petrograd garrison in the plot may well have undermined the morale of the whole officer corps there. When — on 26–27 February — the moment came to give, receive and execute battle orders, many of the officers were not quite sure which side they were on. The fall of Nicholas II was about to take place, but under circumstances so different from those expected that the officers were in a quandary as to what to do. The success of the military rising in Petrograd was due in large measure to their vacillation and absence from barracks at the critical juncture. Hence the Guchkov plot did contribute to the *success* of the Petrograd rising, but we cannot on that account regard it as a *cause* of the mass movement.

As for the third "conspiratorial" theory of the Petrograd rising, we have lent this throughout our unreserved support, more particularly in the chapter on German intervention. The belief that German agents were behind it is as old as the events themselves — indeed older, for the Russian government had suspected and indeed known of the German wartime influence on the labour movement in Russia long before the Petrograd rising. But only in the last ten years or so have certain revelations tended to corroborate these suspicions. We know now for certain that from the very beginning of the war the German government consistently pursued in Russia a *Revolutionierungspolitik*, an essential element of which was the support of an economic strike movement capable, so it was hoped, of gradually escalating into a political revolution. The chief theoretician of this policy, Alexander Helphand, thought the country ripe for revolution as early as 1916. We know for certain that the German government expended considerable sums on fostering the strike movement up to the spring of 1916. For most of 1916 and the beginning of 1917, we lack evidence of direct instigation of labour unrest in Russia by the German agencies. It would, however, be foolish to ignore the existence of such agencies as a factor contributing to the revolution of 1917, which took precisely the form predicted by Helphand as early as the spring of 1915. It seems reasonable either to suggest that the successful popular rising of February 1917 was organised by the same agents as instigated the abortive "trial run" the previous February or to assume that it was a direct sequel to the movement begun in 1916.

A political revolution entailing the fall of the Tsarist régime was the maximum the Germans could hope for in organising and backing Russian labour unrest during the war. The disruption of the war effort brought about by frequent and prolonged strikes was regarded by them as sufficient justification in itself for the support they gave Helphand and similar agents. The revolution came as a windfall much hoped for by some, but hardly expected by any, and necessitated a radical revision of German policy. The problem was now not so much to weaken Russia as an opponent as to effect a separate peace. Again on Helphand's suggestion, the Germans decided the best way to achieve this result would be to bring to power the Bolshevik Party, which alone among major political groups in the new Russia was prepared to conclude an immediate armistice. The dislocation of production could also safely be left to the Bolsheviks, who would effect it as part of the class war. Military sabotage, which Helphand always linked with his strike propaganda, continued to be organised by special German agents trained for work of this kind. But the tenuous and highly conspiratorial links connecting Helphand with the Russian strike movement could now be safely severed, and all record of them be erased. This explains why so little documentary evidence of these links exists.

4. Fomenting or Forestalling the Revolution

The popular rising and the mutiny of the Petrograd garrison resulted in the bloodless collapse of the monarchy only because, as Carr rightly says, liberal circles had decided to exploit them so as to gain their own ends of radical political change. The seditious mass movement originally confined to the capital might by itself have led only to a civil war the outcome of which would have been as questionable as that of the 1905 revolution. Liberal circles, however, did not decide to make use of the popular movement in order to seize power and form a Provisional Government until it became obvious that the Tsarist government could not quell the rising with the troops available in the capital.

For months, indeed for years, by their campaign to denounce and discredit autocracy they had systematically, if unintentionally, paved the way for the success of this rising, and for the country's acquiescence in the fall of the autocracy. There were two aspects to this campaign: one was the historiosophic assumption that autocracy as a form of government was obsolete, and doomed to disappear in Russia, as it had in the other Western countries. The liberals believed that in accordance with some inexorable law of history a modern society, such as Russian society after 1905, would change from an autocracy into a constitutional monarchy, wherein power would first be transferred to the educated and property-owning classes and then, in a process of gradual democratisation, to the people as a whole. Experience of the Soviet régime in the last fifty years has taught us that there was no foundation either for the analogy with West European monarchies or for the belief that autocracy in Russia was obsolete, for autocracy persisted despite the revolution. The very fact that the three men who ruled the country autocratically for many years after 1917 had such totally different characters and backgrounds merely reinforces the view that there are profound reasons why one-man political control could be so easily established and maintained in Russia. The fact that the principle of hereditary succession has been replaced by the elimination of rival successors through political slander and judicial murder in no way affects the issue. To say so is not to give moral sanction to autocracy. It would be paying too great a tribute to nineteenth-century evolutionist optimism to hold that the most viable political form is also the most progressive.

The liberals, as well as making the gratuitous assumption that autocracy was destined to make way for a process of gradual democratisation, justified their demands for an immediate change of régime (war or no war) by levelling at the Tsarist administration countless charges of inertia, ineptitude, inefficacy, arbitrariness and corruption. We have refrained from assessing the degree of justification of these complaints; this does not amount to a denial of the shortcomings of the Tsarist administration. These were obvious, and were comparable to the muddles and abuses of wartime administration in other belligerent countries. But they may be discounted as a revolutionising factor, since the liberals' main line of attack on the régime was not to expose its traditional and its newly-acquired vices and weaknesses, but to declare it incapable of coping with wartime problems so long as it remained autocratic. Not only was absolutism, they claimed, leading the country to disaster through inefficiency: it had, so the liberals alleged, no desire or determination to lead it to victory. That treason was being committed in high places and a shameful separate peace prepared — this became a liberal article of faith and a recurrent propaganda theme developed in the press, at congresses of the Voluntary Organisations and in the Duma itself. This conviction was so strong and so ingrained in the minds of those called upon to play a decisive part in the 1917 drama that it outlived many other delusions. In fact, it became a mainstay of those apologists who, horrified at the consequences of their decisions and actions, sought some kind of justification for them. Thus, with reference to the mounting influence of dark irresponsible forces over the will and judgment of the Tsar in the last days of the monarchy, Rodzyanko wrote in 1919:

> *The influence of Rasputin on the whole circle which surrounded the Empress Alexandra Feodorovna, and through her on the whole policy of the Supreme Power and of the government, increased to unprecedented dimensions. I claim unreservedly that this circle was indubitably under the influence of our enemy and served the interests of Germany . . . I at least have personally no doubt as to the inter-connection of the German Staff and Rasputin: there can be no doubt about it.*

There can be no doubt about the sad delusion of the ex-President of the Duma. There never was anything like a Rasputin circle or a concentration of "dark irresponsible forces" of the type pictured by him. Rasputin's hold over the Empress was certainly not to be underestimated, but neither he nor the Empress herself had any circle of permanent advisers. Instead of the circle in which Rodzyanko asks us to believe there was only a squalid snake-pit, in which various reptilian figures tried to devour each other. As far as the German authorities are concerned, they seem to have been oddly slow to exploit the opportunities offered them by the complex intrigues of these creatures.

And yet it was this legend of a powerful clique of pro-German "dark forces," and not the many proven and documented shortcomings of the government and the High Command, which was used as a lever by the liberals to undermine traditional allegiance to the monarch. It is difficult to believe that people who had access to so much information could in all honesty give credence to the rumours of treason in high places. But such an attitude is quite consistent with the sort of fantasies in which the Russian political opposition had indulged since the turn of the century.

As it became increasingly clear that the attempt of the Progressive Bloc of the Duma and of their allies, the Voluntary Organisations, to seize power by persuading the Tsar to surrender his prerogative to appoint ministers was about to fail, the exasperation of liberal circles assumed a hysterical character. It was a question of giving up a political struggle which had been going on for almost a generation, and submitting to the discipline of a society based on personal allegiance to the monarch, or else of breaking this allegiance and giving support to a violent *coup d'état*. The first alternative was rendered the more difficult because anyone advocating it was immediately denounced as a time-server and a traitor to the cause of progress. The second alternative needed a moral justification difficult to find for a mere struggle for power, which in any case appeared unpatriotic in wartime. The story of treason in high places, with sinister hints at the participation of the Empress in pro-German machinations, provided this justification and lent a patriotic lustre to what in fact was a struggle for power in home politics. This is why, instead of attacking the real shortcomings of the government, liberal circles concentrated on rumour-mongering. Such articles as V. Maklakov's "Mad Chauffeur," and such speeches as Milyukov's broadside on 1 November 1916 in the State Duma, achieved this end to an extent which the authors possibly did not expect.

Once let loose, rumours are difficult to check, particularly in wartime. The very fact that news and information are controlled only enhances the power and increases the circulation of rumours. A hint in the press at matters which it was supposedly not allowed to mention inflamed popular imagination more than a vivid and circumstantial report. For instance, the fact that Rasputin's name was not allowed to appear in the press in the days after the assassination, so that he had to be referred to as "the person living in Gorokhovaya Street," did more to impress the various Rasputin legends on the minds of the people than any actual accounts of his debaucheries. Much of the atmosphere saturated with hatred and slander so typical of the political life of both Russian capitals in 1916 frightened even those who were behind all this rumour-mongering. No wonder that later, when the complete baseless-ness of most of these rumours became obvious to many, and the hyster-ical trance in which Russian society was plunged had passed, memoirists (with the few exceptions of those writing in the Soviet Union) tended to soft-pedal these accusations and to go back to the claim that a change of government was necessary not because of the wickedness but because of the ineptitude of the monarch, his counsel-lors and the régime as a whole.

But how are we to believe that the sense of doom which had hung over the political scene in Russia since the autumn of 1915 was due merely to the tedious wrangle between the government and the Volun-tary Organisations, each complaining that the other hampered and impeded its patriotic efforts? The Voluntary Organisations naturally resented the ban on their all-Russian congresses, and claimed that this hampered their work for the front. The government, on the other hand, answered with possibly more factual justification that any activities of the Voluntary Organisations for the front were tolerated and indeed assisted, but that the exploitation of congresses for purely political, if not directly seditious, purposes could not be allowed, especially in wartime. The sense of doom was a direct result not of this quarrel but rather of the bitterness it engendered, which led to unwarranted mutual attacks and accusations.

5. The Aide-de-Camp Generals' Revolution

As we have seen, a new element was brought into this struggle between the liberals and the government by the gradual involvement of high military circles, mainly the commanders-in-chief of the fronts. The generals, notably Alekseev, Ruzsky and Brusilov, are often accused of having conspired among themselves and with the representatives of the Voluntary Organisations to overthrow Nicholas II. In support of such allegations a statement is quoted which the Emperor is said to have made to his mother when he met her in Mogilev after the abdication. He complained that Ruzsky had adopted an insolent and threatening attitude towards him when urging him to come to a decision. Alekseev's behaviour on the eve of Nicholas II's departure from Mogilev in the early hours of 28 February roused some suspicion among the courtiers. The ease with which he gave in to pressure from Rodzyanko and ap-pealed to the other commanders-in-chief to support the abdication solution produced the impression of duplicity on the part of the "cross-eyed friend" of the Emperor. There is some truth in all this, but it does not support the hypothesis of what is sometimes called the "aide-de-camp generals' revolution." Throughout the war, the generals adopted a strictly non-political attitude. They resisted being drawn into the struggle between the government and the liberal politicians. The reverses and retreats of 1915 had taught them, however, how precarious the supply machinery of the army was, and how easily it could be brought to a stop if the internal political situation deteriorated further. One can safely assume from the few utterances on this subject of the commanders-in-chief that they were, on the whole, against political and constitutional changes in wartime. At the same time they certainly believed that if any such changes were to become inevitable, everything should be done to ensure that they should come about smoothly, without jeopardising the arms and ammunition production, the food and fodder supplies, and the railway transport on which the fighting capacity of the army depended. If Alekseev did not denounce the Moscow plotters, this must have been not because he identified himself with their views, but because arrests and trials of members of the Voluntary Organisations on charges of sedition would certainly have adversely affected arms production and supplies. There is no definite indication that the Emperor himself knew of the existence of these plots, but the degree of his information on the political ferment in the capitals seems to have been much greater than was believed at the time by those innumerable advisers who persisted in futile attempts 'to open the eyes' of the Tsar to the real situation in Russia. It is therefore highly probable that he at least suspected the existence of some of the plots.[2] But he, like Alekseev, preferred to refrain from countermeasures until victory was assured. The aide-de-camp generals did not consider it their duty to ferret out the plotters of a palace coup. Alekseev could easily have lulled his conscience by believing that he had fully complied with his oath of allegiance when he advised the plotters to desist, without, however, denouncing them. To start a political witch-hunt and denounce the plotters to the Minister of the Interior would, it seemed to him, be to take a greater risk from the point of view of the successful prosecution of

[2] In particular those hatched in Tiflis in the entourage of Grand Duke Nikolay Nikolaevich.

the war and of national security in general than to let events take their course. Should the palace coup succeed, the Army would have to face the new situation without having undergone a major crisis. Should it fail, those guilty would perish on the spot.

After the unrest in Petrograd had begun it was easy for Rodzyanko to convince the commanders of the fronts that the Golitsyn government could not cope with the situation. But on 1 March he went further and tried all too successfully to make them believe that if they managed to persuade the Tsar to abdicate, the Duma Committee would take matters in hand and restore order within a few days. Even so the generals, and in particular Ruzsky, showed a total lack of enthusiasm for the abdication solution to the crisis. Yet Nicholas II's consternation at Ruzsky's behaviour is understandable. As the "ghost train" approached Pskov, those on it hoped that they were reaching a safe harbour where the magic of the imperial presence would operate. The Emperor was naturally entitled to expect that his Commander-in-Chief of the Northern Front would ask him what his immediate orders and instructions were. Instead an entirely different atmosphere greeted him on his arrival. Ruzsky took the line that the revolution had already taken place, and that there was nothing for it but to give in to the demands of the Duma, and to empower its representatives to form the new government. The personal desires and preferences of the Emperor do not even seem to have been discussed before the abdication. To raise such a question would have been tactless on the part of the generals, for the tone of the conversation was set by the Emperor with the words: "There is no sacrifice I would not make for the sake of our Mother Russia."

But even when the abdication had been decided upon the generals still believed that they were taking part in an action to save the monarchy and maintain the dynasty. Not until Rodzyanko raised the matter of withholding publication of the manifesto early on 3 March did the generals realise that they had been used to bring about a *coup d'état* which could not have come at a worse moment from a military point of view. Contrary to his tactics of the previous day, Rodzyanko left Ruzsky and Alekseev completely in the dark as to the negotiations concerning the abdication of Grand Duke Michael. And this with good reason. He knew that if the commanders-in-chief at the fronts had been consulted before the momentous decision to renounce the throne was taken by Michael, they would have supported Michael's candidature. As it was, the generals were faced with a *fait accompli* and found themselves discredited in the new order by having shown readiness to support a political solution which was now considered to be both retrograde and abortive.

Allan K. Wildman

The Great Mutiny

One of Leopold Haimson's graduate students at the University of Chicago, Allan Wildman's first monograph was about the workers' movement at the turn of the century. A subtle work of synthesis and analysis, *The Making of a Workers' Revolution* (1967) explored the shift in labor strategy from propaganda to agitation to political struggle. Wildman has taught at the State University of New York at Stony Brook and at Ohio State University and is currently editor of *The Russian Review*. His two-volume work on the soldiers in 1917 breaks with the traditions of Russian military history and treats the revolutionary activity of rank-and-file men in arms as social history. This prize-winning treatment of peasants in uniform illustrates that the same kind of social cleavages that existed between landlords and peasants, industrialists and workers, also appeared between officers and soldiers.

Western and Soviet historiography present basically different conceptualizations of the overturn that brought an end to the Russian monarchy. Whereas Western works tend to portray it as a consequence of the inner decay of a senescent bureaucracy and court that could not cope with the extraordinary demands of war, Soviet works insist that it was an "armed uprising," a "revolutionary assault" of the working class in classic Marxist terms. Yet Soviet historians fail to give any serious proof of the level of conscious preparation that they assume, just as their

Allan K. Wildman, *The End of the Russian Imperial Army: The Old Army and The Soldiers' Revolt (March-April 1917)*. Copyright © 1980 by Princeton University Press. Excerpts, pp. 121–158, 374–380, reprinted with permission of Princeton University Press.

Western counterparts who characterize it as a "fall" or "collapse" pass all too quickly over the hundreds of thousands of workers, soldiers, and ordinary citizens who thronged the streets of Petrograd, burning down police stations, assaulting and arresting policemen, disarming and murdering officers, and breaking into weapons caches and passing out arms.[1] If one lays aside the obvious exaggerations and focuses on the indisputable facts, the viewpoints are not as irreconcilable as they appear at first. There was indeed a breakdown in the functioning of autocratic authority in the February days, climaxing a long process of moral and institutional decay of which the Rasputin affair was only the final episode, and it is certainly reflected in the incapacity to meet the military and economic demands of the war. However, Western accounts usually overlook that the war greatly exacerbated the traditional social cleavages, particularly as its burdens fell chiefly on the politically powerless sectors of the population, whose sense of alienation was rapidly building up to a breaking point in the months before the February Revolution. While the educated and enfranchised social layers ("census Russia") were primarily concerned about the incompetence of the tsarist administration in the conduct of the war, the workers, peasants, and poorer *meshchanstvo*, whether in uniform or not, were becoming profoundly impatient with the war itself.

The reports of Okhrana officials and other surveillance organs reveal a surprising awareness of the potential for revolution in the ugly mood shaping up in the lower-class urban populace. If the mutinies at the front can be regarded as having no serious revolutionary intent, the mounting waves of strikes, particularly in Petrograd, cannot be so lightly dismissed. Though the strikes gained considerable momentum from purely economic causes, the workers had long since been politicized by decades of revolutionary propaganda and frequent clashes with tsarist authorities. Even though it is true that revolutionary organi-

[1] The image of a "fall" finds expression in the works of Pares, Chamberlin, Ferro, and Florinsky. Oliver Radkey, in *The Agrarian Foes of Bolshevism* (New York, 1958), expresses the typical formula as follows: "It was not so much a revolution in the accepted sense of the term as simply the toppling over, under slight external pressure, of a structure that had rotted away." Soviet works follow an undeviating sequence: Lenin's ideological precepts, the assimilation thereof by the party, organizational preparations, the masses' response to the party's influence and the maturing of the "crisis," by which time the party and the masses are primed for revolutionary action.

zations were constantly broken up during the war, and that the generation of workers that had experienced 1905 and the upsurge of 1913–1914 lost its cohesiveness through conscription, the influx from the villages, and a considerable increase in female and child labor, the legacy of the past was still very much alive, as attested by the massive strike on January 9, 1917, commemorating Bloody Sunday. Although most active revolutionary organizations (the Mezhraiontsy, the "Initiative Group" of Mensheviks, and the Petrograd Committee of the Bolsheviks) were crippled by arrests preceding the strikes, the idea caught hold, and more than 150,000 workers from 114 enterprises, including such industrial giants as Obukhov, Putilov, and the Franco-Russian and Nevskii Shipbuilding Works, took a holiday to hold meetings and listen to denunciations of tsarist authority and the war. This strike lasted only one day, but the waves of strikes in individual concerns and in other cities rose in an ever mounting tide until they reached massive proportions in mid-February. On February 14, the day the Duma came back into session, 90,000 workers from 58 enterprises in the capital were out on strike in response to an appeal from the Workers' Group of the Central War Industries Committee.

From the twenty-second on, beginning with the lockout of 26,700 Putilov workers, the strike movement coalesced with general unrest in Petrograd over the lack of bread in the shops. Crowds of workers (particularly female workers), angry housewives, and young people milled through the streets, listening to orators, insulting the police, looting bakeries, and resisting any efforts to disperse or control them. According to official figures, 78,443 workers came out on February 23, 158,583 on the twenty-fourth, and 201,248 on the twenty-fifth (240,000 by another count). Since the mood of the crowds was desperate and showed no signs of abating, the government could only uphold its authority by bringing to bear adequate repressive measures. The regular police force of 3,500 was manifestly inadequate for this purpose, and so the problem inexorably became a military one.

This brings us to the crucial factor in the February Revolution. The tsarist government had at its disposal an unlimited military force, which theoretically should easily have been able to reestablish control. In the capital were the reserve battalions of the fourteen guards regiments, each 6,000 or more strong (they are sometimes referred to as "regiments" because of their size), plus several regular reserve infantry regiments (the First and the 180th; in Krasnoe Selo and Peterhof were the

Petrograd		Suburbs	
Guards Infantry regiments	95,000*	Third, 171st, 176th Infantry regiments	30,000
First, 180th Infantry regiments	22,000	First, Second Machine Gun regiments	17,700
Militia formations	8,000	Marine Guards Equipage Regiment	6,000
Ninth Dragoon Cavalry Regiment	4,700	Artillery, guards, and heavy brigades	10,000
Artillery depot units	9,500	Schools for *praporshchiki*	2,500
Sixth, Guards Sappers regiments	4,800	First, Fourth Don Cossacks regiments	3,200
Electrotechnical units	5,000	Kronshtadt (naval, fortress, and infantry regiments)	80,000
Motorized units (auto, armored car, cycle)	17,000	Miscellaneous (militia; one railroad battalion)	2,000
Aviation units	3,100		
Guards Pontoon Regiment	1,600		
Railroad battalions	2,000		
Military schools	6,500		
Higher academies	1,000		
TOTAL	180,200	TOTAL	151,900

* Based on the average of five regiments of the guards for which reliable figures are available. Sobelev's estimate is based on Kochakov's, which is likely to be inaccurate.

Third, 171st, and 176th), a cycle battalion, an armored car division, the Sixth and the Guards Sappers regiments, and other auxiliary units. The available manpower in the Petrograd garrison was 180,000, with another 152,000 men in the surrounding area; furthermore, it should not have been difficult to detach and entrain additional units (cavalry units were the most feasible) from the Northern Front within a matter of hours. However, the matter was not that simple. The reserve battalions consisted largely of as yet uninstructed new recruits and recuperating veterans who were very reluctant to be returned to duty; also, they were poorly provided with officers and weapons. True, certain formations — the training companies for NCOs (usually one company out of four in each reserve "regiment"), the units from officer training schools, and the armored car and cycle units — were thought to be reliable and were better trained and disciplined. But the overriding, unanswered question was how deeply the general dissatisfaction in the country had penetrated the units that would have to be used. If even a small fraction of the total available force could be depended upon to carry out the task of armed repression resolutely, the government would have no need to worry; but significant defections, or even passivity, within such units would spell disaster.

The government certainly had enough information at its disposal to realize that it had to be prepared for the present contingency. Strikes had assumed threatening proportions since the previous October, and information supplied by Okhrana agents and censorship authorities clearly indicated the dangerous state of the public mind. Furthermore, the incessant clashes of the ministers with the Duma, the unruly press, which constantly harped on German influences, and the various plots by political figures, the court aristocracy, and army officers made it obvious even to the rather dull minds that at this juncture were answerable for the fate of the autocracy that extraordinary measures were necessary to avert disaster. It was characteristic of the times that the four persons most directly charged with responsibility for public order were recent, Rasputin-inspired appointees: A. D. Protopopov, the madcap Minister of the Interior, General M. A. Beliaev, War Minister, General A.P. Balk, Petrograd City Prefect (in command of all police forces), and General S. S. Khabalov, chief of the Petrograd Military District. It is fairly clear that after the death of Rasputin the imperial couple resolved to dismiss or neutralize the Duma, fearing above all popular demonstrations on its behalf.

The military forces in the capital, which heretofore had been under the jurisdiction of General Ruzskii, the commander of the Northern Front, whom the tsarina knew to be implacably hostile to her inner clique, were restored to the administrative jurisdiction of the Petrograd Military District, that is, directly subordinated to Nicholas as Commander in Chief, and put in the hands of General Khabalov, a candidate recommended to the tsarina by Protopopov. . . .

One of the controversies that has not yet been cleared up is whether the strategic deployment of machine guns on rooftops in the capital was a part of the plans for suppressing street demonstrations. There are numerous reports of machine-gun fire from the rooftops during the decisive days of the Revolution (February 27 and 28), and bands of roving soldiers claimed to have cleaned out the "police nests." That Protopopov had secretly trained police detachments in the use of machine guns and purposely provoked street demonstrations to drown the revolution in blood was one of the universally believed legends of the post-February days. A number of investigators (Burtsev, Melgunov, Katkov) have claimed that the rooftop machine guns were a product of the overworked imagination of the public in the grip of fear and confusion during the critical days. Supporting this viewpoint is the fact that the extensive testimony on this question before the Extraordinary Investigative Commission, which included all the leading principals (Khabalov, Beliaev, Balk, Protopopov, and a number of Okhrana and police officials) produced no proof of a prior plan, or even of the existence of special police detachments trained in machine guns or of any orders to put them to use.

The genesis of the popular belief can be fixed with certainty. At a mid-January session of the Special Conference on Defense, Rodzianko accused Protopopov of diverting machine guns sent from England, which were intended for the front, to police units for quelling expected domestic disturbances. In this form the rumor circulated through select political circles well before the revolution and easily worked its way into popular consciousness to account for any unexplained gunfire, of which there was a good deal between February 27 and March 2. Nevertheless, reports of eye (and ear) witnesses on machine-gun fire and the actions of soldiers in removing them from the rooftops are so numerous, that it must be presumed that the reports had some foundation in fact, even if the total number was greatly exaggerated in the general atmosphere of panic and fear of counterrevolution. Though the question cannot be resolved with finality on the basis of the surviving evidence, the myth in its popular form can certainly be discounted, as it presumes a too consciously contrived provocation to square with the pitiful improvisations. . . .

All contemporary witnesses agree that the strikes and street demonstrations that erupted on February 23 came as a surprise both to political groups and to the authorities. Protopopov and Khabalov, gratified that on the opening day of the Duma (February 14) the strikers had remained in their factory districts and that the worker representatives on the Central War Industries Committee had been arrested without major reactions, were convinced that the main danger had passed. The revolutionary groups with contacts in the factory districts (the Bolsheviks, the Mezhraiontsy, and the Menshevik Internationalists) were aware of mounting sentiment for a decisive confrontation, and they scheduled factory meetings with party orators for International Women's Day on February 23 (March 8, N.S.), but hoped to restrain the workers until a major action could be organized and coordinated, possibly for May 1. An interparty steering committee was meeting on the very morning of the twenty-third to discuss future strategy when news arrived that the female workers in the Vyborg Side were already pouring out of the factories and bringing out their male counterparts in nearby factories by means of shouts, stones, and snowballs. Their plea was to support the women of Petrograd in their demand for bread and an end to the killing inflation.

By one o'clock in the afternoon huge crowds, which included housewives, street youths, and ordinary citizens, had collected along the Sampsonevskii Prospect on the far side of the Neva and began pressing toward the Aleksandrovskii Bridge, which would bring them to the major arteries leading to the city center (their goal was Nevskii Prospect, the heart of the "bourgeois district," with the huge Kazan and Znamenskii squares, which were traditional sites for revolutionary demonstrations). At four o'clock a crowd of about four thousand crossed over from the Vyborg Side to the neighboring Petrograd Side (another working-class district between two branches of the Neva) and tried without success to pass over to the center by the Troitskii Bridge. Repeated forays by the police could not break up the perpetually regrouping crowds, but they successfully blocked passage over the bridges. Only late in the afternoon did significant numbers cross over on the ice (dangerous because the river was not completely frozen) and join other demonstrators in the center. A crowd of a thousand or so milled along Liteinyi Prospect (the major artery from the Aleksandrovskii Bridge to Znamenskii Square) and, though easily dispersed by police and Cossack patrols, brought out several factories (a weapons plant and a nail factory with five thousand workers). A crowd of similar size, consisting primarily of women and minors, formed along the Nevskii, but it was also broken up by mounted police and cavalry (two platoons of the Ninth Reserve Cavalry Regiment). By evening many factories in all parts of the capital had heard of the disorders and either came out immediately or held meetings to discuss a course of action for the next day. All over the capital streetcars were halted and the key mechanism removed. Here and there stores were plundered and windows broken, but there were no reports of gunfire or serious injuries.

The reports record that the vast majority of the demonstrators were women and that the only prominent demand was for bread. The women very boldly pressed on police lines, lustily exercising their gift of speech to persuade the guardians of order of the intolerable conditions of their existence. Young boys armed with rocks and snowballs delighted in playing cat and mouse with mounted policemen, but few students, intellectuals, or middle-class persons were observable among the crowds. Although it is true that a large number of housewives and people of the lower classes joined the street crowds and under their protection raided bakeries and grocery shops, the conventional picture that the disorders began as riots in the bread lines must be discarded. Only with the stimulus of large numbers of workers pouring out of the factories onto the street and crying for bread were significant numbers of ordinary citizens emboldened to plunder the shops. On this first day the police predominated in the maintenance of order. The district police chiefs were on the streets directing their forces according to the original plan, and in some cases were subjected to indignities by the crowds. Small patrols of cavalry aided the police in breaking up large crowds, and the military units posted to factories and institutions were strengthened; but otherwise, military forces were held in reserve.

The following day every industrial district of the capital was seized by strikes, and the street crowds gathered early and in imposing numbers (the size had approximately doubled — 158,583 by one official figure, 197,000 by another). It was a repetition of the previous day's events on a citywide scale. Shops were closed, and police posts disappeared from the streets, auguring a major test of strength. A crowd of some ten thousand persons from the Vyborg Side poured over the Aleksandrovskii Bridge and, breaking through a double line of mounted police and cavalry, flooded Liteinyi Prospect. The crowds were pressed into side streets by police with drawn sabers and piecemeal forced back over the bridge. Another crowd tried to bring out the Petrograd Side and pass over the Neva by the Troitskii Bridge, but it too was blocked by heavy cordons of Cossacks and soldiers of the Moskovskii Guards. However, large crowds also formed on the Petrograd Side, on Vasilevskii Island, and in the Kolomenskii and Harbor industrial districts. Clashes with the police and looting were universal. Periodic demonstrations

took place all day on Nevskii Prospect, forming first at the Kazan Square
and then at the Znamenskii (the numbers given are from one to three
thousand). In addition to cries for bread, one now heard: "Down with
the government!" "Down with the tsar!" "Down with the war!" Revolutionary songs and red banners emblazoned with slogans marked the
advent of revolutionary intellectuals, party-affiliated workers, and students. Violent assaults on the police with chunks of ice and heavy
objects (even a few pistol shots) were a typical feature of the day, and
several severe injuries resulted, but again, no firearms were turned on
the demonstrators.

There was a marked increase in the use of Cossacks, cavalry, and
soldiers to disperse crowds and block off streets and bridges, but on this
fateful day it became obvious that the Cossacks were performing their
duties very unwillingly, and in several instances they deliberately
avoided clashes with the crowds. Word of this spread rapidly, and
thereafter an informal alliance, with a specific ritual, was observed
between the two. The crowds cheered and the Cossacks waved back as
they passed harmlessly through them. A young girl is reported to have
boldly stepped out of the crowd to offer a Cossack officer a nosegay,
which he gallantly affixed to his uniform. Whenever the crowds were
able to press up close to idling Cossacks, lively exchanges took place.
One witness recorded the following: "We have husbands, fathers, and
brothers at the front. Here there is only hunger, work beyond our
strength, and humiliation! You also have mothers, wives, and children.
We demand bread and an end to the war!" Usually the Cossacks responded only with significant smiles. If an officer noted his men becoming too involved with the crowd, he would simply order them to
gallop off. Above all, they showed themselves to be quite indifferent to
the insults and indignities directed against the police, which finds bitter
documentation in police reports.

The same illicit fraternization was transpiring, though less con-
spicuously, in infantry units. Sergeant Kirpichnikov, who would become the famous hero of the Volynskii Regiment, was on duty with his
training battalion on Znamenskii Square on this day. He constantly
reassured his officers that everything was under control, while promising the crowds that they would not be fired upon; he also remained
passive as an orator mounted the monument to Alexander III and
harangued the crowd, explaining to his nervous superior officer that the
crowd was simply asking for bread and would soon go away. While the

officers amused themselves in nearby pubs, he allowed people to filter through his cordons and converse with his men.

On the following day, the twenty-fifth, the movement took on the aspect of a general strike, with the forces of order under a virtual state of siege. An additional fifty thousand workers poured into the streets and pressed on the center of the capital from all sides. During the day the students of most institutions of higher learning declared a strike and joined the workers. Stores, schools, factories, and public services were closed down, bringing normal activities to a virtual standstill. The police could no longer cope with the size of the crowds, which circumvented and broke through their lines and regrouped as quickly as they were broken up. Many policemen were assailed by hard objects, toppled from their mounts, disarmed, and beaten by the crowd. The military backup forces were apparently used sparingly, because of their uncertain reliability. The Cossack units on this day refused outright to aid the police and cultivated the cheers of the crowds. Toward the end of the day, a Cossack cut down a policeman with his sword on Znamenskii Square when the latter tried to apprehend demonstrators. The revolutionizing effect of this incident on the street crowds was said to have been extraordinary.[2] Crowds of up to five thousand were forming along the Nevskii all day long. Still, the vast majority of the demonstrators were prevented from reaching the center, and at no time did the police completely lose control.

In spite of the aggressiveness of the crowds, there was remarkably little shooting. The first blood was shed, however, when soldiers of the Ninth Cavalry Regiment opened fire on the Nevskii, supposedly in answer to a pistol shot, leaving eighteen dead and wounded. The police were still under orders simply to break up crowds and control street movements with "cold weapons," and to avoid using firearms. Except for a few pistol shots exchanged for flying bottles and ice chunks, they apparently followed instructions. This day, for the first time, the police attempted to arrest sizable numbers of demonstrators, but in almost every case the arrested, after being temporarily confined in the courtyards of large buildings, were freed by the crowds or sympathetic Cos-

[2] There are numerous, conflicting versions of this incident in the literature, some saying that the policeman was shot, others that he was cut down, others that he was only wounded, and one that his assailant was a Cossack officer who retaliated when a police official struck a Cossack. But on the effect, which is the important point, all agree.

Russian Soldiers and Their Officers During the Revolution of 1917. Rank-and-file soldiers generally backed the soviets, while their officers supported the Provisional Government or restoration of the monarchy. (Culver Pictures)

sacks. The military units other than Cossacks that are reported to have been on duty this day were from the following regiments (usually the training company): the Ninth Cavalry, the Third Guards Riflers, and the Volynskii and Finlandskii Guards Infantry. A Finlandskii detachment was on guard duty at the giant Petrograd Tube Steel Works, where a lieutenant, exasperated by the taunts of a crowd of workers and fearful of their influence on his men, shot down an offending worker point-blank. Kirpichnikov's Volynskiis were again on duty at Znamenskii Square; though his commanding officer, Staff Captain Mashkin, was strangely passive, two junior officers behaved very aggressively toward the street crowds and threatened to shoot. When one of them tried to mount the equestrian statue of Alexander III to seize a red flag from the orator, he was knocked down. Angrily, he demanded that his soldiers seize the culprit, but they claimed "they didn't notice who did it." A confrontation was avoided by the arrival of Cossacks, who interposed themselves and allowed the demonstration to continue.

One can say that on this day all the groups involved — the crowds, the revolutionaries, and the authorities — became aware that something more than simply strikes and street demonstrations was in the making. The crowds, perceiving the confusion and weakness of the police, concentrated on neutralizing the soldiers and Cossacks by friendly approaches. Shliapnikov claims that he advised party workers not to arm themselves, but rather to persuade the soldiers to surrender their weapons and bring over their comrades. Doubtless the demonstrators needed no such instructions: they shouted sympathetically to the soldiers across police lines, engaged them in conversation where possible, and sent messages into the barracks via guards on duty or through fences. By the third day the slogans "Away with the autocracy!" and "Down with the war!" accompanied by red banners and party oratory, had largely replaced the cries for bread.

Only on the twenty-fifth did the authorities in the capital consider the situation serious enough to be reported to the tsar, who had just returned to Stavka. Khabalov, Protopopov, and Beliaev all sent telegrams to Stavka reporting on the street demonstrations and clashes with the crowds, but making assurances that proper measures had been taken to suppress the disorders. Khabalov's report, which cites Okhrana figures for the number of strikers (200,000 on the twenty-fifth), disingenuously claimed that "the attempt of the workers to reach the Nevskii has been successfully thwarted" and that "those who did get through were driven back by Cossacks." Protopopov's report was more alarming in specific details (the murder of the policeman at Znamenskii Square, the attempts by the crowds to fraternize with the soldiers), but assured the supreme commander that "energetic steps are being taken by the military commanders to prevent a repetition of the disorders." The generals at Stavka could not have been misled as to the seriousness of the disorders, however, as Khabalov notified them that several cavalry detachments had been called in from the surrounding area to reinforce the Petrograd garrison.

In reply, Nicholas that same night, issued the fatal order to Khabalov: "I command you no later than tomorrow to put an end to the disorders in the capital, which are impermissible at a time of war with Germany and Austria." Khabalov was thunderstruck. In his mind the order could only be interpreted as a mandate to apply maximum force at once, in other words, to fire on demonstrators who refused to disperse. He was himself inclined to let events run their course in the hope that the crowd would soon tire of endless demonstrations, a not unlikely prospect. With resignation he issued his instructions to the assembled unit commanders:

> *The sovereign has ordered that the disorders be stopped by tomorrow. Therefore the ultimate means must be applied. If the crowd is small, without banners, and not aggressive, then utilize cavalry to disperse it. If the crowd is aggressive and displays banners, then act according to regulations, that is, signal three times and open fire.*

The following day a proclamation signed by Khabalov was posted in the streets: "I forewarn the populace of Petrograd that I have ordered the employment of all weapons and will shirk from nothing to achieve the restoration of order in the capital."

This thoughtlessly taken decision proved fatal for the dynasty. It guaranteed that the movement would not remain within the boundaries of the usual workers' demonstrations, which, though imposing, usually played themselves out, but would become a massive defection of the military arm upon which the autocracy depended for its very existence. Up to this point the soldiers had not been forced to commit themselves irrevocably. Their sympathies were clearly on the side of the demonstrators, and the latter "understood" that they performed their duties under the threat of severe disciplinary reprisals and considerately avoided provoking them. Even many officers showed themselves reluctant to go beyond a token execution of their orders to aid the police. Three days of close contact had amply acquainted the soldiers with the temper of the crowds, and they felt no impulse to restrain their reasonable demands for bread. Being from the same social layer as most of the demonstrators, they shared to a large extent the general hostility to the police, the government, and the endless war. Now, abruptly, they were to be made the instrument of bloody repression against people of their own kind. To refuse, or even to hesitate, meant to be punished with all the force of military law, which could mean the firing squad. Therefore, the only course for those who were not prepared to obey the command to shoot was to mutiny en masse, counting on the safety of numbers.

In times past, the government could have counted on the ingrained habits of discipline, loyalty, and fear to overcome any reticence on the part of the soldiers to fire on unruly crowds. But the present situation was a far cry from 1905, when the thought of disobedience was a horrifying novelty. Many of the old-timers, the over-forty *ratniki* and family men, had absorbed the lessons of 1905 and were determined not to be blindly used again. Recuperating veterans, who were also strongly represented in the reserve units (usually one out of four companies), were greatly embittered over the war, disgusted with the government, and violently antipathetic toward the police, who in their view should have long since been sent to the front in their stead. In other words, all the psychological motives that we have seen in previous chapters predisposed them to side with the demonstrators. True, the younger recruits were less likely to be deeply disaffected by the economic and social grievances so vital to family men, but like young persons generally, they were quick to pick up a mood of defiance from others and thought far less of the risks involved.

Unfortunately, it is virtually impossible to fix the reactions and emotions of the soldiers at the time of the mutiny, as all subsequent accounts are heavily colored by the outcome. Over and above the considerations that predisposed the soldiers to sympathize with the demonstrators, it is very likely that a good many of them had already contemplated the alternatives and inwardly crossed the Rubicon. There had already been a number of instances such as the one at Kremenchug, when punitive units refused to fire on rioters, and rumors concerning them were certainly in circulation. Such an incident had taken place in the Vyborg Side of the capital in the fall of 1916, and many garrison soldiers were doubtless aware of it. During the October strikes workers from the Novyi Lessner plant were assaulted by the police with whips and sabers outside the barracks of the 181st Reserve Regiment. The soldiers, observing the proceedings from the barracks enclosure over a flimsy fence, stormed into the streets to aid the workers. The training company and Cossacks were called out to pacify the mutineers, but they refused orders to open fire. Later, during the anxious days before the opening of the Duma on February 14, 1917, when many soldiers were posted to factories in the capital, an Okhrana agent reported that an unidentified soldier approached the guard detail at an unnamed factory settlement, persuading the men to turn their rifles on the police. Alluding to the incident of the previous fall, the soldier suggested that now was the time to settle accounts. "They gave us two hundred bullets apiece to shoot the strikers," he explained. "It's about time for us, when they give the command to shoot, to knock off the Pharaohs." When workers intervened to suggest that the soldiers needed to be better organized, the soldier indignantly replied that they were already organized and knew what to do: "They've drunk our blood long enough; our people suffer at the front while they stuff their mugs here and take our last crust of bread."[3] Just how widespread such sentiments were is difficult to say, but the alacrity with which many units went over to the uprising suggests considerable psychological preparation.

The decisive test came on the twenty-sixth, a Sunday, when most of the factories were closed. Soldiers, cavalry, and police were deployed in unprecedented numbers throughout the capital in a determined effort to prevent crowds from forming in the center. For most of the day they were successful, but by early afternoon sufficient numbers had filtered through and around the pickets to frustrate the intentions of the police. Here and there soldier cordons, disconcerted by pleas not to shoot, melted with the crowds. By two o'clock in the afternoon shooting began along the Nevskii, first from police revolvers, then from soldier training companies, and, it is reported, from machine guns. The crowds took refuge in doorways and courtyards, and simply reformed when it appeared that the firing had ceased. Finally, crowds boldly pressed on soldier picket lines blocking access to the Nevskii, convinced that the latter would not fire. At first the warning salvos were respected, but soon the crowds were emboldened to ignore them.[4] Around 3:00 p.m. the Pavlovskii training company opened fire directly into a crowd along the Moika Canal, leaving dead and wounded. This action was repeated again at the corner of the Sadovaia and on Znamenskii Square, as a result of which at least forty demonstrators were killed and as many wounded. The total number of casualties on this day must have been well over a hundred, as the police collected sixty bodies and the demonstrators carried off many more. Kirpichnikov is reluctant to admit that his Volynskiis were involved in the heavy bloodletting on the Znamenskii and claims that he instructed his men to fire over the heads of the demonstrators. The officer in charge, Lieutenant Vorontsov, who was thoroughly drunk, berated his men for their poor aim and began firing indiscriminately into the crowd with a soldier's rifle. By five

[3] The men of the first battalion of the Marine Guards Equipage settled among themselves whether they would fire on the people as soon as they heard they were being transferred from the front to Tsarskoe Selo (they well understood the purpose of the move).

[4] The Okhrana report for this day notes: "With preliminary firing into the air, the crowds not only failed to disperse but also greeted the salvos with derision. Only with direct fire into the thick of the crowd was it possible to break them up."

o'clock the hopelessness of the situation had led most demonstrators to disperse. In the opinion of the Bolshevik Kaiurov, the movement had been defeated.

At precisely this moment, however, the soldiers in the Pavlovskii barracks heard that their own training company had fired on the people. Without hesitation they broke into the arms chamber, seized thirty or so rifles, and, against the pleas of their officers, poured out into the streets. A volunteer officer from the street crowds put himself at their head and led them along the Ekaterina Canal toward the Nevskii, where their fellow Pavlovskiis were reported to be shooting. A patrol of mounted police drew up on the opposite side of the canal and, apparently reading the situation, opened fire. The young officer ordered the Pavlovskiis to drop to their knees and return fire, which persuaded the mounted police to gallop off. According to a post-February chronicler, I. Lukash, the police suffered three casualties and the insurgents two, one of which was the unknown officer. The Pavlovskiis resumed their march to the Nevskii, but were soon cut off by a detachment of Preobrazhenskiis under the command of Captain V. N. Timichenko-Ruban, who has left an eyewitness account. According to his version, the roll of the drums signaling a volley was sufficient to disperse the disorganized mutineers; according to Lukash's account (probably less reliable, considering when it was written), the Preobrazhenskiis withdrew after hearing the pleas of the Pavlovskiis not to shoot. In any event, their ammunition was spent and the streets were again in the hands of government forces, so the Pavlovskiis drifted back to their barracks. One can suppose that they hoped thereby to avoid serious reprisals. A guard of Preobrazhenskiis was posted around the barracks (under the command of the same Timichenko-Ruban), and that night twenty or so "instigators" were arrested and marched off to the Peter Paul Fortress. So far as can be determined, this incident did not become known to most other units and therefore was not likely to have inspired the mutiny the following day, as is sometimes claimed, but it was symptomatic of the inner turmoil of garrison soldiers.

As is well known, it was the Volynskii Regiment that set off the avalanche of the twenty-seventh. Most of the accounts are based on Kirpichnikov, and, although there is no reason to doubt his accuracy, he quite naturally dresses up the episode in the rhetoric of a successful revolution. Much of what one would like to know of the thoughts and reactions of the men, the makeup of the units, and the extent of their awareness of outside events remains in obscurity. Kirpichnikov recounts a midnight meeting of the NCOs of his training unit after the officers had departed and the men were in their bunks. They agreed that under no circumstances would they carry out further punitive actions under the command of their officers, and that they should arouse the men an hour earlier the next morning to secure their assent. Supposedly this "sergeants' coup" was carried off smoothly: the men were lined up in the usual order, weapons and ammunition were distributed, and Kirpichnikov then addressed them, receiving affirmative response to his appeal that they obey his orders and not those of the officers. When Captain Lashkevich and his fellow officers arrived at seven o'clock to brief the men on the day's assignment, they faced a flawlessly organized revolt. On a prearranged signal, the men cried from the ranks: "We won't shoot!" Attempts to intimidate them by singling out individuals with threats were met with the ominous pounding of rifle butts on the floor. An appeal to the tsar's explicit order, the text of which was read, failed to produce the desired impression, and the officers, finally sensing their danger, hastily withdrew. This display of officer helplessness apparently cut loose the inner restraints that had hitherto kept the disobedience within orderly channels. The men rushed to the windows and pursued the retreating officers with taunts and catcalls — and Captain Lashkevich was felled by a rifle shot as he crossed the barracks enclosure in the deep snow.

From this point on, the revolt became a disorderly, improvised affair, and can hardly be reconstructed in consecutive order. It is unlikely that the sergeants were providing anything but the most elementary leadership. They could shout orders or suggestions, but the soldiers responded according to their own lights. Hastily dispatched emissaries had no difficulty in persuading other companies of the reserve battalion to follow suit, once it was clear that the officers had been faced down. The fact of the revolt was advertised to the surrounding area by random firing into the air and loud cheers. It was a key circumstance that the Volynskiis shared a huge brick quadrangle and a common court with two other guards units, the Litovskii and part of the Preobrazhenskii (these were the peacetime barracks of the Preobrazhenskii Regiment), their respective areas being separated only by low wooden fences. These units therefore were direct witnesses to the commotion taking place next door and soon followed suit. Raids on the Litovskii arms chamber, it is said, yielded over a thousand rifles, four machine guns, and thirty thousand rounds of ammunition. This armed human mass spilled out into the streets of Petrograd at an hour when neither the demonstrators nor the police were out in force. Thus some twenty thousand leaderless but high-spirited and well-armed soldiers transformed the demonstrations into an insurrection.

From a strategic point of view, the government forces had received an irreparable blow. The Preobrazhenskii barracks were located in the same quarter — between Liteinyi Prospect and a bend in the Neva upstream from the Winter Palace — that enclosed a vast complex of military institutions, arms factories, barracks, and arsenals. According to S. Mstislavskii, a veteran member of the S.R. military organization and a librarian at the General Staff Academy, which was a part of this complex, his small group of officer-revolutionaries expected this quarter to be the "last redoubt" of government forces in the case of an uprising and doubted that it could be taken. Now, at one stroke, this entire area was effectively removed from the government's control and its vast arms stores opened up to the insurgents. In short order the mutinying units brought out the Guards Sappers and the first battalion of the Marine Guards Equipage, and reduced to submission the arsenal of the Artillery Department; likewise, they liberated the prisoners in the House of Preliminary Detention (the Predvarylka, well known to revolutionaries) and subdued all police stations and the barracks of the Mounted Gendarme Division. The military schools, which might have added an element of strength loyal to the government, had not been mobilized during the crisis, and at the General Staff Academy classes were being conducted as usual when they were overtaken by the revolt. Instead of trying to form themselves into some kind of organized units (whether any arms were available is of course an important question), these students and instructors of military science disbanded and went their separate ways. A number of loyal soldiers who had fled for refuge to the premises of the Academy thus had no choice but filter back out inconspicuously and blend with the street throngs. Among other things, the huge building of the regional court was set on fire, which announced to all of Petrograd that the center of the city was in the hands of insurgents. . . .

Simultaneously, on the far side of the Neva in the Vyborg Side, a second uprising was taking place. Factory meetings were being held as usual from early morning, but there was a new note of urgency in the oratory, sounding the conviction that the resistance of the government forces must be overcome at once or the movement would be defeated. The Bolsheviks, who had the strongest organizational roots in the district, were under instructions to urge the workers to make a concerted effort to win over the soldiers and through them to obtain arms. Whether they were persuaded by the Bolshevik orators or were simply following the logic of the situation, the worker-demonstrators did in fact mount an effort in the course of the morning to lift pickets and guard posts and to penetrate the barracks with written appeals or deputations. Several attempts to organize street meetings outside the barracks were broken up by machine-gun fire, which nearly caused the workers to give up the effort. But whether encouraged by news of the revolt on the opposite side or by their success in dissolving military units at several key locations, they persisted in their efforts. Soon they had accumulated enough weapons and soldier defectors to take over police stations, occupy the Finland Station, and liberate the recently arrested political prisoners in the Petrograd Prison of Solitary Confinement (the Kresty). By noon the quarter, except for the barracks of the Moskovskii Guards Regiment, the Bicycle Battalion, and the units guarding the Aleksandrovskii Bridge, was in their hands. Around one o'clock the soldier-mutineers from the Liteinyi district surged across the bridge, overwhelming the units guarding it. The two insurgent forces linked up, occupying a good third of the city and cutting the government forces off from all important reserves of ammunition, weapons, and military supplies (the Sestroretskii rifle factory, a few miles out along the Finland railroad line, the Patronyi Zavod [Ammunition Works], and the "New Arsenal," a huge weapons assembly and storage depot near the Aleksandrovskii Bridge). . . .

It is obvious from the foregoing account that the government forces had lost to the rebels simultaneously with the mutiny in the Liteinyi and Vyborg districts and never succeeded in regaining the initiative. It is a dreary tale of lack of foresight, utterly incompetent leadership, and greatly disproportionate odds. Émigré memoirs and scholarly works lament that had matters been in the hands of energetic commanders, had the staff work prior to the revolt been up to par, or had certain factors been otherwise, the outcome might have been different. Such opinions are hardly surprising on the part of those bred in the old military traditions and the idea of the monarchy. However, it is surprising that such arguments should be vigorously advanced by so serious a contemporary historian as Professor Katkov in his monograph on the February Revolution. He upholds the brave commander of the Cycle Battalion, who maintained the loyalty and fighting capacity of his men for a full twenty-four hours after the outbreak of the mutiny, as an example of what "a determined and popular officer could have done if the commander at the headquarters of the Petrograd garrison had been less disoriented." And he couples this with Sukhanov's statement (and he was not the only one to make this assertion) that on the evening of the twenty-seventh the mutineers would have been helpless against any organized force, the tragedy being that "Tsarism had no such organized force."

The historian, however, cannot attribute decisive significance to fortuitous circumstances or speculate on hypothetical variations of the actual facts. The evidence presented here should substantiate that there were deep and unalterable historical reasons both for the mass defection of the troops and for the inefficacy of the most heroic efforts of energetic officers to give more than a few hours reprieve to the failing government. In effect, to assume that at this juncture there could have been energetic leadership that could have led to an opposite result would be to ignore all the deep-seated social and political reasons that led to the isolation of the monarchy, the deterioration of the quality of its leadership, the enervation of its will to survive, and the alienation of all the important social groups, including those that made up the mechanism of institutional support for the autocracy.

Katkov's point is well taken that even during the mutiny many soldiers displayed ambivalent attitudes and would by no means have been an effective fighting force if faced with disciplined units. As stated before, conflicting motivations during the crisis do not find expression in the documentation, but reasonable conclusions can be inferred nevertheless. The first, of course, was fear of harsh reprisals in case the mutiny should be defeated, and here peasant- and worker-soldiers had a vast fund of historical experience to draw upon. However, there was also evident reluctance on the part of many to go against the code of military discipline, and this cannot simply be attributed to awe before the symbols of tsarist authority. The professionalism and patriotism of conscientious officers could and quite often did inspire respect in their men, particularly at the company level, and also on the part of regimental commanders.[5] One should note, however, that such officers represented a rather small minority, as the great majority looked on garrison duty as a respite or refuge from the hardships of the front and left the day-to-day problems of coping with the disorganized mass of recruits to NCOs. Evidence of the reluctance to go against respected officers can be seen in numerous accounts of apologies to officers for disobeying, friendly warnings, or actual protection against lynching crowds. Many of the units that turned up at the Winter Palace or that declared their "neutrality" undoubtedly did so out of deference to such officers. But this did not necessarily insulate them from the influences that inclined the soldiers generally to the side of revolt. Even with excellent leadership it is doubtful that the forces that showed up at the Palace Square could have been molded into a fighting force, as the example of Captain Kutepov so eloquently shows. Many of the units were there by either misunderstanding or the inertia of obedience to command, and they would not under any circumstances have carried out orders to shoot at fellow soldiers on the rebel side. They could be held there only to the extent that they were ignorant of developments elsewhere in the city, and most of them departed as soon as they were better informed.

Of the psychological factors that might have restrained the soldiers from mutiny, one was certainly no longer effectual, namely, the traditional awe before the person of the tsar. The Rasputin scandal and the rumors of German influence on the tsarina had effectively eroded the last remaining barriers that had hitherto exempted the person of the tsar from the rage directed toward the ministers, the generals, the police, the war, and the shortage of bread. Occasionally the tsar was defended as a well-intentioned but weak person, but the tsarina, who was known to dominate her husband, had indelibly become "that German woman." Proof of the erosion of the prestige of the crown came when appeals to the soldiers to observe the oath of loyalty to the tsar were almost totally ignored in the February days.

---

[5] Col. Ekstrom, commander of the Pavlovskii Regiment, was quite popular with his men, and . . . successfully calmed them after the incident of the twenty-sixth on the Moika, only to be fouly murdered on the street afterwards by angry demonstrators. The commanders of the Moskovskii and Izamilovskii regiments also enjoyed such a reputation and were "reelected" to their posts after the Revolution, albeit only briefly.

Whatever the restraining impulses still intact, they could do no more than delay the process of mass defection, and not in a single instance did they lead to anything like determined resistance. Those few units that actively resisted the rebel forces were training units organized by a few energetic officers before the full impact of the revolt could be felt. An explanation for their resistance is not too difficult to find, for these units consisted primarily of men transferred from the front, who had been recommended by their officers for training as NCOs. This means that they were to some extent motivated by a sense of duty and an ambition to advance in the army. Thus a breach of discipline went strongly against their interests and values (as NCOs, of course, the support payments to their families would be correspondingly greater). Still, they were not immune to the disaffection in the rest of the country, and their special role during the demonstrations was a most unwelcome one. If the Pavlovskii and Moskovskii training units remained subordinate and carried out orders to shoot, the same orders had the opposite effect on other training units, driving them as an organized force over to the side of the revolt. The example of Kirpichnikov's training company was decisive in demonstrating to fellow soldiers that the repressive force they feared most now sided with the people, and it opened the floodgates for the rest of the garrison.

If the training units were the chief potential source of support for the government, other categories of garrison soldiers offset this advantage by the depth of their alienation. The most important of these were the recuperating evacuees (those who had recovered from wounds and illnesses and who were being reassigned to marching companies, usually composing one full company out of the four in reserve units). These soldiers had tasted to the full the bitter dregs of war at the front and were not disposed to return. Hardened by their experiences, they were hostile to discipline and contemptuous of officers as a class. Some of them had been exposed to revolutionary and antiwar propaganda in the hospitals, where surveillance was at a minimum and idle time was spent swapping rumors and stories of Rasputin and the German element. The evacuees enjoyed the reputation of being particularly hostile to barracks routine and training duties, and most officers left them in peace.

Of the new recruits, the most bitter were the over-forties, who had left households behind them in the charge of women and old folks. They were agitated by a pervasive fear that their holdings would be easy prey to the village *kulaks* and *miroeds*, who in their absence dominated the village assemblies, as well as to speculators and venal food supply officials. The desertion rate among this category was extraordinarily high, and they positively revolted at the idea of being sent to the front. How large an element this was in the Petrograd garrison is not subject to precise determination, but it was sizable enough to attract commentary (as an element of "bad luck" for the government). Several authorities, both Soviet and émigré, maintain that a large number of new recruits in the guards regiments were workers from the capital who had lost their exempt status owing to participation in strikes. Thus they supposedly had direct contacts with the workers and were a conduit of the latter's rebellious impulses into the barracks milieu. In certain types of units, such as the automobile and armored car units, the predominance of the worker element is more than a conjecture, and these units did play an important role in the rebellion. The same was true of the Guards Sappers, the Marine Guards Equipage, and the Oranienbaum Machine Gunners. Although a recent Soviet study based on archival data confirms that no substantial change took place in the recruitment patterns into the guards regiments, which, as traditionally practiced, drew from rural regions, the regular infantry regiments (five in all) were drawing recruits exclusively from regions around the capital and thus reflected the urban population structure. Although the share of industrial workers is not strikingly large (3.5 percent), when one adds construction workers (6 percent), petty craftsmen (22 percent), and manual laborers (18.2 percent), it amounts to a total of almost 50 percent, well above the typical 30 percent share of prewar times. The purely agricultural category was represented by a mere 34 percent, as compared with the prewar, nationwide average of 61 percent. Moreover, a goodly number of soldiers in these regiments (four thousand out of nearly forty thousand) were detailed to work in arms assembly plants or to perform guard duty there, and were thus in daily contact with civilian workers. Similarly, it is significant that some of the reserve infantrymen could not be housed in barracks and were quartered with working-class families on the Vyborg Side. One can presume, therefore, that the regular infantry units were in tune with the mood of the lower-class urban populace and felt thoroughly at home on the streets of Petrograd.

Thus, one is safe in concluding that the garrison troops could not possibly have been depended upon in any crisis to serve as a force for the suppression of disorders, and it was the particular blindness of those in authority that they continued to reckon on them. Anyone inclined to think otherwise should contemplate the pitiful remnant of a thousand men cooped up in the Admiralty by midday of the twenty-eighth, and even they were becoming restive. Of that small handful of the autocracy's servants in whose frail hands the last defense of the sinking empire remained, it is perhaps best to say: "Whom the gods would destroy, they first make mad."

. . . The Army was the chief bulwark of the old order, its only major defense against revolutionary challenge and the cement that kept all other institutions in functional relationship to one another. In 1917, as in 1905, the preoccupation of the Army with the tasks of war severely limited its efficacy as an instrument of enforcement and repression. The February Revolution was in effect a test of the viability of that instrument after three years of war had eroded its morale and pushed social tensions to a breaking point. It was tried and found wanting.

The reasons for this failure, though it has been tempting for partisans of the old order to plead the unique circumstances of the war, are represented here as reaching far back into Russia's past. The autocratic system rested on a paradox: it had reshaped Russian society to serve the needs of a strong military state order, but at the same time it had built in severe inequities and tensions that could only be dealt with by further buttressing the military as an internal police force. The carefully circumscribed modernization that the autocracy allowed itself in the last half century of its existence aggravated rather than resolved social tensions, and weakened rather than strengthened the arm of the state designed to cope with them. The Revolution of 1905 had already demonstrated the contradiction inherent in the use of an army of mobilized civilians to quell civil disorders. The peasant and worker masses did not come out of that first revolution unscathed. But the credit for this goes not so much to the revolutionary parties as to the brutalizing experiences of the turmoil, which imparted new images of state authority and society. Unnoticed by cultured society, and even by the majority of the radical intelligentsia, this alienation was not simply away from reactionary tsardom, but also from the world of culture and privilege generally, and events between 1905 and 1914 did little to efface those fundamental attitudes. Thus, taking into consideration the evidence presented here, one can say with reasonable confidence that the peasant-soldiers entered the world war with the conviction that it was an alien enterprise, the patriotic outpourings of cultured society notwithstanding. The strains of the war ultimately produced a mood of intolerable impatience, intensified by every sign of weakness and disorganization in the state order.

The thesis of the present study is that the command authority of the Army was a direct casualty of the February Revolution itself, of the massive groundswell of popular feeling that shattered the autocratic framework, and that it did not simply erode over a period of time. The point scarcely needs demonstrating for the Petrograd garrison and the Baltic ports, where the soldiers' (and sailors') revolt was the most conspicuous mover of events (the others being the strikes and street demonstrations). At the front there was no overt "mutiny" on the same massive order, yet the uninterrupted chain of events, from the first tidings of the abdication to the formalization of soldiers' committees, was just as complete a revolution in authority, leaving the command in a position of sufferance and voluntary recognition at best and sweeping away most of the coercive powers that had formerly ensured obedience to orders. That the soldiers at the front, faced with the presence of the enemy across the wire, were more disposed than their comrades in the rear to observe military routine and to accept replacements for arrested officers should not cause one to overlook the fact that they keenly sensed their own power to impose changes, that they discussed and flouted orders without embarrassment, and that they institutionalized their emancipation from officer tutelage through their committees.

Indicative of the depth of the rupture at the very outset was the behavior of the senior commanders during the crisis. One need not dwell on Katkov's claim that the outcome would have been different had the generals not "betrayed" their monarch. From this author's point of view, an even more chaotic upheaval, with perhaps a more immediately drastic fate for the royal family and its adherents, would have been the result. The generals were concerned above all with maintaining the fighting capacity of the Army and accepted the abdication in order to gain some leverage over events before the front was affected.

But would it have been possible at any subsequent point for the Army command to exert authority either against or on behalf of the Provisional Government in order to arrest the revolutionary course of events? Alekseev did for a time urge Petrograd authorities to stand up to the Soviet, but his truculence found no echo with Rodzianko or Guchkov, or more importantly, with the lower levels of command. Virtually every army and front headquarters and every major garrison, including Stavka, was under siege by the massive, agitated crowds, and the most frequent victims of violent assaults and forced removals were garrison commanders. Katkov blames the breakdown in authority in the garrison centers on the demoralizing consequences of the abdication, whereas by the time the abdication was known, the breakdown was an accomplished fact virtually everywhere. The field commanders, most notably Ruszkii and Dragomirov, advised strongly against repression, cognizant of its utter futility, and by March 11 Alekseev himself yielded to the strategy of accommodation with the revolutionary forces. Without such an accommodation, *a much more violent upheaval would have been the only prospect, and the partisans of authority could not possibly have prevailed.*

In fact, the command's new course of action — unquestioned loyalty to the Provisional Government and acquiescence in the system of dual power in the capital and soldiers' committees at the front — did temporarily succeed in bringing about a new equilibrium and calming of tensions. In late March the illusion took root at the front, as it had earlier in the rear, that the two species of institutions could share power and cooperate in harmony until the convocation of a constituent assembly at some vague future date. The mood of the newly elected soldiers' representatives was often influenced by suggestions of the command that criticized the revolutionary excesses of the rear. For a time it seemed that a united "front" would range itself against the "dual authority" of the "rear" and put pressure on the Soviet to uphold the authority of the Provisional Government for the sake of the war effort. The significance of the ensuing crisis is that it unambiguously demonstrated that two fundamentally different orders of institutions, representing different social layers and embodying irreconcilable goals, were in an unstable relationship and threatened to break apart at any time. The chief landmark of the month of April was that the Soviet clearly established its leadership over the "democratic" layers, which now expected the Soviet to exercise control over the "bourgeois" tendencies of the government. The Soviet's authority had in effect become nationwide, incorporating the committees at the front, as had already been recognized at the All-Russian Conference of Soviets of late March.

The greatest clarity had been achieved on the question of the war: the formula "war to full victory" had been exposed as harboring the annexationist schemes of the bourgeois groups and their spokesman in the Provisional Government, Paul Miliukov, whereas the Soviet position was now broadly understood as expressing the peace aspirations of the working people of all countries and as leading eventually to a negotiated settlement without victors or vanquished. The consequences of this new alignment were to solidify the Soviet position and expose the fragile character of the authority of the Provisional Government, in other words, to demonstrate that the February Revolution was in fact a social compromise that had left the ultimate shape of the new order and all the vexing questions unresolved.

Though initially overshadowed by the cataclysms of the metropolis, the front was very much a part of the overall complexion of power. Having undergone its own revolution, it demonstrated that it could not be enlisted to reverse the arrangements of the center, but only to reinforce them. The cleavage appeared to be strictly between the privileged and the "democratic" elements along the lines of their respective social and political goals. However, the Revolution had mobilized not only the hitherto inarticulate masses, but also the socialist and fellow-traveling intelligentsia. Although the breakdown of old-regime modes of authority and the impulse to replace them with something new must be ascribed to the enormous upsurge of popular energies, the construction of a hierarchy of representative institutions was largely the work of the educated radical intelligentsia, in and out of uniform. At the front, it was the wartime officers, volunteers, clerk-specialists, military doctors, veterinarians, and those workers and peasants, mostly literate, who had had a previous association with the revolutionary movement.

Once the edifice of revolutionary institutions was in place, the "committee class" oriented itself far more toward the politics of the center than toward the aspirations of their own constituency. There was little contact between committees on the army, corps, and division levels and the soldiers in the trenches. Only regimental committees involved themselves in the day-to-day concerns of ordinary soldiers, and even they had problems in comprehending the soldier mass. The most obvious distinctions in attitudes were with regard to the war and — what in the soldiers' minds was closely connected with it — to command authority. The intellectuals, although firmly loyal to the Soviet, were more deeply and permanently affected by the initial wave of "March patriotism" and reinforced the defensist wing of the Soviet leadership, whereas the soldier masses very quickly reverted to their rosy expectations of a speedy peace, in which sense they interpreted all Soviet pronouncements. They asserted their own grasp of things by freely and enthusiastically indulging in fraternization and by stubbornly ignoring or resisting the joint efforts of the command and the committees to put a stop to it. The threatening gulf between electors and elected was masked during most of April by the continuing conflict with the bourgeois groups over war aims; but with the April Crisis and the formation of the Coalition Government, that battle was ostensibly won, and the protective cover was removed. Soviet and state authority had coalesced, and, in the person of the "Socialist People's Defense Minister," pronounced in favor of a new offensive, inflicting on the masses a painful new adjustment of loyalties.

This unpleasant development demonstrated that, apart from the revolution in power and authority, an even more profound revolution in consciousness had taken place in the minds of the soldier-peasant masses, which the democratic intelligentsia initially catered to but did not fully grasp. Quite dramatically, the soldiers became aware of their collective ability to move events and work their will. Unaccustomed to articulate expression and organizational behavior, they deferred to the leadership of their cultural superiors, adopting enthusiastically their revolutionary and socialist rhetoric on the naive assumption that it expressed their own inner promptings.

Even though it was a surprising development that the peasant-soldier could part so easily from his traditional devotion to the person of the tsar, there is no doubt that the erosion had begun long ago (certainly the tsar's prestige had suffered seriously in 1905). The soldiers' reactions to the abdication and subsequent phenomena show that they identified the collapse of the monarchy with the end of the old order, root and branch, which for them meant the end of subjection to the *barin* and the *zemskii nachalnik* (land captains) back home and to the officer at the front. The expectations of land and peace welled up spontaneously as a logical concomitant of the overthrow of the old authorities and cannot, as conventional accounts would still have it, be ascribed to the propaganda of the socialist intelligentsia (or to that of the Germans). Land and freedom, *zemlia i volia*, had always been an indigenous aspect of folk psychology, which the populists had learned to exploit but had by no means invented. At the present juncture, with the war as the only obstacle to the realization of ancient longings, land and peace were similarly joined in an indissoluble bond. The peasants in uniform strongly sensed that the end of the monarchy and of the hierarchical order of authority were the same, whether at the front or in the country at large, and now they and their peers (the workers being honorary peasants) had prevailed over their erstwhile masters. Although no longer fearing the latter's power, the peasant-soldiers did fear their craftiness, their designs to take advantage of the peasant "darkness" to regain their lost position. Thus soldiers determined not to allow their officers to be their intermediaries with Petrograd authority but established their own direct ties, and thus they readily accepted the Soviet version of the conflict over war aims and the accusation that "victory" was a bourgeois code word for annexations. They were immensely reassured by the assertion of Soviet control over the Provisional Government and the prospect of a negotiated peace without further bloodshed. In the soldiers' minds, no return to "normal" military order or resumption of the war on a significant scale was conceivable; only a provisional "holding of the front" and a de facto truce across the trenches were permissible until the proper arrangements could be made. The chronic breaches of discipline in April were almost entirely connected with suspicions of the command's surreptitious preparations for new operations against the wishes of the Soviet.

The ground had thus been well laid for a new crisis, for in fact, peace was beyond the grasp of the new, Soviet-based Coalition Government without a demonstration of force in the shape of a new offensive. The upper-level committees and, with less unanimity, the lower ones were prepared to meet the challenge, and for this purpose they cooperated with the command in restoring military discipline at the front by functioning as adjuncts to the latter's authority. This could not possibly have been more at odds with the mood of the soldier masses, and if the Bolsheviks had not intervened decisively with their peace propaganda at the front in May and June, the very stones would have cried out. The Bolsheviks did not offer the soldiers a new vision of the Revolution, but a more speedy and direct realization of the original one.

The successive efforts of the soldier masses to lay claim to the promissory notes of the Revolution — in their revolt against the offensive, in their response to the Kornilov affair, and finally, in their mighty affirmation of Soviet power and immediate peace — will constitute the body of the sequel, to this volume, in which the fundamental character of the Second Russian Revolution of 1917 will also be reevaluated. For example, I hope to show that it is improperly called the October Revolution, since it occurred not primarily in October, but in the course of the months from November 1917 to February 1918. Certain phases of it should be understood as having occurred much earlier in the year, as for example, in Kronshtadt and the Baltic ports. This Revolution should be regarded as the conquest by the masses of undivided Soviet power, the realization of their vision of direct democracy without compromises with the propertied elements, and the immediate execution of the agenda of the Revolution on land, peace, and workers' control of industry. The Bolsheviks' advance on the crest of this Revolution, and their eventual transformation of it into a party dictatorship, were long-term processes during the course of the Civil War, but that they occurred was a reflection of the bankruptcy of the Bolsheviks' political rivals, who in 1917 would not, or could not, come to terms with the social revolution that in fact had already taken place.

To correct the defects in the traditional perspective on the Russian Revolution, above all, the persistent preoccupation with events in the capital, there is no better arena to study than the Army at the front. The realization of mass control over the representative organs (the committees) and the recognition of Soviet power — with or without Bolshevik majorities — on most sectors within days, on others within a few weeks, of the coup in the capital nullified the possibility of resurrecting the Provisional Government or even of reaching compromise solutions, such as an "all-socialist coalition" or a new republic based on the constituent assembly. Only Soviet power answered to the determination of the mass of uniformed peasants and workers to consummate the Revolution as they understood it. The First Revolution of 1917 was the destruction of the old order and the creation of the soviets to express the will of the masses to the nominal bearers of authority; the Second Revolution was the assumption of unqualified power and the proclamation of the Soviet program.

Soldiers in the Revolution. These regular-army troops, like thousands of others, and sailors as well, played a key role in bringing down the tsarist government and supporting the workers' soviets. (Sovfoto)

PART

II The Deepening of the Revolution

Variety of Opinion

The new political strategy adopted by the moderate leaders of the soviet in early May, that of coalition, not only coincided with a severe economic crisis and exacerbated its political implications, but also began to divide "the Democracy" into leaders and led. . . . Economic deterioration, coupled with the dynamics of the labor struggle (the "second wave" of economic demands in May and June), initiated a process of social polarization that had been largely absent in the first two months of the revolution. The failure of the Provisional Government to deal with the root causes of this crisis — war and economic anarchy — gave political direction to the workers' mounting discontent, further "radicalized" them, and ultimately made them receptive to the Bolshevik slogan of "all power to the soviets."

Ziva Galili

The right-wing bourgeoisie used the anxiety caused by the April events as a starting point for a political attack on the Soviet. For the first time since the beginning of the Revolution, these circles thought the moment opportune for an open, large-scale, organized campaign to provoke a rift between the government and the Soviet. . . . The disorganization of the national life, resulting from a devastating war and the collapse

197

of the old order, they attributed solely to the influence of the Soviet democracy.

Irakli Tsereteli

The agrarian movement was neither a product of external agitation, nor a manifestation of class struggle. It was a phenomenon sui generis — *plebeian, anarchic and anti-centralist. Its archaic features were most evident in the effort to avenge ancient wrongs, in the joy with which the common people destroyed the symbols of their former subjection. . . . With its pronounced levelling tendencies the agrarian movement exemplified the dynamic force behind the Russian revolution itself.*

John L. H. Keep

The extent to which the working-class movement was permeated by a commitment to direct democracy is reflected in the fact that it was not the factory committee per se *which was the sovereign organ in the factory, but the general meeting of all workers in the factory or section. . . . This Rousseauesque concept of sovereignty was established in practice from the first.*

S. A. Smith

At the level of high politics . . . the best hope — and perhaps the last *best hope — for civil liberties, a permanent rule of law, and other traditional liberal goals, was to preserve and protect the Provisional regime. . . . This meant cooperation and close relations [by the Kadets] with Soviet leaders. Social and political stability at a local level also required cooperation with the left. . . . The obvious advantage of moving openly to the right would be a consolidation of anti-socialist political strength, and the development of new abilities to coordinate political and economic pressures against the left. But there was also the obvious danger of further polarizing Russian society as a whole, and the much greater likelihood of civil war.*

William G. Rosenberg

The coalition of the "revolutionary democracy" and the tsentsovoe obshchestvo *(the old ruling classes and the bourgeoisie) on which the Right socialists based their strategy was steadily being eroded away in the summer of 1917. The tremendous pressures on the masses, caused by the war and its stepchild, hunger, drove them to more radical alternatives. . . . No matter how complex or diffused the causes of the material crisis, the nationalities expressed their anger and frustration in the traditional hostility toward their ethnic enemies.*

Ronald Grigor Suny

The Issues

The revolutions of 1917 can be imagined as a series of overlapping revolutions — the liberal revolution of the middle classes and part of the intelligentsia that attempted to create a constitutional order; the workers' revolution with its vision of a more direct democracy that led to the establishment of Soviet Power in October; the peasants' revolution that culminated in the seizure of land and enforced a radical egalitarianism in the countryside; and, finally, the multiple revolts of the non-Russian peoples of the empire that often resulted in separation from Russia and the founding of new nation-states.

Those who initiated the revolution in Petrograd could not have foreseen its radical consequences, and all efforts through 1917 to moderate the demands of various classes and to maintain the precarious alliance of forces that overthrew tsarism failed. By October the country was polarized between the top of society and the bottom, and political leaders on both sides were prepared to accept the risk of civil war. The key questions of the middle period of the revolution center on the reasons for the breakdown of the political consensus that created, first dual power, and later the coalition government. How can we explain the radicalization of the workers, soldiers, and peasants, and the drift to the right of the liberals and the middle classes? How important was the role of political leaders, parties, and propaganda in the process of "deepening the revolution"?

In the first days of the revolution there was both a remarkable agreement among the revolutionary forces on the need to end autocracy and a profound suspicion that divided the workers, particularly, from the Duma politicians. At one end of the Tauride Palace the Duma Committee decided to take power and form a Provisional Government; at the other end of the same building the deputies elected by the workers created the Soviet of Workers' Deputies. The soviet was unwilling either to take power in its own name and risk counterrevolution from conservative and military forces or to join a coalition government that, in their eyes, ought to be "bourgeois." The soviet agreed to support the government "in so far as [poskol'ku, postol'ku] its policy will not run against the interests of the toiling masses," but would also organize itself to defend the class interests of the workers. Thus, dual power (dvoevlastie) was born — two separate loci of power representing two different social groups, neither of which could (or would) govern on their own.

From the outset, however, it was clear to perceptive observers that the two "powers" were not equivalent. The Provisional Government held formal power, was recognized as the actual government of Russia by its allies, and set out to speak in the name of the whole population. The soviet, on the other hand, even though it had been elected only by a part of the workers of the capital, spoke in the name of the working class of Russia and held the real power in the city. Only the Soviet could convince the workers to return to the factories and — once Order No. 1 was accepted by the soldiers — command the soldiers to keep order or fight.

From the first days of the revolution, tensions and suspicions divided the demokratiia *(the lower classes) from the* tsentsovoe obshchestvo *(the propertied classes). Yet at the same time a willingness to work with alien social strata also existed. As Ziva Galili demonstrates, agreement on the length of the working day and wage increases convinced moderate socialists that the alliance of workers and industrialists could survive the euphoria of February. Even the Bolsheviks, before the return of Lenin from exile in April, practiced a politics of relative moderation and shelved their demand for soviet power.*

In this first period of the revolution, up to May, the policy of cooperation was best articulated by the Georgian Menshevik Irakli Tsereteli, who believed that, given the existing level of economic and social development of Russia, only a bourgeois-democratic revolution was possible. Therefore, workers ought to limit their demands and must not take power. On the all-important question of the war, Tsereteli proposed a strategy of "revolutionary defensism" — defense of the country from foreign attack while pursuing a "democratic peace" that would renounce any gains of territory. But just when a broad consensus on economic issues and foreign policy seemed to have been achieved, the first crisis of the revolutionary year broke unexpectedly over the heads of the soviet leaders.

On April 19, the Foreign Minister Pavl Miliukov sent a diplomatic note to the Allies declaring his government's support for their war aims and of "war to a victorious end." His views were shared by many representatives of the upper classes of Russia. By seeming to reject the notion of a "democratic peace" and applauding the imperialist aims of the Allies, Miliukov had challenged the soviet. The next morning crowds went into the streets; workers and soldiers surrounded the Mariinskii Palace, where the government sat, and within days Miliukov was forced to resign.

The members of the Provisional Government demanded that the soviet join them in forming a coalition government. Tsereteli agreed that a coalition would unite the workers with the other "vital forces of the nation" in an effort to combat social disintegration and bring the war to an end. On May 5 soviet representatives joined the coalition government, and the soviet expressed its full confidence in the new government.

The decision to join forces with the representatives of "propertied Russia" linked the moderate socialists with the policies of the Provisional Government and prevented them from reflecting the growing radicalism of their own constituents. The great majority of the soviet followed the Mensheviks and Socialist Revolutionaries, and only Bolsheviks, Menshevik-Internationalists, and anarchists opposed this policy of collaboration. As the war raged on and casualties mounted, however, discontent grew among the soldiers. As inflation eroded whatever wage gains workers had achieved in the first months of the revolution, workers grew increasingly hostile to the industrialists. The government failed to solve the problem of supplying food to the cities and decided to delay major reforms until the war ended and the Constituent Assembly could be convened. While some workers went along with the coalition, growing numbers abandoned both the government and the Mensheviks and Socialist Revolutionaries who supported it.

The April Crisis had exposed the weakness of the Provisional Government and its dependency on the soviet. As the government accepted the soviet's peace policy and other elements of the socialists' program, many in the middle and upper classes grew suspicious of the coalition. Whereas the soviet leaders favored a plan for state regulation of the economy, industrialists opposed such state kontrol' and declared forcefully that "no economic organization other than capitalism is possible in Russia." Workers, on the other hand, turned to a notion of workers' kontrol' — supervision of the overall operation of plants and factories by workers' organizations to prevent sabotage by the industrialists. The Bolsheviks came out in favor of workers' control, and in June demonstrations revealed the mounting support among the lower classes in the city for the Bolsheviks.

Neither the government nor the soviet could find any enthusiasm among the Allied Powers for their peace policy. Unwisely, the government agreed to launch an offensive against the Germans, but Russia's capacity for sustained action had long since dissipated. The failure of the so-called Kerensky Offensive further increased Bolshevik sympathies among the soldiers. In early July radical sailors and soldiers attempted to force the soviet to take power, and when they failed the soviet and the government launched a campaign of repression against the Bolsheviks. Lenin went into hiding; Trotsky went to jail. In August, as the liberals flirted with the military, and the industrialists and officers openly called for suppression of the soviet, General Kornilov tried to march on Petrograd and establish his personal power. Workers and soldiers thwarted the would-be dictator, but the Kerensky government was widely suspected of involvement in the coup attempt. Both the government and the moderate leadership of the soviet were discredited in the eyes of the lower classes. With the coalition government torn between left and right and unable to steer a steady course, workers and soldiers turned to the one major party that rejected the coalition and called for "all power to the soviets." Bolshevik popularity grew month by month until in September they became the dominant party in both the Petrograd and Moscow soviets.

All observers of the revolution agree that a process of deepening the revolution occurred after the initial period of relative harmony and that workers in Petrograd delivered the decisive blow to the February compromise. Chamberlin listed the characteristics of this period as: "loosening of discipline in the army, increasingly radical demands of the industrial workers, first for higher wages, then for control over production and distribution, arbitrary confiscations of houses in the towns and, to a greater degree, of land in the country districts, insistence in such non-Russian parts of the country as Finland and Ukraine on the grant of far-reaching autonomy."[1]

But there is far less agreement on the reasons for this process of radicalization, particularly among workers. Chamberlin suggests that it was the relative weakness of the capitalist class, the lateness of the coming of capitalism to Russia, the influx of peasants into the working class, and the legacy of autocracy that both retarded the development of the labor movement and simultaneously made it more revolutionary.[2] Reversing Marx's expectation that advanced capitalism would create a revolutionary proletariat, Chamberlin assumes that in the normal development of industrial capitalism workers benefit from the rise in the

[1] W. H. Chamberlin, *The Russian Revolution*, I, p. 142.
[2] Ibid., pp. 261–262.

standard of living and are therefore less likely to revolt. "Russia's experience would suggest that the greatest measure of social dynamite is stored up in a proletarian class that has emerged from the well-nigh complete illiteracy and backwardness of the East without yet attaining the standard of living that holds good for the corresponding class in the West."[3] *For many writers, like Chamberlin, workers are to be understood essentially as a form of* homo economicus, *reacting primarily, like their class enemies, the capitalists, to issues of material self-interest.*

Another approach, perhaps best exemplified by John L. H. Keep, holds that categories such as class interests or ideologies are not useful in understanding worker activity, that "such terms as 'bourgeois' and 'capitalist' belonged to the language of revolutionary mythology; they had lost their original roots in socio-economic reality and had become negative symbols."[4] *Rather workers and peasants acted primarily on instinct rather than reason. Their behavior was largely subrational, spontaneously generated, and therefore receptive to manipulation by the Bolsheviks, who were more efficient, ruthless, and systematic than their rivals. Though he feels that "a class-oriented viewpoint came naturally to Russia's industrial workers," Keep considers socialist ideas artificial and external to the workers, something with which the revolutionary intelligentsia infected them.*[5] *He does not explore the possible coincidence of workers' aspirations and Bolshevik aims at the moment of deepening social polarization.*

Much of the research on laboring people in the last several decades has modified the view of workers as either simple rational economic actors or instinctive rebels. Beginning with the ground-breaking explorations of E. P. Thompson on The Making of the English Working Class, *scholars have been sensitized to issues of labor traditions, specific cultures and values, and the complex creation of social perceptions and consciousness. In an impressive series of monographs Russian labor historians, such as S. A. Smith, Diane Koenker, and David Mandel, have dissected the specific claims of Russian workers, and their particular demands and forms of collective behavior, in order to appreciate better their understanding of the workers' interests. Rather than treating the workers as an undifferentiated mass, recent work has disaggregated the working class*

---

[3] Ibid., p. 275.
[4] John L. H. Keep, *The Russian Revolution*, p. 26.
[5] Ibid.

*and drawn distinctions among different sectors within the working class
— women, young people, skilled and unskilled laborers.*

Rather than arguing from an a priori *idea of how workers ideally
ought to have acted or organized, the new labor history has analyzed
both the factors that divided workers one from another and those that
created a sense of cohesion, in terms of the real experience of workers. The
formation of a revolutionary working class in Russia is no longer deduced
from the classic explanation of capitalist development, as in many Soviet
histories, nor is it simply the product of material deprivation or Bolshevik
duplicity. By freeing themselves of the social-scientific models of older
generations and posing questions in new ways, historians have exposed
their readers to the complex ways in which economics, politics, and
culture — in some cases ethnic culture as well as class culture — combined in 1917 to create a revolutionary social consciousness among the
lower classes of urban and rural Russia.*

Ziva Galili

Workers, Industrialists, and Mensheviks

Born and raised on a kibbutz in northern Israel, Ziva Galili grew up in
a community founded by socialist émigrés from Russia. She began her
Russian studies at Hebrew University before continuing under Leopold
Haimson at Columbia. She has taught at Oberlin College and Rutgers
University, edited a collection of interviews of leading Mensheviks, and
completed a major investigation of the "Revolutionary Defensists" in 1917,
their relations with the workers, and the labor policies of the Provisional
Government. Her work has emphasized the psychological and structural
restraints on Menshevik activities during the revolution and has revised
many of the accepted views of Social Democrats in a "bourgeois" revolution. In the article excerpted here she shows how the successes of compro-

"Workers, Industrialists, and Mensheviks" by Ziva Galili y Garcia, *The Russian Review*,
Vol. 44, No. 3 (July 1985) is reprinted by permission. © 1985 by the Ohio State University Press. All rights reserved.

mise and conciliation in labor-management relations in the early months of the revolution influenced the outlook of the Mensheviks throughout the rest of 1917.

One of the stereotypes concerning the Menshevik Party in the revolution of 1917 is that its leaders consistently followed policies that were out of step with existing social relations and the evolving sentiments of the party's working-class constituency. According to this widely-held view, Menshevik strategies — which were essentially directed toward the prevention of sharp conflict in Russian society — ran counter to a process of social polarization that had already begun to unfold on the morrow of the February victory, a process that was evinced in an immediate aggravation of labor relations and a corresponding emergence of workers' radicalism. In addition, the Mensheviks are often blamed for having contributed to the very polarization that they feared, when they sponsored the political arrangement known as "dual power." This arrangement is described in the literature either as an evasion of all political responsibility by the Menshevik leaders of the Petrograd Soviet or else as a form of cooperation between the soviet and the Provisional Government, and thus a precursor of the coalition that would be established two months later, in early May 1917. . . .

Dual Power

The victorious revolution of the Petrograd workers and soldiers gave birth to the novel political arrangement known as "dual power" (*dvoevlastie*). In the literature, the term has often described the varying forms of division of political authority between the Provisional Government and the Soviet of Workers' and Soldiers' Deputies from February to October of 1917. In the following pages, however, "dual power" will denote the specific political agreement that was concluded on March 2 between the Executive Committee of the two-day-old Petrograd Soviet and the Temporary Committee just elected by the State Duma. Fundamental to this agreement was a realization by both the negotiating parties that the long-standing suspicion that separated their respective bases of support in Russian society, as well as the balance of strength that existed between their forces, made it impossible for either to establish singlehandedly the new political order that was to replace the tsarist regime. Thus, it was decided on March 2 that a Provisional Government would be established, that its ministers would be drawn from the parties and the "public organizations" of liberal, propertied, and patriotic Russia, and that the leaders of the soviet would urge their followers to "lend support" to this new government.

While the March 2 agreement left all *formal* state power in the hands of the "liberal bourgeoisie," it did not signal unconditional surrender on the part of "the Democracy," or an abdication of its right to influence the course of the revolution. By deliberately refusing to participate in the cabinet, the moderate socialists of the Executive Committee secured the soviet's freedom to engage in the all-important work of organizing its followers and consolidating them into a united political force. By insisting that in return for their support the new Provisional Government accept an eight-point program, designed to create in Russia "full political freedom and absolute freedom of organization and agitation," the soviet's leaders not only secured sanction for their organizational work but also created a framework for the employment of the soviet's growing force to ensure, through pressure on the government from without, the realization of extensive democratic and social reforms. Finally, by urging their followers to support the new Provisional Government only "insofar as" (*poskol'ku-postol'ku*) it abided by the "obligations" undertaken in relation to the soviet, the leaders had established the formula of *conditional* support for the government, which gave the structure of power in revolutionary Russia its "dual" nature.

"Dual power," then, was a power arrangement between two contending social and political forces that reflected both their interdependence and deep mutual suspicion. The arrangement seemed flexible enough to accommodate both the relative social peace desired by the moderate leaders of the soviet, and the heightened social conflict that they deeply feared. . . .

Workers' Demands

To be sure, the workers of Petrograd responded to their leaders' call for organizational activity with great enthusiasm, and everywhere busied themselves with the establishment of district soviets, shop and factory committees, workers' militias, and with the election of deputies to the Petrograd Soviet. But the *political* victory of the revolution had also brought forth a profusion of workers' resolutions that mixed expressions of support for the soviet with specific demands, addressed to the employers, for changes in the conditions of life and work in the factories. These demands included most often the institution of an eight-hour working day, the rehiring of blacklisted workers, the banishment of certain managerial representatives from the factory, and finally, the establishment of factory committees to control all those aspects of the workers' lives that were not directly connected with production.

The immediate impact of these demands was on the individual factory, yet they should not be considered as merely local economic manifestations. By insisting on these demands — and, after mid-March, the demand for higher wages — the workers were attempting to recreate, on the factory floor, the civic and political gains just made on the national level. "Now, that we have political freedom in the country," declared a resolution adopted on March 11 by 1,000 textile workers, "we must also try to destroy the economic slavery that has survived until now in the area of labor-capital relations." In short, workers saw these demands as vindication of the right to live as was "befitting a worker and a free citizen."

In view of this widespread sentiment, any attempt by the moderate leaders of the soviet to dissuade the workers from pursuing their goals, particularly the demand for an eight-hour working day, must have appeared likely to split the "democratic camp" into leaders and followers. Yet that attempt was made. On March 6, the soviet called on the workers to end the general strike that had been in effect in Petrograd since the last week of February, in spite of the fact that the workers' own demands had not yet been met. Not surprisingly, the workers' reaction, even in those factories that acquiesced and ended their strike, was angry. A meeting on March 8 of twenty-one factories from the Petrograd Side accused the soviet of "ignoring the sentiments of the broad proletarian masses."

> *The meeting proposes to the soviet: (1) that in the future it take such decisions only after a more serious and more thorough discussion and consideration of the sentiments in the [workers'] districts; . . . (2) that it urgently work out and implement radical reforms in the field of*

> *economic life. The meeting recognizes that the agitation against inde-*
> *pendent implementation [by the workers] of the eight-hour working day*
> *and other economic improvements which have already been achieved*
> *is harmful to the general cause.*

By the second week of the revolution, then, a sharp social conflict
concerning the conditions of life and work in the factories seemed to be
in the making, a conflict that affected not only the relations between
workers and employers, but also threatened to create a crisis of trust and
understanding between the soviet's working-class constituency and its
Menshevik-led Executive Committee. Yet the second half of March
would see a dramatic change in the general picture of labor relations,
and with it, a shift in the mood of the workers and the policies of their
Menshevik leaders.

The Industrialists

In the years immediately preceding the revolution significant changes
had taken place in the organization and orientation of Russian industrialists. On the eve of the war a small group of Moscow businessmen had
already emerged as the leaders of the Progressist Party, and had tried to
use innovative, daring tactics in the struggle with the alliance between
tsarism and the nobility that had dominated Russian political life since
1907. A. I. Konovalov, P. P. Riabushinskii and others actively searched
for contacts with the socialist parties, not excluding the Bolsheviks, as a
means of bringing new life to the apparently stymied liberal forces.
Moreover, the confidence shown by these unusual representatives of
the Russian entrepreneurial class continued to grow during the war as
they succeeded in creating for themselves a position of national responsibility in economic affairs (institutionalized in the War-Industrial
Committees) and a place in the vanguard of the anti-tsarist liberal
forces.

By 1916 Konovalov and Riabushinskii seemed ready to launch a
new political initiative. In a series of meetings convened in their Moscow mansions, they urged their fellow industrialists as well as other
activists from the propertied classes to act, in effect, as Russia's "government in the making." Reports filed by secret police informers reveal that
Konovalov's main purpose in these meetings was to urge his listeners to
follow a strategy of building broad, moderate, political alliances. He

warned that the war's end would unleash a "revolutionary storm" and emphasized that this prospect made more urgent the need for the "bourgeois liberals" to cooperate with the more moderate elements of the labor movement as well as be ready to make some concessions to labor's economic demands. Although most Russian industrialists rejected this heterodox appeal to recognize their workers as worthy constituents of the post-tsarist Russian society, Konovalov was able to realize his strategy in the War-Industrial Committees, under whose auspices some fifty-eight worker-elected "Labor Groups" were organized by 1917. While this experiment in labor-enterpreneurial interaction raised the ire of some, many gave their support to Konovalov and his colleagues in gratitude for the lead that they had taken in fighting attempts to increase government regulation of the economy as well as their role in diverting state orders from the industrial mandates of Petrograd and the South — the state's traditional beneficiaries.

In any case, the undeniable differences of interest and perception that had frustrated Konovalov's effort to unite the commercial-industrial elements during the war and that continued to divide these groups in 1917 appeared to have diminished in the days after the February victory. Moreover, in Petrograd, the coming of the revolution had brought forth some dramatic gestures on the part of the commercial-industrial class. Konovalov, whose predictions of revolution had materialized, triumphantly stepped into the post of Minister of Trade and Industry in the new Provisional Government, and a few days later, announced his program of action in the area of labor relations to the nation:

> *The minister believes that the expansion of all kinds of trade unions is one of the chief prerequisites for Russia's economic revival . . . . The minister will strive wholeheartedly to satisfy, as much as possible, the needs of the workers. He hopes, however, for vigorous cooperation on their part.*

Following the example set by Konovalov, the Petrograd Society of Industrialists — always the most "state-oriented" of all Russian industrial organizations — undertook to change its image. Allies of the tsarist regime were ousted from the leadership of the society, and a Provisional Committee was elected whose views were similar to those of the new minister. To be sure, this shift mainly affected the industrialists' potential tactics and could not as yet mitigate the despairing contempt with which most employers regarded the "backwardness" of the Russian worker. Nevertheless, the first act of the reconstituted society marked a milestone in labor relations in Petrograd and in the country at large. On March 9, while some workers were still on strike and others were agitating for the acceptance of their demands, the society invited the soviet to send representatives to negotiate the conditions under which orderly production might be resumed. The agreement reached between the two organizations on March 10 provided for the institution of the eight-hour day, the establishment of workers' committees, and arbitration chambers in all of the factories of the capital. In the following weeks, workers throughout Russia pushed for similar measures in their localities; more often than not, their demands were met.

First Results

In Petrograd, the industrialists' readiness to compromise, evident in the ease and speed with which the March 10 agreement was concluded, resulted in the workers' making considerable gains in the following weeks. During March, the average work day in Petrograd declined from 10.1 hours to 8.4, and wages rose sharply in all but the smallest enterprises of the capital. (In fact, a minimum wage agreement was signed with the Petrograd Society of Industrialists on April 24.) The demand to readmit blacklisted workers to their factories and to oust objectionable managerial representatives were so widely implemented that soon the demand itself disappeared. Factory committees, too, became an almost universal institution. Simultaneously, and presumably as a result of these gains, there was a significant decline in strike activity. For example, the strikes registered by the Factory Inspectorate for the whole of Russia declined from 152 (114,304 strikers) in March to 41 (12,392 strikers) in April.

Of course, there were many instances of employers' resistance, most notably in Moscow, and many cases in which concessions, when made, were based on self-serving political calculation. At a meeting Konovalov held with the representatives of several commercial and industrial organizations on March 16, B. A. Efron of the Petrograd Society of Industrialists explained that the agreement reached in Petrograd on March 10 constituted "a real concession for the purpose of establishing order in the labor situation of the capital" and that the workers themselves understood it to be "only a temporary concession." One reason for the industrialists' readiness to compromise had to do with the workers' ability, once tsarist repression was removed, to bring production to a standstill. Another oft-stated reason for compromise was the industrialists' concern for safeguarding the orderly course of war-related production. . . .

However, the most important explanation for the support of Konovalov's strategy, particularly among the Petrograd industrialists, is to be found in their expectation that economic and political power in post-tsarist Russian society would belong to the commercial-industrial class — an expectation that already seemed realized in the strength of the industrialists' representation in the first cabinet of the Provisional Government. The soviet's self-imposed abstention from governmental power (under the terms of the "dual power" agreement) could only encourage this expectation and the mood of magnanimity that accompanied it. For the time being, many industrialists shared in Konovalov's hope that the workers' freedom to organize, as well as a show of good will on the part of the employers, would save Russia from labor anarchy and direct all future labor relations along more orderly lines. Indeed, an internal memorandum sent on March 14 by the Provisional Committee of the Petrograd Society of Industrialists to all of its members made this point clear. It explained that the eight-hour day was necessary in order to allow for the "workers' spiritual development" and for the construction of labor organizations — the goal of which was to be "the establishment of orderly relations between labor and capital."

It should be kept in mind that none of the workers' demands in the early months seemed to have seriously threatened the long-term goals of the industrialists. Even the issue of factory committees was as yet practically devoid of the aspects of *kontrol'*, or supervision over production, which would be associated with it after May 1917. Typical of the workers' attitude was the resolution adopted by the provisional factory committee of the Radio-Telegraph Factory of the Navy Department:

> *Recognizing the necessity of establishing a permanent factory commit-tee to guide the* internal life of the factory, *we declare ourselves to be the organizational and provisional committee charged with the task of working out our norms and principles for the* internal life of the factory.

The factory committee then defined "internal life" as including the economic conditions of the workers (the length of the working day, wages, and the minimum wage); their general welfare (labor insurance, medical aid, mutual aid funds, and food supplies); their relations with the employer (hiring, dismissals, and labor conflicts); their autonomous organization ("rights, duties, elections"); and measures to ensure orderly production (labor discipline, security measures). Clearly, what mattered most to the workers of the Radio-Telegraph Factory was the creation of their own, autonomous entity within the factory walls that would serve both to organize them and to secure their welfare and rights vis-à-vis the employer. True, they also undertook a measure of responsibility for productivity and in so doing allowed for the later invocation of the right to exercise *kontrol'* over production. In March and April, however, the workers' commitment to productivity did not lead to intervention in management's sphere of competence or even to *kontrol'* over its practices and decisions concerning production. Insofar as there was a struggle in the factories during this early stage, it did not involve the workers' attempt to take over the functions of management, but rather the less objectionable demand of worker autonomy.

Moreover, the manner in which the workers advanced their "economic" demands in March and April was quite reassuring to the advocates of compromise among the industrialists. Workers turned to arbitration more often than to strikes, and they were frequently ready to forego the implementation of the eight-hour working day as long as their right to a shorter day was recognized in principle. This was certainly the case with the highly organized workers of the Donbas mining region (represented in their negotiations with management by 21 local soviets) who admitted that the institution of the eight-hour working day was, for them, a "tactical demand," and stated that under the new conditions of freedom they would perform any overtime needed "for the welfare of the country," provided they were paid time-and-a-half. Thus, while the workers demonstrated a determination to pursue what they considered rightfully theirs, they also displayed remarkable self-restraint and particular concern for the continuation, and even improvement, of production, especially in defense-related enterprises.

Workers' Ambivalence

A basic ambivalence was characteristic of workers' attitudes in the early stage of the revolution. In early March, when the workers were still quite confused about questions of political power, their sentiments were expressed in terms of self-defense; feverish activity to organize in factories and working-class districts revealed a deeply suspicious attitude toward the propertied classes and a strong resolve not to be overborne by them. A general assembly of workers and employees at the Petrograd Cable Factory solemnly stated on March 3 that "the most urgent business of the moment [was to establish] strict *kontrol'* over the ministers appointed by the State Duma . . . who [did] not enjoy the people's trust. [Such] *kontrol'* must be composed of workers' and soldiers' deputies who are represented in the soviet."

Even so, workers did not seem willing to shoulder the task of establishing their own, proletarian government. This response derived not only from a sense of disorganization and unpreparedness, which the workers shared with their leaders, but also from an overriding concern with the achievement of the broadest possible support for the revolution that had just been accomplished. "The success of the revolution," warned the workers of Geisler factory on March 1, "could be secured only on condition of unity among all those who sympathize with the revolutionary uprising."

Indeed, throughout March and April the workers would be torn by ambivalent feelings: by suspicion of the propertied classes and hope for an accommodation with them; by a sense of the revolution as something of their own making and an equally deep appreciation of the role the soldiers had played in the final victory. The workers' urge to achieve full citizenship and human dignity through changes in the structure of relationship in the factory thus contrasted with the ever-present fear of being rebuffed and isolated by the "bourgeoisie" and with an almost desperate search for unity with those whom they saw as their natural allies, the soldiers. . . .

Yet it was not only fear and suspicion that led the workers to practice caution and self-restraint in March and April. The desire to be part of a larger revolutionary collective compelled delegates from the factories of the Petrograd District, for example, to insist, even as they condemned the soviet's call to end the strike on March 6, that the workers of the capital "show class solidarity and submit to the Soviet of Workers' Deputies by resuming work as soon as possible." In regard to the cardinal importance of organizing and uniting around the soviet, the workers were at one with the Menshevik leaders. Indeed, the very formula of "dual power" on which the existence of the soviet and its relationship to the Provisional Government were based — separateness, autonomy, and conditional support, with the soviet free to engage in the organizational work and put pressure on the government of the propertied classes from without — all of this corresponded closely to the workers' own ambivalent feelings about the powerful, educated class of employers. After all, were not the socialist leaders in the soviet (self-proclaimed leaders, to be sure) handling the Provisional Government with the same mixture of suspicion and restraint that the workers in the factories practiced toward management? For this reason the slogan, "unite around the one revolutionary and organizational center — the Soviet of Workers' and Soldiers' Deputies," remained the most popular among the workers of Petrograd throughout April.

Moreover, as the employers' unprecedented readiness for concessions became evident in labor's tangible gains, the workers' patience with the soviet's mediation efforts also grew, while the tensions that had accompanied their quest for unity with their leadership in early March began to disappear. Thus, within the context of "dual power," and with the help of a relatively successful labor struggle, many workers were able to reconcile their goals with the perceived need to accommodate other groups and classes in Russian society. In fact, by allowing for a separate organization and role for each of the "camps" of the revolution, "dual power" had enabled these disparate social forces to accept concessions and accommodations in the present while remaining adamant about their respective goals for the future. Thus, the dual structure of power, which reflected the divergence of these goals, was responsible for at least a temporary lessening of the danger of social polarization.

The Mensheviks as Mediators

As might be expected, the tenor of labor relations that prevailed during much of March and April, and particularly the self-restraint demonstrated by the working class, strongly affected the social and political strategies considered by the Mensheviks. Indeed, the Mensheviks were not merely passive observers; they were the active agents of mediation between labor and capital even while they were the architects of long-range strategies for the success of the Russian revolution.

As demonstrated in the earliest articles in *Rabochaia gazeta*, the prevention of an imminent collision between workers and industrialists was the first concern of the Mensheviks on the scene in Petrograd. This concern was shared by at least two groups of Mensheviks whose expectations of the revolution were otherwise significantly different. Most

Menshevik *praktiki* (the party members from the ranks of the intelligentsia who had spent the years from 1907 to 1914 in the daily practical work of building labor organizations) were still anxious that a serious labor conflict would turn the industrialists and their liberal allies once more against "the Democracy," as had been the case in 1905 and 1914. For these *praktiki*, self-restraint on the part of the workers and the soviet would be the best way of preventing a counterrevolutionary backlash among the propertied classes. However, there were also a few Mensheviks in whom a new hope had been born that there were significant groups among the propertied classes that would cooperate with the socialist leaders of the workers to secure Russia's transition to "full democracy." These Mensheviks had participated in the work of the "public organizations" and had watched these organizations struggle against the tsarist bureaucracy, but for them, too, any hopes of success required that potential labor conflicts be curbed. . . .

Whatever their motives for trying to avert an escalation of labor conflicts, the Mensheviks who assumed the leadership of the soviet initially chose the same tactics: drawing the workers into larger organizational frameworks and using the prestige of such organizations, particularly that of the soviet, to press self-restraint upon the workers. While the soviet's Labor Section moved swiftly to establish ties with the factories of Petrograd — helped by the Secretariat of the now defunct Central Labor Group — *Rabochaia gazeta* reminded its readers that the revolution had been a "political revolution" and that what had been destroyed had been the "bastions of political autocracy," while the "foundations of capitalism" remained standing. The workers were urged to limit their demands to the introduction of the "principle of constitutional relations between workers and administration." In other words, they should concentrate on organizational safeguards, even organizational autonomy, but avoid "economic" demands.

Before long, however, their self-assumed role as guardians of the precarious gains already made by the revolution brought the Menshevik *praktiki* in the Labor Section not only into a kind of cautious confrontation with the workers of the capital, but also into conflict with the other mission to which they had dedicated their best years and of which they were justifiably proud, their mission as champions of the Russian working class and its interests. . . .

As a result of their involvement in labor relations, the leaders of the soviet now found their fears dispelled and their hopes raised. First, there was the conciliatory response of so many employers, as well as the declared dedication of Konovalov, the Minister of Trade and Industry, to an extensive program of new labor legislation and cooperation with the soviet. Now, *Rabochaia gazeta* asserted, "one can rest assured that a peaceful solution to the justified and economically realizable demands of the workers will redound to the advantage of the workers, and with less of an inconvenience for society as a whole, than one [wrought] through thoughtless strikes." Second, and even more reassuring, was the moderation and responsibility shown by the workers — the Mensheviks' strategy of curbing "extremism" now seemed vindicated. Moreover, the painful tension between the moderate leaders and a militant constituency, which had threatened the soviet's unity in early March, appeared to have vanished. . . .

The Issue of Coalition

Between early March and early May, then, a major shift occurred in the political strategy advocated by the moderate Marxists in the soviet; the consensus in favor of "dual power," and the relationship of mutual suspicion between the soviet and the Provisional Government both gave way to an emphasis on cooperation with the "progressive bourgeoisie." This cooperation would eventually lead to the formation of a coalition government (on May 3), in which leaders of "the two camps" in Russian society promised to work together for what was believed to be their common goals. While this shift in political strategy was made possible by the confluence of several developments in late April, there can be no doubt that for the majority of Mensheviks, without whose support a coalition government could not have been formed, the best argument was provided by the experience of managing labor relations in Petrograd in March and April. Men like Bogdanov and Gvozdev, who had hoped all along to find support for their goal of economic and political democratization among the Russian entrepreneurial class, were greatly reassured by the generally subdued tenor of labor relations. Moreover, since they were already functioning, in Sukhanov's words, as a "de facto ministry of labor," working in harmony with Konovalov and his Ministry of Trade and Industry, they could see no reason for remaining outside the government. Then, too, their newly found sense of national responsibility demanded such a course, the more so, since enhanced prestige and an increased influence on labor policy could strengthen the moderate, "mature" majority of the working class against the small element of "extremism" that had begun to make itself evident by late April.

Even I. G. Tsereteli, the leader of the new "Revolutionary Defensist" bloc of Mensheviks and Social Revolutionaries that had held the majority in the soviet since late March, viewed labor relations in Petrograd as a vindication of the strategy of "uniting all the vital forces of the country," which he had formulated during the first two weeks of the revolution in his Siberian exile. As if to buttress his faith in the strength of the liberal bourgeoisie and its readiness to establish in Russia a parliamentary democracy with the full complement of social reform, three of the "bourgeois" ministers with jurisdiction over economic affairs — Konovalov of Trade and Industry, M. I. Tereshchenko of Finance, and N. V. Nekrasov of Transportation — indicated growing enthusiasm for collaboration and consultation with the soviet and its leaders on all major policy decisions. Thus could Tsereteli envision the role of the socialist ministers who joined the coalition government on May 3 as being simply one of *"leading* that part of the bourgeoisie that might *follow* on the path to an increasingly decisive policy in both domestic and foreign affairs, while casting aside . . . those who would not." . . .

New Tensions

On the face of it, and in the eyes of the "Revolutionary Defensist" leadership, the workers seemed to be fully supportive of the change of political strategy that had occurred in early May. At the soviet's Workers' Section only a handful of committed Bolsheviks and Anarchists voted in favor of Trotsky's motion of non-confidence in the coalition government, whereas expressions of support for the decision of May 2 came from all sides. Yet the typical resolution drawn up by workers would invariably greet only the socialist ministers. "As long as you, comrades, are in the government," declared the workers of the Russian Telegraph and Telephone Society on March 10, "we are convinced that all its activity is directed toward the further strengthening of the revolution's achievements." Clearly, the workers' confidence and optimism did not rest in their trust of the good will of the "bourgeois ministers," but rather from a sense of the power invested in their representatives in the soviet and the expectation that this power would be used prudently, yet unflinchingly, in the interests of "the Democracy" and the working class. . . .

However, by early May this first and relatively peaceful stage of social relations was nearing its end. On the political front there was the issue of the war. The workers' suspicions of the "bourgeoisie" had been reinforced in late March by the campaign in the non-socialist press to overturn the soviet's endorsement of peace without annexations and to drive a wedge between the soldiers and the workers. Moreover, a turning point of sorts was reached in late April, when Miliukov's defiance of the soviet's peace formula occasioned the first open crisis of the revolution, in which workers and soldiers were arrayed against propertied, "imperialist" Russia. Perhaps of greater relevance to the workers was the rapid economic deterioration — mostly the result of structural weaknesses, but very much exacerbated by the prolonged war — which minimized the opportunity for new economic gains and undermined the very basis of the workers' livelihood. The workers in small shops and in service branches, who were only now trying to duplicate the achievements of the better organized workers, had to fight harder for more meager raises and were often denied any satisfaction, whereas the stronger groups of workers, which would begin a "second wave" of demands in June designed to make up losses in real wages, were met with recriminations by employers who had lost their earlier generosity. By June, all workers would face a growing threat of factory shut-down, due to the sometimes feigned but often real shortages of fuel or raw materials. The economic crisis further aggravated labor relations, heightened old suspicions, and focused the workers' attention on the question of regulating management — the very question on which the commercial-industrial circles were not likely to concede, especially because the coalition cabinet now included the socialist representatives of the soviet. Indeed, it would be the failure of the socialist ministers to overcome this recalcitrance that would finally point out the actual distance that separated their vision of coalition from the expectations entertained by the workers.

Moreover, the economic crisis that had begun to unfold in May, together with the new political arrangement of coalition, would affect the respective attitudes of workers and leaders in profoundly different ways. The workers viewed their employers' resistance to new economic demands and their professed inability to keep the factories running — particularly when coupled with opposition to economic regulation — as clear signs of treachery. If they still felt unable to take on the powerful industrial class or be responsible for the complicated business of production, they were nevertheless determined to use the power of the soviet, and its membership in the government, to defend their earlier achievements and their livelihood.

As for the Mensheviks, the stage of escalated conflict that had begun in May confronted them once again with the frightening prospect of workers' "extremism" and increased their anxiety about bourgeois counterrevolution. Driven to search ever more desperately for that complex of "vital forces" whose unity they strove to guard at all costs, they naturally addressed their appeal for "responsibility" and "self-restraint" to their working-class constituency. Moreover, their urgency was greater now, because the weight of national responsibility, including the conduct of the war, lay so heavily on the shoulders of their colleagues in the cabinet. To the workers, however, these appeals showed, as nothing else had, the chasm that had begun to separate their understanding of the revolutionary tasks of the working class from that on which the Menshevik leaders were acting.

Thus, the new political strategy adopted by the moderate leaders of the soviet in early May, that of coalition, not only coincided with a severe economic crisis and exacerbated its political implications, but also began to divide "the Democracy" into leaders and led. Each of these developments should be viewed as contributing to the outcome of October. Economic deterioration, coupled with the dynamics of the labor struggle (the "second wave" of economic demands in May and June), initiated a process of social polarization that had been largely absent in the first two months of the revolution. The failure of the Provisional Government to deal with the root causes of this crisis — war and economic anarchy — gave political direction to the workers' mounting discontent, further "radicalized" them, and ultimately made them receptive to the Bolshevik slogan of "all power to the soviets." Finally, the presence of the socialist leaders in the cabinet, which had first raised the workers' expectations, made the failings of the Provisional Government more difficult to bear and more unacceptable. Eventually, the refusal of the Menshevik leadership to break with coalition, to abandon the idea of the "unity of the vital forces," compelled the workers, though much later and with great anguish, to give their support to a new leadership — that of the Bolsheviks.

In retrospect, the general optimism born of the early phase of labor relations appears to have been exaggerated because it equated the modest achievements of the moment with the ambitious goals of social progress, economic advance, and a modicum of national unity. Similarly, the fears and hostilities that grew steadily from May onward appear to have resulted, initially at least, as much from bitter disappointment as from actual danger. Clearly, the responses of both Mensheviks and workers — and the response of the industrialists, as well — to the crises of the revolution were strongly colored by their earlier revolutionary experiences. Indeed, Menshevik tactics in both phases, though different, were informed by the party's main lessons from 1905 and 1914 — that is, that the fate of the Russian revolution depended on a measure of cooperation between the working class and at least some of the educated groups of society (be they Tsereteli's fairly broad "vital forces of the nation" or Dan's more limited "democratic forces" or even Iu. O. Martov's narrower "socialist forces"). If this belief left the Mensheviks ill-suited to lead the workers during the heightened social conflict of the summer and fall of 1917, it should also be credited with having guided their earlier sponsorship of "dual power" and their mediation of labor conflicts — the twin policies that secured for the Mensheviks, however briefly, their position as the leaders of Russia's "Democracy" and as the arbiters of its fragile national unity.

Irakli Tsereteli

The April Crisis

No figure in the revolution has been as greatly underestimated as the Georgian Menshevik Irakli Tsereteli (1881–1959). The son of a prominent Georgian intellectual, Tsereteli was elected a Social Democratic deputy to the Second State Duma in 1907. Arrested along with the other Social Democrats when the Duma was dismissed, Tsereteli spent the next decade in prison and exile. On his return to Petrograd he immediately became the

From Irakli Tsereteli, "Reminiscences of the February Revolution—the April Crisis," in *The Russian Revolution of 1917: Contemporary Accounts*, ed. by Dimitri von Mohrenschildt. Oxford University Press, 1971, excerpts from pp. 146–170.

most prominent Menshevik spokesman, the architect of the policy of "revolutionary defensism," and the force behind the efforts to work together with the middle classes. After the fall of the independent Georgian republic in 1921, Tsereteli lived in France and the United States. His memoirs, *Vospominaniia o fevral'skoi revoliutsii* (Memoirs of the February Revolution) (1963), are an extraordinary description of the politics of the period from February to July 1917. In this excerpt Tsereteli discusses the collapse of the first Provisional Government and the formation of the coalition.

On April 19 the long-awaited notification by Prince Lvov, addressed to me, at last reached the Tavrichesky Palace. I opened the envelope in the presence of Chkheidze, Skobelev, Dan, and several other members of the [Executive] Committee [of the Petrograd Soviet], and read out the text to them. We were stunned by what it contained.

The message apprised us that the Minister of Foreign Affairs [Miliukov] had directed our ambassadors accredited to allied powers to communicate the text of the address "to the citizens" [of Russia] of March 27 to the respective governments. The "address," however, was supplemented with a commentary to the effect that "the general principles stated by the Provisional Government (in its "address to the people of the world") were in full accord with the lofty ideas constantly voiced by many prominent statesmen of the allied powers," and that the Provisional Government "having abiding confidence in the victorious completion of the present war in full accord with the Allies, was firmly convinced that the problems raised by this war would be solved in such a spirit as to lay solid foundations for a lasting peace, and that the progressive democracies of the world, inspired by the same ideals, would find a way to establish the guarantees and the sanctions necessary to prevent new bloody conflicts in the future."

To understand the effect of this note upon us, one has to conjure up the atmosphere of the revolutionary Russia of those days and the campaign then conducted by the Soviet democracy. In our appeals to the socialist parties of the world, in our press, in our resolutions and speeches addressed to the people and the army, we constantly emphasized that the declaration of the Provisional Government of March 27 was the first act, since the beginning of the war, by which one of the belligerent powers renounced all imperialistic war aims. We never tired of urging the public opinion of the democratic countries to support our initiative and to compel their own governments to repudiate imperialistic aims and to work out a new platform for a general democratic peace. It was for these reasons that we had insisted on a formal note to communicate the declaration of March 27 to the Allies.

A fight against this policy of a democratic peace was being waged, both in Russia and abroad, under slogans "war to the victorious end" or "war till the establishment of sanctions and guarantees" imposed on the defeated enemy. And now, in a note ostensibly intended to elucidate the meaning of the act of March 27, Miliukov declared these very slogans, abhorrent to the revolutionary democracy, to be those of the Provisional Government! And this note, which was nothing but a repudiation of the basic principles of the Soviets' foreign policy, was being presented to the revolutionary democracy as a compliance with its request.

The worst of it was that the note had already been dispatched, and the text had been given to the press.

If Miliukov had consciously striven to cause a rift between the Soviets and the government, he could not have used a better method than this document. This was the impression of all those present. Amazement and indignation were shared by all. Chkheidze said nothing for a long while, listening to the angry exclamations of the others. Then he turned to me and said in a low voice, with the accent of deep conviction: "Miliukov is the evil genius of the Revolution."

The news that the text of the note had been received, quickly spread through the Tavrichesky Palace, and members of the Executive Committee dropped in, one after another, to acquaint themselves with the message. Before the opening of the session a kind of improvised conference of those who were present took place. In an animated exchange of opinions not only the members of the left-wing opposition but also some of the majority characterized the note as a provocation, an act of defiance. Feelings were running high. Skobelev, myself, and some others tried in vain to soothe the rising passions. Eager to hear some reassuring information, Bramson asked me whether in my opinion, based on my experience in negotiating with the government, the note had been phrased as it was on purpose, in order to disavow the policy of the Soviet democracy.

To this I replied that, in my judgment, the only member of the government actually intent on opposing a government foreign policy to that of the Soviets, was Miliukov. As for the majority of the ministers, they had, in all our negotiations, displayed the desire to establish a line of conduct in harmony with ours. This being the case, I said, I can explain the adoption of this text by the government only as an act of amazing thoughtlessness on the part of the majority of its members. Very likely Miliukov, with his usual insistence, had kept hammering on the theme that his consent to communicate to the Allies the declaration of March 27 in a formal note was already an enormous concession to Soviet democracy, in which he had acquiesced with great reluctance; and probably as a compensation for this concession he had obtained the assent of the others to the inclusion of his commentary. The other ministers may have assumed that the gratification of our desire to have the "Address" transmitted to the Allies would make us ready to accept the accompanying commentary, to which they apparently had failed to give their close attention.

"All these misunderstandings," said one of the left-wing members of the Executive Committee, "are only possible because we fail to use our full voice in talking to the government. Why has the contact commission failed up to now to urge the government to submit to the Allies the issue of a democratic peace as it was formulated by the Soviet manifesto of March 14?"

"I understand your displeasure with the note," replied Skobelev. "Still, we should not run to extremes. When the Soviet was drawing up its Manifesto, it had to consider only the Russian Revolution, the Russian wide-gauge track. The government, on the other hand, in addressing itself to foreign governments through diplomatic channels, has to keep in mind the conditions in foreign countries, the foreign narrow-gauge track. The cause of a general peace encounters obstacles in the public opinion of these countries, obstacles the Russian Revolution will have to overcome gradually, step by step, if it wants to avoid a collapse. What we find unacceptable in Miliukov's note is not the consideration of existing difficulties but the fact that these difficulties are used as a pretext to substitute the imperialistic slogans for those of the Russian Revolution."

By then most members of the Executive Committee had arrived, and Chkheidze opened the meeting in an atmosphere of extreme tension.

The excitement was due to the awareness that a crisis was imminent. There were no differences of opinion with regard to the note. All were agreed that it could not be accepted by the Executive Committee as satisfactory. The debate, therefore, centered on the question of ways and means to solve the conflict.

At that time the spokesmen for the left-wing opposition were still the Internationalists, to whom the Bolshevik fraction of the Executive Committee [readily] left the initiative of extremist proposals. The Internationalist Yurenev now took the floor to deliver a forceful speech. He insisted that the note had exposed the utter uselessness of negotiations with the government; now was the time for the masses to step in; an appeal to the masses should be our reply to the provocation of the government. Mass action alone would reveal to the government and to the whole world the true will of the Russian Revolution.

Shliapnikov, then a left-wing Bolshevik, also insisted on an appeal to the masses. His spiteful comments on Miliukov and the whole Provisional Government were marked by a deep-rooted class hatred of the bourgeoisie.

But even among the leading majority of the Executive Committee the resentment was so great that some of its members could see no other way out than to call on the masses to demonstrate against the government. Bogdanov [a Menshevik member], normally even-tempered and unruffled, yet capable of impulsive speech and action under stress, was beside himself with rage. Miliukov's note, he said, strikes a blow first of all against us, the representatives of the majority of the Executive Committee. Direct negotiations between the Executive Committee and the Provisional Government have no longer any justification. The time has come for the masses to go into action. Their appearance on the scene is the only thing that would have any real influence on the government.

Members of the Labor Group (Trudoviki) Stankevich and Bramson tried to soothe the storm. There was no need, they said, to exaggerate the importance of the accompanying note. After all, the full text of the declaration of March 27, which contained the repudiation of imperialistic war aims, had been officially communicated to the allied governments. Those acquainted with the situation inside the government realize that Miliukov's commentary was but another of his misplaced stratagems and in no way reflected the views of the government as a whole. Bramson pointed out that even Miliukov's best friends regarded him as a "genius of tactlessness." Was it permissible, because of the tactlessness of a single minister, to gamble with the fate of the national Revolution?

Kamenev, who better than Shliapnikov represented the then dominant tactics of the Bolshevik organization, made a plain attempt to
release the Bolsheviks from the responsibility for an eventual call to the
masses. Miliukov's note, he said, only served to confirm what the
Bolshevik party had maintained all along: that not a democratic peace
but "war to the victorious end" was the true slogan of the bourgeoisie.
Miliukov and his colleagues were representatives of that class and unable to carry out a different policy. An anti-imperialist policy could be
put into effect only after the removal of the present government and
its replacement by a government of the revolutionary democracy. The
Executive Committee was opposed to this. If some of its members were
now supporting an appeal to the masses, they were doing this with the
purpose to compel a bourgeois government to carry out policies alien to
it. The Bolsheviks had no such illusions. However, should a majority of
the Executive Committee decide in favor of such an appeal, the Bolsheviks would support it in a body, since street demonstrations are the
best school for the political education of the masses and the best method
to pave the way for the replacement of the bourgeois government by one
of the revolutionary democracy.

Of the members of the contact commission, Chernov and
Sukhanov were absent. On behalf of the three members present,
Chkheidze, Skobelev, and myself, I declared that, in principle, there
could be no disagreement about the evaluation of the note; it was a clear
violation of the agreement which had made possible our cooperation in
foreign policy with the government. The government ought to give us
some tangible satisfaction, to show to the nation and to the world that its
foreign policy still followed the line laid down by the declaration of
March 27 and not that of Miliukov's accompanying note.

Yet as regards the appeal to the masses, I went on, we disagree not
only with the Bolsheviks, who plan to use street demonstrations for their
propaganda ends, but also with those among our comrades who have no
intention to overthrow the government yet are willing to urge the
masses to fight against it. In the present tense and emotional atmosphere it is not difficult to arouse the masses against the government; yet
it is very doubtful whether these energies once released could be kept
under control and from developing into a civil war. Soviet democracy is
certainly strong enough to overthrow the government; yet it possesses
neither enough solid influence with all circles of the population nor
enough trained democratic cadres to organize on its own a government

that would be indisputably recognized by the majority of the nation and would be able to ensure the fulfillment of the pressing economic and political needs of the country.

This is the situation, I continued, and it compels us to act with caution. Even more so it compels the Provisional Government to proceed cautiously, since it knows that without the support of the Soviets it cannot exist. This being so, we have every reason to presume that even without calling the masses into action we shall be able to make the government comply with the demands we are going to submit to it.

For all these reasons I proposed that, before issuing an appeal to the masses, we attempt to settle the conflict through new negotiations with the government. This proposition, supported by Dan [Menshevik] and Gots [a Socialist Revolutionary], was adopted by the majority.

Nevertheless, the conflict with the government had come to a head, and the consequences of this fact soon became manifest. . . .

During the April demonstrations the chief task of the authorities, the restoration of order, had been performed not by the government but by the Soviet. And to achieve this end, the Soviet had had to resort to extraordinary measures which involved the assumption of certain functions of the executive power.

So long as the crisis lasted and only the energetic action by the Executive Committee appeared able to check the street fighting that might have developed into a civil war, the intrusion of the Soviet into the functions of the government, far from being denounced, was generally welcomed by public opinion and by the Provisional Government itself. As soon as the conflict was settled, however, the problem of strengthening the government was more urgent than ever before.

Even before the April events public opinion had been watching with growing anxiety the increasingly frequent outbreaks of violence and lawlessness in many parts of the vast country already deeply disturbed by the Revolution. In all such cases, whether it was a matter of Anarchists seizing a printing shop, of a military unit refusing to obey orders, or of some provincial committee deciding to declare itself an independent revolutionary authority, the government usually had recourse to the Soviet as an intermediary, relying on this authoritative democratic organization to restore order through moral pressure. Yet, while public opinion prior to the April crisis, had more or less acquiesced in such a situation, accounting for it by the reluctance of the government to use coercion without extreme necessity, now, after the events had exposed the government's impotence, every new manifestation of lawlessness caused a deep sense of alarm. The creation of a strong central power was now demanded by people of every political persuasion.

The democratic section of public opinion regarded a closer bond between the government and the democratic organizations, together with a better coordination between its policies and the aspirations of the revolutionary democracy, as the best way to strengthen the government. Accordingly, a considerable part of this democratic public opinion now demanded, with growing insistency, that the Executive Committee participate in the government.

This trend was strongest in the army organizations. On April 23, at the Tavrichesky Palace, a meeting was organized, composed of delegates from regimental and battalion committees of the Petrograd garrison, to discuss the issue of the attitude to be taken towards the Provisional Government. Bogdanov, addressing the assembly on behalf of the Executive Committee, informed the audience of the settlement of the conflict and of the decision of the Executive Committee to resume its former relationship with the Provisional Government. Yet despite the high prestige of the Executive Committee among the delegates, the majority of the speakers recommended that the former policy be replaced by one of direct participation in the government. A resolution was adopted, expressing the wish "that the Executive Committee submit the problem of the relations between the democracy and the Provisional Government to the assemblies of workers and soldiers for discussion, and that the Executive Committee formulate its opinion regarding the formation of a coalition Cabinet."

This resolution reflected the frame of mind of a large element of the democracy. From every part of the country and of the front, from army organizations and peasants' soviets, a flood of letters and telegrams poured into the Executive Committee, all voicing the desire for a coalition government. Some of the frontline and peasants' organizations went so far as to send special delegations to present this demand to the Executive Committee. This campaign found a favorable response inside the Executive Committee, not only among the Laborites (Trudoviki) and the People's Socialists, who all along had advocated coalition, but also among the Socialist Revolutionaries.

The Provisional Government, on the other hand, was showered with similar demands for the formation of a coalition government, coming from left-wing bourgeois groups, local self-government agencies, the liberal intelligentsia, the civil service, and the officer body.

Once, during those days, I was stopped in the lobby of the Tavrichesky Palace by V. N. Lvov, Procurator of the Holy Synod. He was smiling benignly and seemed greatly pleased by the change in the public mood. Ever since the beginning of the Revolution, he told me, he had advocated the inclusion of Soviet representatives in the government. "Up to now," he said, "you have opposed it. However, the matter can no longer be postponed. It is impossible to govern Russia without the Soviet democracy. Today this is generally understood. Yesterday some young officers from the staff of the Petrograd military district called on us at the Mariinsky Palace and urged us to accept any compromise, provided the Soviets help us to maintain discipline in the army and in the rear. They don't want Guchkov, they don't want Miliukov, all they want is a government enjoying the confidence of the nation. We in the government," continued Lvov, "feel the same way. Come to us with your program, it makes sense, we accept it. But you must join us in the government."

V. N. Lvov went on in that vein for a long time, and from his words it became apparent that Guchkov and Miliukov, who both were opposed to a closer tie with the Soviet, were completely isolated in the government. Listening to him, I recalled a remark once made about him by Prince Lvov in conversation with Skobelev and myself: "V. N. Lvov does not rack his brains about program issues," Prince Lvov had said with a twinkle in his eye, "but he is very useful to the government. He is the most sociable of men, with an extraordinary range of connections. He has an infallible flair for the trends of public opinion."

V. N. Lvov, indeed, reflected the sentiments of the man in the street like a barometer.

However, the temper of the right section of public opinion was vastly different.

The right-wing bourgeoisie used the anxiety caused by the April events as a starting point for a political attack on the Soviet. For the first time since the beginning of the Revolution, these circles thought the moment opportune for an open, large-scale, organized campaign to provoke a rift between the government and the Soviet. Dismayed not only by the weakness of the government but also by the general direction of its domestic and foreign policies pursued in agreement with the

Soviet, these elements, under the guise of opposition to a "diarchy," demanded the elimination of any kind of political control over the Provisional Government. The disorganization of the national life, resulting from a devastating war and the collapse of the old order, they attributed solely to the influence of the Soviet democracy, which they also held accountable for the general yearning for peace, both at the front and in the rear. To counteract the policy of cooperation with the Soviet, these groups, led by the Committee of the Imperial Duma, advocated, as a means of strengthening the government, the adoption by the latter of the program of the rightist bourgeoisie with its militant slogan of "war to the victorious end."

In conformity with this point of view, a prominent member of the Cadet Party, Professor Kokoshkin, submitted to the government the draft of an "Address to the Country," in which the government was to ascribe to the Soviet responsibility for the crisis and was to solicit support, in the administration of the country, from the social elements not connected with the Soviet democracy.

This proposition was vigorously opposed by the majority of the ministers. Not only Kerensky, Nekrasov, and Tereshchenko, who represented the left wing of the Provisional Government, but also Prince Lvov, supported by Konovalov, V. N. Lvov, and Godnev, refused to break with the Soviet democracy. Nekrasov, who kept me informed about the situation inside the government, told me that even the Cadet ministers closest to Miliukov, Manuilov, and Shingaryov, objected to this version of an address to the nation which meant a rupture with the democratic organizations born of the Revolution.

The coming governmental crisis came into the open with the publication, on April 26, of the official version of the "Address of the Provisional Government to the Country." It declared that the Provisional Government had decided to seek a solution of the crisis, as desired by democratic public opinion, by inviting representatives of the Soviet to join the government.

I shall quote here a few passages of this "Address," vividly reflecting the moral atmosphere of that first period of the Revolution. The "Address" began with the enumeration of all the acts of the government in the domestic and foreign fields undertaken in agreement with the Soviet democracy. Next came the following description of the administrative methods applied by the first government of revolutionary Russia:

> *Called into life by a great national movement, the Provisional Government regards itself as the executor and guardian of the people's will. It bases the administration of the state not on force and coercion but on the voluntary obedience of free citizens to the authority created by them. It relies not on physical but on moral force. Ever since the Provisional Government has been established in power, it has not once deviated from these principles. Not a single drop of the people's blood has been shed through its fault, nor has it set up forcible obstacles to any trend of public thought.*

This benign, idealistic faith in the possibility of replacing the coercive functions of power by moral persuasion was characteristic of the initial period of the Revolution, and even the right-wing elements did not reject it at the time. The February upheaval had been christened "the bloodless revolution," and all new Russia took pride in the fact that the downfall of the centuries-old tsarist order had been so painless, without the streams of blood that had accompanied all former revolutions. Not only the socialists but also the bourgeois democracy cherished the hope that a democracy would be able to govern the nation without recourse to the repressive measures identified in the public mind with the tyrannical methods of the past, now loathed by all. For the time being even the rightists had reconciled themselves to this attitude, all the more so because this position of the new authorities had saved the representatives of the old regime, now in the hands of the government, from stern retaliation. . . .

The "Address" was received with notable approval by the greater part of the public. Within the majority of the Executive Committee opinions varied regarding the expediency of joining the government: the Socialist Revolutionaries were in favor of it, the Social Democrats were against. There was agreement, however, about the necessity to respond to the government's step with an expression of confidence and with actions intended to strengthen its authority.

Within the Cadet Party the differences of opinion were more substantial. While the Moscow City Council, on the motion of its Cadet members led by Astrov, went on record in favor of a coalition government, the newspaper *Rech*, inspired by Miliukov, warned against illusions about a coalition: "It is quite possible," wrote the Cadet organ, "that the disease requires a more radical treatment," implying with these words a break with the Soviets and the formation of a strong dictatorial power based on the propertied classes.

This rightist trend found its most effective expression the day after the publication of the "Address," at the anniversary meeting of the Imperial Duma.

The 27th of April was the eleventh anniversary of the convocation of the First Duma. The Committee of the Imperial Duma, headed by the president of the Fourth Duma, Rodzianko, decided to celebrate the day by a solemn meeting of members of the four Dumas at the Tavrichesky Palace, in the "White Hall," former assembly room of the Duma. The declared purpose of the meeting was the discussion of the national issues brought to the fore by the crisis. At the same time the organizers of the anniversary meeting wished to remind the country of the Duma and of the part it had played in the overthrow of tsarism. The public reaction to this would enable them to estimate whether there was a chance that a resurrected Duma — with a bourgeois majority — might become an authoritative permanent organ, to exercise political control over the government in place of the Soviet.

The meeting, coinciding with a moment of general anxiety, aroused keen interest both in the country and beyond its borders. The Provisional Government, led by Prince Lvov, as well as representatives of allied and neutral powers were present. The Executive Committee attended in a body, occupying the box of the Imperial Council. The visitors' gallery was crowded to overflowing, mostly with members of the Petrograd Soviet.

Rodzianko was in the chair. He opened the session with a program speech in which he described the role of the Duma in the overthrow of the old regime and the establishment of the new democratic system. Underscoring in this way the solidarity of the Duma with the Revolution and avoiding any direct criticism of the Soviet, he yet emphasized two basic points on which there was a divergence of opinion between the rightist groups and the Soviets. In foreign policy, he repudiated the campaign for a democratic peace in favor of the old slogan of war to the end, "until full victory over German militarism." In the domestic field, Rodzianko demanded that the Provisional Government be freed from any political control over it: "The country must give its full confidence and voluntary obedience to the single power it has created and which for that reason it has to trust. Active interference in the decisions of the government is inadmissible. The Provisional Government will be unable to fulfill its functions unless it has at its disposal all the might and strength of the supreme power in the state."

These two salient points: the endowment of the Provisional Government with the fullness of power and the restoration of the old war aims, were the recurring theme of all the right-wing speakers at the meeting. They avoided outright polemics against the Soviet democracy; yet the gist of all their speeches was the contention that the salvation of the country was dependent on the elimination of the influence of the Soviet democracy on policy-making, especially in the field of foreign affairs.

The address of Prince Lvov, who spoke on behalf of the Provisional Government, revealed a very different frame of mind. With great political tact he abstained from putting before the assembly the issue of the governmental crisis, which had been so forcefully and candidly expounded in the Government's "Address to the Country" the day before. Prince Lvov spoke of the spiritual essence of the Russian Revolution and made it unequivocally clear that the government of revolutionary Russia would not seek the salvation of the country in the methods recommended by the rightist speakers. With particular force he defended, in the terms of the Slavophile philosophy close to his heart, the orientation of the foreign policy towards a general democratic peace. . . .

The speech of Prince Lvov, obviously intended to stress the inner accord between the policies of the government and the aspirations of the Soviet democracy, had no effect whatever on the right-wing speakers who followed him. Only when speaking of the past, of the Duma's opposition to the old regime, of its part in the February events, and of the first days of the Revolution, did they sound conciliatory notes towards the Revolution. But as soon as the acknowledged leaders of the Duma, Rodichev, Shulgin, Guchkov, and others, touched upon current policies, all the fire of their eloquence was directed against the revolutionary democracy. The culminating point of their attack on the Soviet's policies was the speech by Shulgin.

Shulgin was one of the most eminent and original orators of the Duma. Speaking, now with wistful lyricism, now with irony and restrained passion, he recounted how, under the effect of the defeat of 1915 and the manifest inability of the old system to cope with the situation, he and some other rightist Duma members had sought a rapprochement with the opposition and, together with the whole body of the Duma, had taken part in the overthrow of the old order. "We cannot disavow the Revolution," he said, "we are linked with it, we are welded to it, and for this we bear the moral responsibility." Yet these admissions were made only to give stronger emphasis to the "grievous doubts" with which Shulgin and his friends regarded the system that had emerged from the Revolution. "Despite all the achievements of Russia in these two months," he continued, "the question arises whether Germany may not have made the greater gains. Why is this so? What are the reasons for it? For one thing, the honest and talented government, which we should like to see invested with the plenitude of power, is in reality powerless because it is treated with suspicion. A sentry stationed to watch it was instructed: 'Look out, these are bourgeois, keep a sharp eye on them, and if anything happens, you know your regulations.' Gentlemen, on the 20th of April you had occasion to see for yourselves that the sentry knows his regulations and performs his duty faithfully. Yet it is questionable whether those who have assigned the sentry to his post have done right."

In the same sarcastic, impersonal way, without naming the Soviets directly, Shulgin subjected to ruthless criticism the whole system of the mutual relationship between the government and the Soviet and intimated that the Soviet influence was a source of anarchy and would finally wreck the state. He listed various features of the Soviet foreign and domestic policy, presenting them in an utterly distorted form. Parodying Miliukov's famous speech against Stürmer and the Tsarina, he asked after each of his charges against the Soviets, "what is it, stupidity or treason?" He gave the answer himself: "Each of these actions taken separately is an act of stupidity, but taken all together they add up to treason.". . .

When I interrupted Shulgin from the floor to ask to whom he was directing his accusations, he still did not name the Soviets but referred to "people from the Petrogradskaya Side"[1] acting "under the label of Lenin."

At that moment, however, his assertions were wrong even with respect to Lenin, since the latter, aware of the general hostility to him in the ranks of the revolutionary democracy, had been compelled to disclaim the idea of a separate peace and was still hesitating to incite the

---

[1] One of the main sections of Petrograd in which was located the villa of the well-known ballerina Kshesinskaya. This spacious villa was seized by the Bolsheviks at the beginning of the Revolution and became the headquarters of the Bolshevik Party.

masses to violence, waiting for the time when the majority of the democracy would be won over to the principle of dictatorship.

Yet these circumstances had no significance for Shulgin. Actually he aimed his arrows above Lenin's head at the foe he considered most dangerous, the democracy. After all, Lenin was only preaching dictatorship, while the Soviet democracy, as Shulgin and his set saw it, was already practicing dictatorship in what seemed to them the worst possible form.

Shulgin's vivid and forceful speech, interpreted by the audience precisely in this sense, made a strong impression. The majority of the deputies and a part of the public in the gallery gave him a prolonged, tumultuous ovation.

I took the floor immediately after Shulgin, and my appearance on the rostrum was used by the leftist sector of the Duma and the democratically minded public in the boxes and the gallery to give an even more enthusiastic ovation for the Soviet democracy.

To show how we put our case against the right-wing bourgeoisie before the nation, I shall quote here the essential passages from the stenographic record of my speech:

> . . . *The Soviet stands for control over the Provisional Government because, as a powerful democratic organization, it expresses the yearnings of the broad masses of the population: the working class, the revolutionary army, and the peasantry. The position of the Provisional Government would have been immensely difficult, and at the moment of the Revolution it would have been unable to cope with its task, were it not for this control, were it not for this contact with the democratic elements. (Applause.) The member of the Duma, Shulgin, has said: "You are telling the people — these are bourgeois, keep them under suspicion." There is some truth in this sentence. We do tell the people: "these are bourgeois, this is the responsible organ of the bourgeoisie, the Provisional Government; but to this we add: this is that organ of the bourgeoisie, these are those representatives of the bourgeoisie who have accepted a general democratic platform, who have agreed to defend Russian freedom together with the entire democracy and have decided to make common cause with the democracy." (Stormy applause.)*
>
> *Gentlemen, when we survey the work of the four Imperial Dumas, we note one common feature, their impotence, their utter helplessness in the field of constructive statesmanship, a helplessness to which Deputy Shulgin has called attention. Many have tried to lay a finger on the cause of that impotence. There were frictions, they have said, differences*

of opinion. Of course, there were differences in the Duma; they reflected the differences in the nation, and these differences have been a cause of the failure of all previous revolutionary attempts. But, gentlemen, I wish to call your attention to the following: the left-wing section representing the democracy, the proletariat, and the revolutionary peasantry, that section knew how to combine its class interests with a general democratic platform acceptable to the whole nation, and it has called the bourgeoisie to take its stand on the common democratic platform. And if the bourgeoisie at first failed to respond to this call, it was not because this step would have required it to renounce its class interests, no, it only required it to realize these interests by revolutionary means. Today, in the brilliant light of the Russian Revolution, it has become manifest that this platform is the only one capable of rallying all the live forces of the nation. And so, gentlemen, all the aims of the Russian Revolution, and even its very fate, are dependent on whether the propertied classes will understand that this is a national platform and not one of the proletariat alone. The proletariat, to be sure, has its own ultimate class aims, yet for the sake of the common democratic platform, for which the conditions are already ripe, it abstains for the present from the realization of its own ultimate class aims. Will the propertied classes be able to rise to this level? Will they be able to renounce their narrow group interests and take their stand on the common national democratic platform? (Applause.)

From this general standpoint I dealt with all the questions raised by Shulgin.

Concerning the agrarian violence and the land seizures by the peasants, which Shulgin, without naming the Soviets, had nevertheless attributed to the influence of Soviet agitators, I reminded the audience that the demand for the transfer of the land to the peasantry was by no means a partisan-socialist demand of the Soviets but a national claim of long standing, raised by the Russian democracy whenever it had had the opportunity to speak out freely. While pressing this demand, I said, the Soviets were using their immense authority to impress on the peasants the necessity to carry out this radical land reform in an organized way, through a decision of the Constituent Assembly and not through illegal seizures. Only in the cases of landowners refusing to sow their fields, did the Soviets call for extraordinary measures accomplished not in an arbitrary way, but in full accord with the agencies of the government and the organs of the democracy.

As for the peace campaign which, according to Shulgin, was the primary cause of the disintegration of the army, I reminded the assembly that this campaign was being conducted in agreement with the army organizations which were the sole factor holding the army together since the collapse of the old order. I pointed out that given the general longing for peace, the fighting capacity and discipline of the army that we were striving to strengthen could be maintained only if the troops could be convinced that the government was doing everything in its power to bring closer the conclusion of a general democratic peace. . . .

I told Shulgin that his own position on the main issues of foreign and domestic policy was evidence neither of stupidity nor of treason, but of narrow vision, limited by class prejudice, which prevented him from realizing that propaganda against the democracy was the surest way to strengthen Lenin and his party.

I went on to say, alluding to Lenin's behavior during the April events, that Shulgin's allegation that Lenin had been inciting violence was false. I said:

> *Lenin conducts a campaign based on ideas and principles, and his propaganda feeds on the irresponsible public utterances of Deputy Shulgin and many others from among the so-called moderate propertied elements. This, of course, makes a certain section of the democracy despair of the possibility of an understanding with the bourgeoisie. Lenin's platform is this: Since there exists such a trend in the ranks of the bourgeoisie, since the bourgeoisie is unable to understand the general national exigencies of the moment, it should be eliminated, and the Soviet of Workers' and Soldiers' Deputies should assume the full power. You may dispute Lenin, you may disagree with him. I myself disagree with him since I am deeply convinced that the ideas of Deputy Shulgin cannot be those of the Russian Bourgeoisie. But if I did believe for a moment that these ideas are shared by the entire propertied class, I should have said that there is no other way in Russia to save the conquests of the national revolution than the desperate attempt to proclaim at once the dictatorship of the proletariat and the peasantry. For it is these ideas that involve the only real threat of a civil war. If they should triumph within the Provisional Government, this would be the signal for a civil war.*

I concluded with the expression of my faith that the victory and the consolidation of the all-national revolution in Russia would awaken the forces of a democratic revolution in the whole world:

In my opinion, citizens, members of the Imperial Duma, the present meeting should not create the impression that there is confusion in the ranks of the bourgeoisie, that there is vacillation, that there is a conspiracy in the ranks of the bourgeoisie with the purpose of driving the Provisional Government to irresponsible acts, for I maintain that this would be the first step toward wrecking the Russian Revolution, and wrecking the country itself. Let the Provisional Government continue on the road of understanding it has chosen; let it pursue the ideals of democracy with increased determination, both in its internal and in its foreign policy. If it does this, the democracy will support this revolutionary Provisional Government with the whole strength and weight of its authority, and in a concerted effort of all the live forces of the nation we shall carry our revolution to completion and maybe spread it to the whole world. (Stormy applause at the left and in the center.)

I have never cherished any illusions regarding my oratorical gifts. In the Duma the flower of the Russian intelligentsia was represented, and many of its members in the audience, had, of course, a greater mastery of the spoken word than I. Nonetheless a truthful account of what the revolutionary democracy was striving for and was doing in order to save the country made a stronger impression on the audience than the well-polished oratory of the speakers who opposed our point of view. It is for this reason that my speech called forth quite an unusual ovation, from not only the left-wing section of the Duma, the members of the Executive Committee, and the Soviet, but also from many of that part of the audience which had cheered Shulgin. Rightist Duma members whom I did not know were coming up to me to shake hands. The next day, a bourgeois newspaper with a wide circulation, the *Russkaya Volya*, devoted an editorial to my speech, expressing the view that the salvation of Russia should be sought not in the course of action advocated by the rightist speakers but in that pursued by the leading majority of the Executive Committee.

Let me note, however, two harshly critical comments on my speech. One came from the American Consul, Winship. In a report to the Secretary of State on the anniversary meeting of the Duma, he denounced my views on foreign policy and voiced the opinion that the "sectarian spirit and fanaticism" of the socialists, which he saw reflected in my "fervent defense of Lenin," represented "the greatest danger to Russia at the present moment." "Tsereteli" wrote the American

Mint Employees Demonstrate, May Day, 1917. These government workers, employees of the state mint, participated in the May Day demonstrations that involved hundreds of thousands of people. The banners say "Long Live International Workers Day" and "Long Live Socialism." (Sovfoto)

Consul, "had often delivered fiery speeches against Lenin and his ideas in the Soviet of Workers' and Soldiers' Deputies, yet he proved ready to defend Lenin's cause against the spokesman of the bourgeoisie."

The other sharp criticism, for opposite motives, came from Lenin himself. In an article entitled "I. G. Tsereteli and the Class Struggle," Lenin argued that in assenting to an agreement with a part of the bourgeoisie I had abandoned the principle of class struggle, and in characterizing the dictatorship of the proletariat and the peasantry as a "desperate attempt" I had betrayed the principles of democracy. . . .

This first open attack on the Soviets by the right-wing bourgeoisie did not find the sympathetic public response expected by those who initiated it. Of the two political flanks, the wealthy bourgeoisie on the one side and the Soviet democracy on the other, the middle classes still overwhelmingly preferred the Soviets.

The general interest of the nation continued to be centered on the problem of a reorganization of the government that would ensure for it the greatest possible support by the Soviet democracy.

The position of Kerensky within the government had become very difficult. During the April events he had remained in the background, being unable either to prevent or to mitigate the conflict between the government and the Soviet democracy.

Now, with the other left-wing members of the government, he favored the formation of a coalition and he informed the leaders of the Socialist Revolutionary Party, Chernov and Gots, that he was determined to resign unless the coalition were put into effect.

On the day the government's "Address to the Country" was published, Kerensky issued a letter, composed for him by Chernov, in which he declared that, having joined the government on his own responsibility, in order to serve as a connecting link between the government and the democracy of the laboring classes, he no longer could remain in the government without a formal mandate. The national situation, he wrote, had become so complicated, and the forces of the organized labor democracy had grown to such an extent, that this democracy might no longer be able to avoid responsible participation in the government of the country.

During the first months of the February Revolution, Kerensky had enjoyed an immense, giddy popularity. In the Fourth Duma, he had been the leader of the small group of Laborites (Trudoviki) but after the Revolution he declared that he always considered himself a member of the Socialist Revolutionary Party. At the decisive moment of the Revolution, when the rebellious regiments were marching to the Duma, Kerensky, with characteristic impulsiveness, was instantly fired with such a faith in the victory of the Revolution that he went out to meet the soldiers and declared his solidarity with them in the name of the Duma. He was elected vice-chairman of the Petrograd Soviet and was regarded by the rank and file of the soldiers as closely connected with the Soviet and with a socialist party. Actually, though nominally a member of the Socialist Revolutionary Party, he was by nature a nonpartisan individualist. In his views he was less close to the socialists than to the democratic intelligentsia on the borderline between the socialist and the bourgeois democracy. In the excited atmosphere of the Revolution, his speeches, rather vague, yet echoing the thoughts and feelings of both these groups, aroused a strong enthusiasm at the mass meetings of the soldiers as well as among the plain people outside the Soviets.

Kerensky had the ambition of being a national figure above the parties. It is a curious fact that this man, whose name became the synonym of a weak, spineless government, had a pronounced personal predilection for the exercise of strong, commanding power. Had this tendency been combined with strength of character and organizing ability, he might have played a much more substantial and constructive part in the Revolution than the one he actually performed.

The members of the Executive Committee did not regard him as quite one of themselves. He liked gestures calculated for effect and intended to show his independence of the organization to which he nominally belonged. In his capacity as Minister of Justice, for instance, he released General Ivanov from prison, who in the first days of the Revolution had attempted to lead the troops under his command against Petrograd. When he was denounced for this in the Executive Committee, Kerensky, instead of taking the matter up with this leading organ of the Soviet and explaining his motives, suddenly put in an appearance at a plenary session of the Soldiers' section of the Soviet and delivered a hysterical speech before this mass audience . He spoke of his devotion to the Revolution, of how he had "led the revolutionary regiments to the Duma," of the unjustified criticism directed at him, which he was not going to tolerate, and so on. The audience, uninformed about the whole matter, listened to him sympathetically and, of course, rewarded him with tumultuous applause, which he took as a sign of confidence on the part of the Soviet.

Such incidents caused considerable annoyance to the Executive Committee, and its left-wing members repeatedly proposed that Kerensky be disavowed, a step that certainly would have shaken his political position. However, the majority of the Executive Committee preferred to smooth over such incidents behind the scenes, since, by and large, Kerensky's presence in the government and his popularity were considered valuable assets.

On basic issues, domestic and foreign, Kerensky conformed his attitude to the general line of the Soviet. Miliukov, in his *History*, goes so far as to call him a "Zimmerwaldist." Actually, Kerensky's outstanding characteristic was a kind of high-strung nationalism. The ideology of Russian imperialism and expansion had a stronger appeal to him than, for instance, to Prince Lvov or Nekrasov. Nevertheless, Kerensky, bearing in mind the prestige of the Soviet and the temper of the masses, supported the demand of the Soviet for the revision of the war aims, and defended it in the government against Miliukov, with whom his personal relationship had never been of the best. It hurt his feelings deeply that the Soviet considered his oppositional activities insufficient and used the contact commission to exert a direct influence on the government. . . .

In those April days, when it became known that Kerensky, with the other ministers, had approved Miliukov's note which had provoked the first flare-up of civil war in the streets of Petrograd, his popularity was strongly shaken. The Bolsheviks and some other leftist members of the Executive Committee proposed that Kerensky be deprived of his vice-chairmanship of the Soviet. The majority of the Executive Committee, however, still thought that, despite his weaknesses and shortcomings, he might yet play a positive part for the benefit of democracy. For this reason we protected him against attacks from the left. . . .

Alexander Rabinowitch

The Party Divided

The son of a distinguished atomic scientist, Alexander Rabinowitch grew up knowing several veterans of the Russian revolutionary movement, among them Irakli Tsereteli and Boris Nicolaevsky, archivist of the Social Democrats. After studying at the University of Chicago and Indiana University, he became a professor at Indiana and director of its Russian and East European Institute. Author of two major monographs on the Bolsheviks in Petrograd and a collective volume honoring Nicolaevsky — *Revolution and Politics in Russia* (1972) — Rabinowitch has challenged the established view of the Communist party in 1917 as a disciplined, monolithic organization. In his study of the July Days, the conclusion of which is presented here, he explains the advantages and disadvantages of the relatively open, tolerant, and democratic movement that the Bolshevik party was in 1917.

Text by Alexander Rabinowitch *Prelude to Revolution: The Petrograd Bolsheviks and the July 17 Uprising,* 1968, pp. 229–235. Reprinted by permission of Indiana University Press.

From the time of the October revolution, the writing of Bolshevik Party history has been rigidly controlled by the Communist Party of the Soviet Union in accordance with the changing requirements of politics and ideology. One apparently fixed axiom of Soviet historiography, however, is the basically unified character of the party's leadership during the revolution. Thus, Soviet historians must either ignore such deviations from the revolutionary course prescribed by Lenin as the "right opportunism" of Kamenev and Zinoviev or the leftism of Latsis and Semashko, or present them as the insignificant actions of isolated obstructionists. Consequently, one searches Soviet secondary sources in vain for frank discussions of the very real differences in outlook and policy between the Bolshevik Petersburg Committee and the party Central Committee from April to July, 1917, or the apparently uncoordinated but by no means insignificant activities of the Bolshevik Military Organization during this time. Yet the evidence suggests that precisely these kinds of problem hold the key to an understanding of the Bolshevik role and objectives in the preparation and development of the abortive June 10 demonstration and the July uprising of 1917.

The fissures which plagued the Bolshevik Party throughout 1917 developed almost immediately after the February revolution, when, in spite of the relatively small size of the Petrograd organization (party membership in the capital was then barely over two thousand), conservative and radical wings rapidly emerged. Differing sharply on the crucial issues of the war and the Provisional Government, representatives of these two groups occasionally pursued mutually contradictory policies. Lenin, observing the split in the Petrograd organization at the time of his return to Russia, wasted no time in criticizing this condition. It will be recalled that he warned in his first major speech that the Bolsheviks' former "discipline" and "unity of thought" were missing.

Although Soviet historians today acknowledge some of the disunity prevailing within the party in the aftermath of the February revolution, they suggest that for practical purposes all serious differences were eliminated upon Lenin's return in April. At the First Petrograd City Conference and at the April All-Russian Party Conference, it is true, Lenin succeeded in obtaining formal acceptance of his radical course by an overwhelming majority of the Bolshevik Party. But this was at least partly because his resolutions on the Provisional Government and on the war were ambiguous enough both to allay the immediate fears of the moderates and to inspire the hopes of the radicals. In essence, the major resolutions of the April conferences pointed the party toward the socialist revolution, but left the key questions of how and when unanswered. Right-wing Bolshevik leaders apparently came away from these conferences with the feeling that the extended educational campaign envisioned by Lenin as a prerequisite to transfer of power to the Soviets might not differ much in practice from their own program of action based on their belief in the inevitability of an indefinitely prolonged bourgeois-democratic stage in the revolution. Moreover, they probably hoped that Lenin's position would mellow after longer exposure to Russian conditions. And in the meantime their representation in the Central Committee and on *Pravda*'s editorial board appeared to assure them a significant voice in the formulation of policy. On the other hand, party radicals evidently left the same meetings convinced that Lenin shared their overwhelming impatience and their will to seize power. Thus, while the April conferences confirmed Lenin's ideological and political leadership, fundamental intra-party differences were by no means eliminated. Many basic organizational questions were left unanswered, and more important, the party was provided with only the haziest of blue-prints as a guide for future action.

In the meantime Russian workers, peasants, and soldiers were showing the first signs of disenchantment with the results of the February revolution. In Petrograd the April–June period witnessed the striking spurt in party membership that enabled the Bolsheviks to play such an important role in the subsequent political life of the capital. It is unfortunate that historical literature has paid so little attention to the changing composition of the Bolshevik Party at this time. However, even on the basis of the fragmentary materials available it appears clear that during this period of rapid growth the requirements for party membership were all but suspended in order to obtain a militant mass following in the shortest possible time. At the opening of the April All-Russian Conference party membership in Petrograd was already about 16,000. By late June it had doubled again to reach 32,000, while during these same months 2,000 garrison soldiers joined the Military Organization and 4,000 soldiers became associated with "Club Pravda."

The inevitable price of this enormous growth was a significant increase in problems of control. To be sure, some of these additional members were long-time Bolsheviks returning from exile or emigration, but the bulk were green recruits from among the most impatient and dissatisfied elements in the factories and garrison who knew little, if anything, about Marxism and cared less about party discipline. Thus, besides having to overcome the conservatism of the Central Committee Lenin was now faced with the problem of keeping his thousands of impetuous new followers in the fold (and attracting others), while at the same time controlling them and the increasingly radical Petersburg Committee and Military Organization until a propitious moment for the seizure of power had arrived.

First signs that this would not be an easy task emerged during the April crisis when elements of the Petrograd party organization, without the authorization of the Central Committee, initiated steps to overthrow the Provisional Government. Precisely the same thing occurred during the preparations for the June 10 demonstration. Granted that the full extent of Lenin's aims in connection with the latter is open to question, it appears clear that no more than a peaceful demonstration was authorized by the Central Committee. Yet on June 9 the Military Organization prepared its forces for a possible armed clash, and the powerful Vyborg District Bolshevik Committee, under the leadership of M. Ia. Latsis, armed itself and laid plans to seize vital public services. As we have seen, these activities were halted only at the eleventh hour upon the insistence of conservative members of the Central Committee and the party's delegation in the First Congress of Soviets, without the Bolshevik Petersburg Committee and Military Organization having been consulted. By his own admission, Lenin chose to see the demonstration go by the boards rather than risk an open break with the Soviet. And conscious of the danger of a premature uprising in the revolutionary capital, Lenin now seemed considerably more insistent on the immediate need for organization, patience, and discipline. He emphasized this point in his address at the critical Petersburg Committee meeting of June 11; this was the crux of his message to the All-Russian Conference of Bolshevik Military Organizations, where demands for the immediate overthrow of the Provisional Government were particularly emphatic; and this was a theme of some editorials which Lenin wrote for *Pravda* at this time.

The few weeks between the June crisis and the July days, however, witnessed a sharp rise of unrest in Petrograd factories and military regiments and a concomitant increase in impatience and a desire for direct action on the part of radical elements within the Bolshevik Petersburg Committee and Military Organization. As a result, the divergence between the activities of district and unit level Bolsheviks and the course advocated by the Central Committee widened, and in this process the events of June 18 had special significance.

On June 18 the Bolsheviks were able to turn the mass street demonstration sponsored by the First All-Russian Congress of Soviets of Workers' and Soldiers' Deputies into an impressive expression of support for the Bolshevik program. On that day as well Russian military forces on the Southwestern front launched their long heralded offensive. To Bolsheviks of Kamenev's persuasion the victory exacted by the party in the Soviet demonstration paled considerably beside the Provisional Government's evident success in uniting a large portion of the population behind the dramatic assault of the Russian army. Indeed, to them it seemed more apparent than ever that an extended bourgeois-liberal stage in the revolution could not be avoided and thus that the correct course for the party was a moderate one.

More radically inclined party members from the Petersburg Committee, the Military Organization, and the Kronstadt Bolshevik Committee, on the other hand, drew quite different conclusions from the events of June 18. For people like Podvoisky, Nevsky, Beliakov, Semashko, and Sakharov of the Military Organization and Latsis, Stukov, and Zalutsky of the Petersburg Committee, the mass support for the Bolshevik program which emerged in the June 18 parade seemed evidence enough that the forces already at the disposal of the party were more than adequate for the seizure of power, while the launching of the offensive and the subsequent call for garrison troops were indications that the revolution was in danger. Moreover, not a few Bolsheviks were evidently genuinely concerned about losing the support of the masses if the party proved unwilling to act. At the All-Russian Conference of Bolshevik Military Organizations, in sessions of the Petersburg Committee, in mass rallies at the Kronstadt naval base, and at meetings of the Military Organization they criticized the role of "fireman" being pressed on them by the Central Committee and insisted on the need for immediate direct action. Although on June 20 the leadership of the Military Organization cooperated in squelching efforts by the First Machine Gun Regiment to organize an uprising of the garrison, we have

The Petrograd Massacre. During the "July Days," demonstrators on the Nevskii Prospect were cut down by machine guns manned by soldiers acting under orders from the Provisional Government. (Brown Brothers)

Nevsky's word that on the twenty-second, apparently without authorization from the Central Committee, the Military Organization began to lay plans for an uprising of its own.

A little over a week later the explosive First Machine Gun Regiment touched off the July uprising. Organized with the help of Bolshevik Military Organization members in the First Machine Gun Regiment, it was almost immediately supported by rank-and-file party members throughout the capital and in Kronstadt. Evidently only after the Military Organization, the Executive Commission of the Petersburg Committee, and the Second City Conference had formally approved participation in the movement, and then only very belatedly and reluctantly, did the Central Committee agree to stand at its head. To sum up the Bolshevik role in the preparation and organization of the July uprising, then, it seems that the movement was in part an outgrowth of months-long Bolshevik anti-government propaganda and agitation, that the rank-and-file Bolsheviks from Petrograd factories and military regiments played a leading role in its organization, and that the leadership of the Military Organization and part of the Petersburg Committee probably encouraged it against the wishes of Lenin and the Central Committee.

Finally, it should be noted that Lenin's role in the July events appears to have been a secondary one. His conviction of the need for a socialist revolution, particularly as expressed in the slogan "All power to the Soviets," undoubtedly helped inspire the uprising. Moreover, those radical Bolsheviks from the Military Organization and the Petersburg Committee who joined with the Anarchist-Communists in initiating the July movement may well have been convinced that as Lenin differed with them only in regard to timing, he would ultimately approve of their activities. But in any event judging by available evidence, Lenin appears to have honestly tried to control the rising mood of rebellion in Petrograd until it could be supported in the provinces and at the front. In this task he was unsuccessful. Thus before dawn on July 5, with his forces compromised and with all hope of immediate victory extinguished, Lenin was left with no choice but to sound the call for an ignominious, albeit temporary, retreat.

Lenin emerged from the July experience more convinced than ever of the need for an armed uprising against the Provisional Government. The defeat suffered by the Bolsheviks proved to be much less serious than might have been expected. At the time of the abortive Kornilov affair the party more than recouped its losses. On the last day of August the resurgent Bolsheviks won a majority in the Petrograd Soviet for the first time, and barely two weeks later Lenin was exhorting the Bolshevik leadership in the capital to overthrow the Provisional Government at once. It is significant that during the second half of September and in October, when the Bolshevik Party was once again divided over the question of seizing power, the high command of the Military Organization insisted on the absolute necessity of careful and thorough preparation before taking the offensive against the Provisional Government. Referring to this development in his memoirs, Nevsky recalls that "some comrades felt then that we [the leaders of the Military Organization] were too cautious. . . . But our experience (especially in the July days) showed us what an absence of thorough preparation and a preponderance of strength means." As the October revolution was to show, for the leadership of the Military Organization, as for Petrograd Bolsheviks generally, the lessons of July were not without value.

J. L. H. Keep

The Countryside
in Revolt

John Keep has been a most prolific scholar in both early modern and
twentieth-century Russian history. Born in England, he was lecturer at the
School of Slavonic and East European Studies, University of London,
before becoming professor of Russian history at the University of Toronto.
The author of a number of studies on late-medieval Russia and a major
work on Russia as a garrison state, he has also written *The Rise of Social
Democracy in Russia* and one of the first social histories of the revolution.
In it, he sought to understand the processes of organization that lay within
the chaos and anarchy of the revolution and found that antidemocratic
practices had already existed in revolutionary assemblies before the Bolshevik seizure of power. In this selection from Chapters Twelve and Sixteen,
he attempts to explain the peasant mentalities that led to the spread of
agrarian violence.

Broadly speaking, the pattern of events in Russia's rural areas during the
critical months between February and October 1917 was similar to that
in the towns. The collapse of the old authorities, and the new government's inability to create a viable new administrative structure in their
place, left a vacuum which the peasants themselves, or at least those
who spoke in their name, made haste to fill. The rural population was
suddenly granted an almost limitless freedom to seek its own solution to
besetting problems, above all that of land reform. In this upsurge of
activity the village was greatly stimulated by the example of the towns.
There were, however, several important differences between the "agrarian movement" (to use the customary euphemism) and the offensive in
the urban areas. . . .

Two and a half years of warfare had bred a mood of bitterness and

Selections are reprinted from *The Russian Revolution: A Study in Mass Mobilization*,
by John L. H. Keep, with the permission of W. W. Norton & Company, Inc. Copyright
© 1976 by John L. H. Keep.

frustration in the Russian village. There was a near-total lack of confidence in the empire's political and military leadership, but at the same time a feeling that peasants themselves could do little to bring about any improvement. Everything seemed to depend upon an end to the war, yet this basic question could be solved only from "on high." In some areas an undercurrent of violence made itself felt, but this was still a phenomenon of local and limited significance.

The collapse of the monarchy in February 1917 came to the rural population as a complete surprise. At first the peasants refrained from any overt response. With their natural caution they wanted to take stock of the novel situation in which they found themselves. Most were ready to give the new *vlast'* (central authority), whose nature they but dimly comprehended, time in which to meet their basic demands: for peace, better terms of trade, and above all an immediate start on a far-reaching land reform. A redistribution of wealth in favour of those who worked the land was seen by almost all peasants, especially in the Great Russian areas, as a self-evident necessity, an act of common justice. They were not concerned with the repercussions it would have upon the country's social fabric or its economic potential. If the reform led to the creation of a "peasant Russia," in which the rural areas exercised hegemony over the towns, so much the better; they assumed that the elimination of ancient inequalities would automatically bring about an efflorescence of peasant farming from which the whole population would benefit. With such abundance in the offing townsfolk need suffer no more than a temporary dislocation in the supply of food.

The peasants' mood was thus initially one of self-confidence and optimism. A new age of human brotherhood seemed about to dawn. By and large they were willing to settle accounts peacefully even with their hereditary foes, the large landed proprietors, provided that the latter renounced all the privileges they had enjoyed in the past. The same was true of their attitude towards the independent farmers who had benefited by the Stolypin reforms: if they abandoned their separate plots and reintegrated themselves into the communal village society, they would be accepted as equals and would be allocated a fair share of the land. In the forthcoming "black repartition" their needs, like those of every other household in the community, would stand the same chance of satisfaction. As the peasants envisaged it, equality was to be the guiding principle behind the reform. Each family farm (the basic unit of production) was to receive sufficient land, of varying quality, to support itself. The norm was to be established locally, by balancing the amount of land available against the number of persons to be fed ("eaters," as they were quaintly called), and then was to be revised at intervals as conditions changed to ensure that the principle of equality was maintained. Livestock and agricultural equipment were to be treated similarly. Provision would be made for landless agricultural wage-earners as well as for former members of the commune returning from the towns or from military service, in so far as they wished to claim their rights. The future social order was visualized as one in which all major decisions would be taken at the lowest possible level. The ideal was a kind of "pan-Russian commune" embracing all those elements of the nation endowed with the plain virtues of the countryman — the peasant who earned his living by tilling the soil himself, or with the aid of his family, but without exploiting the labour of others.

We need not examine here how far this attitude reflected the theories of Socialist-Revolutionary intellectuals, which were themselves largely a refinement of ideas circulating at the turn of the century among peasants in those areas where communal ways of thought were still very much alive. That communalism was indeed a living reality in 1917 is clear from the whole history of the agrarian movement, which culminated in a "black repartition" such as had long been advocated by the more militant *narodniki*. This is not to say that the peasants themselves accepted, or even understood, the theoretical implications of Populist "agrarian socialism," but they were closer to the PSR than to any other political party. Nor is this the place to demonstrate that many of these ideas were naive and utopian, or that in economic terms the Populist programme threatened to perpetuate Russia's historic backwardness *vis-à-vis* more industrialized nations. What deserves emphasis here is that communalism served as a kind of talisman to distinguish the peasants from their urban cousins, whose experience in the industrial milieu gave them a different perspective.

Our understanding of these differences of outlook has not, alas, been much advanced by the vast corpus of Marxist (and specifically Leninist) writing that exists on the subject. These observers proceed from the assumption, which cannot be proved, that one is dealing here with two distinct social *classes*, one "proletarian" and the other "petty bourgeois," each distinguished from the other by its attitude to the ownership of property. Unfortunately there is no hard and fast evidence about the strength at this time of proprietorial instincts in either group.

It is probably true that they were very weak among men whose entire lives had been spent at the factory bench (although some of these so-called "hereditary proletarians" may well have aspired to possess a home of their own). At the other end of the spectrum were those peasants who could scarcely conceive of their existence except as owners of a family farm. It is reasonable to assume that such sentiments were more common among the more successful and prosperous villagers, with large families and holdings, but they were certainly not confined to such persons.

In the light of subsequent Soviet agrarian history it is clear that the Marxist approach, based on the concept of social class (determined by relationship to production), is an inadequate tool to comprehend the sociology of the Russian peasantry. Gradations of wealth and status followed a cyclical pattern determined as much by biological as by economic factors. The natural tendency towards material acquisitiveness was offset by a lingering respect for the values characteristic of an earlier age: loyalty to established authorities (especially those that were of peasant origin), family and group solidarity in the face of threats from without, and a sense of the dignity conferred by physical toil. Peasants had had less opportunity to acquire a formal education than their more fortunate kinsmen in the towns, but they displayed a more stable emotional attitude towards their environment, and their indifference or hostility towards certain aspects of modern secular culture was offset by their keener awareness of more basic human concerns.

Reduced to essentials, the motive behind the agrarian movement of 1917 was a desire for greater economic security. It stood greater chances of success than its urban counterpart, for "workers' control" was bound to create anarchy, mass unemployment and impoverishment — and ultimately the imposition of a new system of industrial discipline harsher in many respects than the old. On the other hand small peasant proprietors, tilling their newly acquired additional strips of land under the relatively benign tutelage of the village commune, could feel that they had indeed taken a great step towards controlling their own destiny. This was of course no final solution to the social problem, and disillusionment would come to the village just as it did to the town — but it would come later, and largely as a result of external action by urban activists jealous of the peasants' relative security.

Thus the townsman and the countryman each had a fundamentally dissimilar attitude towards social conflict, although in the short term their aims might seem to coincide. To this basic difference may be added another pertaining to political organization. Village politics were normally simple, in the sense that ideological considerations played scarcely any part. Many communities had no significant internal divisions. Where there was a struggle between rival groups, these were often described as "the old" and "the young": that is to say conservatives as distinct from innovators. Party labels counted for little. If confronted by urban agitators professing different political creeds, the peasants' natural instinct was to stay neutral. "Some say one thing, some say another, but they are all chiefs (*nachal'niki*). We shall be for none of them but shall wait and see later who is right." This was how one peasant, when interviewed many years later, described the atmosphere in a village near Saratov. Hundreds of others were no different.

To be sure, proximity to a town or to a main railway line exposed many rural areas to external influences. Copies of newspapers were available in inns and similar places; they might be read out aloud, and in this way their message could reach even those who were illiterate. Numerous representatives were sent into the provinces by business firms, supply organizations, political parties, soviets and so on. In the late summer they were superseded by a stream of refugees from the hunger-stricken towns. Soldiers and sailors returned home on leave (sometimes without permission) and passed on their impressions of life in the trenches or in the barracks. Often they helped peasants to formulate their own aspirations and to give them concrete organizational shape.

The attitude taken towards deserters from the armed forces varied. Several cases are known where they were handed over to the authorities or even lynched. On the other hand their plight naturally won them a certain amount of sympathy from kinsmen and friends. Members of the armed forces on the run, especially if they had their weapons with them, were natural candidates for leadership in any conflict with the peasants' traditional foes. Soldiers were responsible for the first recorded instance of violence against a landed estate and such behaviour became very frequent later on in the year. F. N. Novikov, a peasant from Borisov county (Minsk province), in the rear of positions occupied by the Third Army, later recalled: "Six healthy young men dressed in soldiers' greatcoats came into our village on three carts. They called us all together and said: 'Get ready, lads, harness your horses. Let's go and sack L . . .' And the peasants went, some on horseback and others on foot. Some went to get rich on the lord's goods while others went to watch." In this way increasing contact with the outside world helped to worsen the social climate in the countryside.

Once violent action had become psychologically acceptable, the question arose of forming organizations able to sustain the dynamism of the movement. The traditional rural institution, the commune, now came into its own. It was the principal unit concerned in the redistribution of property, and in the course of this operation assumed powers that would have been inconceivable in more normal times. It was essentially a defensive rather than an offensive organization, serving to reconcile the interests of its members and to protect them against threats from without. It was an instrument of mediation rather than of combat. Another of its attributes was durability: it was rooted in the fabric of Russian agrarian society and could be eliminated only by the destruction of an entire way of life.

This strength was also a source of weakness. One effect of the communal tradition was to encourage among Russian peasants in 1917 the belief that any organization worthy of the name should aspire to a similar durability and fulfill broadly similar functions. Ordinary folk were sceptical of the merits of the numerous committees and councils that sprang up, modelled on those in the towns, which seemed to serve a merely ephemeral purpose. Such overtly political bodies, they reasoned, were no substitute for duly constituted authorities responsible to an assembly of all "toiling" householders. These democratic instincts did the peasants credit. However, the corollary was that such political organizations were bound to come under the control of outsiders who had no intimate connection with the life of the countryside. Ultimately they would serve as means of subjugating the village to the will of the town.

It was hard for peasants to organize themselves effectively at any level higher than that of the rural district. Communications were still so primitive that men living in different rural districts (*volosti*) within the same county (*uyezd*) could not easily make contact with one another, and at the provincial (*guberniya*) level the problems were correspondingly multiplied. When meetings were held and organizations formed, the decisions they took could only be enforced so long as their spirit coincided with the mood of the villagers. There was a chronic shortage of literate and energetic individuals able to serve as rural cadres. The tasks of coordination and decision-making enevitably passed into the hands of persons who could not easily be held to account for their actions and who took their cue from the urban political parties or soviets. The rural (peasants') soviets were less sophisticated than their counterparts in the towns and were even less rigidly structured. Where their leaders sympathized with the moderate wing of the PSR, some effort might be made to preserve their autonomy, but as the year drew to a close there was increasing pressure for mergers with urban soviets in a common organization directed by the latter's executive personnel. The establishment of centralized control over the countryside by the urban-based Bolshevik regime was to prove to be a lengthy and difficult operation, but the groundwork for later developments was laid during the winter of 1917–18.

It is not easy to categorize the different types of action undertaken by unruly peasants in pursuit of their basic objective, the transfer of all land, together with other natural resources, into the hands of those who worked it. Measures of various kinds were often taken simultaneously, and the sources generally lack precision in this regard. Unsatisfactory as these materials are, they contain a good deal of scattered information about the characteristics of agrarian unrest in 1917 which lends itself to typological classification. One may distinguish between different forms of protest, beginning with the least violent. As was only natural, the peasants generally sought to undermine their enemies' authority and self-confidence by exercising various kinds of pressure before proceeding to sequester their property or to assault their persons.

   The easiest action to take was to deny the proprietors use of the labour force upon which many of them depended to work their land. This labour was of three kinds: prisoners of war, migrants from other districts (including refugees), and local men. The first group was the most obvious target. On 9 April the committee of Shipov district (Yefremov county, Tula province) issued the following peremptory command to Prince Golitsyn, a local squire. "You are hereby informed that by 10 A.M. on 10 April you are required to send to the district office all prisoners of war employed on agricultural work, since they are needed by the citizens of this district. In cases of non-compliance this order will be enforced by the militia with the utmost severity of the law. Send also their effects and the appropriate papers. Signed. . . ." A landowner named Tolmachev, resident in Nizhniy Novgorod province, reported that as a result of the prisoners' removal "the field work which was going ahead rapidly has had to stop and the stables are without hands." In some places the peasants asked only that the captives be paid at the same rate as native agricultural labourers — a demand that was probably motivated less by humanitarian or internationalist sentiments than by a more prosaic concern to maintain current wage levels. In most cases, however, prisoners were prohibited from working for individual proprietors and were made to perform jobs on the peasants' own plots. How extensive this shift was cannot be ascertained. The ministry of Agriculture stated early in 1917 that 600,000 prisoners were engaged on agricultural work. An unofficial survey of ten unspecified provinces made at this time showed that of 41,000 prisoners employed there 19,000 worked on peasant farms and 22,000 on those of individual proprietors. By 1 October the total number of prisoners employed in agriculture had fallen to 431,690, but this figure is not broken down further.

One would like to know more about the prisoners' reactions to this change in their fortunes, their relationship to the new authorities, and their role in spreading "defeatist" ideas in the villages. According to the vivid but sketchy memoirs of a Swedish Red Cross worker, the February revolution led to a number of easements (including, in some places, the introduction of an eight-hour working day), but these were offset by the effects of rising prices and a reduction in the cash element of their remuneration. The prisoners appreciated the muzhiks' kind and simple ways but found it hard to adjust themselves to their low cultural level. As for their peasant masters, they seem to have had no problem in reconciling the temporary employment of these unfortunates with their moral contempt for the principle of hiring labour. It is worth noting that most prisoners were employed in the southern half of the country where some of the inhabitants had forsaken communalist principles.

Whereas prisoners could be expected to fall in fairly readily with the local committees' suggestions, a certain amount of persuasion was sometimes necessary in the case of native agricultural labourers. This was particularly the case with seasonal workers from other provinces who were unsure whether they could expect a share of the sequestered land to offset their loss of wages. In Kirsanov county, Tambov province, in July it was said that "the rye is ripening on the stalk" because local peasants were forcibly preventing migrant labourers from helping with the harvest. In Ranenburg county, Ryazan province — a well-known trouble-spot — activists at first exempted from the employment ban those who looked after the landowners' cattle, but later took more drastic measures, so that the animals had to be slaughtered. In the south-western provinces of Kiev and Podolia, the centre of the sugar-beet industry, and to a lesser extent in the steppe and Baltic provinces, agricultural labourers pressed for higher wages. They also insisted on payment at daily rates in lieu of those fixed in their seasonal contracts.

As a result of these pressures the larger farms, which depended most heavily on hired labour, soon found themselves in grave difficulties. Where the land could not be sown or the crops reaped local peasant activists were presented with a plausible pretext for sequestration, since it was government policy to ensure that not a single dessyatine remained uncultivated. Another consequence of the massive withdrawal of labour was to stimulate tension between different segments of the peasantry.

According to one contemporary analysis of the Main Land Committee's statistics on agrarian unrest between March and August, conflicts involving employment accounted for 268 out of the 2,367 incidents reported, or 11.3 per cent; another 155, or 6.5 per cent, had to do with disputes over rented land. Not too much credence need be placed in these unwarrantedly precise figures, but the overall proportions are probably about right. These were both relatively mild forms of action; if one wonders at the low proportion of disputes over rented land in a rural economy where leasing was so widespread, the explanation is simply that as the year wore on peasants preferred to take more militant measures which made disputes about their contractual obligations obsolete. The effect of these earlier and more limited actions was none the less significant. Those proprietors, particularly in the south-central region, who engaged in such archaic practices as crop-sharing and rack-renting (short-term leases at extortionate rates) soon had to abandon them, and indeed to withdraw from the scene entirely. Many of these men were absentee landlords and their expulsion was no great loss to the economy — although it is only fair to add that some of them were absent only because they were performing military service. These estates were especially vulnerable to peasant action, since the proprietors' strips of arable, pasture or meadow were intermingled with those of the villagers to such an extent that the term estate is really a misnomer.

The simplest and most obvious step which tenants could take was to reduce rent payments, or to cease them altogether. Such unilateral breaches of contract are said to have been most characteristic of the Central Agricultural region. In one instance peasants agreed to pay rent at a fixed percentage (5.5 per cent) of the value of the land, since they calculated that this would provide the owner with a fair return. However, such sophistication and restraint were rare virtues, and even in this instance those concerned soon went on to annul all lease contracts. A more usual practice was to take as the norm the rent charged at some earlier date, such as 1914; sometimes deductions would then be made to take account of "the present needs of the country" or "the high cost of living." In Buguruslansk county, Samara province, the deduction was of the order of seventy-five per cent — a figure later taken over by a congress of peasants from the entire province. In Tambov a committee claiming to speak for the peasants of Kirsanov county lowered rents by a quarter, whereupon some district committees reduced them by a further sixty per cent. In Kharkov province peasants arranged to pay twelve to fifteen roubles in lieu of the forty to fifty roubles charged hitherto.

Where purely nominal sums were paid, such as one to three roubles per dessyatine (when the state land tax alone amounted to three roubles — and this in prosperous Kherson province), the intention was clearly punitive. The Provisional Government might without difficulty have "frozen" rents at the 1916 rate or fixed maximum levels in different regions of the country; this would at least have strengthened the hand of those who were trying to keep unrest within tolerable bounds. The evidence suggests that until mid-summer only a minority of peasants took the radical course of refusing to pay any rent at all or confiscating leased land; even those who did so were not necessarily opposed to the principle of leasing, since they frequently arranged for confiscated land to be rented out to their fellow-peasants. In these circumstances it appears that a firm policy by the government would have had a beneficial effect.

Encouraged by this weakness in high places, peasants proceeded more and more frequently to inventory and to sequester the property of those who did not belong to the village community. This property comprised various categories of land (forest, pasture and meadow, arable), livestock and agricultural implements, crops in the field or in the barn, farm and residential buildings (along with their gardens, orchards and so on), and finally all manner of household and personal possessions. Weakened by depredations of this kind, its residents frightened into acquiescence, a landed estate or individual peasant farm was ripe for complete confiscation, to be followed by the redistribution among the local inhabitants of such property as had not previously been taken.

During 1917, and still more so in the ensuing years, Russia's woods and forests were the scene of a peculiar kind of guerilla warfare that has yet to find its historian. The importance of the timber industry in the country's economic life, always great, was enhanced by the shortage of coal and oil. Wardens were employed to protect the forests against damage, theft or fires, but these guards could hardly be expected to put up effective resistance to massive assaults, especially when those responsible carried firearms and were backed by local sentiment.

The peasants' attitude was ambiguous. On the one hand they wanted to preserve the forests, along with land of other categories, for the people as a whole (which by definition excluded private ownership); on the other hand they looked to them as a means of satisfying their immediate urgent needs. The contradiction was a matter of theory rather than practice. In so far as the peasants appropriated state-owned timber as freely as that in private hands, it may be said that the second motive was more powerful than the first. Their major concern was to prevent private owners from felling timber or removing stocks which they themselves coveted. This was easily done by refusing to let local men work in the forests and by barring the main exits. Sometimes violence was used against recalcitrant timber-workers: in July a crowd of peasants at Smerdyach, Novgorod province, assaulted and injured men preparing timber for delivery to two local entrepreneurs. Even fiercer resistance was offered to any move by owners of wooded property to sell it, for this was interpreted (in some cases no doubt correctly) as "speculation" — that is to say as an attempt to avoid confiscation by exchanging it for cash or other movable assets.

There were complaints by private proprietors that the peasants, while preventing them from exercising their rights, were felling timber extensively themselves. Vorogushinin, a landowner in Cherny county, Tula province, stated that timber worth 12,000 roubles had been felled on his estate, and in nearby Orel the Sharovsk district committee (Sevsk county) allegedly permitted no less than 150,000 roubles worth to be taken from the property of a certain Golynsky. One wonders what was done with such extensive supplies. Some will have been used to repair dwellings, as well as for fuel, but no doubt much of it was put aside in the hope of exchanging it for industrial goods or for foodstuffs from the south. In some areas peasants engaged in a flourishing trade in firewood, which fetched eighty kopecks a pud, or a third as much as rye at the official price.

The grazing of cattle on forest land did considerable damage. Lack of pasture and meadow land had for decades been one of the major weaknesses of Russian agriculture, for the three-field system of cultivation, which was still general, encouraged farmers of all classes to devote an excessive proportion of their land to arable. In the south-central region some unscrupulous squires would lease their hayfields and meadows to the villagers at high rents, taking advantage of the fact that they had no alternative sources of fodder for their cattle. For many of these proprietors the first sign of trouble in 1917 was the appearance on their land of animals that had no right to be there. This step was followed by restrictions upon the landowners livestock, which was sometimes "exchanged" for beasts of inferior quality belonging to peasants. Proprietors were often forbidden to sell their animals. Such measures were but the preliminaries to the wholesale confiscation of livestock and horses belonging to those outside the commune. Sometimes they were offered trivial sums in compensation. At Bolshoy Lomov (Morshchansk county, Tambov province) "a delegate sent by the peasants of Sobinka village appeared at Gorbunov's estate and informed him that the village assembly had decided . . . to requisition his thoroughbreds, paying him one rouble apiece." Gorbunov also lost his woodland, but was apparently left with a portion of his arable.

Unfortunately, although understandably, the reports sent in to the militia about the confiscation of land and crops are seldom precise as to the quantity which was taken; where a figure is given, it is difficult to evaluate its significance without knowing its relationship to the total acreage of land in different categories owned by the individual concerned. This prevents one from assessing accurately the impact of the government's effort to restrict seizures to land left uncultivated. Reports poured in that peasants were appropriating not only uncultivated or fallow land but also arable which had been ploughed and sown. Although the measures adopted by the local land committees were supposed to be temporary, pending the definitive settlement to be authorized by the Constituent Assembly, everyone concerned realized that this was a fiction. It was an axiom of rural life that "he who sowed shall reap." But this axiom was interpreted in a one-sided manner; if peasants sowed privately owned land, the crop was theirs (and by implication the land also); but so too was land sown by the proprietors, whose rights were deemed to have fallen into abeyance. If such appropriations could be speciously represented as having been undertaken for patriotic reasons, to keep the land in cultivation, so much the better; if this pretext were lacking, it was not too difficult to find another. There was virtually nothing the proprietor could do. In some places peasants trooped into the fields, mowed the grass or reaped the corn, and promptly took it off to their own barns; elsewhere they might wait until the crop had been dried and stacked, or even stored, before appropriating it. The situation was well summed up in a report from Lebedyan county, Tambov province, in the latter half of July. "Throughout the county land is being seized. The private proprietors are first placed in a situation that makes it impossible for them to carry on farming, and then the land committees, referring to the general interests of the state, ordain that these lands should be transferred to the peasants."

Another matter on which one regrets the lack of precision in the sources is that of compensation. Some landowners were offered derisory sums for their land or crops, as for their livestock. A sum of two or three roubles per dessyatine was all that the peasants of Kamashkir district (Saratov province) were prepared to give the proprietress Motovilova when they confiscated her land in July — and she could count herself fortunate, since many others got nothing. On the other hand, there were instances where proprietors were given a portion of the crop, evidently to tide them over until the general repartition, or were even allowed to retain a portion of the land. The assumption here was that the community could afford to tolerate in its midst a few ex-landowners who had been "rendered harmless," as it were, by sequestration of most of their belongings. It is impossible to say how widespread this practice was. In the Volga provinces, where some areas had ample land, the peasants were inclined to be liberal, and figures of 80–100 dessyatines are encountered. Normally fifty dessyatines seems to have been regarded as the maximum area permissible in this region. Such compromises did not, however, last long.

Violence had been in the air ever since the spring of 1917, and the restraint shown at first was soon abandoned as the temptations increased. Threats of assault were uttered against proprietors or their dependants, who could not fail to realize that it was only a question of time before they were put into effect. Among the victims, as we have seen, were local officials, even those who had been elected to their post and served without pay; merchants, priests and fellow-peasants deemed disloyal to the community were other likely targets. The group most exposed to popular wrath were the managers in charge of estates whose proprietors were either on active service or resident elsewhere. Some of these men had made enemies by excessive zeal on behalf of their employers, for example in the collection of rents, but even those who had given no such cause for hostility became objects of suspicion. Near Novgorod a farm manager named Kolpakov was expelled from the area for having said, in an address to a peasant meeting, that counter-revolution was a possibility, as after 1905; this remark, intended as a warning against extremism, was taken by his audience as a sign that he wanted a return to the old regime. Elsewhere managers were accused of improperly evading military service and were handed over to the authorities for appropriate action to be taken.

During the spring searches of landowners' homes were carried out on various pretexts in a number of areas. In Voronezh province "the village committee at Gorozhanka, Zadonsk county, arbitrarily inspected the house of N. Mikhaylovskaya, took away some hunting rifles, and sealed up her effects." From this it was but a step to placing suspects under arrest. In July the wife of a serving officer named Ushkanov, who lived alone with two small children at Aleshanka in Orel province, reported that she had become embroiled in a dispute between communal and independent peasants in the locality; when she refused to sign a petition on behalf of the former, she was arrested by a soldier, V.S. Byvshikh, who entered her house along with a group of villagers, whereupon the provincial commissar had intervened to obtain her release. The local activists did not yet control the penal institutions and had nowhere to detain those whom they arrested. This may help to explain why they did not resort more frequently to the practice of taking hostages. The main object of such arrests was probably psychological: to create a climate of insecurity which would oblige landowners and others to surrender their land, and eventually to abandon their homes altogether. . . .

Until September at least most assaults seem to have taken place in the course of armed robberies. It is impossible to draw a clear line between incidents of agrarian protest and ordinary criminal acts. We have already noted that banditry was widespread in Yekaterinoslav province (and by extension throughout the steppe zone); for rather different reasons it was also frequent in areas close to the western front. The object of these attacks was twofold: to intimidate the victims and to obtain funds, goods or foodstuffs. Some proprietors hired guards to protect their homes. These men naturally became a prime target for raiders. Ordinary domestic employees were not exempt either, and some of them lost their lives. In Voronezh province two members of the Shkarin family, who may have been brother and sister, each owned an estate. On the former's land the victims included the manager and his daughter, a housemaid and a guard; on the latter no harm seems to have befallen the servants but the proprietress herself perished.

One early western investigator of these events noted that the murder of managers was "infrequent" and that only an infinitesimal number of proprietors were killed. These homicides must, however, be seen against the background of other forms of violence. It is true that the aroused peasants generally shrank from taking men's lives, as distinct from their property. This may be attributed in part to a residual concern for religious or humanitarian values and in part, more prosaically, to a fear of reprisals. At a guess, the number of landowners or their dependants who lost their lives was probably less than the number of robbers, bandits and deserters who met a similar fate. The militia records abound in instances of the latter kind. Most members of the élite who lost their lives were killed in the course of armed robberies in which some allowance may be made for the aggressors' desperation and anxiety; they were not shot down in cold blood — the fate meted out to countless thousands by Cheka executioners during the years that followed. In 1917 one of the few recorded cases of landowners being lynched occurred in Simbirsk as early as March, when a wealthy proprietor named Gelshert was put to death by a crowd which had been led to believe that he was a traitor. Another source of fatalities in the agrarian context was inter-ethnic conflict, particularly in Perm province, where Russians and Bashkirs sometimes clashed over territorial rights.

By September the rural activists' patience was wearing thin — or perhaps one should say that their appetites had been whetted by the successes they had won. With the harvest all but gathered in, the moment seemed to have come for a final reckoning with the relics of the old agrarian order. The *pogrom*, or violent sacking, of an estate by an irate mob, which had been a relative rarity during the previous months, or at least had been restricted to certain well-defined trouble-spots (notably Spassky county, Kazan province), now came into its own as a characteristic phenomenon. One must hasten to add that even so it was localized in the overcrowded black-soil provinces and had a distinct focus in Tambov. The remoter causes of this wave of destruction and vandalism must be sought in land hunger and other ancient grievances, but the immediate catalyst seems to have been a specific incident: the murder, on 24 August, of Prince Boris L. Vyazemsky, a distinguished local figure noted for his liberal views. A crowd of peasants, said to be five thousand strong, invested his estate at Lotarevo (Usman county), which was one of the most advanced in the region and for this reason had been placed under government protection. Having fortified their courage with alcohol from the prince's cellars, they arrested Vyazemsky and his wife. The former was taken under escort to the nearest railway station, where he was set upon and put to death by soldiers from a passing troop-train. The mob then went on to sack a neighbouring estate. The affair was thought sufficiently serious for a judicial investigation to be held, as a result of which four persons were arrested, but the authorities were forced to hand the men over to the peasants of a neighbouring village.

Attacks followed on several other estates, especially in Kozlov district, in the course of which two of the aggressors were shot by a landowner named K.P. Romanov. This incident added further fuel to the fire. On 12 September the Kozlov section of the landowners' association stated that twenty-four estates had been burned within three days. A correspondent added: "a rumour is spreading among the peasants that unless they take the land by 20 September it will be too late." Another legend was that Kerensky himself (evidently seen as a personal embodiment of the state power) had authorized the seizures. Anonymous letters, evidently written by semi-literates, were said to have circulated in which prospective victims were indicated. When questioned, peasants would say: "Some unknown persons descended upon us, a dozen or so of them on horseback, who fired rifle shots into the air [and said] 'Hey, come out and rob the lords, set fire to the estates. Who is not with us is against us. Whoever does not join in the burning will have it hot from us.'" Among the first estates to be attacked was that of a zemstvo leader named Ushakov, who had contributed to the well-being of the local people by building a school. He had said publicly that the peasants might have his land provided they left him his house and garden. But the mob, "rendered savage by some incomprehensible malice, broke into the house, dragged the furniture into the garden, and while the men, to the sound of a harmonica, set light to the house, the women, in their red skirts and gaily coloured kerchiefs, sat with their feet on a divan, singing and cursing with gusto." The incendiaries also burned stocks of rye, despite Ushakov's pleas that this was earmarked for supply to troops at the front.

On 15 September a detachment of troops, including cossack cavalry and armoured cars, arrived in Kozlov county from Moscow. Martial law was declared and meetings forbidden. At the village of Saburovka the troops succeeded in preventing the destruction of an estate, but elsewhere the disorders flared up anew. The soldiers of the 204th infantry regiment, stationed at Tambov, who had been responsible for some of the trouble, were compelled to lay down their arms, and by 25 September the provincial commissar, K. Shatov, could claim that "order is being restored in all counties. The culprits are being arrested and the property they have seized is being taken from them." There was some substance to the commissar's claim. On 10 October, in his next official fortnightly survey, he could state that there had been no further mass violence. He attributed this to the fact that the local land committees had taken all estates in the province under their supervision for immediate transfer, but it might be equally true to say that the peasant activists could now relax because they had achieved their immediate aim.

This victory had been achieved at a considerable cost. Commissar Shatov stated that in Kozlov county alone fifty-four farms had been sacked, wholly or in part, including sixteen that had been burned. About a third of the losses, it is worth stressing, were suffered by peasants, mostly "separators" from the commune. A more recent calculation for Tambov province as a whole puts the figure at 105 estates and "several dozen" peasant farms. These figures need to be set beside that given in the 1916 census for the total number of "private-proprietorial" farms, which was 3,075.

Tambov was not the only province to be so afflicted. News of the events in Kozlov county, transmitted through the press as well as by word of mouth, soon reached other areas with similar problems. From the village of Zykov in Ryazan province we have an eyewitness account of the destruction of an estate which bears reproduction in full, so vivid is the picture it gives of the way in which the mob proceeded.

At mid-day the village assembly met to decide the fate of our property, which was large and well equipped. The question to be decided was posed with stark simplicity: should they burn the house or not? At first they decided just to take all our belongings and to leave the building. But this decision did not satisfy some of those present, and another resolution was passed: to burn everything except the house, which was to be kept as a school. At once the whole crowd moved off to the estate, took the keys from the manager, and commandeered all the cattle, farm machinery, carriages, stores, etc. For two days they carried off whatever they could. Then they split into groups of 20, divided up the loot into heaps, one for each group, and cast lots which group should get which. In the very middle of this redistribution a sailor appeared, a local lad who had been on active service. He insisted that they should burn down the house as well. The peasants got clever. They went off to inspect the house a second time. One of them said: "What sort of a school would this make? Our children would get lost in it." Thereupon they decided to burn it down [the next day]. They went home quietly leaving a guard of 20 men, who had a regular feast: they heated the oven, butchered a sheep, some geese, ducks and hens, and ate their fill until dawn. . . . Thus the night passed. The whole village assembled and once again the axes began to strike. . . . They chopped out the windows, doors and floors, smashed the mirrors and divided up the pieces, and so on. At three o'clock in the afternoon they set light to the house from all sides, using for the purpose eight chetverti *of kerosene.*

. . .

Whether these events amount to a "peasant war" — the standard term used in Soviet historiography, derived from an expression used at the time by Lenin (who took it from Engels) — must remain a matter of opinion. On one hand violent destruction of estates was restricted to a fairly well-defined region of the country; on the other it represented a climax in the history of the "agrarian movement" (the subsequent redistribution of property being another). For this reason some general remarks on the nature of the phenomenon are in order here.

So far as the motives for these attacks is concerned, one is tempted to say that fear and envy were mixed in equal proportions. Obviously the threat of famine was a potent spur to action, but this was far from a self-sufficient cause (as one recent western writer has argued) — and in any case hunger pangs are not quenched by setting fire to a bulging barn. The fear may well have been enhanced by Kornilov's bid for power, news of which will have reached the peasants in garbled form; correspondingly, the self-evident weakness of the counter-revolutionaries will have helped to stimulate them to violent action. A feeling of "now or never" was widespread. If the communally minded villagers let the opportunity slip, something like the old agrarian order might yet be re-established. One man explained in quaint language what this aim was: "the *muzhiki* are destroying the squires' nests so that the little bird will never be able to return" — the "bird" here being a euphemism for large-scale landed property in general. The era was past when gradual reform might have seemed a preferable alternative: the February overturn had encouraged the peasants to hope that they might at last become masters of their destiny. These feelings were further stimulated by the soldiers and other politically motivated persons who streamed into the villages during the summer. The peasants put their own construction on the information that reached them about events in the towns or at the front. The term *burzhuy* (bourgeois) was used wildly to denote any real or presumed foe of the *muzhik*. Activists preached that it was lawful to make war on the bourgeoisie: so the peasants went into battle in the only way they knew. The individual proprietors bore the brunt of their attacks because they were the most vulnerable of all "outsiders," excluded from the closed world of the commune. The agrarian movement was neither a product of external agitation, nor a manifestation of class struggle. It was a phenomenon *sui generis* — plebeian, anarchic and anticentralist.

Its archaic features were most evident in the effort to avenge ancient wrongs, in the joy with which the common people destroyed the symbols of their former subjection. Only this can explain such wilful and malicious acts as chopping down fruit-trees, ploughing up parks, smashing greenhouses and diverting water from ornamental fish-ponds. When confronted with objects whose value was not understood — libraries, works of art and other cultural objects — the mob followed its instincts, which suggested that these fancies were of no use to ordinary folk and should therefore be destroyed. With its pronounced levelling tendencies the agrarian movement exemplified the dynamic force behind the Russian revolution itself.

Despite this egalitarianism, or perhaps even because of it, there were bound to be conflicts among the beneficiaries. Most obviously, one commune might stand against another when it came to dividing up the confiscated booty. Less obviously, there were gradations of view within the same community, based partly on social position and partly on differences of age, sex and temperament. The activists — where they were local men — were recruited from among the village youth, especially adolescents who faced the disagreeable prospect of military service. The patriarchs and those who walked in their shadow felt threatened by the new spirit of lawlessness and disrespect for authority. A peasant from Putivl county, Kursk province, noted that those households consisting wholly of women did not join in the sacking of estates. (On the other hand in Minsk province one peasant woman soundly abused her spouse for carelessly smashing his share of the loot when other raiders showed more skill.) Conventional ideas on morality and religion, as we have noted, also acted as a restraining force. Sometimes the clergy intervened in an effort to persuade the peasants to reconsider their actions — which might lead to the priest being deprived of his land along with that of the intended victim. Although priests are sometimes said to have participated in village committees, there is no evidence that they sanctioned violence. Fifteen peasants refused to join the villagers of Milshino (Venev county, Tula province), in sacking the estate of Princess Volkonskaya, although they were threatened with reprisals. "There were cases," our informant adds, "where peasants were forcibly dragged to the assembly and given their share of the confiscated property and told 'if anyone is to answer for this, we all shall do so.'"

Were these men kulaks? Unfortunately it is impossible, on the basis of the evidence presently available, to reach firm conclusions about the attitude taken by the more well-to-do peasants (inside and outside the commune) towards the seizure of squires' land. In some cases they identified with their fellow-proprietors; in others they stood aside; on occasion they took part, often under duress; in a very few cases they are said to have taken the initiative — presumably in order to deflect popular wrath from themselves. One eye-witness (the landowner S.P. Rudnev in Simbirsk province) states that none of the wealthier peasants attended the auction of his property because they thought it wrong to enrich themselves at others' expense. There is, however, ample evidence of such persons taking a less altruistic attitude.

As for the victims of the "agrarian movement" these included persons of every social group. The position of the "separators" was if anything even less enviable than that of the great proprietors, for if dispossessed they had no obvious alternative source of subsistence. In Simbirsk province the villagers of Kuranino and Ardatovo are reported to have beaten, arrested and humiliated the local *otrubshchiki*. (The very term, meaning "those who had cut themselves off," was an affront to the commune's egalitarian conscience.) Not far away, at Andreyevo, the wives of three soldiers who owned enclosed farms (*khutora*) were beaten by the villagers and made to sign documents agreeing that their plots should revert to the collective domain. Such instances were by no means rare. Soldiers, too, might have their property confiscated while absent on active service, which meant that their wives and families would be left without any means of sustenance other than their meagre government allowance. It has often been stated, in general accounts of the revolution, that the high rate of desertion from the Russian army during the summer and autumn of 1917 was motivated by a concern among the soldiers that, unless they were present at home, they would suffer a disadvantage when the confiscated land was repartitioned. There is little evidence of such sentiments during this period, although it may well have been a factor after the October revolution, when it became clear that a general redistribution of the land was imminent and had the backing of the new government. . . .

Here we may conclude by noting that the unrest that spread through the rural areas during these months was both cause and consequence of the general state of anarchy in the country: the rebellious peasants took advantage of the government's weakness to press their sectional claims, and this offensive in turn undermined respect for the public authorities. The economic consequences, too, were little less than catastrophic, even though the disturbances were not the *principal* cause of this decline, and were not perceived as such by most city folk. Not only did the peasants consume (or destroy) much of the commercial crop: they also, in their eagerness to sow the confiscated land, neglected their own allotments. Even some of the confiscated land was left fallow, since seed grain was short and there were more exciting things to do. This reduction in the sown area led to a critical situation during the years of civil war. Ironically enough the agrarian movement, which is a *sine qua non* of the Bolsheviks' accession to power, also presented them with their most challenging domestic problem.

Steve A. Smith

The Social Structure of the Labor Movement

A lecturer in history at the University of Essex in Colchester, England, Steve A. Smith has pursued interests both in Russian labor history and in the modern history of China. He was trained at the Centre for Russian and East European Studies at the University of Birmingham, where he worked with Moshe Lewin and Maureen Perrie. In his ground-breaking study of the revolutionary workers of Petrograd, Smith examined the movement for workers' control in the factories and argued that, instead of it being a disruptive, anarchic phenomenon, it was an attempt to maintain production and thwart perceived sabotage by the industrialists. In this selection he dissects the working class in order to understand the varied interests and responses of the skilled "cadre" workers, women workers, and young workers.

The Social Composition of Labour Protest and Labour Organisation

[T]wo broad groups can be discerned within the Petrograd working class in 1917: the proletarianised, skilled, mainly male workers, and the new, younger peasant and women workers. It was the former group of "cadre" workers who built the factory committees and trade unions after the February Revolution. Quantitative data to bear out this contention are lacking, although a survey of fitters at the Putilov works in 1918, conducted by Strumilin, showed that skilled workers dominated all labour organisations and had been the first to join the metal union in 1917. This is borne out by a complaint in the industrialists' newspaper in the spring of 1918 that "it is usually the most skilled workers, they being the most conscious, who participate in the different committees — the factory committees, soviets, etc." The same sentiment was

From *Red Petrograd: Revolution in the Factories 1917–1918*, by Steve A. Smith, 1983, Cambridge University Press. Reprinted with permission.

voiced by A. Gastev at the first national congress of metal workers: "in the unions we operate by basing ourselves on the skilled element of the workforce, for example, the turners and fitters . . . this is the most active section of the working class. The unskilled workers are, of course, less active." Skilled, experienced workers had a greater capacity than new workers to initiate a social movement and to carry out consciously-willed social change. They had more "resources " for organisation: they were better-paid and had more money and time at their disposal; they were at home in the factory and understood how production worked; they had experience of organising strikes and trade unions, of informal shop-floor organisation and of job-control; they were more literate and thus better-placed to participate in political discourse. The shift in the balance of class forces which resulted from the February Revolution created opportunities for "cadre" workers to mobilise these "resources" in order to create an organised labour movement.

The "cadre" workers who built the labour movement, of whatever political persuasion, tended to see the new, inexperienced workers as the "dark" or "backward" masses, who had brought "disorder" and "anarchy" into the labour movement. As early as 1916 the Workers' Group of the War Industries Committee noted that:

> *During the war the composition of the working class has changed; many alien, undisciplined elements have come into the workforce. In addition, the intensification of work, the broad application of female and child labour, uninterrupted overtime and holiday work . . . have increased the number of grounds for conflict of all kinds and these often arise spontaneously. Instead of organised defence of their interests, workers engage in elemental outbursts and anarchic methods.*

A Latvian Bolshevik on the CCFC[1], A. Kaktyn', made a similar point in 1917, blaming "anarchic disorders" on the "not yet fully proletarianised mass of workers consisting of refugees, people from the countryside and others temporarily swept into industry by the war." Employers too ascribed disorders to what they called the "alien element" (*prishlyi element*). At the Franco-Russian works management complained that those who had come to the factory during the war had had a bad effect on the discipline of the workforce as a whole. One must treat the accounts of "disorders" by workers new to industry with a certain caution, for the sources reflect the perceptions and values of the "organisa-

[1] Central Council of Factory Committees.

tion builders," not those of the new workers themselves. We shall see that while the former were by no means unsympathetic to their less experienced comrades, they often underestimated the capacity of new workers for self-activity and political understanding, because the forms of their activity did not fit the leaders' own model of appropriate action.

The "backward masses" (*otstalye massy*) were counterposed to the more "conscious" (*soznatel' nye*) workers. The new workers were perceived as "backward," either because they were apathetic and indifferent to the labour movement and to politics, or because they indulged in uncontrolled militancy (*stikhiinost'*). These characteristics, which at first sight appear mutually exclusive, typified the traditional pattern of behaviour of the Russian peasants: long periods of quiescence punctuated by bouts of rebelliousness (*buntarstvo*). The major task facing "cadre" workers was to convince the new workers of the need for organisation: to break them from their apathy or persuade them of the advantages of planned, sustained pursuit of their goals over sudden bursts of militancy, born of anger and emotion, rather than of calculation. This was not so easy in the spring of 1917, for direct action proved fairly effective in removing hated administrators ("carting out") or in extracting concessions from the employers. As the economic crisis worsened, however, the limitations of sectional, spontaneous actions became more and more apparent. The promotion of the interests of labour as a whole against capital required durable organisation and clearly-formulated goals and strategies. Volatile militancy tended to get in the way of this, and was thus disliked by labour leaders. They sought to channel the militancy of the new workers into organisation or, alternatively, to rouse interest in organisation if workers were bogged down in apathy.

Women Workers

In its first issue, the Menshevik party newspaper did not fail to note that whilst women had courageously faced the bullets of the police during the revolution, not one woman had as yet been elected to the Petrograd Soviet. Observations that working women were not participating in the nascent labour movement were commonplace. A report on the Svetlana factory at the end of March noted that "it is almost exclusively women who work there. They but dimly perceive the importance of the current situation and the significance of labour organisation and proletarian discipline. For this reason, and because of low pay, a certain disorder in production is noticeable." On 22 April fifty women from state factories, including twenty-two from the Pipe works, met to discuss how to organise women. They agreed that "women workers everywhere are yearning to take part in existing labour organisations, but up to now have joined them only in small numbers, on nothing like the same scale as men." As late as June, a woman from the Pipe works described the situation in shop number four, where 2,000 women were employed on automatic machines which cut out and processed fuses:

> *Sometimes you see how the women will read something, and from their conversation it emerges that a desire to step forward has been kindled in their hearts. But to our great regret, there is at present very little organisation among the women of the Pipe works. There are no women comrades among us to fan the spark of consciousness or point out to us the path to truth. We really need a comrade who can speak on the tribune in front of a sea of faces and tell us where to go, whom to listen to and what to read.*

If women workers did act to defend their interests, it was often by means of elemental bouts of direct action. This is apparent from the example of two notoriously "backward" textile-mills on Vyborg Side, where at the end of June two spectacular examples of "carting out" took place. After the textile union began contract negotiations with the textile section of the SFWO, the latter called a halt to further wage-increases in the industry, pending the settlement of the contract. When the director of the Vyborg spinning-mill tried to explain to a general meeting of workers that he was unable to consider their demand for a wage-increase, the women seized him, shoved him in a wheelbarrow and carted him to the canal where, poised perilously on the edge of the bank, he shakily signed a piece of paper agreeing to an increase. When L.G. Miller, the redoubtable chairman of the textile section of the SFWO, heard of this he demanded that the textile union send an official to the mill to sort out the women, but the women refused to listen to the official. The director, therefore, agreed to pay the increase and was fined 30,000 r. by the SFWO for so doing. Only days later, women at the neighbouring Sampsionevskaya mill, where Miller himself was director, demanded a similar increase. When Miller rejected their demand at a general meeting, women workers — who comprised 91% of the workforce — seized him and called for a wheelbarrow ("*Vmeshok i na tachku!*" ["Tie him in a sack and shove him on a barrow!"]). Male apprentices tried to dissuade them, but Miller climbed quietly into the barrow, asking only that the women should not put a sack over his head. Instead they tied it to his feet and, with raucous shouts, wheeled him around Vyborg Side, urging him to agree to a wage-rise. Miller might have been thrown off the Grenadier bridge had not a group of off-duty soldiers intervened. Thoroughly shaken by his ordeal, Miller had to be carried back to the factory, but he remained obdurate, and the women did not receive a wage-rise.

One should not assume from this that women remained outside the orbit of the labour movement. Thanks to the efforts of small numbers of socialist women, working women rapidly began to join the trade unions and to engage in more organised forms of struggle. There are no data on the number of women in the trade unions, but it does not appear that the industries with the highest proportions of women workers were necessarily those with low densities of trade-union membership. In the food and textile industries women comprised 66% and 69% of the workforce, respectively, but trade-union membership stood at about 80% and 70%. Trade-union membership was lowest in the chemical industry — at about 48% — which does seem to have been linked to the fact that the skilled men joined the metal and woodturners' unions, leaving the peasant women machine-operators, who comprised 47% of the workforce, to fend for themselves. In the metal industry, however, men encouraged women workers to join the union, and it is probable that a majority of working women joined trade unions in the course of 1917, although the evidence does not suggest that they participated actively in union life. Women were poorly represented in leadership positions in the unions, even in industries where they comprised a majority of the workforce. Eleven out of twenty members of the first board of the textile union were women, but only two remained after its reorganisation — alongside thirteen men. The Petrograd boards of the metal, leather and needleworkers' unions were equally unrepresentative — each having a solitary woman member.

In the factory committees a similar situation existed. Women comprised a third of the factory workforce, but only 4% of the delegates to the First Conference of Factory Committees. At the Triangle rubber works 68% of the workforce was female, but only two of the twenty-five members of the factory "soviet" were women. At the Nevskaya footwear factory 45% of the workforce was female, but none of the *starosty* was a woman. At the Pechatkin paper-mill 45% of the workforce was female,

but only two out of thirteen *starosty* were women. At the Sampsionevskaya cotton-mill, where 85% of the workforce were women, representation was rather better, for four out of seven members of the committee
were women. This suggests that in industries where women were in the
majority, they may have tended to be less dependent on men — and
more self-reliant.

Those socialist women who devoted so much effort to organising
working women accused the labour leaders of not paying enough attention to the special needs of women. In June A. Kollontai reproached
the delegates to the Third Trade-Union Conference for not taking up
questions of maternity provision and equal pay. In September she wrote
an article for the journal of the Petrograd Council of Trade Unions,
which urged union leaders to treat women "not as appendages to men,
but as independent, responsible members of the working class, having
the same rights and also the same responsibilities to the collective." In
October she spoke to the First All-Russian Conference of Factory Committees warning of the political danger of their remaining indifferent to
the plight of women workers. At none of the conferences of the labour
movement in 1917, however, was there a full discussion of the problems of working women and of their relationship to the organised labour
movement.

At factory level women workers often met with active discrimination from men in their attempts to organise. At the Pipe works a woman
complained. "It happens, not infrequently even now, that the backward
workers, who lack consciousness, cannot imagine that a woman can be
as capable as a man of organising the broad masses, and so they make
fun of the elected representatives of the women workers, pointing their
fingers as though at a savage, and saying with a sneer: 'there go our
elected representatives.'" M. Tsvetkova wrote to the leatherworkers'
journal, complaining about the behaviour of her male colleagues:

> *Instead of supporting, organising and going hand-in-hand with the
> women, they behave as though we are not equal members of the working
> family and sometimes do not bother with us at all. When the question of
> unemployment and redundancies arises, they try to ensure that the men
> stay and that the women go, hoping that the women will be unable to
> resist because of their poor organisation and feebleness. When women
> attempt to speak, in order to point out that the men are behaving
> wrongly and that we must jointly find a solution, the men will not*

allow us to speak and will not listen. It is difficult even for the more conscious women to fight against this, the more so since often the mass of women do not understand and do not wish to listen to us.

Labour leaders, generally, opposed active discrimination against working women (for example, over redundancies). They encouraged them to organise, and the struggles of working women began to assume a more disciplined character, although "spontaneous" militancy by no means disappeared. Labour leaders were genuinely solicitous of the needs of working women as low-paid workers, but less solicitous of their needs as women. They spurned any idea of specific policies for working women, believing that this would be a deviation towards bourgeois feminism. The result was that women joined the labour movement, but played a passive role within it. After October this was to result once more in women becoming apathetic and indifferent.

Peasant and Unskilled Workers

Like women workers, peasant and unskilled workers displayed a preference for direct action over formal organisation, and a certain distrust of labour leaders. At the Metal works a carpenter described the attitude of new workers to the trade unions as follows:

A majority of workers . . . in essence do not belong to the category of true proletarians. These people have come to the factory from the countryside in order to avoid military service and the war, or to assist the rural household with a good factory wage. This element . . . will move only when it feels that it is directly defending its own interests, but it has not grasped the principle of organising the working masses into unions for permanent, day-to-day struggle. They reduce this principle merely to paying subscriptions, and argue that they do not need this extra expense, or frankly admit that they are going to leave the factory as soon as the war is over and return to the countryside.

He also blamed the "cadre" workers for "neglecting the organisation of their less conscious comrades." When the union tried to implement the metalworkers' contract in autumn, over half the workers in the Metal works refused the wage category into which they were placed by the rates commission, inundating the factory committee with demands to be upgraded. In November unskilled painters beat up a representative of the metalworkers' union and refused to release him until he agreed to sign an order granting all workers a wage of twelve rubles a day, back-dated to 5 June.

At the Pipe works the Bolsheviks, whose fortunes were in the ascendant, agitated for new elections to the Vasilevskii district soviet, which were fixed for 17 May. The Petrograd Soviet Executive, however, arranged a meeting at the factory for that day, so the shop stewards agreed to postpone elections. The peasant workers in the foundry were outraged and resolved to press ahead with the elections. Kapanitskii, a shop steward and an SR deputy to the Soviet, was sent to persuade the foundryworkers to change their minds. The official protocol of a general factory meeting describes what happened: "The foundryworkers sat comrade Kapanitskii in a wheelbarrow, beat him and threatened to throw him in the furnace, but then decided to save the furnace for other people. They confined themselves to wheeling him out into the factory yard and then to the river. It was only thanks to the intervention of comrades in shops numbers eight and four that he was released." A few Bolsheviks seem to have provoked or connived in this action. The shop steward of the foundry blamed the violence on a handful of workers, when he made a public apology to the general meeting.

Like women workers, unskilled and peasant workers did begin to organise in 1917. *Chernorabochie* set up a trade union in April, which later merged with the metal union. . . . Similarly, peasant workers and soldiers formed some seventy *zemlyachestva* in the capitals to bring together migrants from the same area and to undertake political agitation among the peasantry. The total membership of the *zemlyachestva* may have been as high as 30,000, and by September the major ones had swung from the SRs to the Bolsheviks.

Young Workers

Workers under the age of eighteen showed a far greater capacity for self-organisation than women or peasant workers, though girls were far less active than boys. They built a youth movement — which acquired a strongly Bolshevik character — in the shape of the Socialist Union of Working Youth (SUWY). Through this, they played a leading role in the political events of 1917 (the July Days and the October seizure of power). Many young workers joined the Bolshevik party and the Red Guards: it has been estimated that 19% of those joining the Petrograd

Bolshevik party were under twenty-one, and no fewer than 28% of Red Guards were of this age. Working youth played a less prominent part in the organised labour movement, however, which seems to have been connected to the fact that workers under eighteen were in a relationship of dependence on adult workers in the workplace.

In the wake of the February Revolution, young workers began to set up committees in the factories, first in the metal works of Vyborg, Narva and Vasilevskii districts, and then spreading to other industries and areas. Out of these factory youth groups there developed district youth organisations and, subsequently, the city-wide youth movement. From the first, these factory youth groups demanded representation on the factory committees. At some of the more politically radical enterprises this demand was conceded. At the Phoenix, Aivaz and Renault works the factory committees allowed young workers two representatives. At the Cable works the committee supported the young workers' demand for the vote at eighteen and called on the Provisional Government to withdraw eighteen-years-olds from the Front if it would not enfranchise them. A majority of factory committees, however, were more reluctant to allow young workers special representation and to take up their demands. Under pressure, committees at the Baltic, Putilov and Gun works allowed youth representatives to sit on the committees but not to vote. Young workers at the Gun works condemned the committee's refusal to allow their representatives voting rights: "We protest because the father-proletariat, in spurning his children, makes it harder for us to become, in the future, experienced, hardened fighters for right, honour and the triumph of the world proletariat and, of course, in the first place, of our own proletariat." At the Kersten knitting mill the factory committee — which was the first in the textile industry to implement workers' control — also refused voting rights to the two representatives of the 660 girls at the mill. The youth committee condemned this policy, but argued that "your representative on our committee may only have an advisory voice since no organisation may interfere in the affairs of youth." In May a conference of factory committees on Vyborg Side agreed that young workers could have voting rights on the committees, but only on matters affecting their economic position.

The trade unions supported the demands for improved wages for young workers and came out in support of a six-hour day for young workers. They were slower to take up demands for the overhauling of the system of apprenticeship and for the vote at eighteen, although Bolshevik-dominated unions supported them. There are no statistics on the age structure of union membership. Young workers seem to have joined the unions, but many officially debarred workers under the age of sixteen from membership. For obvious reasons of age and inexperience, workers under 18 were not represented at leadership level in the unions, but union leaders were by no means old. At the first national congress of metalworkers in January 1918 the average age of delegates was twenty-nine, and at the first congress of leatherworkers, at around the same time, 54% of delegates were under thirty, although only 15% were under twenty-five.

It is clear that the forms of collective action engaged in by most women, peasant and unskilled workers were different from those of "cadre" workers. In general, the former lacked "resources" for sustained, institutionalised pursuit of goals, and turned most easily to forms of "direct action," such as "carting out," wildcat strikes, go-slows. These forms of action were often violent and always sectional, but they were not as irrational as they may seem. "Carting out," for example, entailed a level of communication and coordination, and a conception of appropriate action, though not necessarily a specific plan of action. It was a symbolic action, born of anger and emotion rather than calculation, but it had a certain rationality as a type of "collective bargaining by riot." The evidence suggests that as the economic crisis grew worse, such forms of "direct action" became increasingly less effective — a sign of desperation and weakness, rather than of confidence and strength.

To the leaders of the factory committees and trade unions, spontaneous forms of militancy on the part of the new workers were a threat to the project of building an organised labour movement, and were thus condemned as "backward." The labour leaders sought to direct "spontaneity" into organised channels, for they believed that the pursuit of the interests of workers as a class, and the achievement of far-reaching social and political changes on their behalf required effective organisation and clearly-formulated goals. Whilst spontaneous militancy might be effective in securing the aims of a section of workers in the short term, it could not secure the ends of the working class as a whole. They recognised, moreover, that only formal organisation and planned action could achieve maximum gains at minimum cost. They thus sought to "tame" the volatile, explosive militancy of the new workers, and aspired to bring them within the orbit of the organised labour movement: to teach them habits of negotiation, formulation of demands, the practices of committees and meetings. They seem to have had some success, notwithstanding the unpropitious economic circumstances, in subordinating *buntarstvo* to bargaining.

The labour leaders were sincerely anxious to promote the welfare of those workers less fortunate than themselves. They believed that both new and experienced workers shared the same class interests and could best pursue these through united organisation and struggle. They were, however, unwilling to recognise that there might be contradictions of interest between women and men, youths and adults, or unskilled and skilled. They thus would not give special treatment to any of these groups, for example, by setting up organisations within the unions for women workers or by allowing young workers special representation on the factory committees. Although they justified their position in political terms — the working class is a unity in which there are no diversities of interest — this attitude reflected the social position of the leaders themselves. For within the craft tradition of the "organisation-builders," skill was closely bound up with masculinity and a degree of condescension towards women and youth. Thus in spite of their very best intentions — their determination to involve all workers in the labour movement — the efforts of the labour leaders were stymied by an unconscious paternalism towards those whom they were trying to organise.

Democracy and Bureaucracy in the Trade Unions and Factory Committees

Democracy in the Trade Unions

One usually thinks of "democratic centralism" as the organisational principle espoused by the Bolshevik party, but the principle was accepted by the labour movement as a whole. The Third Trade-Union Conference resolved that "democratic centralism" should underpin the organisational construction of the trade-union movement, in order to ensure "the participation of every member in the affairs of the union and, at the same time, unity in the leadership of the struggle." "Democratic centralism" did not represent a coherent set of organisational rules; it was rather a vague principle of democratic decision-making, combined with centralised execution of decisions taken. The balance between "democracy" and "centralism" was thus not fixed with any precision, and within the trade unions, in the course of 1917, the balance tended to shift away from democracy towards centralism.

The great majority of Petrograd factory workers joined trade unions in 1917, but the data on membership are unreliable, and so one cannot determine the percentage of members in each branch of industry. Rough calculations suggest that the percentage was highest in printing (over 90%); that in the leather, wood and metal industries it was 80% or more; that in the textiles it was around 70%, but that in chemicals it was as low as 48%. In many metal-works general meetings of workers voted to join the union *en bloc*, though in a minority of factories, such as the Metal works the factory committees resisted this "closed shop" policy. In other industries, too, with the exception of chemicals, workers tended to make the decision to join the union collectively rather than individually. On 8 May delegates of the woodturners' union threatened to expel from the factories any worker who refused to join the union.

Union subscriptions were designed to attract all workers, including the low-paid, into the union. Initial membership of the metal union cost one ruble, and monthly dues were graduated according to earnings. Workers earning more than ten rubles a day paid 1 r. 40 k.; those earning less than six rubles, paid 80 k. a month, and apprentices paid 50 k. Union delegates would stand outside the finance-office on pay day to ensure that all workers paid their dues. Initially, most union members seem to have paid their dues: in the metal union the monthly sum of subscriptions rose from 94,335 r. in June to 133,540 r. in July; in the textile union it rose from 4,800 r. in May to 10,000 r. in July. As the economic crisis set in, however, non-payment of union dues became a major problem. In the leather union the monthly sum of dues fell from 18,093 r. in May to 15,167 r. in July. The glass union reported in September that "subscriptions are being paid promptly," but in December reported that only 326 out of 807 members in Petrograd had paid their dues that month.

The collection of monthly dues, the distribution of union publications, the convening of union meetings and the liaison between the individual enterprises and the union hierarchy devolved on factory delegates. These delegates were elected by all the union members in a particular enterprise: in the textile industry delegates were elected on the basis of one delegate for every twenty union members; in the metal industry on the basis of one delegate for every hundred union members. In some of the larger factories union delegates formed councils within the factory, but the main job of delegates was to liaise with other factories in the same industry and district of Petrograd. In the print industry the delegates (*upolnomochennye*) had a similiar job to factory delegates in other industries, except that they also formed the workshop committee. The division between the trade union and the factory committee thus did not exist in the print industry. Union delegates from each enterprise met at city-district level at least once a month to discuss union business, to oversee the activities of the union board and to discuss problems in individual enterprises. In many unions, including the metal, print and leather unions, the delegates elected district boards of the union, which were responsible for liaising between the city board of the union and the individual enterprise and for organising recruitment and the collection of subscriptions. In the metal and print unions some delegates defended the autonomy of the district boards from the city board, fearing that too much centralisation at city level would lead to bureaucratisation of the union.

In principle, if not always in practice, power was vested in the city boards, not the district boards, of the unions. The city boards were elected by city-wide meetings of union delegates (comprising either representatives of city-district delegate meetings or all district delegates *en masse*). On 7 May 535 delegates elected the Petrograd board of the metal union. On 4 June 300 delegates from twenty-six textile mills elected sixteen members to the city board of the textile union. The city board was responsible for coordinating economic struggles, dispensing strike funds, publishing the union journal and for negotiation with the SFWO and the government. In those unions, such as the print, leather and food unions, where professional sections representing individual crafts existed, these were subordinate to the city board. Where district boards existed, these too were subordinate to the city board, though resistance to central control by the district boards was by no means unknown — particularly in the sphere of finance. The members of the city boards — and often the secretaries and treasurers of the district boards — were usually employed full-time by the union.

By the summer of 1917, the Petrograd metal union had almost a hundred full-time officials. Clearly, "bureaucratisation" was under way, although it would be wrong to exaggerate the extent of this. The powers of the city boards were strictly circumscribed, and in all unions the boards in theory were strictly subordinate to the city-wide meetings of union delegates. It was these meetings, rather than the boards themselves, which decided all major policy issues. The boards reported to city delegate meetings at least once a month and members of the boards could be recalled by the delegates. Conflicts arose between the boards and the delegates which reflected the ambitions of the boards to extend their power, and the determination of the delegates to resist this process. The extent of democracy in the unions thus depended on the activism and enthusiasm of the delegates. Where they were remiss in their duties, then not only did the union board develop into an oligarchy but the ordinary members of the union tended to lapse into apathy. This seems to have been an increasing problem in the metal union by the later months of 1917. A worker wrote to the union journal complaining of the behaviour or many factory delegates:

> *If the central and district boards [of the union] are responsible to the meetings of [factory] delegates, then the delegates themselves are responsible to nobody. The majority of delegates, once elected, do not fulfil their duties, they do not recruit members, they do not collect subscriptions and do not even appear at delegate meetings . . . All the time we observe a host of instances where the majority of our members are not aware of the policies and decisions of the central organs . . . Naturally such ignorance at times causes apathy in the membership. Often one feels that the central organs of the union are totally cut off from the mass of the members. This threatens to turn the central organisation into a bureaucracy.*

By the end of 1917 there is growing evidence that power within the union was passing away from the rank-and-file to the full-time officials of the unions. This should not, however, blind us to the fact that before October a significant degree of membership participation in the affairs of the union existed.

Democracy in the Factory Committees

Factory committees were much closer to ordinary workers than trade unions. They embraced all the workers in a single enterprise, whereas the trade unions embraced workers in a branch of industry. The committees represented all workers in a factory regardless of their job, whereas workers in the same factory might be members of different

Red Guards, 1917. Such workers were recruited to serve as defenders of the Revolution. (Sovfoto)

trade unions, despite the principle of industrial unionism. The factory committee represented everyone *gratis*, whereas one had to pay to be a member of a trade union. The committee usually met in working hours on the factory premises, whereas trade unions usually did not. For all these reasons, therefore, factory committees tended to be the more popular organisation. The SR, I. Prizhelaev, wrote: "The factory committees have the crucial merit of being close to the worker, accessible, comprehensible to everybody — even the least conscious. They were involved in all the minutiae of factory life and so are a wonderful form of mass organisation . . . The trade unions are less accessible because they appear to stand further away from the rank-and-file worker." 7,000 workers at the Respirator factory on 3 September described the factory committees as "the best mouthpieces of the working class and the only real and true reflection of the moods of the toiling people."

Every worker could vote in the election of a factory committee, regardless of job, sex or age. Any worker might stand for election, so long as he or she did not perform any managerial function. Some factories, such as the Putilov works, stipulated that workers under the age of twenty might not stand for election. Elections were supposed to be by secret ballot, according to the constitution drawn up by the conference of representatives of state enterprises (15 April), the statutes published by the labour department of the Petrograd Soviet and the model constitution passed by the Second Conference of Factory Committees. Initially, factory committees were elected for one year, but the Second Conference specified that they should be elected for six months only. Factory committees could be recalled at any time by general meetings, and they were required to report on their activities to general meetings at least once a month.

The extent to which the working-class movement was permeated by a commitment to direct democracy is reflected in the fact that it was not the factory committee *per se* which was the sovereign organ in the factory, but the general meeting of all workers in the factory or section. It was this general assembly which passed resolutions on the pressing political questions of the day or decided important matters affecting the individual enterprise. This Rousseauesque concept of sovereignty was established in practice from the first. At the conference of representatives from state enterprises on 15 April it was decided that general meetings of the factory workforce should take place at least once a month and should be called by either the factory committee or by one-third of the workforce. The Second Conference lowered this requirement, by stipulating that one-fifth of the workforce might summon a general meeting, which should be attended by at least one-third of the workers in order to be quorate. The Conference laid down that authority was vested in the workforce as a whole rather than in the committee.

Marc Ferro has argued recently that we should not allow ourselves to be bewitched by the far-reaching democracy of the paper constitutions of the popular organisations of the Russian Revolution: reality was a very different matter. He argues that long before October the popular organisations were undergoing a process of bureaucratisation "from above" and "from below." In the case of the factory committees, Ferro argues that the leadership of the movement became more entrenched and less accountable to the membership. Bureaucratisation "from above" was manifest in a decline in the proportion of delegates at factory-committee conferences elected from the factories and in an increase in the proportion of "bureaucratically appointed" delegates. Bureaucratisation "from below" was evident in the refusal of factory committee members on the ground to submit to re-election, and in the growing practice of inquorate meetings taking decisions. It is not the present purpose to criticise Ferro's work in detail, although scrutiny of his evidence suggests neither that the proportion of "bureaucratically appointed" delegates at the factory committee conferences was on the increase in 1917, nor that they were in a position to influence conference decisions, since many of them did not have voting rights. What is pertinent to the concerns of this chapter is the extent to which factory committees on the ground were subject to re-election prior to October.

Re-elections took place at the Putilov, Electric Light, Pipe, Dinamo, Langenzippen, Skorokhod, Parviainen, Lessner, the Mint, Promet and Okhta shell-works. In other factories individual members of the committees were replaced. At the Baltic works the first committee was self-selected, but it was properly elected in the second half of April. At the end of July a general meeting expressed no confidence in the committee, but the committee did not immediately resign. Only when a further general meeting on 15 September voted for its immediate recall, did it step down. Any party or non-party group was allowed to put up a slate of candidates in the new election, providing it could muster fifty signatures. The slates were then published and voting took place on 18 September by secret ballot. The Bolsheviks won a majority of the forty places. Even if the committees in a majority of factories did not submit for re-election (and it is not clear that this was the case), it was not necessarily a sign of their bureaucratisation, for many had not completed their six-month term of office by October.

Data on the proportion of workers who took part in factory committee elections are exiguous, but they suggest that in most factories a majority of workers took part. At the Pechatkin paper mill in March 57% of workers voted in elections. At the Sestroretsk arms works the committee declared soviet elections void when only half the electorate bothered to vote. It urged workers that: "In view of the seriousness of the present moment, general factory meetings must be well-attended. It is the duty of every worker, as an honest citizen, to attend discussions of all questions concerning both the factory itself and the government in general." On 1 August, when the Sestroretsk works committee was re-elected, 72% of the workers voted. In the same month 88% of workers at Parviainen voted in factory committee elections. In September 69% of workers at New Lessner took part in elections, and in October 74% of workers at the Pipe works.

Surveying the available evidence, it becomes clear that the degree of democracy in operation varied between factories, and that undemocratic practices were by no means unknown. Yet what strikes one about the period prior to October is not the growing bureaucratisation of the factory committees in Petrograd, but the extent to which they managed to realise an astonishing combination of direct and representational democracy.

This is not to dispose of the problem of "bureaucracy," however, for "bureaucracy" and "democracy" need not be polar opposites. It depends in part how one understands "bureaucracy." Max Weber emphasised the inter-relationship of bureaucracy, rationality and legitimate authority (*Herrschaft*), and the factory committees were, to an extent, "bureaucratic" in the Weberian sense. Far from being anarchic, protozoan bodies, the committees were solid, structurally-ramified organisations which functioned in a regular routinised manner. The duties of the committees and their sub-commissions were fixed by rules and administrative dispositions; their activities were spelt out in written records; to a point, the committees followed "general rules which are more or less stable, more or less exhaustive and which can be learned." In other respects, the committees operated in marked contrast to the Weberian model. There was no strict hierarchical system of authority, such that the lower levels of the factory committee movement were subordinate to the higher levels, though this was, arguably, the aspiration of the CCFC. The members of the committees in no way saw themselves as functionaries operating according to fixed rules. They were policy-makers in their own right who viewed their "office" as a means of effecting economic and social change. They were not trained for office and enjoyed no stability of tenure. Finally, they were not appointed by some impersonal organisation, but elected by and accountable to the workers. Nevertheless, in order to implement the goals of workers' control, the committees had begun to develop a degree of bureaucracy and autonomy from the rank-and-file to ensure that spheres of day-to-day, practical activity were left to their discretion. Herein lay a potential for the factory-committee leaders to become a bureaucratic stratum separate from, rather than organically linked to their worker constituency. Moreover, within labour organisations this potential for bureaucratisation existed in a different form, which has been succinctly analysed by Richard Hyman in relationship to trade unionism:

> *There is an important sense in which the problem of "bureaucracy" denotes not so much a distinct* stratum of personnel *as a* relationship *which permeates the whole practice of trade unionism. "Bureaucracy" is in large measure a question of the differential distribution of expertise and activism: of the* dependence *of the mass of union membership on the initiative and strategic experience of a relatively small cadre of leadership — both "official" and "unofficial" . . . the "bad side of leadership" still constitutes a problem even in the case of a cadre of militant lay activists sensitive to the need to encourage the autonomy and initiative of the membership.*

In the Russian labour movement the dependence of the rank-and-file on the initiative and experience of the leadership was particularly acute, in view of the fact that the rank-and-file comprised unskilled or semi-skilled women and peasant workers unused to organisation. The skilled, proletarianised male leaders of the labour movement sought to bind these inexperienced workers into a disciplined unity, so that they might realise their democratic potential and exercise power on their own behalf. In so doing, they ran the constant danger of *dominating* the rank-and-file. As early as autumn, a woman from the Nevka cotton-spinning mill, where 92% of the workforce were women, complained of the behaviour of the overwhelmingly male factory committee: "They have done a lot to organise the dark mass, but now reveal a desire to concentrate all power in their hands. They are beginning to boss their backward comrades, to act without accountability . . . They deal with the workers roughly, haughtily, using expressions like 'To the devil's mother with you!'" Later a leatherworker from the Osipov saddle factory wrote to the leatherworkers' newspaper:

> *Often members of the committees gradually become cut off from the masses, they become alienated from them and lose their confidence. Quite often the masses blame them for becoming autocrats, for taking no account of the mood of the majority of workers, for being too conciliatory. This, it is true, is explained by the peculiar conditions of the present time, by the acerbity of the masses, by their low level of culture; but sometimes the factory committee members themselves provoke such a reaction by their behaviour. They get on their high horse and pay scant attention to the voice of the workers. Sometimes they show little enthusiasm or do very little and this causes discontent among the masses.*

The balance between democracy and bureaucracy in the labour movement depended on the economic and political conditions in society at large. So long as these conditions were favourable to the revolutionary goals which the labour leaders had set themselves, then democratic elements overrode bureaucratic elements, i.e., the conditions were such that the popular forces could check the effectivity of bureaucratic forces. Once these conditions changed radically, as they did after October, bureaucratic elements came to the fore, which fostered the emergence of a bureaucratic stratum dominating the whole of society. After October the Bolshevik leaders of the factory committees, sincerely committed to workers' democracy, but losing their working-class base, began to concentrate power in their hands, excluded the masses from information and decision-making and set up a hierarchy of functions. The trade unions, too, became less accountable to their members, since they were now accountable to the government, and soon turned primarily into economic apparatuses of the state. This may all suggest that bureaucratisation was inscribed in the revolutionary process in 1917, but if so, it was inscribed as a *possibility* only: one cannot pessimistically invoke some "iron law of oligarchy." Democratic and bureaucratic elements existed in a determinate relationship in all popular organisations — a relationship which was basically determined by the goals of the organisations and the degree to which those goals were facilitated by political and economic circumstances. These circumstances were to change dramatically in the autumn of 1917, and it was this change which shifted the balance between the forces of democracy and bureaucracy in favour of the latter.

William G. Rosenberg

Kadets and Kornilov

A graduate of Amherst College and Harvard University, William G. Rosenberg has done fundamental research on various aspects of the revolution and civil war — the liberal Constitutional Democratic party, the railroad workers, the strike movement, and labor in the immediate post-October period. Professor of Russian history at the University of Michigan, Rosenberg has served as director of the Center for Russian and East European Studies. In addition to his monograph on the Kadets, Rosenberg has published *Transforming Russia and China* (1982) (with Marilyn Young), a collection on *Bolshevik Visions* (1984), and *Strikes and Revolution in Russia, 1917* (1989) (with Diane Koenker). His research has demonstrated that the process that created class cohesion through 1917 was reversed after October and that the economic collapse contributed to fragmentation of worker unity and a crisis for the ruling Bolshevik party. In this excerpt from his study of the liberals Rosenberg untangles the web of intentions and consequences that bound the Kadets and Kerensky to General Kornilov's failed attempt to seize power in August 1917.

Liberals could no longer hope to govern by themselves, or even to establish an authoritative, liberal, provisional regime. These possibilities had disappeared with the prolonged crisis in July, and perhaps even before. Social disruption in the countryside, unease and dissension

William G. Rosenberg, *Liberals in the Russian Revolution: The Constitutional Democratic Party, 1917–1921*. Copyright © 1974 by Princeton University Press. Excerpts, pp. 179–228, reprinted with permission of Princeton University Press.

among workers, growing anarchy, and above all, the constant deterioration of Russia's military forces all pressed in the direction of social reforms, particularly in the countryside. They also impelled a rapid end to the war, as well as the election of a popular democratic government through the Constituent Assembly. At the level of high politics, consequently, the best hope — and perhaps the *last* best hope — for civil liberties, a permanent rule of law, and other traditional liberal goals, was to preserve and protect the Provisional regime, just as Kadets had tried to preserve and protect the Second Duma in 1907. This meant cooperation and close relations with Soviet leaders.

Social and political stability at a local level also required cooperation with the left. Kadets all over Russia complained bitterly of "anarchy" and "chaos," but what they were describing in effect was the extent to which political and social administration in the country was coming increasingly under the control of committees, soviets, and other ad hoc local organizations. By the end of July 1917, the influence of these groups could be felt in every city, town, and village, every factory and workshop, every railroad junction, school, and garrison. In one ironic sense, in fact, Russia in the summer of 1917 may have been better organized than at any other time in her history, in that virtually all institutional life was at least to some extent in committee or soviet hands. These groups lacked coordination or even clear policies. They were simply attempting in a chaotic fashion to remedy pressing, deep-rooted social problems on a particularistic and piecemeal basis, with scant regard for questions of political order. Nevertheless, these groups were now clearly managing most Russian affairs at a local level, just as zemstvos had done in many parts of Russia before the revolution; and for Kadets and other liberals to have any positive effect on the country's local affairs, it was necessary to begin working closely and cooperatively with them, and attempt to influence their activities from within.

The problem was, of course, that on a local level most Kadets strongly disagreed with the direction in which the committees and soviets were moving. There was also an enormous amount of mutual distrust, as Kadets appeared increasingly to represent "bourgeois" and gentry interests, while committees and soviets seemed increasingly the tools of radicals like the Bolsheviks. The conflict was, in a word, whether Russia's revolution had meaning primarily in terms of social or political democracy, whether national interests superseded popular ones. In seizing estates and taking control of factories and even army units, the "dark people" and their leaders were corrupting the very values and institutions on which liberals felt their country's future rested.

At the level of high politics, meanwhile, the problem was that liberals who favored conciliation lacked power within the government, or even authority within the party. Nekrasov was now completely discredited among most Petrograd and Moscow party members; and while nominally still a Kadet, was soon to be ceremoniously "disowned" at the ninth party congress. The other Kadet ministers were all virtually handpicked by Miliukov; and despite the divisions in the Central Committee over both the July resignations and the terms for further Kadet participation in the government (as well as a good deal of hostility toward the Kadet leader personally, whose somewhat arrogant personality had become even more abrasive through fatigue and anxiety), Miliukov and his supporters still held sway.

For them, in fact, the July crisis had resulted in a shift away from what earlier could be described as a "centrist" posture, and the assumption of a position much closer to that of the party's clear conservatives like Maklakov, Rodichev, and Izgoev. Having finally been forced into what he regarded as an unacceptable solution to the July crisis, and finally accepting Russian polarization as a present fact rather than future threat, Miliukov was assuming what Leopold Haimson has called a "civil war mentality," one which saw the future of liberal Russia absolutely dependent on the strict — and perhaps forcible — containment of the soviets and committees, rather than cooperation or conciliation. Even the Kadet party's own internal unity was becoming much less important, as would shortly be clear at the ninth congress. As Maklakov argued, there could be no freedom *bez Rodiny*, without, that is, the Great Russian State of the liberal's nationalist conception. If Kadets moved in any direction, it had to be to consolidate and strengthen Russia's "healthy elements."

By the end of July, this had also become the firm view of a majority of provincial party leaders. Pressed by the anxiety and fear of increasing local violence, discouraged by the results of municipal duma campaigns, increasingly harassed by Bolsheviks and other radicals in public meetings, and unable to recruit new cadres, most provincial committee members now felt more strongly than ever that the party had to end its ostensible "nonpartisanship," and ally firmly with right-wing groups. This required the adoption of a much more partisan program, a clearer statement of the Kadets' own national and class biases. . . .

The obvious advantage of moving openly to the right would be a consolidation of anti-socialist political strength, and the development of new abilities to coordinate political and economic pressures against the left. But there was also the obvious danger of further polarizing Russian society as a whole, and the much greater likelihood of civil war. And what then about Russia's role as a great power? Even Kadets like Novgorodtsev, Dolgorukov, Rodichev, and Izgoev shied away from considering open civil combat. Just as most Kadets could never become militant revolutionaries against the tsar, most could not see themselves now as militant counterrevolutionaries against the mass of Russian people.

What seemed to be the logical course for most Kadets in these circumstances was to shift openly from the position of "left-center" (as Miliukov had described it at the eighth congress) to "right center," playing on new hostility toward the Bolsheviks which had developed even in moderate socialist quarters after the July days, identifying the party programmatically with more openly conservative groups, and in particular, giving full support to the army and its forceful new commander, General Kornilov. At best, this might lead party cadres in the provinces to closer associations with groups like the Union of Landowners (completing, in effect, the swing in this direction which had begun as early as April, and perhaps bringing some new sense of personal security); and there was even some possibility that discipline throughout society as a whole could be restored through the use of "loyalist" troops like the cossacks, sanctioned by the government as a result of pressures from the Kadet ministers. Perhaps in these circumstances Kadets could even return a reasonable delegation to the Constituent Assembly (though it would obviously be a minority), whenever that body convened.

As time would tell, however, the optimism underlying such a course for Kadets was bred of despair, rather than a clear perception of viable politics. More important, it meant firing up General Kornilov's own ambitions, which for many liberals would create the greatest dilemma of all.

The ninth Kadet congress, which opened on July 23, just as negoti-ations over a new government were ending, was convened specifically to prepare the party for the Constituent Assembly campaign; and most delegates arriving for the sessions were prepared to convince Miliukov and the Petrograd leadership that the only effective way to enter the electoral struggle was in alliance with clearly anti-soviet groups. . . .

It turned out, however, that Miliukov and most of his colleagues now needed very little convincing. . . .

When Miliukov himself addressed the delegates after the cabinet had been formed, he took little time to align himself clearly with the party's right. Gone was his past role of "unifier." A coalition had indeed been organized with Kadet participation, he argued, contrary to what many Kadets had hoped or been led to expect. . . . But Kadets had entered the cabinet only because Russia had been plunged into a situa-tion where the alternative would have been no government at all. The Petrograd leadership fully recognized Russia's condition, and appre-ciated the needs and desires of provincial delegates. The country was in chaos: "chaos in the army, chaos in foreign policy, chaos in industry, and chaos in nationality questions, which had resulted in the recogni-tion of the Ukrainian Rada and the departure of the Kadet ministers." . . . In sum, Miliukov declared, the Kadet ministers remained deter-mined now as before to defend the country's best interests; they would pull the regime away from soviet domination and strengthen state au-thority "from within." . . . Despite the fact that a number of the approximately 200 ninth congress delegates were still partisans of con-ciliation (including now some prominent new adherents in the Cen-tral Committee like Astrov, Kishkin, and perhaps even Vinaver and Nabokov), the course charted by Miliukov was enthusiastically en-dorsed. (According to *Rech'*, support was "unanimous," though only a voice vote was taken.) Kadets would undertake a new struggle against sectarian left-wing elements, and in the face of "a most critical danger threatening the very existence" of the country, "dedicate all forces to saving the Motherland."

What these forces were the leadership soon made clear. First among them was the army, particularly its officer corps. Traditionally, liberals had insisted that the military be kept out of politics. But now Kadets were clearly anxious to show support for General Kornilov, and argued they had to "agitate" to win soldiers from the radicals. These were extraordinary times, Miliukov declared, and extraordinary times demanded special measures. The official report of the Central Committee's military commission obscured the question somewhat, stating only that "mutual relations between military personnel must be founded on principles of legality and firm military discipline, and correspond to the basic principles of democratic government." But a suggestion that a statement be added to the effect that the army was "nonpolitical" was specifically rejected; and despite a certain ambiguity in the report (which some delegates, in fact, protested), its general meaning was clear. The validity of Nicholas Sukhanov's challenge to Miliukov in April, which assumed the army would become *the* crucial political battleground of revolutionary Russia, was now being formally recognized.

Also clear were the implicit purposes underlying the party's statements on agriculture and industry. Ariadna Tyrkova and V. A. Kosinskii attributed rural unrest directly to Chernov's "socializing adventures." Socialism ran "counter to innate peasant attachment to property." The lack of peasant productivity, the weakening of labor intensity, the decline of peasant willingness to work — all these developments were the result of "socialist experimentation." Tyrkova and Kosinskii even insisted that Kadets take up Stepanov's earlier call and urge the regime to renounce socialism officially: if peasants understood that socialism threatened property in land, they would "follow no other political party but our own. This will lead us out of the horror and chaos which threatens our agrarian life." . . .

The most dramatic indications of the party's move to the right, however, came not on economic matters, but on the nationality issue, and the question of the church. According to Baron Nolde, a member of the government's Juridical Commission and a distinguished professor of law, the Central Committee had resolved "in a final way" to reject the territorial basis as the framework for resolving the nationality question. Kadets would press instead for nationality "unions," to be recognized as quasi-official organizations, and enjoying the prerogatives of administering all *cultural* affairs pertaining to their particular ethnic group.

As Grigorovich-Barskii pointed out — and he was certainly no radical — Nolde's theses meant that Kadets absolutely rejected autonomy for the Ukraine in geographic terms. This not only contradicted what party committees in the Ukraine believed themselves, but made absurd the Kadets' past positions on "other nationality groups," as Barskii described them, like Poland and Finland. But the congress as a whole accepted Nolde's theses as amendments to the party's program. . . .

The question of the church was even more scandalous, at least to left Kadets. Here delegates were not only asked to change the party program so that orthodoxy was designated an "institution of public-legal (*publichno-pravovyi*) character," but also to sanction state aid so that Kadets did not appear "to recommend separation of church and state as the socialist parties do." Such a position corresponded to the programs of prerevolutionary rightist parties, and would obviously appeal to Russia's remaining conservative elements. But it also clearly violated the Kadets' own program (paragraph 2 of which clearly committed Kadets to the separation of church and state); and it implicitly threw into question the whole liberal attitude toward religious discrimination, as several of the delegates pointed out. . . .

For their rightward drifting colleagues, however, the future was clear. Kadets had only to translate the angry, conservative mood of the congress into political force.

Allies on the Right

Immediately after the ninth congress, Rodichev, Kharlamov, and M. S. Voronkov left for Novocherkassk to develop closer ties between Kadets and the Don cossacks, the traditional defenders of state authority. Kharlamov and Voronkov were prominent members of the Kadet committee in Rostov, while Rodichev had now become one of the party's foremost right-wing spokesmen. Kharlamov was also president of the Don Voisko, the cossacks' military administration, in addition to being a member of the party's Central Committee. The task of the three Kadets was to form a Kadet-cossack "united front," and to consolidate efforts for the Constituent Assembly elections. . . .

Meanwhile, Kadets also worked at building their ties with the regular army, or more precisely, the regular army's officer corps. Here, too, contacts had been made in May and June. In early May, when a newly formed Union of Army and Navy Officers held its organizational conference, Rodichev, Shingarev, and Miliukov had all addressed the group as keynote speakers. (Rodichev in particular knew how to strike a responsive chord. "There is a banner," he orated, "under which each citizen must stand in readiness to sacrifice all, even his life — the Holy Banner of Defense of the Motherland!") Prodded by Miliukov, the delegates had passed resolutions condemning "collective decision-making" and the "elective principle," and asserting that the "sole guarantee of national economic welfare" was "access, if not military control, over the Dardanelles Straits."

But before the July interregnum, Kadets had generally followed the party's traditional rule of keeping the army out of politics. An official Kadet pamphlet, "The Army in Free Russia," declared, for example, that armies "in all democratic countries are apolitical . . . independent of parties and governments, and defending the civil liberties of all citizens equally." The Officers Union also made efforts to show its impartiality. Its administrative head was a colonel named Novosiltsev, who openly declared his allegiance to the Kadets, but it also established contacts with the Petrograd Soviet in May and June, and listened attentively to the radical Steklov at its opening conference, along with the Kadets.

All of this changed in July. Shortly after the Kadet ministers resigned, the party's Central Committee organized a special "Military Commission" under Vasili Stepanov. . . .

Meanwhile, Miliukov and other party leaders in Petrograd also developed their contacts with the army's high command. Shortly after Kerensky appointed Lavr Kornilov Supreme Military Commander on July 18, Miliukov was visited by Boris Savinkov, the assistant minister of war and General Kornilov's political commissar. Savinkov's task was to present Kadets with Kornilov's "Program" to extend capital punishment, and implement new disciplinary measures. With Russia still in the midst of the government crisis, he also sounded Kadet opinion on the desirability of creating a three-man military dictatorship, to be composed of Kerensky, Kornilov, and a leading Kadet. Its base of operations would be at army headquarters at Mogilev, rather than Petrograd; and its attention would be focused primarily on problems of military and civil discipline. (Other governmental affairs were to be left to the competence of the vice-ministers and their assistants, who would remain in the capital.)

Miliukov categorically rejected the dictatorship scheme as unworkable and undesirable (though some evidence suggests his attitude was "for the time being").[1] But he and the Kadet leadership enthusiastically supported Kornilov's demands. To mobilize public pressure, they began to develop their contacts with several civilian organizations which were also strongly endorsing Kornilov, particularly the so-called Republican Center, a group which had formed in May to press for strong government, victory over the Germans, and stricter military controls. The Center was not a secret organization, nor did its members generally consider themselves conservatives. In its public statements and declarations, which occasionally appeared in the press, it urged tight control over monarchist groups as well as the satisfaction of "just demands" from the workers. It also urged the rapid convocation of a Constituent Assembly.

The Center maintained close contacts with the army, however, through a special Military Section under L. P. Desimeter, a colonel on the General Staff, and with Petrograd and Moscow commercial circles. In July, it also established close ties for the first time with overtly right-wing organizations like the so-called Society for the Economic Rehabilitation of Russia, a funding group led by the Octobrist and former war minister Guchkov, and Aleksei Putilov, one of Russia's leading industrialists. In addition to moral support for General Kornilov, these people were willing to contribute substantial amounts of money for a campaign in his behalf. They were also more interested than Miliukov in the possibility of a military dictatorship.[2]

The details of this organizational maze are hard to sort out and not very important. The significant point is that the Kadets were the only major political party involved in these groups and discussions, and the

[1] Miliukov may have "entered into personal conversations on the establishment of a military dictatorship with Admiral Kolchak in the beginning of June." Dumova's source is apparently a document of Novosiltsev's, though this is not clear; and she has Novosiltsev learning of this from Kolchak himself, rather than from Miliukov, although the two Kadets were in frequent contact.

[2] The Society for the Economic Rehabilitation of Russia was formed by Guchkov, A. I. Vyshnegradskii, A. I. Putilov, N. A. Belotsvetov, N. N. Kutler, V. A. Kamenka, and A. P. Meshcherskii shortly after Guchkov's resignation as minister of war. Its function was to propagandize, and to fund right-wing agitators, but it was generally inactive in May and June, and had no contact with the Republican Center. According to the Finisov memoirs, in fact, Guchkov was quite unpopular with many army officers, and could not have worked closely with the Center had he wanted to.

only nonsocialist party with officials in the cabinet of ministers. Central Committee figures like Miliukov and Rodichev thus became the political focal point for support of the army generally, a posture they cultivated and welcomed.

As Kartashev, Iurenev, Oldenburg, and particularly the pessimistic Kokoshkin took their posts in the new coalition, they began immediately to champion Kornilov's cause. They pressured Kerensky to accept the general's "program," urged tighter control over committees, and even spoke out forcefully in favor of extending capital punishment, a measure the party still officially opposed. When Kerensky appeared to stall on the question (he was, in fact, quite distrustful of Kornilov, fearing him as a "usurper" and worried about civil war), Kadets also helped arrange a special meeting between the two. And when this failed to produce an agreement, Kokoshkin began attacking Kerensky both for personally trying to assume all governmental power and selfishly protecting his own personal relations with the soviets. On August 11, Kokoshkin went so far as to threaten that the Kadets would again resign if the cabinet did not immediately accept the general's demands. [3]

It was also in their roles both as government officials and local party leaders that many Kadets began extending their contacts with bourgeois organizations like the Trade-Industrialists in the days immediately following the ninth congress, in some places completely discarding even a theoretical commitment to the notion of *nadklassnost'* [being above class interests] and openly defending sectarian class interests. On August 3, when a Trade-Industrialist conference met in Moscow, prominent Kadets from all over Russia were in attendance as speaker after speaker described the chaotic and critical conditions of Russian industry, and attacked the socialist leadership in the government. ("A pack of charlatans," was how the conference president, Riabushinskii, described them: "We ought to say . . . that the present revolution is a bourgeois revolution, that the bourgeois order which exists at the present time is inevitable, and since it is inevitable, one must draw the completely logical conclusion and insist that those who rule the state think in a bourgeois manner and act in a bourgeois manner. . . .") Kadets responded sympathetically, despite the fact that Riabushinskii also criticized party leaders like Shingarev for their constant call "to

---

[3] Kokoshkin's threat came on the heels of a second meeting between Kerensky and Kornilov on August 10, at which time Kornilov presented his program in person.

sacrifice." The conference was "an occasion where the bourgeoisie finally strikes back at the unjustified attacks from the left," according to *Rech'*; while in the cabinet, Kokoshkin and Iurenev took up the Trade-Industrialist call for tight controls on workers' committees. The conference leadership also met with Shingarev, Manuilov, and other Kadets to develop further coordination.

Similar ties were also developed with N. N. Lvov's "Union of Landowners." A plenary session of this group's Central Council was held on July 29–31, where socialists (and particularly Victor Chernov) were denounced in scathing terms. Lvov himself had been a Kadet deputy in the State Duma before the revolution, and a charter member of the party's first Central Committee in 1905. And as we have seen he and the Union had earlier begun to explore the possibility of closer contacts through Grigorovich-Barskii and other landowning Kadets, particularly through the use by the Union of the Kadet provincial press. On July 31, Lvov told his colleagues that he was beginning the work of "organizing groups of industrialists, bankers, Kadets, and others" in order to "boldly defend our interests, because by defending property, we defend statehood. . . ."

All these efforts at liberal consolidation were finally brought into clear focus at a huge Conference of Public Figures, which convened in Moscow on August 8. According to the conservative Kadet E. N. Trubetskoi, who played a prominent role in convening the sessions, the conference was "to gather and strengthen the statesmanlike [*gosudarstvennye*] and nationalist [*natsional'nye*] elements of the country, and to give them an opportunity to express their views on the general state of affairs . . . ," particularly in view of the fact that Minister-President Kerensky had called for a conference of *all* Russian political elements to meet in Moscow on August 12. The meetings were closed to the general public to prevent disruptions. But more than 400 individuals attended, bringing together for the first time since the February revolution representatives from all segments of nonsocialist Russian society. Generals Alekseev, Brusilov, and the cossack general Kaledin were there from the army; Rodzianko and Shulgin from the old Fourth Duma leadership; Riabushinskii and a host of Trade-Industrialists; and Miliukov, Shingarev, Maklakov, Konovalov, and others from the Kadets. Miliukov himself also played a prominent role in the main working committee of the conference, introducing the reports of the Resolutions Committee. To outside observers, and particularly workers, peasants, and soldiers who read the left-wing press, no gathering could have better illustrated the deep social cleavage that now rent Russian society.

The tone of the sessions, moreover, corresponded very closely to the dominant mood of the Kadets' own ninth party congress: "nonpartisan" in the statist and conservative sense this term had come to mean, nationalistic, deeply patriotic in the traditions of old Russia, and passionately supportive of General Kornilov and his efforts to restore strict discipline in the army. "The causes and root of Russia's present evils are evident," one resolution introduced by Miliukov declared:

> *Its sources are the subordination of the great national* [obshche-natsional'nye] *tasks of the revolution to the visionary aspirations of socialist parties. . . . Time will not wait; it is impossible to delay. In the name of Russia's salvation and the rebirth of freedom, the government must immediately and decisively break with all servants of utopia.*

With battle lines thus clearly drawn, scores of reports were then given from all corners of privileged Russia describing with passionate detail the disruption and agony revolutionary change had wrought on a dying way of life.

It is hard to say whether the conference accomplished anything specific. In one sense, its greatest achievement was psychological, bringing together scores of persons who could take some small comfort in knowing many others shared their anxieties and fears. As the sessions closed, Rodzianko, Guchkov, Miliukov, Maklakov, Shingarev, Shulgin, Tretiakov, Riabushinskii, and a number of other "leading public figures" met at a special private session with Generals Alekseev, Brusilov, Iudenich, and Kaledin. They discussed the need for "the most severe measures" for establishing military discipline, and also examined the need for yet another change of government, this time one "which would finally give the possibility of setting up a firm, unlimited [*neogranichennaia*] state authority." This, "in the opinion of the participants" was something "absolutely necessary for the present time." Whether steps were also taken to set such strong ideas in motion is unclear, though not unlikely. According to the Soviet historian N. F. Slavin, who has used archival materials still unavailable to Western scholars, a number of Kadet Central Committee members "categorically" insisted at a meeting on August 11 that "an end must be put to the 'Bolshevik' revolution," while Miliukov emphasized to his colleagues that "the path toward creating a dictatorship was already being followed," and that it was "impossible to change in the middle." Whether or not Slavin is accurate, Miliukov and his supporters at the very least had succeeded in bringing together what their Central Committee leadership now considered the only "healthy elements" in Russia to discuss future tactics, consolidating *tsenzovoe* society as a whole. Openly admitting, in effect, that the country was now thoroughly polarized, they publicly shed at a national level any remaining pretense about their own social and political orientation. . . .

While Kadets received some 17.7 percent of the available local duma seats in elections between July 17 and 30, they received only 12.8 percent from July 31 to August 9. (At the same time, despite the July uprising, there was no real change in the percentage of seats obtained by the Bolsheviks. In twelve elections held in the capital cities of European Russia between July 17 and 30, they received 4.5 percent of all available seats; in the 9 elections between July 31 and August 13, they received 4.8 percent.) According to reports in the Kadet *Vestnik*, Kadet meetings were now increasingly attended by officers, local industrialists, and other clearly "bourgeois" elements, in addition to the party's traditional following among the intelligentsia. But while attendance of this sort very much strengthened the popular conception of local Kadet committees as organs of counterrevolution, it did nothing to increase the party's real political strength. New local dumas were still entirely dominated by the socialists, particularly the SRs.

In addition, Kadet ties with the army command were also seriously flawed, so much so, in fact, that it was very unlikely that even a successful military coup would propel Kadets into power. The full consequences of the party's poor relations with the army would become apparent in the civil war. But even in August 1917, General Alekseev resented the party's "desertion" from the government in July, at the height of the offensive; and Kornilov felt almost all political leaders, Kadets included, were not to be trusted. According to General Brusilov, the majority of officers had sympathy for the Kadets. But some groups, like the Petrograd Officers Council, were clearly hostile, and there was suspicion at all levels about the general competence of civilian administrators. When the local garrison in Rostov participated in a city duma election in July, for example, only 10 of the army's 1,997 votes —

Lenin in Disguise. Using an identification card carrying this photo of himself in makeup and wig, Lenin escaped to Finland in July 1917 to avoid capture by troops loyal to the Provisional Government. He returned in October in time to take power during the Revolution. (Sovfoto)

officers and enlisted men included — went to Kadets. The overwhelming majority here and elsewhere went to socialist bloc candidates, and a good proportion (331 in Rostov) went to the Bolsheviks.

Even the party's vaunted union with the Don cossacks had problems. Not only did the *inogorodnye* react with bitterness to the merger of Kadet and cossack electoral slates; many rank-and-file cossacks themselves were developing great antipathy toward their own officer leadership, emulating their non-cossack comrades throughout the army. A division was thus opening which would prove to have fateful consequences in the Don region during the early months of the civil war, and Kadet activities at "unification" were actually contributing to its development.

But by far the most serious consequence of Kadet efforts to consolidate the right was that they virtually precluded cooperation with moderate socialist leaders, particularly in the Petrograd Soviet and the Executive Committee of the All-Russian Congress of Soviets. While the time had surely passed in mid-August when such cooperation would have significantly increased the authority of the provisional regime, it might have been sufficient to keep counter-revolutionary tendencies under control, and thus preserve such state power as existed until the convocation of the Constituent Assembly. In addition, left-wing radicals were now insisting that Kadets and the right were plotting against the revolution. Demonstrable support for the second coalition would have undermined their arguments, and perhaps even their popular appeal. More important, the moderate socialists themselves were now anxious for liberal cooperation and support. They also felt national unity behind even a weak provisional government would protect the revolution, and lead the way to an authoritative national regime elected by the people themselves.

This became clear at the famous State Conference in Moscow, which was originally conceived after the Kadet resignations in July as a forum for discussing new programs and developing national unity, and which convened on August 12. Initially the Kadets were supportive, even enthusiastic. But as the party moved rapidly to the right, attitudes began to change, particularly among the Petrograd *verkhovniki*. By early August, Kokoshkin, Shingarev, and especially Miliukov felt such a clear difference existed between liberals and socialists that the government would do far better simply to "choose" between one or the other.

As the moderate socialist *Narodnoe Slovo* pointed out, however, this was hardly the road to compromise or national unity. On one hand, Petrograd Kadets were still insisting that the second coalition be "above politics"; on the other, they wanted the regime to commit itself to partisan Kadet positions. And while calling publicly for national "solidification," the Kadet leadership failed to recognize that unity could be achieved only if the party itself established some workable relationship with the Executive Committee of the Soviets. Unity was somehow to be reached only through the implementation of liberal programs.

As the Moscow Conference got underway, debate began to mirror these contradictions. Kadets like Maklakov, Rodichev, and now Miliukov spoke with unbridled hostility against the left and refused to pledge support for Kerensky's regime. So far had Miliukov's own views shifted about the "dangers" of provoking further social polarization, in fact, that the Kadet leader himself wanted to end his own address with an open declaration of *non*-support and failed to do so only by "taking into consideration the mood of some provincial sectors of the party, and the fact that party comrades were still members of the government. . . ." By contrast, Tsereteli, Chkheidze, and other Soviet spokesmen extended the hand of compromise. Tsereteli even embraced the Trade-Industrialist Bublikov in a much noted symbolic gesture; while Chkheidze, who spoke as the official representative of the Soviet Executive Committee, promised he and his colleagues would place "the interest of the whole country, of the revolution, above the interests of classes or specific groups of the population." "The interests of Russia," he also insisted — sounding remarkably like the Kadets themselves — could not be "sacrificed to the importunities of irresponsible or self-interested groups."

The left, moreover, accepted the need for firm state authority, insisting only in the correlation between strength and popularity. But Kadet speakers like Maklakov and Rodichev were still unwilling to associate a strong government with the satisfaction of mass demands. It was true, Maklakov admitted with a typical elitist aside, that the "deep dark masses" were now "quietly casting their votes for party lists." But they were doing this "without understanding" the democratic process; and the regime was mistaken if it believed it "would lose its real strength" if it "parted ways with political parties." On the contrary, if the regime stopped appealing to Russians in political terms, "the masses . . . would instinctively understand who is destroying them . . . and surround those who are leading them to salvation with love, sympathy and loyalty, against which the malignity of political parties would be powerless." The contradiction here, as Tsereteli was quick to point out, was that if the Kadets were right, events themselves would render politics superfluous; masses would "instinctively" reject those who did appeal in "political terms," and follow the liberals.

Similar problems emerged in the discussion about a national program. Here Chkheidze and the Soviet representatives were not only more accommodating than Kadets on specific matters of policy; but the nonsocialists as a whole disagreed among themselves, and had very little to offer in the way of counterproposals. On the question of strengthening the army, both sides agreed that the "salvation of the country and the revolution" depended on the "restoration of the army's military might." (Chkheidze's words.) The left insisted this could be done, however, only by retaining the army's committee structure for all nonmilitary questions, and using it to infuse spirit and morale among the troops. Complete independence of command would have to be enforced in all matters of strategy and tactics; but any return to prerevolutionary methods of discipline would lead to precisely the defeatism and low spirit which so weakened the army in 1915 and 1916. In opposition, Miliukov and the nonsocialists argued that a return to prerevolutionary methods of discipline was the only way the army could be saved, and showed by their rousing reception of General Kornilov that the man whom the Soviet had driven from Petrograd in April was now their national hero. But while Rodzianko wanted an end to *all* political agitation among the troops, which the Kadets could not accept since it would eliminate their efforts as well as the socialists', the Kadets wanted an end to all military committees, which even Kornilov and the high command still recognized as having some role to play in social and economic questions.

Similarly, all speakers agreed that the powers of committees in factories and villages should be clearly defined. But while bourgeois spokesmen like Riabushinskii, Sokolovskii, and even Gruzinov saw real value in some aspects of worker and peasant organizations (Riabushinskii even recalling the role he himself played in setting up labor groups in Moscow), the Duma group called for their total elimination. And here, too, there was paradox. The Duma committee wanted functions exercised by committees and soviets turned over to "legitimate organs of local government." But as Kadet leaders themselves were aware, local elections all over Russia were returning large socialist majorities to these bodies. There was thus as much division and confusion within the nonsocialist camp as a whole on this question as there was antagonism between the liberals and the left.

The left was also more willing to make concessions on questions of finance, taxation, production, and food supply. Despite the sacrifice it implied for the peasants, for example, the Soviet's resolution pledged the left to support the continuation of the grain monopoly and fixed prices. It also called for strict regulation of industrial prices, and for state control over wages. Even more dramatic, the resolution officially pledged Soviet support for private commerce in support of food supply groups, accepted labor conscription as a means to meet industrial shortages "if the need arises," and declared the necessity of repudiating all arbitrary seizures of land in the countryside. But again, the nonsocialists refused to show support for the Soviet's positions, while offering little in the way of alternatives. Kornilov demanded "urgent" measures to meet production needs, but failed to describe specifically what he had in mind. General Kaledin joined the Soviet in calling for labor conscription; but by demanding restrictions on profits as well, he antagonized von Ditmar and other Trade-Industrialists. And while Chkheidze advanced the suggestion both of a mass capital levy and an increase of taxes on articles of mass consumption, Gruzinov and other nonsocialists could only respond with references to their past contributions to the liberty loans. They, too, had no new proposals.

There was, finally, no clear liberal position on the most crucial question of all: whether or not to support Kerensky and the coalition. F. A. Golovin, the former president of the Second Duma, felt support was imperative. Bublikov, Kapatsinskii, Riabushinskii, Sokolovskii and other "bourgeois" speakers agreed, and Nicholas Astrov, speaking for Volkov, Gerasimov, Schepkin, and other Kadets (who now defined themselves as "progressives" and "conciliationists") went so far as to suggest that his "political ear" heard "notes sounding very much like the reconciliation of previously irreconcilable tendencies." Astrov's ear was certainly not cocked in the direction of Maklakov, however, or Rodichev, Kokoshkin, Shulgin, Guchkov, or even Miliukov, whose sympathies lay with right-wing authoritarianism.

In summarizing the results of the Moscow Conference, *Rech'* told its readers the meetings showed Russia divided into two vast "irreconcilable camps." At first glance, these seemed to be "the bourgeoisie and the democracy," though "more attentive analysis" showed that the line ran between "the utopianism of partisanship and the statesmanship of nonpartisans." This was hardly an adequate description, however, or even the only Kadet view. It suggested simply that after months and even years of stressing the need for Russian national unity, of great fear of mass unrest and a deep concern for civil law and order, Miliukov and his supporters among the Petrograd Kadets were girding for civil war. More appropriate would have been the observation that efforts toward accommodation and compromise had been made at the sessions by the moderate socialists and their left-wing liberal supporters, but that right-wing elements offered no positive response. Whether this indicated a "full victory" for the idea of coalition, as Nekrasov told reporters, is very dubious; but equally doubtful is the notion that those who in the past had been the loudest champions of national unity and authority took any constructive steps at the conference to achieve their goals.

"Petrograd Is in Danger!"

Immediately after the Moscow Conference, the situation in Russia began to deteriorate sharply, particularly in Petrograd. Symptomatic of the times, even the newsstand price of *Izvestiia* rose on August 16 from 12 to 15 kopecks, while bourgeois newspapers like *Birzhevye Vedomosti* began to carry long columns of newly vacated apartments, deserted by owners fearful of new disorders. Reports from the front also sounded more ominous. The Germans were now advancing. In several areas, especially along the Baltic, defenses were collapsing entirely. On the night of August 19, Russian troops evacuated Riga. Many now became thoroughly alarmed that the enemy would march on Petrograd itself.

In the midst of these developments, the inhabitants of Russia's capital city held what were destined to be their last free municipal elections under a democratic government. The balloting was scheduled for August 20, to elect a new city duma. And here, too, the results were hardly encouraging for Kadets. Parties approached the campaign with a noticeable lack of enthusiasm. Mensheviks stressed the value of the ballot box in combating the liberals' growing truculence; the Kadets spoke for order and national unity; and radical newspapers like *Proletarii* aimed their editorial guns at "the growing strength of bourgeois-landowner counterrevolutionary dictators," warning workers and soldiers that the Constitutional Democrats were threatening their freedom.

But the Mensheviks were disorganized as a result of an attempt by their internationalist faction to exclude Tsereteli and other defensists from a new city committee; the Bolsheviks had to campaign covertly as a result of the July fiasco; and the SR leadership appeared too busy with state affairs to pay much attention to city business. *Delo Naroda* ran a campaign banner on August 12 and 13, but then virtually ignored the election until just before the balloting on August 20. And on election day, even the SRs admitted the vote could not count for much "while the revolution itself was in danger." The Popular Socialists were even more indifferent. *Narodnoe Slovo* announced the "opening" of their campaign only two days before the election itself.

The elections were also marked by a high degree of absenteeism, especially in the well-to-do Kazanskii and Liteinyi districts. This had characterized other towns in late July and August, particularly Vologda, Voronezh, Viatka, and Ekaterinburg. But nowhere was the voters' indifference more evident than in the revolution's capital. According to *Rech'*, one could walk past a polling station on August 20 and not notice that an election was taking place. And indeed, the total number of ballots cast was some 235,000 less than in district duma elections in May, despite the inclusion of six additional election districts from the city's immediate suburbs.

This hardly encouraged even left Kadets about the feasibility of democratic processes. Predictions of party figures like Vasili Maklakov about Russia not being sufficiently "mature" to utilize the freedoms of liberation seemed to be coming true. According even to the mild-mannered Shingarev, "socialistic instincts" were conquering *"gosudarstvennyi* reason"; what was necessary was "ceaseless cultural work" of the kind Kadets had begun twelve years before.

But the results of the elections revealed that even "ceaseless cultural work" was hardly likely to reverse the course of events. Out of 549,350 ballots (including the suburban vote), socialist candidates (including the Bolsheviks) secured 427,087 or almost 78 percent. The Kadets won only 114,483 or 20.9 percent, a relative decrease of little more than 1 percent from May, but an absolute decrease of 57,262 votes in what was supposed to be the city of their strongest popularity. Most shocking and significant of all was the great increase in Bolshevik support, both in absolute and relative terms. Lenin's followers secured a full 33 percent of the total vote, only 4 percent behind the front running Socialist

Revolutionaries. Not only was this a gain of almost 13 percent over what the Bolsheviks had won in May (relative to the total vote in each election); it represented an absolute increase of 23,688 despite the drastic reduction in the total number of voters. . . . Most of this new strength undoubtedly came from those who had earlier supported socialist moderates. It came primarily in the Alexander Nevskii, Narvskii, Petrogradskii, and Admiralteiskii sections of the cities, where SRs and Mensheviks had been strongest in May; and in the Rozhdest-venskii, where Mensheviks won 19,045 votes (32.1 percent) in the district duma elections, and now returned only 1,688 (4.9 percent). This indicated that workers had become even better organized and politically radical since the July uprising, despite the arrest of Trotsky and other Bolshevik leaders and Lenin's retreat to Finland; while any new liberal and SR supporters either failed for some reason to go to the polls, or had already fled the city. It meant as well, though few Kadets chose to interpret the returns this way, that Kadets and moderate social-ists were both being strongly challenged from the same source, reinforc-ing the desirability of a *sblizhenie* [rapprochement] between liberals and the left which Astrov, Frenkel, and others still advocated. Finally, the elections meant that the new administration of Russia's capital, long dominated by Kadets and a liberal stronghold, would finally be under strong radical influence.

Petrograd was thus "in great danger" according to the Kadet Central Committee. The crucial question was whether any firm authority could possibly be found to save the city, and indeed, the country as a whole.

Plots Against the Government

One obvious possibility for reestablishing firm authority, of course, and one now being talked about freely in liberal circles, was a military dictatorship under General Kornilov. The tumultuous reception the army commander received at the Moscow Conference testified to the popularity of this idea in right-wing circles; while the base for organiz-ing such an effort existed in army groups like the Military League, and civilian societies like the Republican Center. From August 20 onward, even *Novoe Vremia* carried articles warning of anti-government plots (though insinuating the greatest danger in this regard was still from the radical left); while on August 23, the Grand Duke Michael Alexandrovich was placed under house arrest in Gatchina as a precautionary move.

As we have seen, right-wing groups had been considering the possibility of a military dictatorship for quite some time. The Military League and the Union of Officers discussed it as early as May and June, and even talked about it with members of the high command, including Generals Kornilov and Alekseev, and Admiral Kolchak. In July, Boris Savinkov had sounded out Miliukov on the notion; and at the Conference of Public Figures in early August, the subject was mentioned frequently. Kadets themselves discussed the possibility of using troops against the soviets at Central Committee meetings on August 11 or 12, and again on August 20; and they repeatedly explored the question of dictatorship in private conversations.

Within the Central Committee, however, there were several views on the issue, ranging from sympathetic to hostile. The grounds for sympathy were simply that Russia was in imminent danger of collapse, and however much dictatorial methods compromised liberal principles, Russia's survival as a strong, united power was the primary consideration. This meant the application of strict authority and discipline to the country at large by forceful measures. It also meant the elimination of committees and soviets, nationalization of railroads and key military industries, and the exercise of whatever force was necessary to control radicals.

This was Rodichev's view, and it found expression in his exhortation to Kornilov when the General arrived for the Moscow Conference: "Save Russia, and a grateful people will revere you." It was also the view of Tyrkova, Novgorodtsev, Dolgorukov, and others, who argued to the Kadet Central Committee that an imminent (and "inevitable") Bolshevik uprising could be put down only with dictatorial force.[4] Yet other Kadets were more circumspect — even those who considered the Moscow Conference a dismal failure, and who abhorred Nekrasov and Kerensky. The problem was not whether military authoritarianism was

---

[4]These arguments emerged with particular force at Central Committee meetings on August 11, right after the second meeting between Kornilov and Kerensky, and on August 20. Tyrkova told her colleagues on August 20 that Kadets "must support a dictator even more than Kerensky; there is no other way — only through blood" (p. 374).

desirable, but whether it could be extended into a civilian dictatorship — even temporarily, until the convocation of the Constituent Assembly — without hopelessly dividing the nation and precipitating a disastrous civil war.

This was the dilemma Kornilov posed for the liberal moderates: there was little question about endorsing a Kornilov dictatorship *once it had been established*; but most party members in Moscow and Petrograd felt dictatorial efforts could not succeed unless both the cabinet and the Soviet acquiesced voluntarily. This ruled out participation in a conspiratorial coup d'état. As Maklakov himself acknowledged, a unilateral move on Kornilov's part would be "disastrous," serving only to strengthen the Bolsheviks and unite the "very revolutionary democracy that was eroding and defeating the revolution." And when Miliukov himself talked to General Kornilov on August 13, it was this perspective which underlay his insistence that Kadets could not involve themselves directly in any action against Kerensky which "took the form that many in Moscow are discussing."[5] Rather, the party's task was to apply maximum pressure against the second coalition's "triumvirs" — Kerensky, Nekrasov, and Tereshchenko — if not to remove them, at least to assure the adoption of forceful programs like General Kornilov's.

Meanwhile, both the Republican Center and the Union of Officers were stepping up their conspiratorial activities. These groups were now more convinced than ever that Kerensky's regime had to be replaced by one under General Kornilov. Whether their plans involved eliminating Kerensky from power entirely, or simply reorganizing his cabinet under Kornilov's direction, is not clear. Nor is the nature of Kornilov's own personal involvement (though the general almost certainly had a firm hand in discussions at Mogilev, the army's headquarters). What is clear is that while Kadets worked for authoritarian measures within the cabinet, Kornilov's supporters elsewhere contemplated more drastic actions, none of which boded well for the future of the second coalition.

The crux of the anti-government plots involved marching on

---

[5] In his memoirs V. Obolenskii notes that he and others were convinced Miliukov supported Kornilov wholeheartedly; Soviet historians have frequently taken this as evidence of Miliukov's direct involvement in the conspiracy. Support of Kornilov was not incompatible, however, with reservations about a unilateral coup.

Petrograd to put down a Bolshevik "uprising," and under this pretext, replacing Kerensky's cabinet with a "Council of National Defense." (There is abundant evidence as well that many hoped to arrest leaders of the Petrograd Soviet.)[6] The plotters were naturally worried about left-wing resistance, however, fearing the outbreak of civil war and the effect this would have on the front. Consequently, in an apparent effort to persuade Kerensky to yield voluntarily, several of those involved contacted V. N. Lvov, the procurator of the Holy Synod in the first two provisional cabinets, and a centrist with close ties to the regime. While details here are especially vague, it was probably hoped that Lvov could work out some means whereby Kerensky and Kornilov could cooperate, allowing a change of government without forceful opposition. Perhaps Kerensky might even be given a place in Kornilov's Council, at least temporarily.

Meanwhile, Boris Savinkov, Kerensky's assistant minister of war who was still acting as a go-between for the cabinet and Kornilov, had finally worked out a draft of Kornilov's program acceptable to the government. On August 23 he took it to Mogilev, more than a full month after Kornilov himself had first proposed it.[7] The principal stumbling block during this time had been the role of commissars and committees, both in the army and in the country at large. Kornilov was initially willing to have committees retained, recognizing they served some useful functions in keeping the army together. But he wanted their activities sharply circumscribed, something socialists like Victor Chernov objected to on principle, and which other ministers (though not apparently Kerensky himself) feared might unleash new civil disorders.

In accordance with Kornilov's earlier views, Savinkov's "final" version of his program provided for the retention of commissars and com-

---

[6]The following account is distilled from a number of sources, the most important of which are the memoirs of Finisov, Lukomskii, Savinkov, Putilov, Shidlovskii, Vinberg, Miliukov, and Kerensky. There is a great deal of secondary literature on the mutiny, both Soviet and Western. . . . The question of the composition of the new government as well as the arrest of Soviet leaders apparently caused considerable antagonism between the different conspiratorial groups. . . . White goes so far as to suggest that it was this antagonism which "finally disrupted the Kornilovist movement."

[7]There is also evidence that Savinkov was to investigate counter-revolutionary activities at Stavka, and to disperse the Republican Center.

mittees, but limited their functions entirely to nonmilitary affairs. The sources suggest, however, that Kornilov and his aides — particularly General Lukomskii — were less sanguine on this question than even two weeks earlier, and now felt commissars and committees should be eliminated. (This question probably provoked Kornilov's harsh judgments of Kerensky, reported in the latter's *Prelude to Bolshevism.*) In discussions between Savinkov and Kornilov on the question on August 24, Savinkov won out. But even with the committee provisions retained, he and Kornilov both agreed the publication of the program would outrage the left, possibly triggering another mass "Bolshevik" demonstration. This also worried Kerensky. It was therefore apparently decided on all sides that troops should be sent to the capital to deal as necessary with whatever resistance developed, a "precautionary move" which corresponded exactly with the tactical schemes of those hoping to oust the coalition, whether or not Kornilov, Savinkov, or Kerensky himself actually intended it that way.

The somewhat devious V. N. Lvov, meanwhile, having earlier met with Kerensky as an emissary of unnamed right-wing political figures, was himself hurrying out to army headquarters to discover exactly what kind of government Kornilov wanted in place of the coalition. Arriving on August 24, while Kornilov was busy with Savinkov, Lvov cooled his heels until later in the evening, possibly talking in the meantime with members of the Union of Officers or Military League. Then, with Savinkov heading back to Petrograd with Kornilov's agreement on a program preserving the army committees, Lvov confronted the army commander with what he said were Kerensky's own plans for a new cabinet. What these were (or whether they were Kerensky's) is unclear. But Lvov apparently brought word that Kerensky was ready to yield to a directorate or even a dictatorship under Kornilov.[8]

---

[8] According to Lvov's testimony in Chugaev, and his memoirs in *Posledniia Novosti*, No. 186, Nov. 30, 1920, et. seq., he met with Kerensky on August 22 on the prompting of I. A. Dobrynskii, a member of the St. George Cavaliers with close ties to the Republican Center, the Officers Union, and the Moscow industrialists. Lvov says Kerensky authorized him to enter into "negotiations" with Kornilov for a new regime, implying his acceptance of a dictatorship. He also reports that his discussion with Kornilov touched only on a dictatorship, rather than a directorate. Kerensky denies Lvov's account categorically.

What Kornilov himself made of Lvov and this new information, having just met with Savinkov, is hard to determine. Perhaps he was simply pleased to think that the various conspirators had finally convinced Kerensky to come around. Perhaps he thought Kerensky had suddenly gotten new evidence about a possible Bolshevik uprising. In any event, Kornilov certainly preferred the idea of dictatorship to continued coalition; and he undoubtedly said so to Lvov.

Lvov for his part, meanwhile, now had either a general agreement between Kerensky and Kornilov to establish a new cabinet (as he later testified), or simply an open statement of Kornilov's personal desires and intentions (as Kerensky's memoirs would have us believe); and he hurried back to Petrograd to meet again with the minister-president, no doubt convinced he held in his hands the keys to resolving Russia's crisis of authority. If Kerensky himself could now be convinced to accept a change of regime, bloodshed would be avoided. Troops moving toward Petrograd to prevent the disorders which were expected when Kornilov's program was published could be used instead to prevent resistance to the coup. They could also root out radical groups like the Bolsheviks, acting on the pretext of preventing civil war. (At precisely this time, in fact, representatives from the Republican Center were contacting Putilov and other industrialists for funds, planning to stage a Bolshevik "uprising" as a pretext for repressive action if one did not develop on its own.) But when Lvov told Kerensky that Kornilov was actually moving to replace the coalition, Kerensky panicked. Confirming Lvov's account on the wireless with Kornilov (in a conversation during which the hapless general neglected to ascertain exactly what it was in Lvov's message Kerensky was asking him to confirm!), the frenetic minister clapped Lvov in jail, convened his cabinet in emergency session, and declared Kornilov a traitor to the revolution.

What, in all this, was the role of the Kadets? While the details presented here may not be fully accurate, given the contradictions in available source material, they do suffice to indicate that few if any leading party members took personal roles in actively planning or executing the conspiracy, and that official Kadet organizations, such as the Central Committee or the Petrograd or Moscow city groups, stood entirely aloof. Conspiracy was the work of the Republican Center, in conjunction with army groups like the Union of Officers and individual members of the General Staff. Here, military figures like Colonel Novosiltsev, the Kadet leader of the Officers Union, undoubtedly took active roles. And as the competent Bolshevik historian Vera Vladimirova indicated, Kadets were also doubtlessly involved through conversations and discussions with Republican Center leaders, perhaps even being approached by people like Putilov for funds. Discussions along the way must also have touched on realigning the cabinet, a subject constantly preoccupying the Kadets from virtually the first days of the revolution, and something they now very much desired.

But even in terms of their support for such a venture, much less their participation, Miliukov, Kokoshkin, and most of the party's *ver-khovniki* [top leaders] were ambiguous at best, refusing to encourage a unilateral move on Kornilov's part while supporting his goals in the government; and the evidence shows that Kadet supporters close to leading financial circles, like S. N. Tretiakov, president of the Moscow Stock Exchange, unceremoniously rejected requests for funds from Putilov, and kept the Moscow and Petrograd Kadet committees clear of the "conspiracy bankers." Neither Tretiakov nor Miliukov also had a clear idea of exactly what was being planned. . . .

Kadets may not have actively plotted with Kornilov; but their speeches and attitudes clearly encouraged those who did. And more important, they took no steps whatsoever to prevent a mutiny from developing, despite their knowledge that plots were underway, and their political position as Russia's leading nonsocialist party. With little effort, Kadet leaders might have easily contained the mutineers. They could have prevented the "affair" from developing by persuasion, by official pressure, or even by exposure. They thus might have helped Russia avoid what would prove to be a fatal blow to civil liberty and political democracy. Instead they stood silent; and like fellow liberals in other times and places, they bore their own particular responsibility for the sequence of events which followed.

Ronald Grigor Suny

From Economics to Politics

The revolution has traditionally been studied either as the story of central Russia or in discrete investigations of the nationalities. Ronald Grigor Suny has attempted to link the study of ethnic conflict with the broader social and class conflicts affecting the whole of the former Russian Empire. A student of Leopold Haimson, Suny has taught at Oberlin College and the University of Michigan and has done research in the Soviet republics of Armenia, Azerbaijan, and Georgia. He is the author of *Armenia in the Twentieth Century* (1983) and *The Making of the Georgian Nation* (1988). His study of the revolution in Baku, excerpted here, argues that Bolshevism in the peripheries had characteristics distinct from the Bolshevism of Petrograd, that the presence of ethnic fractures determined both the politics of political parties and the eventual ferocity of social conflict.

The coalition of the "revolutionary democracy" and the *tsentsovoe obshchestvo* (the old ruling classes and the bourgeoisie) on which the Right socialists based their strategy was steadily being eroded away in the summer of 1917. The tremendous pressures on the masses, caused by the war and its stepchild, hunger, drove them to more radical alternatives. Before the war Baku had received its food-supplies by ship from the Volga region and by rail from the north Caucasus. But the dislocations of the war had stopped the regular flow of goods into the city, and, with the outbreak of the revolution and the discrediting of local authorities, the peasants of the north Caucasus refused to sell grain to the city at the low fixed prices. They demanded a rise in the official prices, but the government feared that increases in prices would lead to further inflation. A spokesman from Kuba, a provincial city in eastern Transcaucasia, reported:

Ronald Grigor Suny, *The Baku Commune 1917–1918: Class and Nationality in the Russian Revolution*. Copyright © 1972 by Princeton University Press. Excerpts, pp. 102–146, reprinted with permission of Princeton University Press.

The peasants refuse to give grain to the cities because the city robs the peasants. For all urban goods the peasants have to pay exorbitant prices. The peasants will not give grain to the industrialists who think up the prices, will not give to the workers who by their strikes raise the cost of goods. The city will give nothing to the village in exchange for grain.

Efforts by the Baku consumer cooperatives to work with city food-supply organs came to nought. The city government refused to set up a government monopoly on food-supplies and yet discouraged the cooperatives from taking resolute action of their own. The Baku soviet hesitated to get involved in the food question. By May, when the supplies dropped drastically, members of the soviet called for the establishment of a food-supply dictatorship to oversee and coordinate all activity in that field within the city, to stop speculation and hoarding. On the suggestion of Shahumian, Dzhaparidze, and Mandel'shtam, the soviet on May 13 decided to "work out measures" to ease the food shortage. This modest intervention into an area of municipal administration was the first step by the soviet toward assuming the prerogatives of the city duma. It would not be long before people in Baku would consider the institution which most effectively dealt with the food-supply question to be the *de facto* government of the city.

While extending its own influence in the city, the Baku soviet continued to support the IKOO [Executive Committee of Public Organizations] and the Provisional Government. Its loyalty to the *status quo* was displayed in the aftermath of the "July Days." The fall of the first coalition government in Petrograd on July 2 precipitated Bolshevik-led demonstrations by workers and soldiers calling for the transfer of all power to the soviets. Only the Bolsheviks and Martov's Menshevik-Internationalists sympathized with the demands of the crowds. Rumors spread that the Bolsheviks were attempting to seize power, that Lenin was a German agent. The Bolshevik leader was forced into hiding and his party was condemned by the soviet leadership. The crisis ended with the formation of a new coalition with Alexander Kerensky as prime minister, but the crisis for the Bolsheviks continued for another two months. July was the low ebb of popularity for the extreme Left.

In Baku the July Days were greeted with shock and dismay. The Socialist Revolutionary Bekzadian contrasted the milder Bolsheviks of Baku with the more dangerous Petrograd variety: "Here in Baku we still do business with a high-principaled Bolshevism. But there along with

Bolshevism go strange elements. They stir up the water, and someone, unknown as of now, is casting his rod into the water.

Even the Bolsheviks were disturbed by the indications that the Petrograd organization might have attempted to seize power by an armed insurrection. Shahumian rose in the soviet to defend his party: "In the Petrograd events the Bolsheviks were not guilty. They could not hold back the revolutionary masses from a demonstration; this happened against the wishes and without the participation of the Bolsheviks. I am certain that our party did not wage this act. We Bolsheviks have always opposed premature, rash decisions and are against the seizure of power by force of arms!!"

The socialist parties in Baku called a conference of their central committees to discuss the recent events. The Menshevik Bagaturov bitterly attacked the Bolsheviks and called for the transfer of all local power to the IKOO. A motion to that effect by Aiollo was carried, despite strong protests by Bolshevik and Hummet delegates. Attempts to reconcile the majority with the Bolsheviks were futile. The Menshevik Ramishvili's assurance that Lenin, "a fanatic in this matter," is "a man of unusual pride but an honest fighter" fell on deaf ears. Shahumian concluded that no common language existed between the Left and Right socialists: "Either we are traitors or you are counterrevolutionaries. The petty bourgeoisie is already dragging along counterrevolution. We do not hide our views and will not hide them. We are ready for your repressions. But I do not know if your police will be as noble as the police of the Romanovs." . . .

Paradoxically, the Baku soviet, like the Petrograd soviet and the Central Executive Committee, refused to take power formally just when real power was falling into its hands. After the July Days it rejected the only political parties that advocated soviet power, and the Bolsheviks for their part dropped the slogan "All Power to the Soviets." These developments on both the national and the local scenes complicated greatly the question of where power would lie in Baku. For most of 1917 Baku experienced not only *dvoevlastie*, but in effect a tripartite administration. The soviet, the duma, and the IKOO all claimed to have the prerogative of the supreme governing body. None of the three could be said to be "democratic," or even representative, except in a formal sense. The duma was six years old, and by the spring of 1917 a "great tiredness" was felt within it. Members rarely attended, and a quorum could often not be gathered. Just a few days before the outbreak of the

February Revolution, the duma had voted to petition the viceroy of the Caucasus for new elections. Discussion had been held about increasing the number of Moslem members to correspond with the preponderance of Moslems in the local population.[1]

IKOO had never been directly elected by the population and had been conceived as an interim executive to govern only until democratically elected bodies could be convened. Shortly after its creation, the IKOO had ceased to act as if it were subordinate to the duma and in fact, it increasingly became the mouthpiece of soviet policies. By increasing its membership in the IKOO the Baku soviet managed effectively to dominate the local "provisional government."

Even the soviet could not pretend to represent the population of the city but only its workers and soldiers. Moreover, the Moslem poor were hardly represented in the soviet until the fall of 1917. The soviet was, however, the only body in Baku to represent the workers of the oil-field districts and, therefore, to be interested in having those districts officially incorporated into the city.

In the spring and summer of 1917 most politically-minded residents of Baku, including the majority of the socialists, hoped that sometime in the future their city would be governed by a democratically elected duma. The Bolsheviks and Menshevik-Internationalists alone wanted power to be transferred to the soviet. . . . In most other large cities the elections to the duma had already been held, and in some the liberals had not done badly. But in Baku the "democratic" duma would not be elected, for technical reasons, until the end of October, after the Bolshevik revolution.

The authority of all three governing bodies disintegrated in the summer of 1917. Law and order broke down, and the response of the authorities was inadequate. The police chief, Leontovich, resigned early in the summer after his force had been crippled by the loss of former officers now accused of abuses under the old regime. Even ordinary functions of the city government, such as sanitation, had to be taken over by voluntary organizations. . . . A power vacuum existed in

---

[1] By law the Moslems were not permitted to hold more than half the seats in the duma. Moslem liberals and Musavatists had agitated for years for an increase in Moslem representation.

Baku, with no institution willing and able to assert its authority. The threat of hostilities between Armenians and Azerbaijanis hung over the city, and rumors spread that one or the other nationality was arming.

The summer of 1917 witnessed not only a breakdown of law and order and a worsening of the food shortage, but also the first massive appearance of the Moslem poor on the revolutionary stage, in the protests against the food shortage. Hunger, even more than the struggle for a living wage, galvanized the Moslems into mass action.

As early as April a system of rationing by card had been adopted by the City Food Supply Commission. But price-controls had not been put into effect, and speculation continued. The poorer classes suffered most from the inflation, and the psychological result of the crisis was to personalize its causes, to blame the situation on specific groups or individuals, even though the underlying causes were connected with the growing isolation of Baku from its sources of food. Workers began to feel that the chaos resulted from the voracious appetites of merchants who raised prices or of rich people who hoarded food. On June 1, a crowd of about one thousand Azerbaijanis gathered at the city hall, entered the building, and attacked an official whom they mistook for a member of the City Food Supply Commission. Army units had to aid the police in dispersing the angry crowd, which demanded an increase in the grain ration. That same day several thousand Persian citizens stood outside the Persian consulate asking for either an increase in the ration or transportation back to Persia.

In August the Food Supply Commission of Baku Province decided that the grain ration must be cut by one-quarter and that official searches for grain hoards should be organized. The soviet responded favorably to these suggestions, but before it could act the population of the city undertook its own efforts to alleviate the hunger in the city. On August 19, the day the grain ration was cut by a quarter, groups of workers began roaming the streets invading the homes of those they suspected of hoarding grain. The unorganized searches were the spontaneous reaction of one segment of the poorer classes to the latest and most severe crisis in supplies, but they took on an anti-Moslem tone when most of the searches were carried out against Moslems. On August 24, a meeting of three thousand Moslems at the Tazar-Pir Mosque adopted a resolution condemning the searches and protesting the discrimination against the homes of Moslems. That same day the leaders of the political and labor organizations of the city met with workers to discuss the unorganized searches. A clear disagreement between the leadership and the volatile elements among the workers broke into the open. Workers called for the setting-up of a committee to supervise the searches, but the soviet delegates and political leaders opposed all such searches. Workers shouted from the floor, "You have all become completely bourgeois!" Petrukhin, a worker and a former Socialist-Revolutionary who called himself the "representative of the hungry section," shouted: "They tell us to organize. Here we organized and came here hungry. And who has brought us to starvation? the authorities!" . . .

By September the near-starvation of the poorer classes combined with their frustrations at inconclusive negotiations with the oil industrialists to create an explosive situation in the city. As the undirected searches for food turned against Moslem homes, crowds of angry Moslems took to the streets. On September 3, three thousand people in Sabunchiny gathered to protest against the food shortage, and in their resolutions they linked the crisis with the ineffectual policies of the IKOO, the duma, and the soviet and its executive committee. New elections to the soviet were specifically demanded. A week later a crowd of Moslems terrorized the Balakhany food-supply committee. In the soviet the next day a speaker reviewed the situation for the deputies:

> The population of Baku and the industrial districts feels extremely nervous about the supply problems. An intelligent attitude is noticeable among only a few. The dark forces are not sleeping and are using the situation being created to carry on hooligan agitation. Daily at the supply centers excited crowds gather, led by a few constantly active agitators, provoking the crowd to violence. Such phenomena are noticed in the industrial region. Crowds of uninformed Moslems appear with reproaches that no one cares about them. Behind them appears a crowd of similarly uninformed Russian women, claiming that it is mostly the Moslems about whom [the authorities] care.

Once again hunger and economic stress had brought the national communities of Baku to the brink of racial war. No matter how complex or diffused the causes of the material crisis, the nationalities expressed their anger and frustration in the traditional hostility toward their ethnic enemies. Nationalism was the form that the expression of ill-understood economic and social problems took. When the blame was pinned on an Armenian or Russian or Azerbaijani, problems which had seemed rootless and eternal became comprehensible and capable of simple solution. The irony, of course, was that national animosity was not a solution at all but part of the problem. Baku was the victim of its own geography, its ethnic diversity, and the class divisions and hatreds bequeathed to the city in the decades of capitalist industrialization.

Spontaneous as these disorders were, it was impossible to distinguish the mood created by the food shortage from the disgust at the failure to negotiate the labor contract. Just as the hunger was indiscriminate in its victims, so the struggle for a contract had repercussions beyond the oil workers and their families. By September the whole city was in turmoil; the causes had faded into the past, and the authorities had lost control of the population. In a telegram to the Provisional Government, the Congress of Oil Industrialists described the general mood in the city:

> *Starvation threatens the population of Baku and the oil-field districts with all its consequences. . . . In the oil-fields separate strikes have begun; workers demand bread, although the organization of the oil industrialists is completely uninvolved in the business of supplying food. The mood of the masses is threatening. Because of the hunger, not only is a full stoppage of work in the fields inevitable, but excesses and wrecking which will paralyze the whole industry for a long time. The moment is catastrophic in the full sense of the word.*

The industrialists pleaded for governmental intervention, especially for pressure on the north Caucasian authorities to send badly needed food to Baku.

The political shift to the Left which almost all political groups in Baku experienced in September and October was a response to the evident change of mood of the urban masses from reliance on the soviet leaders to spontaneous and often violent action. While hunger lay at the base of this new mood, the growing impatience of the workers with the industry's delay in signing a labor contract was another contributing factor. . . . Reports filtered in from the local courts of conciliation on the principal areas of dissension within the labor community. Workers felt that promises to pay wartime subsidies and bonuses had not been fulfilled. The engineers, as well as the workers, were disgusted with the failure to implement factory legislation to insure safety and improve the general conditions of work. The sometimes brusque treatment of employees by administrators was also resented. These problems, and the difficulties caused by the fall in real wages, were taken up by a soviet commission to work out a project for a labor contract.

The soviet warned the workers not to enter into separate agreements with the industrialists as they had done in the past, since a "collective agreement," a labor contract for all of Baku, would be negotiated. The drillers, oppressed by their unbearable conditions, were especially likely to grasp at the straw of a separate strike or a separate agreement with the owners. Yet another threat to unified action was the workers' old habit of accepting individual subsidies from their employees, rather than insisting on a general salary increase. . . .

The new commission to negotiate a labor contract met on June 16 under the chairmanship of V. I. Frolov. From industry came representatives of the Union of Oil Industrialists, the Zafatem group (the Union of Plant, Factory and Technical Workshop Owners), and the smaller associations of industrialists. The workers were represented by soviet deputies, the Union of Oil Workers, the Unions of Employees and of Sailors, and the Central Bureau of Trade Unions. Before substantive matters could be discussed, the industrialists challenged the right of the soviet deputies to participate. The workers' delegation replied that, in view of the present weakness of the trade unions, the soviet had been forced to take on the negotiations for the labor contract. The industrialists reluctantly recognized the soviet as the spokesman for labor.

Two weeks later, with few concrete decisions taken, the negotiations broke down completely. The Union of Kerosine Factory Owners, along with the Ship Owners and Drilling Contractors, refused to participate in a general labor contract. The workers' delegation walked out of the meeting. . . . Within the soviet a split developed between the more radical elements, who wanted the nationalization of the oil industry or at least a demonstration-strike, and the moderate elements who talked of appealing to the government in Tiflis or Petrograd to mediate the conflict. The soviet finally resolved to call a conference of factory committees and have that body decide on the question of a strike.

The Unions of Baku Oil Industrialists shared the viewpoint of the moderates, like Ramishvili, and telegraphed Prince Lvov and the minister of labor, Skobelev, in Petrograd. They explained that the smaller firms could not satisfy the wage demands of their workers and continue to operate at a profit. That same day (July 5) Ramishvili telegraphed

Skobelev: "The negotiations for the labor contract between the workers and the entrepreneurs have been broken off. The entrepreneurs refuse to negotiate. A general strike is foreseen which is undesirable in view of the national significance of this industry. . . . Intervention by the government is necessary." Not until the end of the month did Ramishvili receive word that Skobelev was leaving for Baku. By that time the situation had been complicated by actions taken by the factory committees.

As requested by the soviet the first conference of factory committees was held on July 6. These committees, the successors to the factory committees that were first set up in May 1905, had reappeared immediately after the February Revolution. Workers at the Nobel Plant, at A. I. Mantashev, and at S. M. Shibaev and Company were the first to elect plant commissions (*zavodskie komissii*). This simplest form of workers' organization spread until all of Baku and the industrial districts were organized in industrial plant commissions (*promyslovo-zavodskie komissii*). Every twenty-five workers elected one representative to the committee. The committees were uniquely responsive to workers' moods and desires because of the frequency of elections to them and their physical proximity to the workers. Not surprisingly, the Bolsheviks were energetic supporters of the factory committees, and the support of many workers, particularly in outlying districts for the Bolsheviks was reflected in the election of Bolsheviks to committee chairmanships. Shortly after the revolution the central factory committees in both Black City and White City, old Menshevik strongholds, elected Bolshevik chairmen.

As in central Russia, the factory committees in Baku mirrored the radicalization of the masses months earlier than the soviet. Their conferences that began in July were the most important forum for the Bolshevik party regulars. At the very first conference Dzhaparidze reported to the 607 delegates that the industrialists had been given three days in which to answer the workers' demands for resumption of negotiations for the labor contract. So far the industrialists had called the system of calculating the wage-rate increases unfair. The Second Union stated that it would agree to a rise in wages only if oil prices were raised. Overestimating the radical temper of the conference, Dzhaparidze called for a one-day work stoppage to show that the workers stood behind the soviet negotiators. The Bolshevik resolution was defeated, and a milder Menshevik–Dashnak–Socialist-Revolutionary resolution

— to have the labor contract put into effect by decree of the soviet and, if the oil industrialists did not respond, for the Provisional Government to decree a minimum wage — was adopted. The conference wished to resort to a strike only when all other means of struggle had been tried and proved unsuccessful. Dzhaparidze in fury announced that the Bolsheviks would abdicate all responsibility for the labor contract in view of the victory of the "conciliatory" policy of the other socialist parties. He demonstratively announced his departure from the commission that was to negotiate the contract. . . .

Ramishvili's attempts to find an agreement acceptable to both the workers and the managers led him to initiate a commission specifically empowered to find a coefficient of the rise in the cost of living on which the wage-rates could be based. The commission was given two weeks to complete its work. After calculations by both sides, the industrialists proposed to raise wages 50 percent. The workers, however, decided that, to keep pace with the cost of living, wages should immediately be doubled. Ramishvili reported to the conference of factory committees on July 21 that the cost of living had actually risen 475 percent since 1914. Since it had been determined that wages had increased much less than half as much as the cost of living (by September 1917, wages had increased only 178 percent over 1913 for the Nobel workers, probably the highest-paid group in the city), even the workers' demand was conservative and would not quite raise the real wage of even the best-paid workers to the 1914 level. As negotiations dragged on and prices continued to rise, the proposed wage-increases became daily less advantageous to the workers.

Nevertheless, two weeks later the commissar of labor announced to the public that the commission had decided on the 50 percent increase. The labor leaders were, indeed, making most modest demands. At the same time Ramishvili called for more time to negotiate with the industrialists, for the original time-limit had long run out. The conference stormed against the proposal, and delegates called for taking the matter to the masses. Their patience had worn thin. But after the initial excitement subsided, the conference resolved to let Ramishvili's commission continue its work. Even the Bolsheviks favored negotiations rather than an immediate strike at this point. All parties stood committed to negotiations for the time being.

On July 26 negotiations resumed, and the meeting continued far into the night. At four in the morning the delegates dispersed with no agreement. The First Union of Oil Industrialists expressed its willingness to recognize a labor contract effective from April 1 and to pay a two-month advance on the basis of the 50 percent increase, but only if oil prices were raised. The Second Union and the drilling-contractors refused to introduce a labor contract until the price-raise had been effected. On receiving the news of the stalemate, the IKS [Executive Committee of the Soviet] telegraphed Petrograd to send a delegation with full powers to settle the dispute. A conference of workers from the oil-fields could hardly be kept under control by Ramishvili, who struggled to keep them from striking and to confine their energies to telegraphing Petrograd for intervention.

In the face of the industrialists' obstinacy, the Bolsheviks met on July 30 to analyze their tactic vis-à-vis the general line of the soviet and the conference of factory committees. The Baku Bolsheviks feared that the "reactionary trend" that was gripping Petrograd, where the Bolshevik leaders were under arrest if not in hiding, would soon reach Baku. They were, therefore, notably cautious in their proposals. A Left minority called for short demonstration-strikes but was disregarded. Fioletov reasoned that intervention by the central government was the only solution. Petrograd, he argued, should "syndicalize" the small and large companies, or simply create a state monopoly over the whole industry. But Shaumian's moderate proposal was adopted by the conference as the tactic for the party: to reject calls for a strike, in view of the unfavorable political and economic situation, and to call on the most "advanced" workers to explain the situation to the others. In the event of a spontaneous strike, however, the Bolsheviks should take the most active part in it in order to give the movement an organized character. This two-pronged approach in effect became the tactic of the Bolsheviks in Baku in August and September, the period of the most rapid expansion of their popularity and influence. Bolshevik success in these months was the result of the coincidence of the party's tactical stance and the interests of the workers. The hope of the Right socialists lay in the success of the negotiations carried on by the government. Once these failed, a strike was inevitable, and equally inevitable was Bolshevik leadership of that strike.

Matvei Ivanovich Skobelev (1885–1930?), minister of labor in the first coalition government, arrived in Baku as trouble-shooter for the Provisional Government. He was determined to stem the tide toward a general strike. For five furious days (August 4–9) he rushed from conference to meeting to private conversation, taking a middle position between two sides with irreconcilable points of view. He tried to identify with the workers but came down heavily on the side of the industrialists. He told the conference of factory committees: "In the spring of 1912 I left the city of Baku as a newly elected member of the Social-Democratic faction of the Fourth Duma. When a few days ago I approached Baku, I wanted to feel myself, not a representative of the government, but as your comrade working with you in the name of the revolution." His solution was simply to adjourn the negotiations to Petrograd and there calmly settle the matter.

Skobelev told the workers that the country was fast approaching a financial crisis, one of the causes of which was the drop in productivity of labor. In his view to ask for higher wages at this time would be inflationary and harmful. To the soviet and the IKOO he explained that he would make sure that the workers received at least the minimum necessary for their existence and promised that the price of oil would not be raised unless the rise in wages was so great as to warrant it. Skobelev soon realized that the workers were firmly committed to receiving an increase of at least 50 percent and could not be easily dissuaded. By the end of his stay in Baku he came out in support of that figure. Meanwhile the industrialists had agreed to raise wages according to that figure if oil prices were raised. A basis for agreement seemed at hand.

Besides wages, agreement over the issue of authority over hiring and firing remained a key to the final agreement, and here Skobelev was notably sympathetic to the managers' viewpoint:

> The entrepreneur will bear the responsibility for the correct operation of the enterprise. . . . He answers not only before the authorities but also before third persons for losses and disorder. It is natural that it is his inalienable right to hire, fire, and transfer employees and workers at his own discretion. . . . The right to hire without any limitations ought to remain with the employer. . . . The government stands firmly on this. . . . The worker has one means to fight the employer — to leave work, and this, in its turn, is the inalienable right of the worker. . . . The labor contract can not take away anyone's private or public rights.

The workers' representatives had earlier decided that hiring and firing, although the prerogative of the owners, should be carried out with the participation of the trade unions and factory committees, which should have the right to reject those hired without their consent. Skobelev addressed himself to this demand of the workers by arguing that, while such an arrangement is desirable, it would be difficult to require that the employers hire only from the unions. On August 9 the conference of factory committees accepted Skobelev's plan to adjourn the negotiations to Petrograd, and that same day the minister left for the north. This seemed to be the only remaining alternative to a strike.

Hopes were raised for an early settlement of the conflict, which was now entering its sixth month, but tensions within the industry had reached the breaking-point and there was no way to restrain individual strikes by groups of workers. In August workers from the Nobel plants, the Neft Company, and the Zafatem enterprises left work. Dock workers, munition workers, more workers from the Zafatem group of firms walked out in the first two weeks of September. With Mandel'shtam's return to Baku the final rounds of negotiations began. They too soon ground to a halt. The oil industrialists balked at relinquishing their complete control over the hiring and firing of employees.

On September 16, a conference of factory committees met jointly with the executive committee of the soviet and listened to a report on the breakdown of the negotiations. Many of the audience called for an immediate strike; others shouted that systematic terror should be directed against the industrialists. Fioletov, speaking as a member of the arbitration commission, cautioned the workers against the use of terror and was shouted down. Angrily he replied: "To whom are you shouting, 'Down!'? For fifteen years I have defended the interests of the workers, and, except for becoming a cripple, have received nothing for it. Against whom will you carry on terror? Here in Baku live only the directors of the plants, the owners are abroad." The Bolsheviks opposed a strike at this time, since the industry had large stocks of oil to fall back on and the workers could not carry on a lengthy walkout. The conference ended by deciding to continue the negotiations until September 22, at which time an ultimatum would be issued and the industrialists given five days in which to accept it or face a strike. The gauntlet had been thrown down.

Each of the major political parties viewed the impending strike as a potential disaster in view of the economic condition of the city, but the wave of spontaneous strikes and the violence expressed in speeches by workers at the conferences indicated to the political leadership of the "democracy" that the alternative to economic suicide would be political suicide. The Dashnaks [Armenian Revolutionary Federation] opposed an immediate strike, but conceded that after all efforts had failed a strike was inevitable. The Mensheviks and Socialist Revolutionaries were also cautious but ready to accede to the pressure from the workers. Even the Musavat [the major Moslem party] was prepared to support the strike. The Bolsheviks took the line that a strike would be a disaster, and that a suitable alternative would be the immediate nationalization of the oil industry by government decree. But if the workers decided on a strike, the conference should lead it. Dzhaparidze feared that "the masses will go past us," and on September 21 he proposed that the conference be declared a strike committee. The proposal was adopted by a large majority.

The strike began at seven in the morning of September 27, 1917. Of the 610 firms that were affected, the workers in 554 (numbering 52,920) struck specifically because the industrialists had refused to sign the labor contract. Another 12,355 workers struck because of the refusal of their administrations to pay the two-month advance or for other reasons. The strike lasted six days, causing the loss of 405,623 worker-days, and was carried on with exemplary order. Gegechkori assured the strike leaders that the legal parts of the labor agreement could be decreed into law by the Ozakom [organ of the Provisional Government in Transcaucasia]. After three days of the strike a delegation of industrialists left Baku for Tiflis and discussions with the Ozakom on the labor contract.

By October 1 the main items of the labor contract had been accepted by the industrialists, particularly a scale of minimum wages ranging from 4r. 35k. to 11r. 75k. a day for the various categories of workers. Many workers wanted to continue the strike until all thirteen points of the workers' ultimatum had been secured, but the moderates appealed for an end to it. Ramishvili pleaded:

> With great joy I came to this meeting; I wanted to congratulate you on your victory, although you have beaten not only the capitalists but me too who was all the time against the strike. But I hear here speeches which dim my joy. Not all of you consider the victory enough. It's not necessary to dissipate our strength, it's not necessary to continue the strike out of blind stubbornness; now it is necessary to end it. That's how true warriors of the working class should act.

The conference decided that local meetings should decide on the question of stopping the strike and that their decisions would be considered at the next meeting. Dzhaparidze summed up the nature of the workers' victory:

> *Our first and principal victory is our organization. This strike proved that we are strong because of our being well organized. There's a famous saying — give me a fulcrum and I will overturn the whole world. It can be paraphrased: give me an organization of workers and I will overturn the whole capitalist world. . . . Our second victory is the recognition of a single labor contract for all workers and employees.*

On October 2 the industrialists finally agreed to accept the preliminary conditions for the labor contract, and the conference-turned-strike-committee announced the end of the strike. In the euphoria that greeted the victory the workers wildly cheered Ramishvili's efforts in the negotiations, as well as Dzhaparidze's leadership of the strike committee. The Bolsheviks greeted the victory as a decisive defeat for the conciliatory policy of their political rivals. The strike had indeed changed forever the balance of political power in Baku. A more radical and uncompromising working class faced a hostile and discredited bourgeoisie, a bourgeoisie — it should be emphasized — whose power survived only as long as it was tolerated by the revolutionary parties.

The political response of the soviet to the continuing crisis was, on the whole, inadequate, and in turn, tended to worsen the situation. The workers looked for new leadership in the factory committees and in the strike committee. The political orientation of Baku had made a complete about-face since July, when Bolshevik orators were shouted down at street meetings. In early September Bolshevik resolutions were passing easily in the factory committees and other workers' gatherings. Whereas in July workers had wanted unity in the ranks of the "revolutionary democracy," by September there were suggestions that the "conciliatory" tactic of the Right socialists was at the root of the crisis. The Bolsheviks hoped to have this new mood of the workers reflected in the soviet, and called for elections. Early in September Shahumian wrote in *Bakinskii rabochii*:

> *Our soviet is perishing! It must be treated and cured. It is necessary to demand new elections. . . .*
>
> *We do not propose this because we think that our party can constitute at present a majority. It's true that there is a significant shift to the left in the ranks of the workers. The collapse of the defensist and conciliationist policy of the Mensheviks and S.R.s, the treacherous character of the slander on the Bolsheviks, and, finally, the Kadet-Kornilov counterrevolutionary conspiracy could not but act on the minds of the workers. The influence of the Bolsheviks and S.R.-Internationalists*

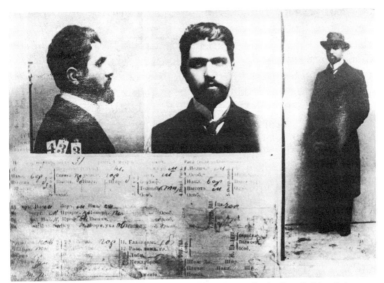

Police Photograph of Stepan Shahumian (1878–1918). The leading Bolshevik in Transcausasia during the Revolution, Shahumian led the Baku Soviet in 1918 and was killed by anti-Bolsheviks in September of that year as one of the ill-fated "26 Baku Commissars."

grows rapidly. But we would prefer in the interests of our party not to hurry and to wait yet a little longer. However, the terrible picture of demoralization and disintegration to which misters Mandel'shtam, Aiollo, and their followers have led the soviet demand the most immediate and decisive measures for its cure.

On September 6, Shahumian proposed a plan by which every five hundred workers or soldiers would elect one deputy, and the soviet approved the formation of a commission to work out procedures for the new elections. The lack of popular confidence in the old soviet was recognized by its members, who now hoped that the organ of the "revolutionary democracy" could be revitalized through new elections.

While the Baku soviet responded to the radicalization of the masses with notable caution, with no more than a call for new elections, the conference of factory committees, then deeply engaged in the struggle for a labor contract, adopted a Bolshevik resolution which condemned the "conciliatory" tactic of the Right socialist parties. The resolution also demanded the transfer of all power to the revolutionary democracy, the end of the war, the arming of the people, the liberation of all Bolsheviks and Internationalists arrested in central Russia, and the abolition of the death penalty. In connection with the financial debacle, the conference of September 18 called for the abolition of private property, workers' control over industry, and the nationalization of large industry. Mandel'shtam and the Mensheviks criticized the resolutions, but to no avail. The conference was the most Bolshevized organ in the city of Baku. Evident in its decisions was the leftist trend in which the workers of Baku had been caught up, a trend to which each of the political parties in the city had to accommodate itself.

Shahumian described the general radicalization of the "revolutionary democracy" in a letter to *Rabochii put'*:

> The Bolshevization noticeable in all of Russia has appeared in the widest dimensions in our oil empire. And long before the Kornilov-shchina. The former masters of the situation, the Mensheviks, are not able to show themselves in the workers' districts. Along with the Bolsheviks the S.R.-Internationalists have begun to get stronger. They have become so strong that they have topped the defensists in their own party, and have formed a bloc with the Bolsheviks in the Soviet of Workers' Deputies and in the districts. The Mensheviks are completely isolated. It must be said that after the Bolsheviks tossed them off, only the most right-wing, definitely Kadetist elements remained in the ranks of the Mensheviks.
>
> Even the sharp turn made by the Tiflis Mensheviks headed by Zhordaniia, expressing themselves unanimously opposed to any kind of coalition with the bourgeoisie and for the immediate end of the war and the taking of power together with the S.R.s in the Caucasus, has not had any effect on the Baku Mensheviks.

The leftist position of the Tiflis Mensheviks, supporting a government of all socialist parties (including the Bolsheviks), was the only feasible alternative to a Bolshevik seizure of power. The Baku Mensheviks, however, made no leftward adjustment in their political program until the eve of the October Revolution. They remained the most conservative socialist party throughout 1917 and on the right wing of Russian Menshevism. As late as October 19, after the Transcaucasian congress of Mensheviks had adopted Zhordania's resolution to form a government of the "revolutionary democracy" and deny confidence to the present coalition, the Baku Mensheviks were unable to rally around

Zhordania's position. . . . There was no doubt that the Mensheviks' rigidity in refusing to break with the coalition government even as it was being discredited in the eyes of the "democracy" was responsible for the rapid falling-off in Menshevik influence among the workers. Only on October 23 did the Baku Committee of Mensheviks vote (8–5, with one abstention) to accept Zhordania's strategic principle. The lateness of the hour was apparent to all, and the subsequent events in Petrograd so altered the political order that the Mensheviks in Baku reverted soon after to their former position supporting collaboration with the Right.

The Socialist Revolutionary Party too suffered an internal crisis as a result of the leftward trend of the workers. On September 2, the day after the soviet readopted the Socialist-Revolutionary–Menshevik–Dashnak resolution on the current movement, the Bibi-Eibat local committee of the Socialist-Revolutionary organization resolved to support the Bolshevik resolution of August 30, and called for new elections to the soviet and the establishment of a firm democratic authority in Baku based on the soviet. Although the committee supported the Provisional Government as well, the tenor of the resolution was clearly far to the left of the Socialist Revolutionary majority and close to the Bolshevik position. . . .

Throughout Transcaucasia the Socialist Revolutionaries were by September losing their predominant position among the Russian soldiers. At the First Congress of Soldiers in Transcaucasia, the Socialist Revolutionaries had managed to have their plank on "socialization of land" adopted and gained control of the territorial council of the Congress. But by September the Tiflis garrison was no longer a Socialist-Revolutionary stronghold and was turning into a Bolshevik one. Only the soldiers at the front were free from Bolshevik influence, thanks to the restrictions on Bolshevik agitators established by the Tiflis authorities. In Baku the soldiers had been meeting regularly on Freedom Square since July, listening to anyone not afraid to take the podium. The meetings started in the heat of the afternoon and went on until midnight. Most popular of the speakers was the young commandant of Baku, Osip Avakian, a nonfactional Social Democrat who in the course of the summer gravitated closer to the Bolsheviks. The oratorical battles on Freedom Square were as decisive as any other part of the political struggle in Baku, for they would ultimately decide which party would win the support of the Baku garrison. Earlier in the year the soldiers were overwhelmingly defensist and supported the Socialist-Revolutionary position. But by September Avakian and his audience were responding sympathetically to the Bolshevik slogans. Only the officer corps and the Armenian volunteer bands continued to support the war. . . . By the end of September Avakian could assure the Bolsheviks: "The soldier is on the outside a Socialist Revolutionary, but inside he is a Bolshevik. . . ."

The Moslem leaders too had reached the end of their patience with the soviet majority that had consistently demonstrated its willingness to underrepresent the Moslem citizens of Baku. The Musavatist newspaper, *Achizsoz*, blamed the socialists for not securing representation of the Moslems more energetically:

> *The leftist parties, having taken in their hands the organization of the revolutionary government, have in their first moves made a great mistake. This mistake is the lack of attention paid to the local population, in this case the Moslems who make up the majority. This is expressed in the absence of representatives of Moslems in significant local organizations, like the IKOO, the Soviet of Workers' Deputies, etc. In some organizations which have less importance Moslem representatives have entered in a meaningless minority, and in the more important have not entered at all.*

Both Topchibashev, a Kadet, and the Musavatist Resul Zade denounced the Kornilov mutiny and linked it with the policy of the soviet leadership, which "has made great mistakes by giving in on important questions to reactionary circles." On September 8, the executive committee of the Baku soviet denied the Musavat a seat in the Bureau for the Struggle against Counterrevolution, thus further alienating the Moslem leadership from the socialist majority. It is not surprising then that at this time the Musavatists began to move closer to the Bolsheviks both on the issue of the war and on the question of Moslem rights.

Midway through 1917 the Moslem leadership in Baku shifted from supporting the military effort made by the Provisional Government to a radical criticism of the war. In May the Committee of Baku Moslem Public Organizations had issued a proclamation which reluctantly admitted that "we cannot yet stop the war." Although all wanted peace, it said, with the enemy in their land they could not lay down arms. As for

Moslem participation in the war and in all future wars, the First All-Russian Moslem Congress had called for the establishment of national Moslem military units with Moslem officers. The proposal was also adopted by the Moslem Military Congress in Kazan in July; but the Provisional Government did not approve the formation of such units until well into October. Until August Moslem leaders, except for the Hummetists, supported the war, as did the Mensheviks, the Socialist Revolutionaries, and the Dashnaks. But by September the Musavat had reversed its position and forcefully expressed its displeasure with the war: "This failure, without a doubt, lies in the lack of boldness to recognize frankly that Russia is already not in a condition to continue this aimless war. This realization is not the fruit of faintheartedness and the closing of eyes to the interest of the country, but comes from the most active and real interests of the revolution, the republic, the motherland, and democracy." This change in attitude made the Musavatists the natural allies of the Bolsheviks on the war issue, though the nationalist rhetoric of the Moslems discouraged the Bolsheviks from close cooperation with Resul Zade and his followers. What was less clear at this moment, but would emerge in a few months as the principal component in Musavat policy, was the party's renewed commitment to an alliance not with the antiwar socialists but with the Ottoman Turks. Freed from their war-time Russian orientation, the Musavatists in the last months of 1917 reasserted the traditional Ottoman orientation which in the prewar years had marked the formation of Azerbaijani nationalism.

Musavat was attracted by the Leninist slogan of "self-determination for all nationalities" and saw in it a basis for cooperation with the Bolsheviks. At the October congress of their party, the Musavat leader Resul Zade reiterated his interest in autonomy for Moslems. The conflict between the Marxist notion of class warfare and the nationalist ideal of the unity of all classes of one nationality was underplayed. Musavat believed that self-determination in eastern Transcaucasia could lead only to Moslem dominance, since the Azerbaijanis were the vast majority of the population; so if the Bolsheviks kept their pledge, then it would be Musavat which would tolerate the Bolsheviks and not vice versa. As long as the Bolsheviks advocated national self-determination and were committed to ending the war, a tacit understanding between the RSDRP (b) and Musavat kept mutual criticism at a minimum.

While remaining the most radical political party in Baku, the local Bolsheviks were more moderate than the Leninists in Petrograd. Shahumian's caution may have been rooted in fears that the launching of a civil war in Baku would trigger off interethnic hostilities. Or he may have carefully calculated the resources of the Baku Bolsheviks and concluded that without a majority in the Soviet and support from the local garrison a seizure of power was unthinkable. . . .

Once the radicalization of the workers and soldiers had become apparent, the Baku Bolsheviks did not hesitate to echo their comrades in the capital and call for a seizure of power by the "revolutionary democracy." On September 12, Dzhaparidze told a conference of Bolsheviks: "If up to this time we have talked about the transfer of power into the hands of the revolutionary democracy, from now on we are going to speak of conquest." Two weeks later the Bolsheviks adopted a resolution which read: "The transfer of power to the democracy cannot be accomplished without a struggle, for which the party should be preparing." The Bolsheviks were confident that their increased influence could be translated easily into political power. At the First Congress of Bolshevik Organizations of the Caucasus, which met at the beginning of October, Shahumian clarified the new militancy of the Bolsheviks:

> *After July 3–5, it was possible to speak only of the conquest of power, not of its transfer.*
>
> *The new government created real anarchy; we cannot remain calm in such a situation. Recognizing that the influence of the Bolsheviks is gaining in many soviets, that even the peasantry is being Bolshevized, that the Ukrainians and even the headquarters of the Mensheviks — Transcaucasia — are expressing themselves against the coalition, finally that unrest is growing everywhere, and land is being seized, etc., our task is to stand at the head of the revolution and to take power into our own hands. . . .*
>
> *Despite all the responsibility we will take on ourselves, not fearing the difficulties and complexities of the work, [we must] go forward boldly toward our tasks which life has given us, and having taken power into our hands carry the revolution to its victorious end. (stormy applause)*

The Baku Bolsheviks, like most of the other leading political parties in the city, had been stimulated by the new radical stance of the masses to shift to a more militant position. In September and October they called for a seizure of power by their party. Yet within the city their deeds did not match their words. If their tactics were measured by what they did, then the Baku Bolsheviks, like most of Lenin's comrades in the Central Committee, remained more moderate than Lenin. Despite the radical rhetoric of September and October, Shahumian and his comrades continued to act as if they sought a peaceful transfer of power to the soviets.

While in the north Lenin was writing frantic letters to his Bolshevik Central Committee urging it to seize power in Petrograd, the Bolsheviks of Baku were cautiously maneuvering the local soviet into a declaration of soviet power. Shahumian managed in the space of one month to reelect the soviet's executive committee (with himself as chairman once again), expand the soviet's membership by introducing delegates from the Bolshevized conference of factory committees, and eliminate two rivals of soviet power — the newly formed Committee of Public Safety and the IKOO. In this way the Bolsheviks achieved predominance in the local soviet without ever winning a majority in elections, and persuaded the soviet to declare itself sovereign in the city without firing a shot. Shahumian's strategy of "peaceful transition" to socialism appeared briefly to be bearing fruit.

Lenin Addressing a Crowd. Note Trotsky listening at the foot of the platform at the right. After Trotsky lost out to Stalin in a bitter struggle for power in the 1920s, he was eliminated from reproductions of this photo that were published in the Soviet Union.

III October

Variety of Opinion

Among Petrograd's workers. . . . the very keen desire for an end to coalition politics and for soviet power was practically unanimous. But a large part of the skilled workers, disheartened by the deepening economic crisis, hesitated before the harsh odds, the threat of political isolation and the spectre of defeat in a civil war.

David Mandel

Lenin's revolution, as Zinoviev and Kamenev pointed out, was a wild gamble, with little chance that the Bolsheviks' ill-prepared followers could prevail against all the military force that the government seemed to have, and even less chance that they could keep power even if they managed to seize it temporarily . . . [Lenin] was bent on baptizing the revolution in blood, to drive off the fainthearted and compel all who subscribed to the overturn to accept and depend on his unconditional leadership.

Robert V. Daniels

The phenomenal Bolshevik success can be attributed in no small measure to the nature of the party in 1917. Here I have in mind neither Lenin's bold and determined leadership, the immense historical signifi-

cance of which cannot be denied, nor the Bolsheviks' proverbial, though vastly exaggerated, organizational unity and discipline. Rather, I would emphasize the party's internally relatively democratic, tolerant, and decentralized structure and method of operation, as well as its essentially open and mass character — in striking contrast to the traditional Leninist model.

Alexander Rabinowitch

Russian working-class political culture was overwhelmingly a socialist political culture. This was the legacy both of a socialist revolutionary movement that predated the rise of a working class and of the influence of Marxist analysis on that emerging working class. . . . The events of the summer of 1917 combined with growing class antagonism to change this socialist consciousness into class consciousness. . . . That the revolutionary unity of March fell apart along class lines can be attributed to economic conditions in Russia but also to the fact that the class framework was after all implicit in socialist consciousness.

Diane Koenker

In view of the deep social tensions within Russian society and of the strength of socialist sentiments among workers, soldiers, and peasants, it is possible that a broadly based socialist regime, that included representation from democratically elected local bodies, municipal and government workers, shopkeepers and people from cooperatives (odnorodnoe sotsialisticheskoe pravitel'stvo), could have been established in Russia even without war. It is difficult to imagine the Bolsheviks' coming to power and creating essentially a one-party government, however, if Russia somehow had withdrawn from the war or had avoided it altogether.

Donald J. Raleigh

They all call themselves Marxists, but their conception of Marxism is impossibly pedantic. . . . "The development of the productive forces of Russia has not attained the level that makes socialism possible." All the heroes of the Second International, including, of course, Sukhanov, beat the drums about this proposition. . . . But what if the situation, which drew Russia into the imperialist world war . . . gave rise to circumstances that put Russia and her development in a position which enabled us to achieve precisely that combination of a "peasant war" with the working-class movement suggested in 1856 by no less a Marxist than Marx himself . . . ?

Vladimir Il'ich Lenin

The Issues

By the fall of 1917 the possibility of a broad coalition supported by the middle classes and the "democracy" had been lost. The inability of the government to prevent the social disintegration in Russia, to bring the war to an end, and to find a firm base of support either in the "democracy" or in the propertied classes had radicalized the lower classes and driven the people of property to find more authoritarian answers. The chance for a military coup had ended with Kornilov's failure. Such a solution of a regime representing "census Russia" would be revived only in the Civil War.

On the left, discussions revolved around alternatives to the Coalition. The Bolsheviks called unequivocally once again for "All Power to the Soviets," the formation of a government that would represent directly the workers, soldiers, and peasants. Leftist Mensheviks like Martov and the Georgians proposed a "homogeneous socialist government," made up of representatives from all the socialist parties, perhaps including elements from the lower-middle classes. The final outcome of the struggle for power was the declaration of Soviet Power and the eventual descent into a one-party, Bolshevik dictatorship. The question why the democratic solution was lost has divided historians broadly between those who look to politics and ideology, Bolshevik will and determination, on the one hand, and those who look to the process of social disintegration and the aspiration toward order, any order, on the other.

Those political historians who have concluded that the collapse of the February regime and the rise of the Bolsheviks can largely be understood as a political failure of the liberal and moderate socialist leaders have often sought their answers in a discussion of the personal qualities of leadership. As Alexander Kerensky put it: "By the will of men, not by the force of the elements, did October become inevitable." Historians like Sergei Melgunov and Robert V. Daniels have emphasized the maniacal determination of Lenin in his drive to power in contrast to the pusillanimity of the government. A common interpretation has been that the Bolsheviks won because of their uncommonly tight organization, which when combined with the fractures among their enemies, greatly aided their victory. In a concise formulation of this classic conception, Merle Fainsod wrote:

> Why then did the Bolsheviks triumph? The Bolsheviks, unlike most of their opponents, were willing to take the initiative and, for all their own disorganization, they represented a relatively disciplined force.

They were greatly aided by division among their opponents, by the general assumption, which all their opponents shared, that the Bolsheviks could not possibly consolidate their authority. The complete disillusionment of the military and the more conservative forces with Kerensky and their refusal to rally around him redounded to the advantage of the Bolsheviks. The cleavages among the non-Bolshevik socialist parties weakened resistance on the left. Finally, the ability of the Bolsheviks to cloak their seizure of power in the legitimacy of Soviet institutions and to make their appeal in terms of such powerful rallying cries as peace, land, and bread provided the political leverage which enabled them to march to power.[1]

Such political analyses, whether state-centered, personality-dependent, or organization-based, have been hard pressed in recent years by the explosion of research on the social history of the revolution. Once the independent generation of worker, soldier, and peasant radicalism is appreciated, explanations relying heavily on organizational structures or personal will may appear inadequate or at least need to be integrated into the larger social context. Alexander Rabinowitch, for one, has done this in his work. He has shown that the Bolshevik party was not as tightly organized as Soviet historians or Cold War models would have us believe. Rather the party of 1917 was relatively open and democratic, and for that reason was able to establish a dynamic relationship between its cadres and the masses. In the chaos of 1917 the Bolsheviks had certain advantages, not the least of which was the clear articulation of a class-based conceptualization of the revolutionary process, one that corresponded both to the developed political culture of workers and resonated their immediate experience. This correspondence between Bolshevik principles and tactics and worker-soldier aspirations was a powerful weapon that the party of Lenin was able to use in its quest for power.

The social history of the revolution has not "left the politics out" but rather has located them in the larger environment of economic collapse, social polarization, and the immediate experience of continuous revolutionary crisis. The Bolsheviks may have succeeded, according to some, because they were the most skillful and duplicitous manipulators of workers' confused desires or, according to others, because they were good politicians in the much more positive sense of both reflecting and heightening the aspirations of significant groups in the population. But certainly any explanation must consider that, given the different responses

---

[1] Merle Fainsod, "Comment," in Richard Pipes, ed., *Revolutionary Russia*, p. 219.

to the war and the economy by the verkhi *(upper classes) and the* nizy *(lower classes), the politics of cooperation favored by the Mensheviks and Socialist Revolutionaries that futilely tried to bring together industrialists and workers, landlords and peasants, officers and soldiers, had little appeal by the late summer of 1917. Since Lenin's return in April, the Bolsheviks had pushed for a government based on the lower classes alone, and this position steadily gained ground among the workers and soldiers until the actual taking of power became relatively easy. Whether one thinks of the February Revolution or the October Revolution as accidental, inevitable, the product of political manipulation, or the consequence of complex historical conjunctures, neither a political history divorced from social context nor a social history devoid of politics can provide a synthesis adequate to explain the events of 1917.*

The results of the 1917 revolution were deep and far-reaching. They changed the nature of the century in which we live. The political revolution of February destroyed the three-hundred-year-old autocratic monarchy, along with its army and bureaucracy. The radical social revolution that followed (and continued through the Civil War) eliminated the old propertied classes, the nobility, and the bourgeoisie. So complete was the disintegration of capitalist industry, so extreme the peasant seizure of the land and destruction of the old landed estates, that, unlike the great revolutions in England in the seventeenth century and France in the eighteenth century, no restoration of the former ruling classes ever occurred in Russia. With the end of legal private capitalism and its replacement, first with state capitalism, then War Communism (1918–1921), still later the New Economic Policy (1921–1928), and eventually a crude state "socialism" (Stalinism, 1928–1953) the possibility of a return to the prerevolutionary order receded further into historical memory.

Though in one important understanding of democracy — political representation and protection of civil rights — the Russian Revolution failed, in another, peculiarly Russian understanding — mobilization of the lower classes into government — the revolution was "democratic." Hundreds of thousands of ordinary people — workers, soldiers, peasants — entered the government, the army, the state apparatus, and the party, and a new ruling class of bureaucrats and party officials, originally from the disenfranchised classes of the past, dominated the Soviet state.[2]

[2] This point is effectively made in the work of Sheila Fitzpatrick, particularly *The Russian Revolution 1917–1932* (Oxford: Oxford University Press, 1984).

Yet perhaps the most lasting achievement of the revolution was the replacement of the tsarist state and the anarchy that followed with the building of a new and authoritarian state — the dictatorship of the proletariat, in Marxist terms. Rather than the radical democracy envisioned by many in 1917 (even by Lenin in his State and Revolution), *the Soviet state that emerged after the Civil War was not elected by the people or ultimately responsible to them in any direct sense. At one and the same time the revolution of 1917 represented the end of oppression, the dawn of social and political liberation, and the metamorphosis of revolutionary energy into a new political dominance. Seventy years would pass before that dictatorial state would embark on a renewed search for a more democratic form of socialism.*

David Mandel

Class Struggle in the Factories

David Mandel is distinct among his generation of students of the revolutionary labor movement in several ways. By discipline he is a historical sociologist; by birth, a native Canadian; by conviction, a Marxist. He was educated at Hebrew University and Columbia University, where he worked with Leopold Haimson, and has taught in England and Canada. His two-volume study on the Petrograd workers is rich in examples taken from Soviet archives, alive with the actual voices of the workers as recorded in memoirs and newspapers. He carefully contrasts the stages through which the workers moved in 1917 — the early "honeymoon" with the industrialists, the break with the liberals and moderates, and the growing sense of isolation after July. In the excerpt here from his second volume, Mandel takes us into the factories and illuminates the mood of Petrograd workers on the eve of the October Revolution.

From *The Petrograd Workers and the Soviet Seizure of Power: From the July Days 1917 to July 1918* by David Mandel, St. Martin's Press, 1984, pp. 264–266, 273–286, 287–309. Reprinted with permission from the publisher.

The months from July to October were a period of contrasts in the labour movement: on the broader political scene (with the exception of the Kornilov affair) — a certain sluggishness, marking time and abdication of initiative to the leaders; in the factories — a continually intensifying struggle for power, with the factory committees under constant pressure from the rank and file. It was here that the workers concentrated their main energies in a desperate effort to avert economic collapse and mass unemployment and to maintain the working class physically and morally intact.

The Factory Committees Under Attack

If the workers' defeat in the July Days gave rise to a more aggressive policy towards labour on the part of the industrialists, Kornilov's defeat did not deter them. It seemed rather to strengthen their determination. In the Kornilov affair the political card had been played and beaten. Command of the economy was the bourgeoisie's last and best trump, although a very risky one since it involved the very core of the class's existence, beyond which there could be no further retreat.

In early September, the industrialists launched a full-scale offensive against the factory committees. Buoyed by Skobelev's circulars restricting committee meetings to extra-work hours and abolishing their *de facto* right of control over hiring and firing (not to speak of control over production), the Committee of United Industry decided that payment of wages to the various elected worker delegates would be discontinued as of 15 September, in contravention of the March agreement between the Petrograd Soviet and the PSFMO [Petrograd Society of Factory and Mill Owners]. The owners even tried to have the military deferments of the factory committee members lifted on the grounds that they were not really engaged in production, threatening to remove even the most prominent members of the CS [Central Soviet] of Factory Committees.

At about this time, the Committee of United Industry outlined its 'Conditions for the Restoration of Industry' in a note to the Minister of Labour. It urged the government to adopt the following measures to regulate worker–management relations: hiring and firing was to be made the exclusive prerogative of management; management was to be given the power unilaterally to impose punishments up to and including dismissal; factory committees, soviets or any other organisations were to be forbidden from interfering with management, and the latter was to be freed of all responsibility to these organisations; and finally, any worker who failed to attain the previous year's level of productivity was to be fired. The note concluded ominously: "Without these measures to influence the worker masses, industry is threatened with complete shutdown."

To the workers it was more than clear that this assault on the factory committees had but one real aim — to remove the last obstacle preventing the industrialists from a massive shutdown. The almost simultaneous resurfacing of the plan to "unload" Petrograd's industry, seen as merely another route towards the same goal, only reinforced this view.

In fact, as the socialist press pointed out, the note was based upon the self-serving premise, adopted soon after the February Revolution, that the chief cause of the declining productivity was the workers' abuse of their newly-won freedom. All the blame that the census politicians had heaped upon the autocracy for the economic dislocation in the months preceding the revolution was quickly forgotten. It did little good to remind the industrialists that productivity had been declining since 1915 due to shortages of fuel and raw materials, the failure to replace worn-out machinery, the physical exhaustion of the workers and the influx of a mass of inexperienced new workers to meet the needs of expanded war production.

The industrialists' formula for curing the economy thus boiled down to putting a leash on the workers. They still showed no readiness to suffer state regulation. When the reformed Factory Conference (*Zavodskoe soveshchanie*), a public body charged with overseeing the economy, finally got on its feet in August, the CS of Factory Committees began to turn to it with considerable success to prevent unjustified closures. As a last resort, the conference could and did sequester factories. However, the industrialists, in disregard of the law, simply boycotted the conference, appealing instead to Pal'chinskii, who now headed the Special Conference of Defence.

For the workers, then, rather than a formula for the restoration of industry, the employers' recommendations were a *carte blanche* for its destruction. And this they were fiercely determined to prevent.

The Struggle for Production — Workers' Control Checked

The mood among the workers was one of growing desperation over the deteriorating situation in the factories, where life had become a continuous series of crises. The gnawing sense of impending disaster became all-pervasive, as workers engaged owners and management in a dogged holding action to save their factories, their livelihood and ultimately, their revolution.

The prospects for success did not appear very bright. Experts told the August Factory Committee Conference that in the coming year Petrograd's industry could at best hope for two-thirds of the quantity of fuel received in the current year, itself one of acute shortage. As for the railroads, the Ministry of Communications was in the same mess as before February. Unless immediate emergency measures were taken, one could expect the system to collapse by the end of September. All speakers warned against optimism: "In deciding how to get out of the catastrophe that threatens us, we can talk only of how to make it less painful." "We see hunger approaching," stated a worker from the Orudiinyi Factory, "unemployment is growing, and all measures to regulate economic life are repulsed. The execution of control also meets resistance on the part of management . . . The country is heading towards ruin, the people are exhausted, labour productivity is falling. We must take measures." Two months later, at the Fourth Conference, Skrypnik could already report: "We are no longer standing in the antechamber of the economic collapse; we have entered the zone of collapse itself." . . .

Vulkan was characteristic of the situation in the factories of Petrograd in several respects. First, in the continuously escalating power struggle between labour and management, the factory committee was being drawn away from its original controlling functions (in the sense of monitoring and overseeing) towards more and more direct intervention into the management of production, particularly in efforts to bolster productivity.

Secondly, in contrast to the situation on the more directly political level, the "masses," the rank and file, were clearly holding onto the initiative, prodding their somewhat reluctant leaders into increasingly militant stands.

Finally, as before, the struggle for production led directly to the question of state power. Vulkan called for state takeover of all factories where production was declining. Its factory committee secretary expressed the general view that real control required a "truly democratic" government and workers' control on the national level. The following discussion will take up these three aspects of the movement.

From Workers' Control towards Workers' Management

The workers first began to intervene directly in management functions in the spring, when some factory committees took it upon themselves to seek out new orders and supplies of fuel and raw materials. But as the Vulkan case show, this was often not enough to ensure that production continued.

The committee of the Parviainen Machine-construction Factory achieved considerable notoriety for its activity in August that saved the jobs of 1,630 workers. These workers were to be fired because, according to the administration, only three-fifths of the required fuel had arrived. In response, the factory committee aided by the CS set up an investigative commission that found that fuel was being consumed in an extremely irrational manner, that a 30 per cent saving could be effected without loss of normal output. After putting up some resistance, the administration was finally forced to confirm these findings. The factory committee also worked out new rules for stokers, machine operators and other workers to eliminate fuel wastage. *Rabochii put'* commented:

> Here the factory committee has already entered onto the path of technical improvement of production. It would be of interest to know what the former Minister of Labour and former social democrat Skobelev would say. Can a factory committee work out these rules . . . during work hours? . . . The workers are creating a new life. The past and present ministers, toadying to the capitalists, only hinder this activity.

In August, the fuel supply at the Sestroretsk Factory outside of Petrograd ran out. The water supply, another source of energy at the plant, was also drawing low. The factory committee took upon itself to dig a canal to a source of water supply on a nearby estate (the landowner protested vigorously, but in vain), which was able to keep the factory going for some time. *Znamya truda* wrote this up in an article entitled "What Would the Factories be Without the Factory Committees?"

These encroachments on management's traditional prerogatives were not the expression of a lust for power on the part of the factory committees or the worker rank and file. Practice was indeed changing, but the basic motive behind the activity of the factory committees remained the same: to keep the factories running. Workers' control in its original monitoring capacity, like dual power in the state, was born of the workers' mistrust of the capitalists. But at the same time it implied a belief that the workers and the owners could cooperate, even if the latter required some rather forceful prodding from time to time. In essence, workers' control meant that the workers entrusted the administration with running the factory, while they reserved for themselves the right to monitor management's activities and to intervene if there was any abuse of this trust. But there was the rub. Workers' control came up against the same obstacle as dual power: the other party refused to cooperate because it felt its interests were opposed to those of the "controlling" workers. In fact, the "controlled" party seemed prepared for the entire enterprise to come to a halt rather than suffer the workers' newly-won power to assert their interests.

The plain fact was that there was no way to "control" an executive that refused at almost any price to be "controlled." The workers reached the conclusion that management was not doing its job in good faith, that it was, in fact, fast losing any interest in maintaining production. In their view, they had no alternative but to move in to fill the void left by management's inactivity or conscious sabotage. "We are told that we must control," complained a Dinamo worker at the August Factory Committee Conference. "But what will we control if we have nothing left but walls, bare walls?" Levin warned the same assembly:

> It is very likely that we stand before a general strike of capitalists and industrialists. We have to be prepared to take the enterprises into our hands to render harmless the hunger that the bourgeoisie so heavily counts upon as a counterrevolutionary force.

Levin himself was far from being an anarchist. After the October Revolution he consistently opposed takeovers that were not absolutely justified by the sabotage or flight of the management.

Not surprisingly, the demand totally to remove the owners from command of the factories began to be raised in this period for the first time on a significant scale. Vulkan, as noted, demanded that the state take charge of all enterprises where productivity was declining. A report on the Soikin Press in *Rabochii put'* also recommended that the state requisition and confiscate all plants being sabotaged or closed. The owner of Soikin had refused to make repairs or to replace worn parts and was found selling his machines piece by piece to speculators. The Kolpino and Obukhovskii District branches of the Metalworkers' Union both recommended that the unions themselves take over the enterprises "as the only radical measure of struggle." The question of confiscation or nationalisation was also being raised in the textile union.

At the time, these were still minority voices in the labour movement, and little came of these demands. The workers' attention was still focused on control, though control in an expanded sense. But it is not difficult to see that full takeover of management was but a few steps away in the logical progression of events that had led from control in the strict sense to control as direct intervention into the management of production.

Factory Committees under Pressure from Below

Reporting on the factory committees, Skrypnik told the Bolshevik CC [Central Committee] in October, "It is felt that the leaders do not entirely express the mood of the masses. The former are more conservative." Both the Vulkan and Putilov cases cited earlier show the worker rank and file as a constant spur to the factory committees. The Lebedev workers' opposition to the CS stand on the evacuation is yet another instance of the often greater militancy of the worker masses when it came to defending the factories.

The shift in the factory committees' activity towards increasingly direct intervention into the management of production occurred largely under pressure from the rank and file exerted against not always enthusiastic factory committee activists. "One notes under the pressure of the workers," wrote the director of the Admiralty Shipyards, "a deviation of the committees from their proper [*pryamoi*] and fruitful activity directed at preliminary [*predvaritel'nyi*] control of the administration, in other words, in the direction of management of the factory."

The background for this was the widespread disappointment with the limited success of workers' control in forestalling the industrial crisis. In retrospect it is clear that this movement played a crucial role in the victory of the October Revolution by postponing the economic collapse for several months. October would not have been possible with a massively unemployed, demoralised and dispersed working class. The fact remains, however, that despite the great popularity of the slogan and the energetic activity of the committees firmly backed by the workers, genuine control, in the sense of full access to documents and systematic monitoring of management, largely eluded the workers before October. One can sense the frustration in the report of the Putilov Factory Committee cited earlier: an affair that could have been put to rest in an hour dragged on for a month, agitating the workers and wasting their energy, simply because management refused to cooperate with the factory committee.

The limited success of the movement was readily admitted. On 26 September at a meeting on the forthcoming dismissal of 5000 Putilov workers, Glebov told his colleagues in the factory committee:

> *The administration has given up and it is hardly likely to take the dismissals upon itself, and in all probability we will have to supervise this dirty work ourselves.[The dismissals were due to a fuel shortage.] To blame in this, of course, are the representatives of the higher ups [verkhy] who refused to allow us close to control.*

Another committee member, Voitsekhovskii, urged: "We must succeed in getting the right to control, and it is about time we put an end to our traipsing about the shops of the factory."

Even in the best of cases the workers only managed to mount a strong holding action, to patch up the leaks temporarily. But everyone could sense the waters rising, and it was obvious that more than patchwork was needed. "At the First Conference [of Factory Committees] we expected to greet the Second amidst brilliant success," lamented Surkov, a delegate to the Second Conference.

> *But the revolutionary wave has stopped, and those for whom it is profitable have been able to exploit this, and as a result our activity has been paralysed to a significant degree. The factory committees have lost their authority [with management].*

Two months later at the Fourth Conference, Zhuk, the delegate from the Schlusselburg Powder Factory, was still trying to fight this disillusionment:

> *Many take a skeptical attitude toward the coming [All-Russian Factory Committee] conference. The conference will give us not vague resolutions but concrete answers to all the cardinal questions that arise in connection with the unprecedented anarchy that has seized all of industry. The conference must solve the question of the factories that are closing and of those where clear acts of sabotage have been exposed. . . . We must carry this out in deeds and not only in words.*

Under these circumstances it is not difficult to understand why the workers were pressing for a more active and direct role of the factory committees in management and for more militant tactics generally.

What does require some explaining, however, is the reluctance often shown by the committees in taking on these new functions and supporting more aggressive tactics.

Most factory committees and their organisations firmly refused formal participation in management, rejecting any responsibility for the state of the factories. In October a conference of representatives of the factory committees and of other labour organisations in Petrograd specifically rejected the idea of sending workers' representatives to participate in the administration of the factories. The same position was taken by the All-Russian Conference of Factories of the Artillery Authority and the Conference of Factories of the Naval Authority:

> Having discussed the question of control by the factory committees over the economic, technical and administrative aspects of production, and considering that responsibility for production lies exclusively with the administration of the factory, [the Conference of Factories of the Naval Authority] recognises for the factory committees through their control commissions the right to be present at all meetings of the administration and to demand exhaustive explanations to questions and to receive them.

This was still control in its original sense. At about the same time the Putilov Factory Committee, backed by the workers, turned down a proposal by Pal'chinskii for a standing conference of representatives of the workers and the administration to "regulate all the work of the factory." It was decided that the factory committee should enter solely for purposes of control but should reject any responsibility for the management of the factory.

There were several interrelated reasons for this position. In part, it was reluctance to take responsibility for a task that the factory committees were not at all sure they could handle, particularly in the current harsh economic conditions. They felt that unless there was absolutely no other alternative, responsibility for the direct day-to-day running of the factory should be left with the administration. The Putilov resolution of 28 September explained:

> Having discussed the question of participation in the institution regulating the entire life of the factory, and taking into account the current state of the factory, which as a result of various causes must be recognised as catastrophic, and that the reorganisation of the administration

of the factory and the regulation of production are an extremely complex affair requiring time, [we resolve:]

1. The workers cannot take upon themselves responsibility for the course of work at the factory in the near future.

2. Representatives of the workers should enter the council being created in order to actively participate in the control and regulation of the entire productive life of the factory and to oppose any attempts to hold up the proper course of factory life mainly on the part of external forces.

Consciousness of the difficulties involved in management was, thus, a restraining factor. On the other hand, the rank-and-file workers, more distant from these problems, tended often to react more spontaneously to events. . . .

But concern for the factory committees' lack of expertise in dealing with the technical and economic difficulties facing the factories was not the major consideration in the refusal of responsibility for production. Prepared or not, it was generally agreed that capital's "Italian strike" would sooner or later leave the workers with no alternative. More important was the fear on the part of the committees that under the coalition government, and in the absence of workers' control on the national level, they would simply lack the power effectively to tackle the problems faced by industry and end up being exploited by the administration and compromised in the eyes of the worker masses. . . .

The same attitudes were expressed at the All-Russian Conference of Factory Committees in mid October in response to a suggestion that the factory committees delegate one member to each department of the administration. According to this proposal, the delegates would have a consultative voice and would make sure that the administration was following a general plan to be drawn up by a proposed central economic organ staffed by a majority of workers' representatives. Chubar' of the Petrograd CS objected that "such a formulation is unfortunate, since it puts the workers in the role of some sort of aides to generals." He referred to the decision of the Conference of Factories of the Artillery Authority against entering the administration.

The members of the factory committee would turn into pushers [tolkachi], whom the administration will use as extra help, itself remaining outside of active work. Such phenomena have already been observed in the practice of the state factories. Besides, if the workers enter the factory administration even with only a consultative voice, in

> *a critical moment (and at present, this can be any moment) the workers will direct all their discontent at the factory committee, blaming it for not having taken measures to prevent the hitches in production. It will, therefore, sow discontent among the workers themselves.*

Chubar' recommended control through a commission entirely separate from management.

Antipov, a worker from the Vyborg District, seconded Chubar', adding that one could indeed observe of late a desire among management to offer the factory committees a place in order to foist upon them responsibility for its own failures.

> *Such a pitting of undeveloped masses against their factory committees can be successful, and in some cases one can already observe a certain straining of relations between the worker masses and their elected organs. A recent meeting in Petrograd of all the representatives of the workers' organisations discussed the issue of entering the factory administration and decided against it.*

The conference vote was 83 to 4 for control through a commission separate from management.

There was, in addition, a related "ideological" issue: by becoming involved in production while the factories were still in effective control of the capitalists, were not the factory committees thereby participating in the exploitation of the workers, even if their motive was to save them from mass unemployment? Although circumstances were forcing the committee activists to go beyond control in the narrow sense, they were nevertheless sensitive to such criticism, which hit at a core value of the "conscious workers" — class separateness from the bourgeoisie.

Lenin himself had reproached the factory committees back in May for acting as the "errand boys" of capital in seeking out fuel and new orders in the absence of soviet power and workers' control on the national level that alone could ensure that their efforts would be in the workers' interests. This was a reproach that union leaders were particularly wont to express. Ryazanov, an old-time trade unionist and one of the moderate Bolsheviks hostile to the activity of the factory committees, told the All-Russian Factory Committee Conference:

> *The union movement does not bear the stain of the entrepreneur, and it is the bad luck of the committees that they seem to be component parts of the administration. The union opposes itself to capital, while*

> *the factory committee involuntarily turns into an agent of the entre-*
> *preneur.*

Similarly, Gastev, a leader of the Petrograd Metalworkers' Union, noted a "touching solidarity [on the part of the factory committees] with the administration." Provincial committees were sending representatives to the government in Petrograd to praise their factories and support the owners' requests for orders and subsidies. "Such a coming together of the factory committees with the administration forced the Petrograd Metalworkers' Union to pass a whole series of resolutions aimed at curtailing this independent activity of the committees or at diverting it into a more defined channel."

The Struggle for Production and the Issue of State Power

The search for a solution to the problems facing the factory committees on both the practical and "ideological" levels thus led them directly to the issue of state power. At the Fourth Factory Committee Conference in October, Skrypnik had some harsh words for those delegates who expressed disappointment with the meagre results of the activity of the factory committees:

> *They apparently flattered themselves with illusions. But our conference*
> *said from the very start that under a bourgeois government we will not*
> *be able to carry out consistent control. The future centre [of factory*
> *committees to be set up by the All-Russian Conference next week] will*
> *find itself in the same conditions, and to speak of a control board under*
> *a bourgeois government is impossible. Therefore, the working class can-*
> *not bypass state power, as comrade Renev [an anarchist] proposes.*

Egorov, a Putilov worker, fully agreed with this assessment:

> *We are only too well acquainted with factory life to deny the need for the*
> *[all-Russian] conference. We know how often the factory committees*
> *turn out to be helpless, knowing how to avert a stoppage of production*
> *in the factories but lacking the possibility of intervening. The conference*
> *can give valuable directives. But we should not fool ourselves that the*
> *conference can get us out of the dead-end. Both private and state*
> *administrations sabotage production, referring us to the Society of Fac-*
> *tory and Mill Owners. They are still strong. The conference must first of*
> *all point out those obstacles which prevent the people of action from*

saving the country. These obstacles are placed before us by the bourgeois government. Only the reorganisation of state power will give us the possibility of developing our activity.

If, as has often been argued, Bolshevik success in the factory committees was due to their allegedly opportunistic support for workers' control, then the anarchists, fervent advocates of factory committee power, for whom the committees played a central role in their vision of the new order, should have shared in this success. But they remained weak in the committees. At the August Factory Committee Conference, Volin, an anarchist from the Shtein Factory, proposed an amendment to the resolution on workers' control: the reference to the "transfer of power to the proletariat" should be deleted. To this Milyutin, speaking for the Bolsheviks, replied: "I decisively disagree with the amendment because it crosses out the essence of the resolution. We are not anarchists and we recognise that a state apparatus is necessary and it must be further developed." Volin's amendment was rejected by an overwhelming majority.

Later Voskov commented on Volin's anarcho-syndicalist model for organising the economy:

Volin has accused us of lacking a broad plan and he pointed to the syndicalist movement in the North American United States. Indeed, the American syndicalists, who, by the way, can all sit around the same table [Voskov had been in emigration in the US], have the broadest of plans, which, however, the workers will not follow. We need a practical plan of work.

But if the anarchists were not making gains among the factory committee activists, their influence among the rank and file in certain districts was finally beginning to grow in this period. Skrypnik reported to the Bolshevik CC in October on the "growth of anarchist influence in the Narva and Moscow Districts." At about this time Gessen told the Bolshevik PC [Petersburg Committee] that in the Narva District "among the backward masses, there is an indifference to politics," while the other Narva representative added that "at the Putilov Factory the anarchists are working energetically, so that it is hard to hold the masses back in an organised structure." In the Rozhdestvenskii District, "the mood has declined in connection with the dismissals due to the evacuations. The influence of the anarchists has increased noticeably."

The picture that presents itself, although the direct evidence is admittedly limited, is one of the growing appeal of the anarchists' direct-action tactics, particularly among the unskilled workers, disillusioned with the political struggle that seemed to be dragging on endlessly somewhere in the centre without any tangible results while the economy continued to deteriorate. The industrial labour force of the Narva, Moscow and Rozhdestvenskii Districts contained a high proportion of unskilled workers, mainly women and wartime workers, who initially had been attracted to the SRs. "Where our influence is weak," went the report from the Petrograd District, "there is political apathy. There a struggle is taking place with the factory committee."

But the contemporary references to the "growth of anarchism" refer to the popularity of the anarchists' tactics rather than their principled rejection of the state and of political struggle. This explains the anarchists' continued weakness in the factory committees, as well as the Bolsheviks' continued success in getting elected to all workers' organisations and the virtually unanimous worker support for soviet power. This is apparently what Gessen meant when he added: "But there is no decline in the authority of our party."

Despite the increasing frequency of "excesses" in worker-management relations, there were still very few takeovers. When they occurred, it was because the administration had shut down or left. At Respirator the workers held several administrators "under arrest" for a few hours. The circumstances are obscure except that the workers were demanding the rescindment of an order issued on 31 August (possibly relating to the Skobelev circulars). In response to the "arrest," the entire administration resigned. The workers decided to continue on their own, asking the government to appoint a commissar "from the juridical point of view" to be responsible for obtaining raw materials from Respirator's idle client factories. The workers also demanded a "democratic trial" of the administration charged with "desertion from the rear." Very typical of such takeovers was an accompanying call for state sequestration, hardly an anarchist-inspired demand.

Workers' control remained first and foremost a practical response to the concrete problems the workers faced and not, as the dominant view in Western historiography has maintained, an anarchistic or antiauthority movement. Even in the state factories, where the right to control was asserted at the very start of the revolution and where the practice of control was most developed, the authority of the state managements was recognised and supported by the factory committees. On 3 October, the factory and shop committees of the Izhorskii Factory met to discuss their relations with the administration. The resolution passed stressed that the committees should cooperate with the director and that:

> *Any order of the foremen, subforemen and senior workers must be unwaveringly executed. In all cases of doubt as to the propriety of an order, one should immediately notify the shop committee without making any independent objections or putting obstacles before the execution of the given order.*

The regulations governing worker–management relations at Orudiinyi asserted the "right of control over all acts of the administration in the area of the mutual relations among workers and in the general course of production." But they left the appointment of higher administrative personnel to management. Moreover

> *Each worker is obliged to execute the legitimate demands of the administrative personnel who are their direct supervisors, maintaining polite address throughout. In case of a disagreement between a worker and a representative of management, the matter is taken up to the shop committee. In extreme cases, it is taken to the factory committee or to the conciliation chamber.*

These rules speak directly against an anarchist interpretation of workers' control. The need for authority was clearly recognised although subject to broad control. The conception, as noted earlier, closely resembled that of the "dual power" established in February on the political level.

The Quiet on the Wage Front

The workers' realisation that there was no salvation from industrial collapse without the seizure of power, along with their preoccupation with keeping the factories open, explains in large part the surprising calm that reigned in the capital in the traditional area of the struggle over wages, when the rest of Russia was experiencing an economic strike wave of unprecedented proportions.

The September Conference of Factory Committees warned the workers against

> *scattered and premature actions that can only be utilised by the counterrevolution. On the contrary, it is necessary to concentrate all the workers' energy on organisational work for the forthcoming solution of*

the question of constructing state power and a swift end to the three-year-old slaughter.

The workers seem to have heeded these warnings. Petrograd witnessed only two major industrial strikes in August–October, the 24–7 September strike of 7,000 workers in the railroad workshops (part of the national railroad strike) and the 16–28 October strike of 25,000 woodworkers. In addition, there were a few small strikes, the most notable being that of 21 printing plants (12–22 August) and a strike of 2,500 paper workers (21 September–4 October). No more than 10 per cent of Petrograd's 417,000 industrial workers participated in strikes in the three-month period preceding the insurrection.

By way of contrast, in the Central Industrial Region around Moscow, even if one includes only the industry-wide strikes of this period, well over 40 per cent (closer to 50 per cent counting the smaller strikes) of the region's 1,030,000 workers took part in economic strikes. These included 110,000 leatherworkers, 300,000 textile workers and 15,000 rubber workers (as well as workers in the railroad workshops and individual metalworking factories).

Not that the grounds or the desire to strike were lacking in Petrograd. Between the opening of negotiations on a collective agreement in the metalworking industry at the end of June and the signing of the agreement six weeks later, the union prevented conflicts in some 180 factories from developing into strikes. At a meeting of the central and district union executives on 1 July, the Bolsheviks successfully spoke against a strike and for a compromise on wages, arguing that all the workers' demands were subsumed in the demand for soviet power and that the workers should conserve their energy towards achieving that goal. . . .

Concern with keeping the factories running and fear that strikes could be turned into lockouts were another source of restraint on the wage issue (which contrasted sharply with the growing militancy over issues concerning production itself). But this too was tied in the workers' minds to the need for state power.

On the Eve

At a meeting of the Bolshevik CC on 16 October, Zinoviev, a member of the party's moderate wing which was opposed to an insurrection, stressed that "the mood in the factories now is not what it was in June. It is clear that there is not such a mood as in June." The previous day at a closed session of the Bolshevik PC, Latsis, party organiser in the Vyborg District and a consistent leftwinger, reported: "In the coming out [*vystuplenie*] the organised apparatus must be in the fore; the masses will support us. It is totally different from before."

On this point, at least, there was agreement: in contrast to the pre-July period, one could not now expect initiatives from the rank-and-file workers in overthrowing the government. It was the turn of the party, grown accustomed, as Latsis put it, to acting as a fire hose, to light the fuse itself.

In attempting to describe and explain the workers' state of mind on the eve of the insurrection, one must be careful to identify the issues as they were debated at the time and not as they have come to be seen in retrospect, as so often occurs in the historiography. The first problem that the workers had to face as the Soviet Congress drew near was whether the soviets should take power at all or whether it made more sense to await the Constituent Assembly (elections for which, after several postponements, were finally set for mid November) in the expectation that its majority would decide on an exclusively revolutionary-democratic government. This second option once again held out the alluring prospect of a peaceful transition of power and the avoidance of political isolation. On the other hand, to wait at least several more weeks meant to allow the present impossible economic and military conditions to deteriorate further.

In essence the debate was whether violence and civil war were inevitable. The moderates — LSRs [Left Socialist Revolutionaries], Menshevik-Internationalists and moderate Bolsheviks (the defencists, who continued to support the coalition, had little worker support and can be ignored for the moment) — argued that a soviet seizure of power, a violent overthrow, were unnecessary (and, in any case, unlikely to succeed) and would only alienate potential allies within revolutionary democracy and lead to civil war. The left countered that some degree of civil war was not only unavoidable but already existed. Even if the Constituent Assembly were to declare itself for a revolutionary government, Kerenskii would certainly not yield power without a fight. Besides, what guarantee was there that the Constituent Assembly would ever meet? Actions, not marking time, would win over the rest of revolutionary democracy.

These issues were set out clearly in the political debate at the All-Russian Conference of Factory Committees in Petrograd on 18 October. Trotsky's report on the "current moment" was received enthusiastically. Not surprisingly, the major part of his speech was devoted to showing that in Russian conditions civil war was unavoidable. Those who compared Russia to the France of 1789, he argued, were blind. France had only the embryo of a proletariat, while in Russia

> *our working class represents a developed organised type of revolutionary class . . . On the other side stands organised capital. This has determined the high degree of class strife. Conciliationism would have a basis if class antagonisms were not so acute . . . There are two extreme wings, and if the revolutionary parties were to draw back from civil war now, the right wing would all the same carry out its attack on the revolution and all its achievements. Desertion by the parties would not avert the civil war. It would merely unfold in an unorganised form, in a haphazard and scattered manner and, one may assume, to the greatest benefit of the propertied classes. Civil war is imposed upon us by the economic situation and by the course of our history.*

Trotsky then turned to the question of the workers' isolation and noted that "between the landowners and the peasantry a civil war is already in progress." Peasant petitioners were arriving daily at the Petrograd Soviet to ask for help against the government's punitive expeditions. Meanwhile, the soldiers at the front were telling the Soviet in no uncertain terms to take power and avert a spontaneous mass desertion at the first snowfall. As for the Constituent Assembly, the bourgeoisie was undermining it by every means it possessed.

> *Only through the seizure of power can the genuinely revolutionary class, the proletariat, and the army that is gravitating towards it, and the insurgent peasantry struggle for the Constituent Assembly . . .*
>
> *You cannot artificially direct historical development along a peaceful path. We must recognise this and say openly to ourselves that civil war is inevitable. It is necessary to organise it in the interests of the working class. This is the only way to make it less bloody, less painful. You cannot achieve this result by wavering and hesitation; only through a stubborn and courageous struggle for power. Then it is still possible, there is still a chance that the bourgeoisie will retreat. By conciliationist wavering you will achieve just the opposite. We cannot allow the demoralisation of the working class through wavering.*

The conference voted by 53 against 5 (9 abstentions) for the following resolution:

> *The government of the counterrevolutionary bourgeoisie is destroying the country, having demonstrated and itself understood its total inability to wage war, which it is dragging out for the sole purpose of smothering the revolution. It does nothing for the struggle against economic dislocation. Just the opposite — its entire economic policy is directed at aggravating the dislocation in the aim of starving the revolution to death and burying it under the debris of general economic ruin. The salvation of the revolution and the goals put forward for it by the toiling masses lies in the transfer of power to the hands of the Soviets of Workers', Soldiers' and Peasants' Deputies.*

This conference reflected the dominant sentiment in the factories of Petrograd. . . .

Dozens of resolutions passed at factory meetings on the eve of the insurrection leave no doubt that when asked to choose between waiting for the Constituent Assembly and seizing power at once through the soviets, the Petrograd workers as a whole were almost . . . unanimous. . . . In fact, a careful search of the press as well as published and unpublished archival material, revealed only one resolution clearly supporting the internationalists' call to use the Soviet Congress not to take power but to prepare the Constituent Assembly. It was passed by the Obukhovskii workers.

Even among workers who voted for LSR candidates, there was a strong tendency nevertheless to support the call for immediate soviet power. Thus, although the Admiralty resolution was passed unanimously, in recent elections here the LSRs had received over one-quarter of the vote. The SR organisations of the Petergof District and of the Sestroretsk Arms Factory themselves called on the congress to take power! . . .

Any lingering doubts about this were laid to rest on 22 October, the "Day of the Petrograd Soviet," the half-year anniversary of the February Revolution. The Petrograd Soviet called for a peaceful review of soviet forces through mass meetings, and eye-witness accounts all concur that the response was overwhelming.

"The day surpassed all our expectations," recalled Lashevich, a Bolshevik soldier activist and delegate to the Petrograd Soviet. 30,000 showed up at the People's House.

Anyone present at that meeting will never forget it. The enthusiasm of thousands of workers and soldiers was so great that one direct appeal and that entire human colossus would have left with empty hands for the barricades, for death.

When Trotsky spoke, "one could actually feel the electricity in the air."

Although the reference to the barricades should perhaps be taken with a grain of salt, that the mood was positive is beyond doubt. Testovskii, another Bolshevik who spoke at two factories on Vasilevskii ostrov, notes: "We spoke frankly before the masses of the coming seizure of power by us and heard only words of encouragement."

Non-Bolshevik observers, hostile to the insurrection, confirm this. According to Mstislavskii,

The Day of the Soviet took place amidst a tremendous upsurge of spirit. Trotsky so electrified the crowd by his speech that thousands of hands rose in a single outburst of emotion at his call, swearing loyalty to the revolution, to struggle for it — to the mortal end.

Sukhanov found the People's House

crammed with an innumerable throng. It overflowed the theatrical halls waiting for the meetings. But there were crowds in the foyers too, in the buffets and corridors . . . [The mood] was definitely elated. Trotsky began to heat up the atmosphere. He described the suffering in the trenches. It was all a matter of mood. The political conclusions had long been known . . .

Around me was a mood close to ecstacy. I felt as if the crowd would rise on its own and sing some religious hymn. Trotsky formulated some brief resolution, something like: we will stand for the cause of the workers and peasants to the last drop of blood. All as one raised their hands. I saw these raised hands and the burning eyes of the men, women and youths, workers, soldiers and typically philistine figures. "Let this be your oath — to support with all your energy and by any sacrifices the Soviet, which has taken upon itself the great burden of carrying through to the end the victory of the revolution, of giving land, bread and peace!" The hands were still in the air . . .

With an unusually heavy heart I watched this truly majestic scene . . . And all over Petrograd it was the same thing. Everywhere final reviews and final oaths. Strictly speaking, this was already the insurrection. It had already begun.

Even the defencist *Rabochaya gazeta*, which for months had been writing of the "disillusionment" and "apathy" of the masses, had to face the reality:

> *And so it has begun. The Bolsheviks gave the signal for the "insurrection." At the Sunday [22 October] meetings, the masses of soldiers and workers, electrified by the "revolutionary" speeches of the Bolshevik leaders, vowed to "come out" at the first call of the Soviet.*

On the face of it, it is hard to accord this with the appraisal of the mass mood, common to both right and left wings of the Bolshevik Party, that "there is no such mood as in June," that the workers were not exactly tearing into the streets. Indeed, despite the resolutions and the enthusiasm of 22 October, they were to all appearances patiently awaiting an initiative from above.

The explanation lies partly in the changed circumstances that confronted the workers after the July Days. In setting out to demonstrate in early July the workers had in mind a peaceful transition of power to the soviets. It was a matter of pressuring the TsIK to declare itself the legitimate government. As Stankevich had told the Soviet back in April, all that was needed was a phone call from the TsIK, and the Provisional Government would be no more. But after July no one could doubt that the transfer of power would require armed struggle, some degree of open civil war. Kerenskii would not hesitate to open fire, as he had clearly shown in July. He would try to disperse any Soviet Congress that decided to take power. This situation called for the deployment of armed forces, which in turn required planning, coordination and leadership. It could not begin spontaneously "from below," as had the July demonstrations. At the start of October the entire Vyborg District had only some 5,000 poorly trained and armed Red Guards. This then was not a time for the mass street scenes of February, April, June and early July. In July, the worst the workers expected was to return empty-handed. But in October all the cards were being played — failure meant a revolution drowned in their own blood.

The Bolsheviks, on their part, were doing everything to dissuade the workers from independent initiatives, warning at every possible turn against premature, unorganised actions. The Soviet had decided to observe 22 October in indoor meetings because it feared that even peaceful demonstrations could turn into a premature and bloody confrontation.

But this is still not the complete picture. The Bolsheviks were obviously not complacent about the workers' mood. Had it been merely a question of changed objective circumstances, they would not have shown such concern that the mood was "not that of June."

True, the workers were more united than ever in their desire for the Soviet Congress to take power. But desire alone would not establish soviet power. The workers would have to seize it by force from the Provisional Government and then fight to defend it. A closer analysis of the workers' attitudes reveals that the virtual unanimity displayed at the meetings did not necessarily signify a uniform readiness to act. For many workers, the problem posed by the July Days had still not been resolved.

One can discern at least four different "moods" among the workers in relation to the insurrection. *Novaya zhizn'* caught something of this in an editorial comment on agitation being conducted in the factories calling on the workers to prepare to come out in active support of the soviets:

> *The mood of the masses, in so far as one can judge it, is not charac-*
> *terised by any definiteness. A certain part apparently is prepared to*
> *come out. Another part is not in an especially militant frame of mind*
> *and is inclined to refrain from active steps. Finally, there is another*
> *group which has a negative attitude toward the coming out or a totally*
> *passive one. It is hard to say what the correlation among these three*
> *groups is. But the active group is hardly a majority.*

The hesitators indeed seemed to be the largest group, strongly for soviet power but with equally strong memories of July and little taste for bloodshed. They would not act until circumstances left no alternative. Hence Trotsky's stress on the inevitability of civil war and the generally defensive tone of Bolshevik agitation regarding the necessity of eventually "coming out."

On 21 October, Sukhanov was called out to speak at a meeting in the Petergof District. He arrived to find about 4,000 workers standing in the yard of the Putilov Works under the autumn drizzle listening to a succession of speakers. Martov told him that they had barely allowed him to finish his talk. "The mood is very strong. Of course, only a minority is active but it is enough to spoil the meeting."

> *I saw myself that the mood was strong. An SR, true, totally un-*
> *talented, was unable to get even two consecutive words out. It was*
> *undoubtedly a minority acting, and even a small one at that — the*

local Bolshevik youth. The majority stood silent with a "vigilant [vyzh-idatel'noe — from vyzhidat' — bide one's time, literally, to wait out] and concentrated" look. The bearded ones were shaking their heads in a puzzled or distracted manner.

These were the same Putilovtsy who had come out 30,000 strong on July 4 to give power to the soviets. They all without exception hated and despised the kerenshchina *[Kerenskii's régime]. But they understood how the July Days had ended. Power to the soviets — an excellent thing. But a coming out? . . .*

Reports from the districts at the 15 October Bolshevik PC meeting give a similar impression of a large group of indecisive workers. Several speakers began by stating that "the mood is extremely complicated" or "it is difficult to appraise the mood." The representative from the Narva District (which in party circles included Petergof) agreed with Suk-hanov: "The general picture is that there is no striving to come out. Where our influence is great the mood is brisk [*bodroe*] and vigilant [*vyzhidatel'noe*] . . . The level of activity [*samodeyatel'nost'*] of the masses had fallen." In the Petrograd District: "Where our influence is strong, the mood is vigilant." Rozhdestvenskii: "The mood is vigilant. If there is a coming out on the part of the counterrevolution, then we will give a rebuff. But if there is a call to come out, then I don't think the workers will go." Vasilevskii ostrov: "Military training is being con-ducted in the plants. There is no mood to come out." And finally, the report from the trade unions:

There is almost not a single union where the mood in our favour has not grown. One does not observe any definite militant mood among the masses. If there is an offensive on the part of the counterrevolution, then a rebuff will be given. But the masses on their part will not take the offensive. If the Petrograd Soviet calls for a coming out, the masses will follow the Soviet.

The picture, in these districts at least, was clear: the worker rank and file would not take the initiative but would respond if attacked.

Of course, as several speakers indicated, it was not easy to gauge these attitudes, particularly since the possibility of an offensive action was not being directly raised before the workers. In fact, until the Bolshevik CC met on 16 October, no decision on an insurrection had yet been taken. And even after it was decided, it seems that a large part of the party rank and file was not informed. As for the Bolshevik leaders, they continued rather demagogically to speak of a "coming out" largely as a necessary response to a possible (or very likely) attack against the soviets or the Congress. Only Lenin did not mince words. He directly called for an immediate insurrection in his letters published in the Bolshevik paper on 19–21 October. As Mstislavskii aptly put it, while Lenin said "necessary!", Trotsky said "inevitable." Undoubtedly the defensive tone of party agitation was based upon the leadership's evaluation of the popular mood.

The traumatic memories of the July Days, when the Petrograd workers suddenly found themselves isolated (even from a part of their own comrades) and defeated by the support of moderate democracy for the government, were a major factor in this indecisive mood. A basic issue for the workers was how much support they could count on in an action against the government. The left wing of the Bolshevik Party was at pains to show how much the situation had changed in three months: all the major soviets had been won over, the army was just about ready for peace at any price and the peasant war was shifting into high gear. The "conciliators" were hanging in the air.

The moderate Bolsheviks and other internationalists, on the other hand, emphasized the workers' continued isolation from the rest of democracy, which was waffling to the left but could be frightened into the arms of reaction by a premature insurrection. Responding to rumours of an impending action, *Novaya zhizn'* warned the workers that the counterrevolution would do everything in its power to make it even bloodier than July. It would be a repeat of the Paris Commune. There would be no food. Furthermore, a bloody civil war would make it impossible to solve the problems facing the revolution. Even among the workers and soldiers of Petrograd the paper warned, only a small hot-headed group would come out. Support would be even weaker in the provinces and at the front. . . .

The other major cause of hesitation was the economic situation. Naumov, a metalworker from the Vyborg District, told the Bolshevik PC on 15 October: "The mood is depressed, there is a hidden dissatisfaction in the masses with the wage rates, the evacuations, the factory dismissals. The mood is exceedingly complex." "The mood has declined," it was reported from the Rozhdestvenskii District, "in connection with the mass dismissals resulting from the evacuation of the factories." Schmidt made the same point in his report on the trade unions to the Bolshevik CC:

The mood is such that one should not expect active [as opposed to defensive] comings out, especially in view of the fear of dismissals. Up to a certain point this is a restraining factor. In view of the existing economic conditions one can expect in the near future colossal unemployment. In this connection the mood is vigilant. All agree that outside the struggle for power there is no way out of the situation. They demand power to the soviets.

The influence of the economic crisis was, thus, twofold. While it lent great urgency to the demand for soviet power, the fear of a general lockout and the rise to prominence of the workers' most basic material concern — their very livelihood — inclined them towards caution and away from bold initiatives.

Aside from the temporisers, another segment of the working class, drawn particularly from among the women, the unskilled and the recently arrived workers, was withdrawing from political life, growing indifferent to the seemingly futile debates surrounding state power, and falling under the influence of anarchist direct-action agitation. In a report at the end of September, the Narva District Menshevik organisation noted:

In the worker milieu the interest in political phenomena has declined. Something like disillusionment is beginning: the masses are already not satisfied with Bolshevism. One observes a growth in the influence of the maximalists and the anarchists. In the worker masses there is not a trace of discipline.

Kollontai, who was active among the women workers, warned the All-Russian Factory Committee Conference in October:

I consider it my duty to make a declaration here on what is taking place among the women workers of Piter, as the most backward and undeveloped part of the working class . . . Fear that indifference which now exists in the midst of the women workers. . . .

Among the originally SR-defensist, and largely unskilled, workers, the time of their conversion to soviet power appears to have played an important role in determining the pre-October mood. Those like the unskilled workers in the Narva–Petergof District, who had participated in the July Days, were becoming increasingly disillusioned with the political struggle. But others who had supported the coalition in July were showing new enthusiasm and energy. Here the movement for soviet power was still fresh. It had no directly experienced defeats or disappointments behind it. . . .

[A]mong the skilled workers of Petrograd, the great majority of whom had been converted to soviet power before July, there was also a significant resolute segment, again centred mainly in machine-construction and other skilled metalworking shops and factories. Although the mood in the Vyborg District (a centre of machine construction) was "totally different from before," it was far from unfavourable to an immediate seizure of power. The PC report noted that "in the masses one observes serious concentration and work. In the district a centre was organised without the knowledge of the district [party] committee. Its organisation occurred from below." With 18 per cent of Petrograd's industrial workers, this district put forth one-third of its Red Guards. In the Kolomna District, with its three large shipyards, "the mood is better than July 3–5." And among the Finnish and Lettish workers, a largely skilled, urbanised group, "the mood is cheerful . . . The[Lettish] comrades will come out not on the call of the Soviet but of the PC. In the July Days our line was left." "The Finns feel that the sooner the better."

Many of these workers, in fact, demanded of the Congress of Soviets of the Northern Region (representing Petrograd, Moscow, Kronstadt, the Baltic Fleet and other northern towns) meeting on 11–12 October to take power immediately itself. . . .

Among the workers prepared for immediate decisive action, the Bolshevik workers undoubtedly constituted the largest single group. A month before the October Revolution the Petrograd organisation counted 43,000 members, of which Stepanov calculates that 28,250 were workers (and 5,800 soldiers belonging to the Military Organisation). Their attitudes towards the seizure of power can be gauged from the October meetings of the PC and from the Third City Conference of 7–11 October.

Opinion in the PC had completely changed since early September, when the majority had felt that the situation called for a peaceful route. Kalinin, who chaired the 5 October session, observed that the "militant line of the majority striving for power is characteristic." Even those who opposed an insurrection admitted there was no alternative. They argued rather that the time was not yet ripe, the chances of success not favourable.

But these moderate voices were severely criticised by most speakers.

"I thought we were all revolutionaries here. But when I heard comrade Volodarskii and Lashevich [who opposed an insurrection], my opinion wavered." "The opinions expressed by comrades Volodarskii and Lashevich," commented another, "are valuable, but there is something negative in them. They have become infected with the spirit of the Smol'nyi Institute." (The reference is to the Bolshevik CC, which was consistently rejecting Lenin's urgent appeals to prepare an insurrection.) . . .

While the record of the political debate at the City Conference has been lost, the resolution passed leaves no doubt as to where the conference stood. It concluded: "All these circumstances say clearly that the moment of the last decisive battle which must decide the fate not only of the Russian but of the world revolution has arrived." Similarly, a meeting of Petrograd party activists at the time of the Congress of the Northern Region resolved:

> *The continuation of the policy of "amassing forces" . . . would only lead to the disillusionment of the masses in the party of the revolutionary proletariat and would lead not only to their refusal to further support the Bolsheviks . . . but also to unorganised comings out by the masses, and in conditions of extreme atomisation and of general disorganisation . . .*
>
> *Hopes attached to the Congress of Soviets are not well founded, inasmuch as solutions to the basic tasks of the revolution are expected from resolutions and not from the struggle of the masses . . . As for the Constituent Assembly, even the most left composition of the Constituent Assembly cannot change anything without the direct and active support on the part of the worker and peasant revolution . . .*
>
> *A defensive policy is incorrect. An offensive is needed to immediately root out the seeds of the counterrevolutionary government.*

Thus, while as late as 16 October the Bolshevik CC was still debating the issue, the Petrograd organisation had for some time already been insisting on an immediate insurrection. In his theses for the Petrograd City Conference, Lenin noted that "in the *verkhy* [the upper levels] of the party, unfortunately one can observe a wavering, as if there is a "fear" of the struggle for power, a tendency to replace it with resolutions, with protests." He specifically appealed to the *nizy*, the lower party ranks, to put pressure on the leaders. Copies of his letters to the CC (which the latter kept secret) were distributed to the PC, the Vyborg and other district organisations. The Moscow organisation was of the same mind as that of Petrograd. Its 10 October City Conference instructed the MC [Moscow Committee] "to bring the revolutionary forces into battle readiness." . . .

Everyone was apprehensive about the prospects of an uprising. But these fears did not paralyse the will of the more militant workers.

The other organisation whose members were solidly on the side of bold action was the Red Guards. Sukhanov, who repeatedly insisted on the indecision of the "average rank-and-file workers," felt compelled to add:

> This did not mean that the Bolsheviks were not able to put together, call out and send into battle as many revolutionary batallions as were necessary. Just the opposite. They were undoubtedly able to do this. They had sufficient numbers of developed active cadres ready for sacrifice. The most dependable were the workers and their red guards. Then the sailors were a fighting force. Worse than the others were the garrison soldiers . . . There was enough fighting material, but only a part of the masses who followed the Bolsheviks were good quality fighting material. On the average the mood was strongly Bolshevik, but rather flabby and unfirm concerning a coming out and insurrection . . .
>
> They had to place their hopes in the workers' red guards. But one could only depend upon their spirit. The fighting abilities of the men, who had never smelled powder or seen a bullet, were more than doubtful.

Mstislavskii concurs that "the sailors, the guards regiments and the red guards — particularly the red guards — rushed to the job."

This attitude among the Red Guards is not surprising. Membership was voluntary and at the time offered few advantages and many risks. Given the overwhelmingly negative assessment of the insurrection's chances in society, there is very little ground to suspect opportunistic motives among the ranks. Skorinko, the Putilov worker, was emphatic on this:

> The conduct of the red guards was above criticism. It is a lie and insolent slander that the red guards got drunk during searches, raped and looted. This did not occur. For at the time, being a red guard promised no material benefits. Just the opposite — given the growing strength of the reaction, it threatened serious troubles. Only conscious workers, dedicated body and soul to the interests of the revolution, joined its ranks.

> Just how highly the factory workers valued their red guards and looked out for their purity is shown by the fact that in certain shops of the Putilov Factory workers were elected by the general assembly. The author of these lines, not without pride, recalls how he was one of the delegates of the turret shop to the red guards.
>
> And if a comrade was found whose presence in the red guards or whose casual conduct shocked everyone, he was expelled from their ranks in disrepute. Of course, I will not speak of the conduct of the red guards afterwards, when a mass of foreign elements [i.e., foreign to the working class] wormed their way into its honest ranks.

Skorinko recalls waking up on the morning of 23 October to find his father, just returned from work, on the floor cleaning his rifle. He had tears in his eyes. Skorinko's mother was about to explode with anger.

> "Your father in his old age has signed up with the windchasers. He won't beat his son for that. And now look what he is up to! Cleaning his rifle. What are you going to do, kill somebody?" my mother asked spitefully . . . "Everyone in the courtyard is laughing at you."

Turning a deaf ear to these taunts, the father told Skorinko that Kerenskii had just shut down the Bolshevik press and was threatening to disarm the workers.

> Accompanied by the weeping and the admonitions of my mother and the ironic looks of the other tenants, my father and I, our rifles over our shoulders, set off for headquarters, where we found extraordinary excitement.
>
> At the headquarters under the tables, on top of the tables and next to the tables we saw a mass of workers whose interests had previously been limited to their family circle now fondly cleaning their rifles, barely keeping themselves from going to the centre to win their workers' power.
>
> Everywhere conversations were in progress. But there were none of the arguments which are a necessity in conversation. To argue at such a moment, when unification was taking place on the other side of the barricades, this the workers felt to be dangerous. Among the hundreds of red guards, among whom there were both Mensheviks and SRs, there was such a community of interest on that day that my father, embracing me, remarked: "Today I feel especially brave. And if everyone feels like me, then tomorrow there will be soviet power, that is — our own."

"*And if the next day we have to give it up?*" *jokingly remarked a company commander as he ran past.*

"*Never! But damn it, even for a day, but it will have been ours,*" *shouted my father, shaking his rifle and evoking enthusiasm from the crowd. "If only for one day, we would show them how we take care of our property . . ."*

In the morning came the soviet's order to get into battle readiness.

During the reading of the declaration, I knew that to show our resolve to struggle for a communist society, we, the armed workers, would do anything. We were high spirited then and madly bold. Who now can doubt that?

Ivan Peskovoi of the Shchetinin Aircraft Factory recalled that the mood of the plant's Red Guards was

so militant that each of us could hardly wait for the coming out. As for our military preparation, it was at the time beneath all criticism. Despite the fact that we had to move against trained soldiers, our revolutionary spirit conquered all.

It was not certainty of victory that moved the Red Guards, but the conviction that there was no other way, mixed with a large dose of revolutionary enthusiasm and class pride, to die with honour, if need be, but not to live in shame.

The Soviet historian Startsev has analysed 3,500 dossiers on Petrograd Red Guards compiled in 1930 for pension purposes. Although, as he himself admits, the sample is far from perfect — some had died by then, others had joined only in the days following the rising, and many members of the moderate socialist parties in 1917 would have preferred to report themselves as unaffiliated — nevertheless, the dossiers do provide valuable, if only approximate, information on the organisation's composition.

About three-quarters of the members were metalworkers. This figure appears less significant in light of the fact that about three-quarters of the male industrial work force were metalworkers. The women who participated in the insurrection served largely as medics.

More interesting are the data on party affiliation. Although 69 per cent of the command positions in the sample were occupied by Bolsheviks, members of that party were actually a minority in the organisation as a whole — 44.3 per cent. The participation of non-Bolshevik workers is confirmed by much other contemporary evidence as well as worker memoirs. It cannot, therefore, be claimed that the insurrection was strictly a party affair or that the Red Guards were acting out of party discipline.

Almost three-quarters of Startsev's sample were under thirty-one years old, 52.2 per cent were under twenty-six and 26.4 per cent under twenty-one. "As always," recalled one worker, "the youth was in front, happy and satisfied."

The youth were indeed in the van. (This was true of the youth of all classes and their struggles in Russia.) But it would be wrong to see the Red Guards as a gang of young leather-jacketed toughs. For one thing, there was a very sizeable contingent of older workers. A little over one-quarter of Startsev's sample was over thirty-one years old and almost half were twenty-six and over. Skorinko's father was forty-eight, married, with a grown son, his own apartment and even a lodger — hardly a shiftless adolescent. "It was interesting," noted Peskovoi, "to look at the composition of the detachment. In it were young workers about 16 years of age and old ones of about 50. Such a mixture made for great cheer and fighting spirit." . . .

This, then, was not the mob of lumpen elements so often portrayed in hostile accounts. Without citing sources, Melgunov (in 1917 a Popular Socialist, close to the Kadet left wing) writes:

> It was not revolutionary cohorts of Bolsheviks that forced their way into the [Winter] palace but an ill-sorted mob, in the full sense of the word, with a mob's interests, excesses and violence, a mob aroused by the martial atmosphere of gunfire, powder and bursting shells. Hooligan elements looted the palace, elements which probably gathered at the palace with the whole demoralised "okhlos," which some researchers of the revolution are inclined to place at the forefront of the events of October.

Yet three pages later, he concedes:

> Five days later a special commission of the City Duma established that the loss of valuable works of art had been small . . . We must be objective. All the rumours of violence and reprisals that appeared in the socialist press and were later recorded in the journals, should be attributed to overwrought nerves . . . This was corroborated by the Duma investigation.

Adamovich, who had been among the workers on the Palace Square on Bloody Sunday 1905, found himself in the same place on the night of 25 October. This time, however, he was a Red Guard and himself doing the shooting.

> *We burst into the palace, ran down the stairs along some sort of corridor. We entered a room — entered and gasped. We had never seen such splendour and luxury. Mirrors, gold, silver. One lad reached his hand toward a clock. He was yanked away. Someone gave him a box on the ear. Laughter and sorrow. We had entered a room and did not know how to get out. Worse than in the deep woods. We were lost and from behind new workers were pushing. We barely made our way out.*
>
> *A shot. What? From whom? By the wall, behind the sofa, a woman was lying — from the [Women's] Battalion of Death. We were already inside the room, and she is taking pot shots, the lout. We ran to the sofa, grabbed her, and she is biting and scratching like a wild kitten. There were ten more of them in the next room. Some in the closet, some under the table, one by the fireplace. They fell to their knees, shaking: "We went for the sake of a crust of bread." We let them get the hell out.*

Estimates of the number of Red Guards in Petrograd on the eve of the insurrection vary wildly from 10,000–12,000 claimed by a Soviet author in 1938 to 40,000 reported by Uritskii at the Bolshevik CC meeting on 16 October. On the basis of archival and memoir materials, Stepanov offers the figure 34,000, which tends to be supported by reports from the districts made to the Bolshevik PC. . . .

The mood among Petrograd's workers on the eve of the October Insurrection, as Naumov had observed, was indeed complex. The very keen desire for an end to coalition politics and for soviet power was practically unanimous. But a large part of the skilled workers, disheartened by the deepening economic crisis, hesitated before the harsh odds, the threat of political isolation and the spectre of defeat in a civil war. Many of the unskilled workers, especially among those who had demonstrated and tasted defeat in July, had grown weary of a political struggle that yielded no tangible results. They seemed indifferent to the entire debate.

In these circumstances, the presence of a resolute minority willing and able to take the initiative was critical. All that was required was for them to begin, to force the issue, to inject a new dynamism into the movement and to make it impossible to procrastinate further. The others would rally. Sukhanov was right: "It was all a matter of mood.

The political conclusions had long been known . . . At the first success, the flabby mood would become firm."

But without this initiative, the very powerful, commonly shared yearning for revolutionary change would have had little real impact. Political stagnation and economic misery would have completely demoralised the workers, paving the way for the counterrevolution. In October the Bolshevik concept of the revolutionary party as the authentic vanguard of the working class was to be put to the crucial test.

Robert V. Daniels

The Leader Decides

To mark the fiftieth anniversary of the October Revolution, Robert V. Daniels of the University of Vermont published an exciting narrative of the events leading up to the Bolshevik coup. Daniels, a Harvard-trained historian and one of the most prolific writers on Soviet political history of his generation, is the author of *The Conscience of the Revolution* (1960), a study of the Communist opposition in Soviet Russia. His *Documentary History of Communism* (1960) provides essential reading for students of Soviet politics. *Red October* argues that Lenin's victory was neither inevitable nor the product of careful Bolshevik planning. Rather it was the fortuitous result of a number of accidents. Central to his understanding was Lenin's lust for power. Daniels argues that Lenin's insistence on the need to seize power before the convening of the Second Congress of Soviets rendered impossible a democratic outcome. In this excerpt he shows how Lenin pressured the reluctant Bolshevik leadership to act before the Congress convened.

When the Petrograd-Helsingfors express train reached the border between Russia proper and Finland on the evening of August 9, 1917, it stopped for the customary check of the passenger's travel documents. As usual, the locomotive — it was number 293, with a Finnish engineer named Yalava and his fireman in the cab — uncoupled and moved off to replenish its supply of water and firewood, while the passenger cars were left standing for the inspection. The fireman this time was not the usual man — though, sturdy and clean-shaven, he could have passed for a typical Petrograd worker. He was a fugitive from justice, travelling with false papers identifying him as Konstantin Ivanov, worker at the Sestroretsk munitions plant. In fact, the man was Lenin, in worker's clothes, with a wig on his well-known pate, fleeing to the separate jurisdiction of Finland to be safer from arrest by Kerensky's police.

The ruse was successful and Lenin reached Finnish territory undetected. He stayed two or three days in a sympathizer's forest cabin near the border. Then, disguised as a Lutheran minister, he was conducted to Helsingfors and hidden safely in the apartment of the socialist police chief. Undaunted by the temporary setback to his hopes, Lenin immersed himself in the revolutionary political theory that had occupied him in earlier periods of exile. In a couple of weeks he had finished his major theoretical opus, published after its author was already ruler of Russia, under the title *State and Revolution*.

This book was a curiously utopian restatement of Marx and Engels on the need to destroy the "bourgeois state machinery" and replace it with the power of "the armed people." Lenin took a phrase Marx used once or twice, "the dictatorship of the proletariat," and made it the cornerstone of his doctrine — expropriation of the landlords and capitalists, suppression of the political rights of "exploiters," replacement of the old bureaucracy with elected officials paid no more than "workmen's wages." Finally, when class differences had been completely abolished, the state could at last be fully democratic — but there would be no more need for it: in the rosy future society of proletarian goodfellowship, the state would "wither away." . . .

At the news of the Kornilov affair Lenin quickly awoke from his reverie of anarchistic theorizing. On August 30 he wrote to the Bolshevik Central Committee in Petrograd, "Events are developing with a speed that is sometimes dizzying. . . . Kornilov's revolt is an altogether unexpected . . . and almost unbelievably sharp turn in the course of events." Lenin was already calculating how to turn the alliance of the Left and the government to his own advantage, though what worried him most was the possibility that his followers would think no further revolution necessary: "One must be extremely cautious lest one lose sight of principles." Some Bolsheviks, he thought, were being carried away by the idea of conciliation. "We are fighting against Kornilov, even *as Kerensky's troops do*, but we do not support Kerensky. *On the contrary*, we expose his weakness. . . . An active and most energetic, really revolutionary war against Kornilov . . . by itself may lead *us* to power, though we must *speak* of this as little as possible in our propaganda (remembering very well that even tomorrow events may put power in our hands, and then we shall not relinquish it)."

Events continued to move, as Lenin said, at dizzying speed. Kerensky made himself Commander in Chief on August 30, and on September 1 his representatives arrested General Kornilov. The same day, still unable to put a new coalition cabinet together, Kerensky announced a temporary "Directory" of five men — himself, Foreign Minister Tereshchenko, the new War Minister General Verkhovsky (promoted for standing with the government against Kornilov), Navy Minister Admiral Verderevsky, and the Menshevik Interior Minister Nikitin. Kerensky also proclaimed what had long been taken for granted — that Russia was officially a Republic.

In the meantime, on August 31, the Bolsheviks for the first time won an absolute majority in the Petrograd Soviet, workers' and soldiers' sections voting together. At issue was a resolution from the Bolshevik Central Committee, drafted by Kamenev (just out of jail), which blamed the Provisional Government for the Kornilov trouble and called for a government "of representatives of the revolutionary proletariat and peasantry." The soviet agreed, by a vote of 279 to 115, 51 abstaining. With this the Bolsheviks had won their strategic base for revolution, no less important than the Commune of Paris in the overthrow of the French monarchy in 1792.

With his characteristic flexibility, Lenin quickly proposed a new tactic to exploit this success. The Bolsheviks' cooperation with the other socialist parties during the Kornilov affair, he suggested in an article he called "On Compromises," could become the model for "a peaceful development of the revolution — a possibility that is extremely rare in history and extremely valuable." For the sake of such an achievement the Bolsheviks would "return to the pre-July demand of all power to the soviets, a government of SRs and Mensheviks responsible to the soviets." For their part, "the Bolsheviks . . . would refrain from immediately advancing the demand for the passing of power to the proletariat and the poorest peasants, from revolutionary methods of struggle for the realization of this demand." With rapid new Bolshevik gains in the soviets, it was natural enough that Lenin should return to his old strategy. Two days later, on September 3, Lenin wrote a postscript to say that because the Mensheviks and SRs had not moved against Kerensky, the peaceful revolution might not be possible after all. Kerensky lost no time in showing his own view of the Bolsheviks: he ordered their press suppressed again on September 2,[1] and followed this with an order on the 4th — quite unenforceable — that all unofficial organizations formed to fight Kornilov give up their arms and dissolve.

What the Mensheviks and SRs did not undertake to do in the wake of the Kornilov fiasco was to start some serious planning of a permanent democratic government. Rather than wait for the Constituent Assembly (the elections and convocation had been postponed by the cabinet from September to November, at the behest of the Kadets), the All-Russian Central Executive Committee issued a call on September 3 for a "Democratic Conference" to convene in Petrograd the following week. It would include participants from every sort of organization around the country — the soviets themselves, local governments, the trade unions, the peasants' cooperatives. In the minds of its sponsors the conference would prepare the ground for a "homogeneously socialist" cabinet (i.e., including all the socialists but no one else) and thus terminate the issue of coalition with the "bourgeois" Kadets that was splintering the moderate socialists.

The Bolshevik Central Committee had to take a stand on the Democratic Conference without any guidance from Lenin. It immediately resolved to get as many Bolsheviks as possible into the conference to make the voice of the workers and poor peasants a strong one. In this direction the party had a stroke of good fortune when Trotsky was released from prison on bail of 3,000 rubles the next day, the 4th. (He took an apartment with his wife and two sons in a bourgeois district where the neighbors were openly hostile — until one day a Bolshevik sailor came to visit and put the fear of the proletariat into them.) Trotsky and Kamenev were quickly appointed to join Stalin and Sokolnikov as

---

[1] The Bolshevik daily had been revived on August 13 as *Proletarii* (*The Proletarian*); suppressed August 24; and reopened August 25 as *Rabochi* (*The Worker*). On September 3 it reappeared as *Rabochi Put* (*The Worker's Path*), the name it bore until the revolution permitted *Pravda* to reappear on the masthead.

editors of the party press, and along with Lunacharsky, Trotsky undertook to harangue an unending series of mass meetings in the wooden theater on the Petrograd Side known as the Circus Modern. He returned to the Petrograd Soviet and at once became the leader of the Bolshevik group.

On September 5 the Moscow Soviet followed the lead of the Petrograd Soviet and passed a Bolshevik resolution for the first time. On the 9th the Petrograd Soviet, on Trotsky's motion, reaffirmed its Bolshevik vote, 519 to 414 with 67 abstaining. Chairman Chkheidze and the moderates who had dominated the soviet's Executive Committee ever since February took this as a vote of no confidence, and resigned. The same day, a regional congress of soviets in Finland — representing mainly the Russian forces there — gave the Bolsheviks a majority and made Antonov their chairman. With this trend clear, Lenin placed his bets squarely on the soviets to create a new revolutionary power and also, as he was explaining at length in *State and Revolution*, to become the basis of the permanent future government.

"The main question of every revolution is, undoubtedly, the question of state power. In the hands of which class power lies — this decides everything," Lenin wrote for *Rabochi Put*. "Either disruption of the soviets and their ignominious death, or all power to the soviets, I said before the All-Russian Congress of Soviets early in June, 1917, and the history of July and August has thoroughly and convincingly confirmed the correctness of these words. . . . The soviets of workers', soldiers', and peasants' deputies are particularly valuable because they represent a new *type* of state apparatus, which is immeasurably higher, incomparably more democratic." In his typically black-and-white fashion he asserted, "Experience has shown that there is no middle road. Either all power to the soviets, and a full democratization of the army, or a new Kornilov affair." In additional articles Lenin disposed of the Constituent Assembly — power should be taken by the soviets beforehand, to guarantee "democratic" elections. And there need be no civil war, contrary to the charges of the party's enemies: "A peaceful development of the revolution is *possible* and *probable* if all power passes to the soviets."

The Bolsheviks in Petrograd took Lenin's return to the slogan of soviets and peaceful revolution as a counsel of moderation. The Petrograd City Committee met on September 10 to allay some objections to Bolshevik participation in the Democratic Conference. Over the protest of Bubnov, the Central Committee member who edited the paper of the Military Organization and was also detailed for liaison with the local Petrograd leadership, the city committee agreed that the party should take part in the conference and make the most of it as a propaganda forum. "It is too early to speak of the struggle for power," said Vladimir Nevsky, a member of the Military Organization where awareness of the odds against an uprising was much keener since July. "We must speak about a long process. . . . Now we need to think about education of the proletariat," added a representative of the workers. On September 12 the Bolshevik papers printed announcements to the workers and soldiers cautioning them not to yield to "provocations" and to refrain from random demonstrations. The Democratic Conference itself got under way the 14th at the Alexandrinsky Theater (now the Pushkin Theater) in Petrograd, and remained in session for more than a week.

For all its high hopes, the Democratic Conference could not arrest the splintering that was taking place among all the moderate political groups. While Kerensky offered — or threatened — to let the socialists form a government, the right wing of the Mensheviks and SRs refused to break with the Kadets. Kamenev promised that the Bolsheviks would support a socialist government — but only until the next Congress of Soviets. Nothing showed how fast the government was sinking more clearly than the reaction of the sailors Kerensky sent to the conference to guard it against the Bolsheviks — they wanted to protect Trotsky instead after they heard him speak. Out of it all, wrote the Menshevik leader Dan, "We got no coalition government, but only a coalition abortion."

The Kornilov affair and the Democratic Conference precipitated a development in the party of the SRs that was highly favorable to the Bolsheviks — the open split between the SR left wing and the rest of the party. Led by the intransigent Boris Kamkov and a frail but dynamic young women, Maria Spiridonova, and fired by a tradition of peasant anarchism, the Left SRs repudiated the Provisional Government and took a stand on land and peace scarcely different from the Bolsheviks. They attracted the lion's share of the SR following in the army; by August they had the upper hand in the Soldier's Section of the Petrograd Soviet. In September they captured the Petrograd city organization of the SR party. After the Democratic Conference the Left SRs were to all intents and purposes an independent party, cooperating closely — they thought — with the Bolsheviks.

The trend toward a new revolutionary crisis was clear to many observers. The American Ambassador David Francis wrote to a friend on September 11, "The greatest menace to the present situation is the strength of the Bolshevik sentiment which, intoxicated with its success (attributable in no small degree to the failure of the Kornilov movement), may attempt to overthrow the present Provisional Government and administer affairs through its own representatives. If such a condition should eventuate, failure will undoubtedly ensue in a short time, but meanwhile there may be bloodshed."

Up to now, for all his revolutionary exhortation, Lenin had said little about the way power was to be transferred to the soviets, the proletariat, and — the Bolsheviks. Emboldened by the manifest upsurge in Bolshevik support around the country, but perhaps fearful that the moderates in the Democratic Conference might produce an attractive alternative, Lenin decided to cast the die. "Having obtained a majority in the Soviets of Workers' and Soldiers' Deputies of both capitals [Petrograd and Moscow], the Bolsheviks can and must take power into their hands," he announced to the Bolshevik Central Committee in the first of two ringing letters written in Helsingfors between September 12 and 14. The masses were with the Bolsheviks, or would be soon enough. If the party waited for the Constituent Assembly, Kerensky would surrender Petrograd to the Germans (a theme from which the Bolsheviks later made great capital). The Bolshevik delegates assembling for the Democratic Conference could function as a party congress; "this congress must (whether it wishes to do so or not) decide the *fate of the revolution*. The main thing," concluded Lenin, was "to place on the order of the day the *armed uprising in Petrograd and Moscow*. . . . We will win *absolutely* and *unquestionably*."

In the companion letter Lenin attacked the theoretical objection that insurrection was not Marxism but "Blanquism" — the conspiratorial heresy of the French socialist Auguste Blanqui. The "vanguard of the revolution" and "all the objective prerequisites for a successful uprising" were ready. He alleged — with no foundation — that the Allies were contemplating a separate peace with Germany so that the Kaiser's forces could stifle the Russian Revolution; but somehow the victorious Bolsheviks could themselves get a truce from Germany — "and to secure a truce at present means to conquer *the whole world*." "We must prove," Lenin went on, "that we accept, and not only in words, the idea of Marx about the necessity of treating uprising as an art." It was the time for "*action,* not writing resolutions"; go to the factories and barracks — "the pulse of life is there"; then, "we shall correctly estimate the best moment to begin the uprising." His conclusion was to the point:

> *Without losing a single moment, organize the staff of the insurrectionary detachments; designate the forces; move the loyal regiments to the most important points; surround the Alexandrinsky Theater [i.e., the Democratic Conference]; occupy the Peter-Paul fortress; arrest the general staff and the government; move against the military cadets, the Savage Division, etc., such detachments as will die rather than allow the enemy to move to the center of the city; we must mobilize the armed workers, call them to a last desperate battle, occupy at once the telegraph and telephone stations, place* our *staff of the uprising at the central telephone station, connect it by wire with all the factories, the regiments, the points of armed fighting, etc.*
>
> *Of course, this is all by way of an example, to* illustrate *the idea that at the present moment it is impossible to remain loyal to the revolution* without treating insurrection as an art.

Smilga, the Bolshevik chief in Helsingfors, took Lenin's letters to Petrograd on the 15th and turned them over to Krupskaya, who had remained in the city. She gave them to Stalin, who read them to the members of the Central Committee assembled in Sverdlov's apartment. The letters were heard with "bewilderment." As Bukharin recalled it:

> *We gathered and — I remember as though it were just now — began the session. Our tactics at the time were comparatively clear: the development of mass agitation and propaganda, the course toward armed insurrection, which could be expected from one day to the next. When I entered, Milyutin came suddenly to meet me and said, "You know, comrade Bukharin, we've received a little letter here."*
>
> *The letter read as follows: "You will be traitors and good-for-nothings if you don't send the whole [Democratic Conference Bolshevik] group to the factories and mills, surround the Democratic Conference and arrest all those disgusting people!" The letter was written very forcefully and threatened us with every punishment. We all gasped. No one had yet put the question so sharply. No one knew what to do. Everyone was at a loss for a while. Then we deliberated and came to a decision. Perhaps this was the only time in the history of our party when the Central Committee unanimously decided to burn a letter of Comrade Lenin's. This instance was not publicized at the time.*

Kamenev proposed replying to Lenin with an outright refusal to consider insurrection, but this step was turned down. Finally it was decided to postpone any decision, and only by the close tally of 6 to 4 with 6 abstentions did the Central Committee resolve to keep one copy of each letter for the record. Word of Lenin's demands quickly spread through the Bolsheviks in the Democratic Conference, but the Central Committee acted for the time being as though nothing had happened.

While Lenin was moving from Helsingfors to Vyborg (still in Finland — not to be confused with the "Vyborg" district of Petrograd where he hid later) to be in somewhat closer touch with his followers, the Bolshevik leaders in Petrograd continued to call for the peaceful assumption of power by the soviets. They were encouraged further by their capture of the Executive Committee of the Moscow Workers' Soviet on September 19, though the man the Moscow Bolsheviks installed as chairman of the soviet was Kamenev's cautious supporter Nogin. Trotsky addressed the Petrograd Soviet on September 20 with the demand that a new nationwide Congress of Soviets be convoked to decide on the transfer of power to the soviets. The next day the soviet passed a resolution to this effect, together with an attack on the Democratic Conference as unrepresentative, and it summoned all the other soviets to mobilize their defenses against the "counterrevolution."

On the 21st, for the first time since the Kornilov affair, the old lines of cleavage reappeared in the Bolshevik Central Committee when some of the members proposed that the party stage a walkout from the Democratic Conference. The cautious wing won a majority and rejected the proposal. Action also had to be taken on the decision by the conference to convoke a provisional legislative body, to be known as the "Council of the Republic." (More familiarly termed the "Pre-Parliament," the Council of the Republic convened October 7, and it was still in session when the Provisional Government was overthrown on October 25.) On the question whether to participate in the Pre-Parliament the Central Committee split almost evenly. Rykov reported for the Bolshevik moderates, and Trotsky for the bolder group. Trotsky prevailed by a vote of 9 to 8 to boycott the Pre-Parliament altogether, but because of the evenness of the division the Committee then decided to refer the whole question to the gathering of Bolshevik members of the Democratic Conference which was scheduled to meet later the same day.

Trotsky and Rykov again presented their respective cases to this larger assemblage. Trotsky was supported, interestingly enough, by Stalin, while Rykov was backed by Kamenev. This time, with the preponderance of less venturesome provincial delegates, the vote went to the opponents of boycotting the Pre-Parliament, by a count of 77 to 50. Nogin expressed the relief of the cautious Bolsheviks: boycotting the Pre-Parliament would be an "invitation to insurrection" that he was not ready to contemplate. A lesser Bolshevik named Zhukov confided to the Mensheviks, "We haven't forgotten the July Days and won't commit any new stupidity." Lenin, now in Vyborg, Finland, was increasingly disturbed at the temporizing of the Petrograd leadership, with one exception that came to his attention: "Trotsky was for the boycott: Bravo, Comrade Trotsky!" Otherwise, "At the top of our party we note vacillations that may become ruinous."

The counsel of caution was strengthened from an unexpected quarter on the 23rd when Zinoviev began attending the Central Committee meetings for the first time since the July Days. The experience of the summer had brought him to the conclusion that any attempt at an uprising would end as disastrously as the Paris Commune of 1871; revolution was inevitable, he wrote at the time of the Kornilov crisis, but the party's task for the time being was to restrain the masses from rising to the provocations of the bourgeoisie. This drastic change of mood on the part of the man recently so close to Lenin was perhaps intensified by chagrin that he had been displaced by Trotsky as the Bolsheviks' number-two leader. Though he was still wanted by the police, Zinoviev joined Kamenev to lead an unyielding campaign against Lenin's call for armed insurrection.

While the Bolsheviks debated the Pre-Parliament, the All-Russian Central Executive Committee of the soviets was wrangling over the Bolshevik demand for a new Congress of Soviets. The Bolsheviks wanted a congress in two weeks, and threatened to call their own if the CEC did not act. The CEC yielded on September 23 and issued a call for the Second All-Russian Congress of Soviets to convene in Petrograd on October 20.

Lenin was irked that this date was so far off and wrote, "The Congress of Soviets has been postponed [sic] till October 20. At the tempo of Russian life at present, this almost means postponing it to the Greek Calends," i.e., indefinitely. But the Bolsheviks in Petrograd began immediately to exploit the opportunity which the calling of the Soviet Congress gave them. On September 24 a conference of the Central Committee, the Petrograd City Committee, and the Bolshevik members of the Democratic Conference heard a report by Bukharin on the impending "open clash of classes" and the aim of "all power to the soviets." The conference resolved that it was now the task of the "party of the proletariat" to fight off the bourgeoisie and secure the transfer of power to the soviets. Work in the Pre-Parliament would only be "auxiliary" to this. But still nothing was being said in these secret gatherings about armed insurrection.

Monday September 25 saw a crystallization of leadership on both sides, government and revolutionary. Kerensky was finally able to announce the formation of a new provisional cabinet, more than half new men, largely from the Kadets and other moderate groups, plus three Mensheviks and two SRs. The same day the Petrograd Soviet resumed business, now that its leaders were no longer involved in the Democratic Conference, and finally elected a new Executive Committee to replace the body that had resigned September 9. The results, reflecting six months of revolutionary upsurge, were as follows: Workers' Section — Bolsheviks, 13; SRs, 6; Mensheviks, 3; Soldiers' Section — Bolsheviks, 9; SRs, 10; Mensheviks, 3. Bolsheviks held exactly half the total, and with the support of the left-wingers among the SRs, had a good working majority. The first step of the new majority was to install Trotsky as chairman of the soviet. (A week or two later the Soldiers' Section elected as its leader Andrei Sadovsky, an activist of the Bolshevik Military Organization.) Predictably the soviet passed a resolution offered by Trotsky condemning the counterrevolutionary nature of Kerensky's new coalition cabinet, and calling on the masses to struggle through the soviets for revolutionary power.

This was still not enough for Lenin. From Vyborg he wrote to Smilga in Helsingfors that the Petrograd Bolsheviks "have declared war on the government" but did nothing except "pass resolutions." He reiterated his demand that the party prepare for an armed uprising, with emphasis on the role of the soldiers and sailors in Finland, whom Lenin now thought most reliable to the Bolshevik cause. "History has made the *military* question now the fundamental *political* question. I am afraid that the Bolsheviks forget this . . . , hoping that 'the wave will sweep Kerensky away.' Such hope is naive: it is the same as relying on chance. On the part of the party of the proletariat this may prove a crime." He would not consider waiting for the newly summoned Congress of Soviets to take decisive action. Instead he demanded "all power to the Petrograd Soviet *now*, later to be transferred to the Congress of

Soviets. Why should we tolerate three more weeks of war and Kerensky's 'Kornilovist preparations?' "

Along with this Lenin composed a long article, "Will the Bolsheviks Retain State Power?", to apply his propositions of *State and
Revolution* — destruction of the "bourgeois" state, and management of
capitalist enterprise by the workers — to the immediate situation in
Russia. The masses, Lenin argued, "will support a purely Bolshevik
government"; the police machinery of the old government could be
replaced by the soviets, and the banking system could be taken over and
used as the lever to control industry. Power had to go to one class or
another; civil war was inevitable; and victory was within the Bolshevik
grasp: "There is no force on earth which can prevent the Bolsheviks, *if
only they do not allow themselves to be cowed* and are able to seize
power, from retaining it until the final victory of the world socialist
revolution."

THE PARTY PERSUADED

For all his fulminations against the counterrevolution and the petty-
bourgeoisie, Lenin had not succeeded by the end of September in
moving his own party toward the goal of a violent seizure of power. On
September 29 the Central Committee did no more than pick candidates
for the anticipated election to the Constituent Assembly and approve a
statement by Zinoviev on the Congress of Soviets. Published the next
day as an "Appeal of the Central Committee of the RSDWP (B) to the
Workers, Soldiers, Sailors and Peasants with a Summons to Struggle for
the Transfer of Power into the Hands of the Soviets," Zinoviev's document put the Bolsheviks squarely behind the Congress of Soviets and
the Constituent Assembly, and depicted Kerensky and the proposed
Pre-Parliament as a counterrevolutionary threat to both. Welcoming
new allies — the left wings of both the Mensheviks and SRs "whom we
call on to struggle hand in hand with us for the interests of the workers
and peasants, for a democratic peace, for the power of the Soviets" —
Zinoviev cautioned against premature "isolated actions."

This was exactly the attitude Lenin meant to condemn. The same
day, the 29th, he decided to spell out as much of his insurrectionary
reasoning as he dared in published form. The article, entitled "The
Crisis Has Matured," was printed in *Rabochi Put*, minus one section
that the editors cut out and lost and a particularly frank conclusion

which Lenin marked only for "distribution" to the party leadership. "There is no room for doubts," Lenin wrote for the public. "We are on the threshold of a world proletarian revolution." And it was, he made clear, the mission of the Russian Bolsheviks to take the lead in this revolution. He enumerated again all the circumstances that made Russia ripe for a new revolution — "a peasant uprising is growing"; "the counterrevolutionary forces are approaching the last ditch"; "we witness finally the vote in Moscow where fourteen thousand out of seventeen thousand soldiers voted for the Bolsheviks." Everything pointed to revolution, save the irresolution of the Bolshevik leaders themselves. Lenin's great fear was that his lieutenants would content themselves with a legal approach to power:

> There is not the slightest doubt that the Bolsheviks, were they to allow themselves to be caught in the trap of constitutional illusions, of "faith" in the Congress of Soviets and in the convocation of the Constituent Assembly, of "waiting" for the Congress of Soviets, etc. — that such Bolsheviks would prove miserable traitors to the proletarian cause.

In Germany two sailors had been shot for leading a food protest at Kiel. Lenin took this as a revolutionary signal for the Bolsheviks to do their international duty. "To 'wait' for the Congress of Soviets, etc., under such conditions means *betraying internationalism*, betraying the cause of the international socialist revolution."

All this obvious revolutionary agitation appeared in print on October 7, more than a week after it was written. In the addendum reserved for party eyes only, Lenin bore down on the resistance to his views:

> What, then, is to be done? We must aussprechen, was ist [*Lenin liked to use German for emphasis*], "say what is," admit the truth, that in our Central Committee and at the top of our party there is a tendency in favor of awaiting the Congress of Soviets, against an immediate uprising. We must overcome this tendency or opinion.
> Otherwise the Bolsheviks would cover themselves with shame forever; they would be reduced to nothing as a party.
> For to miss such a moment and to "await" the Congress of Soviets is either absolute idiocy or complete betrayal.

This suggests how slender was Lenin's regard for the revolutionary institution of the soviets, when he felt the pressure of time to strike against Kerensky's government before it could put down the rampaging peasants. "Weeks and even days now decide everything." October 20, the date set for the Congress of Soviets, was too late. In a footnote Lenin wrote, "To 'call' the Congress of Soviets for October 20, in order to decide upon the seizure of power — is there any difference between this and a foolishly 'announced' uprising? Now we can seize power, whereas October 20–29 you will not be allowed to seize it." . . .

While the Bolsheviks wrestled with Lenin's demands for action, volatile new fuel was spilled on the revolutionary fires of Petrograd by the leaders of the Provisional Government. At a closed meeting during the night of October 4–5, Kerensky's cabinet discussed the danger of a German offensive against Petrograd, following the enemy's successful amphibious operation to occupy the Baltic islands off Estonia. Nikolai Kishkin, the Kadet Minister of Welfare, brought in a plan to transfer the seat of government to Moscow and declare Petrograd part of the zone of military operations. The Petrograd Soviet and the Central Executive Committee, being private organizations, would be left to fend for themselves.

The idea of moving the capital was taken by the socialist members of the cabinet as a transparent plot to cut off revolutionary influence on the government and the forthcoming Constituent Assembly. They protested vigorously, and in consequence the cabinet made no decision at all, but put the transfer plan off until the Pre-Parliament could consider it. However, the discussion quickly leaked out to the public, in a version that had the Provisional Government plotting to surrender Petrograd to the Germans so that the enemy forces could extinguish the fire on the hearth of the revolution. As in the summer of 1792 in France, the menace of invasion and the fear of treason combined to panic the capital into a new revolutionary mood, and the Bolsheviks quickly made the most of it. *Rabochi Put* carried the evacuation story on October 6, and Trotsky went into a session of the Soldiers' Section of the Petrograd Soviet the very same day with a resolution, adopted unanimously:

> *The Soldiers' Section of the Petrograd Soviet of Workers' and Soldiers' Deputies categorically protests against the plan to transfer the Provisional Government from Petrograd to Moscow, since such a transfer would mean abandoning the revolutionary capital to the whim of fate.*
>
> *If the Provisional Government is not able to defend Petrograd, then it should either conclude peace or yield its place to another government.*
>
> *The move to Moscow would mean desertion from a responsible post of battle.*

All the past week Lenin had been writing more notes and letters to rouse support for his uprising among the top Bolshevik Party committees. He got more response in Moscow, where the romantic Bukharin and his old school friend Osinsky spoke vigorously for radical action. Sensing this mood, Lenin suggested again that Moscow might show the way to insurrection while Petrograd faltered. He jotted down some theses for the planned party congress (before he learned it was postponed) to reiterate his opposition to participating in the Pre-Parliament and his concern about "vacillations . . . at the top of our party, a 'fear,' as it were, of the struggle for power, an inclination to substitute resolutions, protests, and congresses in place of this struggle." This was written before the opposition by Zinoviev and Kamenev became a matter of record, and it shows Lenin's feeling that practically the whole party leadership wanted to avoid an armed test of strength. Lenin repeated his stress on a revolution through the soviet — "a refusal now on the part of the Bolsheviks to transform the soviets into organs of uprising would be a betrayal both of the peasantry and of the cause of the international socialist revolution." But he refused adamantly to let the uprising depend on the Congress of Soviets. He feared exposing the party's plans by tying them to the date of the congress, but more fundamentally he asserted,

> It is necessary to fight against the constitutional illusions and against hopes placed in the Congress of Soviets, to reject the preconceived idea of "waiting" for it at all cost. . . . The Bolsheviks have in their hands the soviets of both capital cities; if they refused to carry out this task and became reconciled to the convocation of the Constituent Assembly (which means a concocted Constituent Assembly) by the Kerensky government, they would reduce all their propaganda for the "power to the soviets" slogan to empty phrases and, politically, would cover themselves with shame as a party of the revolutionary proletariat.

In other words, soviets were good organs of power as long as they were certain to respond quickly under Bolshevik control; but as a practical matter, if delay or weakness were entailed, they should be disregarded.

Lenin's latest letters were taken to a meeting of the Petrograd City Committee on the evening of October 5. With good reason Lenin sensed that this body would support him more readily and give him leverage against the Central Committee. But his directive for insurrection was eloquently opposed by Moisei Volodarsky, a former Interdis-

"but its fate will be decided momentarily. . . . In the history of the revolutionary movement I know of no other examples in which such huge masses were involved and which developed so bloodlessly. The power of the Provisional Government, headed by Kerensky, was dead and awaited the blow of the broom of history which had to sweep it away. . . . The population slept peacefully and did not know that at this time one power was replaced by another."

In the midst of Trotsky's speech, Lenin appeared in the hall. Catching sight of him, the audience rose to its feet, delivering a thundering ovation. With the greeting, "Long live Comrade Lenin, back with us again," Trotsky turned the platform over to his comrade. Side by side, Lenin and Trotsky acknowledged the cheers of the crowd. "Comrades!" declared Lenin, over the din:

> *The workers' and peasants' revolution, the necessity of which has been talked about continuously by the Bolsheviks, has occurred. What is the significance of this workers' and peasants' revolution? First of all, the significance of this revolution is that we shall have a soviet government, our own organ of power without the participation of any bourgeois. The oppressed masses will form a government themselves. . . . This is the beginning of a new period in the history of Russia; and the present, third Russian revolution must ultimately lead to the victory of socialism. One of our immediate tasks is the necessity of ending the war at once.*
>
> *We shall win the confidence of the peasantry by one decree, which will abolish landlord estates. The peasants will understand that their only salvation lies in an alliance with the workers. We will institute real workers' control over production.*
>
> *You have now learned how to work together in harmony, as evidenced by the revolution that has just occurred. We now possess the strength of a mass organization, which will triumph over everything and which will lead the proletariat to world revolution.*
>
> *In Russia we must now devote ourselves to the construction of a proletarian socialist state.*
>
> *Long live the world socialist revolution.*

Lenin's remarks were brief; yet it is perhaps not surprising that on this occasion most of his listeners did not trouble themselves with the question of how a workers' government would survive in backward Russia and a hostile world. After Lenin's remarks, Trotsky proposed that special commissars be dispatched to the front and throughout the country at once to inform the broad masses everywhere of the successful uprising in Petrograd. At this someone shouted, "You are anticipating the will of the Second Congress of Soviets," to which Trotsky immediately retorted: "The will of the Second Congress of Soviets has already been predetermined by the fact of the workers' and soldiers' uprising. Now we have only to develop this triumph."

The relatively few Mensheviks in attendance formally absolved themselves of responsibility for what they called "the tragic consequences of the conspiracy underway" and withdrew from the executive organs of the Petrograd Soviet. But most of the audience listened patiently to greetings by Lunacharsky and Zinoviev, the latter, like Lenin, making his first public appearance since July. The deputies shouted enthusiastic approval for a political statement drafted by Lenin and introduced by Volodarsky. Hailing the overthrow of the Provisional Government, the statement appealed to workers and soldiers everywhere to support the revolution; it also contained an expression of confidence that the Western European proletariat would help bring the cause of socialism to a full and stable victory. The deputies then dispersed, either to factories and barracks to spread the glad tidings, or, like Sukhanov, to grab a bite to eat before the opening session of the All-Russian Congress.

Dusk was nearing, and the Winter Palace was still not in Bolshevik hands. As early as 1:00 p.m. a detachment of sailors commanded by Ivan Sladkov had occupied the Admiralty, a few steps from the Winter Palace, and arrested the naval high command. At the same time, elements of the Pavlovsky Regiment had occupied the area around the Winter Palace, bounded by Millionnaia, Moshkov, and Bolshaia Koniushennaia streets, and Nevsky Prospect from the Ekaterinsky Canal to the Moika. Pickets, manned with armored cars and anti-aircraft guns, were set up on bridges over the Ekaterinsky Canal and the Moika, and on Morskaia Street. Later in the afternoon, Red Guard detachments from the Petrograd District and the Vyborg side joined the Pavlovsky soldiers, and troops from the Keksgolmsky Regiment occupied the area north of the Moika to the Admiralty, closing the ring of insurrectionary forces around the Palace Square. "The Provisional Government," Dashkevich would subsequently recall, "was as good as in a mousetrap."

Noon had been the original deadline for the seizure of the Winter

Palace. This was subsequently postponed to 3:00 and then 6:00 P.M., after which, to quote Podvoisky, the Military Revolutionary Committee "no longer bothered to set deadlines." The agreed-upon ultimatum to the government was not dispatched; instead, loyalist forces gained time to strengthen their defenses. Thus in the late afternoon, insurgent troops watched impatiently while cadets on the Palace Square erected massive barricades and machine gun emplacements of firewood brought from the General Staff building.

By 6:00 P.M. it was dark, drizzly, and cold, and many of the soldiers deployed in the area around the palace hours earlier were growing hungry and restless. Occasionally, one of them would lose patience and open fire at the cadets, only to be rebuked with the stern command, "Comrades, don't shoot without orders." On the Petrograd side, the Bolshevik Military Organization leader Tarasov-Rodionov, for one, was beside himself worrying about what was happening in the center of the city. "I had the urge," he later wrote, "to drop everything — to rush to them [the Military Revolutionary Committee] to speed up this idiotically prolonged assault on the Winter Palace." During these hours, Lenin sent Podvoisky, Antonov, and Chudnovsky dozens of notes in which he fumed that their procrastination was delaying the opening of the congress and needlessly stimulating anxiety among congress deputies.

Antonov implies in his memoirs that unexpected delays in the mobilization of insurgent soldiers, faulty organization, and other problems of a minor yet troublesome nature were the main reasons it took so long to launch the culminating offensive on the government. In support of this view, there are indications that, for one reason or another, last-minute snags developed in connection with mobilizing some elements of the Preobrazhensky and Semenovsky regiments for the attack. More important, most of the sailor detachments from Helsingfors that the Military Revolutionary Committee was counting on for its assault did not arrive until late evening or even the following day. (In one case, a trainload of armed sailors was delayed in an open field outside Vyborg for many hours after the locomotive had burst its pipes; the Vyborg stationmaster, sympathetic to the government, had purposely provided the sailors with the least reliable locomotive available.) . . .

Podvoisky, in his later writings, tended to attribute continuing delays in mounting an attack on the Winter Palace to the Military Revolutionary Committee's hope, for the most part realized, of avoiding a bloody battle. As Podvoisky later recalled: "Already assured of victory, we awaited the humiliating end of the Provisional Government. We strove to insure that it would surrender the face of the revolutionary strength which we then enjoyed. We did not open artillery fire, giving our strongest weapon, the class struggle, an opportunity to operate within the walls of the palace." This consideration appears to have had some validity as well. There was little food for the almost three thousand officers, cadets, cossacks, and women soldiers in the Winter Palace on October 25. In the early afternoon the ubiquitous American journalist John Reed somehow wangled his way into the palace, wandered through one of the rooms where these troops were billeted, and took note of the dismal surroundings: "On both sides of the parqueted floor lay rows of dirty mattresses and blankets, upon which occasional soldiers were stretched out; everywhere was a litter of cigarette-butts, bits of bread, cloth, and empty bottles with expensive French labels. More and more soldiers, with the red shoulder-straps of the Yunkerschools, moved about in a stale atmosphere of tobacco smoke and unwashed humanity. . . . The place was a huge barrack, and evidently had been for weeks, from the look of the floor and walls." . . .

Whatever obstacles confronted the Military Revolutionary Committee in its assault on the Winter Palace on October 25 pale by comparison with the difficulties facing members of the Provisional Government, gathered in the grand Malachite Hall on the second floor of the palace. Here Konovalov convened a cabinet session at noon, an hour after Kerensky's hurried departure for the front. Present were all of the ministers except Kerensky and the minister of food supply, a distinguished economist, Sergei Prokopovich, who, having been temporarily detained by an insurgent patrol in the morning, was unable to reach the Winter Palace before it was completely sealed off in the afternoon. Fortunately for the historian, several of the participants in this ill-fated last meeting of Kerensky's cabinet penned detailed recollections of their final hours together; these tortured accounts bear witness to the almost complete isolation of the Provisional Government at this time, and to the ministers' resulting confusion and ever-increasing paralysis of will. . . .

By now, at the Peter and Paul Fortress, Blagonravov, under continual prodding from Smolny, had decided that the final stage of the attack on the government could be delayed no longer, this despite the fact that difficulties with the cannon and the signal lantern had not yet been fully surmounted. At 6:30 P.M. he dispatched two cyclists to the General Staff building, and in twenty minutes they arrived there armed with the following ultimatum:

> *By order of the Military Revolutionary Committee of the Petrograd Soviet, the Provisional Government is declared overthrown. All power is transferred to the Petrograd Soviet of Workers' and Soldiers' Deputies. The Winter Palace is surrounded by revolutionary forces. Cannon at the Peter and Paul Fortress and on the ships* Aurora *and* Amur *are aimed at the Winter Palace and the General Staff building. In the name of the Military Revolutionary Committee we propose that the Provisional Government and the troops loyal to it capitulate. . . . You have twenty minutes to answer. Your response should be given to our messenger. This ultimatum expires at 7:10, after which we will immediately open fire. . . .*
>
> Chairman of the Military Revolutionary Committee Antonov
> Commissar of the Peter and Paul Fortress G. B.

. . . Along with the news of the Military Revolutionary Committee's ultimatum, the ministers also learned that large numbers of previously wavering cadets from Oranienbaum and Peterhof now intended to leave the palace. Besides, the original deadline set by Antonov was already close to expiration. The ministers hurried back to the Malachite Hall at once to consider the question of whether or not to surrender. Looking out at the crowded Neva and the Peter and Paul Fortress, one member of the cabinet wondered aloud, "What will happen to the palace if the *Aurora* opens fire?" "It will be turned into a heap of ruins," replied Admiral Verderevsky, adding sanguinely: "Her turrets are higher than the bridges. She can demolish the place without damaging any other building."

Still, all the ministers, including Verderevsky, were agreed that surrender in the prevailing circumstances was unthinkable. They resolved simply to ignore the ultimatum, and Kishkin, Gvozdev, and Konovalov immediately rushed off to coax the cadets to remain at their posts. In his diary, Minister of Justice Pavel Maliantovich attempted to explain the cabinet's decision. He suggested that although at this point the ministers had lost hope of holding out until the arrival of outside help, they believed strongly that legally the Provisional Government could hand over its authority only to the Constituent Assembly. They felt a solemn obligation to resist until the very last moment so that it would be clear beyond doubt that they had yielded only to absolutely overwhelming force. That moment had not yet come, Maliantovich affirmed, hence the cabinet's decision to give no reply to the Military Revolutionary Committee and to continue resistance. . . .

For their part, the ministers now dispatched the following radio-telegram to the Russian people:

> *To All, All, All!*
> The Petrograd Soviet has declared the Provisional Government overthrown, and demands that power be yielded to it under threat of shelling the Winter Palace from cannon in the Peter and Paul Fortress and aboard the cruiser Aurora, anchored on the Neva. The government can yield power only to the Constituent Assembly; because of this we have decided not to surrender and to put ourselves under the protection of the people and the army. In this regard a telegram was sent to Stavka. Stavka answered with word that a detachment had been dispatched. Let the country and the people respond to the mad attempt of the Bolsheviks to stimulate an uprising in the rear of the fighting army.
>
> . . .

. . . At 9:40 P.M. Blagonravov finally returned to the fortress and signaled the *Aurora* to open fire. The *Aurora* responded by firing one blank round from its bow gun. The blast of a cannon shooting blanks is significantly greater than if it were using combat ammunition, and the ear-splitting reverberations of the *Aurora*'s first shot were felt throughout the capital. The blast impelled gawking spectators lined up on the Neva embankments to flop to the ground and crawl away in panic, and it contributed to the further thinning out of military forces inside the Winter Palace. (Many cadets finally abandoned their posts at this point and were followed shortly afterward by a number of the women soldiers.) Contrary to legend and to Verderevsky's prediction, the *Aurora*'s shot did no physical damage.

After the *Aurora*'s action the artillerists at the Peter and Paul Fortress allowed time for those forces who wished to do so to leave the palace. During this interim, the officer of the watch on the *Amur* spotted a string of lights at the mouth of the Neva and sounded the alarm: "Ships approaching!" As their silhouettes came into view, old deck hands on the *Amur* triumphantly identified the arriving vessels as the destroyers *Samson* and *Zabiiaka*, accompanied by some of the other ships from Helsingfors.

At around 11:00 P.M. Blagonravov gave the order to commence

shooting in earnest. Most of the shells subsequently fired exploded spectacularly but harmlessly over the Neva, but one shattered a cornice on the palace and another smashed a third-floor corner window, exploding just above the room in which the government was meeting. The blast unnerved the ministers and influenced at least a few of them to have second thoughts about the wisdom of further resistance. Meanwhile, from the walls of the Peter and Paul Fortress, Tarasov-Rodionov watched the spectacular fireworks, whose tremors momentarily drowned out the sound of the rifle and machine gun fire and the droning of lighted streetcars crawling single file across the Troitsky and Palace bridges, and wondered at the incredibility of it all, of "the workers' soviet overthrowing the bourgeois government while the peaceful life of the city continued uninterrupted." . . .

While all this was going on, Lenin remained at Smolny, raging at every delay in the seizure of the Winter Palace and still anxious that the All-Russian Congress not get underway until the members of the Provisional Government were securely behind bars. Andrei Bubnov later recorded that "the night of October 25 . . . Ilich hurried with the capture of the Winter Palace, putting extreme pressure on everyone and everybody when there was no news of how the attack was going." Similarly, Podvoisky later remembered that Lenin now "paced around a small room at Smolny like a lion in a cage. He needed the Winter Palace at any cost: it remained the last gate on the road to workers' power. V. I. scolded . . . he screamed . . . he was ready to shoot us."

Still, the start of the congress had been scheduled for 2:00 P.M. By late evening, the delegates had been milling around for hours; it was impossible to hold them back much longer, regardless of Lenin's predilections. Finally, at 10:40 P.M., Dan rang the chairman's bell, formally calling the congress into session. "The Central Executive Committee considers our customary opening political address superfluous," he announced at the outset. "Even now, our comrades who are selflessly fulfilling the obligations we placed on them are under fire at the Winter Palace."

John Reed, who had pushed his way through a clamorous mob at the door of the hall, subsequently described the scene in Smolny's white assembly hall as the congress opened:

> In the rows of seats, under the white chandeliers, packed immovably in the aisles and on the sides, perched on every windowsill, and even the

edge of the platform, the representatives of the workers and soldiers of all Russia awaited in anxious silence or wild exultation the ringing of the chairman's bell. There was no heat in the hall but the stifling heat of unwashed human bodies. A foul blue cloud of cigarette smoke rose from the mass and hung in the thick air. Occasionally someone in authority mounted the tribune and asked the comrades not to smoke; then everybody, smokers and all, took up the cry "Don't smoke, comrades!" and went on smoking. . . .

On the platform sat the leaders of the old Tsay-ee-kah [Central Executive Committee] . . . Dan was ringing the bell. Silence fell sharply intense, broken by the scuffling and disputing of the people at the door. . . .

According to a preliminary report by the Credentials Committee, 300 of the 670 delegates assembled in Petrograd for the congress were Bolsheviks, 193 were SRs (of whom more than half were Left SRs), 68 were Mensheviks, 14 were Menshevik-Internationalists, and the remainder either were affiliated with one of a number of smaller political groups or did not belong to any formal organization. The dramatic rise in support for the Bolsheviks that had occurred in the previous several months was reflected in the fact that the party's fraction was three times greater than it had been at the First All-Russian Congress of Soviets in June; the Bolsheviks were now far and away the largest single party represented at the congress. Yet it is essential to bear in mind that, despite this success, at the opening of the congress the Bolsheviks did not have an absolute majority without significant help from the Left SRs.

Because delegates, upon arrival at Smolny, were asked to fill out detailed personal questionnaires, we can ascertain not only the political affiliation of most of them, but also the character of each of the 402 local soviets represented at the congress and its official position on the construction of a new national government. Tabulation of these questionnaires reveals the striking fact that an overwhelming number of delegates, some 505 of them, came to Petrograd committed in principle to supporting the transfer of "all power to the soviets," that is, the creation of a soviet government presumably reflective of the party composition of the congress. Eighty-six delegates were loosely bound to vote for "all power to the democracy," meaning a homogeneous democratic government including representatives of peasant soviets, trade unions, cooperatives, etc., while twenty-one delegates were committed to support of a coalition democratic government in which some propertied elements, but not the Kadets, would be represented. Only fifty-five delegates, that is, significantly less than 10 percent, represented constituencies still favoring continuation of the Soviet's former policy of coalition with the Kadets.

As a result of the breakdown in relative voting strength, moments after the congress opened fourteen Bolsheviks took seats in the congress Presidium alongside seven Left SRs (the Mensheviks, allotted three seats in the Presidium, declined to fill them; the Menshevik-Internationalists did not fill the one seat allotted to them but reserved the right to do so). Dan, Lieber, Broido, Gots, Bogdanov, and Vasilii Filipovsky, who had directed the work of the Soviet since March, now vacated the seats at the head of the hall reserved for the top Soviet leadership; amid thunderous applause their places were immediately occupied by Trotsky, Kollontai, Lunacharsky, Nogin, Zinoviev, Kamkov, Maria Spiridonova, Mstislavsky, and other prominent Bolsheviks and Left SRs.

As if punctuating this momentous changeover, an ominous sound was heard in the distance — the deep, pounding boom of exploding cannon. Rising to make an emergency announcement, Martov, in a shrill, trembling voice, demanded that, before anything else, the congress agree to seek a peaceful solution to the existing political crisis; in his view, the only way out of the emergency was first to stop the fighting and then to start negotiations for the creation of a united, democratic government acceptable to the entire democracy. With this in mind, he recommended selection of a special delegation to initiate discussions with other political parties and organizations aimed at bringing to an immediate end the clash which had erupted in the streets.

Speaking for the Left SRs, Mstislavsky immediately endorsed Martov's proposal; more significantly, it was also apparently well received by many Bolsheviks. Glancing around the hall, Sukhanov, for one, noted that "Martov's speech was greeted with a tumult of applause from a very large section of the meeting." Observed a *Delo naroda* reporter, "Martov's appeal was showered with torrents of applause by a majority in the hall." Bearing in mind that most of the congress delegates had mandates to support the creation by the congress of a coalition government of parties represented in the Soviet and since Martov's motion was directed toward that very end, there is no reason to doubt these observations. The published congress proceedings indicate that, on behalf of the

Bolsheviks, Lunacharsky responded to Martov's speech with the declaration that "the Bolshevik fraction has absolutely nothing against the proposal made by Martov." The congress documents indicate as well that Martov's proposal was quickly passed by unanimous vote.

No sooner had the congress endorsed the creation of a democratic coalition government by negotiation, however, than a succession of speakers, all representatives of the formerly dominant moderate socialist bloc, rose to denounce the Bolsheviks. These speakers declared their intention of immediately walking out of the congress as a means of protesting and opposing the actions of the Bolsheviks. The first to express himself in this vein was Iakov Kharash, a Menshevik army officer and delegate from the Twelfth Army Committee. Proclaimed Kharash: "A criminal political venture has been going on behind the back of the All-Russian Congress, thanks to the political hypocrisy of the Bolshevik Party. The Mensheviks and SRs consider it necessary to disassociate themselves from everything that is going on here and to mobilize the public for defense against attempts to seize power." Added Georgii Kuchin, also an officer and prominent Menshevik, speaking for a bloc of moderately inclined delegates from army committees at the front: "The congress was called primarily to discuss the question of forming a new government, and yet what do we see? We find that an irresponsible seizure of power has already occurred and that the will of the congress has been decided beforehand. . . . We must save the revolution from this mad venture. In the cause of rescuing the revolution we intend to mobilize all of the revolutionary elements in the army and the country. . . . [We] reject any responsibility for the consequences of this reckless venture and are withdrawing from this congress."

These blunt statements triggered a storm of protest and cries of "Kornilovites!" and "Who in the hell do you represent?" from a large portion of the assembled delegates. Yet after Kamenev restored a semblance of order, Lev Khinchuk, from the Moscow Soviet, and Mikhail Gendelman, a lawyer and member of the SR Central Committee, read similarly bitter and militantly hostile declarations on behalf of the Mensheviks and SRs respectively. "The only possible peaceful solution to the present crisis continues to lie in negotiations with the Provisional Government on the formation of a government representing all elements of the democracy," Khinchuk insisted. At this, according to Sukhanov "a terrible din filled the hall; it was not only the Bolsheviks who were indignant, and for a long time the speaker wasn't allowed to continue." "We leave the present congress," Khinchuk finally shouted, "and invite all other fractions similarly unwilling to accept responsibility for the actions of the Bolsheviks to assemble together to discuss the situation." "Deserters," came shouts from the hall. Echoed Gendelman: "Anticipating that an outburst of popular indignation will follow the inevitable discovery of the bankruptcy of Bolshevik promises . . . the Socialist Revolutionary fraction is calling upon the revolutionary forces of the country to organize themselves and to stand guard over the revolution. . . . Taking cognizance of the seizure of power by the Bolsheviks . . . , holding them fully responsible for the consequences of this insane and criminal action, and consequently finding it impossible to collaborate with them, the Socialist Revolutionary fraction is leaving the congress!"

Tempers in the hall now skyrocketed; there erupted a fierce squall of foot-stamping, whistling, and cursing. In response to the uprising now openly proclaimed by the Military Revolutionary Committee, the Mensheviks and SRs had moved rightward, and the gulf separating them from the extreme left had suddenly grown wider than ever. When one recalls that less than twenty-four hours earlier the Menshevik and SR congress fractions, uniting broad segments of both parties, appeared on the verge of at long last breaking with the bourgeois parties and endorsing the creation of a homogeneous socialist government pledged to a program of peace and reform, the profound impact of the events of October 24–25 becomes clear. One can certainly understand why the Mensheviks and SRs reacted as they did. At the same time, it is difficult to escape the conclusion that by totally repudiating the actions of the Bolsheviks and of the workers and soldiers who willingly followed them, and, even more, by pulling out of the congress, the moderate socialists undercut efforts at compromise by the Menshevik-Internationalists, the Left SRs, and the Bolshevik moderates. In so doing, they played directly into Lenin's hands, abruptly paving the way for the creation of a government which had never been publicly broached before — that is, an exclusively Bolshevik regime. In his memoir-history of the revolution, Sukhanov acknowledged the potentially immense historical significance of the Menshevik-SR walkout. He wrote that in leaving the congress "we completely untied the Bolsheviks' hands, making them masters of the entire situation and yielding to them the whole arena of the revolution. A struggle at the congress for a united democratic front *might* have had some success. . . . By quitting the congress, we ourselves gave the Bolsheviks a monopoly of the Soviet, of the masses, and of the revolution. By our own irrational decision, we insured the victory of Lenin's whole 'line'!"

All this is doubtless more apparent in retrospect than it was at the time. At any rate, following the declarations of Kharash, Kuchin, Khinchuk, and Gendelman, several radically inclined soldier-delegates took the floor to assert that the views of Kharash and Kuchin in no way represented the thinking of the average soldier. "Let them go — the army is not with them," burst out a young, lean-faced soldier named Karl Peterson, representing the Latvian Rifle Regiment; his observation would soon be only too evident to all. At this the hall rocked with wild cheering. "Kuchin refers to the mobilization of forces," shouted Frants Gzhelshchak, a Bolshevik soldier from the Second Army at the front, as soon as he could make himself heard. "Against whom — against the workers and soldiers who have come out to defend the revolution?" he asked. "Whom will he organize? Clearly not the workers and soldiers against whom he himself is determined to wage war." Declared Fedor Lukianov, a soldier from the Third Army, also a Bolshevik, "The thinking of Kuchin is that of the top army organizations which we elected way back in April and which have long since failed to reflect the views and mood of the broad masses of the army."

At this point Genrikh Erlikh, a representative of the Bund (the Jewish social democratic organization), interrupted to inform the congress of the decision of a majority of City Duma deputies, taken moments earlier, to march en masse to the Winter Palace. Erlikh added that the Menshevik and SR fractions in the Executive Committee of the All-Russian Soviet of Peasant Deputies had decided to join the Duma deputies in protesting the application of violence against the Provisional Government, and invited all congress delegates "who did not wish a bloodbath" to participate in the march. It was at this point that the Mensheviks, SRs, Bundists, and members of the "front group" — deluged by shouts of "Deserters!" "Lackeys of the bourgeoisie!" and "Good riddance!" — rose from their places and made their way out of the hall.

Soon after the departure of the main bloc of Mensheviks and SRs, Martov, still intent most of all on facilitating a peaceful compromise between the moderate socialists and the radical left, took the floor to present a resolution on behalf of the Menshevik-Internationalists. His resolution condemned the Bolsheviks for organizing a coup d'état before the opening of the congress and called for creation of a broadly

based democratic government to replace the Provisional Government.
It read in part:

> *Taking into consideration that this coup d'état threatens to bring about
> bloodshed, civil war, and the triumph of a counterrevolution . . . [and]
> that the only way out of this situation which could still prevent the
> development of a civil war might be an agreement between insurgent
> elements and the rest of the democratic organizations on the formation
> of a democratic government which is recognized by the entire revolution-
> ary democracy and to which the Provisional Government could pain-
> lessly surrender its power, the Menshevik [Internationalist] fraction
> proposes that the congress pass a resolution on the necessity of a peaceful
> settlement of the present crisis by the formation of an all-democratic
> government . . . that the congress appoint a delegation for the purpose
> of entering into negotiations with other democratic organs and all the
> socialist parties . . . [and] that it discontinue its work pending the
> disclosure of the results of this delegation's efforts.*

It is easy to see that from Lenin's point of view, passage of Martov's
resolution would have been a disaster; on the other hand, the departure
of moderates offered an opportunity which could now be exploited to
consolidate the break with them. Not long after Martov resumed his
seat, congress delegates rose and cheered the surprise appearance of the
Bolshevik City Duma fraction, members of which, pushing their way
into the crowded hall, announced that they had come "to triumph or
die with the All-Russian Congress!" Then Trotsky, universally recognized as the Bolsheviks' most forceful orator, took the platform to
declare:

> *A rising of the masses of the people requires no justification. What has
> happened is an insurrrection, and not a conspiracy. We hardened the
> revolutionary energy of the Petersburg workers and soldiers. We openly
> forged the will of the masses for an insurrection, and not a conspiracy.
> The masses of the people followed our banner and our insurrection was
> victorious. And now we are told: Renounce your victory, make conces-
> sions, compromise. With whom? I ask: With whom ought we to compro-
> mise? With those wretched groups who have left us or who are making
> this proposal? But after all we've had a full view of them. No one in
> Russia is with them any longer. A compromise is supposed to be made,
> as between two equal sides, by the millions of workers and peasants
> represented in this congress, whom they are ready, not for the first time
> or the last, to barter away as the bourgeoisie sees fit. No, here no*

*compromise is possible. To those who have left and to those who tell us
to do this we must say: You are miserable bankrupts, your role is played
out; go where you ought to go: into the dustbin of history!*

Amid stormy applause, Martov shouted in warning, "Then we'll
leave!" And Trotsky, without a pause, read a resolution condemning
the departure of Menshevik and SR delegates from the congress as " a
weak and treacherous attempt to break up the legally constituted all-
Russian representative assembly of the worker and soldier masses at
precisely the moment when their avant-garde, with arms in hand, is
defending the congress and the revolution from the onslaught of the
counterrevolution." The resolution endorsed the insurrection against
the Provisional Government and concluded: "The departure of the
compromisers does not weaken the soviets. Inasmuch as it purges the
worker and peasant revolution of counterrevolutionary influences, it
strengthens them. Having listened to the declarations of the SRs and
Mensheviks, the Second All-Russian Congress continues its work, the
tasks of which have been predetermined by the will of the laboring
people and their insurrection of October 24 and 25. Down with the
compromisers! Down with the servants of the bourgeoisie! Long live the
triumphant uprising of soldiers, workers, and peasants!"

This bitter denunciation of the Mensheviks and SRs and blanket
endorsement of the armed insurrection in Petrograd was, of course, as
difficult for the Left SRs, left Mensheviks, and Bolshevik moderates to
swallow as Martov's resolution was for the Leninists. Kamkov, in a
report to the First Left SR Congress in November, when these events
were still very fresh in mind, attempted to explain the thinking of the
Left SRs at this moment, when the gulf dividing Russian socialists
widened, when in spite of Left SR efforts the Military Revolutionary
Committee had been transformed into an insurrectionary organ and
had overthrown the Provisional Government, and when the moderate
socialists had repudiated and moved to combat this development:

*As political leaders in a moment of decisive historical significance for
the fate of not only the Russian but also the world revolution, we, least
of all, could occupy ourselves with moralizing. As people concerned
with the defense of the revolution we had first of all to ask ourselves what
we should do today, when the uprising was a reality . . . and for us
it was clear that for a revolutionary party in that phase of the Russian revolution that had developed . . . our place was with the revolu-*

*tion. . . . We decided not only to stay at Smolny but to play the most
energetic role possible. . . . We believed we should direct all of our
energies toward the creation of a new government, one which would be
supported, if not by the entire revolutionary democracy, then at least by
a majority of it. Despite the hostility engendered by the insurrection in
Petrograd . . . knowing that included within the right was a large mass
of honest revolutionaries who simply misunderstood the Russian revolution, we believed our task to be that of not contributing to exacerbating
relations within the democracy. . . . We saw our task, the task of the
Left SRs, as that of mending the broken links uniting the two fronts of
the Russian democracy. . . . We were convinced that they [the moder-
ates] would with some delay accept that platform which is not the
platform of any one fraction or party, but the program of history, and
that they would ultimately take part in the creation of a new government.*

At the Second Congress of Soviets session the night of October
25–26, loud cheers erupted when Kamkov, following Trotsky to the
platform, made the ringing declaration: "The right SRs left the congress but we, the Left SRs, have stayed." After the applause subsided,
however, tactfully but forcefully, Kamkov spoke out against Trotsky's
course, arguing that the step Trotsky proposed was untimely "because
counterrevolutionary efforts are continuing." He added that the Bolsheviks did not have the support of the peasantry, "the infantry of the
revolution without which the revolution would be destroyed." With this
in mind, he insisted that "the left ought not isolate itself from moderate
democratic elements, but, to the contrary, should seek agreement with
them."

It is perhaps not without significance that the more temperate
Lunacharsky, rather than Trotsky, rose to answer Kamkov:

*Heavy tasks have fallen on us, of that there is no doubt. For the effective
fulfillment of these tasks the unity of all the various genuinely revolutionary elements of the democracy is necessary. Kamkov's criticism of us
is unfounded. If starting this session we had initiated any steps whatever to reject or remove other elements, then Kamkov would be right.
But all of us unanimously accepted Martov's proposal to discuss peaceful ways of solving the crisis. And we were deluged by a hail of declarations. A systematic attack was conducted against us. . . . Without
hearing us out, not even bothering to discuss their own proposal, they
[the Mensheviks and SRs] immediately sought to fence themselves off
from us. . . . In our resolution we simply wanted to say, precisely,*

honestly, and openly, that despite their treachery we will continue our
efforts, we will lead the proletariat and the army to struggle and victory.

The quarrel over the fundamentally differing views of Martov and Trotsky dragged on into the night. Finally, a representative of the Left SRs demanded a break for fractional discussions, threatening an immediate Left SR walkout if a recess were not called. The question was put to a vote and passed at 2:40 A.M., Kamenev warning that the congress would resume its deliberations in half an hour. . . .

It was now well after midnight, and the situation of the cabinet in the Winter Palace was growing more desperate by the minute. The steady dwindling of loyalist forces had by this time left portions of the east wing almost completely unprotected. Through windows in this section of the building, insurgents, in increasing numbers, were able to infiltrate the palace. In their second-floor meeting-room, many of the ministers now slouched spiritlessly in easy chairs or, like Maliantovich, stretched out on divans, awaiting the end. Konovalov, smoking one cigarette after another, nervously paced the room, disappearing next door from time to time to use the one phone still in service. The ministers could hear shouts, muffled explosions, and rifle and machine gun fire as the officers and cadets who had remained loyal to them fought futilely to fend off revolutionary forces. Their moments of greatest apprehension occurred when the artillery shell from the Peter and Paul Fortress burst in the room above and, somewhat later, when two grenades thrown by infiltrating sailors from an upper gallery exploded in a downstairs hall. Two cadets injured in the latter incident were carried to Kishkin for first aid.

Every so often Palchinsky popped in to try to calm the ministers, each time assuring them that the insurgents worming their way into the palace were being apprehended, and that the situation was still under control. Maliantovich recorded one of these moments: "Around one o'clock at night, or perhaps it was later, we learned that the procession from the Duma had set out. We let the guard know. . . . Again noise. . . . By this time we were accustomed to it. Most probably the Bolsheviks had broken into the palace once more, and, of course, had again been disarmed. . . . Palchinsky walked in. Of course, this was the case. Again they had let themselves be disarmed without resistance. Again, there were many of them. . . . How many of them are in the palace? Who is actually holding the palace now: we or the Bolsheviks?"

Contrary to most accounts written in the Soviet Union, the Winter Palace was not captured by storm. Antonov himself subsequently recounted that by late evening "the attack on the palace had a completely disorganized character. . . . Finally, when we were able to ascertain that not many cadets remained, Chudnovsky and I led the attackers into the palace. By the time we entered, the cadets were offering no resistance." This must have occurred at close to 2:00 A.M., for at that time Konovalov phoned Mayor Shreider to report: "The Military Revolutionary Committee has burst in. . . . All we have is a small force of cadets. . . . Our arrest is imminent." Moments later, when Shreider called the Winter Palace back, a gruff voice replied: "What do you want? From where are you calling?" — to which Shreider responded, "I am calling from the city administration; what is going on there?" "I am the sentry," answered the unfamiliar voice at the other end of the phone. "There is nothing going on here."

In the intervening moments, the sounds outside the room occupied by the Provisional Government had suddenly become more ominous. "A noise flared up and began to rise, spread, and draw nearer," recalled Maliantovich. "Its varying sounds merged into one wave and at once something unusual, unlike the previous noises, resounded, something final. It was clear instantly that this was the end. . . . Those sitting or lying down jumped up and grabbed their overcoats. The tumult rose swiftly and its wave rolled up to us. . . . All this happened within a few minutes. From the entrance to the room of our guard came the shrill, excited shouts of a mass of voices, some single shots, the trampling of feet, thuds, shuffling, merging into one chaos of sounds and ever-mounting alarm."

Maliantovich adds that even then the small group of cadets outside the room where the ministers sat seemed ready to continue resistance; however, it was now apparent to everyone that "defense was useless and sacrifices aimless" — that the moment for surrender had finally arrived. Kishkin ordered the commander of the guard to announce the government's readiness to yield. Then the ministers sat down around the table and watched numbly as the door was flung open and, as Maliantovich described it, "a little man flew into the room, like a chip tossed by a wave, under the pressure of the mob which poured in and spread at once, like water, filling all corners of the room." The little man was Antonov. "The Provisional Government is here — what do you want?" Konovalov asked. "You are all under arrest," Antonov replied, as

Chudnovsky began taking down the names of the officials present and preparing a formal protocol. The realization that Kerensky, the prize they sought most of all, was not in the room, drove many of the attackers into a frenzy. "Bayonet all the sons of bitches on the spot!" someone yelled. Maliantovich records that it was Antonov who somehow managed to prevent the cabinet from being lynched, insisting firmly that "the members of the Provisional Government are under arrest. They will be confined to the Peter and Paul Fortress. I will not allow any violence against them."

The ministers were accompanied from the Winter Palace and through the Palace Square by a selected convoy of armed sailors and Red Guards and a swearing, mocking, fist-shaking mob. Because no cars were available, they were forced to travel to their place of detention on foot. As the procession neared the Troitsky Bridge, the crowd surrounding the ministers once again became ugly, demanding that they be beheaded and thrown into the Neva. This time, the members of the government were saved by the apparently random firing of a machine gun from an approaching car. At the sounds of the shots, machine gunners at the Peter and Paul Fortress, believing themselves under attack, also opened fire. Ministers, escorts, and onlookers scattered for cover. In the ensuing confusion, the prisoners were rushed across the bridge to the safety of the fortress.

The ministers were led into a small garrison club-room, lighted only by a smoky kerosene lamp. At the front of the room they found Antonov, seated at a small table, completing the protocol which Chudnovsky had begun preparing at the Winter Palace. Antonov read the document aloud, calling the roll of arrested officials and inviting each to sign it. Thereupon, the ministers were led to dank cells in the ancient Trubetskoi Bastion not far from where former tsarist officials had been incarcerated since February. Along the way Konovalov suddenly realized he was without cigarettes. Gingerly, he asked the sailor accompanying him for one and was relieved when the sailor not only offered him shag and paper but, seeing his confusion about what to do with them, rolled him a smoke. Just before the door of his cell banged shut, Nikitin found in his pocket a half-forgotten telegram from the Ukrainian Rada to the Ministry of Interior. Handing it to Antonov, he observed matter of factly: "I received this yesterday — now it's your problem."

At Smolny, meanwhile, the Congress of Soviets session had by now resumed. Ironically, it fell to Kamenev, who had fought tooth and nail against an insurrection for a month and a half, to announce the Provisional Government's demise. "The leaders of the counterrevolution ensconced in the Winter Palace have been seized by the revolutionary garrison," he barely managed to declare before complete pandemonium broke out in the hall. Kamenev went on to read the roll of former officials now incarcerated — at the mention of Tereshchenko, a name synonymous with the continuation of the hated war, the delegates erupted in wild shouts and applause once more. . . .

Apparently at this point at least a portion of the Menshevik-Internationalist fraction reentered the hall, and its spokesman, Kapelinsky, tried to turn the delegates' attention to Martov's idea of recessing the congress while a delegation was sent to sound out all socialist organizations about the creation of a representative democratic government. Before long, many of the delegates who now either ignored or booed Kapelinsky would regain interest in seeking an accommodation with moderate groups. But for the moment, in their initial ecstasy over the apparently painless triumph over the Kerensky regime, they were in no mood to do so. For the Bolsheviks, Kamenev summarily dismissed Kapelinsky's plea with the claim that the moderate socialists had only themselves to blame for the fact that Martov's proposal to search for peaceful ways of dealing with the crisis had not been implemented. At the same time, he proposed that Trotsky's resolution condemning the Mensheviks and SRs be tabled, thus leaving the door partly open for the resumption of relations with them.

As the Menshevik-Internationalists again walked out of the hall, Lunacharsky rose to present, for the congress' immediate adoption, a manifesto written by Lenin "To All Workers, Soldiers, and Peasants," endorsing the Petrograd uprising; decreeing the transfer of supreme political authority into the hands of the congress and of local soviets everywhere in Russia; and, in the most general terms, outlining the immediate plan of the new soviet regime. This historic proclamation, ultimately the source of Soviet political authority, read:

> To All Workers, Soldiers, and Peasants:
>   The Second All-Russian Congress of Soviets of Workers' and Soldiers' Deputies has opened. It represents the great majority of the

soviets, including a number of deputies of peasant soviets. The prerogatives of the Central Executive Committee of the compromisers are ended.

Supported by an overwhelming majority of the workers, soldiers, and peasants, and basing itself on the victorious insurrection of the workers and the garrison of Petrograd, the congress hereby resolves to take governmental power into its own hands.

The Provisional Government is deposed and most of its members are under arrest.

The Soviet authority will at once propose a democratic peace to all nations and an immediate armistice on all fronts. It will safeguard the transfer without compensation of all land — landlord, imperial, and monastery — to the peasant committees; it will defend the soldiers' rights, introducing a complete democratization of the army; it will establish workers' control over industry; it will insure the convocation of the Constituent Assembly on the date set; it will supply the cities with bread and the villages with articles of first necessity; and it will secure to all nationalities inhabiting Russia the right of self-determination.

The congress resolves that all local authority shall be transferred to the soviets of workers', soldiers', and peasants' deputies, which are charged with the task of enforcing revolutionary order.

The congress calls upon the soldiers in the trenches to be watchful and steadfast. The Congress of Soviets is confident that the revolutionary army will know how to defend the revolution against all imperialistic attempts until the new government has concluded a democratic peace which it is proposing directly to all nations.

The new government will take every measure to provide the revolutionary army with all necessities, by means of a determined policy of requisition from and taxation of the propertied classes. Care will be taken to improve the position of the soldiers' families.

The Kornilovites — Kerensky, Kaledin, and others — are endeavoring to lead troops against Petrograd. Several regiments, deceived by Kerensky, have already joined the insurgents.

Soldiers! Resist Kerensky, who is a Kornilovite! Be on guard!

Railwaymen! Stop all echelons sent by Kerensky against Petrograd! Soldiers, Workers, Employees! The fate of the revolution and democratic peace is in your hands!

Long live the Revolution!

> The All-Russian Congress of Soviets of
> Workers' and Soldiers' Deputies
> Delegates from the Peasants' Soviets

the city, and killing anyone who opposed it." The Moscow Soviet's chairman Viktor Nogin brought the first accurate report to the October 26 meeting of the Soviet executive committee. Nogin, a member of the Bolshevik Central Committee, had opposed the insurrection and now stressed the defensive nature of the seizure of power, lamenting that all socialist parties would not rally behind the presidium of the Congress of Soviets.

> *Individual representatives of the Mensheviks and SRs told me that they would not separate from us in this responsible and difficult moment of the Russian Revolution. I was certain that during the October revolution, as happened in February, all socialists would be in one camp, that other parties would not break with us, would not betray us, leaving us alone to walk into the fire. I was certain that at the Congress of Soviets all parties would try to unite and find a common language.*

But the Mensheviks and some SRs had demonstratively walked out of the congress, leaving moderate Bolsheviks like Nogin indeed alone to walk into the fire.

This isolation contributed to the embattled mentality of the leaders of Moscow's October. Convinced that the Bolshevik party alone could not rule, but that the seizure of power, once begun, must be played out to the end, Moscow Bolsheviks reluctantly made preparations to support the rising in the capital city. Their reluctance, the sense of betrayal by the old comrades with whom they had amicably quarreled through the summer, their exaggerated fear of the forces of the opposition all contributed to the indecision that prolonged the struggle for power in Moscow.

For ten days, starting on October 25, local power hung in the balance. The sequence of events of those days, elements of which are so exhaustively recalled by every contemporary memoirist, are not easily reconstructed. The parties of the class struggle soon lined up behind two "fighting centers." The Moscow Soviet elected its own Military Revolutionary Committee on October 25, primarily for defensive purposes, while the opponents of soviet power rallied behind a Committee of Public Safety, which drew its members from the city duma. Significantly, there were no representatives of the Provisional Government on the committee formed presumably to defend that government. Neither group appeared to want to take action; both claimed their purposes were defensive only. Indeed, the goal of both sides was to ensure the convo-

cation of the Constituent Assembly, still seen by all parties as the
ultimate arbiter of the fate of the revolution. The banner headline of the
Bolsheviks' *Sotsial-Demokrat* announcing the soviet victory in Petrograd in fact proclaimed, "The Convocation of the Constituent Assembly Is Guaranteed: Power has been Transferred to the Soviets."

Since neither side wished to begin offensive operations, military
action began in Moscow only on October 27 after two days of unsuccessful negotiations between representatives of the Military Revolutionary Committee and the Committee of Public Safety. Street skirmishing
between progovernment military cadets (*junkers*) and revolutionary soldiers began on the night of October 27 with an exchange of fire in Red
Square. The Kremlin, at first in the hands of troops loyal to the Soviet,
was surrendered (some said by deception) to the Committee of Public
Safety. During the next two days, the military position of the Soviet side
deteriorated, and defenders of soviet power feared imminent annihila-
tion. On October 28, Nogin bravely set out from Soviet headquarters
on Tverskaia street to the nearby duma building in order to negotiate.
On the way he was arrested, taken to the military barracks opposite the
Kremlin, insulted, and threatened with bayonets before being released.
His chauffeur later reported overhearing plans of these same troops to
blow up the Kremlin. In the Soviet headquarters that night, secretaries
were busy destroying papers; the Military Revolutionary Committee
prepared to go down fighting. In the cramped one-room office of the
Central Bureau of Trade Unions, union activists decided to issue a call
for a general strike. They had no typewriter but would not have used it if
they had, for fear the sound of typing would reveal their presence to the
armed students who had laid siege to the area.

Also on the twenty-eighth, neutral elements led by the all-Russian
railway union executive committee (Vikzhel) attempted to negotiate an
end to the fighting. Both protagonists in Moscow agreed to a twenty-
four-hour cease-fire; Vikzhel, members of the Menshevik and SR parties, the Orthodox church's Metropolitan of Moscow all tried to reach
some compromise that would avert the feared civil war. Moderate
socialists continued to insist on an interim government formed from all
socialist parties — from the Popular Socialists to the Bolsheviks. (This
position was not unacceptable to many Bolsheviks; Nogin, Zinov'ev,
Kamenev, Rykov, and Miliutin even resigned from the Central Committee in part because party leaders refused to accept a broad-based
coalition of socialists, albeit under the structure of the soviets.) But the

ism. The Sokol'niki party secretary refused to allow local youth-group members to join the Red Guard and remained seated on a box of rifles to emphasize her point. But the youths dislodged her from her seat and set off anyway to join the action. Eduard Dune, sent to Moscow as part of the Tushino Red Guard, was amazed to find his co-worker Evel' in the thick of the fighting. Evel', who was currently scandalizing his mates by courting a nonproletarian office employee, had been rejected by the Tushino Red Guard because of his "hooliganism." Now, free of any chain of command, Evel' was fighting where he pleased — more "hooliganism," recalled Dune, not without a touch of envy.

Most Red Guards did not participate in any action. Memoirs suggest the main activities of these combatants were searching for arms and patrolling factories and other vulnerable points in the outlying working-class districts. Closer to the action, women served mostly as messengers between raion and central headquarters and as nurses. Most of the fighting took place in the city center and in the adjacent neighborhoods of Zamoskvorech'e. This raion boasted the city's largest Red Guard contingent of perhaps 1,500, but the most important military units here were in fact soldiers from several reserve infantry regiments and from a detachment of about 850 veterans of the front only just released from imprisonment for revolutionary behavior. (These were the soldiers marching through Red Square to the aid of the Military Revolutionary Committee on October 27 who became the first targets of the Committee of Public Safety's military cadets.)

The military objectives of the Red Guard in Moscow (as in Petrograd) were first, the main centers of communication — bridges, newspaper offices, telegraph and telephone stations — and second, stores of arms. Since neither side fielded large military detachments, there were no sieges, pitched battles, or assaults on barricaded enclaves. Late in the fray, the Military Revolutionary Committee gained control of some artillery and used it to shell the Kremlin from the vantage point of the Sparrow Hills several miles away. At the same time, outlying units of Red Guards uncovered reserves of arms in the railway yards near Sokol'niki; these they provided to Red Guards now arriving from provincial towns and factory settlements to aid in the struggle. It is possible that by the end of the fighting, the Military Revolutionary Committee could count on up to 30,000 armed supporters, but by then they were not really needed.

More difficult to uncover is the situation in the factory districts surrounding the center. With the heaviest concentration of the fighting directed at central focuses of local power, there was nothing really for the workers in the outskirts to do. Workers in the southernmost Danilovskii district feared those cossacks last reported on the march from Kaluga and set up barricades to prevent their entry into the city. But most Red Guards mustered their units in their factory courtyards and waited for something to happen. On the critical October 28, the Military Revolutionary Committee finally called for a general strike to obstruct the forces of the Committee of Public Safety, but there had been little industrial activity in any case; traffic was hindered by the dangerous situation in the city center, and who could work when the sound of gunfire could be heard rattling through the old city? A bizarre sense of holiday prevailed. Some workers gathered at their plants in order to hear the latest political news; others arrived to drink with their fellows. A Red Guard courier recalled arriving wounded at a plant whose workers were drinking and playing cards. They laughed at first at her appeal for help; but when they saw she was bleeding, they volunteered to form a squad and fight the opposition.

The prevailing climate of nonparticipation in the factory districts can be read two ways. There were those workers, like Eduard Dune's father, a Menshevik, who did not himself volunteer but who sympathized with the cause his son had gone to defend. The card players and the defenders of Danilovka might also be included in this category, and there were surely many more. But the prevalent passivity was read another way by the Menshevik and SR press: in Zamoskvorech'e, reported the SRs' *Trud*, the Military Revolutionary Committee's cause was unpopular, and Bolshevik leaders could not rouse the workers to active participation. The Mensheviks' *Vpered* (both of these parties were of course officially extremely hostile to the insurrection) charged that Bolsheviks had to threaten repressive measures in order to enlist Zamoskvorech'e workers in the fighting brigades.

I believe that the passivity of most Moscow factory workers during October can indeed be seen as a commentary on their attitudes about soviet power and its forcible seizure. I have argued above that resolutions were easily passed when no more serious commitment was called for. Politically, the majority of the city's working population probably favored soviet power, but not so strongly that they were willing to risk civil war or to die for it. Those workers and soldiers who joined the fighting, like the SR Sablin above, did so out of a belief that they were

ants and their emerging revolutionary institutions, but his view of the working class seems shaped by the Menshevik historical bias predominant in the West: the Russian working class was so recently formed from the peasantry that workers' political responses in 1917 were insufficiently mature.[1] Cultural activities could not possibly be carried on by workers such as these, for example, so Keep asserts that " 'education and culture' was often a euphemism for political propaganda." Such workers' political activity, in Keep's interpretation, was determined almost exclusively by economic need — the lower the wage and bread ration, the more radical the political response. Moreover, Keep, like Chamberlin, stresses the radicalism of the unskilled: untutored peasant-workers were quick to respond to radical solutions like factory seizures. Finally, Keep describes the radicalized working class in October: "Driven to near-despair by the economic crisis, their nerves kept on edge by incessant propaganda, they responded uncritically to the appeals of a party that promised untold blessings once 'soviet power' had been achieved." Keep devotes more attention to the activities of workers than previous historians, and he has assembled much information on the scope of the labor movement. But his workers seem to proceed toward their reflex radicalism in one great wave, and the complexities within the working class which might tend to soften his view are ignored.

Such are some conventional views of workers when they are treated as part of the more general social and political history of 1917. How has this more specialized study of Moscow workers added to or altered this view?

First of all, the view that the workers are one uniform mass must be rejected. Urbanized workers possessed different values from those of workers recently migrated from the countryside; workers in small shops faced organizational constraints different from those confronted by workers in large plants; workers living in purely working-class neighborhoods formed different attitudes from those of workers living in socially mixed neighborhoods. Metalworkers, because of these and other characteristics, behaved differently in 1917 from textile workers; former Petrograd metalworkers even behaved differently from Muscovite

---

[1] Keep's view can be traced in part to his use of sources. He treats Soviet sources with due skepticism, but seems to accept the reliability of the bourgeois press in 1917. He reserves his greatest skepticism, however, for sources generated by the workers themselves. For example, he rejects the value of using workers' resolutions as historical evidence.

metalists. Printers, despite a similar urban background, generally rejected the metalists' positions on political issues.

The range of diversities and antagonisms among workers themselves has been demonstrated over and over in the preceding pages. The workers in artisanal trades were the ones who most quickly organized trade unions after February. Urbanized metalworkers were the earliest to advocate soviet power; textile workers who lived near metalworkers later on endorsed soviet power but for primarily economic reasons. Metalworkers least of all cast their votes for the hugely popular peasant-oriented Socialist Revolutionary party in the June city duma election. Workers in small plants tended to be more generous toward soldiers than were workers in large plants. Workers with relatively high wages tended to strike more often and more easily than poorly paid workers.

Nonetheless, having analyzed the molecular structure of the working class in more detail than previous studies, does not this study arrive at the familiar conclusion that there was by October a radicalized, unified working class? The workers were radical, yes, in the sense that many of them supported soviet power in one way or another. They were unified, too, in the sense of common class identity. But such adjectives oversimplify the important political and social processes of 1917; and by examining these processes, this study can add to the prevailing views of the revolution.

This study has emphasized revolutionary dynamics as well as the revolution's October result. The workers who took to the streets in February were the very same individuals who had supported soviet power in the autumn, but they had changed in many ways. Eight months of relative political freedom may not be long compared to the evolution of Anglo-American civic traditions, but they permitted a modicum of intensive political education for the Moscow working class. The experience of electing deputies, debating resolutions, discussing contributions, and choosing political parties all helped to educate workers and to develop their political as well as class consciousness. Workers learned how to differentiate among political parties. They learned how to conduct meetings, how to express themselves. They learned how to evaluate the opinions and behavior of their own colleagues and of those outside their class.

Not all workers learned at the same rate; they certainly did not all arrive at the same political conclusions. The militant metalworkers at the Moscow telephone works soon adjusted their extremist positions to keep pace with political development. . . . Lenin, Trotsky, and Chamberlin appear to attribute organizational weakness to the organizations themselves, to the organizations' insufficient radicalism, to their failure to respond to grass-roots political changes. In fact, the organizational history of 1917 reveals the legacy of the relatively rapid formation of the Russian working class and the years of repression by the tsarist political system. Perhaps a revolution teaches political and class consciousness in eight months, but organizational success took not just consciousness, but practice as well. Such practice had been limited to the urban cultural institutions that had attracted Moscow's workers before 1917; only after February did organizational practice finally become available at all levels of working-class life. A newspaper report in June from the suburb of Tushino announced that even the children were organizing. In 1914, children there played war games, but now they played at democracy. Tushino children constructed red banners with such slogans as "Long live free children," they conducted singing processions through the Provodnik factory, and they held "formal meetings, elected chairmen and committees."

The urbanized segment of the labor force provided the critical element in whatever organizational stability existed in 1917; when the Tushino children grew up, they would add to that element. But ironically, the success of soviet power and then the demands of the civil-war emergency took just these experienced cadres out of the factories and the city, and in the 1920s the slow process would have to begin again, under new conditions. The further implications of the workers' organizational immaturity will not be explored here, but many questions arise. Hannah Arendt has suggested that the collapse of independent workers' institutions after October (very well documented by John Keep) contributed to an atomization of society which weakened resistance to Stalin's consolidation of power. Did the failure of these working-class institutions in fact facilitate the rise of Stalin or someone like him to centralized, absolute rule? Clearly the questions raised by this approach to the Russian Revolution suggest new items for the agenda of study of postrevolutionary Soviet society.

The primary focus of this study has been the workers of Moscow in order to understand the role of workers in 1917 and to explain the complex processes that culminated in the October revolution. But an equally important goal has been to examine the revolution outside the capital city of Petrograd; and while this study has not explored the revolutionary experience of Moscow in its entirety, some new insights nonetheless emerge.

Both 1917 revolutions in Moscow are usually viewed as slow-motion instant replays of the Petrograd revolutions. "The overturn in Moscow was only an echo of the insurrection in Petrograd," writes Trotsky of February. In October Moscow's workers continued to be more backward than Petrograd's; they lacked fighting experience, and therefore the insurrection in the second capital was not so quickly successful. The social, economic, and political analyses of the preceding chapters, however, indicate not that Moscow's working class was more backward, but that it was more socially complex than Petrograd's. Skilled metalworkers played an important role in the revolution wherever they were, but these workers were not the only ones involved in the revolution, and the degree of a city's revolutionary zeal cannot be linked only with the numerical or proportional size of its skilled metalist work force. Moscow's workers, as has been seen, interacted with one another and with members of other social classes, producing more muted and less impulsive responses to such events as the April crisis and the July insurrection.

The experience of Moscow suggests that there was more than one model of the revolutionary process in 1917 rather than time-lagged variants of the Petrograd model. Further work on other Russian cities and regions in 1917 might well produce a new reassessment of the significance of Petrograd and of the process of the revolution. If Petrograd, as the center of government, had had Moscow's mixed social composition, would the capital city have been polarized along class lines so early? Was there an alternative to the sharp class antagonisms that Petrograd transmitted to less-polarized provinces? Did this example of polarization affect the development of class consciousness in Moscow and elsewhere? Or was Petrograd's radicalism, and Moscow's moderation, due as much to the attraction of the capital's factories for underground socialist revolutionaries as to its social composition? At any rate, like different strata of workers, Moscow and Petrograd interacted in 1917; it is important to remember that one did not merely follow the other.

A final goal of this study has been to demonstrate the value and feasibility of social history in its application to the Russian Revolution. The results of this approach have modified common perceptions of the role and significance of workers in 1917; they have indicated the complexity of the revolutionary process. There is more work to be done, however, in order to understand the revolution and its consequences. Further studies of this and other revolutions must continue to look at processes, at complexities, at contradictions. The example of Moscow in 1917 can supply some building blocks for future work and future comparisons: the categories of peasant versus worker, socialist versus class consciousness, artisanal versus factory work can be applied to other contexts. In time, historians and readers will have a new synthesis and a deeper understanding of the Russian Revolution and the process of social change.

Donald J. Raleigh

The Revolution on the Volga

If one considers Moscow a "second capital" and Baku a city of the ethnic periphery, Raleigh's study of the Volga town of Saratov was the first look at the revolution in an ethnically Russian provincial setting. A student of Alexander Rabinowitch at Indiana University, Raleigh has taught at the University of Hawaii and the University of North Carolina. The editor of *Soviet Studies in History,* he is the translator of Burdzhalov, and is currently extending his study of Saratov into the Civil War period. Combining political and social history, Raleigh shows that Saratov was neither behind Petrograd in its radicalism nor simply following patterns set in central Russia. In his conclusion, presented here, he shows that the nature of Bolshevism differed from region to region and should not be simply equated to the best-known images that flow from Petrograd.

Reprinted from Donald J. Raleigh, *Revolution on the Volga: 1917 in Saratov.* Copyright © 1986 by Cornell University. Used by permission of the publisher, Cornell University Press.

Concentrating almost exclusively on Petrograd and to a lesser extent on Moscow, Western historical writing on the revolution until recently has ignored popular moods and attitudes in the country at large. For this reason alone, provincial Russia needs to be brought into our understanding of the revolution. When we look beyond the confines of Petrograd, it becomes clear that many interpretations of 1917, when translated into a local setting, are glaringly inadequate. This investigation of Saratov challenges those a priori evaluations of October that explain what happened in terms of Lenin's and Trotsky's unscrupulousness (and their opponents' fateful mistakes) or in terms of conspiracy, historical accident, or political manipulation. This investigation belies the arguments of historians who maintain that the Bolsheviks came to power in October because of the discipline and conspiratorial nature of the party itself, which imposed its will on a reluctant, indifferent, or politically immature people. This investigation also brings into question Soviet historians' image of a tightly knit, centralized party and of a meticulously planned insurrection in October. Such interpretations often color one's assessment of the course of Soviet history and less consciously weigh upon attitudes toward the Soviet Union today. Moreover, Western monographs and general histories tend to suggest that provincial Russia was nothing more than a torpid partner to developments in the capital cities. If this work on Saratov draws attention to revolutionary politics in provincial Russia, raises questions about standard accounts of the revolution, and contributes to a broader understanding of what took place in 1917, it has served its purpose.

The tsarist political system with all of its shortcomings had provided rich soil for the growth of an opposition movement. The autocracy had alienated much of the professional middle class. It had failed to satiate the peasants' hunger for land. It had hampered workers' attempts to mitigate the social ills of industrialization and the arbitrariness of authority relations at the workplace. Then came war. The socioeconomic disequilibrium and extraordinary movement of people caused by it and the government's suspicion of public initiative during the war furthered discontent, exacerbating antigovernment feelings even within official circles.

Dealing a death blow to the centralized state structure, the February Revolution swept away all of the impediments that had kept the

Russian masses out of the country's political life; now an array of other considerations led to October. The moderate socialists' theoretical conceptualization of the revolution as bourgeois-democratic undermined their party programs after February: in Saratov it caused them to abandon the legitimacy of the popular organs set up in 1917; and it eventually led to a rupture between party leaders and the rank and file, who came to share the Bolsheviks' call for an all-soviet government. Although riddled with compromises, retreats, setbacks, and confusion, the Bolshevik party offered the most consistently plebian program to the Russian people, and rode to power at the top of self-legitimized popular organs — soviets, factory committees, trade unions, Red Guard detachments, soldier committees, and the rest. In Saratov as in Petrograd, Moscow, and Baku, the Bolshevik platform of land, peace, and bread and the slogan "All Power to the Soviets" appealed increasingly to common people, whose expectations often had soared to unreasonable levels while their economic situation deteriorated. The Bolsheviks' combination of tactical flexibility with a militant class interpretation of Russian political life (in the inclusive Russian sense of the upper classes, *verkhi*, pitted against the lower elements, *nizy*) proved successful in a fluid setting characterized by economic ruin, growing anarchism, and a tottering structure of voluntary authority relationships. The October Revolution *was not so much a Bolshevik Revolution as a triumph of all radical groups* that had broken decisively with those elements that supported further coalition with the bourgeoisie — Bolsheviks, Left SRs. SR Maximalists. Menshevik Internationalists, and anarchists. This convergence of purpose explains the spread of Soviet power throughout Saratov province.

Two broad political contests actually took place in 1917. The first involved the competition between Russian socialism and Russian liberalism. It found expression in the system of dual power that surfaced after the February Revolution. The second involved the competition between radical socialism and moderate socialism. It found expression in the battle over whether or not an all-socialist government could rule Russia. To understand the dynamics of the move toward a class solution to the question of Russia's political future posed by the February Revolution, it is necessary to weigh the impact of popular attitudes in Saratov toward political power and toward the new plebian institutions formed after the fall of the autocracy. For the first time since the Revolution of 1905, the people were brought into politics; what is most striking about their behavior is the degree to which socialist ideas and rhetoric had shaped it during the preceding generation. This conclusion raises further doubts about the viability of a democratic representative government for Russia. Ronald G. Suny has noted that "despite frequent claims of detachment and objectivity, scholars often make their judgments about the revolution and the Soviet Union against the standard of quite different European and American experiences." It is time for us to explore the implications of the fact that Russia's political evolution differed from our own.

The unresolved question of Russia's political future acquired an institutionalized form in the compromise system of dual power embodied in the parallel existence of the Provisional Government and the Petrograd Soviet, which soon spoke out on behalf of the newly formed popular organs established throughout the country. When translated into a provincial setting, the dual authority fashioned in Petrograd took on new shape. The weakness of Russian liberalism was much more apparent in Saratov and throughout much of provincial Russia in general, where political power had already been concentrated in the hands of local soviets in April. The dilemma posed by this unexpected situation could remain unresolved as long as the forces of "the democracy" and of the propertied elements appeared to be working for the same common goals. Why was this, and why did the truce ultimately break down?

First, the Provisional Government and its provincial counterparts, the public executive committees, claimed to be the legitimate heirs to the Imperial Duma, pending convocation of a constituent assembly. The Petrograd Soviet did not challenge this fundamental interpretation of the revolution. Second, at the local level the socialists had entered the public executive committees from the very beginning, and often played the most important role in them of the various political groups. In Saratov, socialists took over the public executive committee, which became an extension of the Soviet. Socialist sympathies prevailed overwhelmingly at the local level and it was tacitly understood that any permanent solution to the problem of political power would reflect this reality. (In the July Duma elections, the socialist parties polled 82.3 percent of the popular vote.) Third, the moderates believed that Russia could not sustain social revolution until objective historical conditions had ripened.

But Lenin's return to Russia in April and the collapse of the Provisional Government over the Miliukov Affair, which pushed the Mensheviks and Socialist Revolutionaries into a coalition with the liberals, exposed the fragility of the compromise. Now only the Bolsheviks maintained that Russia could move immediately to establish a socialist government without the participation of the country's propertied elements. Insisting that his party should not support the Provisional Government, Lenin lobbied for a transfer of power to the soviets; this turned out to be one of the most important tactical positions taken by a political party in 1917. The leaders of the moderate socialists, seeking to prevent social war, saw their historical mission as that of harmonizing the discordant political voices raised throughout the country. Entering the coalition ministry, they believed that they were saving war-torn Russia from a counterrevolutionary restoration and from the demagogic appeals of the Bolsheviks. In retrospect, however, the moderate socialists' co-optation into the bourgeois government blurred the meaning of dual power at both the national and the local level and failed to resolve the differences they had with Russian liberalism. More important, it forced the Rakitnikovs, Chertkovs, and Topuridzes eventually to reject their own revolutionary programs, revealing the extent to which many of the moderate leaders had come to accept nonradical, compromise — democratic — politics. The Russian political center remained socialist, but in becoming respectable it had lost its revolutionary fire.

Ironically, after their entry into the government the moderates tried to curb the power of the soviets in internal affairs. In striving to revive the prestige of the Duma, the moderates sacrificed their mass support and took the country one step closer toward civil war. As various election results in Saratov strongly suggest, once the failure of the Kornilov Affair indicated that a peaceful resolution to the question of political power was unlikely, some of the less radical socialists moved into the liberal camp, while the more militant elements within these parties now embraced Bolshevism or formed separate factions that agreed with the Bolsheviks that only a transfer of power to the soviets could save Russia. A vote for Bolshevism in local terms stood for an all-soviet socialist government, but since only the Bolshevik party and splinter groups from the other parties advocated a transfer of power to the soviets, it perhaps is not surprising that the new regime eventually turned into an exclusively Bolshevik one. It was Chertkov, a local Menshevik leader, former chairman of the Saratov Soviet and president of the City Duma, who led the struggle in Saratov against a transfer of power to the soviets.

In view of the deep social tensions within Russian society and of the strength of socialist sentiments among workers, soldiers, and peasants, it is possible that a broadly based socialist regime that included representation from democratically elected local bodies, municipal and government workers, shopkeepers and people from cooperatives (*odnorodnoe sotsialisticheskoe pravitel'stvo*), could have been established in Russia even without war. It is difficult to imagine the Bolsheviks' coming to power and creating essentially a one-party government, however, if Russia somehow had withdrawn from the war or had avoided it altogether. The war split apart Russian socialism and led to the terrible economic situation that magnified social tensions. Moreover, without war there would have been no Saratov garrison, and the soldiers, after all, played an enormous role in establishing Soviet power. The ambiguous political structure set up in March combined with efforts to continue fighting, on the one hand, and the Bolsheviks' rejection of it and of the Provisional Government, on the other, contributed immensely to the events of October. The collapse of the First Provisional Government in April had exposed both the divisions between upper- and lower-class Russia and the tactical differences within the socialist camp, which became more pronounced during debates over the June offensive and further strained as a result of the July uprising in Petrograd and the move toward Soviet power in Tsaritsyn. Meanwhile, the democratic elements had begun shifting to the left as the coalition government failed to end the war and halt the ongoing economic ruin. In early August the Bolsheviks began to recover from temporary setbacks caused by the abortive July uprising, while the Menshevik and SR organizations experienced growing apathy and disillusionment within their ranks. Left-wing factions in both groups, often composed of the rank and file, moved willy-nilly toward a Bolshevik government by accepting the need to break decisively with the bourgeoisie.

Efforts to suppress Bolshevism in July, followed by the failure of a military restoration in August, shattered hopes for a liberal or peaceful solution to the question of Russia's political future. Force failed to curb the revolutionary tide and the disintegration of state power; instead the threat of counterrevolution revitalized the soviets, whose deputies across much of Russia now elected Bolshevik and other leftist representatives. Isolated from the lower classes, the liberals remained politically vulnerable. Dissension ripped Russian socialism apart. In the popular view the Bolsheviks became inseparably associated with Soviet power, whereas

the moderate socialists, clinging stubbornly to coalition with the bourgeoisie and to their belief in the righteousness of a revolutionary war against the Central Powers, lost credibility.

Although they faced determined opposition from moderate leaders, the Saratov Bolsheviks controlled the Soviet's executive bodies in September. Throughout the month workers and soldiers passed resolutions demanding a transfer of power to the soviets, the dissolution of the State Duma, and the arming of workers. Across Russia people expected a promulgation of Soviet power at the upcoming Second Congress of Soviets; others feared a Bolshevik coup in the name of the soviets beforehand. In either case, the strength of the Bolsheviks and other leftist groups within the context of the soviets was manifest. The Bolsheviks won in Saratov because they stood for Soviet power and in this regard enjoyed institutional legitimacy. Once Soviet power was challenged, civil war began in earnest.

What has this study told us about the nature of local Bolshevism? Saratov Bolshevism bore the telltale marks of local conditions. Since the turn of the century a strong measure of comradeship had united the opposition movement in Saratov and weakened the impact of partisan politics, which were a pervasive element of émigré politics. Interaction among local activists, party centers, émigré groups, and exiles had created a fluid relationship. Conditioned by the peculiarities of the Volga underground, Saratov Bolshevism had developed a healthy respect for local needs, which affected its response to party tactics in general.

In his two-volume investigation of the Petrograd Bolsheviks, Alexander Rabinowitch stressed the historical significance of the "dynamic relationship that existed in 1917 within the top Bolshevik hierarchy, as well as between it, the ostensibly subordinate elements of the party, and the masses." Rabinowitch also called attention to the relatively flexible structure of the party as it emerged from the underground and to its tactical responsiveness to the prevailing mass mood. As in Petrograd, the price of the same uneven but ultimately large growth in membership of the Saratov Bolshevik organization was a proportionate increase in problems of control at all levels. The problem of control was evinced in the tactical debates taking place within the Saratov committee itself and in its relations with the center and neighboring party organizations. At the provincial level the Saratov Bolsheviks' efforts to contain their

Tsaritsyn comrades' radical inclinations strained relations between leaders in the two cities. At the regional level the Saratov Bolsheviks failed to establish an oblast committee because of the rivalry between the Saratov and Samara organizations. (Samara's Kuibyshev as well as Tsaritsyn's Minin considered Antonov too conciliatory.) To be sure, the Saratov committee strove to adhere to policy guidelines formulated in Petrograd. But first it had to ascertain what they were and decipher the mixed signals it sometimes received from the center before adapting the measures to local conditions. The party center presented a far from confident image to provincial leaders, and the many debates that rocked the Central Committee (over Lenin's April Theses, the June demonstrations, the July Days, the vitality of the soviets, political power, and later the question of an insurrection) complicated politics along the banks of the Volga. At times the Saratov committee ignored directives from Petrograd (e.g., it refused to drop the slogan "All Power to the Soviets" after the Sixth Party Congress in July deemed it inappropriate). Likewise, the Tsaritsyn Bolsheviks came close to effecting a purely local seizure of power: the Astrakhan Bolsheviks remained part of a united Social Democratic organization until October; and the Samara Bolsheviks actively participated in the deliberations of the city's public executive committee until late fall.

Much has been written about the rapid radicalization of the Petrograd masses. This study has shown that the deepening of the revolution in Saratov, as in Baku, did not lag behind developments in Petrograd to any great extent. In fact, the early consolidation of power in the hands of the Saratov Soviet and simultaneous collapse of the Public Executive Committee suggest that provincial populations often had to deal with one of the most important issues of the Revolution before it was resolved at the national level. Events in Tsaritsyn show that given the right circumstances, provincial populations could be as leftist in their political orientation as inhabitants of the capital. Petrograd Bolsheviks captured only 10 percent of the votes in elections to the city soviet in July 1917 but more than 50 percent in September elections. Scoring similar successes at approximately the same time, Saratov Bolsheviks, too, benefited from the perceived threat of counterrevolution and from the tottering economy and breakdown in law and order.

Because of the failure of traditional pillars of authority before 1917, workers, soldiers, and peasants had placed considerable hope in the

ability of their own, unrepresentative class institutions to effect change. Even though many questions remain unanswered regarding Saratov's working class, some recent findings on the political behavior of the Moscow and Petrograd proletariat appear to hold true for Saratov workers, who became radicalized in 1917 by participating in a frustrating struggle to improve their economic position. The crumbling economic structure caused by the war turned workers against the government and eventually against those socialist parties that supported it. Profound suspicion toward the propertied elements and industrialists expressed itself in workers' efforts to better their economic situation already in March, and as crisis after crisis broke out, workers came to perceive Soviet power as a rational solution to their economic straits and to political impasse.

Not to be viewed as a monolithic social group, Saratov's work force responded variously to the political climate of 1917. Skilled workers — and not "dark," semipeasant unskilled types — were the first to become radicalized. Workers evacuated from Russia's Baltic and Polish provinces as early as April advocated Soviet power. But one must not ignore skilled local workers in the metal-processing industry, in the railroad yards and on tram lines, and in the large mechanized food- and lumber-processing plants, who contributed to the Saratov labor movement many militant working-class activists. Unskilled workers toiling in the above-mentioned industries, especially in those in which revolutionaries had carried on underground agitational work the longest (flour milling, tobacco processing, vegetable oil, and transportation), also became swept into the labor movement and by fall helped swell Bolshevik ranks. In Tsaritsyn, for example, lumber workers and dock hands fell under the influence of their more militant comrades in the large metalworks and of the unruly frontoviki.

The Saratov garrison and within it the frontoviki particularly played a greater role than the working class in turning the tide in favor of Soviet power locally. The impact of the garrisons was even more important in the uezd towns, where Soviet power was first recognized by radicalized soldiers. Strong before February, antiwar feelings gradually infected the entire Saratov garrison once institutional vehicles for expressing soldiers' aspirations were set up and the old command structure ceased to exist. The continuation of the war soon became the most important issue as far as the masses of soldiers were concerned, and after the moderate socialists, especially the Socialist Revolutionaries, entered the coalition ministry in May, the door to victory was left wide open for any group that denounced the war. The garrison's conversion to Bolshevism began when the SR party joined the liberals in pressing for the continuation of the war to a victorious end. To those in the barracks and trenches there was little difference between a revolutionary war and an imperialist one. The June offensive and the conservative resurgence in July and August meant a revival in discipline and the postponement of any hopes of returning to the countryside to share in the division of land. Visits to home villages for furloughs or for field work, combined with the impact of the frontoviki and of a swell of deserters, deepened the soldiers' discontent. Spreading tales about horror and carnage at the front, the evacuated soldiers now refused to fight. There was no one to make them. The soldiers were, as one government report put it, "the irresponsible masters of the situation."

Although the Saratov garrison did not turn into a Bolshevik stronghold until fall, the move to the left deprived the opposition of any potential armed force and strengthened at a critical moment those groups that advocated a transfer of power to the soviets. Bolshevik popularity among soldiers remained tenuous, however. Saratov Bolshevik leaders, fully aware of the fragility of their hold over the garrison and the lack of cadre within the officer corps, avidly promoted a workers' Red Guard. As the events of the October Revolution in Saratov and the uezd towns show, the Bolshevik leaders' apprehensions over the reliability of the soldiers was warranted. Their Bolshevism was only skin deep.

Because the economic life of Saratov was based on the production, processing, and distribution of agricultural products, the peasant movement also left its mark on local developments. The magnitude of the Saratov peasant uprising sharpened political debates in the towns, resulting in a rupture between the peasants' self-propelled move toward satiating their land hunger and the call of the populist leaders for restraint. By fall the peasants' reluctance to sell grain had created food shortages in Saratov and upset deliveries to more industrialized provinces.

The broad forces that shaped agrarian relations and attitudes in Saratov province since the mid-nineteenth century explain what took place in the villages in 1917. The cumulative impact of the activities of several generations of revolutionaries, strained economic relationships, and the vitality of the commune account for the immediate move on the part of the peasantry against the economic advantages of the estate

owners and Stolypin peasants. Launching their assault against the land-owners already in March, the peasants quarreled over rents and the use of prisoners of war for farmwork. They seized forestland. The chronology and scope of the peasant movement in Saratov challenges widely accepted views in Western historical writing, which date the beginning of the agrarian movement for April and May.

In the Saratov countryside the February Revolution led to the spontaneous establishment of peasant organizations that promoted the interests of the communal peasants. Examination of the varied activities of the peasant executive committees shows that the mood of the countryside was far less cautious and patient than that of the urban-based leaders of the populist parties. In this regard subsequent developments in the Saratov villages underscored the weakness of the SR party's leadership. Once the moderate socialists entered the coalition government they became accountable for its hesitant agrarian program. Government efforts to curb the power of the peasant executive committees by establishing land committees and food-supply committees failed. Local activists and often government officials themselves, becoming increasingly sympathetic to the peasants' demands, pressured authorities to resolve the land question promptly. The failure to do so had the same consequence as the government's inability to end the war: it alienated a large element of the population and seriously challenged the hold the populist parties had over the villages. In the less remote rural areas populism split apart, and local-based militants now reached the same conclusion that many workers and soldiers had come to accept: only an all-soviet socialist government could end the war, distribute land, and set the economy right. Left SRs carried resolutions at the Second Saratov Province Peasant Congress, held in September, calling for an immediate transfer of land to those who tilled it and the establishment of an all-soviet government.

Despite the separate sets of demands, aspirations, and attitudes of Russian workers, soldiers, and peasants, then, a combination of factors brought the lower classes together, providing, as Michal Reiman so aptly put it, a "dividing line for . . . social upheaval." The class organs created by the February Revolution — soviets, factory committees, trade unions, military committees, soldiers' committees, armed guards, peasant committees, volost committees, and rural soviets — created a rival form of political representation outside conventional middle-class politics. Virtually all of these bodies viewed the legitimate institutions with distrust and suspicion, and sought to set up some sort of supervision or control over them. As the year progressed and the successive governments failed to solve the pressing socioeconomic problems, people came to believe that the propertied elements were acting in their own best interests. By the fall of 1917 the wide strata of workers, soldiers, and peasants had concluded that only an all-soviet government could solve the country's problems.

Vladimir Il'ich Lenin

Our Revolution

No history of 1917 can avoid the "question" of Lenin. Trotsky once asked, If there had been no Lenin, would there have been an October Revolution? Not surprisingly, he answered that another leader would have been found. Perhaps he had himself in mind. Though the figure of Lenin dominates our field of vision on the revolution, the effect of much of the recent writing on the revolution has been to reduce Lenin to human dimensions and to place him within the broader social dynamics of the revolution. Vladimir Il'ich Ulianov (1870–1924) was born in the Volga town of Simbirsk (now Ulianovsk) and educated as a lawyer. Joining the Social Democrats (Marxists) in the early 1890s, Ulianov (Lenin) developed his own perspective on the formation of workers' consciousness. Workers, he argued, required the intervention of socialist intellectuals in order to move beyond "trade-union consciousness" to full socialist consciousness. In his influential book *What Is to Be Done?* (1902), Lenin outlined his plan for a centralized underground party that could lead the working class to revolution. In 1903 the Russian Social Democratic Workers' Party split into the moderate Menshevik wing and the more radical Bolshevik wing, led by Lenin. In 1917 Lenin devised the strategy of militant opposition to the Provisional Government and the call for "All Power to the Soviets" that became increasingly popular among urban workers. In October he became chairman of the new Soviet government, a post he held until his premature death in January 1924. Here are two short articles by Lenin on his own understanding of the revolution.

The first article, "Vybory v uchreditel'noe sobranie i diktatura proletariata," was first published in Kommunisticheskii Internatsional, Nos. 7–8, December 1919. The second article, "O nashei revoliutsii (po povodu zapisok N. Sukhanova)," was first published in *Pravda* No. 117, May 30, 1923.

"The development of the productive forces of Russia has not attained the level that makes socialism possible." All the heroes of the Second International, including, of course, Sukhanov, beat the drums about this proposition. They keep harping on this incontrovertible proposition in a thousand different keys, and think that it is the decisive criterion of our revolution.

But what if the situation, which drew Russia into the imperialist world war that involved every more or less influential West-European country and made her a witness of the eve of the revolutions maturing or partly already begun in the East, gave rise to circumstances that put Russia and her development in a position which enabled us to achieve precisely that combination of a "peasant war" with the working-class movement suggested in 1856 by no less a Marxist than Marx himself as a possible prospect for Prussia?

What if the complete hopelessness of the situation, by stimulating the efforts of the workers and peasants tenfold, offered us the opportunity to create the fundamental requisites of civilisation in a different way from that of the West-European countries? Has that altered the general line of development of world history? Has that altered the basic relations between the basic classes of all the countries that are being, or have been, drawn into the general course of world history?

If a definite level of culture is required for the building of socialism (although nobody can say just what that definite "level of culture" is, for it differs in every West-European country), why cannot we begin by first achieving the prerequisites for that definite level of culture in a revolutionary way, and *then*, with the aid of the workers' and peasants' government and the Soviet system, proceed to overtake the other nations?

January 16, 1923

II

You say that civilisation is necessary for the building of socialism. Very good. But why could we not first create such prerequisites of civilisation in our country as the expulsion of the landowners and the Russian capitalists, and then start moving towards socialism? Where, in what books, have you read that such variations of the customary historical sequence of events are impermissible or impossible?

Napoleon, I think, wrote: *"On s'engage et puis . . . on voit."*

Rendered freely this means: "First engage in a serious battle and then see what happens." Well, we did first engage in a serious battle in October 1917, and then saw such details of development (from the standpoint of world history they were certainly details) as the Brest peace, the New Economic Policy, and so forth. And now there can be no doubt that in the main we have been victorious.

Our Sukhanovs, not to mention Social-Democrats still farther to the right, never even dream that revolutions could be made otherwise. Our European philistines never even dream that the subsequent revolutions in Oriental countries, which possess much vaster populations and a much vaster diversity of social conditions, will undoubtedly display even greater distinctions than the Russian revolution.

It need hardly be said that a textbook written on Kautskyan lines was a very useful thing in its day. But it is time, for all that, to abandon the idea that it foresaw all the forms of development of subsequent world history. It would be timely to say that those who think so are simply fools.

January 17, 1923

Lenin

Suggestions for Additional Reading

Since the classic studies by Sukhanov, Trotsky, and Chamberlin, the literature on Russia in 1917 has expanded tremendously. This brief bibliographical note does not include any of the works excerpted in this volume or referred to in the introductions or notes. Also, it is limited to literature available in English.

On the prerevolutionary socialist and labor movements, one might consult:

Abraham Ascher, *Pavel Axelrod and the Development of Menshevism* (Cambridge, MA: Harvard University Press, 1972).

Paul Avrich, *The Russian Anarchists* (Princeton, NJ: Princeton University Press, 1967).

Samuel H. Baron, *Plekhanov, the Father of Russian Marxism* (Stanford, CA: Stanford University Press, 1963).

Victoria E. Bonnell, *Roots of Rebellion: Workers' Politics and Organizations in St. Petersburg and Moscow, 1900–1914* (Berkeley, CA: University of California Press, 1983).

Leopold H. Haimson, *The Russian Marxists and the Origins of Bolshevism* (Cambridge, MA: Harvard University Press, 1955).

John L. H. Keep, *The Rise of Social Democracy in Russia* (Oxford, England: Oxford University Press, 1963).

Leonard Schapiro, *The Communist Party of the Soviet Union* (New York: Random House, 1959).

Allan K. Wildman, *The Making of a Worker's Revolution: Russian Social Democracy, 1891–1903* (Chicago: University of Chicago Press, 1967).

For discussions of the historiography of the Russian revolutions, see:

David Anin, "The February Revolution: Was the Collapse Inevitable?" *Soviet Studies*, XVIII, 4 (April 1967), pp. 435–457.

James Billington, "Six Views of the Russian Revolution," *World Politics*, XVIII, 3 (April 1966), pp. 452–473.

Ronald Grigor Suny, "Toward a Social History of the October Revolution, *American Historical Review*, LXXXVIII, 1 (February 1983), pp. 31–53.

General books on the Russian revolutions of 1917 include:

Marc Ferro, *The Russian Revolution of 1917* (London: Routledge and Kegan Paul, 1972); and *October 1917: A Social History of the Russian Revolution* (London: Routledge and Kegan Paul, 1980).

Daniel H. Kaiser, ed., *The Workers' Revolution in Russia, 1917: The View from Below* (New York: Cambridge University Press, 1987).

Marcel Liebman, *The Russian Revolution* (London: Jonathan Cape, 1970).

On the Provisional Government and the Soviet, one might look at:

Robert Paul Browder and Alexander F. Kerensky (eds.), *The Russian Provisional Government, 1917: Documents*, 3 vols. (Stanford, CA: Hoover Institution Press, 1961).

Ziva Galili, *The Menshevik Leaders in the Russian Revolution: Social Realities and Political Strategy* (Princeton, NJ: Princeton University Press, 1989).

Virgil D. Medlin and Steven L. Parsons, eds., *V. D. Nabokov and the Russian Provisional Government, 1917* (New Haven, CT: Yale University Press, 1976).

Rex A. Wade, *The Russian Search for Peace, February–October 1917* (Stanford, CA: Stanford University Press, 1969).

On social groups and movements, see:

Oscar Anweiler, *The Soviets: The Russian Workers, Peasants and Soldiers Councils, 1905–1921* (New York: Pantheon, 1974).

Graeme J. Gill, *Peasants and Government in the Russian Revolution* (London: Macmillan, 1979).

Diane Koenker and William G. Rosenberg, *Strikes and Revolution in Russia, 1917* (Princeton, NJ: Princeton University Press, 1989).

Evan Mawdsley, *The Russian Revolution and the Baltic Fleet: War and Politics, February 1917–April 1918* (New York: Barnes and Noble, 1978).

Oliver Henry Radkey, *The Agrarian Foes of Bolshevism* (New York: Columbia University Press, 1958).

William G. Rosenberg, "The Democratization of Russia's Railroads in 1917," *American Historical Review*, LXXXVI, 5 (December 1981), pp. 983–1008.

Carmen Sirianni, *Workers' Control and Socialist Democracy: The Soviet Experience* (London: Verso, 1982).

Norman E. Saul, *Sailors in Revolt: The Russian Baltic Fleet in 1917* (Lawrence: The Regents Press of Kansas, 1978).

Rex A. Wade, *Red Guards and Workers' Militias in the Russian Revolution* (Stanford, CA: Stanford University Press, 1984).

On the non-Russian areas, see:

Andrew Ezergailis, *The 1917 Revolution in Latvia* (New York: Columbia University Press, 1974).

Zvi Y. Gitelman, *Jewish Nationality and Soviet Politics: The Jewish Sections of the CPSU, 1917–1930* (Princeton, NJ: Princeton University Press, 1972).

John Reshetar, *The Ukrainian Revolution, 1917–1920: A Study in Nationalism* (Princeton, NJ: Princeton University Press, 1952).

Ronald Grigor Suny, *The Making of the Georgian Nation* (Bloomington and Stanford: Indiana University Press and Hoover Institution Press, 1988).

The Constituent Assembly Elections
and the Dictatorship of the Proletariat

The symposium issued by the Socialist-Revolutionaries, A *Year of the Russian Revolution. 1917–18.* (Moscow, Zemlya i Volya Publishers, 1918), contains an extremely interesting article by N. V. Svyatitsky: "Results of the All-Russia Constituent Assembly Elections (Preface)." The author gives the returns for 54 constituencies out of the total of 79.

The author's survey covers nearly all the gubernias of European Russia and Siberia, only the following being omitted: Olonets, Estonian, Kaluga, Bessarabian, Podolsk, Orenburg, Yakut and Don gubernias.

First of all I shall quote the main returns published by N. V. Svyatitsky and then discuss the political conclusions to be drawn from them.

I

The total number of votes polled in the 54 constituencies in November 1917 was 36,262,560. The author gives the figure of 36,257,960, distributed over seven regions (plus the Army and Navy), but the figures he gives for the various parties total up to what I give.

The distribution of the votes according to parties is as follows: the Russian Socialist-Revolutionaries polled 16.5 million votes; if we add the votes polled by the Socialist-Revolutionaries of the other nations (Ukrainians, Moslems, and others), the total will be 20.9 million, i.e., 58 per cent.

The Mensheviks polled 668,064 votes, but if we add the votes polled by the analogous groups of Popular Socialists (312,000), *Yedinstvo* (25,000), Co-operators (51,000), Ukrainian Social-Democrats (95,000), Ukrainian socialists (507,000), German socialists (44,000) and Finnish socialists (14,000), the total will be 1.7 million.

The Bolsheviks polled 9,023,963 votes.

The Cadets polled 1,856,639 votes. By adding the Association of Rural Proprietors and Landowners (215,000), the Right groups (292,000), Old Believers (73,000), nationalists — Jews (550,000), Moslems (576,000), Bashkirs (195,000), Letts (67,000), Poles (155,000), Cossacks (79,000), Germans (130,000), Byelorussians (12,000) — and the "lists of various groups and organisations" (418,000), we get a total for the landowning and bourgeois parties of 4.6 million.

We know that the Socialist-Revolutionaries and the Mensheviks formed a bloc during the whole period of the revolution from February to October 1917. Moreover, the entire development of events during that period and after it showed definitely that those two parties together represent petty-bourgeois democracy, which mistakenly imagines it is, and calls itself, socialist, like all the parties of the Second International.

Uniting the three main groups of parties in the Constituent Assembly elections, we get the following total:

Party of the proletariat (Bolsheviks)	9.02 million	= 25	per cent
Petty-bourgeois democratic parties (Socialist-Revolutionaries, Mensheviks, etc.)	22.62 "	= 62	"
Parties of landowners and bourgeoisie (Cadets, etc.)	4.62 "	= 13	"
Total	36.26 million	= 100 per cent	

Here are N. V. Svyatitsky's returns by regions.

Votes Polled (thousands)

Regions[1] (and armed forces separately)	S.R.s (Russian)	Per cent	Bolsheviks	Per cent	Cadets	Per cent	Total
Northern	1,140.0	38	1,177.2	40	393.0	13	2,975.1
Central-Industrial	1,987.9	38	2,305.6	44	550.2	10	5,242.5
Volga-Black Earth	4,733.9	70	1,115.6	16	267.0	4	6,764.3
Western	1,242.1	43	1,282.2	44	48.1	2	2,961.0
East-Urals	1,547.7	43(62)[2]	443.9	12	181.3	5	3,583.5
Siberia	2,094.8	75	273.9	10	87.5	3	2,786.7
The Ukraine	1,878.1	25(77)[3]	754.0	10	277.5	4	7,581.3
Army and Navy	1,885.1	43	1,671.3	38	51.9	1	4,363.6

[1] The author divides Russia into districts in a rather unusual way: *Northern:* Archangel, Vologda, Petrograd, Novgorod, Pskov, Baltic. *Central-Industrial:* Vladimir, Kostroma, Moscow, Nizhni-Novgorod, Ryazan, Tula, Tver, Yaroslavl. *Volga-Black Earth:* Astrakhan, Voronezh, Kursk, Orel, Penza, Samara, Saratov, Simbirsk, Tambov, *Western:* Vitebsk, Minsk, Mogilev, Smolensk. *East-Urals:* Vyatka, Kazan, Perm, Ufa. *Siberia:* Tobolsk, Tomsk, Altai, Yeniseisk, Irkutsk, Transbaikal, Amur. *The Ukraine:* Volhynia, Ekaterinoslav, Kiev, Poltava, Taurida, Kharkov, Kherson, Chernigov.
[2] Svyatitsky obtains the figure in brackets, 62 per cent, by adding the Moslem and Chuvash Socialist-Revolutionaries.
[3] The figure in brackets, 77 per cent, is mine, obtained by adding the Ukrainian Socialist-Revolutionaries.

From these figures it is evident that during the Constituent Assembly elections the Bolsheviks were the party of the proletariat and the Socialist-Revolutionaries, the party of the peasantry. In the purely peasant districts, Great-Russian (Volga-Black Earth, Siberia, East-Urals) and Ukrainian, the Socialist-Revolutionaries polled 62–77 per cent. In the industrial centres the Bolsheviks had a majority over the Socialist-Revolutionaries. This majority is understated in the district figures given by N. V. Svyatitsky, for he combined the most highly industrialised districts with little industrialised and non-industrial areas. For example, the gubernia figures of the votes polled by the Socialist-Revolutionary, Bolshevik, and Cadet parties, and by the "national and other groups", show the following:

In the Northern Region the Bolshevik majority seems to be insignificant: 40 per cent against 38 per cent. But in this region non-industrial areas (Archangel, Vologda, Novgorod and Pskov gubernias), where the Socialist-Revolutionaries predominate, are combined with industrial areas: Petrograd City — Bolsheviks 45 per cent (of the votes), Socialist-Revolutionaries 16 per cent; Petrograd Gubernia — Bolsheviks 50 per cent, Socialist-Revolutionaries 26 per cent; Baltic — Bolsheviks 72 per cent, Socialist-Revolutionaries — 0.

In the Central-Industrial Region the Bolsheviks in Moscow Gubernia polled 56 per cent and the Socialist-Revolutionaries 25 per cent; in Moscow City the Bolsheviks polled 50 per cent and the Socialist-Revolutionaries 8 per cent; in Tver Gubernia the Bolsheviks polled 54 per cent and the Socialist-Revolutionaries 39 per cent; in Vladimir Gubernia the Bolsheviks polled 56 per cent and the Socialist-Revolutionaries 32 per cent.

Let us note, in passing, how ridiculous, in face of such facts, is the talk about the Bolsheviks having only a "minority" of the proletariat behind them! And we hear this talk from the Mensheviks (668,000 votes, and with Transcaucasia another 700,000–800,000, against 9,000,000 votes polled by the Bolsheviks), and also from the social-traitors of the Second International.

II

How could such a miracle have occurred? How could the Bolsheviks, who polled one-fourth of the votes, have won a victory over the petty-bourgeois democrats, who were in alliance (coalition) with the bourgeoisie, and who together with the bourgeoisie polled three-fourths of the votes?

To deny this victory now, after the Entente — the all-mighty Entente — has been helping the enemies of Bolshevism for two years, is simply ridiculous.

The point is that the fanatical political hatred of those who have been defeated, including all the supporters of the Second International, prevents them from even raising seriously the extremely interesting historical and political question of why the Bolsheviks were victorious. The point is that this is a "miracle" only from the standpoint of vulgar petty-bourgeois democracy, the abysmal ignorance and deep-rooted prejudices of which are exposed by this question and the answer to it.

From the standpoint of the class struggle and socialism, from that standpoint, which the Second International has abandoned, the answer to the question is indisputable.

The Bolsheviks were victorious, first of all, because they had behind them the vast majority of the proletariat, which included the most class-conscious, energetic and revolutionary section, the real vanguard, of that advanced class.

Take the two metropolitan cities, Petrograd and Moscow. The total number of votes polled during the Constituent Assembly elections was 1,765,100, of which Socialist-Revolutionaries polled 218,000, Bolsheviks — 837,000 and Cadets — 515,400.

No matter how much the petty-bourgeois democrats who call themselves socialists and Social-Democrats (the Chernovs, Martovs, Kautskys, Longuets, MacDonalds and Co.) may beat their breasts and bow to goddesses of "equality", "universal suffrage", "democracy", "pure democracy", or "consistent democracy", it does not do away with the economic and political fact of the *inequality* of town and country.

That fact is inevitable under capitalism in general, and in the period of transition from capitalism to communism in particular.

The town cannot be equal to the country. The country cannot be equal to the town under the historical conditions of this epoch. The town inevitably *leads* the country. The country inevitably *follows the town*. The only question is *which class*, of the "urban" classes, will succeed in leading the country, will cope with this task, and what forms will *leadership by the town* assume?

In November 1917, the Bolsheviks had behind them the vast majority of the proletariat. By that time, the party which competed with the Bolsheviks among the proletariat, the Menshevik party, had been utterly defeated (9,000,000 votes against 1,400,000, if we add together 668,000 and 700,000–800,000 in Transcaucasia). Moreover, that party was defeated in the fifteen-year struggle (1903–17) which *steeled*, enlightened and organised the vanguard of the proletariat, and *forged* it into a genuine revolutionary vanguard. Furthermore, the first revolution, that of 1905, prepared the subsequent development, determined in a *practical* way the relations between the two parties, and served as the general rehearsal of the great events of 1917–19.

The petty-bourgeois democrats who call themselves socialists of the Second International are fond of dismissing this extremely important historical question with honeyed phrases about the benefits of proletarian "unity." When they use these honeyed phrases they forget the historical fact of the *accumulation of opportunism* in the working-class movement of 1871–1914; they forget (or do not want) to *think* about the causes of the collapse of opportunism in August 1914, about the causes of the split in international socialism in 1914–17.

Unless the *revolutionary* section of the proletariat is thoroughly prepared in every way for the expulsion and suppression of opportunism it is useless even thinking about the dictatorship of the proletariat. That is the lesson of the Russian revolution which should be taken to heart by the leaders of the "independent" German Social-Democrats, French socialists, and so forth, who now want to evade the issue by means of verbal recognition of the dictatorship of the proletariat.

To continue. The Bolsheviks had behind them not only the majority of the proletariat, not only the *revolutionary* vanguard of the proletariat which had been steeled in the long and persevering struggle against opportunism; they had, if it is permissible to use a military term, a powerful "striking force" in the metropolitan cities.

An overwhelming superiority of forces at the decisive point at the decisive moment — this "law" of military success is also the law of political success, especially in that fierce, seething class war which is called revolution.

Capitals, or, in general, big commercial and industrial centres (here in Russia the two coincided, but they do not everywhere coincide), to a considerable degree decide the political fate of a nation, provided, of course, the centres are supported by sufficient local, rural forces, even if that support does not come immediately.

In the two chief cities, in the two principal commercial and industrial centres of Russia, the Bolsheviks had an overwhelming, decisive superiority of forces. Here our forces were *nearly four times* as great as those of the Socialist-Revolutionaries. We had here *more than the Socialist-Revolutionaries and Cadets put together*. Moreover, our adversaries were split up, for the "coalition" of the Cadets with the Socialist-Revolutionaries and Mensheviks (in Petrograd and Moscow the Mensheviks polled only 3 per cent of the votes) was utterly discredited among the working people. *Real* unity between the Socialist-Revolutionaries and Mensheviks and the Cadets against us was quite out of the question at that time.[4] It will be remembered that in November 1917, even the leaders of the Socialist-Revolutionaries and Mensheviks, who were a hundred times nearer to the idea of a bloc with the Cadets than the Socialist-Revolutionary and Menshevik workers and peasants, even those leaders thought (and bargained with us) about a bloc with the Bolsheviks *without* the Cadets!

We were *certain* of winning Petrograd and Moscow in October–November 1917, for we had an overwhelming superiority of forces and the most thorough political preparation, insofar as concerns both the assembly, concentration, training, testing and battle-hardening of the Bolshevik "armies," and the disintegration, exhaustion, disunity and demoralisation of the "enemy's" "armies."

And being certain of winning the two metropolitan cities, the two centres of the capitalist state machine (economic and political), by a swift, decisive blow, we, in spite of the furious resistance of the bureaucracy and intelligentsia, despite sabotage, and so forth, were able with the aid of the central apparatus of state power to *prove by deeds* to the *non*-proletarian working people that the proletariat was their only reliable ally, friend and leader.

III

But before passing on to this most important question — that of the attitude of the proletariat towards the non-proletarian working people — we must deal with the *armed forces*.

---

[4] It is interesting to note that the above figures also reveal the unity and solidarity of the party of the proletariat and the extremely fragmented state of the parties of the petty bourgeoisie and of the bourgeoisie.

The flower of the people's forces went to form the army during the imperialist war; the opportunist scoundrels of the Second International (not only the social-chauvinists, i.e., the Scheidemanns and Renaudels who directly went over to the side of "defence of the fatherland," but also the Centrists) by their words and deeds strengthened the subordination of the armed forces to the leadership of the imperialist robbers of both the German and Anglo-French groups, but the real proletarian revolutionaries never forgot what Marx said in 1870: "The bourgeoisie will give the proletariat practice in arms!" Only the Austro-German and Anglo-Franco-Russian betrayers of socialism could talk about "defence of the fatherland" in the imperialist war, i.e., a war that was predatory on both sides; the proletarian revolutionaries, however (from August 1914 onwards), turned all their attention to revolutionising the armed forces, to utilising them *against* the imperialist robber bourgeoisie, to converting the unjust and predatory war between the two groups of imperialist predators into a just and legitimate war of the proletarians and oppressed working people in each country against "their own," "national" bourgeoisie.

During 1914–17 the betrayers of socialism *did not make preparations* to use the armed forces *against* the imperialist government of *each* nation.

The Bolsheviks prepared for this by the whole of their propaganda, agitation and underground organisational work from August 1914 onwards. Of course, the betrayers of socialism, the Scheidemanns and Kautskys of all nations, got out of this by talking about the *demoralisation* of the armed forces by Bolshevik agitation, but we are *proud* of the fact that we performed our duty in demoralising the forces of our class enemy, in winning away *from him* the armed masses of the workers and peasants *for the struggle* against the exploiters.

The results of our work were seen in, among other things, the votes polled in the Constituent Assembly elections in November 1917, in which, in Russia, the armed forces also participated.

The following are the principal results of the voting as given by N. V. Svyatitsky:

Number of Votes Polled in the Constituent Assembly Elections,
November 1917
(thousands)

Army and Navy units	S.R.s	Bolsheviks	Cadets	National and other groups	Total
Northern Front	240.0	480.0	?	60[6]	780.0
Western "	180.6	653.4	16.7	125.2	976.0
South-Western "	402.9	300.1	13.7	290.6	1,007.4
Rumanian "	679.4	167.0	21.4	260.7	1,128.6
Caucasian "	360.0	60.0	?	—	420.0
Baltic Fleet	—	(120.0)[5]	—	—	(120.0)[5]
Black Sea Fleet	22.2	10.8	—	19.5	52.5
Total	1,885.1	1,671.3 +(120.0)[5]	51.8 +?	756.0	4,364,5 +(120.0)[5]
		1.791.3			+?

Summary: the Socialist-Revolutionaries polled 1,885,100 votes; the Bolsheviks polled 1,671,300 votes. If to the latter we add the 120,000 votes (approximately) polled in the Baltic Fleet, the total votes polled by the Bolsheviks will be 1,791,300.

The Bolsheviks, therefore, polled a *little less* than the Socialist-Revolutionaries.

And so, by October-November 1917, the armed forces were *half Bolshevik.*

If that had not been the case we could not have been victorious.

We polled nearly half the votes of the armed forces as a whole, but had an overwhelming majority on the fronts *nearest to the metropolitan cities* and, in general, on those not too far away. If we leave out the Caucasian Front, the Bolsheviks obtained on the whole a majority over

[5] The figure is approximate. Two Bolsheviks were elected. N. V. Svyatitsky counts an average of 60,000 votes per elected person. That is why I give the figure 120,000.
[6] No information is given as to which party polled 19,500 votes in the Black Sea Fleet. The other figures in this column evidently apply almost entirely to the Ukrainian socialists for 10 Ukrainian socialists and one Social-Democrat (i.e., a Menshevik) were elected.

the Socialist-Revolutionaries. And if we take the Northern and Western fronts, the votes polled by the Bolsheviks will amount to *over one million*, compared with 420,000 votes polled by the Socialist-Revolutionaries.

Thus, in the armed forces, too, the Bolsheviks already had a *political "striking force,"* by November 1917, which ensured them an overwhelming superiority of forces at the decisive point at the decisive moment. Resistance on the part of the armed forces to the October Revolution of the proletariat, to the winning of political power by the proletariat, was entirely out of the question, considering that the Bolsheviks had an enormous majority on the Northern and Western fronts, while on the other fronts, far removed from the centre, the Bolsheviks had the time and opportunity to *win the peasants away from the Socialist-Revolutionary Party.*

IV

On the basis of the returns of the Constituent Assembly elections we have studied the three conditions which determined the victory of Bolshevism: (1) an overwhelming majority among the proletariat; (2) almost half of the armed forces; (3) an overwhelming superiority of forces at the decisive moment at the decisive points, namely: in Petrograd and Moscow and on the war fronts near the centre.

But these conditions could have ensured only a very short-lived and unstable victory had the Bolsheviks been unable to win to their side the majority of the *non*-proletarian working masses, to win them from the Socialist-Revolutionaries and the other petty-bourgeois parties.

That is the main thing.

And the chief reason why the "socialists" (read: petty-bourgeois democrats) of the Second International fail to understand the dictatorship of the proletariat is that they fail to understand that

> *state power in the hands of one class, the proletariat, can and must become an instrument for winning to the side of the proletariat the non-proletarian working masses, an instrument for winning those masses from the bourgeoisie and from the petty-bourgeois parties.*

Filled with petty-bourgeois prejudices, forgetting the most important thing in the teachings of Marx about the state, the "socialists" of the Second International regard *state power* as something holy, as an idol, or as the result of formal voting, the absolute of "consistent democracy" (or whatever else they call this nonsense). They fail to see that state power is simply an *instrument* which *different* classes can and must use (and know how to use) *for their class aims.*

The bourgeoisie has used state power as an instrument of the capitalist class against the proletariat, against all the working people. That has been the case in the most democratic bourgeois republics. Only the betrayers of Marxism have "forgotten" this.

The proletariat must (after mustering sufficiently strong political and military "striking forces") overthrow the bourgeoisie, take state power from it in order to use that *instrument* for *its* class aims.

What are the class aims of the proletariat?

Suppress the resistance of the bourgeoisie;

Neutralise the peasantry and, if possible, win them over — at any rate the majority of the labouring, non-exploiting section — to the side of the proletariat;

Organise large-scale machine production, using factories, and means of production in general, expropriated from the bourgeoisie;

Organise socialism on the ruins of capitalism.

In mockery of the teachings of Marx, those gentlemen, the opportunists, including the Kautskyites, "teach" the people that the proletariat must first win a majority by means of universal suffrage, then obtain state power, by the vote of that majority, and only after that, on the basis of "consistent" (some call it "pure") democracy, organise socialism.

But we say on the basis of the teachings of Marx and the experience of the Russian revolution:

the proletariat must first overthrow the bourgeoisie and win *for itself* state power, and then use that state power, that is, the dictatorship of the proletariat, as an instrument of its class for the purpose of winning the sympathy of the majority of the working people.

How can state power in the hands of the proletariat become the instrument of its class struggle for influence over the non-proletarian working people, of the struggle to draw them to its side, to win them over, to wrest them from the bourgeoisie?

First, the proletariat achieves this *not* by putting into operation the old apparatus of state power, but by *smashing* it to pieces, levelling it with the ground (in spite of the howls of frightened philistines and the threats of saboteurs), and building a *new* state apparatus. That new state apparatus is adapted to the dictatorship of the proletariat and to its struggle against the bourgeoisie to *win* the non-proletarian working people. That new apparatus is not anybody's invention, it *grows* out of the proletarian class struggle as that struggle becomes more widespread and intense. That new apparatus of state power, the new *type* of state power, is *Soviet power*.

The Russian proletariat, immediately, a few hours after winning state power, proclaimed the dissolution of the old state apparatus (which, as Marx showed, had been for centuries adapted to serve the class interests of the bourgeoisie, even in the most democratic republic) and transferred *all power to the Soviets*; and only the working and exploited people could enter the Soviets, all exploiters of every kind were excluded.

In that way the proletariat at once, at one stroke, immediately *after* it had taken state power, *won* from the bourgeoisie *the vast mass* of its supporters in the petty-bourgeois and "socialist" parties; for that mass, the working and exploited people who had been deceived by the bourgeoisie (and by its yes-men, the Chernovs, Kautskys, Martovs and Co.), *on obtaining Soviet power*, acquired, *for the first time*, an instrument of mass struggle for their interests against the bourgeoisie.

Secondly, the proletariat can, and must, at once, or at all events very quickly, win from the bourgeoisie and from petty-bourgeois democrats *"their" masses*, i.e., the masses which follow them — win them *by satisfying their most urgent economic needs in a revolutionary way by expropriating the landowners and the bourgeoisie*.

The bourgeoisie *cannot* do that, no matter how "mighty" its state power may be.

The proletariat *can* do that on the very next day after it has won state power, because for this it has both an apparatus (the Soviets) and economic means (the expropriation of the landowners and the bourgeoisie).

That is exactly how the Russian proletariat *won the peasantry* from the Socialist-Revolutionaries, and won them literally *a few hours after* achieving state power; a few hours after the victory over the bourgeoisie in Petrograd, the victorious proletariat issued a "decree on land", and in that decree it entirely, at once, with revolutionary swiftness, energy and devotion, *satisfied* all the most urgent economic needs of the *majority* of the peasants, it expropriated the landowners, entirely and without compensation.

To prove to the peasants that the proletarians did not want to steam-roller them, did not want to boss them, but to help them and be their friends, the victorious Bolsheviks did not put a *single word of their own* into that "decree on land," but copied it, word for word, from the peasant mandates (the most revolutionary of them, of course) which the *Socialist-Revolutionaries* had published in the *Socialist-Revolutionary* newspaper.

The Socialist-Revolutionaries fumed and raved, protested and howled that "the Bolsheviks had stolen their programme," but they were only laughed at for that; a fine party, indeed, which had to be defeated and driven from the government in order that everything in its programme that was revolutionary and of benefit to the working people could be carried out!

The traitors, blockheads and pedants of the Second International could never understand such dialectics; the proletariat cannot achieve victory if it does not win the majority of the population to its side. But to limit that winning to polling a majority of votes in an election *under the rule of the bourgeoisie*, or to make it the condition for it, is crass stupid-ity, or else sheer deception of the workers. In order to win the majority of the population to its side the proletariat must, in the first place, overthrow the bourgeoisie and seize state power; secondly, it must in-troduce Soviet power and completely smash the old state apparatus, whereby it immediately undermines the rule, prestige and influence of the bourgeoisie and petty-bourgeois compromisers over the non-proletarian working people. Thirdly, it must *entirely destroy* the influ-ence of the bourgeoisie and petty-bourgeois compromises over the *majority* of the non-proletarian masses by satisfying their economic needs *in a revolutionary way at the expense of the exploiters*.

It is possible to do this, or course, only when capitalist development has reached a certain level. Failing that fundamental condition, the proletariat cannot develop into a separate class, nor can success be achieved in its prolonged training, education, instruction and trial in battle during long years of strikes and demonstrations when the oppor-tunists are disgraced and expelled. Failing that fundamental condition, the centres will not play that economic and political role which enables the proletariat, after their capture, to lay hold of state power in its entirety, or more correctly, of its vital nerve, its core, its node. Failing

only as a screen to conceal the dictatorship of the landowners and capitalists.

Another turn towards Bolshevism began and peasant revolts spread in the rear of Kolchak and Denikin. The peasants welcomed the Red troops as liberators.

In the long run, it was this vacillation of the peasantry, the main body of the petty-bourgeois working people, that decided the fate of Soviet rule and of the rule of Kolchak and Denikin. But this "long run" was preceded by a fairly lengthy period of severe struggle and painful trial, which have not ended in Russia after two years, have not ended precisely in Siberia and in the Ukraine. And there is no guarantee that they will end *completely* within, say, another year or so.

The supporters of "consistent" democracy have not given thought to the importance of this historic fact. They invented, and are still inventing, nursery tales about the proletariat under capitalism being able to "convince" the majority of the working people and win them firmly to its side by voting. But reality shows that only in the course of a long and fierce struggle does the stern experience of the *vacillating* petty bourgeoisie *lead it* to the conclusion, after comparing the dictatorship of the proletariat with the dictatorship of the capitalists, that the former is better than the latter.

In theory, all socialists who have studied Marxism and are willing to take into account the lessons of the nineteenth-century political history of the advanced countries recognise that the *vacillation* of the petty bourgeoisie between the proletariat and the capitalist class is inevitable. The economic roots of this vacillation are clearly revealed by economic science, the truths of which have been repeated millions of times in the newspapers, leaflets and pamphlets issued by the socialists of the Second International.

But these people cannot apply those truths to the peculiar epoch of the dictatorship of the proletariat. They substitute petty-bourgeois-democratic prejudices and illusions (about class "equality," about "consistent" or "pure" democracy, about solving great historic problems by voting, and so forth) for the *class struggle*. They will not understand that after capturing state power the proletariat does not thereby cease its class struggle, but continues it in a different form and by different means. The dictatorship of the proletariat is the class struggle of the proletariat conducted with the aid of an instrument like state power, a class struggle, one of whose aims is to demonstrate to the non-proletarian sections of the working people by means of their long experience and a long list of practical examples that it is more to their advantage to side with the dictatorship of the proletariat than with the dictatorship of the bourgeoisie, and that there can be no third course.

The returns of the Constituent Assembly elections held in November 1917 give us the main background to the picture of the development of the Civil War that has raged for two years since those elections. The main forces in that war were *already* clearly evident during the Constituent Assembly elections — the role of the "striking force" of the proletarian army, the role of the vacillating peasantry, and the role of the bourgeoisie were already apparent. In his article N.V. Svyatitsky writes: "The Cadets were most successful in the same regions where the Bolsheviks were most successful — in the Northern and Central-Industrial regions." Naturally, in the most highly developed capitalist centres, the intermediary elements standing between the proletariat and the bourgeoisie were the weakest. Naturally, in those centres, the class struggle was most acute. It was there that the main forces of the bourgeoisie were concentrated and there, only there, could the proletariat defeat the bourgeoisie. Only the proletariat could rout the bourgeoisie, and only after routing the bourgeoisie could the proletariat definitely win the sympathy and support of the petty-bourgeois strata of the population by using an instrument like state power.

If properly used, if correctly read, the returns of the Constituent Assembly elections reveal to us again and again the fundamental truths of the Marxist doctrine of the class struggle.

These returns, incidentally, also reveal the role and importance of the national question. Take the Ukraine. At the last conferences on the Ukrainian question some comrades accused the writer of these lines of giving too much "prominence" to the national question in the Ukraine. The returns of the Constituent Assembly elections show that in the Ukraine, as early as November 1917, the *Ukrainian* Socialist-Revolutionaries and socialists polled a majority (3.4 million votes + 0.5 = 3.9 million against 1.9 million polled by the Russian Socialist-Revolutionaries, out of a total poll in the whole of the Ukraine of 7.6 million votes). In the army on the South-Western and Rumanian fronts the Ukrainian socialists polled 30 per cent and 34 per cent of the total votes (the Russian Socialist-Revolutionaries polled 40 per cent and 59 per cent).

Under these circumstances, to ignore the importance of the national question in the Ukraine — a sin of which Great Russians are often guilty (and of which the Jews are guilty perhaps only a little less often than the Great Russians) — is a great and dangerous mistake. The division between the Russian and Ukrainian Socialist-Revolutionaries as early as 1917 could not have been accidental. As internationalists it is our duty, first, to combat very vigorously the survivals (sometimes unconscious) of Great-Russian imperialism and chauvinism among "Russian" Communists; and secondly, it is our duty, precisely on the national question, which is a relatively minor one (for an internationalist the question of state frontiers is a secondary, if not a tenth-rate, question), to make concessions. There are other questions — the fundamental interests of the proletarian dictatorship; the interests of the unity and discipline of the Red Army which is fighting Denikin; the leading role of the proletariat in relation to the peasantry — that are more important; the question whether the Ukraine will be a separate state is far less important. We must not be in the least surprised, or frightened, even by the prospect of the Ukrainian workers and peasants trying out different systems, and in the course of, say, several years, testing by practice union with the R.S.F.S.R., or seceding from the latter and forming an independent Ukrainian S.S.R., or various forms of their close alliance, and so on, and so forth.

To attempt to settle this question in advance, once and for all, "firmly" and "irrevocably," would be narrow-mindedness or sheer stupidity, for the vacillation of the non-proletarian working people on *such* a question is quite natural, even inevitable, but not in the least frightful for the proletariat. It is the duty of the proletarian who is really capable of being an internationalist to treat *such* vacillation with the greatest caution and tolerance, it is his duty to leave it to the non-proletarian masses *themselves* to *get rid* of this vacillation as a result of their own experience. We must be intolerant and ruthless, uncompromising and inflexible on other, more fundamental questions, some of which I have already pointed to above.

VI

The comparison of the Constituent Assembly elections in November 1917 with the development of the proletarian revolution in Russia from October 1917 to December 1919 enables us to draw conclusions concerning bourgeois parliamentarism and the proletarian revolution in every capitalist country. Let me try briefly to formulate, or at least to outline, the principal conclusions.

1. Universal suffrage is an index of the level reached by the various classes in their understanding of their problems. It shows how the various classes are *inclined* to solve their problems. The actual *solution* of those problems is not provided by voting, but by the class struggle in all its forms, including civil war.

2. The socialists and Social-Democrats of the Second International take the stand of vulgar petty-bourgeois democrats and share the prejudice that the fundamental problems of the class struggle can be solved by voting.

3. The party of the revolutionary proletariat must take part in bourgeois parliaments in order to enlighten the masses; this can be done during elections and in the struggle between parties in parliament. But limiting the class struggle to the parliamentary struggle, or regarding the latter as the highest and decisive form, to which all the other forms of struggle are subordinate, is actually desertion to the side of the bourgeoisie against the proletariat.

4. All the representatives and supporters of the Second International, and all the leaders of the German, so-called "independent," Social-Democratic Party, actually go over to the bourgeoisie in this way when they recognise the dictatorship of the proletariat in words, but in deeds, by their propaganda, imbue the proletariat with the idea that it must first obtain a formal expression of the will of the majority of the population under capitalism (i.e., a majority of votes in the bourgeois parliament) to transfer political power to the proletariat, which transfer is to take place later.

All the cries, based on this premise, of the German "independent" Social-Democrats and similar leaders of decayed socialism against the "dictatorship of a minority," and so forth, merely indicate that those leaders fail to understand the dictatorship of the bourgeoisie, which actually reigns even in the most democratic republics, and that they fail to understand the conditions for its destruction by the class struggle of the proletariat.

5. This failure to understand consists, in particular, in the following: they forget that, to a very large degree, the bourgeois parties are able to rule because they deceive the masses of the people, because of the yoke of capital, and to this is added self-deception concerning the nature of capitalism, a self-deception which is characteristic mostly of the

petty-bourgeois parties, which usually want to substitute more or less disguised forms of class conciliation for the class struggle.

"First let the majority of the population, while private property still exists, i.e., while the rule and yoke of capital still exist, express themselves in favour of the party of the proletariat, and only then can and should the party take power" — so say the petty-bourgeois democrats who call themselves socialists but who are in reality the servitors of the bourgeoisie.

"Let the revolutionary proletariat first overthrow the bourgeoisie, break the yoke of capital, and smash the bourgeois state apparatus, then the victorious proletariat will be able rapidly to gain the sympathy and support of the majority of the non-proletarian working people by satisfying their needs at the expense of the exploiters" — say we. The opposite will be rare exception in history (and even in such an exception the bourgeoisie can resort to civil war, as the example of Finland showed).

6. Or in other words:

"First we shall pledge ourselves to recognise the principle of equality, or consistent democracy, while preserving private property and the yoke of capital (i.e., actual inequality under formal equality), and try to obtain the decision of the majority on this basis"—say the bourgeoisie and their yes-men, the petty-bourgeois democrats who call themselves socialists and Social-Democrats.

"First the proletarian class struggle, winning state power, will destroy the pillars and foundations of actual inequality, and then the proletariat, which has defeated the exploiters, will lead all working people to the *abolition of classes*, i.e., to socialist *equality*, the only kind that is not a deception" — say we.

7. In all capitalist countries, besides the proletariat, or that part of the proletariat which is conscious of its revolutionary aims and is capable of fighting to achieve them, there are numerous politically immature proletarian, semi-proletarian, semi-petty-bourgeois strata which follow the bourgeoisie and bourgeois democracy (including the "socialists" of the Second International) because they have been deceived, have no confidence in their own strength, or in the strength of the proletariat, are unaware of the possibility of having their urgent needs satisfied by means of the expropriation of the exploiters.

These strata of the working and exploited people provide the vanguard of the proletariat with allies and give it a stable majority of the population; but the proletariat can win these allies only with the aid of an instrument like state power, that is to say, only after it has over-thrown the bourgeoisie and has destroyed the bourgeois state apparatus.

8. The strength of the proletariat in any capitalist country is far greater than the proportion it represents of the total population. That is because the proletariat economically dominates the centre and nerve of the entire economic system of capitalism, and also because the proletariat expresses economically and politically the real interests of the overwhelming majority of the working people under capitalism.

Therefore, the proletariat, even when it constitutes a minority of the population (or when the class-conscious and really revolutionary vanguard of the proletariat constitutes a minority of the population), is capable of overthrowing the bourgeoisie and, after that, of winning to its side numerous allies from a mass of semi-proletarians and petty bourgeoisie who never declare in advance in favour of the rule of the proletariat, who do not understand the conditions and aims of that rule, and only by their subsequent experience become convinced that the proletarian dictatorship is inevitable, proper and legitimate.

9. Finally, in every capitalist country there are always very broad strata of the petty bourgeoisie which inevitably vacillate between capital and labour. To achieve victory, the proletariat must, first, choose the right moment for its decisive assault on the bourgeoisie, taking into account, among other things, the disunity between the bourgeoisie and its petty-bourgeois allies, or the instability of their alliance, and so forth. Secondly, the proletariat must, after its victory, utilise this vacillation of the petty bourgeoisie in such a way as to neutralise them, prevent their siding with the exploiters; it must be able to hold on for some time *in spite of this vacillation*, and so on, and so forth.

10. One of the necessary conditions for preparing the proletariat for its victory is a long, stubborn and ruthless struggle against opportunism, reformism, social-chauvinism, and similar bourgeois influences and trends, which are inevitable, since the proletariat is operating in a capitalist environment. If there is no such struggle, if opportunism in the working-class movement is not utterly defeated beforehand, there can be no dictatorship of the proletariat. Bolshevism would not have defeated the bourgeoisie in 1917–19 if before that, in 1903–17, it had not learned to defeat the Mensheviks, i.e., the opportunists, reformists, social-chauvinists, and ruthlessly expel them from the party of the proletarian vanguard.

At the present time, the verbal recognition of the dictatorship of the proletariat by the leaders of the German "Independents," or by the French Longuetists, and the like, who are *actually* continuing the old, habitual policy of big and small concessions to and conciliation with opportunism, subservience to the prejudices of bourgeois democracy ("consistent democracy" or "pure democracy" as they call it) and bourgeois parliamentarism, and so forth, is the most dangerous self-deception — and sometimes sheer fooling of the workers.

December 16, 1919

OUR REVOLUTION

(apropos of N. Sukhanov's Notes)

I

I have lately been glancing through Sukhanov's notes on the revolution. What strikes one most is the pedantry of all our petty-bourgeois democrats and of all the heroes of the Second International. Apart from the fact that they are all extremely faint-hearted, that when it comes to the minutest deviation from the German model even the best of them fortify themselves with reservations — apart from this characteristic, which is common to all petty-bourgeois democrats and has been abundantly manifested by them throughout the revolution, what strikes one is their slavish imitation of the past.

They all call themselves Marxists, but their conception of Marxism is impossibly pedantic. They have completely failed to understand what is decisive in Marxism, namely, its revolutionary dialectics. They have even absolutely failed to understand Marx's plain statements that in times of revolution the utmost flexibility is demanded, and have even failed to notice, for instance, the statements Marx made in his letters — I think it was in 1856 — expressing the hope of combining a peasant war in Germany, which might create a revolutionary situation, with the working-class movement — they avoid even this plain statement and walk round and about it like a cat around a bowl of hot porridge.

Their conduct betrays them as cowardly reformists who are afraid to deviate from the bourgeoisie, let alone break with it, and at the same time they disguise their cowardice with the wildest rhetoric and braggartry. But what strikes one in all of them even from the purely theoretical point of view is their utter inability to grasp the following

Marxist considerations: up to now they have seen capitalism and bourgeois democracy in Western Europe follow a definite path of development, and cannot conceive that this path can be taken as a model only *mutatis mutandis*, only with certain amendments (quite insignificant from the standpoint of the general development of world history).

First — the revolution connected with the first imperialist world war. Such a revolution was bound to reveal new features, or variations, resulting from the war itself, for the world has never seen such a war in such a situation. We find that since the war the bourgeoisie of the wealthiest countries have to this day been unable to restore "normal" bourgeois relations. Yet our reformists — petty bourgeois who make a show of being revolutionaries — believed, and still believe, that normal bourgeois relations are the limit (thus far shalt thou go and no farther). And even their conception of "normal" is extremely stereotyped and narrow.

Secondly, they are complete strangers to the idea that while the development of world history as a whole follows general laws it is by no means precluded, but, on the contrary, presumed, that certain periods of development may display peculiarities in either the form or the sequence of this development. For instance, it does not even occur to them that because Russia stands on the borderline between the civilised countries and the countries which this war has for the first time definitely brought into the orbit of civilisation — all the Oriental, non-European countries — she could and was, indeed, bound to reveal certain distinguishing features; although these, of course, are in keeping with the general line of world development, they distinguish her revolution from those which took place in the West-European countries and introduce certain partial innovations as the revolution moves on to the countries of the East.

Infinitely stereotyped, for instance, is the argument they learned by rote during the development of West-European Social-Democracy, namely, that we are not yet ripe for socialism, that, as certain "learned" gentlemen among them put it, the objective economic premises for socialism do not exist in our country. It does not occur to any of them to ask: but what about a people that found itself in a revolutionary situation such as that created during the first imperialist war? Might it not, influenced by the hopelessness of its situation, fling itself into a struggle that would offer it at least some chance of securing conditions for the further development of civilisation that were somewhat unusual?

were seen to be sabotaging the revolution as well as the factories. That the revolutionary unity of March fell apart along class lines can be attributed to economic conditions in Russia but also to the fact that the class framework was after all implicit in socialist consciousness. Capitalists began to behave as Marx said they would: no concessions to the workers, no compromise on the rights of factory owners. Mensheviks and SRs tried to straddle both sides of the class split; this appeal can be seen in the mixed social composition of their supporters. The Bolsheviks, however, had offered the most consistent class interpretation of the revolution, and by late summer their interpretation appeared more and more to correspond to reality. The language of class struggle provided workers who had no theoretical understanding of Marx with a familiar conceptual tool with which to understand the actions of the Provisional Government; the continued failure of the government to solve the problems of the war and the economy, translated into class terms became deliberate sabotage by the workers' natural class enemy. By October, the soviets of workers' deputies, as the workers' only class organ, seemed to class-conscious workers to be the only government they could trust to represent their interests. The combination of theory and experience had produced Moscow's class consciousness.

The class consciousness of October, however, by the same logic as it developed, represented that particular historical moment. Once the theoretically articulate workers left the city with the Red Army, once the dictatorship of the proletariat had eliminated the sense of struggle against the ruling capitalist class, the set of circumstances which had produced class consciousness in 1917 would change. If the class-pure Bolsheviks, once in power, were also to fail to provide political responsiveness and economic security, if nonclass ties such as regional, ethnic, or occupational bonds were to assert more appeal than class solidarity, perhaps the consolidation of the Moscow workers around their class representative, the Bolshevik party, might eventually have weakened. More research is needed on the working class during the civil war and the early years of soviet power; it should be carried out with an eye toward the complexities of the revolutionary process which have been demonstrated here.

Finally, by looking beyond one-dimensional notions of radicalization and by examining the roots of the October revolution, another significant aspect of the revolution has emerged which deserves far more study than it has received: the failure of organizational development to

positions, gained concreteness in the struggle to enact political reform in the 1830s. In the process, workers gained a collective self-consciousness based on their political traditions as well as their economic position in society; the result — English class consciousness.

This process was not and could not have been the same for Russian workers in 1917; Thompson's brief is that class "happened" in England in a fashion peculiar to England. This study of Moscow workers in 1917, however, indicates some elements that contributed to Moscow working-class consciousness by October.

Russian working-class political culture was overwhelmingly a socialist political culture. This was the legacy both of a socialist revolutionary movement that predated the rise of a working class and of the influence of Marxist analysis on that emerging working class. Furthermore, a democratic socialist political and economic order seemed the logical next step for Russia, where the state had always been closely involved in economic activity and where the activity of public organizations during the war had legitimized popular participation in economic administration. The workers' economic-control resolutions of May and June, and the June duma elections, demonstrated this socialist consciousness; the resolutions stipulated active state and public intervention in the economy, and in the elections workers voted almost exclusively for the three parties bearing the socialist label.

This socialist consciousness was not yet class consciousness, consciousness of class struggle. The prevailing sentiment of Moscow workers during the first few months of the revolution was for national unity in the defense of the revolution, exemplified in workers' appeals for solidarity with the army. Of the three socialist parties, the Bolsheviks offered the most class-oriented position, and they were relatively less popular during this period than the Socialist Revolutionaries and Mensheviks, who stood for compromise and solidarity with all elements of revolutionary Russia. Strikes during the period almost all were called to demand wage increases, an indication that workers were willing to function within a multiclass framework.

The events of the summer of 1917 combined with growing class antagonism to change this socialist consciousness into class consciousness. Economic strikes became less successful, and capitalists seemed less willing to treat workers as equal partners in labor-management relations. The coalition government failed to enact the minimal socialist demands of workers, and the onus fell first on the capitalists, who technically unprepared for an offensive against the government. In these circumstances tactically cautious party leaders in Petrograd, headed by Trotsky, devised the strategy of employing the organs of the Petrograd Soviet for the seizure of power; of masking an attack on the government as a defensive operation on behalf of the Soviet; and, if possible, of linking the formal overthrow of the government with the work of the Second Congress of Soviets.

On October 21–23, using as an excuse the government's announced intention of transferring the bulk of the garrison to the front and cloaking every move as a defensive measure against the counter-revolution, the Military Revolutionary Committee of the Petrograd Soviet took control of most Petrograd-based military units, in effect disarming the Provisional Government without a shot. In response, early on the morning of October 24, Kerensky initiated steps to suppress the left. Only at this point, just hours before the scheduled opening of the Congress of Soviets and in part under continuous prodding by Lenin, did the armed uprising that Lenin had been advocating for well over a month actually begin.

The argument has been made that the belated uprising of October 24–25 was of crucial historical importance because, by impelling the main body of Mensheviks and SRs to withdraw from the Second Congress of Soviets, it prevented the creation by the congress of a socialist coalition government in which the moderate socialists might have had a strong voice. In so doing, it paved the way for the formation of a soviet government completely controlled and dominated by the Bolsheviks. The evidence indicates that this was indeed the case. A more crucial point, however, is that only in the wake of the government's direct attack on the left was an armed uprising of the kind envisioned by Lenin feasible. For it bears repeating that the Petrograd masses, to the extent that they supported the Bolsheviks in the overthrow of the Provisional Government, did so not out of any sympathy for strictly Bolshevik rule but because they believed the revolution and the congress to be in imminent danger. Only the creation of a broadly representative, exclusively socialist government by the Congress of Soviets, which is what they believed the Bolsheviks stood for, appeared to offer the hope of insuring that there would not be a return to the hated ways of the old regime, of avoiding death at the front and achieving a better life, and of putting a quick end to Russia's participation in the war.

Diane Koenker

Moscow's October

The almost-exclusive focus on Petrograd has been expanded in recent decades by regional and local studies. One of the most important is Diane Koenker's investigation of the workers of Moscow. A student of William G. Rosenberg at the University of Michigan, Koenker brought a clear, social-scientific vision to her research. Combining the insights of labor history and sociology, she constructed a convincing portrait of the revolutionary experience that led Moscow workers to a high degree of class cohesion and consciousness by October. Koenker has taught at Temple University and the University of Illinois, has written a study of strikes in 1917 with William Rosenberg, and is currently researching the role played by printers in the early years of Soviet power. In this excerpt she illustrates the social and political logic that led to a conscious, though hardly monolithic, working class by the fall of 1917.

We are for those who know how to make life cheaper.
Zamoskvorech'e Voter in November

The "October Days"

The month of October in Moscow offered little hope that the twin economic and political crises could be peacefully resolved. With winter closing in, shortages of food and fuel became even more threatening. Grain shipments continued to dwindle; the daily bread allowance was to fall to a meager half-funt (about eight ounces) again on October 24. The causes of such shortages were complex, but many workers felt that the government and its supporters deliberately sabotaged the economy in order to consolidate their own political and economic positions. This deep sense of suspicion and hostility underlay the development of the strike movement in October; it was further fueled by the shrill attacks of

Diane Koenker, *Moscow Workers and the 1917 Revolution*. Copyright © 1981 by Princeton University Press. Excerpts, pp. 329–367, reprinted with permission of Princeton University Press.

the liberal press on the Bolshevik-led soviets and by the sudden onset of an apparent currency shortage in mid-October; this latter meant that workers and employees could not receive their wages.

Elsewhere in Russia newspapers reported ongoing confrontations between the bourgeoisie and the proletariat; the true complexity of class relations and the political situation was disguised by the now-habitual application of the categories and the rhetoric of class struggle. In Ivanovo-Voznesensk on October 21, "a worker-host is raising its fighting banner" against the "enemy — capital." This is how the local strike committee announced the start of a strike by 300,000 textile workers in the Ivanovo-Voznesensk region. In the Donbass coal-producing area, continuing conflicts between workers and managers had nearly halted production altogether. At the end of September at the request of the mine owners the government had dispatched cossacks to the area to help preserve order. On October 19, as noted above, cossacks routed the Soviets of Soldiers' and Workers' Deputies in Kaluga. The refusal of garrison units to obey their marching orders had been the primary reason for the punitive expedition of cossacks, but as in Moscow, mutual hostility between the soviets and the local bourgeoisie had exaggerated the level of tension. Both the Bolshevik-dominated soldiers' soviet and the Menshevik-led workers' soviet fell victim to the cossacks' force, sowing the seeds of panic in the Moscow population. On October 21, the following terse communication from Tula appeared in *Izvestiia*:

> *Kaluga is in the hands of Cossacks. The Soviets are dispersed, arrested; there have been casualties. We are defenseless. Punitive units are moving on Tula, Briansk, Novozybkov. Strength: one armored car, rapid-fire machine guns, and a regiment of dragoons.*

The Bolsheviks' *Sotsial-Demokrat* screamed, "Today Kaluga, tomorrow Moscow!" On the same day, the front page of *Izvestiia* carried a report of the formation of a "black guard" organized and armed by the bourgeoisie.

In Petrograd, the situation also appeared to be drawing to a confrontation between classes. Writing on October 18 in Maxim Gorky's paper *Novaia zhizn'*, the Bolshevik Kamenev openly dissented from the party's decision to stage an uprising; this was the first time that the rumored coup had received public confirmation. Meanwhile, Kerensky had laid plans to send to the front the revolutionary units of the Petrograd garrison, and in response the Petrograd Soviet had authorized the formation of a committee to coordinate the city's defense against an anticipated counterrevolutionary assault. This Military Revolutionary Committee, composed primarily but not exclusively of Bolsheviks, began to function on October 20; its task was to assume control of the city's military forces, that is, to keep the Kerensky government powerless in its own capital. Alexander Rabinowitch has argued that the Bolshevik Central Committee, knowing that the Petrograd working population would support a soviet seizure of power only in self-defense, intended to provoke Kerensky into an attack on the Military Revolutionary Committee, the Bolsheviks, and the Soviet. The Kerensky cabinet indeed responded to the challenge by ordering the arrest of Bolshevik leaders free on bail from imprisonment for their July-days activities, forcibly closing the Bolshevik party newspapers on October 24, and calling up loyal troops to report for duty at the Winter Palace. The Military Revolutionary Committee began to act — twenty-four hours later its representative Trotsky announced to the Petrograd Soviet that the Provisional Government had been overthrown.

Moscow, as elsewhere, had been expecting some sort of resolution to the crisis of power. Central authority was collapsing; banditry continued to prevail in the suburbs; and in the central residential districts, homeowners were forming their own vigilante squads. The presence of thirty thousand garrison troops was no guarantee of order; on the contrary, the regional military commander had ordered the troops' weapons to be locked up to prevent their uncontrolled use.

Everyone expected that the Second All-Russian Congress of Soviets would respond to the growing grass-roots demand for the soviets to take power. Already on October 15, textile union leader Rykunov tried to placate restive union delegates: "It may be that in the near future we will have to take power into our hands, and we cannot shirk from this, since it is a question of existence." The Moscow Soviet on October 19 had asserted its authority over the economic sphere by "decreeing" an end to economic strikes. A wide spectrum of Moscow workers was now endorsing the demand for soviet power.

Nonetheless, the news from Petrograd was met with great trepidation both outside and inside the halls of the Moscow Soviet headquarters. A self-styled Plekhanovite socialist recalled the news that circulated throughout privileged Moscow on the day after the coup: "Before noon of that day, Moscow knew for a certainty that Petrograd was in the grasp of a reign of terror. A marauding mob was plundering

to enact a more general decree on censorship which enraged not only the printers but also provoked the resignation from the Central Committee and government by Nogin and others.

It is easy to see the spark of self-interest which motivated the printers to oppose the Moscow Soviet's infringement on freedom of the press. But one must remember that the printers, by the nature of their work, shared the Menshevik party's sense of working-class isolation. Soviet power, held by a minority, would inevitably lead to civil war and dictatorship, argued the Menshevik leaders in the Soviet. Workers at the big Sytin printing plant in Zamoskvorech'e echoed this fear, resolving by a vote of 980 to 20 on October 30 that they did not want to criticize the workers' and soldiers' movement but that they could not actively support a movement that would lead to the ruin of the working class.

Thus working-class support for the soviet seizure of power in Moscow was by no means unanimous, but neither was there significant opposition. Workers in two machine-building plants in addition to the printers passed resolutions critical of the Bolsheviks' actions, but the majority of workers simply stood aside while power hung in the balance and then resumed their day-to-day tasks of working, finding food, and keeping warm.

One characteristic stood out among the vocal minority of the Moscow work force. This was the strong desire, despite the sharp rise in class hatred, for a compromise solution to the fighting and to the struggle for power. Most of the moderate socialists indeed worked hard for a peaceful outcome, one that would not necessarily give power to the Bolshevik party alone. That the conflict had led to bloodshed was blamed by all on the intransigence of the "other side," the Committee of Public Safety. The railway union and the union of post and telegraph workers (not considered heretofore because, as employees, they were not represented in the Moscow Soviet) actively worked for a negotiated settlement. This sentiment was much stronger in Moscow — thanks to its mixed class composition — than elsewhere.

Even in victory, the soviet partisans voiced little hostility toward the vanquished. True, left-wing Bolsheviks like Avanesov thought nothing of imprisoning their foes; and Nikolai Bukharin, when asked what would happen to the millions of middle-class Russian peasants who did not realize their interests corresponded to the workers', was said to have replied, "We will arrest them." But the dominant mood among Moscow Bolsheviks, both party leaders and rank and file, was more conciliatory. Aleksei Rykov, a moderate like Nogin (and who much later allied with Bukharin in the "Right Opposition" to Stalin's leadership) declared himself to be an enemy of repression and terror and guaranteed full freedom of elections to the Constituent Assembly. "As soon as the Constituent Assembly convenes, power will be transferred to it." . . .

In preparation for the Constituent Assembly elections scheduled for November 18–20, the solemn organ of the bourgeoisie, *Russkie vedomosti*, had constantly intoned warnings about the evils of Bolshevism. Its leading article on November 19, the second day of voting in the assembly, employed terms like "Bolshevik anarchy" and "Bolshevik usurpation" and warned against adopting even the compromise position of the moderate socialists.

> *There are two paths before the country: The path of deepening class struggle and destruction of the state on one side, and the path of the consolidation of Russia and the establishment of firm state power on the other.*

For Kadet as well as Bolshevik partisans, there was no middle choice.

The results of the Constituent Assembly elections again clearly revealed this polarization. The Bolsheviks received approximately 353,000 votes (including 90 percent of the garrison), or 47.9 percent of the total. The Kadet party won 35.7 percent of the vote, about 260,000 ballots, which represented a substantial increase over September when the party had won 102,000 votes and 26 percent of the total. Such an increase appeared to be a moral victory for the party of "firm state power," and *Russkie vedomosti* inferred from the returns that "the growth of bolshevism in the last two months has virtually stopped." Such a conclusion ignored the plain fact that after the soviet seizure of power, the Bolshevik party surpassed its September vote by 153,000 votes, or 75 percent! . . .

The most significant feature of the election was of course the division of votes between Kadets and Bolsheviks. In percentage of total vote, the remaining parties did even more poorly than in September, as Table 9-2 indicates. The Socialist Revolutionaries, who emerged as the largest party in the overall Russian vote with 40 percent, played no role at all in the urban elections. In all provincial capital cities together, the SRs won just 14 percent of the vote, the Bolsheviks 36 percent, the Kadets 23 percent. The cities were the center of class antagonisms, and

mesh with the more moderate Moscow social and political climate. But metalworkers and machine workers continued to act as opinion leaders; and when they lived and worked near other workers with less political experience, like the textile workers, the two groups together combined to act in very forceful ways. These are examples of the internal dynamics that the monolithic view of the working class tends to ignore.

Once the dynamics of the revolutionary process receives careful attention, other new aspects of 1917 emerge. One of the most important here is the overwhelming evidence not of workers' notoriously irrational militancy but in fact of its opposite. The behavior of Moscow's workers in 1917 suggests a working class that was both highly rational in its responses to the political and economic pressures of 1917 and extremely patient as well. The leather workers' strike of August and September provides a good example. The best-known episodes of this protracted strike were the workers' espousal of soviet power on October 19 and the seizure of two factories by striking workers when the leather workers, in Chamberlin's analysis, demonstrated the widespread desire to "pull down the temple of private property." In fact, the majority of workers did not seize their plants; rather, they took the more moderate, disciplined step of asking the Soviet, as a legitimate organ, to sequester leather plants in order to force a settlement. The history of the strike helps explain some of the frustrations that finally provoked 1,000 out of 22,000 strikers to seize their factories. The workers had been ready to accept in August the settlement that the owners finally acceded to in October; the union throughout the strike had been more willing to compromise than the intransigent owners. Finally, the behavior of the leather workers during the strike indicates some of the lessons learned during revolutionary 1917. Leather workers were relatively nonurbanized, prime candidates for "irrational" and "undisciplined" behavior, yet their strike was a model of organization. Such a strike would have been improbable six months earlier.

The basic rationality and patience of Moscow workers can be seen in the resolution and contribution processes as well as in many aspects of the strike movement. Workers' resolutions, . . . were remarkable for their sensibility rather than their maximalism. Workers' contributions, many from factories not otherwise politically active in 1917, indicated a sizable social base for restraint; these workers supported their institutions and supported their leaders, often in opposition to the more vocal minority who sponsored political resolutions. This was not just political inertia; this support for institutions represented support for the cause of working-class unity, a cause that almost all politicized workers in Moscow endorsed. Finally, the logic of working-class behavior can also be seen in two aspects of the strike movement. . . . first that workers who tended to strike most were those with the highest wages. These workers had the reserves to withstand a strike; they knew they were valuable enough to an employer to expect a speedy victory. Secondly, strikes in general and wage strikes in particular diminished over the course of 1917. As inflation increased and output declined, Moscow workers did not struggle hopelessly for higher wage demands, but instead they chose both to strike for control over their jobs and to seek broader political solutions for their problems.

One must therefore reject the image of the Russian working class as uniformly irrational, poorly educated, and incapable of independent participation in the political process. One must reject in particular the myth that the revolution in the cities was carried out by dark semipeasant masses "who did not understand the real meaning of the slogans they loudly repeated." Yes, of course, many Moscow workers were more rural than urban; but when one looks at the participation levels of different segments of the urban labor force, the fact that skilled urban cadres, not the unskilled peasant mass, were the leading political actors can be seen over and over again. These workers possessed experience, political connections, and the degree of economic security which enabled them to function freely and easily in the political life of 1917. Thus metalists and printers participated most frequently in the prerevolutionary strike movement. Metalists led the labor force in the frequency of political resolutions, and they catalyzed their neighboring nonurban textile workers to vote Bolshevik in the June duma elections. Urban workers also led the strike movement, further evidence that strikes in 1917 were much more than spontaneous reactions to immediate threats.

The revolutionary working class takes on new complexity in this context. The existence, demonstrated here, of a leading, politically experienced segment of the working class uniting over time with other varying but less mature segments, plus the existence of a dynamic revolutionary process suggest new approaches to the familiar and important problems of radicalization, Bolshevization, class consciousness, and organization.

What was the nature of the radicalization process that occurred within the working class in 1917? Chamberlin describes the increasing radicalism of workers' demands from higher wages to workers' control during the strikes, and from dual power to soviet power in the political arena. Trotsky clouds the issue by claiming that the radicalism of the masses ("a hundred times to the left of the Bolshevik party," in Lenin's famous phrase) was for the most part an unconscious radicalism. Radicalism becomes almost an innate characteristic of workers by virtue of their working-class position.

This study examines how and why the radicalization process occurred. Radicalization was an incremental process, which took place in response to specific economic and political pressures, and it reflected the political maturation of an increasing number of workers. Factory take-overs and independent declarations of workers' control are commonly cited as evidence of radicalization. "The activity of factory committees . . . thoroughly destroyed in the minds of the workers any respect for the rights of private ownership," writes Chamberlin. Keep asserts that delegates favoring workers' control at the Petrograd factory committee conference "took this slogan in its literal sense, as meaning a real transfer of power to the men's chosen representatives. . . . " But the workers of the Trekhgornaia manufacture did not become radicalized because they now gathered once a week to make decisions about hot water in the dormitories and about personality conflicts on the shop floor. Rather, radicalization took place when the factory management announced a long-term suspension of work for lack of fuel and the factory committee found ample reserves in a neighboring district. Radicalization took place when other workers read about these incidents or heard about them in the factory or in the neighborhood tavern. The radicalization of October, when even the Bolsheviks admitted they were hard pressed to restrain workers from independent acts of violence, was the culmination of the months of revolutionary experience, not the sudden blossoming of maximalist desires and class hatred that workers had secretly harbored all along. "Radical" metalworkers and Bolshevik activists were now at odds with "radical" textile and leather workers because organizational maturation had not kept pace with political developments. The newly politicized workers did not have the capability to express their outrage in the same disciplined way as the radical urban cadres of March and April.

The partisan analogue of radicalization in 1917 was Bolshevization. Here too the study of Moscow workers suggests the complexity of the Bolshevik rise to power. "Bolshevization" is too often used in a purely formulaic way; a district soviet passes a Bolshevik-sponsored resolution on the economic crisis — presto, they are Bolshevized. The Bolshevization of Moscow workers, and presumably elsewhere in Russia, was rather more complex. The process by which the majority of workers identified their interests with the Bolshevik party program was a product of rational, logical choices that corresponded to the changing political and economic nexus.

This process has been seen here in a dozen different ways. In resolutions, workers often endorsed Bolshevik positions without committing themselves to the party on all political questions. The May economic resolutions, the Liberty Loan opposition campaign, the death-penalty issue were all Bolshevik political positions that won support — but for the positions, not for the party. The Moscow Conference strike illustrates the important division between party and policies: even though the majority of workers shared the party's view of the State Conference, the Bolsheviks could not call out workers simply on their own authority but had to rely on that of district soviets and the trade union leadership. Finally, the evolution of the demand for soviet power exemplifies the Bolshevization process. Soviet power was supported by Moscow workers for the practical results they expected it to bring: economic management the workers could trust, honest attempts to make peace, and a guaranteed convocation of the Constituent Assembly. By October, a wide spectrum of workers favored soviet power; but since only the Bolshevik party advocated this power as part of their political program, support for soviet power inevitably translated into support for the Bolshevik party.

These reconsiderations of the meaning of radicalization and of Bolshevization in turn lead to a new consideration of the meaning of class consciousness in the Russian revolution. How closely bound were the political processes of 1917 with the formation of working-class consciousness? Had the Moscow working class by October become a class "for itself" as well as a class "in itself"?

E. P. Thompson concludes his magisterial *Making of the English Working Class*, with a discussion of the elements that contributed to the English workers' very specific sense of class consciousness. These elements, such as the Radical party's political culture of the early 1800s. William Cobbett's rhetoric about social justice, and the Owenites' vision that the people themselves could change their social and economic

Party	June	Percent	September	Percent	November	Percent
Kadet	108,781	18	101,846	26	260,279	35
Socialist Revolutionary	374,885	61	54,410	14	61,394	8
Menshevik	76,407	12	15,787	4	19,790	3
Bolshevik	75,409	12	199,337	51	353,282	47
Democratic-Socialist bloc (Plekhanovites)	—	—	413	—	33,366	4
Total	615,393	100	387,280	100	746,809	100

TABLE 9-2 Electoral Results by Party in Three 1917 Elections

the Moscow elections confirmed this. Roving reporters captured a sense of the motivations of voters which sounded strikingly similar to comments in September. "Citizens, vote for the Bolshevik list!" appealed an agitator in Zamoskvorech'e. "The Bolsheviks will give you everything. The Kadets will give you tsar and police." . . .

Conclusion

> A revolution teaches, and teaches fast.
> *Leon Trotsky*

The role of the Russian working class has hardly been minimized in existing studies of the 1917 revolution. Standard works on the subject agree that workers helped to spark the February revolution, that workers underwent a significant radicalization during the course of 1917, and that this radicalization contributed to the success of the soviet seizure of power in October. The assessment of the workers' role has varied according to the perspective of the historian; "radicalized" workers have been heroes or unwitting villains, but none of the conventional histories has adequately explored or explained this process of radicalization.

Consider three excellent histories of the Russian Revolution. Leon Trotsky's *History of the Russian Revolution* appeared in English in 1932. Trotsky's emphasis on the workers in 1917 derives from his Marxist principles, and he treats workers as revolutionary heroes. Trotsky admits that the Russian working class was not steadfastly revolutionary from the beginning of 1917, primarily because of the influx of non-proletarian elements during the war. But the events of 1917, together with Bolshevik leadership, combined to radicalize the Russian workers. Reviewing the April demonstrations, the July days, the Kornilov mutiny, and October, Trotsky writes, "under these events, so striking in their rhythm, molecular changes were taking place, welding the heterogeneous parts of the working class into one political whole." The strike takes on special importance in Trotsky's view: the "increasing" number of strikes both indicated workers' increasing radicalism and served to initiate the more backward workers into the realities of class conflict. Trotsky's working class, however, remains more or less monolithic. He writes of "molecular processes in the mind of the mass" which led to soviet power in October, but his chosen metaphor suggests that the processes were too minute and too obscure to be analyzed; all that can be seen are the results (a conscious revolutionary class in October) and some of the forces that produced them (strikes, capitalist offensives, and the Bolshevik party). The workers are crucial in Trotsky's history, but they remain obscure "masses" with the merest hints of heterogeneity and of internal, "molecular" dynamics.

William Chamberlin offers the Russian Revolution without Marxism and without Trotsky's self-justification. He too finds a radicalization of the mass in 1917. Like Trotsky, he sees the strike as an important indicator of the radicalization of workers since strikers proceeded first from peaceful conflicts over wages and hours, then to local implementation of workers' control, and finally to support for the Bolshevik program of soviet power. In Chamberlin's study, which deals with other aspects of 1917 besides the workers' movement, this radicalization is uniform across the entire working class. The radical outcome is then explained by the composite characteristics of a peculiarly Russian model proletarian:

> The predestined standardbearer of the social revolution according to Marx proved to be . . . the Petrograd metal worker or the Donetz miner, sufficiently literate to grasp elementary socialist ideas, sufficiently wretched to welcome the first opportunity to pull down the temple of private property.

Finally and quite recently, John Keep has offered a history of the revolution from a social perspective. Keep focuses on workers and peas-

Moscow Military Revolutionary Committee said it would only agree to a compromise in which the Committee of Public Safety acknowledged the fact of soviet power and of the decrees on land and peace voted by the Congress of Soviets after the seizure in Petrograd. By this time, it was clear that the preponderance of military force was on the side of the Military Revolutionary Committee, and there was less need for them to compromise. They rejected another attempt of Mensheviks and SRs to negotiate a cease-fire on November 1. Early on November 3, the Kremlin was retaken by soviet forces; at four o'clock that afternoon the last bastion of the Committee of Public Safety's strength, the Alexander military school in Lefortovo, also surrendered. Military victory in Moscow belonged to the soviets.

Political victory was not so certain. Despite the decisions taken by the Congress of Soviets in Petrograd to enact the Bolshevik program of land, peace, and workers' control, the Bolshevik party assured fellow socialists that the Constituent Assembly would proceed as scheduled. The Moscow Military Revolutionary Committee continued to function as the city political center until November 9, when the first plenary session of the Moscow Soviet since October 25 was held.

The discussion at the session reflected the degree of confusion about both the actual events of the Moscow fighting and the immediate consequences of soviet power as well. Each political party had been internally sundered by the bloody events just ended. Moderate Bolsheviks such as Nogin were countered by hard-line party members who shared the sense of extreme class isolation and hostility that had been building within the Moscow work force. Responding to Menshevik denunciations of Bolshevik political terror at this meeting, V. A. Avanesov exclaimed to loud applause,

> *We do not have a policy of terror, but we do have a policy of carrying out the will of the people, and this policy we will not disavow. If this policy means that we will have to send ten or twenty factory owners to prison, then so we will send them.*

. . .

. . . Moscow did not rise in order to seize power for the soviets, but to defend the soviets from the counterrevolution. Despite the crescendo of sentiment for soviet power among Moscow workers in the last weeks before October 25, there were few among these workers who advocated or even expected that this power would be seized by force. Consequently, when the Military Revolutionary Committee began its operations under a veil of great confusion about the stakes involved, Moscow workers were not ready to mobilize. By and large, throughout the October days they stayed near their factories, watching and waiting.

The Workers in October

The level of working-class participation is open to dispute, of course, and so is the significance of this participation. Did those workers who remained out of the fighting do so out of indifference to the soviet cause or because there was no need for mass participation given the nature of the contest? Unfortunately, the plethora of participants' memoirs devoted to these crucial days almost all stress very personal, adventuristic aspects of the fighting; they provide little evidence of the level of activity of Moscow's workers from October 25 to November 3. But one can still try to assess this activity using the evidence at hand.

First, there were the Red Guards, those workers commanded by the Military Revolutionary Committee who actively fought in the streets of Moscow, many of whom lost their lives. Throughout the summer, individual factories had organized armed or semiarmed units of young men, usually for the defense of their own factories. After the Kornilov mutiny, these units were augmented by fighting squads, formally Red Guards, organized under the aegis of factory committees, raion soviets, or Bolshevik party committees. Most were poorly armed; the dominant theme of Red Guard memoirs about October is not the use of weapons but rather the search for them. By October 25, when the Red Guard had become a formal adjunct of the Moscow Soviet, there were probably about 6,000 guards in the entire city. They were predominantly young, for married workers were discouraged from joining. Probably about half were Bolsheviks of mostly recent vintage; the non-Bolsheviks tended to be members of no party. Of seventy-two factories known to have furnished Red Guard units, about half were metal and machine producers. (All of the units reported to have formed before July were from such plants.)

The overwhelming impression offered by their memoirs is that these Red Guards were very young, undisciplined, and radical but not doctrinaire; for them the October revolution was the great adventure in their lives, as going to war in 1914 had been for a generation in Western Europe. Some older Bolsheviks recognized and feared this adventur-

TABLE 9-1	A Model of Working-Class Participation in the October Days in Moscow		
	Workers Against Soviet Power Prior to the Constituent Assembly		*Workers for Immediate Soviet Power*
Combatants	Red Guards moderate Bolsheviks Left SRs United Social-Democrats urban workers		Red Guards Left Bolsheviks urban workers
Noncombatants	Mensheviks SRs printers (urban workers)		non-Red Guard resolution-passers moderate Bolsheviks (Nogin) rural migrants

now defending the very survival of the soviets as legal institutions. By the time this fact had filtered into the working-class districts, victory was nearly in hand, and potential defenders did not need to make a decision about going to the aid of the soviet. . . .

The distinction between political support for soviet power and participation in the October fighting can perhaps best be made with the help of Table 9-1. The range of attitudes with respect both to armed combat and to the subsequent arrangement of power can be grouped under four separate positions. Both participants and nonparticipants in the street fighting could each support immediate soviet power or oppose soviet power at least before the Constituent Assembly. It seems clear from the wording of October soviet-power resolutions, from studies of working-class and Bolshevik activist attitudes in Petrograd, that many politically active workers fought for soviet power only as a defensive reaction to the perceived attack on the soviets by the Kerensky government. I would guess, in fact, that most of the Red Guards in Moscow, especially the older, urbanized, experienced ones, fought primarily for defensive reasons. . . .

I would assert that this position of nonparticipatory support for immediate soviet power was the dominant one among Moscow workers. The events of 1917 had created a climate, as already seen, in which power to the soviets, the working-class representative, appeared as the only solution to the multiple crises of power, food, production, and war. But this belief was not so strongly held as to motivate many workers to volunteer for the barricades. I have argued above that nonurban workers were the least politicized of the Moscow factory work force, and it must surely have been these apolitical workers who, although accepting the basic concepts of the class-struggle view of society, stood aside when the time came to test their beliefs. Many workers at the Trekhgornaia textile manufacture (and surely elsewhere) actually left the city during the October fighting. The Trekhgornaia factory committee on November 7 gave the absent workers one week to return without jeopardizing their jobs, but the textile workers returned slowly because the deadline was extended by ten more days on December 1. Here is one concrete example of the passive role played in October by those apolitical, little-urbanized workers who remained aloof from the revolution throughout 1917. . . .

Among the workers, printers were the only organized group to oppose and not just to ignore both the fighting and the transfer of power to the soviets. [T]he only published resolutions protesting the October insurrection came from the printshops. Few printers — mostly the very young — were known to have joined the Red Guard. In Presnia, where printers had actively joined the 1905 rising, one printshop was reported to have furnished a Red Guard unit, but it consisted of only five men. This same shop, despite electing a Bolshevik as its Soviet deputy on September 23, voted overwhelmingly (293 to 7) during the October days for the Menshevik resolution calling for the creation of an all-socialist democratic power.

Exacerbating the printers' already well-known antipathy toward the Bolsheviks was the decision made by the party's "fighting center" (not the Military Revolutionary Committee, which had not yet been elected) on October 25 to close down the city's bourgeois press. Troops were apparently dispatched to the presses of the four major bourgeois dailies, which action prompted angry meetings by the printers thus prevented from working: not even Tsar Nicholas had so seized printing presses, declared a resolution from the workers of the large Levenson shop. It was only a short time before the new soviet government felt compelled

Here was a true doctrine of the historical decisiveness of the *coup d'état*, belying all the economic proof of inevitable proletarian victory. For moral support, Lenin referred with some exaggeration to the troubles of the German navy at Kiel: "It cannot be doubted that the mutiny in the German navy is a sign of the great crisis of the rising world revolution." But the real mission was for the Russians: "Yes, we shall be real betrayers of the International if, at such a moment, under such favorable conditions, we reply to such a call of the German revolutionists by mere resolutions."

He repeated his charge that Kerensky was plotting to deliver Petrograd to the Germans, now with more plausibility, for one of the Sunday morning papers had reported a speech by the conservative ex-president of the Duma, Rodzianko, calling for just this. Lenin wrote, "We must not wait for the All-Russian Congress of Soviets, which the Central Executive Committee may postpone till November; we must not tarry, meanwhile allowing Kerensky to bring up still more Kornilovist troops. Finland, the fleet, and Reval [now Tallinn, the Estonian capital and naval base] are represented at the Congress of Soviets [i.e., the Northern Soviets]. Those, together, can bring about an immediate movement towards Petrograd. . . ." He was improvising a new strategy — attack on the capital by pro-Bolshevik soldiers and sailors from the Baltic bases, instead of primary reliance on a coup inside Petrograd. "Such a movement has ninety-nine chances in a hundred of bringing about within a few days the surrender of one section of the Cossack troops, the destruction of another section, and the overthrow of Kerensky, since the workers and the soldiers of both capitals [Petrograd and Moscow] will support such a movement. Delay means death." . . .

By the following day, October 10, the Bolshevik Party had finally been goaded to the decisive fork in the road. The Petrograd city conference of Bolsheviks, meeting in the Smolny Institute between sessions of the soviet, finally endorsed Lenin's mood — without any specifics — by urging "the replacement of the government of Kerensky, together with the stacked Council of the Republic, by a workers' and peasants' revolutionary government." Later that evening, as a cold mist rolled in from the Gulf of Finland, Lenin left the Fofanova apartment, disguised with wig and eyeglasses and still clean-shaven. He was headed for his first formal meeting with the Bolshevik Central Committee since the July Days.

Most histories represent this meeting of October 10 as the time when the Bolsheviks actually decided to seize power. The session had been planned five days earlier — before Lenin returned to Petrograd — as a party conference. But because Lenin would now be present to raise the issue of insurrection, the meeting was restricted to the twelve members of the Central Committee present in Petrograd. They gathered in an apartment on the ground floor at 32 Karpovka Street, a drab brick building on the Petrograd Side. Of all places, this was the home of the Menshevik writer Sukhanov, whose sensitive, tubercular wife, Galina Flakserman, was a Bolshevik of a dozen years standing. She persuaded her unsuspecting husband to stay overnight near his newspaper office in the center of town across the Neva, so that the Bolshevik Central Committee might utilize her unwatched premises. And the Central Committee needed the whole night; with occasional respite for tea and sausages, the twelve men argued for all of ten hours, well into the dawn. They sat in the dining room, with its one window opening on the courtyard carefully covered. Across the canal in front, there was enough coming and going at the John-of-Kronstadt nunnery to divert any attention from the Sukhanovs' unusual visitors.

Only the sketchiest minutes of this meeting were kept, but enough to show how Lenin reasoned and raged to get support for insurrection. Sverdlov began with a routine report on the equivocal political mood among the frontline armies. Then he gave the floor to Lenin for a "Report on the Present Situation." Here is the entire record of the meeting from this point on, as translated from the published proceedings of the Central Committee:

> *Lenin takes the floor.*
>
> *He states that since the beginning of September a certain indifference towards the question of uprising has been noted. He says that this is inadmissible, if we earnestly raise the slogan of seizure of power by the soviets. It is, therefore, high time to turn attention to the technical side of the question. Much time has obviously been lost.*
>
> *Nevertheless the question is very urgent and the decisive moment is near.*
>
> *The international situation is such that we must take the initiative.*
>
> *What is being planned, surrendering as far as Narva and even as far as Petrograd, compels us still more to take decisive action.*
>
> *The political situation is also effectively working in this direction. On July 16–18, decisive action on our part would have been defeated*

Command posts were to be set up in the barracks of the Pavlovsky Regiment and the Second Baltic Fleet Detachment, the former to be directed by Eremeev and the latter by Chudnovsky. A field headquarters for overall direction of the attacking military forces, to be commanded by Antonov-Ovseenko, was to be established in the Peter and Paul Fortress.

Even as these preparations for the seizure of the last bastions of the Provisional Government in Petrograd were being completed, Lenin, elsewhere at Smolny, was nervously watching the clock, by all indications most anxious to insure that the Kerensky regime would be totally eliminated before the start of the Congress of Soviets, now just a scant few hours away. At about 10:00 A.M. he drafted a manifesto "To the Citizens of Russia," proclaiming the transfer of political power from the Kerensky government to the Military Revolutionary Committee:

25 October 1917

To the Citizens of Russia!
  The Provisional Government has been overthrown. State power has passed into the hands of the organ of the Petrograd Soviet of Workers' and Soldiers' Deputies, the Military Revolutionary Committee, which stands at the head of the Petrograd proletariat and garrison
  The cause for which the people have struggled — the immediate proposal of a democratic peace, the elimination of landlord estates, workers' control over production, the creation of a soviet government — the triumph of this cause has been assured.
  Long live the workers', soldiers', and peasants' revolution!

The Military Revolutionary Committee
of the Petrograd Soviet
of Workers' and Soldiers' Deputies

The seminal importance Lenin attached to congress delegates being faced, from the very start, with a *fait accompli* as regards the creation of a soviet government is clearly illustrated by the fact that this proclamation was printed and already going out over the wires to the entire country even before the Military Revolutionary Committee strategy meeting described above had ended.

If October 25 began as a day of energetic activity and hope for the left, the same cannot be said for supporters of the old government. In the Winter Palace, Kerensky by now had completed arrangements to meet troops heading for the capital from the northern front. A striking indication of the isolation and helplessness of the Provisional Government at this point is the fact that the Military Revolutionary Committee's control of all rail terminals precluded travel outside of Petrograd by train, while for some time the General Staff was unable to provide the prime minister with even one automobile suitable for an extended trip. Finally, military officials managed to round up an open Pierce Arrow and a Renault, the latter borrowed from the American embassy. At 11:00 A.M., almost precisely the moment when Lenin's manifesto proclaiming the overthrow of the government began circulating, the Renault, flying an American flag, tailed by the aristocratic Pierce Arrow, roared through the main arch of the General Staff building, barreled past Military Revolutionary Committee pickets already forming around the Winter Palace, and sped southwestward out of the capital. Huddled in the back seat of the Pierce Arrow were the assistant to the commander of the Petrograd Military District, Kuzmin; two staff officers; and a pale and haggard Kerensky, on his way to begin a desperate hunt for loyal troops from the front, a mission that was to end in abject failure less than a week later. . . .

Elsewhere by this time, insurgent ranks had been bolstered by the liberation from the Crosses Prison of the remaining Bolsheviks imprisoned there since the July days. A Military Revolutionary Committee commissar simply appeared at the ancient prison on the morning of October 25 with a small detachment of Red Guards and an order for the release of all political prisoners; among others, the Bolsheviks Semion Roshal, Sakharov, Tolkachev, and Khaustov were immediately set free. At 2:00 P.M. the forces at the disposal of the Military Revolutionary Committee were increased still further by the arrival of the armada from Kronstadt. One of the more than a thousand sailors crammed on the deck of the *Amur*, I. Pavlov, subsequently recalled the waters outside Petrograd at midday, October 25:

> *What did the Gulf of Finland around Kronstadt and Petrograd look like then? This is conveyed well by a song that was popular at the time [sung to the melody of the familiar folk tune* Stenka Razin*]: "Iz za ostrova Kronshtadta na prostor reki Nevy, vyplyvaiut mnogo lodok, v nikh sidiat bol'sheviki!" [From the island of Kronstadt toward the River Neva broad, there are many boats a-sailing — they have Bolsheviks on board.] If these words do not describe the Gulf of Finland exactly, it's only because "boats" are mentioned. Substitute contemporary ships*

and you will have a fully accurate picture of the Gulf of Finland a few hours before the October battle.

At the entrance to the harbor canal the *Zaria svobody*, pulled by the four tugs, dropped anchor; a detachment of sailors swarmed ashore and undertook to occupy the Baltic rail line between Ligovo and Oranienbaum. As the rest of the ships inched through the narrow channel, it occurred to Flerovsky, aboard the *Amur*, that if the government had had the foresight to lay a couple of mines and emplace even a dozen machine guns behind the parapet of the canal embankment, the carefully laid plans of the Kronstadters would have been wrecked. He heaved a sigh of relief as the motley assortment of ships passed through the canal unhindered and entered the Neva, where they were greeted by enthusiastic cheers from crowds of workers gathered on the banks. Flerovsky himself was in the cabin of the *Amur* ship's committee below decks, discussing where to cast anchor, when a mighty, jubilant hurrah rent the air. Flerovsky ran up on deck just in time to see the *Aurora* execute a turn in the middle of the river, angling for a better view of the Winter Palace.

As the men on the *Aurora* and the ships from Kronstadt spotted each other, cheers and shouts of greeting rang out, the round caps of the sailors filled the sky, and the *Aurora*'s band broke into a triumphant march. The *Amur* dropped anchor close by the *Aurora*, while some of the smaller boats continued on as far as the Admiralty. Moments later Antonov-Ovseenko went out to the *Amur* to give instructions to leaders of the Kronstadt detachment. Then, as students and professors at St. Petersburg University gawked from classroom windows on the embankment, the sailors, totaling around three thousand, disembarked, large numbers of them to join the forces preparing to besiege the Winter Palace. A member of this contingent later remembered that upon encountering garrison soldiers, some of the sailors berated them for their cowardliness during the July days. He recalled with satisfaction that the soldiers were now ready to repent their errors.

Important developments were occurring in the meantime at Smolny. The great main hall there was packed to the rafters with Petrograd Soviet deputies and representatives from provincial soviets anxious for news of the latest events when Trotsky opened an emergency session of the Petrograd Soviet at 2:35 P.M. The fundamental

The Cruiser *Aurora* on the Neva River, 1918. This ship, manned by sailors loyal to the Bolsheviks, shelled the Winter Palace, headquarters of the Provisional Government, during the October Revolution. (Sovfoto)

transformation in the party's tactics that had occurred during the night became apparent from the outset of this meeting, perhaps the most momentous in the history of the Petrograd Soviet. It will be recalled that less than twenty-four hours earlier, at another session of the Petrograd Soviet, Trotsky had insisted that an armed conflict "today or tomorrow, on the eve of the congress, is not in our plans." Now, stepping up to the speaker's platform, he immediately pronounced the Provisional Government's obituary. "On behalf of the Military Revolutionary Committee," he shouted, "I declare that the Provisional Government no longer exists!" To a storm of applause and shouts of "Long live the Military Revolutionary Committee!" he announced, in rapid order, that the Preparliament had been dispersed, that individual government ministers had been arrested, and that the rail stations, the post office, the central telegraph, the Petrograd Telegraph Agency, and the state bank had been occupied by forces of the Military Revolutionary Committee. "The Winter Palace has not been taken," he reported, *because we had no majority with us. Since then, our upsurge has been making gigantic strides.*

The absenteeism and the indifference of the masses can be explained by the fact that the masses are tired of words and resolutions.

The majority is now with us. Politically, the situation has become entirely ripe for the transfer of power.

The agrarian movement also goes in this direction, for it is clear that enormous efforts are needed to subdue this movement. The slogan of transferring the entire land has become the general slogan of the peasants. The political background is thus ready. It is necessary to speak of the technical side. This is the whole matter. Meanwhile we, together with the defensists, are inclined to consider a systematic preparation for an uprising as something like a political sin.

To wait for the Constituent Assembly, which will obviously not be for us, is senseless, because it would make our task more complex.

We must utilize the regional congress [of the Northern Soviets] and the proposal from Minsk to begin decisive action.

Comrade Lomov takes the floor, giving information concerning the attitude of the Moscow regional bureau and the Moscow Committee, as well as about the situation in Moscow in general.

Comrade Uritsky states that we are weak not only in a technical sense but also in all other spheres of our work. We have carried a mass of resolutions. Actions, none whatever. The Petrograd Soviet is disorganized, few meetings, etc.

On what forces do we base ourselves?

The workers in Petrograd have forty thousand rifles, but this will not decide the issue; this is nothing.

The garrison after the July Days cannot inspire great hopes. However, in any case, if the course is held for an uprising, then it is really necessary to do something in that direction. We must make up our mind with regard to definite action.

Comrade Sverdlov gives information concerning what he knows about the state of affairs throughout Russia.

Comrade Dzerzhinsky proposes that for the purpose of political guidance during the immediate future, a Political Bureau be created, composed of members of the C.C.[2]

---

[2] This "Politburo" never functioned — it never even met (the fate of more than one revolutionary committee). It should not be confused with the Politburo created in 1919, the direct ancestor of the present ruling group in the USSR.

After an exchange of opinion, the proposal is carried. A Political Bureau of seven is created (the editors plus two plus Bubnov).

A resolution was accepted, reading as follows:

RESOLUTION

The Central Committee recognizes that the international situation of the Russian Revolution (the mutiny in the navy in Germany as extreme manifestation of the growth in all of Europe of the worldwide socialist revolution; the threat of a peace between the imperialists with the aim of crushing the revolution in Russia) as well as the military situation (the undoubted decision of the Russian bourgeoisie and of Kerensky and Co. to surrender Petrograd to the Germans) and the fact that the proletarian parties have gained a majority in the soviets; all this, coupled with the peasant uprising and with a shift of the people's confidence towards our party (elections in Moscow); finally, the obvious preparation for a second Kornilov affair (the withdrawal of troops from Petrograd; the bringing of Cossacks to Petrograd; the surrounding of Minsk by Cossacks, etc.) — places the armed uprising on the order of the day.

Recognizing thus that an armed uprising is inevitable and the time perfectly ripe, the Central Committee proposes to all the organizations of the party to act accordingly and to discuss and decide from this point of view all the practical questions (the Congress of Soviets of the Northern Region, the withdrawal of troops from Petrograd, the actions in Moscow and in Minsk, etc.).

Ten express themselves for it, and two against.

The question is then raised of establishing a Political Bureau of the C. C. It is decided to form a bureau of seven: Lenin, Zinoviev, Kamenev, Trotsky, Stalin, Sokolnikov, Bubnov.

As day broke on the 11th of October Lenin finally had reached the objective he had been fighting for for an entire month: the Bolshevik Central Committee had yielded in principle and acknowledged the aim of armed uprising.[3] It did nothing more in the direction of deliberate

---

[3] Trotsky, in his book on Lenin and in other recollections, recounts an exchange with Lenin that supposedly took place at this meeting but is not in the published minutes. Conceivably it was the night before. Trotsky says that he brought up the new project of the soviet military committee and urged the Congress of Soviets as the occasion for the uprising. "Vladimir Ilyich inveighed against this date horribly. The question of the Second Congress of Soviets, he said, was of no interest to him; what meaning did the congress have? . . . The rising must be begun absolutely before and independent of the

that fundamental condition, there cannot be the kinship, closeness and bond between the position of the proletariat and that of the non-proletarian working people which (kinship, closeness and bond) are necessary for the proletariat to influence those masses, for its influence over them to be effective.

V

Let us proceed further.

The proletariat can win state power, establish the Soviet system, and satisfy the economic needs of the majority of the working people at the expense of the exploiters.

Is that sufficient for achieving complete and final victory? No, it is not.

The petty-bourgeois democrats, their chief present-day representatives, the "socialists" and "Social-Democrats," are suffering from illusions when they imagine that the working people are capable, under capitalism, of acquiring the high degree of class-consciousness, firmness of character, perception and wide political outlook that will enable them to decide, *merely by voting*, or at all events, to *decide in advance*, without long experience of struggle, that they will follow a particular class, or a particular party.

It is mere illusion. It is a sentimental story invented by pedants and sentimental socialists of the Kautsky, Longuet and MacDonald type.

Capitalism would not be capitalism if it did not, on the one hand, condemn the *masses* to a downtrodden, crushed and terrified state of existence, to disunity (the countryside!) and ignorance, and if it (capitalism) did not, on the other hand, place in the hands of the bourgeoisie a gigantic apparatus of falsehood and deception to hoodwink the masses of workers and peasants, to stultify their minds, and so forth.

That is why only the proletariat can *lead the working people* out of capitalism to communism. It is no use thinking that the petty-bourgeois or semi-petty-bourgeois masses can decide in advance the extremely complicated political question: "to be with the working class or with the bourgeoisie." The *vacillation* of the non-proletarian sections of the working people is inevitable; and inevitable also is their own *practical experience*, which will enable them to *compare* leadership by the bourgeoisie with leadership by the proletariat.

This is the circumstance that is constantly lost sight of by those who worship "consistent democracy" and who imagine that extremely important political problems can be solved by voting. Such problems are actually solved by *civil war* if they are acute and aggravated by struggle, and the *experience* of the non-proletarian masses (primarily of the peasants), their experience of comparing the rule of the proletariat with the rule of the bourgeoisie, is of tremendous importance in that war.

The Constituent Assembly elections in Russia in November 1917, compared with the two-year Civil War of 1917–19, are highly instructive in this respect.

See which districts proved to be the least Bolshevik. First, the East-Urals and the Siberian where the Bolsheviks polled 12 per cent and 10 per cent of the votes respectively. Secondly, the Ukraine where the Bolsheviks polled 10 per cent of the votes. Of the other districts, the Bolsheviks polled the smallest percentage of votes in the peasant district of Great Russia, the Volga-Black Earth district, but even there the Bolsheviks polled 16 per cent of the votes.

It was precisely in the districts where the Bolsheviks polled the lowest percentage of votes in November 1917 that the counter-revolutionary movements, the revolts and the organisation of counter-revolutionary forces had the greatest success. It was precisely in those districts that the rule of Kolchak and Denikin lasted for months and months.

The vacillation of the petty-bourgeois population was particularly marked in those districts where the influence of the proletariat is weakest. Vacillation was at first in favour of the Bolsheviks when they granted land and when the demobilised soldiers brought the news about peace; later — against the Bolsheviks when, to promote the international development of the revolution and to protect its centre in Russia, they agreed to sign the Treaty of Brest and thereby "offended" patriotic sentiments, the deepest of petty-bourgeois sentiments. The dictatorship of the proletariat was particularly displeasing to the peasants in those places where there were the largest stocks of surplus grain, when the Bolsheviks showed that they would strictly and firmly secure the transfer of those surplus stocks to the state at fixed prices. The peasants in the Urals, Siberia and the Ukraine turned to Kolchak and Denikin.

Further, the experience of Kolchak and Denikin "democracy," about which every hack writer in Kolchakia and Denikia shouted in every issue of the whiteguard newspapers, showed the peasants that phrases about democracy and about the "Constituent Assembly" serve

take, it is enough to recall that throughout 1917 many of the Bolsheviks' most important resolutions and public statements were influenced as much by the outlook of right Bolsheviks as by that of Lenin. In addition, moderate Bolsheviks like Kamenev, Zinoviev, Lunacharsky, and Riazanov were among the party's most articulate and respected spokesmen in key public institutions such as the soviets and the trade unions.

In 1917 subordinate party bodies like the Petersburg Committee and the Military Organization were permitted considerable independence and initiative, and their views and criticism were taken into account in the formation of policy at the highest levels. Most important, these lower bodies were able to tailor their tactics and appeals to suit their own particular constituencies amid rapidly changing conditions. Vast numbers of new members were recruited into the party, and they too played a significant role in shaping the Bolsheviks' behavior. Among these newcomers were many of the leading figures in the October revolution, among them Trotsky, Antonov-Ovseenko, Lunacharsky, and Chudnovsky. The newcomers included tens of thousands of workers and soldiers from among the most impatient and dissatisfied elements in the factories and garrison who knew little, if anything, about Marxism and cared nothing about party discipline. This caused extreme difficulties in July when leaders of the Military Organization and the Petersburg Committee, responsive to their militant constituencies, encouraged an insurrection, against the wishes of the Central Committee. But during the period of reaction that followed the July uprising, in the course of the fight against Kornilov, and again during the October revolution, the Bolsheviks' extensive, carefully cultivated connections in factories, local workers' organizations, and units of the Petrograd garrison and the Baltic Fleet were to be a significant source of the party's durability and strength.

The importance to the Bolshevik success of the dynamic relationship that existed in 1917 within the top Bolshevik hierarchy, as well as between it, the ostensibly subordinate elements of the party, and the masses, was illustrated immediately after the July uprising. At the time, Lenin believed that the Provisional Government was effectively controlled by counterrevolutionary elements; overestimating the government's capacity to damage the left, he was convinced, moreover, that under the influence of the Mensheviks and SRs the existing soviets had been rendered powerless. Hence he demanded that the party abandon its orientation toward a possible peaceful transfer of power to the soviets and shift its attention toward preparations for an armed uprising at the earliest opportunity. Other leaders, many of whom had particularly close ties with workers and soldiers and were also active in the Central Executive Committee and the Petrograd Soviet, refused to discount completely the Mensheviks and SRs as potential allies and the soviets as legitimate revolutionary institutions. While the slogan "All Power to the Soviets" was officially withdrawn by the Sixth Congress in late July, this change did not take hold at the local level. Moreover, the congress did not deemphasize efforts to win the soviets, and they continued to be a major focus of party activity throughout the month of August.

As it turned out, the impact of the post–July Days reaction against the left was not nearly as serious as originally feared. To the contrary, the repressive measures adopted by the government, as well as the indiscriminate persecution of leftist leaders and the apparently increasing danger of counterrevolution, served simply to increase resentment toward the Kerensky regime among the masses and stimulated them to unite more closely around the soviets in defense of the revolution. The Bolsheviks, working in cooperation with Mensheviks and SRs primarily through revolutionary committees created by the soviets, played a leading role in the quick defeat of Kornilov. In the capital, the Petrograd Soviet, distinctly more radical in composition and outlook, emerged from the Kornilov experience with its power and authority greatly enhanced. In response, the Bolsheviks in early September formally resurrected their main pre–July slogan, "All Power to the Soviets."

Probably the clearest example of the importance and value of the party's relatively free and flexible structure, and the responsiveness of its tactics to the prevailing mass mood, came during the second half of September, when party leaders in Petrograd turned a deaf ear to the ill-timed appeals of Lenin, then still in hiding in Finland, for an immediate insurrection. To be sure, on October 10 the Bolshevik Central Committee, with Lenin in attendance, made the organization of an armed insurrection and the seizure of power "the order of the day." Yet in the ensuing days there was mounting evidence that an uprising launched independently of the soviets and in advance of the Second Congress of Soviets would not be supported by the Petrograd masses; that the seizure of power by the Bolsheviks alone would be opposed by all other major political parties, by peasants in the provinces and soldiers at the front, and possibly even by such mass democratic institutions as the soviets and trade unions; and that in any case the party was

The reading of this historic manifesto was interrupted again and again by thundering waves of delirious cheers. After Lunacharsky had finished and a semblance of order was restored, Kamkov announced that, with a minor change, the Left SRs would support its adoption. The change was immediately accepted. A spokesman for the tiny Menshevik-United Internationalist fraction declared that if the proclamation would be amended to provide for the immediate organization of a government based on the broadest possible elements of the population, he would vote for it as well; however, when this suggestion was ignored, he announced that his followers would abstain. Finally, at 5:00 A.M., October 26, the manifesto legitimizing the creation of a revolutionary government was voted on and passed by an overwhelming margin, only two deputies voting against and twelve abstaining. A misty gray dawn, typical of Petrograd in late fall, was breaking as congress delegates drifted slowly out of Smolny. Upstairs, exhausted Military Revolutionary Committee leaders stretched out on the floor of their crowded command post to catch some sleep, many of them for the first time in several days. Lenin had gone off to the nearby apartment of Bonch-Bruevich to rest and draft a decree on land reform for adoption at the next session of the congress. The Bolsheviks had come to power in Petrograd, and a new era in the history of Russia and of the world had begun. . . .

The central question of why the Bolsheviks won the struggle for power in Petrograd in 1917 permits no simple answer. To be sure, from the perspective of more than half a century, it is clear that the fundamental weakness of the Kadets and moderate socialists during the revolutionary period and the concomitant vitality and influence of the radical left at that time can be traced to the peculiarities of Russia's political, social, and economic development during the nineteenth century and earlier. The world war also inevitably had a good deal to do with the way the 1917 revolution in Petrograd turned out. Had it not been for the Provisional Government's commitment to pursue the war to victory, a policy which in 1917 enjoyed no broad support, it surely would have been better able to cope with the myriad problems that inevitably attended the collapse of the old order and, in particular, to satisfy popular demands for immediate fundamental reform.

As it was, a major source of the Bolsheviks' growing strength and authority in 1917 was the magnetic attraction of the party's platform as embodied in the slogans "Peace, Land, and Bread" and "All Power to the Soviets." The Bolsheviks conducted an extraordinarily energetic and resourceful campaign for the support of Petrograd factory workers and soldiers and Kronstadt sailors. Among these groups, the slogan "All Power to the Soviets" signified the creation of a democratic, exclusively socialist government, representing all parties and groups in the Soviet and committed to a program of immediate peace, meaningful internal reform, and the early convocation of a Constituent Assembly. In the late spring and summer of 1917, a number of factors served to increase support for the professed goals of the Bolsheviks, especially for transfer of power to the soviets. Economic conditions steadily worsened. Garrison soldiers became directly threatened by shipment to the front. Popular expectations of early peace and reform under the Provisional Government dwindled. Concomitantly, all other major political groups lost credibility because of their association with the government and their insistence on patience and sacrifice in the interest of the war effort. In the wake of the Kornilov affair, among the lower strata of the Petrograd population the desire for an end to coalition government with the Kadets became very nearly universal.

That in the space of eight months the Bolsheviks reached a position from which they were able to assume power was due as well to the special effort which the party devoted to winning the support of military troops in the rear and at the front; only the Bolsheviks seem to have perceived the necessarily crucial significance of the armed forces in the struggle for power. Perhaps even more fundamentally, the phenomenal Bolshevik success can be attributed in no small measure to the nature of the party in 1917. Here I have in mind neither Lenin's bold and determined leadership, the immense historical significance of which cannot be denied, nor the Bolsheviks' proverbial, though vastly exaggerated, organizational unity and discipline. Rather, I would emphasize the party's internally relatively democratic, tolerant, and decentralized structure and method of operation, as well as its essentially open and mass character — in striking contrast to the traditional Leninist model.

As we have seen, within the Bolshevik Petrograd organization at all levels in 1917 there was continuing free and lively discussion and debate over the most basic theoretical and tactical issues. Leaders who differed with the majority were at liberty to fight for their views, and not infrequently Lenin was the loser in these struggles. To gauge the importance of this tolerance of differences of opinion and ongoing give-and-

suppressed during Stalin's heyday, but after the de-Stalinization of 1956 Soviet historians resurrected it — as proof of another of Stalin's errors, overestimating Trotsky! In fact they are right, though the whole party shared Stalin's accolade at the time: Trotsky in October was at the height of his career as the flaming revolutionary tribune, yet he shied away from the outright insurrection that Lenin demanded. Trotsky exemplified the feelings of the main body of the Bolshevik leadership, eager for power yet afraid either to take a military initiative or to face Lenin's wrath. Trotsky talked revolution but waited for the Congress — until the moment of Lenin's return to Smolny. Then, like most of the party leadership, he persuaded himself that he had been carrying out Lenin's instructions all along; any statement he had made about waiting for the Congress became, in retrospect, a political lie "to cover up the game." But in truth there was far more lying about the October Revolution after the event than before.

How important was the matter of waiting for the Congress of Soviets? What difference would it have made if Kerensky had not precipitated the fighting and the Congress had assembled peacefully to vote itself into power? Lenin, for one, believed it made a vast difference, and his view is underscored from the opposite direction by the conduct of the Mensheviks and Right SRs after the uprising. They were bitter and intransigent and unwilling to enter a meaningful coalition where they might have balanced the Bolsheviks. The Bolsheviks — a majority of them, at least — were emboldened by the smell of gunpowder, and ready to fight to the end to preserve the conquests of their impromptu uprising. The same was true of the Left SRs, reluctant though they had been for violence. Many moderates, on the other hand, were so enraged that they were prepared to join hands with the Ultra-Right, if need be, to oust the Bolshevik usurpers. If the Congress had met without insurrection — a large "if" — Russia would have remained for the time being on the course of peaceful political compromise; with prior insurrection a fact, Russia was headed on the path to civil war and dictatorship.

The October Revolution gave the impetus to the whole subsequent development of the Soviet Russian regime and the worldwide Communist movement. If the revolution had not occurred as it did, the basic political cleavage of Bolsheviks and anti-Bolsheviks would not have been so sharp, and it is difficult to imagine what other events might have established a similar opportunity for one-party Bolshevik

accept and depend on his own unconditional leadership.

To this extent there is some truth in the contentions, both Soviet and non-Soviet, that Lenin's leadership was decisive. By psychological pressure on his Bolshevik lieutenants and his manipulation of the fear of counterrevolution, he set the stage for the one-party seizure of power. But the facts of the record show that in the crucial days before October 24th Lenin was not making his leadership effective. The party, unable to face up directly to his browbeating, was tacitly violating his instructions and waiting for a multi-party and semi-constitutional revolution by the Congress of Soviets. Lenin had failed to seize the moment, failed to avert the trend to a compromise coalition regime of the soviets, failed to nail down the base for his personal dictatorship — until the government struck on the morning of the 24th of October.

Kerensky's ill-conceived countermove was the decisive accident. Galvanizing all the fears that the revolutionaries had acquired in July and August about a rightist *putsch*, it brought out their utmost — though still clumsy — effort to defend themselves and hold the ground for the coming Congress of Soviets. The Bolsheviks could not calculate, when they called the Red Guards to the bridges and sent commissars to the communications centers, that the forces of the government would apathetically collapse. With undreamed-of ease, and no intention before the fact, they had the city in the palms of their hands, ready to close their grip when their leader reappeared from the underground and able to offer him the Russian capital in expiation of their late faintheartedness.

The role of Trotsky in all this is very peculiar. A year after the revolution Stalin wrote, "All the work of the practical organization of the insurrection proceeded under the immediate direction of the chairman of the Petrograd Soviet, Comrade Trotsky. It can be said with assurance that for the quick shift of the garrison to the side of the soviet and the bold insurrectionary work of the MRC the party is indebted firstly and mainly to Comrade Trotsky." This passage was naturally

Party seize the moment and hurl all the force it could against the Provisional Government. Certainly the Bolshevik Party had a better overall chance for survival and a future political role if it waited and compromised, as Zinoviev and Kamenev wished. But this would not yield the only kind of political power — exclusive power — that Lenin valued. He was bent on baptizing the revolution in blood, to drive off the fainthearted and compel all who subscribed to the overturn to

plans, and even its theoretical submission to Lenin was won at the cost of a bitter majority-minority division. Everyone soon knew who the two were who voted against the resolution that Lenin had scribbled out on a piece of notebook paper. They were his oldest and truest lieutenants, Zinoviev and Kamenev. The opposition of these two kept the party leadership in turmoil and gave Lenin his main political worry right up to the eve of the uprising. It is significant that Zinoviev and Kamenev still figured in the proposed Politburo (though this body never functioned). They had more strength than the vote showed, including at least four of the ten Central Committee members who were not present. In a complete vote the opposition would have had better than 25 per cent of the Central Committee, with particular strength in Moscow, where Bolshevik opinion on the insurrection was more clearly polarized pro and con.

It was cold and raining when the twelve Bolshevik leaders filed out of the Sukhanov apartment. Lenin had no overcoat; Dzerzhinsky offered his own, and when Lenin protested, said, "It's an order of the Central Committee, Comrade!" For once, Vladimir Ilyich submitted to party discipline. . . .

The Myth and the Reality

Since the days of the October uprising itself, it has been difficult for either side to take stock of the extraordinary series of accidents and missteps that accompanied the Bolshevik Revolution and allowed it to succeed. One thing that both victors and vanquished were agreed on, before the smoke had hardly cleared from the Palace Square, was the myth that the insurrection was timed and executed according to deliberate Bolshevik plan.

The official Communist history of the revolution has held rigidly to an orthodox Marxist interpretation of the event: it was an uprising

---

congress." Trotsky appears to have stuck by his sense of the political appeal of the soviets. "In the end," he noted, "three groups were formed in the Central Committee: the opponents of the seizure of power by the party . . . ; Lenin, who demanded the immediate organization of the rising, independent of the soviets; and the last group who considered it necessary to bind the rising closely with the Second Congress of Soviets and in consequence wished to postpone it until the latter took place."

of thousands of workers and peasants, the inevitable consequence of the international class struggle of proletariat against bourgeoisie, brought to a head first in Russia because it was "the weakest link in the chain of capitalism." At the same time it is asserted, though the contradiction is patent, that the revolution could not have succeeded without the ever-present genius leadership of Lenin. This attempt to have it both ways has been ingrained in Communist thinking ever since Lenin himself campaigned in the name of Marx for the "art of insurrection."

Anti-Communist interpretations, however they may deplore the October Revolution, are almost as heavily inclined to view it as the inescapable outcome of overwhelming circumstances or of long and diabolical planning. The impasse of the war was to blame, or Russia's inexperience in democracy, or the feverish laws of revolution. If not these factors, it was Lenin's genius and trickery in propaganda, or the party organization as his trusty and invincible instrument. Of course, all of these considerations played a part, but when they are weighed against the day by day record of the revolution, it is hard to argue that any combination of them made Bolshevik power inevitable or even likely.

The stark truth about the Bolshevik Revolution is that it succeeded against incredible odds in defiance of any rational calculation that could have been made in the fall of 1917. The shrewdest politicians of every political coloration knew that while the Bolsheviks were an undeniable force in Petrograd and Moscow, they had against them the overwhelming majority of the peasants, the army in the field, and the trained personnel without which no government could function. Everyone from the right-wing military to the Zinoviev-Kamenev Bolsheviks judged a military dictatorship to be that most likely alternative if peaceful evolution failed. They all thought — whether they hoped or feared — that a Bolshevik attempt to seize power would only hasten or assure the rightist alternative.

Lenin's revolution, as Zinoviev and Kamenev pointed out, was a wild gamble, with little chance that the Bolsheviks' ill-prepared followers could prevail against all the military force that the government seemed to have, and even less chance that they could keep power even if they managed to seize it temporarily. To Lenin, however, it was a gamble that entailed little risk, because he sensed that in no other way and at no other time would he have any chance at all of coming to power. This is why he demanded so vehemently that the Bolshevik

the night of October 24–25 in that center of revolutionary radicalism, Fletovsky was later to recall:

> *It is doubtful whether anyone in Kronstadt closed his eyes that night. . . . The Naval Club was jammed with sailors, soldiers, and workers. . . . The revolutionary staff drew up a detailed operations plan, designated participating units, made an inventory of available supplies, and issued instructions. . . . When the planning was finished. . . . I went into the street. Everywhere there was heavy, but muffled traffic. Groups of soldiers and sailors were making their way to the naval dockyard. By the light of the torches we could see just the first ranks of serious determined faces. . . . Only the rumble of the automobiles, moving supplies from the fortress warehouses to the ships, disturbed the silence of the night.*

Shortly after 9:00 A.M. the sailors, clad in black pea jackets, with rifles slung over their shoulders and cartridge pouches on their belts, finished boarding the available vessels: two mine layers, the *Amur* and the *Khopor*; the former yacht of the fort commandant, the *Zarnitsa*, fitted out as a hospital ship; a training vessel, the *Verny*; a battleship, the *Zaria svobody*, so old that it was popularly referred to as the "flatiron" of the Baltic Fleet and had to be helped along by four tugs; and a host of smaller paddle-wheel passenger boats and barges. As the morning wore on these vessels raised anchor, one after the other, and steamed off in the direction of the capital.

At Smolny at this time, the leaders of the Military Revolutionary Committee and commissars from key locations about the city were completing plans for the capture of the Winter Palace and the arrest of the government. Podvoisky, Antonov-Ovseenko, Konstantin Eremeev, Georgii Blagonravov, Chudnovsky, and Sadovsky are known to have participated in these consultations. According to the blueprint which they worked out, insurrectionary forces were to seize the Mariinsky Palace and disperse the Preparliament; after this the Winter Palace was to be surrounded. The government was to be offered the opportunity of surrendering peacefully. If it refused to do so, the Winter Palace was to be shelled from the *Aurora* and the Peter and Paul Fortress, after which it was to be stormed. The main forces designated to take part in these operations were the Pavlovsky Regiment; Red Guard detachments from the Vyborg, Petrograd, and Vasilevsky Island districts; the Keksgolmsky Regiment; the naval elements arriving from Kronstadt and Helsingfors; and sailors from the Petrograd-based Second Baltic Fleet Detachment.

rule. Given the fact of the party's forcible seizure of power, civil violence and a militarized dictatorship of revolutionary extremism followed with remorseless logic.

Alexander Rabinowitch

The Bolsheviks Come to Power

In this selection Rabinowitch, like Daniels, shows the confusion and disorganization that surrounded the Bolshevik seizure of power. But he does not go so far as Daniels, who claims that October was an accident, but rather shows the sources of Bolshevik armed support. Rabinowitch concludes that the Bolshevik organization worked to enhance their strategy in 1917 but in precisely the opposite way from the familiar view that centralization and discipline marked their activities.

At the main bases of the Baltic fleet, activity began long before dawn on the morning of Wednesday, October 25. The first of three large echelons of armed sailors, bound for the capital at the behest of the Military Revolutionary Committee, departed Helsingfors by train along the Finnish railway at 3:00 A.M.; a second echelon got underway at 5:00 A.M., and a third left around midmorning. About the same time, a hastily assembled naval flotilla, consisting of a patrol boat — the *Iastrev* — and five destroyers — the *Metki, Zabiiaka, Moshchny, Deiatelny,* and *Samson* — started off at full steam for the roughly two hundred-mile trip to Petrograd, with the *Samson* in the lead flying a large banner emblazoned with the slogans "Down with the Coalition!" "Long Live the All-Russian Congress of Soviets!" and "All Power to the Soviets!" Activity of a similar kind was taking place at Kronstadt. Describing

Excerpted from Alexander Rabinowitch, *The Bolsheviks Come to Power*, Chapter 15, pp. 273–304, 310–314. Reprinted by permission of W. W. Norton & Company.

The Imperial Winter Palace, St. Petersburg. This neoclassical building, designed by Bartolomeo Rastrelli, was the home of the tsars from the mid-eighteenth century until the Revolution. It now houses the Hermitage museum, which contains thousands of priceless paintings, sculptures, jewels, and other art treasures. (UPI/Bettmann Newsphotos)

trict man and a popular leader in the soviet. "There are two sides to this question," Volodarsky warned. "I think that we, a party of genuine revolutionaries, could in no case take power and hold out more than one or two months." Petrograd and Finland were not the whole country. "We must not force events. . . . This policy is doomed to certain collapse. . . . We can take power only in a state of desperation." The masses would have to learn that it was the government who opposed the Congress of Soviets and the Constituent Assembly. Then the Bolsheviks could act, but for the time being, "Ilyich's course seems to me extremely weak."

Volodarsky was backed up by Lashevich of the Military Organization, another man who had sobered up since July: "The strategic plan proposed by Comrade Lenin is limping on all four legs. . . . Let's not fool ourselves, comrades. Comrade Lenin has not given us any explanation why we need to do this right now, before the Congress of Soviets. I don't understand it. By the time of the Congress of Soviets the sharpness of the situation will be all the clearer. The Congress of Soviets will provide us with an apparatus; if all the delegates who have come together from all over Russia express themselves for the seizure of power, then it is a different matter. But right now it will only be an armed uprising, which the government will try to suppress." In any case the party would not have to wait long. "We are sitting on a volcano. Every morning when I get up I wonder, 'Hasn't it begun yet?' "

Smilga was present to defend Lenin's view — "Actually we have long been in power already." But even this young firebrand toned down the insurrectionary line a little: it did not mean "the seizure of power tomorrow," but only the basic strategy. Both he and Sokolnikov, who spoke for the Central Committee, emphasized the role that the Congress of Soviets would play, quite contrary to Lenin's warning about "constitutional illusions." Said Sokolnikov, "The Congress of Soviets in itself constitutes the apparatus which we can use," while the transfer of the government from Petrograd to Moscow would provide "the excuse for battle." "If only Lenin were here," someone lamented. . . .

While democratic Russia was debating itself to death, out at the border checkpoint of Beloostrov the same Konstantin Ivanov who fled to Finland in August was returning in the same disguise, once again with engineer Yalava in locomotive 293. With his bodyguard Rakhia, Ivanov-Lenin got off the train when it reached the Udelnaya suburban station in the northern outskirts of Petrograd. They were met at the station by another Finnish Bolshevik named Kalske, the man Zinoviev was staying with not far away. Lenin's first move was to go with Kalske to see Zinoviev. "Entering the apartment and meeting Comrade Zinoviev," Kalske recalled, "he began an animated conversation, and at least as far as I recall Vladimir Ilyich was not entirely happy with the tactics of the comrades who had been leading our party." . . . .

To the Bolshevik contingent assembling to dominate the Congress of Northern Soviets, Lenin sent a special appeal:

> *Comrades! Our revolution is passing through a highly critical time. This crisis coincides with the great crisis of a growing worldwide socialist revolution and of a struggle against it by world imperialism. The responsible leaders of our party are confronted with a gigantic task; if they do not carry it out, it will mean a total collapse of the internationalist proletarian movement. The situation is such that delay truly means death.*